CONFLICT LANDSCAPES

Conflict Landscapes explores the long under-acknowledged and under-investigated aspects of where and how modern conflict landscapes interact and conjoin with pre-twentieth-century places, activities, and beliefs, as well as with individuals and groups.

Investigating and understanding the often unpredictable power and legacies of landscapes that have seen (and often still viscerally embody) the consequences of mass death and destruction, the book shows, through these landscapes, the power of destruction to preserve, refocus, and often reconfigure the past. Responding to the complexity of modern conflict, the book offers a coherent, integrated, and sensitized hybrid approach, which calls on different disciplines where they overlap in a shared common terrain. Dealing with issues such as memory, identity, emotion, and wellbeing, the chapters tease out the human experience of modern conflict and its relationship to landscape.

Conflict Landscapes will appeal to a wide range of disciplines involved in studying conflict, such as archaeology, anthropology, material culture studies, art history, cultural history, cultural geography, military history, and heritage and museum studies.

Nicholas J. Saunders is Professor of Material Culture at Bristol University, UK, and co-director of the Great Arab Revolt Project. Between 1998 and 2004, he was British Academy Senior Research Fellow at University College London, making the first anthropological study of the material culture of the First World War.

Paul Cornish is a Senior Curator at the Imperial War Museum. He is currently working on the creation of a new permanent Second World War gallery to open in 2021, having previously been involved with the construction of the First World War gallery, which opened in 2014.

CONFLICT LANDSCAPES

Materiality and Meaning in Contested Places

Edited by Nicholas J. Saunders and Paul Cornish

LONDON AND NEW YORK

First published 2021
by Routledge
2 Park Square, Milton Park, Abingdon, Oxon OX14 4RN

and by Routledge
605 Third Avenue, New York, NY 10158

Routledge is an imprint of the Taylor & Francis Group, an informa business

British Library Cataloguing-in-Publication Data
A catalogue record for this book is available from the British Library

Library of Congress Cataloging-in-Publication Data
A catalog record has been requested for this book

ISBN: 978-0-367-71153-5 (hbk)
ISBN: 978-0-367-69019-9 (pbk)
ISBN: 978-1-003-14955-2 (ebk)

Typeset in Bembo
by Deanta Global Publishing Services, Chennai, India

CONTENTS

ILLUSTRATIONS

Figures

Table

CONTRIBUTORS

Alessandro Bezzi has a 2006 MPhil from the University of Padua, and was a founder member in 2005 of Arc-Team, an Italian company which specializes in archaeology and cultural heritage. He has archaeological fieldwork experience in Europe, the Caucasus, and the Middle East. He has academic teaching experience in Italy, Austria, Sweden, and Germany. His publications are mainly focused on digital archaeology, FLOSS (free/libre and open-source software), and field archaeology. He works for Arc-Team with a special focus on archeorobotic devices.

Luca Bezzi has a 2005 MPhil from the University of Padua, and the same year founded Arc-Team, an Italian company which specializes in archaeology and cultural heritage. He has worked on several archaeological campaigns in Europe, the Caucasus, and the Middle East. He has academic teaching experience in Italy, Austria, Sweden, and Germany. His published articles mainly focus on digital archaeology, FLOSS (free/libre and open-source software), field archaeology, and anthropology. Apart from his work at Arc-Team, his research interests are related to underwater archaeology and speleoarchaeology.

Mark A. Burchell is a former Royal Marine Commando who received his PhD at the University of Bristol. He is a professional anthropologist at the Defence Science and Technology Laboratory (Dstl), Porton Down, UK. His current research area is organizational ethnography focusing on cultural integration of cross-government departments. He also researches and publishes on conflict anthropology, particularly concerning the body as material culture.

Vincent Carpentier is an archaeologist responsible for supervising operations with INRAP and is a scholar at the Centre Boüard-CRAHAM (UMR 6273 CNRS/University of Caen, Normandy). He has a PhD in history and archaeology and is a specialist in the Middle Ages and coastal societies. He has directed many excavation projects in north-western France, and focuses on the historical and archaeological study of Second World War remains in Normandy and abroad.

Gilly Carr is a senior lecturer in archaeology at the University of Cambridge. She is also a Fellow in Archaeology at St Catharine's College, a partner of the Cambridge Heritage Research Centre, and a member of the UK delegation of the International Holocaust Remembrance Alliance (IHRA). Her research interests include conflict archaeology and post-conflict heritage, and she has carried out extensive long-term fieldwork in the Channel Islands since 2006. Dr Carr's most recent book, *Victims of Nazism in the Channel Islands: A Legitimate Heritage?* was published in 2019.

Paul Cornish is a Senior Curator at the Imperial War Museum. He is currently working on the creation of a new permanent Second World War gallery to open in 2021, having previously been involved with the construction of the First World War gallery which opened in 2014. He has co-organized five IWM-based international conferences on the material culture of conflict with Nicholas J. Saunders and co-edited the volumes *Contested Objects* (2009), *Bodies in Conflict* (2014), and *Modern Conflict and the Senses* (2017), all published by Routledge. He is co-editor of the Routledge series *Material Culture and Modern Conflict*.

Jacek Czarnecki is a polemologist and journalist. He studied DEA Strategie et Politique at the Université Paris 1 Panthéon-Sorbonne. He was a war correspondent for more than 15 years, and today is a radio journalist and a special parliamentary correspondent at Radio Zet. He is committed to protecting the material heritage of the First World War in Poland as part of his interest in modern conflict archaeology. He is particularly interested in the beginnings of aerial reconnaissance and the use of aerial photography in 1915 on the Eastern Front and is currently completing his doctoral thesis on this topic.

Paola Filippucci is a Fellow and Lecturer in Social Anthropology at Murray Edwards College, Cambridge, and a member of the Heritage Research Centre at the Department of Archaeology, University of Cambridge. Since 2000, Dr Filippucci's research has focused on war commemoration and post-war reconstruction in the former battlefields of the First World War on the Western Front in France (Argonne and Verdun) on which she has published several articles. She is currently completing a monograph on her research in Argonne. As a member of No Man's Land, she participates in archaeological excavations of Great War sites in Belgium and France.

Salvatore Garfi has been a professional archaeologist since 1974, working on projects ranging from the prehistoric to the contemporary. He has worked in Egypt, Southern Arabia, and elsewhere in the Middle East besides working in Wales and England. Since 2010, he has specialized in the archaeology of modern conflict, and his PhD was on late-twentieth-century conflict in Western Sahara. He was a postdoctoral Leverhulme Fellow in the School of Cultures, Languages, and Area Studies, University of Nottingham (2015–2018), and co-founder of the International Brigades Archaeology Project (IBAP) in Spain from 2014 to 2015. His book *Conflict Landscapes: An Archaeology of the International Brigades in the Spanish Civil War* was published in 2019.

Emmanuel Ghesquière is an archaeologist responsible for supervision operations with INRAP, and a scholar of the mixed research unit 6566 'Atlantic civilizations and archaeo-sciences' (UMR 6566 of the CNRS). He has a PhD in Prehistory and is a specialist in the Mesolithic of Normandy. He recently directed several excavations of military sites related to the Battle of Normandy, in particular, that of a large camp of a Canadian infantry division at Fleury-sur-Orne, south of Caen.

Wouter Gheyle is a scientific researcher at Ghent University. His main interest is landscape archaeology and the use of remote sensing in archaeology. His PhD (2009) combined these in an interdisciplinary survey and analysis of archaeological sites in the Altai Mountains in Russia. His research interests extend to the historical aerial photography and archaeology of modern conflicts, primarily the First and Second World Wars. In this, he is especially interested in combining non-invasive techniques, such as the analysis of LiDAR-data and geophysical prospection alongside aerial photography as a powerful way of documenting conflict heritage.

Rupert Gietl has a 2005 MPhil from the University of Vienna, and in the same year was a co-founder of Arc-Team, an Italian company which specializes in archaeology and cultural heritage. He has archaeological fieldwork experience in Europe, the Caucasus, and the Middle East, and teaching experience in Italy and Austria. His publications are mainly on digital archaeology, field archaeology (related to different projects), and modern conflict archaeology (mainly the First World War). He works for Arc-Team with specific interests in modern conflict archaeology, glacial archaeology, and high mountain archaeology.

Ville Hemminki is a student in archaeology at the University of Helsinki and is interested in the heritage and memory of Lapland. The German occupation and legacies of war are his particular research topics.

Benoît Labbey is an archaeologist supervising operations with INRAP who previously worked as a guide at the Caen Memorial. Since 2015, he has contributed to the inventory of remains of the Second World War as part of the Collective Program of Research organized by the DRAC Normandie and the University of Caen. His works focus on the history and archaeology of the Atlantic Wall and the daily lives of troops during the Battle of Normandy.

Cyril Marcigny is an archaeologist supervising operations with INRAP and a scholar in the mixed research unit 'Atlantic civilizations and archaeo-sciences' (UMR 6566 of the CNRS). A PhD in Prehistory, he is a Bronze Age specialist. He has directed many excavations in north-western France and has been involved in the archaeological and methodological study of remains of the Second World War in Normandy, in the sectors of La Hague, Port-en-Bessin, and Longues-sur-Mer. Since 2015, he has directed the excavation and mapping of a network of quarries located at Fleury-sur-Orne, south of Caen, which were used as shelters for hundreds of civilians fleeing the bombings of Caen in June and July 1944.

William Mitchell is the Project Archaeologist for the Centre of Archaeology at Staffordshire University. He has over 15 years of experience in development-led and research-centred archaeological projects and has undertaken archaeological projects at Holocaust sites across Europe. He publishes widely on a range of topics, from William Shakespeare to Heritage Lottery-funded community-led archaeology projects. In 2016, he published *Finding Shakespeare's New Place: An Archaeological Biography* (co-authored with Paul Edmonson and Kevin Colls).

Gabriel Moshenska is an associate professor in public archaeology at the Institute of Archaeology, University College London, UK. He works on the public and community archaeology of First and Second World War sites in Greater London, as well as historical research on Civil Defence and the Home Front. Recently he has taken part in the work of the project 'Lapland's Dark Heritage' in Sápmi, northern Finland.

Guy De Mulder is a professor in the Department of Archaeology, Ghent University, Belgium, where he received his PhD in Archaeology in 2011. From 2011 to 2015, he was a doctoral assistant at the Department of Archaeology and was appointed as a research professor BOF in October 2016. His PhD was on the cremation rites of the Late Bronze Age and Early Iron Age cemeteries in the Scheldt basin. His current projects are focused on material studies, such as the relation between typochronology and radiocarbon dating, on the protohistoric archaeology of the Balearic Islands, and more recently on conflict archaeology. Together with Jean Bourgeois, he is leading the Centre for Historical and Archaeological Aerial Photography (CHAL), a long-term partnership between Ghent University, the Province of West-Flanders, and the In Flanders Fields Museum (2014–2023).

Giuseppe Naponiello is a professional archaeoanthropologist at Arc-Team with a special interest in archaeological web-technologies. He is a 3D web technology and cybersecurity expert and has worked on archaeological projects in Europe, the Caucasus, and the Middle East (Iran). His teaching experience focuses on cybersecurity, DBMS (database management systems), and web-GIS in Italy and Austria. His research has focused on archaeological web-GIS and DBMS with FLOSS (free/libre and open-source software).

Volker K. Pachauer is currently finishing his doctoral thesis entitled 'Fortification and Representation' at Graz University of Technology. From 2011 to 2017, he was a university assistant, then a lecturer at the Institute for Urban and Architectural History, Graz. His research is focused on the architectura militaris of the nineteenth and twentieth centuries, functional buildings, historicism, and railway infrastructure, with a special geographical interest in Italy, Bosnia, Croatia, and Montenegro. He is a member of the ICOMOS National Committee Austria and a founding member of the Austrian Society for Fortification Research. He lectures on fortification and bunker architecture of the nineteenth and twentieth centuries.

Anita Pinagli has worked for many years as a field archaeologist and is currently the vice auditor and scientific director of Landscapes – a small community-based cultural and historical association in Friuli-Venezia Giulia, north-eastern Italy. Throughout her career, she has worked on several community-based projects, specializing in analyzing the level of engagement between local communities and archaeo-historical conflict landscapes. She graduated from the National University of Ireland, Galway, with a BA in Archaeology in 2010, and received her MA in Landscape Archaeology from the same university in 2013.

Gertjan Plets is an assistant professor in archaeology and heritage studies at Utrecht University. His research bridged methods from anthropology, archaeology, and cultural history to study contemporary engagements with the material past. Before his tenure at Utrecht, Gertjan was at Stanford University where he contributed to the research lab of Lynn Meskell, exploring the role of cultural heritage in global politics. He has published on a variety of issues related to heritage and memory politics in Siberia, World Heritage politics, and the funding of heritage preservation abroad by the Kremlin in the Middle East.

Alexander J. Potočnik is a Slovenian historian and currently a doctoral student at Monash University in Melbourne. Amongst his many English-language publications are *Slovenian Fortifications* (2008), *Fortifying Europe's Soft Underbelly* (2012), *Hemingway's Trail of the Novel: A Farewell to Arm* (2013), *Erwin Rommel's Blue Max* (2014), and the important article 'The Rupnik Line', published in *Fort – the International Journal of Military Architecture* (2001).

Jeffrey S. Reznick is the Chief of the History of Medicine Division of the US National Library of Medicine in Bethesda, Maryland, and an Honorary Research Fellow in the Centre for War Studies of the University of Birmingham, UK. He is the author of *John Galsworthy and Disabled Soldiers of the Great War* (2009) and *Healing the Nation: Soldiers and the Culture of Caregiving in Britain during the Great War* (2005), as well as numerous articles which explore medical, material, and memorial cultures of 1914–1918.

Nicholas J. Saunders is Professor of Material Culture at Bristol University, UK, and co-director of the Great Arab Revolt Project. Between 1998 and 2004, he was a British Academy Senior Research Fellow at University College London, making the first anthropological study of the material culture of the First World War. He has undertaken research in France, Belgium, Bosnia, Jordan, Mexico, Peru, and the Caribbean, and currently in Slovenia with the Soča/Isonzo Valley Conflict Landscapes Project. He is also researching the First World War material culture of the Chinese Labour Corps on the Western Front. He has published widely on the anthropology and archaeology of modern conflict, including *Trench Art* (2003), *Matters of Conflict* (2004), *Killing Time: Archaeology and the First World War* (2007), and *Desert Insurgency: Archaeology, T.E. Lawrence, and the Arab Revolt* (2020). With Paul Cornish, he has edited *Contested Objects* (2009), *Bodies in Conflict* (2014), and *Modern Conflict and the Senses* (2017). He is co-editor of the Routledge series *Material Culture and Modern Conflict.*

John M. Scott has a BA and an MA in Anthropology from the University of Northern Colorado, and a PhD from the Department of Archaeology and Anthropology, University of Bristol, UK. He is Principal Investigator at Metcalf Archaeological Consultants, Inc., Colorado, USA, with whom he has over 30 years' experience. He has led archaeological projects throughout the Rocky Mountains, the Great Plains, and the south-western USA, as well as conducting research in the West Indies, Jordan, and Peru. His current research interest is inventory and mapping of the 10th Mountain Division's Second World War battle-zone in the Italian Apennines and their training landscape at Camp Hale in Colorado's Rocky Mountains.

Oula Seitsonen (Sakarin-Pentin Ilarin Oula) is an archaeologist and geographer currently working at the University of Helsinki on the archaeology and heritage of the Second World War in Finland, and at the University of Oulu on the domestication of reindeer in Sápmi, Finnish Lapland. His PhD thesis (2018) was the first in Finland on twentieth-century conflict archaeology, and investigated the legacy of Nazi German wartime presence in northern Finland as part of the project Lapland's Dark Heritage. His wide range of interests includes prehistoric pastoralists in Fennoscandia, East Africa, and Mongolia, GIS-based mobility studies, and contemporary archaeology of twenty-first-century refugees.

Mary Shepperson is an archaeologist specializing in ancient Mesopotamian architecture. She is currently a Research Associate at the University of Liverpool, based jointly in the Department of Archaeology and the School of Architecture. She is an active field archaeologist and has excavated extensively in the Middle East, including five projects in Iraq. On the Charax Spasinou Project, she acts as the senior field archaeologist, responsible for test excavations at the site. She has a PhD from University College London and an undergraduate degree from Cambridge University.

Birger Stichelbaut obtained his PhD in archaeology (FWO 2005–2009) at Ghent University in 2009. Since then, he coordinates aerial photographic research as a postdoctoral researcher. His research focuses on the study of material remains and landscapes of war using non-invasive remote sensing techniques and mainly historical aerial photographs. Besides scientific research he is also involved in the In Flanders Fields Museum in Ypres working on 'Landscape as the Last Witness', and where he recently curated a major exhibition on First World War conflict archaeology.

Caroline Sturdy Colls is a Professor in Conflict Archaeology and Genocide Investigation and Director of the Centre of Archaeology at Staffordshire University. Her research primarily focuses on the application of interdisciplinary approaches to the investigation of Holocaust landscapes and twentieth-century mass violence. Her monographs include *Adolf Island* (forthcoming, with Kevin Colls), *Holocaust Archaeologies: Approaches and Future Directions* (2015), the *Handbook of Missing Persons* (2016, edited with Steven Morewitz) and *Forensic Approaches to Buried Remains* (2013, co-authored with John Hunter and Barrie Simpson). In 2016, she received the European Archaeological Heritage Prize for her contribution to modern conflict archaeology.

Suzie Thomas is an Associate Professor in Cultural Heritage Studies at the University of Helsinki. She is interested in issues around contested and 'dark' heritage, and in non-professional interactions with material heritage. She was a member of the Lapland's Dark Heritage research team (2014–2018), which investigated the material legacies of the Second World War in Finnish Lapland. Her PhD from Newcastle University was on the relationships between archaeologists and metal detectorists in England and Wales.

Simon Verdegem is an archaeology project leader for the Belgian company Ruben Willaert BVBA. He has a master's degree in history (2005) and also a master's in archaeology (2007) from Ghent University. He began working as an archaeologist in 2008 and gained wide experience excavating sites of all periods across Flanders. Since 2012, he has excavated and directed excavations of various sizes on First World War sites in Flanders. He is one of the organizers of an annual conference on Conflict Archaeology in Flanders, contributed to the exhibition *Traces of War* on First World War archaeology at the In Flanders Fields Museum in Ypres, and was one of the initiators of the DigHill80 project.

Graeme Were is the Chair and Professor of Anthropology in the Department of Anthropology and Archaeology at the University of Bristol. His research interests include museum anthropology, digital heritage, and material culture studies, with a regional specialism in Papua New Guinea and Vietnam. His most recent book is *How Materials Matter: Design, Innovation, and Materiality in the Pacific* (2019).

John B. Winterburn is a landscape and modern conflict archaeologist, with extensive knowledge of southern Jordan gained over 14 years. Combining fieldwork with archive research, satellite imagery and aerial photography, he investigated the Late Ottoman period landscapes of the Hejaz Railway and the Arab Revolt for his PhD at Bristol University. He continues this work and more recently has investigated prehistoric linear features in Jordan. He is a Research Associate for the Endangered Archaeology in the Middle East and North Africa project at the University of Oxford.

Anna Izabella Zalewska is an archaeologist and historian, and professor at the Maria Curie-Skłodowska University in Lublin, Poland. Her specialities include methodology, public history, critical heritage studies, memory studies, landscape studies, and the archaeology of contemporary times. Her work promotes the social and scientific value of all types of traces and carriers of memories about troubled pasts – as material warnings. It includes 'gas-scapes' – landscapes which saw the use of chemical weapons. This led to her involvement in the Advisory Board of Outreach and Education of the intergovernmental Organization for the Prohibition of Chemical Weapons, which was awarded the Nobel Peace Prize in 2013. She has published several books and over 100 articles on the uses and abuses of history, memory, and heritage.

INTRODUCTION

Paul Cornish and Nicholas J. Saunders

The industrialized nature of modern conflict presents a material and psychological intensity hitherto unknown in the dramatic shifts of human behaviour in history's previous wars. This phenomenon, beginning in the early twentieth century, has led to a dramatic transformation of landscape through the agency of destruction, and created new places, at the time, for decades afterwards, and still today as a volatile ongoing process. Such landscapes did not exist before the First World War, but after 1918, and in various forms, they are everywhere.

An interdisciplinary reassessment of the character and role of conflict landscapes is one result of recent advances in our ability to conceptualize, investigate, and understand the contemporary and recent historical past, as well as the more distant one of prehistory. Inextricably bound up with issues of memory, identity, emotion, sacrifice, and wellbeing, the landscape dimensions of modern conflict – from the First World War to the Second, from Korea to Vietnam and ongoing struggles in Gaza, Syria, and Ukraine – are everywhere apparent. They are increasingly studied not just for academic, political, and military reasons, but for their associations with cultural, public, pragmatic, and sustainable environmental reasons too – for scientific solutions to current problems and future threats.

The transformative power of modern war's technological capacity, and its ability to move across disciplinary as well as political and moral boundaries, demands a rigorous response informed by global studies of the kind in this volume. The long under-acknowledged and under-investigated aspects of where and how modern conflict landscapes interact and connect with pre-twentieth-century places, behaviours, and beliefs, as well as with individuals and groups, are addressed here in varied ways. The aim is to push ajar new doors to investigating and understanding the often unpredictable power and legacies of landscapes which have seen (and often still viscerally embody) the consequences of mass death and destruction. In other words, to show through landscape analysis the power of destruction to preserve, refocus, and reconfigure the past.

Characterizing this interdisciplinary reassessment of modern conflict landscapes has been the emerging perspective of the personal and individual – the theoretically nuanced bottom-up analysis of conflict-related material culture (e.g. Saunders 2003; Moshenska 2019; Carr 2014), reconfigured sensorial worlds (e.g. Leonard 2019; Winterton 2012; Saunders and Cornish 2017), archaeology (e.g. Moshenska 2013; Košir et al. 2019; Saunders 2010), and landscape itself (e.g. Bender and Winer 2001; Saunders; Kobialka et al. 2017) to mention just a few recent examples. These contributions and many others would have been almost impossible just 20 years ago, and have benefitted from and intersected with a growing interdisciplinarity across many traditional subjects, and a host of new scientific advances, from remote-sensing LiDAR to DNA technologies. All of these, each in their own manner, have contextualized and enriched the study of conflict landscapes in ways previously unimaginable. But, to start at the beginning.

Landscape as we know it has not always been with us. It is a human construct of relatively recent origin. In the Western world at least, consciousness of landscape as a 'thing' dates only back as far as the early modern era. We know this from the appearance of landscape in painting. In the sixteenth century, the natural and built environment began to feature in paintings as something more than a mere backdrop to biblical and mythological scenes or (in books of hours), the seasonal pursuits of lords and peasants. Some art historians assign the first full blossoming of this tendency to the work of Joachim Patinir (1480–1524). His astonishing images certainly promote landscape at the expense of the 'action' that he is depicting and he appears to have been the first to perfect the use of colour to create a sense of depth and distance. He also established the use of an elevated putative 'viewpoint', the basis of the artistic trope subsequently known as *Weltlandschaft*. But the 'cut and paste' approach he took to assembling the different elements of the landscape, coupled with the sheer chromatic intensity of his works, lends them a surreal and dreamlike quality. For a more fully developed and, perhaps, 'modern' representation of landscape we need to jump forward forty years to the works of Pieter Bruegel (1525–1569) (see Hagen and Hagen 2000).

Bruegel's paintings offer us naturalistically rendered landscapes; although he did not entirely eschew the 'Photoshop' technique of his predecessors. While he was inspired by local country scenes (most notably in Pajottenland, west of Brussels), he distorted them. And he frequently framed his landscapes with dramatic mountains, based on scenery he had seen during a journey to Italy in the early 1550s. But within this framework, his landscapes have a truth and solidity that goes beyond the visual. While (arguably for the first time in Western art) his landscapes would work as compositions if denuded of human presence, it is the people that give them meaning. Usually, the paintings contain a message, frequently veiled, relating to proverbial or biblical axioms or to the political situation of his own time and place.

But beyond this, there are clear interactions between man and his environment on view. In Bruegel's work, man is reliant upon the landscape that he inhabits but, while it might give him succour in good times, this environment can also be harsh and unpredictable. It is also a place of *conflict*. Biblical armies march across Bruegel's mountain landscapes; children are massacred by soldiers in a snow-covered village square. And this was not just a representation of a 'historical' conflict landscape but a barely disguised reference to his own times.[1] This brings us directly to the substance of this book, for Bruegel was demonstrating that landscape, as Barbara Bender put it, is 'not a record but a recording' – it is '*time materializing*'. Furthermore, it is also '*always subjective*' (Bender 2002: 103).

The creation of landscapes through the application of human instinct, intellect, emotion, and memory is as old as time itself; although, as noted above, our knowing participation in it is of relatively recent date. As for landscapes of *conflict* – they are everywhere, and always have been. As Margaret MacMillan said, apropos her 2018 Reith Lectures 'we like to think of war as an aberration, as the breakdown of the normal state of peace. This is comforting but wrong. War is deeply woven into the history of human society'.[2] Thus, conflict landscapes abound. As this book powerfully demonstrates, their existence and their development are founded on the people who interacted (and who continue to interact) with them. Just as in Bruegel's painted world, it is people that give landscapes their meaning – whether they be his Netherlandish villagers, or, in this volume, modern Sámi reindeer herders (Seitsonen and Moshenska; Stichelbaut et al.), the ethnically mixed population on Italy's northern borders (Bezzi et al.; Pinagli et al.) or the Saharawi of Western Sahara (Garfi).

And just like the Flemish old masters, people persistently select elements of their environment to create landscapes that suit their own purposes or requirements. In effect, they (to use a nowadays much abused and devalued word) curate their own landscapes. These landscapes exist more in the minds of their creators, rather than in actual topography. They are created when people make a selective engagement with what is around them (Layton and Ucko 1999: 1). This might be due to a wish to remember or un-remember aspects of heritage considered 'dark' (Seitsonen and Moshenska) or it might be a way of coping with their own, current experience of conflict (Carr). Incidentally, the focus on landscape as a relief from incarceration described by Carr has a sinister contemporary counterpart in the stamps that had to accompany parcels sent to prisoners in the Theresienstadt ghetto. Introduced in 1943, when nobody could have retained any doubts about its nature and purpose, these stamps depict not the grim little fortress-town but a peaceful view of the surrounding Bohemian countryside.[3] Envisionings of essentially similar landscapes could evidently serve wildly different purposes depending on whether you were the incarcerated or the incarcerator.

Other conflict landscapes are constructed to answer the varying requirements of conflict. This can occur on a massive scale, when vast chunks of the environment, or existing landscapes, are remade or overbuilt for the purposes of military training (Scott) or military control (Garfi; Winterburn). A recurrent feature of the military reconfiguration of landscape is fortification. This might serve more than one purpose – in some cases to create a barrier to the transit of enemy forces (Pignali et al.; Shepperson; Verdegem), in others to ensure the safe movement of friendly forces (Winterburn) and, in some instances, both of these things (Stichelbaut et al.). Some of these defences remain 'invisible in plain view', such as parts of Mussolini's inter-war *Vallo Alpino* and elements of its communist Yugoslavian counterpart the Rupnik Line in Slovenia – a fact which has helped preserve them to become tourist attractions.

Conflict has also prompted the re-purposing or modification of landscapes for therapeutic purposes (Reznick). This brings to mind a more unexpected therapeutic use of landscape that appears in the film *War Neuroses* made by Major Arthur Hurst in 1917–1918.[4] The scenes purporting to show shell-shock sufferers displaying their symptoms are a standard feature of TV documentaries, but fewer people are familiar with the last sequences of the film in which Hurst's patients 'complete' their cure when, among the hills and hedges of South Devon countryside, they carry out a mock attack on an imaginary German strongpoint. As part of this curious (not to say shocking) therapy, the pastoral landscape is re-imagined as the Western Front (see also Cornish, this volume, for a similar landscape becoming a *new* Western Front). The inextricability of mind, body, and landscape – all damaged by conflict – is painfully evident here.

This volume's focus on conflict terrains created since 1914 acknowledges also that the First World War represents a caesura in the artistic – and by extension everyone's – engagement with landscape (Saunders 2014: 23). In particular, the profound level of destruction wreaked upon the environment of the static Western Front found artists struggling to respond. Paul Nash was horrified by the landscape of the Ypres Salient where 'the stinking mud becomes more evilly yellow, the shell holes fill up with green-white water, the roads and tracks are covered in inches of slime, the black dying trees ooze and sweat and the shells never cease' (Gough 2010: 152).

Representing such scenes in paint became his self-appointed mission (Gough 2010: 152). At the same time others, like photographer Frank Hurley (ibid.: 153–154) and painter CRW Nevinson struggled to represent the sheer emptiness of the modern battlefield – as exemplified in the latter's *After a Push*.[5] And, as William Orpen said, 'one could not paint the smell' (although it has been plausibly claimed that he did) (Gough 2010: 175, 185). This conflict landscape manifested a degree of hideous grandeur that had never before been witnessed. Across Europe artists such as Nevinson, Dix, Braque, and Vallotton – to name but a handful – felt impelled to alter their style of painting to encompass what they had witnessed. As Samuel Hynes (1990: 195) observed, 'a Modernist method that before the war had seemed violent and distorting was seen to be realistic on the Western Front. Modernism had not changed, but reality had'.[6] And the creations of these painters and photographers achieved a hold over our imaginations which has proved enduring and influential.

The First World War also precipitated the re-making of our perception and understanding of landscape in another fundamental context – that of our ability to see it from an aerial perspective (Stichelbaut and Chielens 2014). *Weltlandschaft* paintings had long adopted an imagined elevated viewpoint that spread the landscape out before the viewer's gaze, but now things were taken, literally, to a new level. Initially, such a grasp of landscape was limited to those who flew or had access to aerial photographs. But now, in the twenty-first century, digitized aerial photographs and particularly free public access to satellite imagery has created a 'completely new mental map' of our environment (Saunders and Cornish 2016: xxx). To this latter facility – extraordinary to those of us old enough to remember life without it – can now be added access to LiDAR imagery, a bird's-eye view which penetrates vegetation cover to reveal the physical landscape beneath (e.g. Crutchley and Crow 2018; Gheyle et al. 2018). Both of these resources, together with GIS mapping software, have supported and even driven new archaeological research (Bezzi et al.; Stichelbaut and Moshenska).

The First World War furthermore initiated a wave of political change that had a strong and lasting effect on the way that some landscapes have been perceived by those who inhabit them. Artificial borders were drawn across great tracts of the Middle East in the wake of the dissolution of the Ottoman Empire, and their significance has been enduring (Shepperson; Saunders; Barr 2012). In Europe, the collapse of the Russian and Austro-Hungarian empires re-drew borders and created new nations. The inhabitants of these new, largely ethnically based states, had little reason to engage with the warscapes in which the old empires had foundered, and still less cause when, after another war, they became part of the Soviet 'empire' (Cornish and Saunders 2019: xviii). On the Austrian-Italian frontier, concepts of landscape twisted and turned as fortifications were turned one way, then the other and then back again, as political control changed (Pignali et al.).

Landscapes also evolve in concert with the understanding and memories of the people who inhabit them. At a fundamental level, different groups of people might begin such an engagement from very different starting points. For example, the Sámi understanding of the land that they inhabit is completely different from that of 'outsiders' who view it as a wilderness (Seitsonen et al.). Visitors will generally engage with the landscape in a different way from its inhabitants, although both might claim some sort of 'ownership' of it (Filippucci; Miles 2016: 120–130). These relationships provide rich material for archaeologists – some of whom choose to incorporate (sometimes contested) public engagement into their projects (Seitsonen in preparation; Zalewska and Czarnecki) – once again proving the nature of landscape as a recording, not a record.

Inevitably, the outcome of archaeological and anthropological investigations might end up challenging the understanding of the landscape held by those who claim 'ownership' of it. For example, the contested view of how war-torn Ypres should be dealt with after 1918 – left as a memorial to German aggression or rebuilt in its Medieval splendour; similarly, when a project at the site of

Bergen-Belsen concentration camp suggested the presence of mass burials that did not feature in the landscape-consciousness of the curators of that 'Site of Memory' (Sturdy Colls and Mitchell). Or, in the limestone mountains of the Croatian-Bosnian borderlands, where

> While a (former) Partisan might perceive the mountains as a site of fierce fighting and victory over the fascists, a Serbian dweller might rather be reminded of Ustaša [Croatian ultra-nationalist group] crimes and the eviction of Serbs. In turn, many Croats who have lost family members or friends in executions or mass killings perceive the place primarily as a site of Partisan atrocities and – depending on context – one of historic threat from Ottoman Turks followed by eventual victory.
>
> *(Schäuble 2011: 50)*

Or indeed, in Vietnam, where 'Beyond the tombs, cemeteries, and war monuments are many spaces in between, sublayers of ancient remains, a "wilderness" haunted not only by traces of chemicals or munitions but also of ghosts from these contested pasts' (Biggs 2018: 14).

The historiography of conflict events intimately linked to landscape is also open to challenge and change. In this volume, each of the two World Wars provides the basis for such revisionist analyses – two by archaeologists and two by non-archaeologists. Perhaps surprisingly, the two Second World War examples both relate to one of the best-known landscapes of that war – the 1944 Normandy battlefield. Because of its dense historiography and frequent popular representation in film and on television, the campaign there seems to have drawn more than its fair share of 'myth', or at least an encrustation of commonly accepted tropes which are challenged here by archaeology (Carpentier et al.; Cornish). Two famous incidents of the First World War are subjected to a similar evaluation, informed by an intimate knowledge of the landscape in which they took place: the German gas attack at Bolimów (Zalewska and Czarnecki) and Erwin Rommel's part in the 1917 Battle of Caporetto, itself retrospectively affected by Rommel's Second World War activities (Potočnik).

Conflict landscapes of all eras are characterized by death and suffering – of civilians as well as soldiers, by apparently historical as well as obviously fictional accounts, by truth and propaganda, by forgetfulness, and by commemorative monuments and activities. What makes the landscapes of modern conflict so different is the ability of these places to autonomously yet randomly kill and maim decades, probably centuries, after the event itself – either by the detonation of volatile munitions or the poisoning of soil, water, and crops. When coupled with the sheer quantity of the dead in many conflicts, and the atomizing ('disappearing') effects of industrialized technologies on the human body, modern conflict landscapes are revealed as a unique and defining invention of the twentieth century, with which we interact in a diversity of ways, and whose interdisciplinary study has only just begun.

Notes

1 Although discussion continues as to the extent to which Bruegel was making *specific* allusion to the contemporary Spanish attempts to suppress political and religious separatism in the Netherlands.
2 www.bbc.co.uk/mediacentre/latestnews/2017/reith-lectures-margaret-macmillan
3 https://collections.ushmm.org/search/catalog/irn76777
4 IWM Film MGH 3600
5 www.iwm.org.uk/collections/item/object/20212
6 Although Nevinson, counterintuitively, temporarily abandoned his Futurist style for a more conventional one.

References

Barr, J. (2012) *A Line in the Sand: Britain, France and the Struggle That Shaped the Middle East*. London: Simon and Schuster.

Bender, B. (1993) Stonehenge – Contested Landscapes (Medieval to Present-Day). In B. Bender (ed.), *Landscape: Politics and Perspectives*, pp. 245–279. Oxford: Berg.

——— (2002) Time and Landscape. *Current Anthropology* 43 (4): 103–112.

Bender, B. and M. Winer (eds.) (2001) *Contested Landscapes: Movement, Exile and Place*. Oxford: Berg.

Biggs, D. (2018) *Footprints of War: Militarized Landscapes in Vietnam*. Seattle: University of Washington Press

Carr, G. (2014) *Legacies of Occupation: Archaeology, Heritage and Memory in the Channel Islands*. New York: Springer.

Cornish, P. and N.J. Saunders (2019) Preface. In U. Košir, M. Črešnar and D. Mlekuž (eds.), *Rediscovering the Great War*, pp. xvi–xix. London: Routledge.

Crutchley, S. and P. Crow. (2018) *Using Airborne Lidar in Archaeological Survey: The Light Fantastic*. Swindon: Historic England.

Gheyle, W., B. Stichelbaut, T. Saey, N. Note, H. Van den Berghe, V. Van Eetvelde, M. Van Meirvenne and J. Bourgeois. (2018) Scratching the Surface of War. Airborne Laser Scans of the Great War Conflict Landscape in Flanders (Belgium). *Applied Geography* 90: 55–68.

Gough, P. (2010) *A Terrible Beauty: British Artists and the First World War*. Bristol: Sansom.

Hagen, R.M. and R. Hagen. (2000) *Bruegel: The Complete Paintings*. Köln: Taschen.

Hynes, S. (1990) *A War Imagined: The First World War and English Culture*. London: Bodley Head.

Kobiałka, D., M. Kostyrko and K. Kajda. (2017) The Great War and its Landscapes between Memory and Oblivion: The Case of Prisoners of War Camps in Tuchola and Czersk, Poland. *International Journal of Historical Archaeology* 21 (1): 134–151.

Košir, U., M. Crešnar and D. Mlekuž (eds.) (2019) *Rediscovering the Great War: Archaeology and Enduring Legacies on the Soca and Eastern Fronts*. London: Routledge.

Layton, R. and P.J. Ucko (1999) Introduction: Gazing on the Landscape and Encountering the Environment. In P.J. Ucko and R. Layton (eds.), *The Archaeology and Anthropology of Landscape: Shaping Your Landscape*, pp. 1–20. London: Routledge.

Leonard, M. (2019) A Sensorial No Man's Land: Corporeality and the Western Front during the First World War. *The Senses and Society* 14 (3): 258–270.

Miles, S. (2016) *The Western Front: Landscape, Tourism and Heritage*. Barnsley: Pen & Sword.

Moshenska, G. (2013) *The Archaeology of the Second World War*. Barnsley: Pen & Sword.

——— (2019) *Material Cultures of Childhood in Second World War Britain*. London: Routledge.
Saunders, N.J. (2001) Matter and Memory in the Landscapes of Conflict: The Western Front 1914–1999. In B. Bender and M. Winer (eds.), *Contested Landscapes: Movement, Exile and Place*, pp. 37–53. Oxford: Berg.
——— (2003) *Trench Art: Materialities and Memories of War*. Oxford: Berg.
——— (2010) *Killing Time: Archaeology and the First World War* (second edition.). Stroud: History Press.
——— (2014) Bodies in Trees: A Matter of Being in First World War Landscapes. In P. Cornish and N.J. Saunders (eds.), *Bodies in Conflict*, pp. 22–38. London: Routledge.
Saunders, N.J. and P. Cornish. (2016) Preface. In B. Stichelbaut and D. Cowley (eds.), *Conflict Landscapes and Archaeology from Above*, pp. xix–xxxi. London: Routledge.
——— (eds.) (2017) *Modern Conflict and the Senses*. London: Routledge.
Schäuble, M. (2011) How History Takes Place: Sacralized Landscapes in the Croatian-Bosnian Border Region. *History and Memory* 23 (1): 23–61.
Seitsonen, O. (2021) *Archaeologies of Hitler's Arctic War*. London: Routledge.
Stichelbaut, B. and P. Chielens. (2014) *In Flanders Fields: The Great War Seen from the Air, 1914–1918*. New Haven, CT: Yale University Press.
Winterton, M. (2012) Signs, Signals and Senses: The Soldier Body in the Trenches. In N.J. Saunders (ed.), *Beyond the Dead Horizon: Studies in Modern Conflict Archaeology*, pp. 229–241. Oxford: Oxbow.

PART I

The First World War

1

THE DEAD AND THEIR SPACES

Origins and meanings in modern conflict landscapes

Nicholas J. Saunders

Landscape is complex and slippery, a concept rather than a single place in historical time, a cultural image as well as a physical location (Daniels and Cosgrove 1988: 1). It is, fundamentally, a palimpsest of multi-vocal overlapping layers possessing different meanings for those who choose and engage with an aspect important to them. Each layer represents a physical engagement with space and time, and thus a world of social experience and imagination. Landscapes possess memory-making and memory-evoking qualities that connect to our cultural, emotional, and spiritual lives (Basso 1996), and so can serve as sensuous metaphors of identity. In this sense, every landscape embroiders the past with the present.

How much more so for landscapes of modern conflict, those bloody markers of industrialized war, the defining human activity of the twentieth century; created by the suffering and death of those whose remains have become part of the terrain – sometimes indistinguishable from, and at one with, the shattered earth and debris of war. These landscapes possess arguably the most intense and enduring legacies of pain, suffering, redemption, sacrifice, and in a world of materiality, of broken objects large and small. Such places are not simply the fossilized remnants of battle-space, but rather volatile dynamic entities, constantly changing their shape and significance for successive generations who engage with them in new and often unpredictable ways. Conflict landscapes are proactive, stationary yet ever-changing, and open to many kinds of interpretation and representation.

As Schäuble (2011: 52) observes for the Second World War Partisan landscapes of the Croatian-Bosnian borderlands,

> The land does not allow its inhabitants to forget and is in turn also not allowed to forget as the people of the region persistently charge the territory

with commemorative meaning and erect monuments and religious shrines to that effect.

Volatility is a characteristic here – for while in the immediate aftermath of the conflict the dead haunted the memories of the living, 'since the 1980s the living seem to haunt the dead in an attempt to secure them as allies for their changing political endeavours' (ibid.: 53).

Here, I explore modern conflict landscapes from the perspective of the First World War as the event which created and perpetuated the idea and the reality of such places, so different in intensity and scale to the landscapes of pre-twentieth-century conflict. I do so in part because the legacies of 1914–1918 include the effects which the multidimensional nature of that war have had on many if not most subsequent conflict landscapes (e.g. González-Ruibal 2008; Garfi 2019), of which, as I write, the area around Idlib in north-western Syria is the most recent (Anon. 2020). I do not deal here with other kinds of First World War landscapes – those focused on military training, the Home Front of munitions factories and other economic wartime activities (Saunders 2010: 202–212; Brown 2017; Cocroft and Stamper 2018), and cemeteries, though these are equally the result of modern conflict. For my purposes, I deal with battle-zone landscapes and draw mainly on the evidence of three case studies – the Western Front (France and Belgium), the Italian Front (Italy and Slovenia), and the Middle East (Jordan). Each of these reveals distinctive elements which illustrate the complex and enduring nature of historically recent conflict landscapes and their infinite capacity to shape-shift meaning, significance, emotion, and cultural and political resonance.

At once physical and metaphysical, all landscapes are made by and for people, and those of the First World War still conceal many of the individuals who created them between 1914 and 1918, either as undiscovered bodies, body parts, or millions of microscopic bone fragments. In such places, literally and figuratively, human beings and landscape have become one. Lying sometimes just centimetres beneath the modern land surface, these landscape makers sometimes return, bursting forth into the modern world by virtue of urban construction, motorway building, accidental explosions of ordnance, and sometimes archaeological excavations. Here, time, space, history, memory, and chance intertwine, most notably (and emotionally) perhaps when families who had forgotten or never knew of their First World War ancestors are informed that they have been found. At such times, a paradox is born – absence becomes presence with a phone call or email, a name is erased from the list of the missing, and temporal and geographical distance collapses (see Saunders 2017).

The human cost of creating First World War landscapes was often described day by day, sometimes hour by hour, in memoirs and regimental (and private) war diaries, producing what must be some of the most exhaustively documented, personalized, and spiritualized locations ever to be considered for archaeological, anthropological, and historical study. Despite this, the remains of those who undertook these acts of destruction/creation often remain lost or unidentified, so many that they became something new – 'the missing', remembered on monuments and in cemeteries – but 'made present' by absence, by anonymity rather than by name. Here was, and remains, a landscape of intense sorrow and pain, yet also of 'nothingness' – no bodies to grieve over, only the landscape itself to bear witness (Dyer 1994; van Emden 2019; and see Chielens et al. 2006). As Jennifer Iles (2006: 177) observed,

> The people who once went to battle there have disappeared, yet their spaces remain ... [and quoting Hilaire Belloc] 'More than dust goes, more than wind goes; ... But what is the mere soil of the field without them? What meaning has it save for their presence?'

The Western Front

Arguably, never before in human history has a landscape impressed itself onto human memory so deeply or in such myriad ways as the Western Front. Since 1914, it has been shaped by war, peace, renewed conflict, and a post-1945 political reconfiguration forged at least in part by a transnational desire not to repeat the wars of the recent past. Today, this landscape continues to be re-invented (and redeveloped) at an accelerating pace, and integrated piecemeal into a common European and possibly world heritage (Miles 2016: 18–19; Himpe 2018: 180–181).

In recent years, the Western Front has been reassessed as far more than a century-old battlefield; rather, it is a battle-zone composed variously of industrialized slaughterhouses, vast tombs for 'the missing', places for returning refugees and contested reconstruction, popular tourist destinations, locations of memorials and cemeteries, pilgrimage destinations, sites for archaeological research and cultural heritage development, and, not least, still deadly places full of unexploded shells and bombs (Saunders 2001: 37). The Western Front, and the less well investigated Eastern and Italian Fronts, are indeed palimpsests – prime examples of landscape as ongoing process, colliding with and implicating the lives of countless individuals since their inception (see Hirsch 1995: 22–23).

There is no greater proof of this than the Western Front today, after more than four years of Centenary events (2014–2018), which have seen the creation of multiple new layers of landscape in the form of commemorative monuments (including trees), cemeteries, war walk routes, signage, school visits, archaeological investigations, museums and art galleries and their exhibitions, hotels/cafés, souvenirs, confectionery, food and drink, books, films, and television programmes. Each of these represents new or reconfigured ways of seeing and understanding the First World War in this region.

The Western Front landscape which existed before 2013–2014 is now 'buried' beneath that which exists in 2020, at least in part, and in a not dissimilar way to how the immediate post-war landscape of 1919 was covered over, rebuilt, re-valued, and re-presented by often contested layers of the inter-war period (and beyond) (Clout 1996; Various 2020; Vermeulen 1999). The Western Front demonstrates beyond doubt that a conflict landscape is a hybrid of the original geographical location, geological nature (e.g. Devos et al. 2017; Doyle 2017), the cultural landscape at the time of the military event, that event itself, and the various ways in which it lives on in memory and is physically reconfigured so that real worlds and memory worlds are brought into alignment.

War landscape 1914–1918

Military actions along the Western Front took place in largely medieval landscapes, finely balanced between architectural splendour (e.g. churches, cathedrals, and civic buildings) and rural features (e.g. moated farms, fields, and centuries-old drainage systems). These landscapes themselves lay on top of (and sometimes were visibly integrated with) the remains of a deeper prehistoric past, such as the Butte de Warlencourt on the Somme (Saunders 2004: 10–11). War changed rich agricultural terrain into a factory of industrialized death (Bernède 1997:91), as the landscape was 'drenched with hot metal', cut by trenches, swathed in barbed wire, poisoned with gas, soaked with human and animal blood, and disfigured by shattered buildings, shell craters, and blasted trees. This new layer of death and destruction quickly overlaid traditional pre-war landscapes, but mainly only in a narrow front-line zone beyond which physical destruction was either minimal or non-existent, though social life could be greatly disrupted (Giono 2004 [1931]). This could lead to a surreal experience where total devastation could lie almost adjacent to areas of untouched bucolic beauty.

This new landscape was created by men for whom the physical and psychological intensities of their experiences produced otherworldly places where 'the bizarre mixture of putrefaction and ammunition, the presence of the dead among the living, literally holding up trench walls from Ypres to Verdun, suggested that the demonic and satanic realms were indeed here on earth' (Winter 1995: 68–69). As the French *poilu* Louis Barthas recalled, 'On both sides of the trench, uncovered by earth slides, appeared skulls, feet, leg bones, skeletal hands, all mixed up with rags, shredded packs, and other shapeless debris' (Barthas 2014: 32). And animals joined the *danse macabre* – crows, eager to reach the flesh of dead French soldiers 'even pushed the helmets back from the heads of the dead … [and] pulled at the beard until the area between beard and chest hair was exposed … [and began] pecking at once, tearing off the skin' (Giono 2004 [1931]: 92).

Sensing and navigating this terrain was a dangerously novel experience, where, if vision was denied, it could be replaced by other senses such as smell, touch, and sound (Howes 1991; Leonard 2019; Winterton 2012; Saunders and Cornish 2017). Soldiers quickly developed new skills, identifying by sound different kinds of artillery shells as they travelled through the air, and recognizing the tell-tale odour of a buried corpse before (or without ever) seeing it. This re-education of the senses was critical for survival; as Private Alexander Paterson remembered, he had to develop 'an expert knowledge of all the strange sounds and smells of warfare, ignorance of which may mean death' (Paterson 1997: 239). And new, life-saving habituated movements were learnt, as soldiers were often reduced to crawling and slithering, feeling and smelling their way around trenches, dugouts, and in subterranean tunnels, where 'Your hands feel the clay wall, cold, sticky, sepulchral. This earth weighs on you from all sides, wrapping you in dismal solitude, touching your face with its blind, mouldy breath' (Barbusse 2003: 256; and see Leonard 2016). In other words, these landscapes were a new haptic universe as well as a new physical world. Even the soldier's quotidian experience of 'time' didn't escape and was recalibrated through the body by the widespread adoption of 'at a glance' wristwatches over unwieldy pocket watches.

And that wasn't all. In and around this new landscape, enveloping it above and below, was another lethally reconfigured medium, air. As Latour (2006: 105) observed, nobody knew that air was part of the body's sensorial spheres until the Germans launched their chlorine gas attack outside Ypres on 22 April 1915 (and see Zalewska and Czarnecki this volume). Air itself had been weaponized (Sloterdijk 2009 [2002]: 9–46), carrying also the stench of death, the sounds of dying, and the palpable heat of killing, and becoming the unnervingly 'invisible killer' which left no trace – concussion. At Beaumont Hamel on the Somme,

> In one underground room ... nearly fifty of the enemy were found lying dead in their bunks, all unwounded, and as though asleep. They had been killed by the concussion of the air following on the burst of a big shell at the entrance.
>
> *(Masefield 2003: 108)*

The fragmentation of human bodies, matériel, and earth joined together as if by alchemy to shatter reality, to reconfigure the sensorium, and to create new smellscapes, touchscapes, and soundscapes. These 'scapes' were short-lived worlds, glimpsed today mainly in diaries and war poetry, but invisible in the photographs and films which have survived, and which, of course, represent their own very different images and understandings of landscape. In such places, many men 'were physically and symbolically folded into landscape and emerged remade' (Saunders 2004: 9); there was, as Stéphane Audoin-Rouzeau (1992: 81) observed, 'a close connection, an osmosis between the death of men, of objects, of places' (Figure 1.1).

Draping these new deathly landscapes with the familiarity of home, and thereby creating a landscape within a landscape, was the soldiers' habit of naming trenches and places with a bewildering array of terms, from Thunder and Moonray to Poppy Post and Hawthorn Ridge (Chasseaud 2006: 46–55). German, French, and British troops did this, though the latter's habit of naming after London streets and landmarks has received the most attention, such as Regent Street and Piccadilly Circus (ibid.: 62). Even the deep archaeological

FIGURE 1.1 Men-objects-landscape: the French 87th Regiment at Cote 34 Verdun 1916. Source: © Public Domain, https://commons.wikimedia.org/w/index.php?curid=602064.

past was reborn in this way, with Caesar's Camp and Dolmen amongst others (ibid.: 48). German soldiers took an overtly heroic perspective, naming their locations after Nordic mythology such as *Wotan* and *Brunnhilde*, creating 'a sort of mythologised cultural and psychological space' (ibid.: 47).

Post-war landscape 1919–present

After the war, it was clear that in destroying one past, many new futures had been and were being created. In the decades which followed, new landscapes would be physically and figuratively piled one on top of the other (sometimes cutting into a deep archaeological past). Each of these landscape layers was infused with new meanings, and while many – such as those of pilgrimage, commemoration, land reclamation, and urban reconstruction – appeared quickly, others – such as the landscapes of archaeology, heritage, and ethnic presence – would lie dormant for decades before emerging.

These new post-war landscapes demonstrate a fundamental truth about such places – that their afterlives endure far longer than the events which gave them birth, and far beyond the living memory of those involved. If war itself is unpredictable, then so is its aftermath, manifested in different views of what shape the future should take. The contested nature of the post-1918 Western Front, and indeed all post-conflict terrains, emerges from different groups engaging with the matter of landscape in different ways (Layton and Ucko 1999: 1), whether simply the earth itself, or memorials, cemeteries, and new structures placed upon it. These differences arise from diverse experiences of individuals 'being in' *their* landscape, and the sense of place, identity, and belonging that this can produce (Tilley 1994: 15; Seaton 2000). The Western Front, therefore, is not only a historical battle-zone and testament to twentieth-century industrialized war; as with Stonehenge, the Soviet gulags, or Gaza, it is 'something political, dynamic, and contested, something constantly open to renegotiation' (Bender 1993: 276).

The reconstruction of the medieval Belgian town of Ypres is a case in point, as it illustrates competing memories and ideas concerning the shape of the future townscape (Anon. 1999; Various 2020). The architect Eugène Dhuicque said, 'leave the ruins as they are. Why should the thirteenth or fourteenth centuries be of more value than the four years of the World War' (Vermeulen 1999: 10). A similar view was expressed by the British military authorities and veterans' associations, who believed the ruins should be holy ground held in memoriam for soldiers who had died in the Ypres Salient (see Willson 1920). Despite this, post-war Ypres looked backwards rather than forwards, and was dominated by 'much pre-war town-scaping ... [which produced] an ersatsz replica of what was lost forever' (Derez 1997: 450). The debate continues today: 'Ieper is a lie, a missed opportunity. [It could have been] ... the first modern city of this century, a symbol of regrowth, forgiveness and inventiveness'. Instead, 'people prefer the sheltering past to the present and future' (Vermeulen 1999: 9–10).

Ironically, these two landscapes now lie nested one inside the other: the rebuilt mainly thirteenth-century Cloth Hall – the attempt to re-present a glorious medieval past – houses the In Flanders Fields Museum and its chronicling of the First World War which destroyed that past. This landscape relationship has recently been acknowledged by a joint initiative with Ghent University, which has seen the museum bring the war landscape into the museum via innovative audio-visual presentations, and take the museum out into the landscape via apps for mobile phones and tablets, where historical aerial photographs are used to enable GPS augmented-reality walks, and keyed into the planting of 305 memorial trees along the old front lines (Stichelbaut and Chielens 2016; IFFM n.d.) (Figure 1.2). It is perhaps a moot point to what extent these activities represent new landscape and/or museological layers.

Arguably the war's most singular and powerful contribution to defining a modern conflict landscape, so different from all humanity's previous conflicts, was the post-war presence of potentially lethal volatile munitions which could act autonomously. This meant that 'landscapes could now kill and maim indiscriminately, long after conflict had been resolved, and long after the original protagonists had passed away and direct memory of events faded' (Saunders 2001: 46–47). Here was the darker side of the post-war layers of Western Front

FIGURE 1.2 Museum in the landscape: memorial trees outside Ypres, part of a social media–augmented walk. Source: © author.

landscapes, and one which characterized many subsequent twentieth- and twenty-first-century wars; wartime killing had stopped, but war-related deaths had not. Post-war fatalities and injuries are still often elided in accounts of the human cost of war, and of creating this particular layer of the conflict landscape.

Along the Western Front, areas that had between 80 and 100 per cent of the land destroyed were considered too dangerous ever to rebuild or reoccupy. These *zones rouges* formed a new contested landscape, where governments and the military wanted to retain the war-torn terrain as a testament to German aggression and the sacrifice of so many men, and to recognize the land as forever unsafe (Saunders 2001: 42). Local people disagreed, repeatedly challenging such official assessments, with the effect of ever-downward revisions of such areas in the decade after the armistice (Clout 1996: 28–29).

Some areas, however, remain lethal and can contain long-abandoned settlements – the *villages détruits* – such as the French Army training area of Camp de Suippes in Champagne, some 13,500 hectares acquired by the French state in 1922 and containing the remains of five destroyed villages. There is also Moronvilliers, a small village annihilated by the war and later used for French nuclear weapons testing for 50 years, 'adding radioactive waste to the unexploded First World War shells, poison-gas residue and unrecovered bodies' (Isitt 2019: 202). A marker for modern war, this recalls Vietnam today, where digging in such places risks 'being maimed by unexploded ordnance, finding human remains, or perhaps being exposed to toxic residues' as well as to the ghosts of 'wandering souls' (Biggs 2018: 15). More recently in France, tourists, locals, and farmers have all been killed by century-old munitions, as have the *démineurs* of the bomb disposal units, and private collectors too. Whole houses have exploded in Belgium and France in recent decades due to the mishandling of First World War ordnance.

During the inter-war years, children and adults living by the old battlefields were maimed and killed while playing in trenches and dugouts with unexploded bombs and shells, or while scavenging the area for scrap metal for their families to sell to make ends meet (Debaeke 2010: 16, 75–76, 114) or from which to make trench art souvenirs for tourists (Saunders 2003: 146–147) (Figure 1.3). For children and their parents, these areas were peacetime landscapes of civilian trauma, tragedy, and loss (Debaeke 2010: 104–105, 133–134) that is seldom acknowledged or added to the cost of the war in general, or to the price asked for inter-war souvenirs sold to battlefield visitors. Local grief was thereby sublimated to that of pilgrims and tourists who, by purchasing these items, sought to validate their relationship with their own war dead.

At the same time, and in uncomfortable proximity, the search for British and Empire dead was undertaken initially by British military personnel and then the Imperial War Graves Commission (IWGC), subsequently the Commonwealth War Graves Commission (CWGC). Bodies were located, exhumed, and transferred to new concentration cemeteries by Graves Registration Units, a process which inevitably created a new mortuary landscape of smaller abandoned and 'empty' battlefield cemeteries, and the new architectural manicured

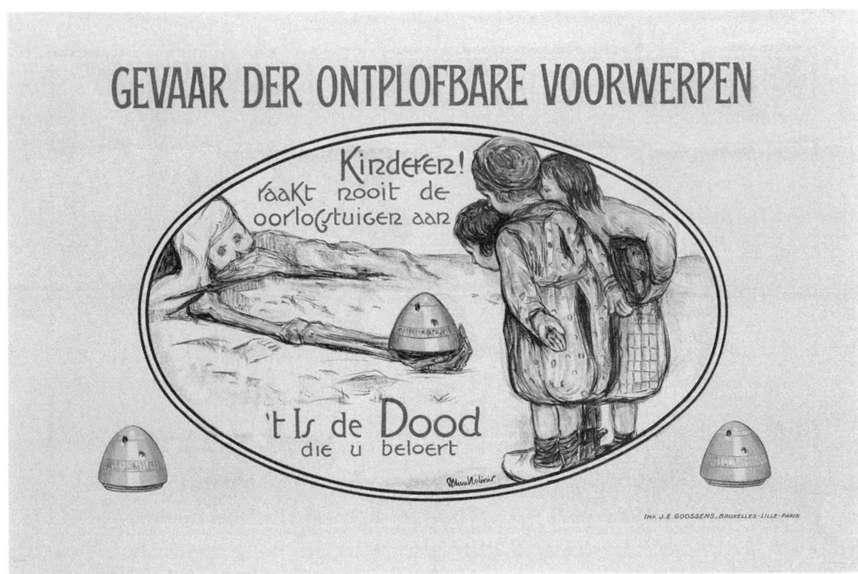

FIGURE 1.3 Inter-war warning to Belgian children not to pick up ordnance. Source: © In Flanders Fields Museum, Ypres.

cemeteries of Portland stone (Longworth 1967; Crane 2013). Even here there were strange new landscape formations – cartographic images of destruction and death, where, for example, it was estimated that some 330,000,000 cubic metres of trenches scarred the French landscape as did some 375,000,000 square metres of barbed wire, with an estimated total of 794,040 buildings destroyed or damaged (Clout 1996: 46, 49). These sat alongside the Graves Registration Units' Body Density Maps which, for example, just south of High Wood on the Somme revealed an almost incomprehensible 808 bodies found in an area of less than 90 by 90 metres (Isitt 2019: 133). Between November 1918 and September 1921, these units exhumed and reburied more than 200,000 bodies. This landscape of moved bodies included national cemeteries for French, German, and Belgian troops as well as those from Britain's dominions, and quickly became part of the commemorative geography of battlefield tourism (see discussion below).

The claws of this conflicted past reach out to the present in unsuspected ways in soils poisoned by gas attacks and artillery barrages. In Belgian Flanders, and along the old Eastern and Italian Fronts, soil and water sources have been polluted by century-old lead shrapnel balls and other military metals (Souvent and Pirc 2001; Van Meirvenne et al. 2008; Laterza et al. 2018; Note et al. 2018). In 2012, 544 communes of the Pas-de-Calais had their tap water declared unsafe for children and pregnant and breastfeeding women (Isitt 2019: 203). Trees grow and prove toxic to humans because wood polluted by high levels of wartime lead are used for oak wine casks and have caused lead poisoning in northern France. Here,

> The tree is an agent, sucking up toxic wartime chemicals through its roots, incorporating them in the fibre of its trunk, and releasing them into wine, where they are then absorbed into the human body. In this complex way, artefactual wartime poison is transformed and carried by natural entities (trees) for a century, then becomes embodied in humans via cultural actions of tree felling, cask making, and wine production and consumption.
>
> *(Saunders 2014: 33)*

In addition to such physical changes to the terrain, the period 1919 to 1939 saw the creation of a vast emotional and monumental landscape of memory, loss, and commemoration as tens of thousands flocked to the old battlefields to remember, honour (and perhaps search for) their loved ones (Lloyd 1998; Evanno and Vincent 2019). While pilgrim-visitors' associations were less with the physical landscape than a symbolic one full of memories glimpsed through letters, postcards, and souvenirs sent home, these visitors nevertheless reshaped the landscape, physically altering it to accommodate the flow of the bereaved. Indeed, the financial basis for reconstruction in the war-devastated regions was strengthened by the money brought into local economies by pilgrimage tourism. The irony was that battlefield visitors' finances paid for the change in the appearance of the landscape – their presence actually distancing them from what they most desired to see.

These short-lived and liminal landscapes were frozen in time by the photographs which illustrated the ubiquitous Pickfords and Michelin Battlefield Guides (see Eksteins 1990), and that portrayed the terrible destruction wrought on villages and cities, cathedrals and countryside. Battlefield visitors tramped across the landscape looking for places associated with their loved ones, seeking to correlate photographs with reality but increasingly encountering disjunction as reconstruction changed the face of the land again (e.g. Elise Guyot quoted in Clout 1996: 44). Battlefields were being cleared, villages rebuilt, and permanent cemeteries and memorials constructed, distancing the 'authentic' battle-zone landscape the foreign visitors desired from the reconstructions so longed for by local inhabitants (Osborne 2001: 79). Many pilgrims had to contend not only with their missing loved ones but also with the vanishing landscape that their loved ones would have known. In this sense, people and places were now missing – both were, at least in part, out of time and out of place.

Moving beyond stable pre-war categories of space, place and time, post-war traumas conjured imaginary landscapes to a bewildering degree. At Carrefour de la Rose outside Boezinge near Ypres, prehistoric megaliths and a sixteenth-century calvary were brought from Brittany to create a monument to the old Breton reservists of the French 45th and 87th Divisions who suffered a devastating German gas attack here on 22 April 1915 (Saunders 2010: 71–72). The resulting monument, augmented by characteristically Breton pine trees, broom, and heather, became a focus for inter-war Breton family pilgrimages and is a geologically and archaeologically/culturally 'impossible' landscape created to conform to Breton post-war memory and commemoration.

Even more unexpected perhaps, and albeit on a smaller scale, were representations of traditional landscapes from Chinese culture and mythology inscribed onto artillery shell-cases by the Chinese Labour Corps (CLC) to sell as striking trench art souvenirs to battlefield pilgrims and tourists (Saunders 2012). These metallic landscapes were complex reifications, bringing together Chinese responses to the geographical and human devastation around them (and which, in part, they were here to clean up) and meshing with the pilgrim-tourist landscape which supplied the purchasers of such artworks. The Western Front continues to be imagined a century after the events. Along the line of the A1 motorway from Calais to Lille (and partly following the old 'no man's land'), was an imagined ribbon of a hundred million poppies – a scarlet floral tribute to those who died at the Battle of the Somme in 1916 – a vast landscape of war remembrance that was never created (Saunders 2013: 1–2).

There was also a curious geographical and cultural expression of 'identity landscape' during the inter-war years, inasmuch as the reconstruction which so disoriented battlefield pilgrims/tourists was also partly funded with money and goods raised by British towns. In the 1920s, the British League of Help for the Devastated Regions of France paired some 80 British towns with 95 French communities (Osborne 2001; Lewis 2006). After sacrificing their menfolk, many now aided in rebuilding the devastated landscapes, formalizing the process by officially pairing themselves with French towns, such as Birmingham and Albert, and Ipswich and Fricourt. Once again, British money changed the face of the battlefields which the bereaved tried increasingly in vain to experience in person, yet which also some could feel a degree of co-identity with through their own charitable donations.

Although most attention has focused on the inter-war battlefield visits of bereaved civilians, ex-soldiers too undertook these journeys (e.g. Relph and Saunders 2019). Henry Williamson on two battlefield tours in 1925 and 1927 kept a record of his thoughts which he reworked for his 1929 book *The Wet Flanders Plain*. His was a landscape inhabited by the ghosts of fallen comrades, and so visiting it was an emotional repayment of debt. 'I must return to my old comrades of the Great War – to the brown, the treeless, the flat and grave-set plain of Flanders – for I am dead with them, and they live in me again' (Williamson 2004: 200).

The Second World War buried these memorial landscapes under new layers of killing and destruction, and from 1945 until the early 1960s the Western Front all but disappeared from popular consciousness. It was a blank period, few visitors and little public interest – a strange era of forgetfulness, waiting, it seems, to be revived. This happened in 1964 with the BBC's epic series *The Great War*, which inspired a revival of battlefield tourism and an accumulation of new landscape layers. From the mid-1960s, and especially after the mid-1990s, visitor numbers burgeoned, as did the diversity of material culture: reconstructed (and sometimes completely bogus) trenches were created as tourist traps, new and revamped cafés and café-museums appeared, as did hotels and book, souvenir, and chocolate shops – all participating in the production of new commercial landscapes of war remembrance, and often signalled by the ubiquitous red poppy (Saunders 2013). These developments were reinforced by the availability of original and recently made war memorabilia, trench art, T-shirts, bags, and badges and confectionery in the shape of British Tommy helmets and poppies – all reifications of the tourist experiential landscape.

After 2000, the Western Front was increasingly dominated by an expanding battlefield tour company market, incorporating schoolchildren visits (Figure 1.4), whose adherence to cross-channel ferry and Eurotunnel schedules made tour itineraries commercially edited landscapes of the war (see Miles 2016: 27–45). And tourists themselves, knowingly and unwittingly, created new experiential places by virtue of 'being in' the landscape (Iles 2008, 2012). They participated in and accelerated the production of new kinds of personal and public memories through engaging with locations whose commercial potential was then developed by the creation of 'new' sites and monuments which subsequent visitors could mistakenly view as part of a genuine wartime landscape, raising the issue of authenticity once again. And then there are the 2014–2018 Centenary levels mentioned above. The tourist layers of the last 30 years or so have selectively

FIGURE 1.4 Schoolchildren visit the Thiepval Monument to the Missing, the Somme, May 2006. Source: © author.

reshaped the landscapes of the First World War, inter-war, and Second World War years.

From the late 1990s, another war landscape appeared on the Western Front as an increasingly professional archaeological engagement (Saunders 2001, 2010: 1–30). It had two parts. First was the ground-level landscape of excavation, previously the domain mainly of serious-minded amateur diggers and others who were little more than looters. In Belgian Flanders and on the Somme, significant benchmark research was undertaken by French, Belgian, and British archaeologists (e.g. Desfossés et al. 2008; Robertshaw and Kenyon 2008; Brown and Osgood 2009; Verdegem this volume; Verdegem et al. 2013; Stichelbaut 2018) – a tacit acknowledgement that First World War archaeology, as part of an interdisciplinary modern conflict archaeology, had come of age (Figure 1.5). Such activities attracted television companies keen to film these investigations and thereby create their own distinctive televisual landscapes (Saunders 2010: 19–20). Yet, even scientific archaeology faced distinctive First World War challenges, which saw 'excavators, landowners, and innumerable tourists struggling to imagine today's verdant woods and fields as monochrome images of Hell, just as returning refugees in 1919 struggled to see devastated landscapes as fertile pastures and farms' (Saunders 2002: 10).

The research potential of engaging with conflict landscapes at ground level is shown by the archaeological investigation of features diagnostic of modern war – shell holes/bomb craters – their survival in the Western Front landscape, and

FIGURE 1.5 Three landscapes in one, France: front-line 1916 trench on the Somme; ongoing excavation, ongoing reconstruction, and initial presentation as a tourist attraction in 2007. Simulacra in the authentic. Source: © author.

their century-long influence on land use and now on heritage valuations (Van den Berghe et al. 2018). The relationship between shell holes and First World War archaeology is insightful; in May 1915, at Gallipoli, Turkish bombardment of Allied French positions created shell damage which ultimately revealed the remains of the ancient Greek city of Elaious, which was then excavated (Mackie 2010: 218–223).

Beyond 1914–1918, the archaeological (excavation) potential of using modern bomb craters to more quickly investigate the deep stratigraphy of ancient sites has been shown at Qasr Shemamok in Iraq, and its long occupation from Assyrian to Ottoman times (Calini et al. 2019). Its most recent fortification by Saddam Hussein's forces was bombed in April 2003 by American F15 or F16 planes, producing six craters, the excavation of one of which – apart from being a case study in 'bombturbation' (Hupy and Schaetz 2006), was an 'operation [which] brought us to experience in a concrete way the correlation between the traces of the most ancient and the most recent past' (Calini et al. 2019: 232–233; and see Mackie 2010).

The second part was the above-ground landscape, which involved the technological innovations of LiDAR and GIS which, amongst other things, enabled century-old wartime aerial photographs to be digitized and manipulated with and supplemented by modern remote sensing imagery in computer software (e.g. Stichelbaut and Chielens 2014; Stichelbaut and Cowley 2016; Taborelli et al.

2017; Van den Berghe et al. 2018; Gheyle et al. 2018; and see Bezzi et al. this volume). LiDAR imagery can be startling – a bird's-eye view which penetrates vegetation cover to reveal the physical landscape beneath (Figures 1.6a and b).

These developments created a whole new research agenda – a digital landscape layer of conflict (in fact many overlapping layers) which added ever more kinds of meaning and value to battle-zone investigations, to inform and guide archaeological excavations of medieval and prehistoric as well as First World War sites, to help define heritage priorities, and to present all these to the public in innovative audio-visual, augmented reality, and social media ways (Stichelbaut and Chielens 2016).

These developments have produced a challenging layering of vertical space and distance, where archaeological trenching investigates previous wartime trenches, guided by 100-year-old trench maps produced from contemporary aerial photographs (now digitized and georectified by GIS) and which themselves overlaid and incorporated far older pre-war ditches, channels, and defensive

FIGURE 1.6 a and b Landscape revealed: the Bellewaarde Ridge outside Ypres – showing (a) the landscape today, and (b) 1915–1917 craters on the ridge and faint traces of cratered landscape in undisturbed grassland north of the wood. Source: (a) Orthophoto – open data Department Information Flanders; (b) Sky View factor visualization of high-resolution Digital Terrain Model II Flanders. Source: © author.

FIGURE 1.6 Continued

earthworks stretching back into history. Here, technology brings together different kinds of evidence to reveal long-forgotten relationships between people, material culture, and landscape, though not always without cost (see Saunders 2009).

Over the last 20 years, the Western Front has undergone an increasingly analytical layering of landscapes, each layer embodying a different social experience and use of space, and sitting on and sometimes cutting into previous layers from yesterday to prehistory. Investigating these layers, often with new technologies, contributes a more nuanced understanding of conflict landscapes of the Western Front, and beyond. Indeed, the idea and potential of doing interdisciplinary modern conflict archaeology at all, and particularly in relation to older, more established archaeological periods, has moved beyond the First World War in France and Belgium as the varied chapters in this volume demonstrate (and see e.g. Košir et al. 2019a; Shapland and Stefani 2017; Yioutsos 2017).

The Soča/Isonzo Front

The multi-layer conflict landscape described for the Western Front also existed in the battle-zone of the Soča/Isonzo Front along the border of modern Italy and

Slovenia. Arguably the layering can be seen more clearly here, as the northern and central parts of the Soča Valley are comparatively rural and remote, without high levels of urban development. Also, the density and diversity of investigations and literature which characterizes the well-documented Western Front are largely absent for the Soča Valley – the lack of overwhelming detail facilitating the initial identification of suggested palimpsestic layers.

The fighting on the Soča/Isonzo Front was some of the bloodiest of the First World War, with 12 battles between the Italians and the Austro-Hungarians and their German allies between May 1915 and October 1917 (Schindler 2001; Thompson 2008). The initial conflict landscape created by these actions preserves a unique anthropological and archaeological record of a multinational and multi-ethnic war waged across topographically diverse terrain. The subsequent post-war layers began with the 1918 annexation of the Soča/Isonzo Valley by Italy. This subsequently enabled Mussolini to remobilize the Italian war dead and create a commemorative landscape of Fascist monuments during the inter-war years, notably the ossuaries at Kobarid (Italian *Caporetto*), Redipuglia, and Oslavia. Further layers were added during the Second World War, and then again under Communist rule in Yugoslavia. Here, post-1918 conflict landscapes have been embedded within those of the First World War, creating a complex layering of modern warfare and enduring legacies similar to but also different from those along the Western Front.

Archaeological and anthropological investigations along the Soča Valley between 2009 and 2013 began identifying, documenting, and analyzing the area's conflict landscape, through historical research, reconnaissance, excavation, topographic assessments, and ethnographic interviews. The valley landscape was initially conceptualized as having 13 layers in order to capture as much evidence as possible, each layer characterized by a different engagement with space, and manifesting a distinct configuration of material culture, rather than being strictly chronologically distinct. A detailed description of these layers is given elsewhere (Saunders et al. 2013), but a brief outline here demonstrates the approach and contributes to our understanding of how such landscapes are created and how they might best be investigated.

Austro-Hungarian militarized landscape pre-1914

Austro-Hungarian militarized landscape 1914–1915

Austro-Hungarian/Italian conflict landscape May 1915–October 1917

Austro-Hungarian/German/Italian conflict landscape (Caporetto) October 1917

Post-war clearance, civilian recycling, and returning refugees re-settlement landscape 1920s and 1930s

Post-war body retrieval, old cemetery clearances, and new cemetery mortuary landscape 1920s and 1930s, including the building of monumental Italian ossuaries

Italian construction of new militarized landscape of the *Vallo Alpino* 1936–1943

Second World War Italian/German/Allied conflict landscape 1940–1945

Post–Second World War memorial-commemorative landscape 1945–1950s. First World War landscape (especially cemeteries) forgotten and abandoned 1945–1970s
Further clearance of First World War *matériel* by enthusiasts, re-enactors, and militaria collectors landscape 1960s–1990s
Memorial heritage (cemeteries and memorials), renovation, and artistic commemoration landscape 1980s–present
Open-air museums, restoration, and 'Walks of Peace' landscape 2000–present
Commemorative events and archaeological research landscape 2010–present

The first layer represents Austro-Hungarian Army presence before 1914, as evidenced for example by the 1882 construction of Fort Kluže (Simić 2005: 106), while the second layer, from 1914 to May 1915, saw new trenches, shelters, and military roads constructed on Mengore Hill (Klavora 2004: 26–31). Layer three includes the remains of the 11 large-scale Italian offensives between 1915 and 1917 (Schindler 2001: 41–265), with layer four belonging to the combined Austro-Hungarian and German attack on 24 October 1917 ('The Battle of Caporetto') and its aftermath – a rapid 18-kilometre advance on the first day, and the withdrawal of Italian forces on 28 October to the Piave River some 200 kilometres west of the Soča Valley (Schindler 2001: 243–265; Simić 1998: 178, 226). As Austro-Hungarian and German troops advanced into Italy, behind them in the Soča Valley special salvage companies (*Sammelkompanien*) were already collecting abandoned weaponry and war debris, a process that extended into 1918 (Lipovec 2013: 9, 198–100) so that by war's end some battle-zones had already been cleared.

Layer five, the immediate post-war era of the 1920s, saw returning refugees clearing more war debris, collecting and selling metals, and rebuilding their homes along the devastated valley (Pirih 2005: 38). This changed the landscape irrevocably, as removing, burying, and recycling elements of the preceding (and sometimes already partially cleared) war layers meant that pristine battlefields largely ceased to exist – a crucial factor in understanding the character of and relationship between layers. The sixth layer, distinct from yet contemporary with the fifth, was created by the Italian Army moving the dead from battlefields and battlefield cemeteries to larger concentration cemeteries and ossuaries along the valley. It is ambiguous for several reasons: battlefield cemeteries were not always totally cleared of human remains, Austro-Hungarian cemeteries were reconfigured and grave markers re-inscribed by the Italians (Košir 2019: 187) (Figure 1.7); the new mortuary landscape was smaller than its predecessor as at war's end there were about 2,591 (or 2,876, sources vary) battlefield cemeteries, but only 349 after consolidation (of which only 64 have been restored today) (Fortunat Černilogar 2005: 94). Also, Mussolini's monumental ossuaries housed Italian dead transferred from their original (and often individually named) battlefield graves to the anonymizing charnel houses at Kobarid, Redipuglia, and Oslavia (ibid.: 95). Layer six's mass movement of

FIGURE 1.7 Four landscapes in one, Slovenia: Austro-Hungarian wartime cemetery of Brje pri Komnu 4, rebuilt with graves re-inscribed post-war by Italians, Slovenian renovation 2003, and Czech commemorative ribbon 2012–2013. Source: © author.

dead bodies was paralleled by that of the living – thousands of Italians joining pilgrimages to ossuaries which quickly became the foci of fascist political rallies during the inter-war years.

A seventh layer partly overlapped with the sixth from the 1930s until 1943. In some remote areas of the upper Soča Valley were built sections of the Alpine Wall (*Vallo Alpino*), a new Italian fortification system (Anon. n.d.; Bernasconi and Muran 2009) (Figure 1.8). In some locations, it overlaid or was incorporated into remnants of the First World War conflict landscape, such as the system of concrete extensions to the tunnel that leads to Fort Hermann above Fort Kluže (Simić 2005: 303).

The Second World War created layer eight, less extensive than preceding ones, but sometimes having an intimate relationship with them. For example, German troops dug trenches around their small First World War ossuary near Tolmin, repurposing it as a fortified position, and also altered some elements of Fort Kluže (Klavora 2000: 47; Simić 2005: 303). The ninth layer, between 1945 and the 1970s, saw new cemeteries and memorials to the partisans and the national liberation movement – marking the guerrilla war of 1941–1945 between Italians, Germans, local fascists, and Yugoslav partisans. This period also marked the nadir of interest in First World War cemeteries and places, which were abandoned to deterioration (Košir 2019: 189–190).

FIGURE 1.8 Camouflaged 'natural' landscape bunker of the late 1930s Italian Alpine Wall (*Vallo Alpino*) superimposed on the First World War landscape of the Tolminka Valley, part of the Soča Valley conflict landscape. Source: © author.

The tenth layer emerged during the 1980s as a nascent First World War heritage landscape with commemorative sites being conserved and some military cemeteries renovated. The result was a patchwork, some sites altered, others not, but there was an important shift in public perception. The tenth layer's changes were obvious to local people but could easily be misinterpreted by others who might consider all such sites as equally conserved, renovated, or perhaps even mainly in their original condition. The issue of perceptions of authenticity parallels the situation on the Western Front during the 2000s, where an increasing influx of visitors stimulated 'new' and/or reconstructed places which later visitors mistook for the original or near-original war landscape.

The eleventh layer was partly a consequence of Slovenia's 1991 independence when interest in the First World War gathered momentum and militaria collectors began clearing the battlefields (especially at high altitudes) of remaining *matériel* for sale at militaria fairs and for adding to personal collections and private museums (Košir 2019: 190, 193; Kravanja 2018; Repic 2018). Old battlefield landscapes were largely emptied of their remaining objects which, by being moved, were recycled/re-categorized into a new museological landscape. When combined with the effects of battle-zone clearance and recycling of materials of the 1920s, it is clear that such areas today are mostly not pristine survivals from 1915–1918, but the result of a century's selective alteration.

More recently, the twelfth layer has been added, composed of modern heritage-related activities. In 2000, the Walks of Peace Foundation was established and initiated a programme of restoring First World War military features and memorials (Koren 2008). Six open-air museums have so far been created, including those at Kolovrat and Mrzli Vrh (ibid.: 103–105, 140–145). Elsewhere, other restorations have sometimes been problematic, for instance, at the Austro-Hungarian cemetery at Dutovlje on the Carso (Košir 2019: 193).

The power of the present to rejuvenate and re-inscribe the past is shown by two even more recent developments which arguably form a thirteenth layer. First is the trend to hold official and unofficial commemorative events at First World War locations, sometimes leaving ephemeral (but occasionally permanent) material reminders. The largest of these to date was a re-enactment on 17 September 2017 which took place on the actual battlefield of Kolovrat and commemorated the events of 24 October 1917 (part of the Battle of Caporetto) (Košir et al. 2019b: 104–105). Significantly, and almost certainly, some of the century-old fallen still lie beneath the grassy slopes where the re-enactment took place. The second development was the beginning of modern scientific archaeological investigations of the First World War along the Soča/Isonzo Valley in 2010, and which is ongoing (see Košir et al. 2019a; Saunders et al. 2013).

All of these layers of conflict- and post-conflict-related activity from the beginning of the twentieth century to the present reveal the diversity and complexity of the Soča/Isonzo Valley as a modern conflict landscape, likely accentuated by its status as a long-contested border region. In attempting to classify and understand these layers and the social worlds they represent, we gain important insights into the formation of many other conflict landscapes and the ongoing processes by which such places constantly change their shape and significance.

The Middle East

The Middle East offers different First World War perspectives on the formation and character of modern conflict landscapes. Here, I draw on the archaeological evidence of British-Arab actions against the Ottoman Turkish Hejaz Railway line from Damascus to Medina which were a central feature of the Arab Revolt of 1916–1918 (Saunders 2020). Not only was the Revolt nested within the First World War, but it was also a meeting of traditional Bedouin tactics and modern technology to create what was, in effect, the world's first modern guerrilla landscape. Given the influence of guerrilla tactics on twentieth-century conflict, the Arab Revolt offers sharp insights into the character of many post-1918 conflict landscapes – not least the rapid advance of Islamic State in the same region in 2014 and using the same tactics as the British in 1917–1918.

There are key differences between the conflict landscapes of southern Jordan and the Western Front: the first is geological, as the stony desert allows mainly for a thin surface layer in this conflict zone, and so archaeologically there is horizontal rather than vertical stratigraphy, with traces of conflict being ephemeral and fragile (Figure 1.9). A second difference is the asymmetric nature of the conflict – hit-and-run tactics leaving only marginal traces. Yet, while both of the above argue against good preservation, there are countervailing factors. First, the remoteness of the area produced well-preserved sites along the Hejaz Railway, a geographical fact reinforced by several cultural ones: the lack of interest in recent historical archaeology in an area of rich prehistoric, classical, and Islamic remains; the non-recognition of the post–AD 1750 period, and thus the First World War, as archaeological. One significant result of this mix of issues is that guerrilla actions measured only in minutes, or an hour, have left traces of conflict which have endured for more than a century.

There are many examples of this along the route of the Hejaz Railway; the Hallat Ammar ambush illustrates the process of conflict landscape formation and its easily misinterpreted character particularly well. On 19 September 1917, T.E. Lawrence and a group of Bedouin and British soldiers blew up a railway bridge and Turkish train at Kilometre 587 in what is today a remote demilitarized zone between Jordan and Saudi Arabia. The birth pangs of this landscape were captured by Lawrence:

> there followed a terrific roar, and the line vanished from sight behind a jetted column of black dust and smoke a hundred feet high and wide. Out of the darkness came shattering crashes and long, loud metallic clangings

FIGURE 1.9 Horizontal stratigraphy at Wadi Rutm Turkish Army Camp (c. 1917–1918), southern Jordan. Turkish star-and-crescent army button, padlock, two broken spoons, and a prehistoric flint tool. Source: © author.

> of ripped steel, while many lumps of iron and plate, with one entire wheel of a locomotive, whirled up suddenly black out of the cloud against the sky, and sailed musically over our heads to fall slowly and heavily into the desert behind.
>
> *(Lawrence 2003: 407)*

There followed a one-sided firefight in which the attackers suffered one killed and a handful wounded, while the Turks lost about 70 dead, 30 wounded, and 80 taken prisoner in a scene of carnage and plunder which lasted less than ten minutes (ibid.: 405–407). These events were immortalized by Lawrence in *Seven Pillars of Wisdom* and then visually as the iconic scene in David Lean's 1962 Hollywood epic *Lawrence of Arabia*. For a century, three versions of events circulated – the historical, the literary, and the cinematic – all layered one on top of the other, and each with its own distinctive landscape.

In 2013, there was an archaeological investigation of the site, by which time, despite its isolation, it was no longer the pristine remains of the Arab Revolt, but rather a layering of the intervening century's activities, disturbing, overlaying, and obscuring the original events (Figure 1.10). These included immediate post-ambush repairs and fortification by the Turks, subsequent abandonment and then short-lived reuse of the railway, later conflict with Saudi Arabia, an

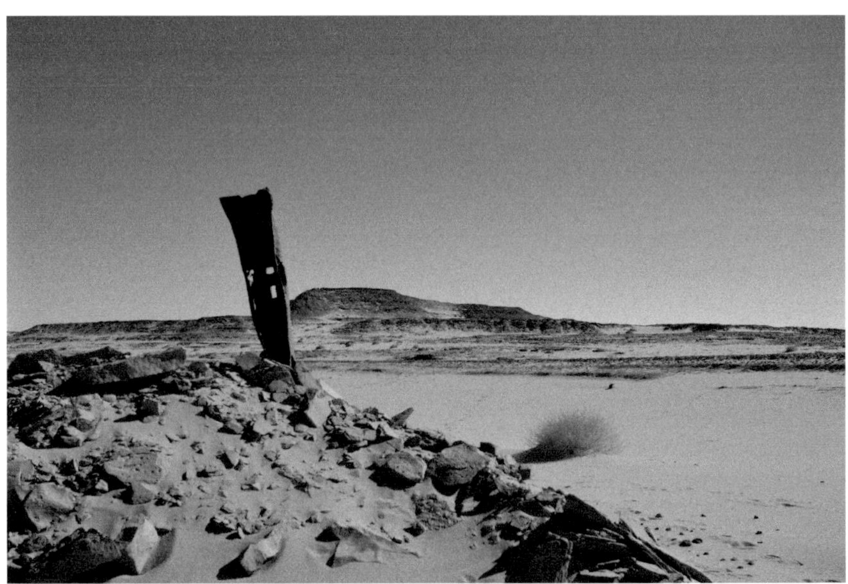

FIGURE 1.10 Hallat Ammar 1917 ambush site, southern Jordan. A shattered railway sleeper with the ambush-site railway embankment in the middle distance and a post-ambush hill-top Turkish fort dominating the horizon. Source: © author.

abortive 1960s refurbishment of railway infrastructure including a second repair and rebuilding of track and bridge, plus significant bulldozer clearance of the area. In one sense this was the archaeology of ten minutes, but in another sense, it was anything but.

The Hallat Ammar ambush is an extreme example to make a point concerning the character of a modern conflict landscape, including here the role of cinema in creating and perpetuating a powerful popular view of events. Nevertheless, even an outline profile of such a place in southern Jordan reveals a rich corpus of interleaving elements requiring careful interpretation. These include,

- Remains of the traditional Ottoman Hajj route
- Remains of the construction era of the Hejaz Railway 1900–1908
- Remains of Turkish railway defences and Arab-British raids on the railway between August 1917 and September 1918
- Remains of Turkish repairs to the railway in the wake of Arab-British attacks
- Evidence of short-lived post-war repair and reuse of the railway between 1919 and the mid-1920s
- Evidence of abandonment and robbing in the late 1920s to early 1960s
- Vernacular architecture composed of re-used railway sleepers and rails in Arab houses
- Abortive refurbishment of the railway during the 1960s
- Partial rebuilding of the railway during the 1970s to carry phosphate trains
- Bulldozing and robbing of Hejaz Railway sites from the 1970s to the present

Despite the fame of T.E. Lawrence, his *Seven Pillars of Wisdom*, the Hollywood film, and the iconic Hejaz Railway, most of this conflict landscape has not been touristified; it remains unprotected by heritage legislation, and open to irreversible damage from urban development, robbing for building materials, and ad hoc digging and bulldozer destruction in search of gold. The Arab Revolt conflict landscape of 1916–1918 is distinctively configured (see Winterburn this volume) by its role in shaping the Middle East and by bequeathing guerrilla warfare to the world, but also shares its volatile palimpsestic nature with the Soča/Isonzo Valley and the Western Front.

Conclusions

The world's first industrialized global war created the first modern conflict landscape. Later conflicts added new dimensions: civilian strife in the Spanish Civil War, blitzed cities, the Holocaust, atomic devastation in the Second World War, Cold War nuclear proliferation, and more recently, satellite imagery, GIS, and robot and drone technologies; but the First World War forged the template.

Until 1914, conflict landscapes shared most of their characteristics with other landscapes – physical places whose symbolic dimensions endured only as long as individual or group memory permitted. Pre-twentieth-century battlefields did not arbitrarily generate new lethal conditions, though new meanings and significances could always be given by those who occupied them. From Megiddo (Armageddon) to Agincourt, from Marathon to Waterloo, historic battlefield landscapes were deadly mainly only to the combatants and only while fighting continued. The First World War changed this forever by creating proactive landscapes that killed and maimed autonomously and indiscriminately for decades (now more than a century) afterwards.

Apart from the deadly physical legacy, there was the sheer number of dead, missing, and wounded, which required a unique memorializing response across the world as monuments, cemeteries, and annual commemorative events to remember the fallen. To these names (actual and 'unknown') were subsequently added those who died in later conflicts, making war memorials miniature palimpsests, and always incomplete – leaving space for future names – memorials as 'ongoing process' rather than finished business.

What emerges from the First World War is that its battlefields are fundamentally different from all previous kinds of war-zone spaces. A modern conflict landscape is not a single stable place in history, but a volatile metaphysical location capable of countless iterations over time – united only by death, suffering, and loss, for victor and vanquished alike, though propaganda spinning can make them appear different. A modern conflict landscape then is indeed a concept, an ever-changing set of actions and consequences, rooted in a place and a primary event, but once born/created, it is let loose on history and its followers.

A landscape of modern conflict possesses elements common to all such battle-zone places back into history – bodies and body parts, weapons and their fragments, personal belongings, possibly a monument, and a variable presence in ideology and cultural and political memory, ranging from invisibility to a founding myth (see Saunders et al. 2019). Issues of tourism, pilgrimage, heritage, and damage to authenticity are also variously shared by these historical battle-zone landscapes. To these however are added five key elements uniquely created by the First World War – *none of which are present in pre-modern conflict landscapes, but most of which exist variably in all post-1918 conflict terrains.*

- A landscape which can autonomously kill and maim decades (probably centuries) after conflict has ended and protagonists are long dead, due to unexploded ordnance
- A landscape which can poison its inhabitants long after conflict ends due to 'invisible' contamination of soil, water, and crops
- A landscape which is archaeologically variable; the constant is evidence of modern conflict, while the variable is evidence of (usually) earlier archaeology – Palaeolithic, Bronze Age, Iron Age, Classical Antiquity, or medieval.

Each landscape is thus a unique combination of modern and pre-modern remains arranged in a distinctive 'conflict layer'

- A landscape which creates/perpetuates the concept of 'the missing'
- A landscape which, contextualized by the nineteenth-century rise in nationalism, can be endlessly politicized, reinterpreted, and buttressed by ideology, and subsequently by ideas of heritage

Whatever else the First World War reveals about a modern conflict landscape, it demonstrates that such a landscape is not a safe or stable entity with one unchangeable set of meanings and values. In southern Jordan, it is the landscape of imperial Ottoman collapse and the rise of modern guerrilla warfare. On the Western and Italian fronts, it variously incorporates dangerous areas of unexploded munitions and environmental poisoning and heritage and tourism places where 'new attractions' can be simulacra which obscure the authentic, alienating those elements that gave the place its original value and meaning. A modern conflict landscape also has a unique relationship with the deeper past through its stratigraphic relationship with earlier archaeologies. No single modern conflict landscape possesses all the characteristics explored here, but there can be no doubt that such locations can be physically dangerous and metaphysically volatile for a far longer time than the military events which created them. Such places did not exist before 1914; today they are everywhere.

References

Anon. (1999) Verwoest Gewest, Ieper 1919-. *In Flanders FieldsMagazine* 1 (2): 12–15.

Anon. (2020) *Northwestern Syria Offensive* (December 2019-March 2020). Wikipedia. https://en.wikipedia.org/wiki/Northwestern_Syria_offensive_(December_2019%E2%80%93March_2020) Accessed 5 May 2020.

Anon. (n.d.) *A Guide to the Fortifications of the Italian Alpine Wall in Eastern Alps and Carso (1920–1943).* www.valloalpino.com/index_en.htm Accessed 5 September 2013.

Audoin-Rouzeau, S. (1992) *Men at War 1914–1918: National Sentiment and Trench Journalism in France during the First World War.* Oxford: Berg.

Barbusse, H. (2003 [1926]). *Under Fire.* London: Penguin.

Barthas, L. (2014) *Poilu: The World War I Notebooks of Corporal Louis Barthas, Barrelmaker 1914–1918* (transl. E.M. Straus). New Haven, CT: Yale University Press.

Basso, K.H. (1996) *Wisdom Sits in Places: Landscape and Language among the Western Apache.* Albuquerque: University of New Mexico Press.

Bender, B. (1993) Stonehenge – Contested Landscapes (Medieval to Present-Day). In B. Bender (ed.), *Landscape: Politics and Perspectives*, pp. 245–279. Oxford: Berg.

Bernasconi, A. and G. Muran. (2009) *Il testimone di cemento – Le fortificazioni del 'Vallo Alpino Littorio' in Cadore, Carnia e Tarvisiano.* Udine: Editore La Nuova Base Editrice.

Bernède, A. (1997) Third Ypres and the Restoration of Confidence in the Ranks of the French Army. In P.H. Liddle (ed.), *Passchendaele in Perspective: The Third Battle of Ypres*, pp. 324–332. London: Leo Cooper.

Biggs, D. (2018) *Footprints of War: Militarized Landscapes in Vietnam.* Seattle: University of Washington Press.

Brown, M. (2017) *First World War Fieldworks in England*. Research Report Series 61- 2017. Portsmouth: Historic England and WYG Planning & Environment.

Brown, M. and R. Osgood. (2009) *Digging up Plugstreet: The Western Front unearthed*. Yeovil: Haynes Publishing.

Calini,I., J-J Herr and M.G. Masetti-Rouault. (2019) Craters at Qasr Shemamok (Kurdistan, Iraq) Opportunities and Problems for Excavations. In J. Bessenay-Prolonge, J-J. Herr, M. Mura and A. Havé (eds.), *Archéologie des Conflits/ Archéologie en Conflits: Documenter La Destruction au Moyen-Orient et en Asie Centrale*, pp. 225–248. Paris: Routes de L'Orient Revue de L'Orient Ancien, Actes II.

Chasseaud, P. (2006) *Rats Alley: Trench Names of the Western Front 1914–1918*. Stroud: Spellmount.

Chielens, P., D. Dendooven and H. Decoot (eds.) (2006) *De Laatste Getuige: Het oorlogslanschap van de Westhoe*. Tielt: Lanoo.

Clout, H. (1996) *After The Ruins: Restoring the Countryside of Northern France after the Great War*. Exeter: University of Exeter Press.

Cocroft, W. and P. Stamper (eds.) (2018) *Legacies of the First World War: Building for Total War 1914–1918*. Swindon: Historic England.

Crane, E. (2013) *Empires of the Dead*. London: William Collins.

Daniels, S. and D. Cosgrove. (1988) Introduction: Iconography and Landscape. In S. Daniels and D. Cosgrove (eds.), *The Iconography of Landscape*, pp. 1–10. Cambridge: Cambridge University Press.

Debaeke, S. (2010) *Oud Ijzer: De frontstreek bedolven onder levensgevaarlijke oorlogsmunitie*. Brugge: De Klaproos.

Derez, M. (1997) A Belgian Salient for Reconstruction: People and *Patrie*, Landscape and Memory. In P.H. Liddle (ed.), *Passchendaele in Perspective: The Third Battle of Ypres*, pp. 437–458. London: Leo Cooper.

Desfossés, Y., A. Jacques and G. Prilaux. (2008) *L'archéologie de la Grande Guerre*. Rennes : Éditions Ouest-France.

Devos, A., P. Taborelli, T. Damien, N. Bollot, A. Blanc, G. Fronteau, S. Laratte, O. Lejeune, Y. Desfosses and M. Embry. (2017) La Grande Guerre sur La Côte D'Île-De-France, en Champagne Crayeuse er en Argonne Journées d'Études d'Automne 8- Octobre 2016. *Bulletin Inf. Géol. bass. Paris* 54 (3): 3–19.

Doyle, P. (2017) *Disputed Earth: Geology and Trench Warfare on the Western Front 1914–1918*. London: Uniform Press.

Dyer, G. (1994) *The Missing of the Somme*. London: Penguin.

Eksteins, M. (1990) *The Rites of Spring: The Great War and the Birth of the Modern Age*. Boston: Houghton Mifflin.

Evanno, Y-M. and J. Vincent (eds.) (2019) *Tourisme et Grande Guerre. Voyage(s) sur un Front Historique méconnu (1914–2019)*. Ploemeur: Éditions Codex.

Fortunat Černilogar, D. (2005) Kje Stoji jim Grobni križ? In P. Svoljšak, D. Pirih, D. Fortunat Černilogar and L. Galić (eds.), *Tolminsko mostišče II*, pp. 85–105. Tolmin: Tolminski muzej.

Garfi, S. (2019) *Conflict Landscapes: An Archaeology of the International Brigades in the Spanish Civil War*. Oxford: Archaeopress.

Gheyle, W., B. Stichelbaut, T. Saey, N. Note, H. Van den Berghe, V. Van Eetvelde, M. Van Meirvenne and J. Bourgeois. (2018) Scratching the Surface of War. Airborne Laser Scans of the Great War Conflict Landscape in Flanders (Belgium). *Applied Geography* 90: 55–68.

Giono, J. (2004 [1931]) *To the Slaughterhouse*. London: Peter Owen Publishers.

González-Ruibal, A. (2008) Time to Destroy: An Archaeology of Supermodernity. *Current Anthropology* 49 (2): 247–279.

Himpe, K. (2018) Protecting the Scars: A Century of Heritage Policy. In B. Stichelbaut (ed.), *Traces of War: The Archaeology of the First World War*, pp. 170–181. Veurne: Hannibal Publishing.

Hirsch, E. (1995) Introduction: Landscape: Between Place and Space. In E. Hirsch and M. O'Hanlon (eds.), *The Anthropology of Landscape: Perspectives on Place and Space*, pp. 1–20. Oxford: Clarendon Press.

Howes, D. (1991) Introduction: 'To Summon All the Senses'. In D. Howes (ed.), *The Varieties of Sensory Experience*, pp. 3–21.Toronto: University of Toronto Press.

Hupy, J.P. and R.J. Schaetzl. (2006) Introducing 'Bombturbation', a Singular Type of Soil Disturbance and Mixing. *Soil Science* 171 (11): 823–836.

IFFM (n.d.) www.inflandersfields.be/en/in-flanders-fields-museum-e/oorlogslandschap-e/

Iles, J. (2006) Recalling the Ghosts of War: Performing Tourism on the Battlefields of the Western Front. *Text and Performance Quarterly* 26 (2): 162–180.

——— (2008) Encounters on the Fields – Tourism to the Battlefields of the Western Front. *Journal of Tourism and Cultural Change* 6 (2): 138–154.

——— (2012) Exploring Landscapes After Battle: Tourists at Home on the Old Front Lines. In J. Skinner (ed.), *Writing the Dark Side of Travel*, pp. 182–202. New York: Berghahn.

Isitt, T. (2019) *Riding in the Zone Rouge: The Tour of the Battlefields 1919 – Cycling's Toughest-Ever Stage Race*. London: Weidenfeld & Nicolson.

Klavora, V. (2000) *Plavi križ: Soška fronta: Bovec 1915–1917* (second edition). Celovec: Mohorjeva družba.

——— (2004) *Koraki skozi meglo: Soška fronta: Kobarid, Tolmin 1915–1917*. Celovec: Mohorjeva družba.

Koren, T. (2008) *The Walk of Peace: A Guide Along the Isonzo Front in the Upper Soča Region* (transl. B. Klemenc). Kobarid: The 'Walks of Peace in the Soča Region Foundation'.

Košir, U. (2019) Legacies of the Soča Front – From Rubbish to Heritage (1915–2017). In U. Košir, M. Črešnar and D. Mlekuž (eds.), *Forgotten Fronts, Enduring Legacies: Archaeology and the Great War on the Soča and Eastern Fronts*, pp. 181–198. London: Routledge.

Košir, U., M. Črešnar and D. Mlekuž (eds.) (2019a) *Forgotten Fronts, Enduring Legacies: Archaeology and the Great War on the Soča and Eastern Fronts*. London: Routledge.

Košir, U., N.J. Saunders, M. Črešnar and G. Rutar. (2019b) Between Tourism and Oblivion: Rombon and Kolovrat – Conflict Landscapes on the Soča Front, 1915–2017. In U. Košir, M. Črešnar and D. Mlekuž (eds.), *Forgotten Fronts, Enduring Legacies: Archaeology and the Great War on the Soča and Eastern Fronts*, pp. 90–108. London: Routledge.

Kravanja, B. (2018) Learning by Collecting: Amateur Collectors and Their Shifting Positions in the Isonzo Front Heritagization and Tourism Adaptation. *Folklore* 73: 95–116.

Laterza, V., C. Turetta, J. Gabrieli, W.R.L. Cairns, E. Balliana, C. Baroni, S.M. Cristina, A. Bondesan and C. Barbante. (2018) Chemical and Lead Isotope Characterisation of First World War Shrapnel Balls and Bullets Used on the Alpine Austrian–Italian Front. *Scientia Militaria: South African Journal of Military Studies* 46 (1): 163–187.

Latour, B. (2006) Air. In C.A. Jones (ed.), *Sensorium. Embodied Experience, Technology, and Contemporary Art*, pp. 105–107. Cambridge, MA: MIT Press.

Lawrence, T.E. (2003) *Seven Pillars of Wisdom, a Triumph. The Complete 1922 Text.* (Second edition with amendments. Jeremy and Nicole Wilson). Fordingbridge: Castle Hill Press.

Layton, R. and P.J. Ucko. (1999) Introduction: Gazing on the Landscape and Encountering the Environment. In P.J. Ucko and R. Layton (eds.), *The Archaeology of Landscape: Shaping Your Landscape*, pp. 1–20. London: Routledge.

Leonard, M. (2016) *Beneath the Killing Fields: Exploring the Subterranean Landscapes of the Western Front.* Barnsley: Pen & Sword Archaeology.

——— (2019) A Sensorial No Man's Land: Corporeality and the Western Front During the First World War. *Senses and Society* 14 (3): 258–270.

Lewis, B.F. (2006) *Adoptive Kinship and the British League of Help: Commemoration of the Great War through the Adoption of French Communities.* PhD dissertation, Department of History, University of Reading.

Lipovec, A. (2013) *Vedno kot pri Bovcu/Always Like at Bovec.* Logatec: Vojni muzej Logatec.

Lloyd, D.W. (1998) *Battlefield Tourism: Pilgrimage and the Commemoration of the Great War in Britain, Australia and Canada, 1919–1939.* Oxford: Berg.

Longworth, P. (1967) *The Unending Vigil.* London: Constable & Co.

Mackie, C.J. (2010) Archaeology at Gallipoli in 1915. In A.M. Tamis, C.J. Mackie, and S. Byrne (eds.), *Philathenaios: Studies in Honour of Michael J. Osborne*, pp. 213–225. Athens: Greek Epigraphic Society.

Masefield, J. (2003 [1917]) *The Old Front Line.* Barnsley: Pen & Sword.

Miles, S. (2016) *The Western Front: Landscape, Tourism and Heritage.* Barnsley: Pen and Sword.

Note, N., W. Gheyle, H. Van den Berghe, T. Saeya, J. Bourgeois, V. Van Eetvelde, M. Van Meirvenne and B. Stichelbaut. (2018) A new Evaluation Approach of World War One's Devastated Front Zone: A Shell Hole Density Map Based on Historical Aerial Photographs and Validated by Electromagnetic Induction Field Measurements to Link the Metal Shrapnel Phenomenon. *Geoderma* 310: 257–269.

Osborne, B.S. (2001) In the Shadows of Monuments: The British League for the Reconstruction of the Devastated Areas of France. *International Journal of Heritage Studies* 7 (1): 59–82.

Paterson, A. (1997) Bravery in the Field? In J.E. Lewis (Introd.), *True World War One Stories: Sixty Personal Narratives of the War*, pp. 239–46. London: Robinson Publishing.

Pirih, D. (2005) Kam so vsi ti Fantje šli… In P. Svoljšak, D. Pirih, D. Fortunat Černilogar and L. Galić (eds.), *Tolminsko mostišče II*, pp. 27–43. Tolmin: Tolminski muzej.

Relph, M. and N.J Saunders. (2019) The Italian Front on the Soča (Isonzo): A British Officers' Military Tour in 1923. In U. Košir, M. Črešnar and D. Mlekuž (eds.), *Rediscovering the Great War: Archaeology and Enduring Legacies on the Soča and Eastern Fronts*, pp. 9–26. London: Routledge.

Repic, J. (2018) Memorialization of the First World War in the Landscape of the Julian Alps. *Folklore* 73: 7–18.

Robertshaw, A. and D. Kenyon. (2008) *Digging the Trenches: The Archaeology of the Western Front.* Barnsley: Pen & Sword.

Saunders, N.J. (2001) Matter and Memory in the Landscapes of Conflict: The Western Front 1914–1999. In B. Bender and M. Winer (eds.), *Contested Landscapes: Movement, Exile and Place*, pp. 37–53. Oxford: Berg.

——— (2002) Excavating Memories: Archaeology and the Great War, 1914–2001. *Antiquity* 76 (1): 101–108.

——— (2003) *Trench Art: Materialities and Memories of War.* Oxford: Berg.

——— (2004) Material Culture and Conflict: The Great War, 1914–2003. In N.J. Saunders (ed.), *Matters of Conflict: Material Culture, Memory and the First World War*, pp. 5–25. London: Routledge.

——— (2009) Ulysses' Gaze: The Panoptic Premise in Aerial Photography and Great War Archaeology. In B. Stichelbaut, J. Bourgeois, N. Saunders and P. Chielens (eds.), *Images of Conflict: Military Aerial Photography & Archaeology*, pp. 27–40. Newcastle upon Tyne: Cambridge Scholars.

——— (2010) *Killing Time: Archaeology and the First World War* (second edition). Stroud: Sutton.

——— (2012) Travail et Nostalgie sur le Front de l'Ouest : l'Art des Tranchées Chinois et la Première Guerre Mondiale. In Li Ma (ed.), *Les travailleurs chinois en France dans la Première Guerre mondiale*, pp. 435–451. Paris: CNRS.

——— (2013) *The Poppy*. London: One World.

——— (2014) Bodies in Trees: A Matter of Being in Great War Landscapes. In, P. Cornish and N.J. Saunders (eds.), *Bodies in Conflict: Corporeality, Materiality and Transformation*, pp. 22–38. London: Routledge.

——— (2017) Materiality, Space and Distance in the First World War. In N.J.Saunders and P. Cornish (eds.), *Modern Conflict and the Senses*, pp. 29–42. London: Routledge.

——— (2020) *Desert Insurgency: Archaeology, T.E. Lawrence and the Arab Revolt*. Oxford: Oxford University Press.

Saunders, N.J. and P. Cornish (eds.) (2017) *Modern Conflict and the Senses*. London: Routledge.

Saunders, N.J., N. Faulkner, U. Košir, M. Crešnar and S. Thomas. (2013) Conflict Landscapes of the Soča/Isonzo Front, 1915–2013: Archaeological-Anthropological Evaluation of the Soča Valley, Slovenia. *Arheo* 30: 47–66.

Saunders, N.J., J. Frolik and V. Heyd. (2019) Zeitgeist Archaeology: Conflict, Identity, and Ideology at Prague Castle, 1918–2018. *Antiquity* 93 (370): 1009–1025.

Schäuble, M. (2011) How History Takes Place: Sacralized Landscapes in the Croatian-Bosnian Border Region. *History and Memory* 23 (1): 23–61.

Schindler, J.R. (2001) *Isonzo: The Forgotten Sacrifice of the Great War*. Westport, CT: Praeger.

Seaton, A.V (2000) 'Another Weekend Away Looking for Dead Bodies…' Battlefield Tourism on the Somme and in Flanders. *Tourism Recreation Research* 25 (3): 63–77.

Shapland, A.and E. Stefani (eds.) (2017) *Archaeology Behind the Battle Lines: The Macedonian Campaign (1915–1919) and its Legacy*. London: Routledge.

Simić, M. (1998) *Po Sledeh Soške Fronte*. Ljubljana: Založba Mladinska Knjiga.

——— (2005) *Utrdbi pod Rombonom: predstraža soške fronte: Razplet svetovnega spopada med utrdbami in topovi na Bovškem*. Ljubljana: Rombon.

Sloterdijk, P. (2009) *Terror from the Air*. Cambridge, MA: MIT Press.

Souvent, P. and S. Pirc. (2001) Pollution Caused by Metallic Fragments Introduced Into Soils Because of World War I Activities. *Environmental Geology* 40: 317–323.

Stichelbaut, B. (ed.) (2018) *Traces of War: The Archaeology of the First World War*. Veurne: Hannibal Publishing.

Stichelbaut, B. and P. Chielens. (2014) *In Flanders Fields: The Great War Seen from the Air, 1914–1918*. New Haven, CT: Yale University Press.

——— (2016) The Aerial Perspective in a Museum Context: Above Flanders Fields 1914–1918. In B. Stichelbaut and D. Cowley (eds.), *Conflict Landscapes and Archaeology from Above*, pp. 279–291. Farnham: Ashgate Publishing.

Stichelbaut, B. and D. Cowley (eds.) (2016) *Conflict Landscapes and Archaeology from Above*. Farnham: Ashgate Publishing.

Taborelli, P., A. Devos, S. Laratte, Y. Desfossés and J. Brenot. (2017) Typologie et Organisation Spatiales des <<Polemo-Formes >>de la Grande Guerre Revelees par l'outil Lidar et les Plans Directeurs. Application a la Champagne et a L'Argonne. *Revue de Géographie Historique* 10: 1–33.

Thompson, M. (2008) *White War: Life and Death on the Italian Front 1915–1919*. London: Faber & Faber.

Tilley, C. (1994) *A Phenomenology of Landscape, Places, Paths and Monuments*. Oxford: Berg.

Van den Berghe, H., W. Gheyle, N. Note, B. Stichelbaut, M. Van Meirvenne, J. Bourgeois and V. Van Eetvelde. (2018) Revealing the Preservation of First World War Shell Hole Landscapes Based on a Landscape Change Study and LiDAR. *Geografisk Tidsskrift – Danish Journal of Geography* published online 3 December: 1–14.

Van Emden, R. (2019) *Missing: The Need for Closure after the Great War*. Barnsley: Pen & Sword.

Van Meirvenne, M., T. Meklit, S. Verstraete, M.D.E. Boever and F. Tack. (2008) Could Shelling in the First World War Have Increased Copper Concentrations in the Soil Around Ypres? *European Journal of Soil Science*, 59 (2): 1–8.

Various. (2020) *From the Ashes: Reconstruction of Flanders Fields after the Great War*. Bruges: Westtoer apb.

Verdegem, S., J. Billemont, and S. Genbrugge. (2013) *Archeologisch onderzoek Mesen Aquafin Collector*. ADEDE Search & Recovery Rapport 28. Ghent.

Vermeulen, B. (1999) Ieper is a lie. *In Flanders Fields Magazine* 1 (1): 9–11.

Williamson, A. (2004) *Henry Williamson and the First World War*. Stroud: Sutton.

Williamson, H. (1929) *The Wet Flanders Plain*. London: Faber.

Willson, Lt. and Col, H.B. (1920) *Ypres: The Holy Ground of British Arms*. Bayaert: Bruges.

Winter, J. (1995) *Sites of Memory, Sites of Mourning: The Great War in European Cultural History*. Cambridge: Cambridge University Press.

Winterton, M. (2012) Signs, Signals and Senses: The Soldier Body in the Trenches. In N.J. Saunders (ed.), *Beyond the Dead Horizon: Studies in Modern Conflict Archaeology*, pp. 229–241. Oxford: Oxbow.

Yioutsos, N-P. (2017) The Last Occupation of Asine in Argolis. *Opuscula – Annual of the Swedish Institutes at Athens and Rome* 10: 164–189.

2

CUTTING THE LANDSCAPE

Investigating the 1917 battlefield of the Messines Ridge

Simon Verdegem

How are modern conflict landscapes created, how can we investigate them, and what might they tell us of the relationships between people, technology, and the shape of the traces they leave behind? The archaeological consequences of industrialized war incorporate the remains of battle-zone landscapes whose investigation reveals the physical relationships between prior military planning, the reality of war on and in the ground, the vagaries of preservation, and the excavation strategy. Here, these issues are explored through the excavation of a distinctive First World War conflict landscape on the Western Front – the century-old remains of the Battle of Messines on 7 June 1917. The investigation throws light on the battle and its consequences by giving insights into the small-scale formation processes of a large-scale landscape.

Between 26 March and 21 December 2012, archaeological excavations were undertaken at Messines in advance of the laying of a new system of underground sewage pipes. The Flemish Heritage Agency recommended that the entire route of this system be excavated. As far as is known, the excavation area touched on the medieval defences of the town and some medieval residential traces, but above all, it included many remnants of the First World War (Figure 2.1). In this, of course, it shared a common element with many cities, towns, villages, and rural landscapes along the Western Front of 1914–1918 (Saunders 2001).

Messines was in the front area during the entire war, and its landscape is thus the record of overlapping military actions (Edmonds 1948). In 1914 the front line was fixed on the Messines Ridge and German troops had dug themselves in around the town. An extensive trench network was developed in the following three years, until Allied troops captured the stronghold in June 1917 (Passingham 1998). Following the Battle of Messines, the front shifted two kilometres to the

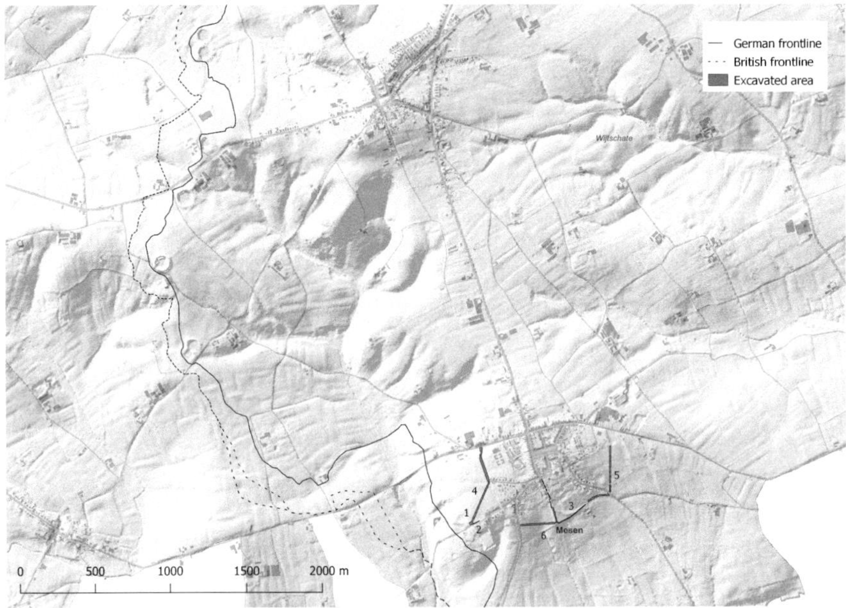

FIGURE 2.1 Map of Messines Ridge with the location of the excavation in relation to the front lines between 1914 and 1917. The location of the features discussed in the text is indicated by a number: (1) *Eckert Graben*, (2) German concrete bunker, (3) tunnel system, (4) temporary trench 7 June 1917, (5) machine gun position, and (6) ammunition collection point. Source: © Simon Verdegem; source geographical data: © Geopunt Vlaanderen.

east, and Messines was incorporated into the Allied positions. However, this was short-term, as the Germans were back in the spring of 1918 following their last major offensives. The Battle of Messines of 10–11 April 1918 saw a German breakthrough along a six-kilometre front and the recapture of Messines, though this too was short-lived as the Allies retook the town for the final time on 29 September (Baker 2011).

Due to the linear nature of the research area, an archaeological cross-section was made of the former battlefield around the town, cutting across the different lines of the German trench network, including the June 1917 battlefield and, importantly, the post-battle British trench network. All these different elements were uncovered during the excavation and provided insights into the organization and development of trench networks and the layout of a battle in a trench war. In addition, excellently preserved structures provided much information on construction methods, layout, and maintenance of a trench system. In other words, the investigation provided a tightly focused view of a palimpsest conflict landscape, moving between the small (and very human) scale and the larger area.

Origin of the Messines stronghold

The First World War had such a profound impact on the Messines landscape that by November 1918 every pre-war landmark had been wiped out as a result of more than four years of artillery bombardment – another widespread occurrence along the Western Front. This was evidenced in a dense concentration of bomb craters, which in some places coalesced to form a continuous whole. In between these craters, and indeed beneath them, all kinds of remarkably well-preserved structures came to light during excavation. The majority of the examples, and also the best-developed of them, comprising trenches and other features, were made by German soldiers and were part of a trench network that was continually improved and expanded during the occupation period to create an almost impregnable stronghold.

The first confrontation between German and British troops on the ridge took place on 21 October 1914. British cavalrymen had taken positions east of the town and stood their ground there. After the fighting, the British were ordered to dig in and improve their positions in advance of a possible new attack. The German commanders wanted to drive the British off the ridge at all costs and repeatedly sent their troops forwards. Every German attack failed, despite their numerical majority. After three days of battle, on 23 October 1914, the Germans realized that the enemy positions were too strong. Success would only be possible if a renewed attack were supported by heavy artillery. When attempts to break through in other places along the front also failed, the German artillery was brought into position (Oldham 2000: 13–16).

On 30 October, the German bombardment began, though the artillery's extended deployment was such that the barrage had little effect. In the afternoon, the German 26th (Württemberg) Division rushed to Messines where dismounted units of the British 1st Cavalry Brigade, the 9th Lancers (2nd Cavalry Brigade), and two companies of the Indian 57th Rifles were located on the east side of the town. The concentrated British gunfire repulsed the attackers again and again. The Germans reacted with another artillery bombardment targeting the church, houses, and the defenders all day and all night. The next day, the German Grenadier Regiment 119 and the Infantry Regiment 125 unexpectedly stormed the town, but while some positions were taken, a breakthrough was not achieved; the artillery bombardment continued without respite. A second German assault was more successful, and the British cavalry and the 2nd Inniskilling Fusiliers retreated to houses in the west of the town centre – a line which had to be held if they weren't to be driven from the ridge completely. Both sides brought in reinforcements. On the British side, the 2nd King's Own Scottish Borderers and the 2nd King's Own Yorkshire Light Infantry appeared from the west and the London Scottish from the north (Oldham 2000: 17; Sheldon 2010: 239–241).

The latter unit was brought to the nearby village of Wijtschate by London buses and from there they planned to take the main road to Messines. The heavy fighting precluded this, however, and they detoured, eventually moving up the western slope to the town with the intention of launching a counter-attack. The British were only noticed when they appeared at the top of the ridge, and they immediately came under intense German fire. The losses were immense, with the London Scottish losing more than half of its men. Finally, on 1 November, the British decided to evacuate their ridge-top lines and retreat down into the valley (Oldham 2000: 18).

On 6 and 7 November 1914, more Allied counter-attacks were launched to recapture the town, some by French troops, but Messines remained in German hands and the front line stabilized on and around the ridge; soldiers started to dig in. Messines became part of the *Wytschaete-Bogen*, a line that made a bulge towards the British positions, parallel to the British lines known as the Ypres Salient. The strategic importance of this position should not be underestimated. From the higher ground they occupied, the Germans were able to dominate many British positions in the wider vicinity of Ypres. Every movement was watched by German observers. If the British wanted to force a breakthrough in the Ypres Salient, they first had to drive the Germans off the Messines Ridge. However, this was no easy task. In succeeding years the German fortifications were expanded, and a system of defence in depth was adopted to prevent any breakthrough. Messines was gradually developed into an impressive stronghold with an extensive network of different types of trenches, bunkers, hiding places, and tunnels.

Messines, Ypres, and geology

The town of Ypres – the centre of the war in Flanders between 1914 and 1918 – is surrounded by a vast plain with few or no distinct features. The subsoil of this plain consists of thick clay layers that are covered by other sediments and deposits. To the east of the town, there is a higher ridge that – between Passchendaele in the north and Messines in the south – curls in an arc around the town. Although this ridge is on average no higher than 50 metres, it dominates the otherwise flat landscape (Doyle 2017: 54).

The plain itself consists mainly of clay, as part of the Kortrijk Formation, which is virtually impenetrable to water. Rain and groundwater, therefore, lodge above the clay, which has an immediate effect on the permeable sediments of sand and loam which form the topsoil layers. This geology creates varying degrees of saturation depending on the amount of precipitation. When combined with poor drainage exacerbated by artillery bombardment, heavy rainfall produces extremely high rates of saturation (Doyle 2017: 56–58).

East of Ypres, the heights have a different soil structure than the plain, with higher percentages of sand to heavy clay creating better drainage. Nevertheless, flooding could still occur, and the complex soil structure of alternating sand and clay could lead to problems when digging was required and a watery layer encountered (Doyle 2017: 67–73).

The German soldiers who had dug themselves in around Messines were on the flanks of the ridge and although their position was undoubtedly more favourable than that of the Allied units in the valley below, they too were confronted with these water-rich aquifers. Different structures examined during the archaeological investigation reflect this constant struggle against water in the way they were built and rebuilt. Militarily and geologically, therefore, Messines was part of the strategic situation of Ypres, and the two towns shared a conjoined importance, if not a common fate.

Eckert Graben: the biography of a trench

At Messines, the first trenches were built where the troops had come to a standstill in 1914, and principally by the German Army. Some of these trenches were abandoned over time for strategic reasons, others expanded, and new ones constructed. Each of these three variants was investigated. A total of ten different German fighting and communication trench segments were excavated; some were simple trenches without revetment, or at most, with a few long floorboards laid directly on the ground. Other trenches were built using well-thought-out construction methods for both soil and wall revetment. Several examples clearly revealed adaptations caused by the threat of groundwater, with two or more levels of floorboards on top of each other not being exceptional. Particularly revealing was that here the evolution in construction method could be observed, from simple long trench boards at the bottom of the trench to transversely placed timbers that look like a copy of British duckboards.

The best-preserved German trench was *Eckert Graben* (Uhlan Support to the British), a support trench west of Messines that was initially dug in 1914 and modified several times in the following months and years. During the excavation, 19 metres of this trench were investigated, and due to its excellent preservation, it was possible to dissect the construction of the trench completely (Verdegem et al. 2013: 87). A striking feature was the variety of construction methods and the need for continuous modifications, repairs, and improvements. It turned out that it had been necessary to increase the floor level – sometimes twice – and it was established that several types of wall revetment were used systematically (Figure 2.2).

The deepest level of the trench was between 150 and 200 centimetres below ground level. At this depth, the first-floor level was laid with long boards that were placed on the ground without any provision for drainage and were only supported by short transverse beams at the ends. However, one of the aquifers had already been reached, and it was undoubtedly not long before the bottom of the trench was flooded. It is difficult to determine when the first adjustments were made, but in the next construction phase provisions were made to drain the incoming groundwater (Verdegem et al. 2013: 88–94).

During these adjustments, the trench level was raised by 20 to 60 centimetres so that it rose above the level of the water at the bottom of the trench with

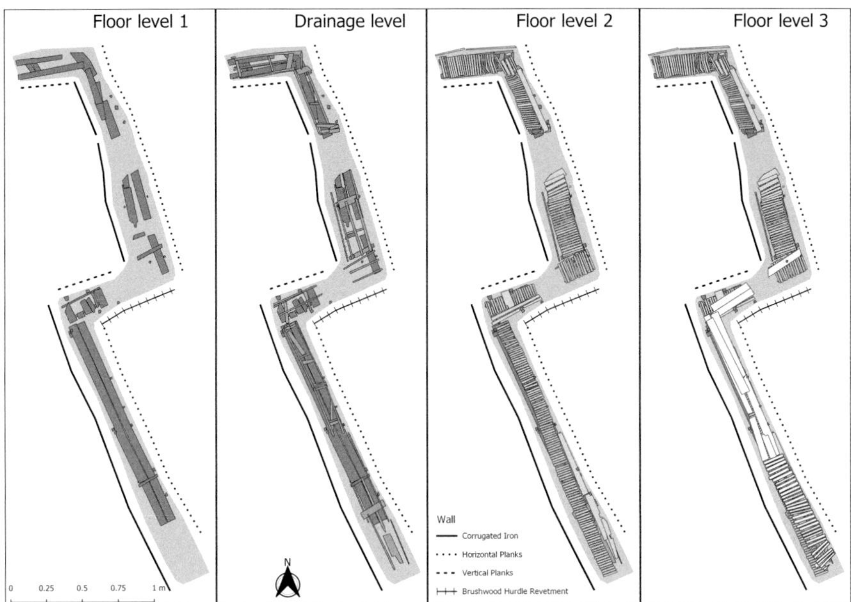

FIGURE 2.2 Detailed map of *Eckert Graben* with the different floor levels and wall revetment. Source: © author.

enough space for drainage. For this purpose, a wooden frame was built to support the floorboards – beams and slats without uniform dimensions placed every metre and fitted up to the trench wall. There they were supported by planks placed on their narrow side against the trench wall. Depending on the height that had to be bridged, one or more planks were used. A system similar to the British duckboards was used for the floor level, but whereas the latter employed prefabricated elements, the German timbers were nailed to the load-bearing beams on site. This technique was probably more labour-intensive but had the advantage of being more flexible. For example, crossbars of different lengths – 40 and 60 centimetres – were used, depending on the width of the trench (Figure 2.3).

Even so, this higher level proved insufficient – at least in the southern half of the trench segment investigated, which was located lower down the slope. Here, consequently, a second round of adjustments was made to cope with the water problem. Wear and tear or destruction of the underlying level was certainly not the cause, as excavation showed it to be virtually undamaged. This new adjustment used two techniques, the first of which was the duckboard-like system. The second is seen in the north part of the trench, where planks of different lengths and widths were used and arranged in such a way, sometimes one on top of another, that the trench bottom was completely covered. The way in which these planks were placed betrays a certain time pressure in raising the trench level. No effort had been made to cut the planks to the correct size or in mitre. This was

FIGURE 2.3 Detail photo of the second level in *Eckert Graben*. Source: © author.

something that recurred in most of the German trenches that were investigated (Verdegem et al. 2013: 88–94). It is abundantly clear that the German troops here had to fight a constant battle against water. During the initial construction, the trench was dug down to a level lower than the groundwater table. Subsequently, the problem of flooding took on such proportions that adjustments became necessary.

The wall revetment seen in *Eckert Graben* was also well preserved and was investigated extensively. Studying *Eckert Graben*'s wall covering revealed a wide variety of construction techniques: horizontal planks, vertical planks, brushwood hurdle revetment, and corrugated iron. For most of the trench, the original shoring was still present. Only in a few places had it been necessary to carry out repairs. In some places, the wall revetment had partially or completely disappeared as a result of artillery fire or poor conservation. Nevertheless, it was possible to identify a certain system in the placement of the different types of construction (Figure 2.2).

Initially, the variety of wall revetment within a relatively short stretch of trench gave the impression that it was not a planned construction, but rather a make-do effort in the chaos of the battle. However, further investigation and mapping of the trench gave a completely different picture. First and foremost, all types of revetment were found to extend to the bottom of the trench, deeper than the elevated floor levels. This implied that they were inserted during the initial construction of the trench. In addition, a recurring pattern appeared where a certain type of shoring was used. The wall of the trench on the front side was provided with corrugated sheets at the traverse and at the fire bay. The opposite wall was covered with horizontal planks. The walls of the short sections of the trench between the traverse and the fire bay were covered with vertically placed planks and the brushwood hurdle revetment, the former method being on the side of the front with the hurdle on the opposite side (Verdegem et al. 2013: 95–99).

Concrete bunker

The development of the trench network on the Messines Ridge was not limited to the trenches themselves. Underground shelters also took on a more permanent character. During excavation, a good example of a concrete bunker was uncovered. The combination of this with the deeply preserved access trench again provided considerable insight into the techniques used.

The bunker was located just behind *Eckert Graben* and must have been connected to it. However, as it was underground, its existence was unknown to the Allies and could not be detected by Allied aircraft. Consequently, it was not mapped on the British trench maps. Because it was so deep, it was in the water-saturated soil layers, which explains why it was made of concrete rather than wood. The bunker was not built from prefabricated concrete blocks but was poured on the spot into a mould that was then removed from the inside. The imprint of the mould's wooden planks was clearly visible on the interior walls. On the outside, corrugated sheets were used for the formwork. The walls, the floor, and the roof were concrete, but the roof had not been preserved, though its remains were still in and around the bunker. The construction was 450 centimetres long and at least 350 centimetres wide. The walls were 70 to 80 centimetres thick at the front and back, while the side walls were at least 100 centimetres thick. At the back, the wall was interrupted over a distance of 80 centimetres by a doorway that provided access to the bunker (Verdegem et al. 2013: 136–137).

The interior of the bunker was 300 by 200 centimetres and had a wooden floor. Wooden planks parallel to the longitudinal axis rested on three transverse planks. In this way, a space was created between the concrete floor and the wood to ensure that the plank floor could be kept more or less dry. In the southeast corner, a round hole (⌀ 30 centimetres) was provided as a sump. In the doorway, three steps led to the slightly higher trench. The steps were also cast in concrete and covered with wooden planks that covered both the horizontal and vertical surfaces of the steps. The doorway itself was clad in heavy upright wooden beams, two on either side, which served as doorposts. On the inner, southern beam of the doorpost, the lower hinge pin had been preserved, indicating that the bunker had an inwards-swinging door (Verdegem et al. 2013: 138–139). The bunker entrance was accessible via a deep trench that was not perpendicular to the door opening but made a slight bend, which ensured that there was no direct line of fire from the trench into the bunker (Figure 2.4).

This access trench was equipped with revetment on both its walls and floor. The trench level consisted of long planks that ran parallel to the direction of the trench. Two wide planks (approximately 25 centimetres wide) and one narrower plank (approximately 10 centimetres) formed a tread of 60 centimetres wide. A drainage channel was visible beneath the gangways (Verdegem et al. 2013: 139–140). Because the trench had been laid so deep, a considerable part of the wall sheeting had been preserved. Two types of shoring alternating with each other were identified. On the one hand, there were two-metre-long wooden planks placed horizontally against the wall and supported every metre by upright beams. On the other hand, corrugated iron sheets were placed against the wall, which was stopped by the same type of beams (Verdegem et al. 2013: 140).

FIGURE 2.4 Overview of the rear side of the bunker with the access trench. Source: © author.

FIGURE 2.5 Detail photo of the access trench with the wall cabinets for the *Stielhandgranate* (left) and the rifle rack at the bottom (right). Source: © author.

In addition to gaining a large amount of information about the construction method of such a trench, the excavation also yielded interesting insights concerning its use and organization. At the T-junction, a heavy beam was found at the bottom of the trench that was placed against the southern wall. In the beam were six U-shaped cut-outs, the right size for a rifle butt to fit. From this rifle rack, it was deduced that the bunker could hold up to six soldiers. In the opposite wall, two niches, placed next to each other, were visible (Verdegem et al. 2013: 141); these were completely covered with wood inside and served as cupboards, one of which was unopened and filled with 11 armed *Stielhandgranate*, ready for use (Figure 2.5).

Tunnel system

A third part of the German trench system is the underground tunnel complex south of the town. Such features form part of a distinctive subterranean conflict landscape that has only recently attracted scholarly attention (Barton et al. 2010; Leonard 2016). Four different segments were encountered within the research area (Figure 2.6), though the size of the entire complex is not clear. One of the tunnels was still open and continued beyond the research area. The others were closed and were twice found to house a time capsule of First World War objects.

These tunnels were not dug from above and then covered over but built from below. The construction timber for these tunnels was of prefabricated custom-made elements that fitted together like pieces of a jigsaw puzzle via a mortise connection with an open hole. All elements were equally wide and thick so that the construction could be divided into a series of identical segments. Each segment consisted of four different parts: a ceiling, a floor, and two types of wall pieces (Verdegem et al. 2013: 149–152).

Tunnel 1 was the most westerly of the four and ran from the south in a straight line to the north-northwest (Verdegem et al. 2013: 158–160). The investigated segment was 450 centimetres long, 90 centimetres wide and 120 centimetres high. In the south, the tunnel had collapsed, but to the north, it continued ten to 15 metres outside the research area (Figure 2.7), where another collapse blocked the road (Figure 2.6). Tunnel 2, five metres further east (Verdegem et al. 2013: 136–145), ran parallel to Tunnel 1 from the south but made a right angle to the northeast after 250 centimetres and stopped 170 centimetres further on. The inner space of the southern part was identical to Tunnel 1, but after the bend, the tunnel became larger with a width of 120 centimetres and a height of 150 centimetres. The lack of shoring at the dead end of the tunnel was striking (Figure 2.6).

Tunnel 3 was 250 centimetres east of Tunnel 2 (Verdegem et al. 2013: 161–164). From the north, it ran parallel to Tunnel 1, but after about 300 centimetres it made a right angle to the northeast followed by another in a southwest direction. The width was different from that of the first two tunnels. The first part parallel to Tunnel 1 was also about 90 centimetres wide, but after the first bend, it

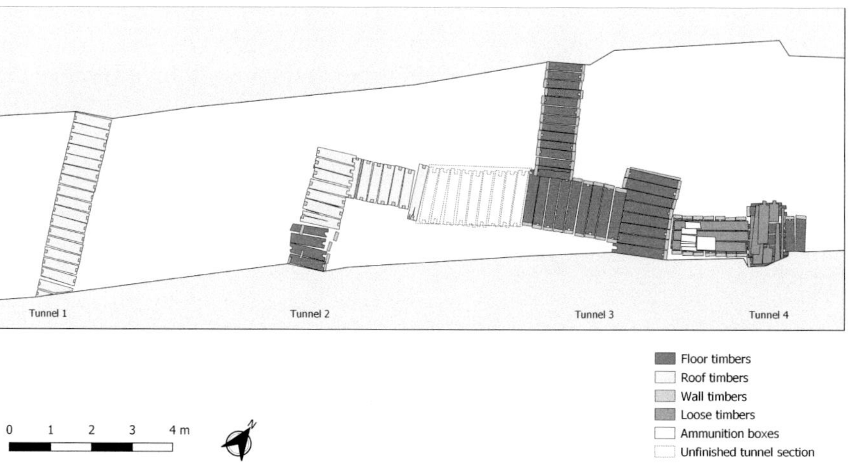

FIGURE 2.6 Detailed map of the tunnel system. Source: © author.

FIGURE 2.7 Inside Tunnel 1 looking north into the preserved section of the tunnel outside the excavation area. Source: © author.

widened to about 120 centimetres. Tunnel 3 had collapsed over its entire length within the research area. The damage was much greater than in the collapsed part of Tunnel 2 and had a severe impact on the state of preservation of the wall shelves, making it impossible to determine the height of the tunnel. The western wall at the end of the second section was also never covered, a finding that suggested that the intention was to extend the tunnel in a westerly direction and to connect it to Tunnel 2 (Figure 2.6). In other words, the tunnel complex was still under construction when it was abandoned or destroyed. This was confirmed by the discovery in Tunnel 3 of a set of tools in a recess, still standing against the wall of the tunnel as it had been left by the German soldiers. It included a shovel, a pickaxe, and a hoe, which were all provided with a shortened handle to be able to work more conveniently in the narrow tunnels (Figure 2.8).

Tunnel 4, east of Tunnel 3, was a dead-end segment of the tunnel system that went further south, and of which only the T-shaped end could be examined (Verdegem et al. 2013: 165–167). Its state of preservation, like that of Tunnel 3,

FIGURE 2.8 German tools left behind against the wall of Tunnel 3. Source: © author.

was poor due to collapse over its entire length. As a result, only the floorboards were well preserved. It soon became clear why the tunnel ended in a 'T' shape. Both arms of the 'T' turned out to be storerooms in which extra shelves were provided. In one of the two rooms, several ammunition boxes were found in situ. In addition to three wooden boxes with rifle cartridges for the Mauser rifle, there were also several metal boxes with belts for the MG08 machine gun (Figure 2.6).

7 June 1917: the Battle of Messines

The German positions on the Messines Ridge dominated the area. The heights made it possible to observe every Allied movement in the Ypres Salient to the north. If the Allies were to force a breakthrough there, they first had to drive the Germans from the ridge. With this necessity in mind, the plan that led to the Battle of Messines was born. The German positions would be destroyed by the detonation of 19 underground mines. As early as the autumn of 1915, preparations had been started with the intention of launching the attack in 1916. By this time most of the planned mines were ready (Passingham 1998: 5–10). But the battles on the Somme proved tougher than expected and absorbed so much manpower that the attack had to be postponed.

During the placing of these mines, there was an underground war between the British tunnellers and the German *Mineure* which created a unique subterranean landscape. It was a sensorially intense (Leonard 2019) and nerve-wracking struggle in which the Germans went in search of the British tunnels and mine chambers, with the intention of destroying them. This was done by placing charges aimed at causing the British tunnels to collapse. Sometimes the groundwater itself was weaponized, directed by the Germans through shafts into the British tunnels and flooding them. The result of these counteractions was the elimination of one of these mines, which had been placed beneath La Petite Douve farm (Passingham 1998: 83–87).

In mid-May 1917, the preliminary Allied bombardment started in preparation for the attack planned for 7 June. The goal was to disrupt the German organization, destroy the defences, and take out their artillery batteries. For this purpose, 2,266 guns and howitzers were set up, which worked according to a meticulous fire plan. In the last week before the attack, no fewer than 3.5 million shells were fired. In the meantime, the effects of the shelling were investigated by means of nocturnal raids on the enemy trenches. In most cases, it was reported that the first line was almost non-existent and remained virtually unmanned. The Germans had indeed already switched to a minimum occupation and attached more importance to the intermediate zone between the first and second line where they expected an attack to get stuck (Passingham 1998: 39–47).

It was 3:10 am on 7 June 1917 when a brief silence was broken by the simultaneous eruption of the underground mines. Subsequently, the cannonade was resumed. An interplay of artillery, mortars, and machine guns had to cut off the supply lines and erect a protective shield behind which the Allied infantry could advance. The town centre of Messines was the attack area assigned to the New Zealand Division, which kept to the timetable while remaining protected by the artillery curtain. German strong-points were neutralized before the defenders had a chance to respond. The first Allied wave reached all its targets and consolidated its positions by constructing new trenches. Behind them, the second wave had the heavier task of clearing the town centre. There the resistance grew from the many German bomb-proof cellars and shelters. In the meantime, other Allied units moved around the centre to assault the enemy positions in the east. After about two and a half hours, the targets on the eastern slope had been reached and the new positions were quickly consolidated, knowing that a German counterattack was imminent. This came shortly after noon but failed with much bloodshed. The New Zealanders were well prepared and had placed their machine guns and artillery in predetermined positions. Most of the German troops did not even come close to the Allied positions (Passingham 1998: 108–125).

In the afternoon, the Allied attack was restarted with the aim of taking the German positions known as the *Oosttavernelinie*. The fighting became tougher and lasted until 14 June. The battle would go down in history as one of the most successful British attacks of the entire war. The losses were fewer than expected, although Allied casualties likely matched the 25,000 suffered by the Germans, who had at last been driven from the ridge. This essential first step in launching an offensive in the Ypres Salient led to the start of the Third Battle of Ypres on 31 July, which would last until 10 November but failed to deliver the hoped-for Allied breakthrough. Nevertheless, peace returned to the Messines Ridge for the rest of 1917.

A significant point for understanding the nature of modern conflict landscapes is that the huge German effort to build an impregnable stronghold at Messines was wiped out in a matter of hours when the New Zealanders stormed the ridge on 7 June 1917. Success was a combination of a disoriented and demoralized enemy due to prolonged artillery bombardment along with the mine explosions, on the one hand, and excellent artillery and infantry coordination, on the other, which ensured that the defenders had no time to man their posts after the Allied bombardment had ceased. The consequences of the preliminary Allied shelling could be seen in the excavated German trenches. The walls of *Eckert Graben* showed heavy damage. In one place the wall was completely shattered by an almost direct hit by a shell, of which the detonator was still stuck in the wood. The walls of *Blauer Graben* – a communication trench that was excavated north of *Eckert Graben* – had been pushed in at various places. Part of *Flechsig Graben* – a fighting trench at the edge of the town centre – was blown away by a large calibre shell. *Emil Graben* – a communication trench south of the town – and the other investigated trenches were also affected, as well as the access trench to the concrete bunker, the wall of which had been folded up in two places. Archaeological investigation at Messines uncovered the processes and consequences of the Allied attack, chronicling in intricate detail the formation of a landscape of total destruction and defeat for the Germans.

Military history and archaeology combine to reveal detailed insights into the events of 7 June 1917. The attack was prepared step by step and the attacking waves advanced to a predetermined line. There they stopped and let another wave pass on its way to the next objective. The troops that had reached their position consolidated it by digging temporary trenches, the investigation of which revealed a remarkable degree of irregularity in their construction. The depth and width fluctuated significantly, even on the relatively short segments of trench under investigation. This is unsurprising in view of the fact that they were built in the heat of the battle and did not immediately have a permanent function.

Other traces too reveal details from which the large-scale organization and planning of the Allied operation can be deduced. By the time the New Zealanders had reached the German line east of Messines town centre, their first day's objectives had been achieved, and were followed by a stop before the offensive's second phase was launched. The newly captured line was consolidated because a typically swift German counter-attack was expected. As part of these preparations, it had been decided in advance where artillery and machine guns would be placed. One of these positions was most probably cut by the excavation area east of the town, where a foxhole flanked on both sides by slightly curving trench segments was discovered. The central pit was dug deep and provided with a shallow plateau on the front side intended for a machine gun. The large number of spent .303 cartridge cases and fragments of empty machine gun belts found there clearly supports this interpretation. The adjacent trench segments were much shallower and probably served to cover the other members of the team who had to assist the gunner. A petrol tin used to carry water for, or condense steam from, the water-jacket of the Vickers machine gun and an empty ammunition box was also found there (Verdegem et al. 2013: 206–210). This was the archaeological signature of military planning and of the German counter-attack which unfolded, a nuanced material record of just a small part of the conflict landscape's creation.

Another archaeological discovery substantiated the meticulous planning of the attack. To ensure that the attacking troops did not run out of ammunition, reserve supplies were brought closer to the front so that soldiers could maintain their momentum. These reserves were made available at collection points identified by signboards visible at a distance. We investigated what was likely one such collection point. Large quantities of rifle ammunition were found in a bomb crater south of the town, which yielded .303 cartridges on chargers that were clearly put in cotton bandoliers, and a wooden box with a belt for the Vickers machine gun together with some lids of opened boxes of the same type. The presence of an indented pole was noted in the middle of this stack of cartridges and interpreted as the remnant of the signal post intended to lead runners to this location (Verdegem et al. 2013: 213–216).

The Allied post-battle trench system

After the battle, Messines became an Allied hinterland, and the ridge gradually returned to being a quieter sector. The newly conquered terrain was used to defend the new front line, for which a new trench system was constructed between the remains of the old German lines. Archaeological excavations identified and investigated this oft-ignored and under-documented aspect of a battle-zone landscape.

Allied trenches were found to the west, south, and east of the town, and were clearly more systematically constructed than the quickly dug ad hoc lines from the time of the attack. They are distinguished from the latter by their straight walls and flat bottoms with duckboards in most cases. Some examples were provided with an additional excavated area beneath the gangways to serve as a drainage channel.

Excavations also revealed informative differences between these new Allied trenches and their German predecessors. Although the Allies did indeed work on their post-battle Messines trench system, it is clear that these were not heavily reinforced. Compared to the permanent character of the German trenches, the new Allied ones are far more temporary in nature, with construction materials hardly used, other than for reinforcing the soil structure.

Conclusion

Because of the linear nature of the research area, one large test trench was excavated around Messines. This had its advantages because it cut through the different lines of the German trench network, the battlefield of June 1917, and the later post-battle British trench network. As a result, all these different elements were uncovered during the investigation, which gave many important insights into the organization and development of individual trenches, the trench networks, and the character of a trench warfare battle. The excavation was unique in itself and because of the extraordinary preservation of many of the uncovered structures (and their contents). It offers a distinctive contribution to our knowledge of the formation of modern conflict landscapes.

References

Baker, C. (2011) *The Battle for Flanders: German Defeat on the Lys, 1918*. Barnsley: Pen & Sword.

Barton, P., P. Doyle and J. Vandewalle (2010) *Beneath Flanders Fields. The Tunellers' War.* Stroud: Spellmount.

Doyle, P. (2017) *Disputed Earth. Geology and Trench Warfare on the Western Front 1914–1918*. London: Unicorn Press Group.

Edmonds, J.E. Brig.-Gen. (1948) *History of the Great War. Military Operations: France and Belgium: 1917*. London: MacMillan.

Leonard, M. (2016) *Beneath the Killing Fields: Exploring the Subterranean Landscapes of the Western Front*. Barnsley: Pen & Sword.

——— (2019) A Sensorial No Man's Land: Corporeality and the Western Front during the First World War. *The Senses and Society* 14 (3): 257–270.

Oldham, P. (2000) *De Heuvelrug van Mesen: Mesen, Wijtschate, Sint-Elooi*. Erpe: De Krijger.

Passingham, I. (1998) *Pillars of Fire. The Battle of Messines Ridge June 1917*. Cheltenham. History Press.

Saunders, N.J. (2001) Matter and Memory in the Landscapes of Conflict: The Western Front 1914–1999. In B. Bender and M. Winer (eds.), *Contested Landscapes: Movement, Exile and Place*, pp. 37–53. Oxford: Berg.

Sheldon, J. (2010) *The German Army at Ypres 1914 and the Battle for Flanders*. Barnsley: Pen & Sword Military.

Verdegem, S., Billemont, J. and Genbrugge, S. (2013) *Archeo Rapport 28: Mesen-Collector Aquafin*. Gent: ADEDE Archeologische Rapporten.

3

GARDEN LANDSCAPES OF THE GREAT WAR

Jeffrey S. Reznick

G is for the gardens that look fresh and green,
H is for huts where they grow in between.[1]

Nearly two full years into the Great War and towards the height of the contemporary European food shortage, an announcement entitled 'Economy in Hospital Gardens' appeared in the *Hospital*, one of Britain's leading contemporary professional journals. Here, readers learned about a new series of Royal Horticultural Society pamphlets intended for 'amateur and cottage gardeners with a view to the encouragement of economy by increasing the home production of vegetables and fruit, and maintaining existing gardens inexpensively during the war'. The announcement continued, stating that

> [m]any of those hospital managers whose institutions possess gardens or grounds that have not been properly developed would do well to study these pamphlets. The one which covers the general principles and contains the most useful collection of practical hints is entitled 'Economy in the Garden', price threepence. Its instructions are detailed and practical, and if followed out would increase the yield or save the expense of maintaining the grounds of most institutions which possess them.
>
> *(Anon. 1916a: 484)*

In offering such a perspective this article points to essential connections between garden landscapes of the 1914–1918 period and the contemporary 'war machines' of Britain and America which served to ensure adequate manpower and *matériel* for military combat and civilian defence.[2] Scarcity and rationing widely characterized these systems, and this was especially the case in the context of food production and consumption.[3] While scholars have paid substantial attention to the war-garden movements that emerged from these conditions to become hallmarks of wartime life and postwar memory, they have done so with a limited focus on the prevalence of garden landscapes and the activity of gardening, and how contemporaries used both as means by which to heal men made sick by and broken in battle and to sustain food-economy and morale among soldiers and civilians alike. In dialogue with these studies and advancing Great War and related scholarship which reveals the important relationships between agricultural-related labour and programmes of rehabilitation for convalescent and permanently wounded soldiers, this chapter demonstrates how garden landscapes of the Great War were of a piece with other 'contested landscapes' described in this volume and elsewhere.[4]

Hospital gardens and soldier gardening on the British home front

Garden landscapes and the activity of gardening in and around hospitals on the British home front received substantial attention from institutional administrators and medical and voluntary-aid authorities. Among the best examples of this phenomenon was the First Eastern General Hospital, Cambridge, where officials framed their thinking about the institution's gardens and gardening activities predominantly in terms of the physical layout of the hospital itself. In the eyes of its architects, administrators, and staff, the First Eastern was a model of modern institutional efficiency (Figure 3.1). The site was situated entirely on a single level with two central passages connecting each ward block to the hospital kitchens and to administrative offices located at the northern end of the institution. As Ward Muir, an orderly at the hospital, described the arrangement: 'Corridor branches out of corridor – A Corridor, B Corridor, C Corridor, D Corridor, each with its perspective of doors opening into wards; and shorter corridors leading to store-rooms and the like' (Muir 1917: 47). This design provided 'ease of mobility' for all, and especially for hospital staff who could serve meals quickly, administer treatments easily, and supervise patients with minimal effort. For the soldier-patient, Muir explained, he who is:

> on crutches can go anywhere without fear of tripping, the patient in a wheeled chair can propel himself anywhere, the orderlies can push wheeled stretchers or dinner-wagons anywhere … [T]he patient or orderly who has dwelt in a hospital where, though distances are shorter, staircases are involved – or where every trifling coming-and-going of goods or stretchers necessitates the manipulation of a lift – blesses those level, smooth corridors, with their facile access to any ward, to operating theatres, kitchens, stores, X-ray room, massage department, etc.
>
> *(ibid.)*[5]

Such efficiency through design also characterized the interior of the ward blocks, each of which was significantly larger than the standard 30-bed ward of a large

FIGURE 3.1 Architectural sketch of the First Eastern General Hospital and environs which structured the 'ward gardens' depicted in postcards associated with the institution. Source: Griffiths ca. 1917–1918. Reproduced with permission of Cambridge Collection, Cambridge Central Library.

civilian hospital. Rectangular in shape and flanked on opposite sides by two rows of 25 beds and lockers, all the wards of the First Eastern had a wide central aisle through which doctors, nurses, and orderlies moved freely from bed to bed. At the end of this aisle was the nursing sister's writing desk, from which she could monitor up to 50 patients in her ward (Griffiths 1917–1918). Through these arrangements, the wards of the First Eastern structured a curative regime comparable to that established in traditional pavilion hospitals. Consisting of a long, rectangular-shaped room with high ceilings, the pavilion was lined with large windows on opposite sides, against which two rows of beds were positioned at right angles. Access to the ward was at one end only, past the nursing sister's desk and the service rooms. The opposite end of the ward housed the patients' washing facilities.[6]

Traditional pavilion hospitals had practical values that complemented their medical virtues. They economized on space and provided efficient supervision of staff and patients by institutional authorities. As Florence Nightingale explained in 1858, when the pavilion was already becoming the standard architectural feature in hospitals across western Europe and in Britain, the idea of this method of organization made 'each ward a cul-de-sac of the main circulation system; thus, each was like a separate mineratureature [*sic*] hospital, the sister's domain, where intruders would always be noticed' (Nightingale 1859: 6–8). In this regard pavilion hospitals shared a common purpose with lock hospitals, where authorities sought to instil moral values into working-class female syphilitics by subjecting them to surveillance and to 'lessons in deference, respectability and personal cleanliness'.[7]

The pavilion style was therefore prominent at the First Eastern as its ward blocks ran east–west on the cricket ground and therefore utilized the natural progression of the sun and wind as key elements in the treatment of patients by open air. The north side of each ward was 'protected by louvres', yet open 'close to the roof to ensure free circulation of air throughout'. The south side opened entirely into verandahs and small gardens, 'except for a low open railing at the floor level and ordinary sun blinds', which were used to regulate the amount of sunlight streaming into the ward. This arrangement provided soldier-patients with 'a stepless exit' into the hospital gardens (Anon. 1915a: 343).[8] Here, they could continue their fresh-air treatment either by lounging on the lawn or by 'ample exercise and abundance of simple amusements, including sports and games' (Anon. 1915b: 72). Addressing the subject of the ward-bordered garden generally, the *Hospital* once claimed that it 'promotes the return to vigorous life' (Anon. 1914a: 25–26).[9] In addition to promoting health in this way, the hospital garden had important economic value as a site in which to grow vegetables for the institution and to encourage economy in food production and consumption. Institutions also used hospital gardens as a source of medicinal herbs for certain treatments (Anon. 1916b, 1916c).

Authorities at the First Eastern and elsewhere also understood their gardens as means by which to help maintain morale among soldiers and civilians alike. Official picture postcards of the institution evoked an idyllic past that served the present by sustaining a presumed, universally held hope that days past and serene with garden scenes could help Britain's heroes, and what's more, the country itself, survive the present and unprecedented social and cultural upheaval[10] (Figure 3.2). Serving a similar function, garden-themed lapel pins produced and distributed by the Woman's Auxiliary Force became a material means by which patriotic citizens could display publicly their pride in and financial support of hospitals for sick and wounded men and these men themselves (Figure 3.3). Taken together, such efforts helped to yield a distinct public view of the wartime 'culture of caregiving' as a focus of intense public pride, indeed a means by which those who remained at home to experience the war in their own way could articulate their appreciation of those who were 'doing their bit' overseas and those who had returned home sick, wounded, or had given the lives for King and Country. This focus in turn helped to define both a bridge and a gap between soldiers and civilians, and it was an integral part of fulfilling Prime Minister David Lloyd George's promise that Britain would be a country 'fit for heroes to live in'.

The popularity of gardens and the activity of gardening – for the intertwined purposes of therapy, morale, and economy – was not unique to the First Eastern,

FIGURE 3.2 Postcard. First Eastern General Hospital, Cambridge, Ward Garden, ca. 1915–1918. Source: © private collection.

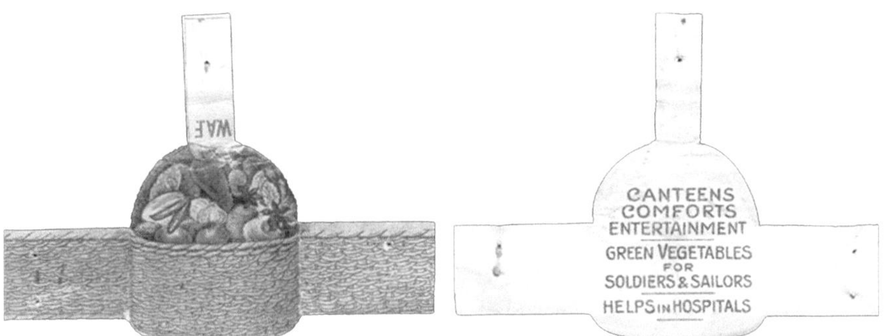

FIGURE 3.3 Women's Auxiliary Force (WAF) garden-themed lapel pin (recto, left; verso, right) produced and sold to support the care of sick and wounded soldiers, ca. 1914–1918. Source: © private collection.

as an illustration in *The Magazine* of the Fourth Northern General Hospital plainly suggested (Figure 3.4). Meanwhile, authorities in Netley's Red Cross Hospital engaged soldier-patients in decorative and practical gardening. 'The extent of the latter', according to a 1917 summary of work produced by the hospital,

> may be gauged by the fact that 2 1/4 tons of potatoes, 450 cabbages, 50 vegetable marrows, 200 curly kale, 8 bushels of runner beans, 2 1/2 bushels

THE GARDENING SEASON IS IN FULL SWING

FIGURE 3.4 'The gardening season is in full swing'. Source: Anon. 1917c. Reproduced with permission of Leeds University Library.

> of broad beans, 2 bushels of dwarf beans, 4 1/2 bushels of peas, 2 bushels of turnips, 100 beetroot, and over 1,000 head of lettuce have been provided for the use of the hospital, and 100 sticks of celery will shortly be available. There has also been a splendid supply of flowers.
>
> *(Anon. 1917a)*

Moreover, in Blackpool's Military Convalescent Hospital, authorities reported that 'all the space between the huts is cultivated, and looks very gay with flowers'. Additionally, they observed '6 to 8 acres of vegetable garden, 18 acres of oats, and 6 acres of turnips etc., making a total of 24 acres' (Anon. 1917b). And as the official pictorial 'souvenir' of Summerdown military convalescent hospital revealed, gardens marked the landscape of that institution and figured prominently in its curative regime for convalescent soldiers (Figure 3.5).

British arrangements on the Western Front

Gardens and gardening were also prominent features of British convalescent facilities located in France. This was especially the case at Number 13 Convalescent Depot, known as Trouville Hospital Centre. Tens of thousands of British and Colonial servicemen passed through this unit from the time it opened until its closure in 1919 during demobilization. Located near the beaches of the Channel coast, Trouville encompassed a variety of facilities intended to ensure the quick return to duty of sick and wounded soldiers, including four voluntary-aid rest

Photos by COMPTON, High Street.
16

SHOWING THE GARDENS.

FIGURE 3.5 'Showing the gardens'. Source: Anon. 1916d. © Private collection.

huts – an Expeditionary Force Canteen, YMCA Hut, Salvation Army Hut, and Soldiers' Christian Association Hut – alongside a bathhouse, athletic ground, dining hall, eye and dental institutes, barber, chaplaincy, drill shed, and miniature rifle range. Vegetable and flower gardens complemented these facilities. According to the official diary of the institution, 'gardening in the Camp provided exercise and interest' (Anon. n.d.a). Moreover, a contemporary film produced by the War Office Cinema Committee featured the gardens located between Trouville's Nissen huts, and in so doing, the production suggested the popularity of gardening among many convalescent men (WACC n.d.).

Gardens and gardening became prominent features of life in Trouville's counterpart institutions. At Number 7 Convalescent Depot located near Boulogne, authorities once sponsored an 'agricultural show'. In competition with other area depots, the institution won first prize for 'the best cropped vegetable garden and farm, second prize for the best pair of farm horses and three first prizes for carrots, onions and turnips' (OWD 1918). At Number 3 Convalescent Depot located near Le Treport, authorities used gardening to keep 'convalescent-fit men' busy while they were under 'observation' (OWD 1915). At Number 11 Convalescent Depot located near Buchy, authorities placed an entire team of gardeners under a chief gardener. Together, the group 'cultivated over an acre of garden' (OWD 1917). Authorities at Britain's Command Depots also saw gardening as suitable employment for soldiers (Anon. n.d.b). And similar arrangements took shape at Britain's Number 6 General Hospital where '200 trees, shrubs, and 10,000 bulbs' surrounded the institution thanks to the officially sanctioned gardening efforts of soldier-patients and staff (OWD 1916).

America's hospital gardens overseas and at home

Within months following America's formal entry into the war, American hospitals in Britain and France and on the American home front all began to construct their own garden landscapes as part of the American 'war machine' generally, and more specifically in response to European food shortages, the need to engage hospital staff and convalescent soldiers in morale-boosting activity, and the need to rehabilitate permanently wounded soldiers. American Red Cross officials assessed the initial overseas plan in August 1918, revealing that:

> The venture has not merely been an excellent measure of monetary economy. It has also been an excellent tonic for the morale of the staffs and a useful exercise for the convalescent patients. Soldiers who wished to do work in the gardens have been placed under the supervision of the medical staff and the work which they could best do has been assigned to them by doctor's prescription, so that the garden work provides suitable relaxation and really beneficial exercise for the men in conjunction with their hospital treatment. The work is treated as a recreative agency to bring back the men to a normal, mental and physical state.
>
> *(Anon. 1918a)*

Examples of such success abroad included American Base Hospital Number 8, where patients and staff cultivated dozens of acres of wheat, rye, and oats alongside peas, carrots, lettuce, beans, and beets. In August 1918 alone, the crops yielded 2,800 pounds of vegetables for the institution (Anon. 1918b). And across the English Channel, 'a considerable portion of the 186 acre estate' of the American Red Cross Farm at Sarisbury Hospital saw cultivation by convalescent soldiers (ibid.: 6).[11] One of the largest efforts of its kind among American institutions in England, Sarisbury involved 15 acres being dedicated to 'garden vegetables for the use of the hospital' as well as 'all the milk, cream, and butter from the dairy [going] to the hospital' (Anon. 1918c).

Many military hospitals located on the American home front also included gardens on their grounds and gardening in their patient regimens. At General Hospital Number 8, Otisville, New York, market-gardening courses occupied many 'tuberculous men' (Crane 1927: 199). These courses involved 'hotbed construction, the making of flats, sowing seeds, transplanting, the use of farm implements, problems in farm management, etc.'. The authorities of the institution had a 'farm of 75 acres at their disposal', with which they 'planned to produce a large portion of the market stuff for the hospital consumption' (ibid.). The overall scheme was 'to accomplish three distinct things…namely, occupational therapy, vocational training, and the greatest production of foodstuff possible for the use of the hospital' (ibid.).

The soldier-patients of Convalescent Hospital Number 1, Lawrenceville, New Jersey, engaged courses on 'agriculture, horticulture, and dairying, [and] care of plants in greenhouse' (ibid.: 253). Originally established by the Army, this 500-acre institution was eventually transferred to the Federal Board for Vocational Education after 'it was found that the number of men who desired to take such a course was too small to justify the maintenance cost' (ibid.). The Board 'conducted it as a receiving station and school of practical farming (from April 1, 1919) until August 5, 1919, just prior to the time when the land-grant colleges were ready to admit the students' (ibid.). According to the official history of the US medical department during the war:

> While the total enrolment was less than 200, this farm-hospital school would undoubtedly have been an efficient agency in caring for the convalescent farm-minded men had the war continued longer. It returned men to the farm better fitted for farm activities and bridged the gap between hospital discharge and the opening of established educational institutions.
>
> *(ibid.)*

Finally, at the Base Hospital at Camp Grant, Illinois, authorities drew on 'hospital and exchange funds, together with funds received from the Red Cross and other welfare organizations' to purchase 'seeds, plants, and farming machinery' for the institution (Reed 1923: 216). The 'entire hospital grounds [were eventually] seeded in grass and laid out in appropriate flower beds' (ibid.). The arrangement 'not only enhanced the beauty of the hospital and added to the contentment and satisfaction of the patients and personnel, but had a decided advantage in that they prevented the raising of dust' (ibid.). Moreover,

> the use of hospital funds permitted the operation of a hospital garden upon a neighbouring 10-acre plot. This garden provided a large percentage of the fresh vegetables used in the mess and netted a clear profit in hospital funds through the saving of approximately $4,000.
>
> *(ibid.)*

Beyond helping to promote institutional economy, boost morale, and improve the health of soldier-patients deemed able to return to the war front, gardens and gardening figured prominently in British and American rehabilitation schemes for permanently disabled men. The most significant example of this phenomenon in Britain was arguably the landscape garden created by the surgeon Sir John Lynn Thomas at the Prince of Wales Limb Fitting Centre in Cardiff (Figure 3.6). Including hills, dales, and sloping paths edged with thick planks of wood, this site helped to teach limbless men how to walk again. Thomas and his colleagues intended this garden to be inspirational while the specific layout of the paths helped to achieve a practical goal: 'to remind the men not to kick out sideways with the artificial leg' (Anon. n.d.c).

As Thomas recognized the therapeutic value of his distinctive garden landscape, the physical educator R. Tait McKenzie saw the activity of gardening, alongside such fields as carpentry and draughting, as useful occupational therapy

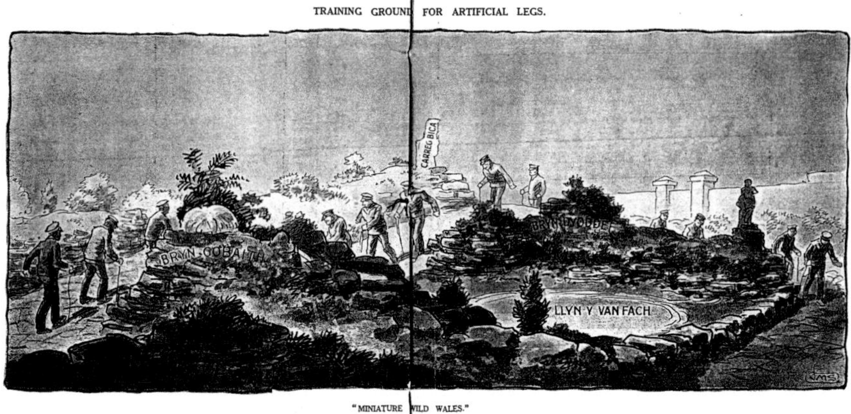

FIGURE 3.6 'Training ground for artificial legs'. Source: Anon. 1918e, after p 10. Reproduced with permission of Cardiff Central Library.

for disabled men. McKenzie explained that the 'purpose of occupational therapy was threefold', namely:

> 1. Physical: To carry on the improvement in muscular strength and control, obtained by treatment, and to apply it to the varied movements that the carpenter uses in handling his tools or the gardener in cultivating his land; 2. Vocational: To give him an education directed to make him able to keep a set of books, or take a position in business where the handicap of a missing leg or an amputated arm will not be felt; 3. Moral, or self-disciplinary: To give courage to being life over again, sometimes in a new trade or business. To give him that self-respect that makes him want to stand on his own two feet, and not be dependent on charity or the efforts of others, to give him ambition to shake off the deadening effects of his long period of enforced idleness, and to undertake the necessary training for a trade or occupation from which he can make a living.
>
> *(Mackenzie 1918: 10)*

Along these lines, therapeutic gardening programmes for disabled soldiers developed in institutions across Britain. At Alder Hey Hospital, Knotty Ash, Liverpool, men could participate in gardening workshops in addition to classes in painting, typewriting, and cinematograph operating (Hutt 1917: 86). Medical authorities at St Dunstan's Hostel for Blinded Soldiers and Sailors saw 'market-gardening' to be one occupation among many that could be 'useful in [the men's] future lives for pleasure or profit'. Other classes involved instruction in Braille, typewriting, net-bag making, boot repairing, mat making, net making,

FIGURE 3.7 Disabled soldier in a greenhouse at Walter Reed General Hospital, ca. 1918–1919. Source: Anon. 1918–1919. Image courtesy of the National Museum of Health and Medicine, Forest Glen, Maryland.

basket making, joinery, massage, and poultry farming (St Dunstan's 1916: 2–3).[12] At Enham Village Centre, authorities offered similar curative and retraining schemes to disabled men. Here,

> some are being taught shorthand and typewriting, book-keeping, or otherwise fitted for various commercial callings, others are undergoing complete courses of instruction in wood-, metal, or leather-work and the like, while others for whom out-door occupations are desirable and appropriate are being thoroughly trained as gardeners or for agricultural pursuits, including dairying and poultry keeping.
>
> *(Anon. 1918d: 7)*

Comparable arrangements developed in America, one of the most extensive being at Walter Reed General Hospital in Washington, DC. Here, agricultural occupational therapy workshops included courses in 'truck farming out of doors, vegetable forcing under glass, growing of flowers, and text-book studies' (Reed 1923: 311–313). As contemporary photos suggest, men with and without artificial limbs took part in vegetable and flower gardening, presumably to enable their successful reintegration into civilian society (Figure 3.7).

Conclusion

Whereas the 'war gardens' of civilian society became known and were *remembered* after the war as 'victory gardens', the garden landscapes of British and American hospitals became vacant and forgotten environments as their associated facilities were demobilized and forgotten by societies that wished to leave behind four years of death, disablement, and destruction (Lawson 2005: 170ff; Reznick 2004: 137ff).[13] Whether oriented to economic, social, or therapeutic ends, the wartime work achieved by soldiers and medical staff in and around military hospital gardens – and no less the promising *rhetoric* of work extolled through these environments – meant little by the end of the conflict as so many returned soldiers on both sides of the Atlantic were swept out of the labour market. Ironically, the 'waste land' in which they found themselves was not unlike the abandoned military hospital garden that once played its own role in helping to make a land 'fit for heroes'.

Acknowledgements

In addition to thanking Paul Cornish and Nicholas Saunders for their critical feedback, the author is grateful to several colleagues for their assistance in locating and investigating the provenance of sources used in this essay, including Katrina Coopey of Cardiff Central Library; Richard Davies of Leeds University Library; Christopher Jakes of the Cambridgeshire Collection, Cambridge Central Library; Michael Rhode of the US Navy BUMED Office of Medical History (formerly of the Otis Historical Archives of the National Museum of Health and Medicine, Armed Forces Institute of Pathology); and Andrew Nichols and Susan Robbins Watson of the Hazel Braugh Records Center and Archives of the American Red Cross. With the experience and expertise of these colleagues and further research, the author made a substantial effort to trace the copyright holders of the material reproduced here which is not understood to be in the public domain. Should holders step forward after publication, due acknowledgement will gladly be made.

Notes

1 MCSC, 'The Hospital Alphabet', *The Magazine of the Fourth Northern General Hospital, Lincoln* (November 1916): 23.
2 For an excellent treatment of this subject see Pick (1993).
3 A useful discussion of these subjects in the British context appears in DeGroot (1996: 86ff). In the American context, see Schaffer (1991: 34ff).
4 See Reznick (2004); Dewey (1989); Hayden-Smith (2014); Hickman (2013); Lawson (2005); Linker (2011); Perry (2014); and Weiss (2008). On the relationship between gardens and memorial spaces related to the Great War, see especially Gough (1998) and Morris (1997).
5 Muir added that the ward blocks at the Third London were built along the same lines at the First Eastern and were 'put up at a remarkable pace…[as] an open field vanished in less than a month and [a] 'Bungalo Town' [of fifty huts] appeared'.

6 On the pavilion hospital, see especially Forty (1980).
7 See Walkowitz (1980: 59–60); Andrew (1991); Rosenberg (1979).
8 This description also points out that 'in cases of a southern gale the beds nearer the southern front can be drawn further back [into the ward]'.
9 However, such praise did not come without occasional warning of the infectious potential of this outdoor space. See, for example, Anon. (1914b).
10 Useful discussions of the pastoral tradition in World War I Britain, and particularly the broader relationship between war and nature, appear in Khan (1988: 56ff). See also Fussell (1975: 235ff and passim).
11 See also Anon. (1918c).
12 See also Anon. (1915c).
13 On the 'generation of 1914', see especially Wohl (1979).

References

Andrew, D. (1991) Two Medical Charities in Eighteenth-Century London: The Lock Hospital and the Lying-In Charity for Married Women. In J. Barry and C. Jones (eds.), *Medicine and Charity before the Welfare State*, pp. 82–97. New York: Routledge.

Anon. (n.d.a) History of Trouville Hospital Centre (Number 13 Convalescent Depot). In *Official War Diary*, Number 13 Convalescent Depot. National Archives (United Kingdom), War Office 95/4121.

Anon. (n.d.b) *War Office Documents, World War I Medical Arrangements*. NA WO 222/1.

Anon. (n.d.c) *Typescript Memoir Relating to Wartime History of St. Thomas's School of Physiotherapy and Wartime Physiotherapy Programs Generally*. London: Metropolitan Archives.

Anon. (1914a) Hospital Gardens. *Hospital* 10 October: 25–26.

Anon. (1914b) The Infectious Hospital Garden. *Hospital* 2 May: 117.

Anon. (1915a) *Builder*, 12 November: 343.

Anon. (1915b) Hospital Provision: Its Difficulties and Limitations. *Hospital* 23 October: 72.

Anon. (1915c) *The British Red Cross Society and The Order of St. John of Jerusalem in England: What We Are Doing To-Day for Sick and Wounded Sailors and Soldiers*. London: British Red Cross Society Pamphlet, October: 10.

Anon. (1916a) Economy in Hospital Gardens. *Hospital* 26 August.

Anon. (1916b) Medicinal Herb Cultivation in Hospital Gardens. *Hospital* 22 April: 77.

Anon. (1916c) A New Use for Hospital Gardens: The Cultivation of Medicinal Herbs. *Hospital* 26 August: 492.

Anon. (1916d) *Souvenir: Summerdown Military Convalescent Hospital. Profits Devoted to Camp Funds*. Eastbourne: Henry J. Capon.

Anon. (1917a) *British Red Cross Society, Red Cross Hospital, Netley, Summary of Work for 30 September 1917*. London: British Red Cross Society.

Anon. (1917b) *Joint War Committee Minutes, 21 June 1917*. London: Library of the Order of St. John.

Anon. (1917c) *Magazine of the Fourth Northern General Hospital, Lincoln*, May: 90.

Anon. (1918a) Wounded Make Good Hospital Gardeners. *American Red Cross Bulletin* 2: 2.

Anon. (1918b) Hospital Farms in France and England. *American Red Cross Bulletin* 4: 6.

Anon. (1918c) To Teach Soldiers Intensive Farming: Convalescent Americans Will Be Pupils at Sarisbury Farm. *American Red Cross Bulletin* 14: 1.

Anon. (1918d) *What of the Afterwards: A Problem for Patriots*. London: The Village Centres; London: Chiswick Press.

Anon. (1918e) *Miniature Wild Wales*. The Prince of Wales' Hospital for Limbless Sailors and Soldiers, Wales and Monmouthshire, Cardiff: The Story of the Hospital Opened by H.R.H. The Prince of Wales, K.G., Wednesday, February 20th, 1918. Cardiff: n.p.).

Anon. (1918–1919) *Otis Historical Archives, Reeve Collection, WWI 280*. Washington, DC: United States Army.

Crane, A.G. (1927) Physical Reconstruction and Vocational Education. In M.W. Ireland (ed.), *The Medical Department of the United States in the World War*, volume 13, p. 199. Washington, DC: U.S. Government Printing Office.

DeGroot, G.J. (1996) *Blighty: British Society in the Era of the Great War*. New York: Longman.

Dewey, P.E. (1989) *British Agriculture in the First World War*. New York: Routledge.

Forty, A. (1980) The Modern Hospital in England and France: The Social and Medical Uses of Architecture. In A.D. King (ed.), *Buildings and Society: Essays on the Social Development of the Built Environment*, pp. 61–93. New York: Routledge and Kegan Paul.

Fussell, P. (1975) *The Great War and Modern Memory*. New York: Oxford University Press.

Gough, P. (1998) War Memorial Gardens as Dramaturgical Spaces. *International Journal of Heritage Studies* 3(4): 199–214.

Griffiths, J. (1917–1918) *Hospitals: Yesterday, Today and ...Tomorrow*. Unknown.

Hayden-Smith, Rose (2014) *Sowing the Seeds of Victory: American Gardening Programs of the World War 1*. Jefferson, NC: McFarland.

Hickman, C. (2013) *Therapeutic Landscapes: A History of English Hospital Gardens*. Manchester: Manchester University Press.

Hutt, C.W. (1917) *The Future of the Disabled Soldier*. New York: William Wood and Company.

Khan, N. (1988) *Women's Poetry of the First World War*. Lexington, KY: University Press of Kentucky.

Lawson, L.J. (2005) *City Bountiful: A Century of Gardening in America*. Berkeley: University of California Press.

Linker, B. (2011) *War's Waste: Rehabilitation in World War I America*. Chicago: University of Chicago Press.

McKenzie, R.T. (1918) *Reclaiming the Maimed*. New York: Macmillan Company.

Morris, M.S. (1997) 'Gardens 'For Ever England': Landscape, Identity and the First World War British Cemeteries on the Western Front. *Ecumene* 4(4): 410–434.

Muir, W. (1917) *Observations of an Orderly; Some Glimpses of Life and Work in an English War Hospital*. London: Simpkin, Marshall, Hamilton, Kent, and Co., Ltd.

Nightingale, F. (1859) *Notes on Hospitals: Being Two Papers Read before the National Association for the Promotion of Social Science, 1858*. London: John W. Parker and Son.

OWD. (1915) *Official War Diary*, Number 3 Convalescent Depot, 29 August 1915. NA WO 95/411.

OWD. (1916) *Official War Diary*, Number 6 General Hospital, 29 January 1916. NA WO 95/4077.

OWD. (1917) *Official War Diary*, Number 11 Convalescent Depot, 31 May 1917. NA WO 95/4121.

OWD. (1918) *Official War Diary*, Number 1 Convalescent Depot, 25 August 1918. NA WO 95/411.

Perry, H. (2014) *Recycling the Disabled: Army, Medicine, and Modernity in WW1 Germany*. Manchester: Manchester University Press.

Pick, D. (1993) *War Machine: The Rationalisation of Slaughter in the Modern Age*. New Haven: Yale University Press.

Reed, F.W. (1923) *Military Hospitals in the United States*. (Volume 5 of M.W. Ireland (ed.) series, 'The Medical Department of the United States in the World War'). Washington, DC: U.S. Government Printing Office.

Reznick, J.S. (2004) *Healing the Nation: Soldiers and the Culture of Caregiving in Britain during the Great War*. Manchester: Manchester University Press.

Rosenberg, C. (1979) Florence Nightingale on Contagion: The Hospital as Moral Universe. In C. Rosenberg (ed.), *Healing and History*, pp. 116–136. New York: Folkestone, Dawson.

Schaffer, R. (1991) *America in the Great War: The Rise of the Welfare State*. New York: Oxford University Press.

St. Dunstan's. (1916) *Report of St. Dunstan's Hostel for Blinded Soldiers and Sailors for the Year Ended March 26th, 1916*, pp. 2–3. Blinded Soldiers and Sailors Care Committee. London: Bankers.

WACC. (n.d.) *How We Treat Our Wounded*. War Office Cinema Committee. Imperial War Museum Film Archive. B/W, 1 Reel, 10 minutes, silent, no intertitles.

Walkowitz, J. (1980) *Prostitution and Victorian Society: Women, Class, and the State*. New York: Cambridge University Press.

Weiss, E. (2008) *Fruits of Victory: The Woman's Land Army of America in the Great War*. Lincoln, NE: Potomac Books.

Wohl, R. (1979) *The Generation of 1914*. Cambridge, MA: Harvard University Press.

4

CONFLICT GAS-SCAPE

Chemical weapons on the Eastern Front, January 1915

Anna Izabella Zalewska and Jacek Czarnecki

Introduction

The Great War of 1914–1918 is, to this day, a living and painful scar on the collective memory of the western world. Its status as a watershed event and as the harbinger of 'total war' is ingrained in the memory of many societies, at local, national, and supra-national levels. It is also a conflict that left deeper traces in the 'archive of the earth' than any other before it. Much has been written about the practices and dynamics of memory concerning the millions of soldiers who perished. Most of this attention has been focused on the trench warfare fought in Flanders, Champagne, and Lorraine. The materiality of this familiar Western Front warscape has been subjected to in-depth interdisciplinary scrutiny (e.g. Saunders 2004; Schofield 2005; Desfossés et al. 2009; Saunders and Cornish 2009; Stichelbaut 2018).

However, there are spaces where the memory of the causes, course, and consequences of what Michael S. Neiberg, in describing the events of 1914–1918, calls the 'dance of the furies', has been contested (Neiberg 2013). Chief among them are the regions of Eastern Europe affected by the conflict, and which include parts of modern Poland. From our perspective, rooted in these landscapes which constituted three-quarters of the entire Eastern Front in 1914–1915, it is surprising that public awareness of military operations there remains patchy, and that memory of the events barely survives. This is arguably even more surprising given the radical extent to which the war scarred these landscapes. And these physical wounds are echoed by hidden scars left in our collective psyche. Closer analysis reveals complex reasons behind this war amnesia in cultural memory, of which the main one is the heavy burden of post–First World War conflicts and their legacies and memories which Central/Eastern Europe carries. The layering of conflict-related matter, places, and memories is a testament to the continuous physical and semantic transformations which this area has experienced (see Zalewska 2013, 2019; Czarnecki 2019; Zalewska, Czarnecki, Kiarszys 2019).

In the first part of this chapter, we briefly discuss the historical and spatial conditions that led to the creation of a landscape of military operations in central Poland relatively near to the capital Warsaw. We focus on issues related to the landscape and elaborate on themes that have hitherto been contested. Our second focus is on the first phase of positional warfare, from December 1914 till March 1915, and on selected aspects entangled with the landscape's natural-cultural features. Finally, we present the reasons for, and circumstances and consequences of, employing archaeology as a trigger for searching for and understanding what we call the Eastern European gas-scape. This area of over 440 square kilometres is now becoming an evocative memory-scape due to the fact that it was investigated archaeologically and historically during the last decade.

The primary process: war comes to central Poland

In 1914, a significant part of the Eastern Front was located in the territory of modern Poland. It consisted of roughly 800 kilometres of frustration and hope in equal amounts (i.e. meadows, forests, towns, and villages converted into battlefields, and young men pressed into service). At the time, Poland had been under occupation for 120 years by three partitioning powers: Russia, Prussia, and Austria-Hungary. Many Poles surmised that the defeat of one or more of these powers would allow Poland to rebuild its independence among the charred ruins – a hope that did eventually come to pass. The military engagements on the region's Rawka and Bzura Rivers can hardly be described as the strategic nexus of the war in 1914. Nonetheless, they were fought over an area of key strategic importance, the centre of the 'Vistula Land' and the 'distant outskirts' of Warsaw (Figure 4.1). The significance of the nearby city was described in October 1914 by Bernard Pares, one of the embedded war correspondents and the official British Observer with the Russian Armies in the Field:

> The Germans tried to force their way up here from the south, close to the Vistula, and got to within some nine miles from Warsaw. If they had captured the town (about 900,000 inhabitants, of whom 300,000 are Jews), and occupied the Vistula bridges, they would have established an enormous political and military advantage, which could not have been reversed without the greatest difficulty. Though Warsaw was beyond their line of defence, the Russians made every effort to hold it.
>
> *(Pares 1915: 37)*

This description dates to the first German attack on the capital of so-called 'Russian Poland' during the 'Warsaw-Ivangorod Operation'. At a great cost in lives, the Russian Army not only stopped this thrust but pushed the German Army back to the borders of the Reich and thereby directly threatened German

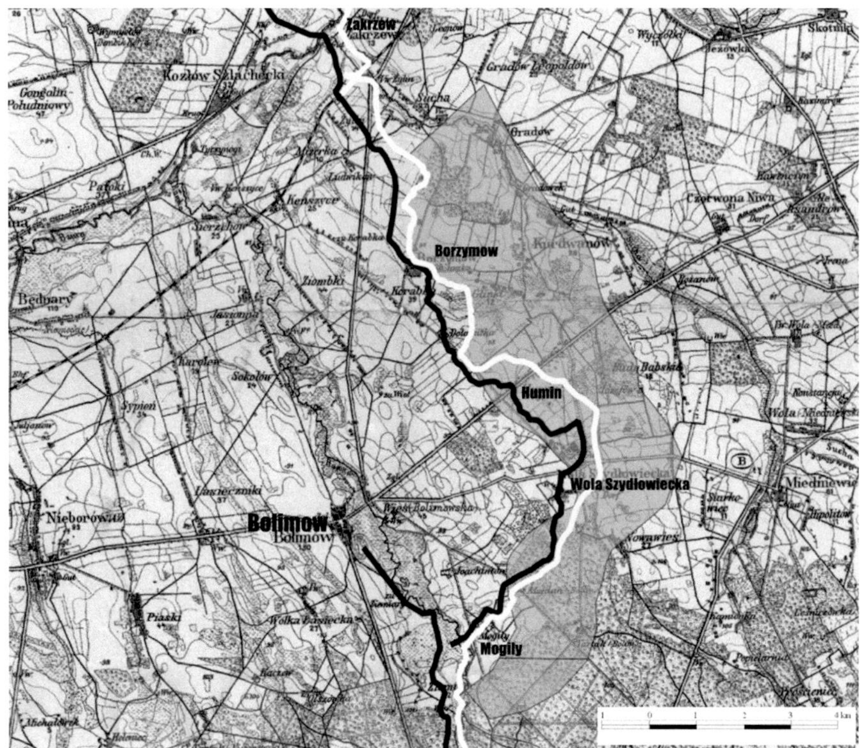

FIGURE 4.1 The front line in the Bolimów outpost sector, from Ziemiary (south) to Zakrzew (north). The Germans launched four gas attacks here between January and May 1915 (BArch HStAS M410). Source: © authors' elaboration of data on the German map from 1915, from the private collection of Jacek Czarnecki.

territory. The Germans responded by bringing additional divisions from the Western Front as reinforcements and re-engaging the Russian defences to once again threaten Warsaw in December 1914. The Tsar's armies withdrew to pre-designated positions dug in along the eastern banks of the rivers Bzura, Rawka, Pilica, and Nida. The location of this front line which, unknown to the two opposing forces at the time, would become the site of extended positional warfare, was far from accidental.

From landscape to warscape: the Rawka and Bzura battlefield

When it comes to the art of war, landscape was, and to a large extent still remains, one of the key factors determining the manner of engagement and organization of the front line. Also, in the Rawka and Bzura region, the way that military operations were conducted was directly affected by the area's topography. The region of Mazovia in central Poland features gently rolling terrain, rising only about 90–110 metres above sea level. When preparing their backup defences, the Russian Army took full advantage of the natural lay of the land, aligning their fortifications with the eastern banks of the local rivers. These eastern banks were, in the case of the Rawka and Bzura Rivers, tall and steep, while the western banks were predominantly flat and marshy. The riverside escarpments could rise up to between three and eight metres above the water level, which provided the defenders with an unobstructed view of the approaches and a perfect field of fire. Furthermore, in spring, autumn, and during part of the winter, the western banks of the Rawka and Bzura tended to overflow, while in summer they turned to marshy meadows, all of which rendered them unfit as a site for field fortifications.

Despite being defensible and difficult to attack, this landscape had one weak point. On the upper reaches of the Rawka River (north of the village of Bolimów) the eastern bank became as flat and marshy as the western for approximately 10 kilometres. For this reason, the Russian Army moved their defences away from the river – to an area where the level of groundwater allowed for more maintainable earthworks and trenches. After the first month of fighting, the line rested against the fortified villages and landed estates in the region, starting from the Mogiły manor, through the villages of Wola Szydłowiecka, Humin, Borzymów, and Sucha, all the way to the estates of Żylin and Zakrzew in the north (Figure 4.2).

In the creation of this warscape, any potentially advantageous element of the landscape was likely to be subjected to military repurposing. These elements included smaller rivers (e.g. the Sucha) and streams, woods and coppices, the aforementioned manor houses, and other parts of the rural infrastructure. The original primary functions and meanings of these landscape elements were either transformed or ignored; their characteristics were destroyed by their conversion into defensive positions and outposts. In the initial stage of the battle, the Russian Army's fortifications on the banks of the Rawka and Bzura Rivers were highly susceptible to the forces of nature, which rendered them barely defensible, as observed by the Russian historian Andrei Nieznamov:

> The 'pre-prepared' positions comprised a line of trenches flooded by autumn rains, without any proper shelters or entanglements in the approaches. On the right flank, between the Vistula and the outlet of the Rawka and Bzura – the line was protected by the broad overflow area of the Bzura, but in the section of the upper Rawka the lines were anything but impregnable. Our 'pre-prepared' defense line also did not extend 'backwards', not only was there no second line of fortifications but not even any communication trenches. The reserve forces of the 1st Army manning the Rawka positions, tasked on December 16 and 17 with securing the withdrawal of our forces, were unable to improve the military

FIGURE 4.2 Map showing the central Polish section of the Eastern Front. The black square indicates the approximate area covered by the Great War conflict landscape of 1914–1915 and investigated archaeologically and historically during the last decade. Source: map © J. Czarnecki.

> quality of the positions under these conditions, and only barely managed to clear them of snow and mud.
>
> *(Nieznamow 1922: 31)*

This description of the defensive line, written after the war, is corroborated by a telegram dated 6 December (19 December) 1915.[1] It was dispatched by the 2nd Army chief of staff, General Kiprian Kondratowicz, to the command of the North-Western Front as an urgent report:

> The works on fortifying the positions are conducted with great intensity. The engineering units aided by local residents were unable to complete any of the preliminary fortification works before the arrival of the main corps force to the right bank of the Rawka. The works were initiated only under the commands of the corps engineer, by the army's own efforts.
>
> *(РГВИА Фонд 2019, О. 1. Д. 72)*

Manpower and firepower

The failure of the Russians to deal effectively with the forces of nature in this landscape encouraged their enemies to take action. From mid-December 1914, the German forces made repeated efforts to break through this 'dry' front line section referred to as the 'Bolimów outpost' with the hope of overcoming the Russian defences and advancing towards Warsaw. Six divisions of the German Ninth Army were concentrated in this region. Their opposition initially consisted of eight divisions (in December 1914), but by January that number had increased to 15 (HStAS m33/3 533), though some of these were likely in name only. For instance, on 14 January 1915, the 55th Infantry Division was composed of only 10,473 soldiers commanded by 145 commissioned officers, rather than the statutory 18,288 soldiers and 378 officers (РГВИА Фонд 2019, О. 2. Д. 32). The 5th Siberian Rifle Division fared even worse with only 9,464 of its 18,767 men still capable of fighting. Of the initial 387 officers, only 100 remained in the division by mid-January (РГВИА Фонд 2019, О. 2. Д. 32). Admittedly, during the period of stagnation and positional warfare on the Eastern Front in central Poland, the condition of the German troops was hardly any better (Figure 4.2). On 21 December 1914, the regiments of XIII Army Corps fighting in the regions of Żylin and Sucha could muster only a third of their statutory force. Of the official 3,400 officers and soldiers per regiment, the 119th Grenadier Regiment counted only 970 men, the 125th Infantry only 900 men, and the 121st and 122nd approximately 1,100 men each, including recently received reinforcements (HStAS M33/2 Bu 87: 317). Despite this shortage of manpower, the Germans attacked during December 1914 and January 1915. Their advance brought further people, places, and things into the warscape.

In mid-January 1915, the German command began preparations for two large-scale military operations to be launched on the Eastern Front. The first, and most important from the perspective of German commanders, would be an offensive in the Mazurian Lake District of East Prussia (today, the eastern part of the Warmia and Mazuria region of Poland). The second would be an operation on the Rawka and Bzura Rivers, the main purpose of which was to divert Russian attention from the German preparations in East Prussia. As described by General Ludendorff: 'In order for the Russians to believe that we would continue the offensive [towards Warsaw], the 9th Army was to launch a full-scale attack in the region of Bolimów at the end of January' (Ludendorff 1919: 121).

FIGURE 4.3 German 15-centimetre Howitzer sFH 02 in position on the Rawka in the area of Borzymów. Source: © collection of J. Czarnecki.

To focus attention on the Rawka, the Ninth German Army planned a full-scale infantry attack supported by 600 artillery pieces (Figure 4.3). This was to be the greatest artillery barrage of its time, concentrated along a front line of only 10–11 kilometres. The eminent artillery general Hans von Schabel was present at Rawka, aiding the attack, and recorded a conversation with the commander of the Ninth Army, General August von Mackensen.

> He welcomed me with the words: 'do you realize you will be commanding 596 guns in total? That has never happened before in the history of the world. I congratulate you on your task. You must be so proud. We did not have that many guns throughout the whole war of 1866'.
>
> *(Kaliński 2015: 113)*

The earth itself still bears witness to this heavy concentration of firepower. After 100 years, 18% of the 30,800 archaeological finds uncovered in the ARM's research area consisted of artillery shell fragments.

From landscape to gas-scape

The barrage planned for the winter Battle of Bolimów was most notable for the fact that this mass of conventional shells was accompanied by various 'experimental munitions' containing tear-producing and irritant gases. The artillery units operating in the Rawka region were issued with at least 18,000 shells containing two chemical agents: o-Dianisidine (in German, *Dianisidinsalz*) – a substance inducing violent spasms of sneezing, which the Germans referred to as *Niespulver* – and Xylyl bromide (also known as *T-stoff* ['Substance-T']), which caused a strong lachrymal reaction. The shells containing the irritant sneeze-inducing gas had first been used by the Germans during the battle of Nueve Chapelle in France in October 1914. During that initial test, approximately 3,000 Ni shells (*Ni-Geschosse*), officially known as *10.5 cm Schrapnell Ni* (Hanslian 1925: 9), were fired. The attack failed to produce the expected results. Nevertheless, by the end of December 1914, both 'Ni shells' and 'T shells' – officially the *15 cm Gr. 12 T* – were delivered to the Rawka front line. They would be fired, respectively, by the 10.5-centimetre light field howitzer and 15-centimetre heavy field howitzer (Figure 4.3).

The earliest mention of chemical weaponry deployment on the Eastern Front is likely provided in the *War Journal of the 9th Army*. An entry under 4 January reads: '1st Reserve Corps requested permission to use "Ni" shells during the attack on Russian trenches between the Mogiły manor and the edge of the forest' (*Kriegstagebuches der 9. Armee Zeit*: 5.1–31.1). For 15 January, a Ninth Army officer entered a report regarding gas shell use on 17 January, after the attack of the 17th Army Corps troops on the so-called 'Hill 95' in the vicinity of the village of Humin. The effects of the chemical weapons were described thus:

> The gas shells had a fairly good effect yesterday, as the physically strong Russians could not bear to stand the gas spreading in the shelled trenches, nor outside them. The riflemen abandoned their positions – covering their faces with their hands – and the captured prisoners (1 officer, 90 soldiers) remained intoxicated until the evening. [...] Immediate recapture of the positions was impossible due to the gas lingering there for a long time. However, the enemy's panicked escape from the trenches proves the possibility of effectively using those shells in the future.
>
> *(BArch PH 5-II/281: 20)*

Also, the 13th Army Corps fighting in the northern section of this outpost tested 'T shells' no later than 20 January. This is confirmed in the entry reading: 'Our artillery "T" shelled the identified enemy positions' (HStAS M33/2 Bu 88 281). The subsequent mentions of the use of chemical weaponry refer to 22 January, and the 26 January entry in the *War Journal of the 13th Corps* reads:

> 14.00 hours, 4th battery of the 13th Field Artillery Regiment (Mizerka Group), commanded by Major Goecke and Captain Breidert, commenced experimental barrage. [...] [Russian] Soldiers fled the trenches. Then, field artillery initiated the special barrage. Some men fled once the "T" shelling began.
>
> *(HStAS M33/2 Bu 88 281)*

The aforementioned accounts evidence the fact that gas ammunition was in the Rawka region as early as 1915. The conciseness of those accounts, compared to the relatively more descriptive character of other reports, indicates that the German command wished to keep these uses of chemical weaponry secret.

The deliberate contestation of these events is further corroborated by the fact that while the *War Journal of the 13th Corps* (HStAS M33/2 Bu 88) reported in detail the exact time and artillery units involved in the respective attacks, there was no mention of the qualitative or quantitative inventory of 'T shells' or the extent of their use. While each artillery report was accompanied by drawings detailing the respective bombardments, there was only one piece of material evidence (see Figure 4.4) for the use of 'T shells', in the form of a sketch. It is highly doubtful that this could be an accident.

Another entry, dated 23 January 1915, and apparently 'accidentally' left in the *War Journal of the Ninth Army*, concerns the delivery of gas shells to that army's depots: 'Of the newly introduced shells [9.], the Army received 1,200 heavy (15cm) and 6,000 light (10cm) gas shells' (BArch PH 5-II/281).

The fact that only one of many such deliveries is mentioned can be inferred from the number of shells mentioned. As claimed by both generals Ludendorff (1919:121) and Hoffman (2013: 51) in their memoirs, the Ninth Army was issued a total of 18,000 gas shells, whereas the quoted entry mentions only 7,300 items, approximately a third of the entire publicly admitted allotment. It seems likely that this discrepancy results from a deliberate attempt during 1915 to obscure the use of these new munitions – a necessity that no longer prevailed when the two generals wrote their post-war memoirs. This perception is reinforced by

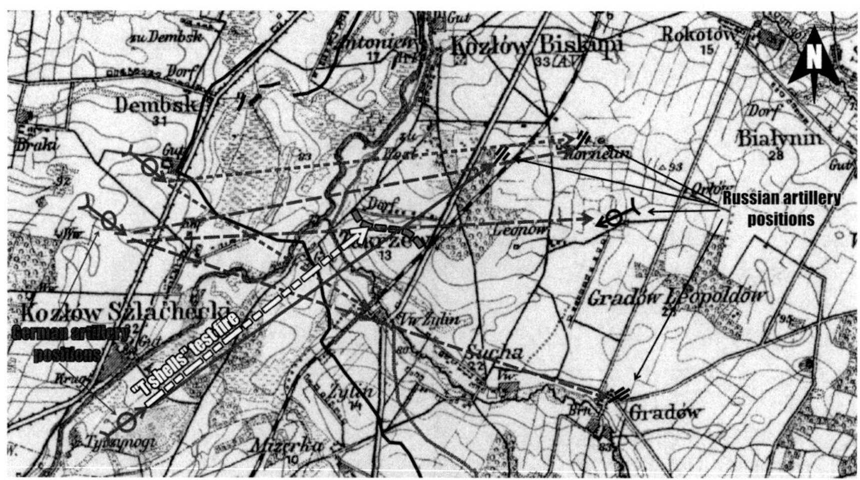

FIGURE 4.4 A sketch illustrating the topographic context of the artillery barrage of 26 January 1915, with marked directions of the attacks undertaken with 'T shell' chemical weapons. Source: © authors' elaboration of primary data from HStAS M33/2 Bu 88: 245; map © J. Czarnecki.

the absence of any mention in Ninth Army and 13th Army Corps documents of the continued use of thousands of 'T' and 'Ni' shells between 31 January and 5 February, even though reports concerning the effectiveness of this new weapon must have been forwarded to all command levels.

Questioning the significance of the gas barrage of 31 January 1915

The German offensive on the Rawka began on 31 January 1915. The attack with gas shells was preceded by a regular artillery barrage. This alternation of conventional and chemical bombardment continued for six days. In the memoirs of two leading wartime officers, the results of the gas were reported as underwhelming. Much of the subsequent historiography of the battle has followed their lead. Erich Ludendorff, responsible for Eastern Front strategy at the time, recalled in his memoirs that 'the weather was too cold for a gas attack, though that as yet we did not realize' (Ludendorff 1919: 122). Ludendorff's chief of staff, Max Hoffmann, personally observed the gas attack launched between 9:00 and 9:45 am (Kaliński 2015: 121), recalling that:

> In the morning of January 31, I arrived in Bolimów and observed the gas attack and the battle from the church tower. Judging by what General Schabel had told me about the gas shells, I assumed that the use of such an amount of munitions, which seemed truly enormous to us, would have far more serious effects [...] At the time, they did not realize that *extreme cold* can impact the effectiveness of the gases. The tactical outcome, apart from the heavy losses suffered by the Russians, was that we managed to even out some of the positions.
>
> *(Hoffmann 2013: 52, emphasis added)*

However, if we correlate the alleged 'extreme cold' with the available meteorological information, it is difficult not to question this explanation for the 'ineffectiveness' of the chemical attack. Analyzing German weather reports for the days preceding the battle and during it, it becomes apparent that the temperatures in the region could not have been as low as suggested. From the *War Journal of 13th Corps* (HStAS M33/2 Bu 88), which includes information about temperatures and weather forecasts, we know that on 29 January, the temperature was approximately −6 degrees Celsius and it was snowing lightly. On 31 January, the temperature was around −5 to −6 degrees Celsius, and on 2 February it was −4 to −5. Furthermore, the claims that the 'extreme cold' weakened the effects of the gas seem to be contradicted by the Germans' own reports, both those officially included in war journals and others unofficially published after the war in various regimental chronicles. These suggest that the gas shells proved effective during the tests of 16 and 26 January. Also, the descriptions of how the gas worked during the clashes of 31 January and afterwards, as provided by German and Russian soldiers, suggest that the gas was indeed effective and caused severe lachrymation, coughing, and headache. The surviving Russian archives include telegrams sent by the Second Army chief of staff, General Kondratowicz, who reported to the North-Western Front Command that: 'There have been reports from various places along the frontline that upon impact, the German shells release some sort of suffocating and acrid gas that severely affects the eyes, there are suspicions it may be formalin' (РГВИА Фонд 2019, О. 1. дело 72, telegram of 31(18) January 1915 at 1:30 pm).

On the German side of the front line, the advancing soldiers of the 128th Infantry Regiment described the gas effects as follows: 'shells filled with gas poisoned the air so badly the [captured] Russian trenches could only be manned by volunteers' (Richter 1931: 109). The author of the 49th Infantry Regiment's war history described a gas attack thus:

> Our artillery has just started firing the T (gas) shells. This was to be the final 10 minutes. [...] We were only bothered by the tear inducing gases rained on us by the artillery which did not know we were already on the attack. [...] Some men could not handle the T gas and wanted to run back. We did not know gas masks back then.
>
> *(Duncker and Eisermann 1927: 49)*

These descriptions differ from the version first disseminated by the generals and later repeated in historiography as to the reduced volatility of the gases due to low temperatures. German archives also include another account pertaining to the artillery barrage and the effects of gas weapons. *The War Journal of the 9th Army* sums up the events of 31 January 1915 as follows:

> The effects of yesterday's attack, particularly the artillery barrage, was underwhelming. The results obtained by firing the howitzers against the enemy's earthworks and terrain obstacles in the local theatre seems disproportionate to the amount of munitions spent. Just the 26 heavy howitzer batteries fired a total of 18,345 rounds today, and the 6 210mm mortars fired 1286 times. Also, as reported today by the 17th Army Corps command, the intoxicating gas ammunition proved more of an obstacle to our own soldiers.
>
> *(BArch PH 5-II/281: 49)*

To recapitulate, in our opinion there are certain well-founded doubts regarding the truthfulness of the accounts of generals Ludendorff and Hoffmann, which were subsequently widely cited by historians and which reduced the significance of the event to a single-sentence footnote. But the knowledge not publicly admitted or mentioned in the post-war memoirs of the generals must nonetheless have been perfectly clear to all the German staff officers at the time: namely that the Russian defences in the Rawka region were too strong for the Germans to break through even with all the artillery and chemical weaponry at their disposal. The allegations, by high-ranking officers, of a weather-related technical failure of the gas might have stemmed from a wish to deflect attention from their own inadequate planning. This must have resulted in an intensification of the work on gas deployment in combat situations. This development was conducted in two key directions – improvement of tear gases as well developing new lethal agents (see Szöllösi-Janze 2015; Kaliński 2015; Zalewska and Czarnecki 2014).

Positional warfare on both the Western and Eastern Fronts effectively prevented significant advances, thereby rendering a swift end of the hostilities unlikely. The Central Powers were ill-equipped to fight a long war, so the Germans continued to develop their chemical warfare capabilities, seeking a 'breakthrough weapon' that would get soldiers out of the trenches. It is not widely remembered that the resulting chemical agents were deployed on the Eastern Front as well as in the well-documented West (e.g. Haber 2002; Lepick 1998; Szöllösi-Janze 2015; Zanders 2015). After the fiasco of the January gas bombardment on the Rawka, the Germans decided to deploy new, and this time lethal, gases. Three gas-cloud attacks (with the agent released from cylinders rather than contained in shells) were made. One of these (in May) employed a huge number of gas containers – almost twice the number used in the more famous gas attack at Ypres on the Western Front. In a subsequent attack (in June), a significant number of German soldiers were poisoned, some fatally, due to a change in wind direction. The fact that these major chemical attacks are largely ignored in the conventional historiography of the war is a significant factor in shaping the contours of the memory-scape that developed out of the warscape of the Rawka and Bzura. For further analysis of these gas-cloud attacks, see Zalewska (2013, 2016, 2019), Zalewska et al. (2014), Kaliński (2015), and Zalewska and Czarnecki (2016).

Archaeology searching for a contested present

The transformation of landscape into warscape had human consequences. When the front line stood in the Rawka-Bzura region, local people were pressed into constructing field fortifications, and later they contested this wartime appropriation and began repairing and healing the landscape. This post-depositional transformation of field fortifications and support infrastructure, as well as of war cemeteries and other burial places, began in the autumn of 1915. It continued until 1918 when locals displaced by German occupiers began returning to their ruined homes and were forced to live initially in the shelters and dugouts left behind by the soldiers (Figure 4.5). Our studies revealed, unexpectedly, that this was the most radical stage in the conversion of the *warscape* into a *memory-scape*. Subsequently, changes occurred at a slower pace, as warscape memories faded and its remnants became displaced and erased.

Descendants of those who returned to the war-ravaged area[2] reported that even the trees left standing in the forests could not be used as building material as they were riddled with bullets and shrapnel. When under German occupation

FIGURE 4.5 Public lectures, archaeological exhibitions, and active learning *in situ* workshops in direct contact with the warscape encouraged interest, empathy for the fallen, and a reflexive engagement with the material remains of the Great War. Source: © A. I. Zalewska.

(from late summer 1915 onwards), the military authorities forced local residents to clear recyclable materials from the trenches, in particular, scrap metal and ammunition casings. Civilians were also employed and/or forced to collect the dead from the surrounding fields and orchards and bury them alongside those still lying in the trenches. Once the front line had been cleared of human remains, farmers filled in the trench lines, smaller shell craters, and some of the mine crater remains of underground warfare. They began cultivating the land and returned to their pre-war lives. Even at this early stage, contestation of the events on the Rawka and Bzura, including efforts to erase the material traces, was evident in actions undertaken and words spoken. These took the form of memoirs, the rare diaries of an eye-witness, and also stories handed down in families and that survive today.

All efforts aimed at restoring the landscape to its original pre-war condition and roles can be regarded as a form of contesting war and its material consequences (see Zalewska et al. 2014; Czarnecki 2019; Kiarszys 2019; Zalewska, Czarnecki and Kiarszys 2019). Efforts to blur the legacy of war – a matter of social and agricultural necessity – were so effective that after a hundred years, modern technologies were required to locate and identify its traces. Archaeology, however, proved more than capable of simply mapping material remains; it also facilitated research into the material memory of this regional warscape. Indeed, this was one of the principal goals of the project entitled *Archaeological Restoration of the Memory of the Great War: Material traces of the life and death in the trenches of the Great War in the region of the Rawka and Bzura rivers* (abbreviated: ARM). This research was conducted between 2014 and 2018 and combined scientific research with social and cultural activities. It also provided the context for the realization of three principal goals of the endeavour:

- To restore the memory of the First World War's Eastern Front.
- To enrich our knowledge about the lives and deaths of soldiers in the trenches.
- To inform the general public's awareness and understanding of the significance, scale, and material consequences of the military operations undertaken in the Rawka and Bzura region 100 years ago.

The research deployed remote sensing methods, including analysis of archive aerial photographs from 1915 (see Czarnecki 2019) and numerical analyses of terrain models derived from LiDAR (Zalewska et al. 2015; Zalewska and Kiarszys 2015; Kiarszys 2019), as well as an archaeological surface survey. We enhanced the perception of the landscape at cognitive and social levels, as a tangible witness and indeed as the sole witness of itself. This was achieved by determining the specificity, quality, dispersion, and preservation of movable artefacts and immovable monuments – closely related to each other and jointly constituting the (currently unwanted, under-valued, and poorly known) Polish heritage of the Great War. The results of these historical and archaeological investigations have been presented elsewhere (see Zalewska 2017, 2019; Zalewska et al. 2015, 2017, 2019). Here, we focus on the problem of investigating the experimental use of chemical weapons in combat, the outcome of which was contested as early as 1915 (as shown above), and which we suggest is still contested after 100 years.

The volatile nature of the chemicals used in January 1915 meant that they were unlikely to have left any physical traces, and neither would the lethal chlorine used subsequently. This was confirmed by Dr Śliwakowski from the Organic Industry Institute, who is also a member of the Scientific Advisory Board of Organization for the Prohibition of Chemical Weapons – OPCW (Śliwakowski and Chałas 2019). Nevertheless, having completed the historical stage of the ARM project, we investigated whether it might be possible to detect traces of irritants such as xylyl bromide or o-nitrobenzyl. Analysis of samples from five locations of confirmed gas attacks in the vicinity of Joachimów-Mogiły and Wola Szydłowiecka, near Bolimów, revealed no traces of the irritants or any products of their decomposition. However, the volatility of chemical agents was not the primary cause of the absence of irrefutable evidence of such attacks. The incomplete historical data was due to a decision made by people, not nature.

A further strand of human intervention that has eroded the remains of the warscape is the persistent phenomenon of militaria hunting, or battlefield looting, a feature of many First and Second World War locations in Europe and beyond. This has been present in the Rawka and Bzura region since the 1970s. Even though such activities have been illegal in Poland since 2003, they continue largely unhindered. Easy public access to NMT and LiDAR results, as well as modern detecting equipment, has made the problem more widespread. Numerous traces of illegal diggings conducted at combat locations (i.e. trenches and no man's land) and at the burial sites of Russian or German soldiers were documented by our project in the Rawka and Bzura region.

As we have tried to show, many factors contributed to the current condition of the warscape in central Poland, a condition due in large part to the significant episodes that transformed this landscape into a gas-scape. However, as archaeology has revealed, within a century of the war's end, multiple layers of subsequent material and discursive practices were overlaid onto that landscape, superimposing their own traces.

Excavation followed the surface survey and located and identified the remains of soldiers killed on the battlefield. We also identified unknown and unregistered military cemeteries, as well as traces of backfilling and levelling which had altered the features of the post-war landscape. These discoveries raise many new interpretative issues for future research. Our perception of a general lack of public understanding of the material traces of the war and our awareness of the significant changes that the landscape had undergone in recent times encouraged us to engage with a very different type of archaeological practice[3] (Figure 4.5).

The project had two distinct parts. Locally, it entailed the organization of workshops for young residents of the local Bolimów Commune and the joint preparation of educational materials and other resources (e.g. a quiz on the Great War remains in the Rawka River basin and educational tools helpful in field games and *in situ* workshops). At the transnational level, it entailed the preparation of a publication discussing the history of the 1915 use of chemical weapons in central Poland for translation into English. The goal was to stimulate the local desire to provide *in situ* protection for the area's unique monuments and the material remains of specific events of 1915, and to disseminate knowledge of those events in order to ensure a future free from weapons of mass destruction and encourage conservation and cultural tourism. Summing up, the project allows us to make a number of observations and conclusions which are significant in the context of the critical heritage studies, memory studies, and curation of war memorials, and the study of the processes of investigating the remains of the troubled past. In other words, it allows us to analyze the First World War's conflict landscapes in all their complexity from an interdisciplinary perspective.

Some final remarks

The importance and urgency of the socially sensitive and public-oriented project briefly described above stems from the fact that the landscape of the Rawka and Bzura region is – in common with human memory – subject to a continual fading of the remaining physical traces. In many places, these have been erased almost completely, and often intentionally. This is why the current condition and the ongoing transformation of the Rawka and Bzura landscape are in need of painstaking and interdisciplinary documentation. The post-war places and objects that were, are, or might become 'carriers of memory' are subject to continuous evolution. Their changes are influenced by a variety of factors and processes – both anthropogenic and natural. This chapter has identified three distinct stages in this evolution:

1. *Primary (pre-depositional) stage*, i.e. from 1914 to July 1915, when the significance of events was questioned while they were still unfolding. For example, the January tests with gas shells were concealed or camouflaged as insignificant and those that could not be 'denied' were described as unsuccessful and therefore generally not discussed. The effectiveness of this type of contestation is evidenced in the still prevalent belief that 18,000 shells failed to 'work' due to cold temperatures. Meanwhile, as archival resources have revealed, it is evident that those early experiments with weapons of mass destruction were not merely about 18,000 shells rendered ineffective by weather conditions, but about consistently testing the usability of the weapon in this particular time and place. The trials resulted in the further escalation of the use of chemical weapons, which culminated in attacks whose scale far exceeded those deployed at the Second Battle of Ypres – a fact conveniently forgotten by the world.
2. *Secondary (depositional and post-depositional) stage*, i.e. between 1915 and 1918. This comprised the immediate aftermath when the front line moved on from the Rawka and Bzura region, and the immediate post-war period when the historical significance and status of war cemeteries and battlefield features were elided and efforts were made to return the landscape to its pre-war condition and function. This led indirectly to a situation where to reflect on central Poland's former gas-scape is in fact to reflect on the absence (or rather absent presence) of wartime interments of fallen soldiers and (seemingly) the non-existence of traces of war.
3. *Secondary (post-depositional) stage*, i.e. from 1918 until 'yesterday' (since Poland regained its independence and the landscape marked with material traces of the Great War became what it is today, a phenomenon that is open to enquiry and which needs to be studied and interpreted before its historical significance can be understood). It therefore satisfies the most classic definition of 'archaeologicality': to investigate what it was and what it has become and assess whether or not it is worth researching, and whether it can offer any social value (as a material warning against future conflicts).

These stages emphasize the point that the complex and difficult transformations of the conflict landscape continue and that its significance and evocative character demand wider recognition. This is why the current condition and the ongoing transformation of the remains of the gas-scape in central Poland require thoughtful, attentive, and trans-disciplinary research by archaeologists, historians, anthropologists, and others, as well as pro-social, inclusive, and participatory culture-forming activities.

As we have tried to demonstrate in this chapter, the contested past and experienced war landscapes along with the constantly evolving memory of them can be investigated and discussed in a variety of ways and on a number of levels, from archaeological and historical research and scientific reports and monographs to *in situ* workshops, public presentations, exhibitions, youth competitions, and popular science publications (Figure 4.5).

What matters most, however, is direct contact with the relics of field fortifications, artefacts, and the final resting places of soldiers in official war cemeteries and in places only recently gaining that status through the efforts of archaeologists and so-called grave finders. The directness of contact with the experienced place confirms the belief that despite continuous transformations, the gas-scape created in January 1915 might serve as a trigger for future research, a warning from the past to the future, and a truthful light shed on the present.

Acknowledgements

The results of this research are the outcome of the project entitled *Archaeological Restoration of the Memory of the Great War: Material traces of the life and death in the trenches of the Eastern Front and the transformations of the battlefield landscape in the region of Rawka and Bzura*, financed with a grant from the National Science Centre awarded under decision number DEC-2013/10/E/HS3/00406. Observations in the field of education, pro-conservation activities, and the dissemination of knowledge about the contacts between the troubled recent past and the present have been made on the basis of observation from implementing the project titled *Experienced places as spaces of maintaining historical monuments, protecting the difficult 20th century heritage, and educating for peace*, which is part of a scholarship from the Minister of Culture and National Heritage awarded to the senior author.

Notes

1 All the dates obtained from Russian documents (included in the citations) are given in two versions: a) according to the Julian calendar, i.e. as given in the source material, and b) in brackets – according to the Gregorian calendar used in the entire western world. The discrepancy is 13 calendar days, e.g. the date of 18(31) January will refer to 18 January according to the calendar used by the Russians at the time and 31 January according to the western calendar which was also used by Poles living under the partition rule, in this case under Russian occupation. Unfortunately, many English, French, or German translations and/or analyses seem to contain numerous mistakes resulting from the failure to account for the discrepancy between calendars used by the opposing sides of the conflict.

2 Interviews with selected residents of the research area whose family histories were marked by the First World War were one of the stages of the ARM project.

3 An outreach programme entitled *Experienced places as spaces of maintaining historical monuments, protecting the difficult 20th century heritage, and educating for peace*, the main goal of which was to demonstrate the global significance of local monuments related to the Great War in the territory of today's Poland. In this chapter we refer especially to the initial use of weapons of mass destruction in combat in January 1915, which, while significant in world history, was soon forgotten. We are investigating whether or not these events can be examined and remembered through the work of archaeologists, historians, anthropologists, and the 'last witnesses' so that the former gas-scape can achieve the status of archaeological finds and monuments.

References

Czarnecki, J. (2019) Archiwalne zdjęcia zwiadowcze – rozpoznanie lotnicze oraz rola samolotów w czasie bitwy nad Rawką i Bzurą 1914–1915. In A. Zalewska (ed.), *Archeologiczne przywracanie pamięci o Wielkiej Wojnie w rejonie Rawki i Bzury (1914–1915)*, pp. 181–196. Warszawa: Wydawnictwo IAiE PAN.

Desfossés, Y., A. Jacques and G. Prilaux. (2009) *Great War Archaeology*. Rennes: OUEST-FRANCE.

Duncker, H. and H. Eisermann. (1927) *Das Infanterie-Regiment v. Kluck (6. Pomm.) Nr. 49 im Weltkriege 1914–1918*. Oldenburg: Gerhard Salling.

Haber, L.F. (2002) *The Poisonous Cloud*. Oxford. Clarendon Press.

Hanslian, R. (1925) *Der Chimische Krieg*. Berlin: S. Mittler & Sohn.

Hoffmann, M. (2013 [1925]) *Wspomnienia. Wojna Wśród Niewyzyskanych Sposobności*. Reprint. Oświęcim: Wydawnictwo Napoleon V.

Kaliński, S. (2015) *Bolimów 1915*. Warszawa: Bellona.

Kiarszys G. (2019). *Zastosowanie lotniczego skanowania laserowego w projekcie Archeologiczne Przywracanie Pamięci o Wielkiej Wojnie*. In: A.I. Zalewska (ed.). *Archeologiczne Przywracanie pamięci o Wielkiej Wojnie w rejonie Rawki i Bzury (1914-1915)*, pp 155-170. Warszawa: IAE PAN

Lepick, O. (1998) *La Grande Guerre Chimique*. Paris: Presses universitaires de France.

Ludendorff, E. (1919) *My War Memories, 1914–1918*. London: Hutchinson.

Neiberg, M.S. (2013) *Wybuch pierwszej wojny światowej oczami Europejczyków*. Kraków: Wydawnictwo Uniwersytet Jagieloński.

Nieznamow, A. (ed.) (1922) *Стратегический очерк войны 1914–1918*, vol. III. Moskwa.

Pares, B. (1915) *Day By Day With The Russian Army 1914–1915*. London: Constable.

Richter, W. (1931) *Das danzinger Infanterie Regiment 128, cz. I*. Zeulenroda: Sporn Verlag.

РГВИА Фонд (RGVIA) (2019) O. 1. дело 72. Telegram of January 31(18), 1915 at 1:30 pm. Rossijskij Gosudarstvennyj Voenno-Istoričeskij Arhiv - Russian State Military Historical Archive.

Saunders, N.J. (ed.) (2004) *Matters of Conflict. Material Culture, Memory, and the First World War*. London: Routledge.

Saunders, N.J. and P. Cornish (eds.) (2009) *Contested Objects. Material Memories of the Great War*. London: Routledge.

Schofield, J. (2005) *Combat Archaeology. Material Culture and Modern Conflict*. London: Duckworth.

Śliwakowski, M. and A. Chałas. (2019) Poszukiwanie śladów użycia substancji drażniących. Analiza próbek z rejonu walk prowadzonych w czasie I wojny światowej w okolicach Bolimowa. In A. Zalewska (ed.), *Archeologiczne przywracanie pamięci o Wielkiej Wojnie w rejonie Rawki i Bzury (1914–1915)*, pp. 113–116. Warszawa: Wydawnictwo IAiE PAN.

Stichelbaut, B. (2018) *Traces of War: The Archaeology of the First World War*. Veurne: Hannibal Publishing.

Szöllösi-Janze, M. (2015) *Fritz Haber, 1868–1934: Eine Biographie*. München: C.H. Beck.

Zalewska, A.I. (2013) Roadside Lessons of Historicity. The Roles and the Meanings of the Material Points of References to The Great War and in Shaping Historical Sensitivity and Awareness. *Sensus Historiae* XIII (4): 69–85.

——— (2016) The 'Gas-scape' on the Eastern Front, Poland (1914–2014): Exploring the Material and Digital Landscapes and Remembering Those 'Twice-Killed'. In B. Stichelbaut and D. Cowley (eds), *Conflict Landscapes and Archaeology from Above*, pp. 147–165. Farnham: Ashgate.

——— (2017) Archaeology of the Contemporaneous Times and the Power(Lessness) of Physical Traces of the Great War in Poland. *Ochrona Zabytków* 2 (271) LXX 2/2017: 47–77.

——— (2019) Historia użycia przez armię niemiecką broni masowego rażenia (*Massenwirkung*) w rejonie Rawki i Bzury w styczniu 1915 roku. In A.I. Zalewska (ed.), *Archeologiczne Przywracanie pamięci o Wielkiej Wojnie w rejonie Rawki i Bzury (1914–1915)*, pp. 97–110. IAE PAN:Warszawa.

Zalewska, A.I and J. Czarnecki. (2016) *Ślady i Świadectwa*. Warszawa: Fundacja Przydrożne Lekcje Historii

Zalewska, A.I., J. Czarnecki and M. Jakubczak. (2015) Archaeological Revival of Memory of the Great War. The Role of LiDAR in Tracing of the Boundaries of the Planned Cultural Park, The Rawka Battlefield (1914–1915) – in Memory of War Victims. *Archaeologia Polona* 53: 407–412.

Zalewska, A.I., J. Czarnecki and S. Kaliński. (2014) *Wielka Wojna nad Rawka (1914–1915) i materialne po niej pozostałości*. Warszawa:Fundacja Przydrożne Lekcje Historii & IAIE PAN.

Zalewska, A.I., J. Czarnecki and G. Kiarszys. (2019) *Krajobraz Wielkiej Wojny. Front nad Rawką i Bzurą (1914–1915) w świetle teledetekcji archeologicznej i źródeł historycznych*. Warszawa: Fundacja Przydrożne Lekcje Historii & IAIE PAN.

Zalewska, A.I. and G. Kiarszys (2015) Sensing the Material Remains of the Forgotten Great War in Poland. Sensibly or Sensationally – The dilemma in Front of Presenting Results of the Airborne Laser Scanning Visualizations. In A.G. Posluschny (ed.), *Sensing the Past. Contributions from the ArcLand Conference on Remote Sensing for Archaeology*, pp. 72–73. Arcland/Habelt-Verlag: Bonn.

——— (2017) Absent Presence of Great War Cemeteries in the Municipality of Bolim.w, Central Poland. In A.I. Zalewska, J.M. Scott and G. Kiarszys (eds.), *The Materiality of Troubled Pasts: Archaeologies of Conflicts and Wars*, pp. 55–81. Warszawa-Szczecin: Fundacja Przydrożne Lekcje Historii & Uniwersytet Szczeciński.

Zanders, J.P. (ed.) (2015) *Innocence Slaughtered: Gas and the Transformation of Warfare and Society*. Chicago: Uniform Press/University of Chicago Press.

Archives

Bayerisches Hauptstaatsarchiv München – Geheimes Hausarchiv
Bundesarchiv-Militararchiv in Freiburg im Breisgau (BArch)
Hauptstaatsarchiv Stuttgart (HStAS)
Rossijskij Gosudarstvennyj Voenno-Istoričeskij Arhiv (RGVIA – РГВИА)

5

CONTROVERSY IN THE JULIAN ALPS

Erwin Rommel, landscape, and the 12th Battle of the Soča/Isonzo

Alexander J. Potočnik

Introduction

Relationships with the landscape are personal as well as cultural, perhaps never as tellingly as during conflict. Human movement across and through a wartime landscape is critical to survival as well as to victory or defeat, and the more extreme the terrain, the more difficult it can be to master. One of the most challenging of such landscapes is the Julian Alps in present-day Slovenia and Italy, which played a central role in the First World War between Italy and the Austro-Hungarian and German armies. It was here that one of the most militarily dramatic and controversial events of the war took place in October 1917, involving a young Erwin Rommel and his ability to pursue tactical and strategic goals in the Alpine landscape. This episode, it seems, is an insightful example of how the 'battle-zone landscapes of modern industrialized war are unique locations for the creation and expression of individual identity' (Saunders 2009: 37).

The Julian Alps are part of the Ljubljana Gap area. Contrary to its literal meaning, it is not a single space but rather a network of valleys, basins, and passes that traverse the peaks, forming the last promontory of the high Alps and the lower Pre-Alpine Hills. This network connects the plain of the River Po in northern Italy with the Pannonian Plain to the northeast. It is also the easiest access to Italy and as such was used as an entry route for Italy-bound northern peoples during the period of great migrations.[1]

The strategic importance of this passage and efforts to control it can be discerned from the overlay of borders between major European nations for the last two millennia (Figure 5.1). When compared to the stability of the borders on the ridges of the Carnic Alps and the Karawanks and on the rivers Kolpa and Sotla, the shifting borders within the Ljubljana Gap area and the concentration

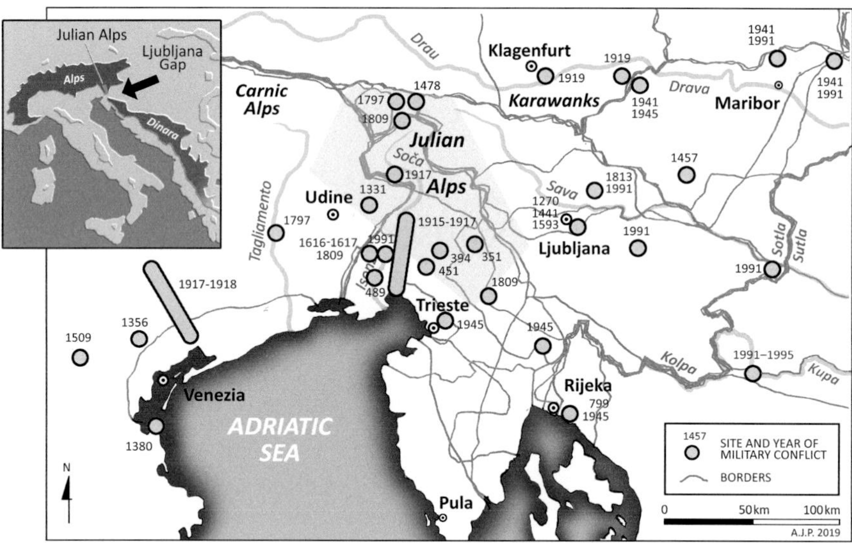

FIGURE 5.1 The Ljubljana Gap area marked with shifting borders and significant military conflicts during the last 2,000 years. Source: © author.

of significant military conflicts which took place there suggest that this was a heavily contested landscape throughout history.

The battle of Frigidus, with an outcome that in AD 394 established Christianity as the only religion of the previously pagan Roman Empire, may have been the one with the most far-reaching consequences for European history. However, the First World War battlefront along the River Soča/Isonzo that led to over a million casualties (Gradnik 1977: 212) was certainly the bloodiest. In the years 1915–1917, the Italians launched 11 offensives with the aim of breaking through the Ljubljana Gap onto the Pannonian Plain to conquer either the Austrian capital, Vienna, or the Hungarian capital, Budapest.

In October 1917, the combined Austro-Hungarian and German forces launched a counter-offensive, the 12th Battle of the Soča/Isonzo. In Italy and in Anglophone history this became known as the Battle of Caporetto, from the nearby town of Caporetto (Italian), also known as Karfreit (German) or Kobarid (Slovenian). By contrast to the Italians, who had concentrated their efforts in the Vipava River Valley and on the Kras/Carso Plateau further south, the Austrians chose the Upper Soča Valley, high in the Julian Alps, as the location for their break-through attempt. One of the participants of the battle was the then-Lieutenant Erwin Rommel. During the battle, he demonstrated great leadership skills and an ability to read and use the landscape to his advantage. After the war, he summed up his experiences in his 1937 book *Infantry Attacks*.

Rachel Woodward has remarked on the scarcity of literature written by military personnel as those most involved in looking at military landscapes (Woodward 2014: 48). It is perhaps hardly surprising then that Rommel's book has received a lot of attention through the years.[2] More surprising perhaps is the recent questioning of both his book and his actual role in the battle. The contradictory views imply the retention of certain traits of a contested landscape,[3] which the Julian Alps were even before the outbreak of hostilities in 1915; during the late nineteenth century, the Julian Alps were a place where national identities competed as they underwent a period of consolidation that required the establishment of ethnically defined frontiers.

The Julian Alps as a symbolic battlefield

If battlefields can be regarded in part as places for the construction of national identity (Woodward 2014: 42), then the battlefields of the European Alps certainly qualify. In his article 'The Mountains Roar', Tait Keller explores their role in the development of German national consciousness. Climbing mountain peaks demands courage, strength, energy, and the desire to fight for victory, while the 'alpine landscape itself conferred power and bravery' (Keller 2009: 255). For the Germans, who, in the middle of the nineteenth century, were divided into many political entities, the struggle for Alpine peaks represented, apart from freedom and spiritual renewal, the embodiment of 'Greater-German' ideals of cultural unity (ibid.: 256). In this context, Keller notes that the German and Austrian Alpine Associations formally united in 1873 (ibid.: 271).

Slovenians, then part of the Austro-Hungarian Empire, appreciated the Alps in a similar way,[4] and consequently, the Julian Alps became a symbolic battlefield. As a response to the intrusion of the German association into Slovenian mountains, the Slovenian Alpine Association (PZS) was formed in 1893.[5] The material manifestation of the contest was the speedy construction of mountain huts to secure the best starting points for tours. The first two huts were built by the Slovenian Mountaineering Association in 1894 on Lisec and under Mt Ojstrica (Mikša 2013). The contest reached a climax in 1895 when Jakob Aljaž, a priest from Mojstrana, purchased a plot on the peak of Mt Triglav, the highest in the Julian Alps, and erected a shelter in the shape of a tower[6] (Figure 5.2). During the early twentieth century, Mt Triglav became Slovenia's national symbol, depicted on the coat of arms[7] (Figure 5.3). A second legacy of the contest was that the use of mountain huts and shelters became a part of Slovenian national tradition.

The last people to become involved in this symbolic fight for the peaks of the Julian Alps were the Italians. Whether or not the depiction of a great fist-fight between Italian, Slovenian, and German mountaineers on the summit of Mt Triglav in 1895 – which featured in the 1980s Austrian-Slovenian biographic TV series about the mountaineer, Julius Kugy – is historically accurate or not, it illustrates the 1980s' perception of the historic rivalry.[8]

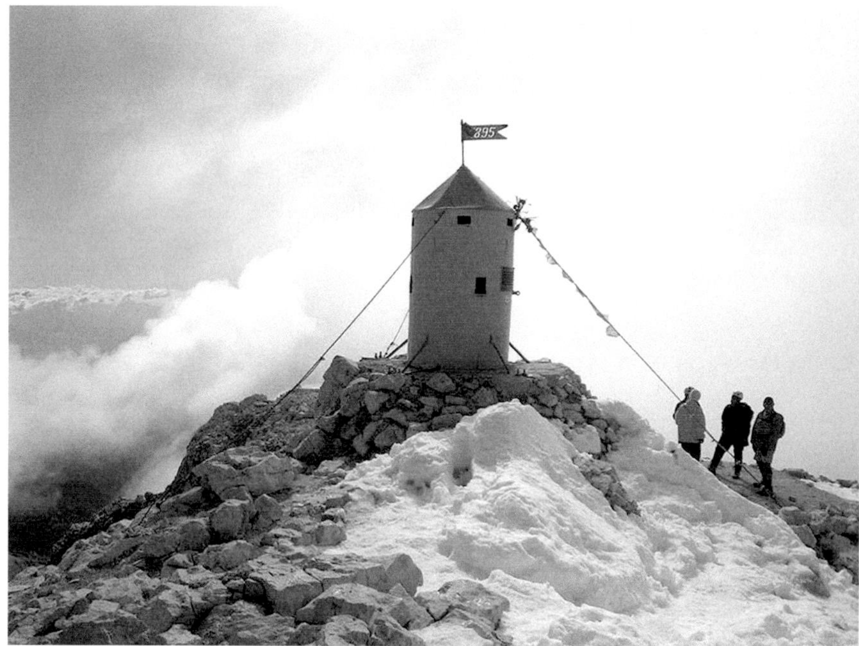

FIGURE 5.2 Aljaž Tower (*Aljažev stolp*) on the summit of Mt Triglav. Jakob Aljaž gifted the tower to the Slovenian Alpine Association (PZS) with a desire to preserve the Slovenian face of Slovenian mountains. Source: © David Edgar, Wikipedia, Creative Commons.

FIGURE 5.3 Coats of Arms of Slovenia featuring Mt Triglav. Left: 1945–1991. Right: the current Coat of Arms of the Republic of Slovenia, designed by Marko Pogačnik. Source: Wikipedia, public domain.

The 12th Battle of the Soča/Isonzo

With the Italian attack on Austria-Hungary in May 1915, the Julian Alps became a real battlefield and later the site of the 12th Battle of the Soča/Isonzo. On the morning of 24 October 1917, the major role was played by the Austro-German Battle Groups 'Krauss' and 'Stein', which executed a pincer movement from the towns of Bovec and Tolmin respectively. They managed to isolate Italian forces within a river bend – trapped on the peaks of Polovnik and Krasji vrh. The 12th German and 50th Austrian Divisions of the Stein Group advanced past Kobarid, reaching the gorge of the River Natisone. Because of their rapid progress,[9] the battle was nicknamed 'The Miracle of Caporetto'. Their advance was stopped in the Natisone Gorge at Stupizza.

On the morning of 25 October, Austro-German forces were poised to converge on Cividale, the gateway to the Friuli Plain. But to do so they first had to neutralize Italian positions at the Kolovrat Ridge and Mt Matajur. This was the task of the *Alpenkorps*, of which Rommel's WGB (Royal Württemberg Mountain Battalion) was part. During the day, the *Alpenkorps* breached the main defensive line on Kolovrat while the Italians retreated to Mt Matajur and attempted to man the last pre-prepared defence, called the San Martino line. On 26 October, Italian attempts to regroup on this last line were thwarted and the Italian defences started to collapse. The fall of Mt Matajur forced the defenders of Stupizza to retreat. Attempts to halt the attackers, first at Cividale and then at the River Tagliamento, failed. The Austro-German advance was only stopped at the River Piave, just 20 kilometres from Venice, on 9 November 1917 (Figure 5.4).

The Italian historian, Paolo Gaspari, claims that the speedy advance of Battle Group Stein through the gorge of the Natisone River in order to reach the Friuli Plain at Cividale was always the plan of the commanding German General Otto von Below (Gaspari 2016: 103).[10] This means that the choice of seemingly impassable Alpine landscape (Figure 5.5) was not illogical and that von Below chose a route along an ancient, well-established traffic corridor, part of one of the ancient passages through the Ljubljana Gap that follows the Cividale–Kobarid–Tolmin–Škofja loka (Bischoflack)–Celje (Cilli, Celeia) route (Kosi 1998: 20). The route is nicknamed 'The Old Celtica' (or 'Keltika') (Figure 5.6). Since it is unlikely that von Below was familiar with the local history, the planning of the offensive along the ancient trade route indicates the proficiency of his military planners in reading the landscape.

Gaspari's claim explains why von Below attributed such importance to the conquest of Mt Matajur that he promised the *Pour le Mérite* medal[11] to the first officer to reach the peak. Mt Matajur rises sharply above the Natisone Gorge, commanding complete control of the passage. Gaspari also raises the issue of whether attacks on the nearby mountains, such as Mts Rombon, Polovnik, Stol, Kolovrat, and Globočak, were only of a tactical nature – necessary to tie down Italian forces and prevent them from regrouping to block the main thrust along the Natisone.

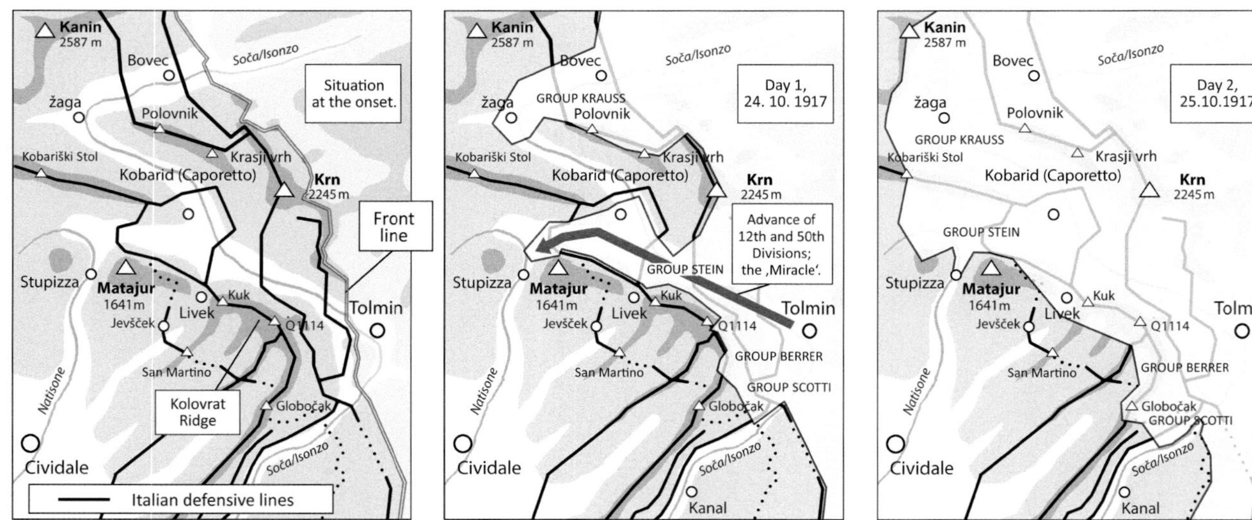

FIGURE 5.4 The pre-battle situation and the first two days of the Battle of Caporetto in October 1917. Source: © author. Adapted from V. Gradnik, P. Gaspari, esercito.difesa.it/storia.

FIGURE 5.5 Mountains of the upper Soča/Isonzo, seen from Mrzli vrh on the northern slopes of Mt Matajur, a slope of which is the wooded mass on the left. Source: © author.

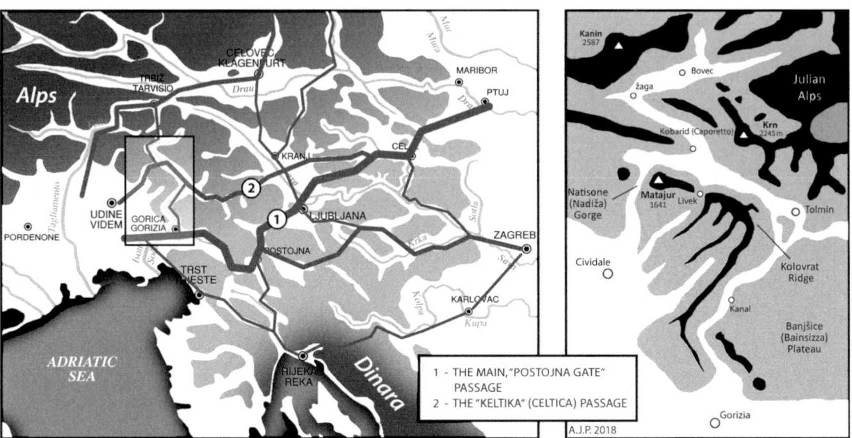

FIGURE 5.6 Left: the terrain of the Ljubljana Gap and most-used passages, according to Miha Kosi. Right: insert indicating the area of the 12th Battle of the Soča/Isonzo. Source: © author.

An earlier Austrian plan to breach the front at Tolmin and advance westwards towards Cividale (Wilks, 2001: 14) and von Below's promise of *Pour le Mérite* to the conqueror of Mt Matajur seem to support this notion of following the ancient route. But the actual deployment of forces does not indicate that the passage through the Natisone Gorge was given particular preference. It could also be argued that it was the unexpectedly fast advance of the 12th and 50th divisions along the valley and the strong Italian resistance on the Kolovrat Ridge that shifted attention to the push through the Natisone Gorge. In any case, securing Mt Matajur meant protecting the flanks of the advancing army and its conquest was considered of great importance.

Evaluation of Rommel's role – from Gradnik to Gaspari

The 12th Battle took place on what is today mostly Slovenian soil, but until the 1990s neither the Slovenian nor the global public knew much about Rommel's role in the fighting. Rommel's biographies, such as *Rommel* (Douglas-Home 1973) and *The Trail of the Fox* (Irving 1978) merely mentioned his participation in the First World War, concentrating instead on Rommel's much-better-known North Africa campaign of the Second World War.

The 1977 description of Rommel's 1917 engagement by the Slovenian historian Vladimir Gradnik is brief and inaccurate:

> The units of the right column of the German Alpine division, cooperating with a half of a battalion of the German 12th division, commanded by the then Lieutenant and later General Rommel, have around midday advanced through the villages of Ravne and Livek towards Mount Kraguvenca and along the way captured, almost without a fight, over 2000 prisoners.
>
> *(Gradnik 1977: 253)*

As we have seen, Rommel in fact belonged to the Royal Württemberg Mountain Battalion. In his 2001 book *Isonzo*, the military historian John Schindler admiringly describes Rommel's advance towards Mt Matajur and contrasts the number of captured Italians with Rommel's own minimal losses (Schindler 2001: 255–256). Unlike Gradnik, he quotes precise details, but he does not deal with the relationship between Rommel's advance and developments elsewhere on the battlefield.

In *Rommel and Caporetto*, published in the same year as Schindler's book, John and Eileen Wilks focus on Rommel at the Soča/Isonzo front and offer an in-depth analysis of the entire 12th Battle. The authors hint at Rommel's notable role, but hesitate to give him full credit: 'The advance of the XIVth Army during the first three days of the offensive was made all along its front by all the front-line divisions, and would have surely been made had Rommel and the WGB not been present'. They continue, 'The Rommel detachment was but a small part of a much greater whole, but there remain at least three very striking aspects of Rommel's performance' (Wilks and Wilks 2001: 114). These are given as Rommel's undoubted military skill, the fact that his unit was the fastest advancing, and the capture of the Italian 20th Bersaglieri Regiment, a unit that was, unlike other surrendering Italian units, prepared to carry on the fight (ibid.).

Wilks and Wilks fail to see the connection between Rommel's capture of the 20th Bersaglieri Regiment and the whole-scale engagement the next day. The 20th Regiment was sent to occupy the reserve line of San Martino. Had it fulfilled the task and linked up with units on the slopes of Mt Matajur, then, in theory at least, the battle would not yet have been lost. But by capturing the regiment and occupying Jevšček, Rommel prevented the Italians from utilizing the San Martino line. It therefore comes as no surprise that the next day, realizing that they had been cut off, the Italian units surrendered one after another.

In the more recent *White War*, Mark Thompson cites from Rommel's own *Infantry Attacks* – 150 captured officers and 9,000 men at a cost of six dead and 30 wounded – and comments on Rommel's skill in exploiting the landscape: 'Operating in harmony with the landscape, moving at extraordinary speed, Rommel's men have swooped along the hillsides, weaving across the ridge between Italian strongholds, mopping up resistance as they go, protected as well as empowered by their own momentum' (Thompson, 2008: 315).

My interpretation that Rommel was not merely a participant but rather a key contributor to the outcome of the 12th Battle was published first in Slovenian (Potočnik 2013: 185–194) and later in English (Potočnik 2014: 119–134). This interpretation emerged during the preparation of the Slovenian language edition and was the result of an analysis of Rommel's *Infantry Attacks* (1942) that was necessary to produce pictorial maps of the upper Soča/Isonzo landscape, the Italian defensive positions, and the movement of Rommel's unit.[12]

In the summer of 2014, an animated diorama of the 12th Battle was unveiled in the Kobarid Museum by Željko Cimprič. He undertook a detailed analysis of the movement of all participating units to produce a projection of moving lights on a large-scale model of the upper Soča/Isonzo Valley. It corresponds with Rommel's own description, on which I had based my hypothesis of Rommel's role.

The most recent major work on this topic is Gaspari's *Rommel a Caporetto* (2016). Based on in-depth research, Gaspari is scathing of the attention given to Rommel and his role in the breach of the front. Gaspari writes,

> In history books printed in Great Britain and in almost all Italian television programs, the lieutenant and his genius is described in such a way that there is an impression that the breakthrough and the overwhelming advance can be traced back to his manoeuvre, as if he had conceived it himself and the rest of the army had just followed his footsteps.
>
> *(Gaspari 2016: 70)*[13]

Gaspari thus agrees with John and Eileen Wilks that Rommel was just a cog in a large and efficient military machine, and stresses that the German units were better trained, better armed, and better led, while Italian defence lines were undermanned (Wilks and Wilks 2001: 37).

Drawing on numerous testimonies, Gaspari adds names and faces to Italian participants who have been so far regarded only as a nameless mass of surrendering soldiery. He describes their often-overlooked struggles and confirms the impression that, despite shock and heavy losses, the Italian army was, until the end of the battle's second day, still a functioning fighting force. However, this admirable detail does not diminish the scope of Rommel's contribution. Gaspari is clearly 'setting the record straight' by stressing the contributions of other combatants rather than denying Rommel's particular role.[14] Gaspari's book is a seminal work and the data he presents provides an opportunity to re-evaluate my interpretation.

Rommel's contribution to victory

Rommel's WGB unit, and the *Alpenkorps* to which it belonged, were part of the Stein Battle Group. The *Alpenkorps*' main objective was to secure the Kolovrat Ridge. WGB was supposed to guard the flank of the *Leib-Regiment* (Bavarian Guard Regiment). On the first day of the battle (24 October), the Italian first defensive line was obliterated by an artillery barrage and captured with almost no fighting. On the flank of the *Leib-Regiment*, Rommel's detachment advanced up the slope of Mt Hlevnik, a ridge branching northwards from Kolovrat. Stopped at the second Italian line, Rommel used a gorge they had traversed earlier to reach unnoticed a higher section of the front line where they were not expected. Here he used a deception: pretending that they were Italians, Rommel's soldiers breached the Italian second line without firing a single shot. It is possible that this caused the collapse of the entire Italian line in that sector, but this cannot be confirmed.[15]

Less disputed are Rommel's achievements on the second day of the battle (25 October). While the other units were encountering stiff Italian resistance, Rommel's unit found a weak spot[16] and breached the third Italian defence line running along the top of the Kolovrat Ridge. This too was achieved without firing a shot, but to secure the breach, Rommel's unit had to subdue the garrison on the nearby peak of Nagnoj. Again he utilized the terrain to conceal his movements and surprise his opponents. By 11:00 am, the units of WGB and the *Leib-Regiment* were streaming through the opening. While other German units advanced westwards along the ridge towards Mts Kuk and Livek (Luico), Rommel, acting on his own initiative, led his unit southwards into the Livek Valley and blocked the Livek–Polava road. His men cut the telephone lines connecting the Italian units in Livek with the divisional Headquarters in Cepletischis (Čepleišišče).

Realizing that the line on the Kolovrat Ridge was collapsing, and unable to obtain reserves, the commander of the Italian 62nd Division, General Giuseppe Viora, ordered the 20th Bersaglieri Regiment to retreat and occupy the reserve line running from the slopes of Matajur through the village of Jevšček onto the peak of San Martino (Gaspari 2016: 106). In an attempt to fulfil this order, the regiment ran into Rommel's ambush. The Italians only surrendered after a notable fight. Later that day, the Italian garrison of Livek, unable to use the Livek–Polava road, retreated to Mt Matajur. Rommel and his detachment ascended to the village of Jevšček where he exchanged fire with the Italian units approaching from the direction of Mt Matajur before encamping for the night.

Jevšček was part of the San Martino reserve line, which means that earlier that day Rommel's detachment prevented the 20th Bersaglieri Regiment from occupying it and now it prevented another Italian unit[17] from manning part of the line beyond Jevšček. In effect, he prevented the Italians from consolidating on the last pre-prepared defensive line (Figure 5.7).

On the morning of the third day (26 October), Rommel's detachment managed to dislodge the Italians from trenches above Jevšček and from the nearby peak of Kraguvenca.[18] By doing so, it cut off all the Italian units on the Matajur massif. Rommel could have now fortified himself on Kraguvenca and waited, but instead, he pressed on towards the peak of Matajur. Units of the Italian 62nd Division were, until then, fighting off the advances of the German 12th Division up the northern slopes. Once the soldiers of Rommel's detachment appeared from behind their backs, they surrendered en masse. Authors writing about the

FIGURE 5.7 The well-prepared trenches above Jevšček were part of the San Martino reserve line that the Italian 62nd Division failed to utilize due to the rapid advance of Rommel's detachment into the Livek Valley on 25 October 1917. Source: © author.

12th Battle of the Soča/Isonzo attribute these massive surrenders to war weariness and low morale. But it should be kept in mind that the concept of 'fighting until the last man' was a characteristic of the Second World War, particularly on the Eastern Front. During the First World War, it was acceptable to surrender if one's unit was cut off from the rest of the army – which was the case with the Mt Matajur garrison once Rommel's detachment conquered Kraguvenca.

While Rommel was heading towards the peak of Matajur, the rest of the WGB, the *Leib-Regiment*, and other units of the *Alpenkorps* were breaking the Italian resistance at Cepletischis (Čepleišišče), just south of Polava. Their breakthrough forced the Italian defenders at Stupizza (Stupica) to abandon the defence of the Natisone Gorge (Gaspari 2016: 152) and retreat towards Cividale.

To sum up, on 24 October, using a deception, Rommel's unit breached the second Italian line. On 25 October, Rommel breached the third line by finding a weak spot and then outmanoeuvred the Italians during the fight for Nagnoj, which created a gap used by other German units to advance towards Mt Matajur. He then descended into the Livek Valley, blocked the Livek–Polava road and cut Italian communications. By capturing the 20th Bersaglieri Regiment on the Livek–Polava road and the village of Jevšček, Rommel twice that day thwarted Italian attempts to occupy the San Martino reserve line. On the morning of 26 October, he captured Kraguvenca and thus effectively cut off Italian troops at Mt Matajur (Figure 5.8).

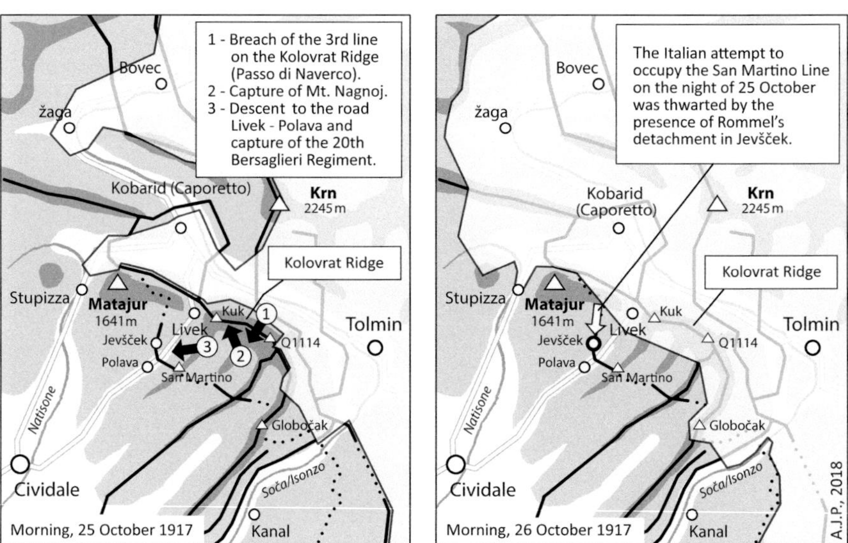

FIGURE 5.8 Rommel's activities on the Kolovrat Ridge and on the Livek–Polava road. The organization of Italian defences is mainly based on original Italian plans published in Gaspari (2016: 39, 43). Source: © author.

A study of Rommel's actions reveals at least four instances[19] when he took advantage of opportunities for action offered by gorges, knolls, and similar landscape features[20] to avoid detection and circumvent his opponents. In two of these instances, he reversed a seemingly hopeless situation and regained tactical initiative by making instant, considerable changes to the original plan, and in the other two instances, he made strategic decisions that had a considerable impact on the course of the battle.[21] An innate ability to make sense and take advantage of such natural features at speed is clearly on display, as is Rommel's own psychology of taking risks and ignoring or at least drastically reconfiguring his orders (Figure 5.9).

Controversy about Rommel's role

Conflict, landscape, military orders, personalities, and reputations made the German victory a contested event even before the battle was over. Rommel and his superior, Major Theodor Sproesser, lodged a complaint in order to be awarded the *Pour le Mérite* medals, which happened only after the battle at Longarone later that year. According to Wilks and Wilks (2001: 188), the official German history of the battle, compiled by General Krafft, praised the advances of the 12th German and 50th Austrian divisions along the valley but neglected the actions of the *Alpenkorps*. An attempt by Sproesser to change the narrative was unsuccessful.

Rommel's own *Infantry Attacks* can be regarded as a continuation of Sproesser's effort. The examples describing how to efficiently use to one's advantage the given terrain are accompanied by Rommel's own crude but clear sketches that underline the importance of graphic presentations of the landscape.[22] The 'social life', and indeed the 'military life' of this book endured beyond the First World War and Rommel himself as, in the wake of the Second World War, it was used as a textbook in military schools in Germany and the United States. The power of the book lay in its first-hand account of how to use landscape, albeit framed perhaps by Rommel's belief that it 'justified' the award of the *Pour le Mérite*.

That Rommel's published account is as contested as the conflict landscape with which it deals is shown by Gaspari, who uses the book's alleged shortcomings rather than Rommel's actions to downplay his contribution in the battle. Gaspari's view is that *Infantry Attacks* is a self-promotional work that often manipulates facts to magnify the author's own role (e.g. Gaspari 2016: 41). Gaspari reproaches Rommel and his book for being 'unreliable' (ibid.: 110), claims that 'All Rommel's fervour has only propaganda value, mitigated only by antitheses and oxymorons'[23] (ibid.: 81), and concludes that 'The Swabian lieutenant attributed to himself some extraordinary leadership skills'[24] (ibid.: 71).

Gaspari's opinion is not without substance. Most researchers regard the number of captured Italians as the measure of Rommel's success. Yet there is a question as to whether his conquest of Mt Matajur on 26 October, during which he took the largest number of prisoners,[25] was necessary. The desired effect could

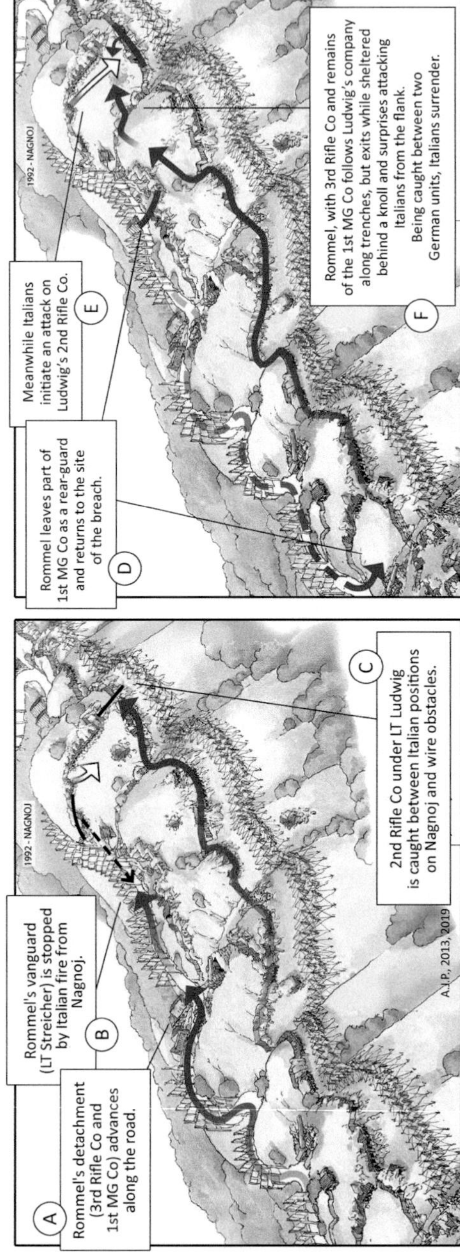

FIGURE 5.9 Reconstruction of the attack on Nagnoj after breaching the line on Kolovrat on 25 October 1917. Source: © author.

also have been achieved simply by holding fast at Mt Kraguvenca. It must be conceded that Rommel could have rushed towards the peak of Mt Matajur in order to satisfy his personal ambitions and obtain the medal promised by von Below, and thus it was an act of vanity. Arguably, however, it can be suggested that without Rommel's speedy intervention the fighting would have lasted longer and the death toll would have been much higher.

It is also possible that, on the second day of the battle, Rommel acted intuitively and was not aware that, by blocking the Livek–Polava road, capturing the 20th Bersaglieri Regiment, and occupying Jevšček, he thwarted an attempt by General Viora to regroup his forces on the reserve line at San Martino. Yet, it is fair to assume that thwarting that attempt was indeed the effect of his action. It should be said that 24 hours earlier, on the morning of 25 October, other Austrian and German units, such as the *Leib-Regiment* and the 1st *Jäger* battalion, had fought hard on the Kolovrat Ridge. Nevertheless, it was the breach made by Rommel's detachment between 9:00 and 11:00 am that was exploited for the further advance of the *Alpenkorps* towards Matajur.[26]

The only action with a questionable impact is Rommel's breach of the second Italian line on the first day of the battle (24 October). According to Rommel's own description, it was a brilliantly executed manoeuvre that may have facilitated the collapse of all Italian defences at Mt Hlevnik. Such a claim, however, cannot be substantiated. Gaspari's impatience with Rommel, which corresponds interestingly to the story that Rommel and his wife Lucie were chased out of Longarone when visiting in a private capacity during the 1930s, may well be explained by the fact that Italians still consider 'Caporetto' an unprecedented disaster. What may be more surprising is that Gaspari's views have been readily embraced on the Slovenian side, though earlier history may be playing a role here. It is possible that Slovenian attitudes to Rommel's actions in the Soča/Isonzo Valley are the legacy of the late nineteenth-century symbolic conflict enhanced by the Second World War narrative. In other words, the events of October 1917 may have been reconfigured by those of the preceding century and those of the succeeding conflict.

Landscape of discomfort

Landscape can be defined in part as a 'palimpsest of overlapping places which possess different meanings for different groups of people who select an aspect which interests them most' (Saunders 2018: 211). Recent archaeological-anthropological research on the Soča/Isonzo has defined 13 different landscape layers, with the tenth, dated to the 1980s, described as the one in which 'the Soča Valley re-emerged as a nascent heritage landscape with conservation and commemorative sites' (Saunders et al. 2013: 54). Slovenia today is regarded as a tourist destination. Heritage and tourism are interwoven to the extent that Icomos[27] was obliged to define and regulate their interrelationships in documents such as the International Cultural Tourism Charter (Icomos 1999). But while Saunders et al. note a significant increase in battlefield tourism along the old Western Front, especially during the 2014–2018 Centenary years, such activities are far rarer along the Soča/Isonzo, though Kolovrat is an exception, probably due to its association with Rommel (Košir et al. 2019).[28]

Franja Hospital is a secret, makeshift Second World War hospital constructed in a gorge near Cerkno in the Julian Alps, not far from the Soča/Isonzo Valley, and which has been damaged by torrential floods on several occasions. Reconstructions affected the authenticity of the monument and thus prevented it from being listed on the UNESCO list of world heritage sites.[29] Franja is nevertheless a notable monument to the resilience and ingenuity of the war's Slovenian partisans during the world's second global conflict. It attracts many school excursions, but it is virtually unknown outside Slovenia. It is an important national monument, but it is not a globally recognized 'tourism brand', while Erwin Rommel's name is. It would therefore not be unreasonable to expect that tourism stakeholders would welcome Rommel's 'global story' as a vehicle to attract attention to 'local stories' such as Franja. But it appears that in 2017, one such attempt was discouraged.

Rommel spent the night from 25 to 26 October in a house in Jevšček that is now owned by Mr Stanislav Šekli (Jože Šerbec, personal communication). In 2017, with the support of the Kobarid Museum, Mr Šekli marked the one-hundredth anniversary of the occasion by mounting a memorial plaque on his house. The reaction of the national media was stern. In an article titled 'Memorial marker yes, mythicising of German General no!' published in *Delo*, the country's main daily newspaper, the journalist Blaž Močnik warned against praising Rommel. He evoked the memory of the Second World War and quoted Jože Šerbec,[30] who said that, for Slovenians, Rommel is a contradictory personality, responsible for the deaths of 2,000 partisans and an equal number of civilians (Šerbec, cited in Močnik 2017).[31]

Before 1991, such an article would have been understood as a signal by the authorities that the topic was off-limits. In his 2018 article about the 12th Battle, Marko Simić echoed Gaspari by stating at the outset that:

> Rommel's endeavours in the battle of Kobarid (Caporetto, ed.) have become a real myth, but in fact the success of his unit was only a result of a consistent execution of infiltration tactics, carried out also by other German and Austro-Hungarian units.

Simić then devoted eight pages to German infiltration tactics, and only at the end a single sentence to Rommel (see Figure 5.10):

> The Germans had already during the first day of the battle reached Kobarid. Here, commanding three companies of the Württemberg Mountain Battalion, Lieutenant Rommel on the morning of 26 October, after two days of characteristic infiltration fighting during which he circumvented

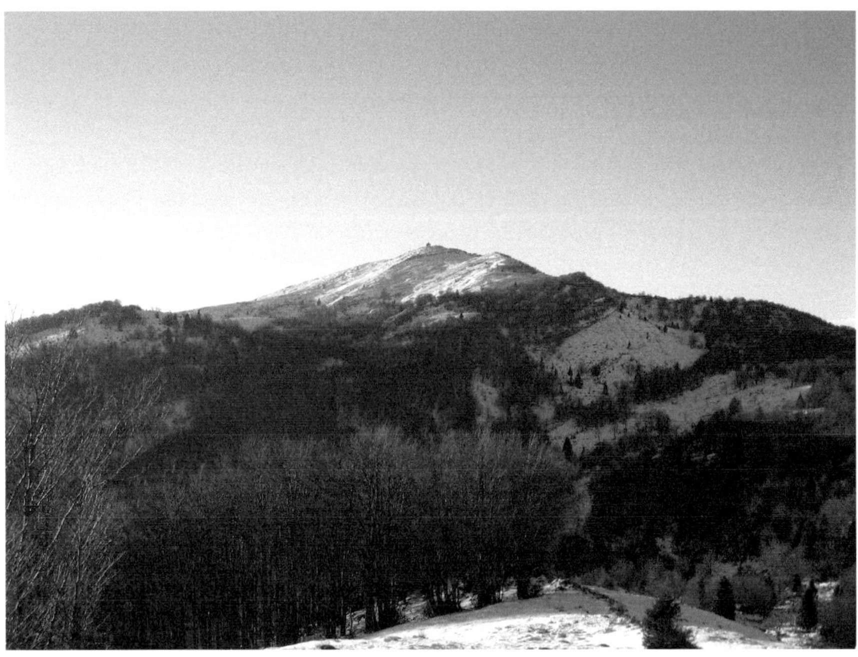

FIGURE 5.10 The peak of Mt Matajur from Mrzli vrh on the eastern slope. This was also the direction of the advance of Rommel's detachment. Source: © author.

> and then conquered several Italian regiments, captured Mt Matajur. The Italians now couldn't do anything else but retreat.
>
> *(Simić 2018: 24–32)*[32]

Conclusion

Given the nature of conflict landscapes, and their ability to contest received and create new identities, it is pertinent to ask whether Rommel's role in the First World War events of 1917 on the Soča/Isonzo front have been affected by his actions in the Second World War. Such a view might be more easily understood if the latter conflict had been part of the Slovenian national narrative since 1945. Yet, except for translations of Rommel's biographies published by Slovenian publishers in the 1970s,[33] Rommel does not feature much in the abundant Slovenian literature about the 1941–1945 war. However, there are two connections which might help explain this conundrum. As commander of 'Army Group B', Rommel in September and October 1943 planned operations 'Istrien' (Giron 2004: 214)[34] and 'Wolkenbruch'[35] (Butorović 1975: 328). The aim of these operations, which were carried out by the 2nd SS Armoured Corps led by SS General[36] Paul Hausser, was to neutralize Slovenian and Croatian partisans in the North Adriatic hinterland. According to the Slovenian historian Tone Ferenc (1967: 378), Hitler personally ordered extremely harsh treatment of partisans and civilians. If tried by a Yugoslav court, Rommel would probably have been found guilty of complicity.[37] Paul Hausser, on the other hand, lived to work as a historian on the US payroll and died in 1972 aged 92.

There seems little doubt that military operations along the Soča/Isonzo Valley in October 1917 created a conflict landscape which in various ways remains contested today. In terms of military history (the actual events), the immediate aftermath (the Italian retreat to the Piave river), the role of Erwin Rommel (his deferred award of the *Pour le Mérite* and the later publication of *Infantry Attacks*), the views of the Battle of Caporetto as a 'miracle' for the Austro-German forces and a national catastrophe for the Italians, and the long afterlife of all of these through and beyond the Second World War combine to create a complex multilayered landscape. As for Rommel, his actions in this landscape can be seen as creating a unique, enduring, and contested identity.

As we have seen, the Julian Alps, as part of the Ljubljana Gap, has been a contested landscape for millennia, a situation reinforced by the symbolic confrontation between Germans/Austrians and Slovenians for access to the peaks at the end of the nineteenth century. Two subsequent world wars have shaped the present-day borders, and the peace that followed should have secured the stability of these borders and put to rest old animosities. But has it?

Among souvenirs sold throughout Italy, there is a tea towel depicting a map of Italy within its pre-war borders. As recently as June 2019 the Slovenian Foreign Ministry protested against the appearance of a similar map on the Facebook site of an Italian politician, Lorenzo Giorgi.[38] In Slovenia, any mention of Rommel's achievements in the First World War is counteracted by a reminder of his questionable role in the Second. One may be forgiven for regarding the Julian Alps as a still-contested landscape and believing that within it, the forces that plunged the world into two cataclysmic conflicts have not entirely been put to rest.

Acknowledgements

I wish to thank Alistair Thomson and Nicholas J. Saunders for their support and guidance, members of the Monash Historical Studies Writing Group – Margaret Coffey, Bernard Keo, Jennifer Lord, Rosa Martorana, Eugenia Pacitti, Anisa Puri, and Julia Smart – for welcome comments, and Elsie Hill for patient proofreading. I would also like to thank Anna Frangipane for providing Italian language sources. Finally, I would like to express my great respect for the work of Paolo Gaspari. Disputing one particular view should by no means be regarded as disrespect for the tremendous amount of research he has carried out.

Notes

1 The Visigoths in 401, the Ostrogoths in 489, the Huns in 452, and the Lombards in 568.

2 The importance of the book resonates in the 1970 film *Patton*, in which George C. Scott as Patton, observing his troops battling Rommel's, yells, 'Rommel, you magnificent bastard. I've read your book!'
3 The term 'contested landscape' in relation to armed conflict is explored in detail in Saunders (2001). Here, I use it in a somewhat broader sense.
4 Slovenian mountaineer Valentin Stanič (1774–1849) reached the top of Grossglockner as early as in 1700 (Mikša, 2013).
5 See PZS history at the website: www.pzs.si/vsebina.php?pid=21
6 See the website Slovenska Biografija: www.slovenska-biografija.si/oseba/sbi127893/
7 In the coats of arms of both the Socialist Republic of Slovenia, a part of socialist Yugoslavia from 1945 to 1991, and the Republic of Slovenia, Mt Triglav is the central motif.
8 The authors of the TV series produced by Slovenian and Austrian state broadcasters were Željko Kozinc and Helmut Andics; the director was Marjan Ciglič.
9 On 24 October, the 12th German and 50th Austro-Hungarian Divisions of the Battle Group Stein advanced 27 kilometres.
10 Gaspari writes,
Il 24 ottobre ci fu l'inatteso sfondamento di Caporetto – 27 cilometri – lungo l'Isonzo, ma fu il 25 il giorno in cui s'impose sul campo di bataglia il piano strategico di von Below con la manovta convergenta della 12a divisione e dell'Alpenkorps per prendere il Matajur e permettere lo sbocco in pianura dell'armata.
The unexpected breakthrough of Caporetto – some 27 kilometres – took place on 24 October, but 25 October was the day on which von Below's strategic plan of taking Matajur by a converging manoeuvre of the 12th division and of the Alpenkorps, thus allowing the army to reach the plain, was carried out on the battlefield.
(author trans.)
11 The *Pour le Mérite* was Germany's highest award, and bestowed for extraordinary personal achievement. Established in 1740 by King Frederick II of Prussia, it was discontinued after the end of the First World War in November 1918.
12 Although this evaluation of Rommel's role differed from previous works, reviews were favourable (e.g. Rugeli 2013).
13 *Nel libri di storia della Grande guerra stampati in Gran Bretagna, e in quasi tutte le trasmissioni televisive italiane, si menziona il tenente e si fa risalire al suo genio la manovra dello sfondamento e dell'avanzatta travolgente, quasi che l'avesse ideata lui stesso e il resto dell'esercito avesse seguito solo le sue orme, tranne a Plezzo dove ci fu l'attaco con il gas.*
Great War history books printed in Great Britain and almost all Italian television broadcasts speak of the Lieutenant and attribute the manoeuvre of the breakthrough and the overwhelming advance to his genius, as if he alone had conceived it and the rest of the army had just followed his footsteps, except for Bovec where the gas attack took place.
(author trans.)
14 Two examples. On page 110, Gaspari claims that the 20th Bersaglieri regiment was fired upon also by other units (most notably the Leib Regiment) and that not only Rommel's detachment, but other units too took some prisoners. While this may indeed be the case, the fact remains that without Rommel's blockade the capture of the 20th regiment would not have taken place at all. On page 147, Gaspari claims that Mt Matajur was attacked simultaneously by multiple units from three directions: north, east, and south. That, however, does not change the fact that the defenders of Mt Matajur put up stiff resistance until the afternoon of 26 October when Rommel's unit appeared from the south – from behind.
15 The reaction of Major von Bothmer, the commander of the Leib Regiment, to Rommel's actions indicates that Rommel's activities on 24 October were significant.
16 According to Gaspari (2016) the spot is called *Passo di Naverco*. Most of the place names on Kolovrat are of Slovenian origin, but are mainly quoted in Italian literature, hence the Italian form of the name.

17 According to Gaspari, that was the 3rd Regiment of the 90th Salerno Brigade (Gaspari 2016: 124).
18 The name of the hill is disputed. According to present-day Slovenian topographic maps, it is either *Strmola* or *Breza*, while Kraguvenca is marked as a rise further to the west. But Rommel himself quotes this hill as Kraguvenca, as do some Italian maps.
19 Using the gorge at Hlevnik on 24 October (specifically a ravine at the site of the breach), the knoll at Nagnoj on 25 October, and a side slope of Glava under the peak of Mt Matajur on 26 October.
20 These landscape features presented Rommel with opportunities to achieve the goal in accordance with Gibson's (1966) theory *of 'affordances'*. If these were to be used as 'tools' (Norman 1988) to win the battle, then they not only present but were also perceived as such and used accordingly by Rommel.
21 The descent into the Livek Valley on 25 October and the continuing advance towards the peak of Mt Matajur on 26 of October.
22 For the role of graphic presentations of a conflict landscape see Birket Rees (2016: 59–82).
23 '*Tutto il fervorino di Rommel ha solo un valore propagandistico appena mitigato da antitesi e ossimori*'. English: 'All Rommel's fervour has only a propagandistic value, even if mitigated by antitheses and oxymorons' (author trans.)
24 '*Il tenente svevo si mise di suo una straordinaria capacità di comando*'. English: 'The Swabian lieutenant attributed to himself an extraordinary leadership capacity' (author trans.).
25 Estimated to have been around 4,500 (Rommel 1937).
26 A fact discernable in Gaspari (2016: 68).
27 Icomos – International Council on Monuments and Sites.
28 This is probably also due to excavation, clearance, and reconstruction at the site from 2001, the subsequent inauguration of an open-air museum on 14 October 2007, and its accessibility by car (Kosir et al. 2019: 101). In 2017, the October 1917 German-Austrian breakthrough on Kolovrat was re-enacted on-site with explosions and machine-gun fire, and was watched by several thousand spectators (ibid.: 105).
29 According to the website of the Idrija Museum; attempts to list the site continue.
30 Mr Jože Šerbec was the director of the Kobarid Museum at the time.
31 '*V resnici gre pri nas za kontradiktorno osebnost. Čeprav takrat ni stopil na slovenska tla, je na Hitlerjevo osebno povelje iz Belluna z nekakšnimi elitnimi nemškimi enotami čistil zaledje severnega Jadrana in Istre, posledica je bila 2000 mrtvih partizanov in prav toliko civilistov*'. English: 'Here [in Slovenia] he is indeed a controversial personality. Even though at the time he did not set foot on Slovenian soil, following Hitler's personal order he cleansed, with some sort of elite German troops, the hinterland of the Northern Adriatic and Istra. The consequences were 2,000 dead partisans and an equal number of civilians' (author trans.)
32 Slovenian:
Nemci so že prvega dne bitke zasedli Kobarid, nadporočnik Rommel pa je tu na čelu oddelka treh čet Wuertemberškega gorskega bataljona 26. Oktobra dopoldne, po dveh dnevih značilnega infiltracijskega bojevanja, med katerim je obšel in nato premagal več italijanskih polkov, zasedel vrh Matajurja. Italijaniom je preostal le še umik.
33 Douglas-Home (1973), Irving (1978).
34 Page 209 in the digitalized version: www.znaci.net/00003/689.pdf
35 English: 'Cloudburst'.
36 *Obergruppenführer.*
37 There is a parallel attitude to Rommel in the UK – on the one hand the gentlemanly 'Desert Fox', the only German hero of 1960s British war films, who ends up plotting against Hitler. And on the other hand (less well known) an ambitious climber who ingratiated himself with Hitler, and whose Afrika Korps included an Einsatz Kommando that was intended to wipe out all the Jews in Palestine once Rommel got there.

38 Unsigned article, *Slovensko zunanje ministrstvo ostro obsodilo Giorgijev zemljevid*, Primorski dnevnik, Trst, 5.6.2019.

References

Birket-Rees, J. (2016) Capturing the Battlefield: Mapping and Air Photography at Gallipoli. In A. Sagona, A. Antonio, M. Atabay, C.J. Mackie, I. McGibbon and R. Reid (eds.), *Anzac Battlefield, A Gallipoli Landscape of War and Memory*, pp. 59–82. Cambridge: Cambridge University Press.

Butorović, R. (1975) *Sušak i Rijeka u NOB*. Rijeka: Centar za historiju radničkog pokreta i NOR Istre, Hrvatskog primorja i Gorskog kotara. znaci.net/00003/7xx.php?bk=799.

Douglas-Home, C. (1973) *Rommel*. London: Excalibur Books/George Weidenfeld & Nicolson Ltd.

Ferenc, T. (1967) *Kapitulacija Italije in narodnoosvobodilna borba v Sloveniji jeseni 1943*. Maribor: Zalozba 'Obzorja'.

Gaspari, P. (2016) *Rommel a Caporetto, le gesta degli Italiani e dei Tedeschi tra il Kolovrat e il Matajur*. Udine: Gaspari editore.

Gibson, J.J. (1966) *The Senses Considered as Perceptual Systems*. Boston: Houghton Mifflin.

Giron, A. (2004) *Zapadna Hrvatska u drugom svjetskom ratu*. Rijeka: Adamić. Digital version: www.znaci.net/00003/689.htm

Gradnik, V. (1977) *Krvavo posočje*. Koper: Založba lipa.

ICOMOS (1999) *International Cultural Tourism Charter, Managing Tourism at Places of Heritage Significance*. www.icomos.org/charters/tourism_e.pdf

Irving, D. (1978) *The Trail of the Fox*. Hamburg: Hoffman und Campe Verlag.

Keller, T. (2009) The Mountains Roar: The Alps During the Great War. *Environmental History* 14: 253–274.

Kosi, M. (1998) *Potujoči srednji vek : Cesta, popotnik in promet na Slovenskem med antiko in 16. stoletjem*. Ljubljana: Zbirka ZRC, 20.

Košir, U., N.J. Saunders, M. Črešnar and G. Rutar. (2019) Between Tourism and Oblivion: Rombon and Kolovrat – Conflict Landscapes on the Soča Front, 1915–2017. In U. Košir, M. Črešnar and D. Mlekuž (eds.), *Forgotten Fronts, Enduring Legacies: Archaeology and the Great War on the Soča and Eastern Fronts*, pp. 90–108. London: Routledge.

Mikša, P. (2013) *Slovensko Planinstvo*, web site PZS, https://zgodovina.pzs.si/

Močnik, B. (2017) Obeležje da, mitiziranje nemškega feldmaršala ne. *Delo*, 29.08.2017.

Norman, D. (1988) *The Design of Everyday Things*. New York: Basic Books.

Potočnik, A.J. (2013) *Po sledeh Erwina Rommla*. Logatec: Ad Pirum.

——— (2014) *Erwin Rommel's Blue Max or Just What Did Rommel Do to Deserve the Highest German Military Medal*. Ljubljana: CreateSpace/Amazon.

Rommel, E. (1937) *Infanterie Greif an*. Potsdam: Feldpostausgabe, Ludwig Voggenreiter Verlag.

——— (2009) *Infantry Attacks*. Minneapolis: Zenith Publishing.

Rugelj, S. (2013) *Recenzija Bukla, Bukla, 100, 2013*. www.bukla.si/knjigarna/zgodovina/20-stoletje/po-sledeh-erwina-rommla.html

Saunders, N.J. (2001) Matter and Memory in the Landscapes of Conflict: The Western Front 1914–1999. In B. Bender and M. Winer (eds.), *Contested Landscapes: Movement, Exile and Place*, pp. 37–53. Oxford: Berg.

——— (2009) People in Objects: Individuality and the Quotidian in the Material Culture of War. In C. White (ed.), *The Materiality of Individuality*, pp. 37–55. New York: Springer.

——— (2018) Traces of Being: Interdisciplinary Perspectives on First World War Conflict Landscapes. In S. Daly, M. Salvante and V. Wilcox (eds.), *Landscapes of the First World War*, pp. 209–224. Cham: Palgrave Macmillan.

Saunders, N.J., N. Faulkner, U. Košir, M. Črešnar and S. Thomas. (2013) Conflict Landscapes of the Soča/Isonzo Front, 1915–2013: Archaeological-Anthropological Evaluation of the Soča Valley, Slovenia. *Arheo* 30: 47–66.

Schindler, J.R. (2001) *Isonzo – The Forgotten Sacrifice of the Great War*. Westport: Praeger.

Simić, M. (2018) Bitka pri Kobaridu kot mejnik v razvoju nemške napadalne doktrine med prvo svetovno vojno. *SLO, Slovenski zgodovinski magazin, special edition, 100 letnica od konca prve vojne*, 24–33.

Thompson, M. (2008) *The White War*. London: Faber and Faber.

Unsigned Article (2019) *Slovensko zunanje ministrstvo ostro obsodilo Giorgijev zemljevid, Primorski dnevnik*. Trst: Zadruga Primorski dnevnik.

Wilks, J. and E. Wilks. (2001) *Rommel and Caporetto*. Barnsley: Leo Cooper, Pen & Sword Books.

Woodward, R. (2014) Military Landscapes: Agendas and Approaches for Future Research. *Progress in Human Geography* 38 (1): 40–61.

Websites

Website of the Idrija Museum: www.muzej-idrija-cerkno.si/index.php/sl/lokacijerazstave/stalne-razstave/partizanska-bolnica-franja.html

Website of **the Slovenian Alpine Association** (PZS): www.pzs.si/vsebina.php?pid=21

Website of Slovenian Biography (Slovenska Biografija): www.slovenska-biografija.si/oseba/sbi127893/

6

FIRST WORLD WAR LANDSCAPES ON THE ALPINE FRONT LINE

New technologies between wish and (augmented) reality

Alessandro Bezzi, Luca Bezzi, Rupert Gietl, and Giuseppe Naponiello

Whoever hikes today over the green Alpine pastures and follows the ridges of the Dolomite mountain range in northern Italy no longer hears the echo of gunfire and machine guns that filled the valleys and mountains between 1915 and 1918. A veil of oblivion has been drawn almost everywhere over the old positions of this war-front of rock and ice. Almost ten years ago, archaeologists began to lift this veil. It was the start of a daunting task.

The 2014–2018 commemorative years of the centenary have spawned an abundance of diverse cultural and scientific initiatives along the south-western front of the First World War. The mountain front is peculiar for two main reasons: first, its presence in the narrative tradition started by the war's participants in the early post-war years (Schemfil 1926; Berti 1936) and which still resonates today, and second, the particularly good condition of the former front line stretching from the Swiss border to the Adriatic Sea (Figure 6.1). While many scars of the war on the Western Front were removed after 1918 or are now hidden underground, many positions on the Alpine front until a few years ago appeared as if the last soldiers had only just left their century-old positions.

One hundred years of change

Where such positions were within easy reach of the villages in the valleys, there was active re-use of raw materials after the end of the war, a post-war recycling common to all fronts. This began on the Dolomite front immediately after the Italian retreat in November 1917. For example, the 'Eisenreich group' (border subsection 10c of the Austro-Hungarian front division – Western Carnic Ridge) reported on 12 November 1917:

> The following items were collected and deposited at the collection points: 7 sandbags with Rifle ammunition, […] 20 hand grenades, 10 flare cartridges,

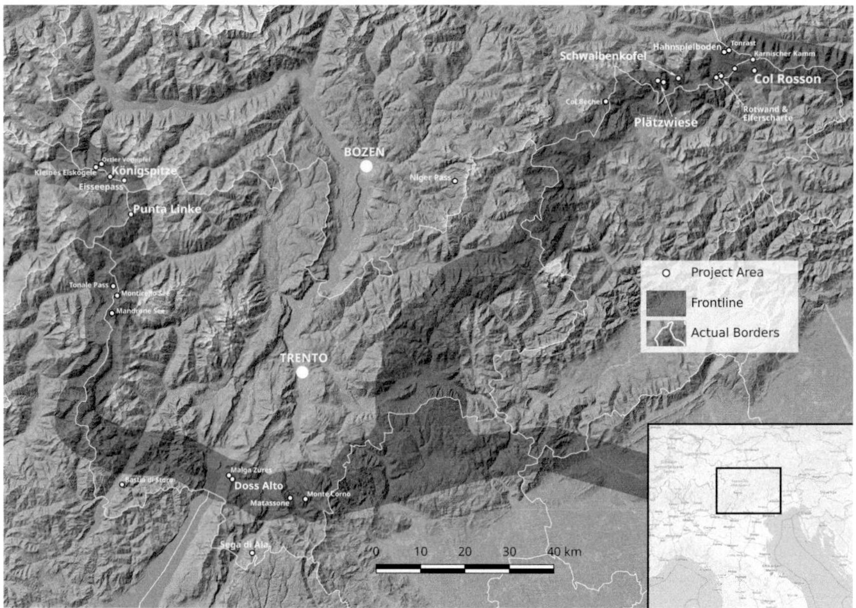

FIGURE 6.1 The western part of the Italian front line during the First World War. The white dots mark archaeological projects carried out by Arc-Team Archeology between 2012 and 2019. The projects with names in larger font size are discussed in this chapter. Source: © Arc-Team.

> 2 infantry rifles, 200 empty sandbags, 5 field spades, 5 empty infantry cable drums, 2 pairs of shoes, 1 fur vest, 1 straw sack, 1 cushion, 1 wash basin.
>
> *(Austrian State Archive)*

Immediately after the war, the residents of the front areas also took back confiscated or stolen items of furniture, as is reported, for example, in the local oral history record of the destroyed town of Sexten. In the 1920s, the removal of larger metal objects began. During the Abyssinian War in 1935–1936, the price of scrap metal in Italy skyrocketed, and even small quantities were worth collecting. In more accessible sections of the front, timber was also recycled, so that soon only the foundation terraces of the formerly extensive military camps were visible. Everything that could not be carried away was exposed to the forces of nature; a harsh climate, erosion in the high mountains, and the spreading vegetation in lower areas gnawed away at the monuments.

Since the 1970s, this process has been ameliorated by the establishment of open-air museums on numerous sections of the front. Their goal was to counter the decay of the front-line structures at particularly heavily contested points and to make the events of the war both tangible and understandable in the spirit of peace work.

The post-war search for human remains of the fallen ran parallel to the recycling of raw materials. Many bodies lay in rocky terrain, were covered with snow and ice, or had been buried in improvised front-line cemeteries. In the first post-war years, the *Polizia Mortuaria* (a service devoted to the management of dead bodies, rather than a police force) developed a lively activity that had to remain unfinished in view of the enormous challenge. To make up for this, at least in part, a 'bounty' of 25 lire (now around 23 euros) was offered to encourage the recovery of human remains. However, it was only paid when a skull was handed over. Unfortunately, this also led to wild excavations in the cemetery areas and the subsequent loss of the identity of numerous fallen soldiers (Giacomel 2004: 114). Official work on the front cemeteries reached a climax during the Second World War. As part of the South Tyrol Option Agreement between Italy and the German Reich, the cemeteries of the First World War on the mountain front were merged and reorganized according to the nationality of the fallen. It is significant that all of these war-related activities altered, destroyed, and created new levels (and sometimes kinds) of conflict landscapes, albeit focused on reconfiguring mortuary-commemorative issues of the First World War.

After the Second World War, private collecting began along the front, concentrating on all kinds of militaria. The search for remnants of war gained an economic impetus, with the value of many objects increasing steadily as the events of 1915 to 1918 receded into history. Fuelled by the commemorative activities and publicity of the centenary of the First World War, these activities reached a peak in May 2016, when the online valuation of a cap badge of the Austrian 165th Landsturm battalion exceeded 1,000 euros for the first time.

Cultural heritage preservation

Such was the situation at the beginning of the new millennium, when heritage authorities began, for the first time, to engage with the physical legacy of the First World War's Alpine front. A similar situation pertained around the same time on the Western Front of France and Belgium, and to a lesser extent on the Soča/Isonzo front on the Slovenian–Italian border. In the former, these developments were accompanied by, and in part derived from, the beginnings of a modern scientific archaeological engagement with First World War landscapes (Saunders 2010: 1–30).

Depending on the country or region, the approach was different, not least concerning how the First World War had been processed historically and politically, and how badly an area had been affected by the war. In Switzerland, the question of what age an object or structure must be in order to be of interest and qualify as heritage is legally irrelevant. This made it easy, for example, for the Swiss authorities to document the remains of the First World War on their part of the border triangle west of the Stilfser Joch Pass (Reitmaier 2014: 355).

Between 2001 and 2004, several decrees were passed in Italy concerning the status of First World War remains. These decrees form the legal basis for the archaeological study of legacies from the period 1915 to 1918. In Lombardy, Veneto, and Friuli-Venezia Giulia, the regional branches of the Ministry of Culture are responsible, while in Trentino and South Tyrol the autonomous regional offices are responsible. Most of the affected areas are concentrated here and the officials responsible were suddenly confronted with an enormous amount of new monuments to deal with. Initially, the institutions were neither technically nor financially prepared for this challenge (Gietl et al. 2015: 4). In addition, the law allows a wide range of interpretations in its application or non-application, which has led to rather passive behaviour by the state monument-protection authorities. Although individual researchers tried to fill this vacuum, the field in the regions of Lombardy, Veneto, and Friuli-Venezia Giulia has so far largely been left to private associations (see Pinagli et al. this volume).

In contrast, the Trentino Heritage Office set high standards with a series of ambitious conflict archaeology projects relating to the First World War. The most important and difficult projects were the de-icing and conservation of the glacier positions on the Corno di Cavento and the Punta Linke, at an altitude of over 3,000 metres above sea level (Nicolis 2011: 14, 2017).

Slovenia is the site of the extensive material remains of the fiercely contested Soča/Isonzo front and has been protecting all war relics older than 50 years since 2008 (Mlekuž et al. 2016: 127; Košir 2019). The Federal Monuments Authority Austria only started a pilot project to protect some selected front sections on the Carnic Ridge in the commemoration years, an undertaking which has not yet been completed.

The archaeological situation

The material remains of the First World War in the mountains are of many kinds and include: trenches, caverns, barracks, cemeteries, paths, water supply lines, telephone and power lines, inscriptions, graffiti, uniforms and equipment, written documents, etc. This heterogeneity requires interdisciplinary cooperation between the sub-disciplines of monument conservation, especially between archaeology, architectural history, and art monuments. Due to a lack of capacity, the monument authorities limit themselves mainly to the supervision of construction work in the front area, as well as to the salvage and documentation of particularly outstanding objects. It was clear from the beginning that complete protection and preservation of all military legacies from the period 1915–1918 would be impossible. It was therefore all the more important to obtain a detailed overview of the situation 100 years ago and use this data to plan further, targeted measures to direct visitor flows and to monitor sensitive areas.

In the years before 2012, we had been working on our own initiative concerning the feasibility of undertaking a large-scale documentation of the mountain front. The goal was to document the conflict landscape through the use of modern surveying technology. This could only be achieved if the chosen method was as time-saving and economical as possible. We based our approach on the following premises:

- In a limited project area, all visible objects and structures should be fully documented. The archaeologists in the field make no subjective choice between supposedly important or unimportant monuments (Figure 6.2).

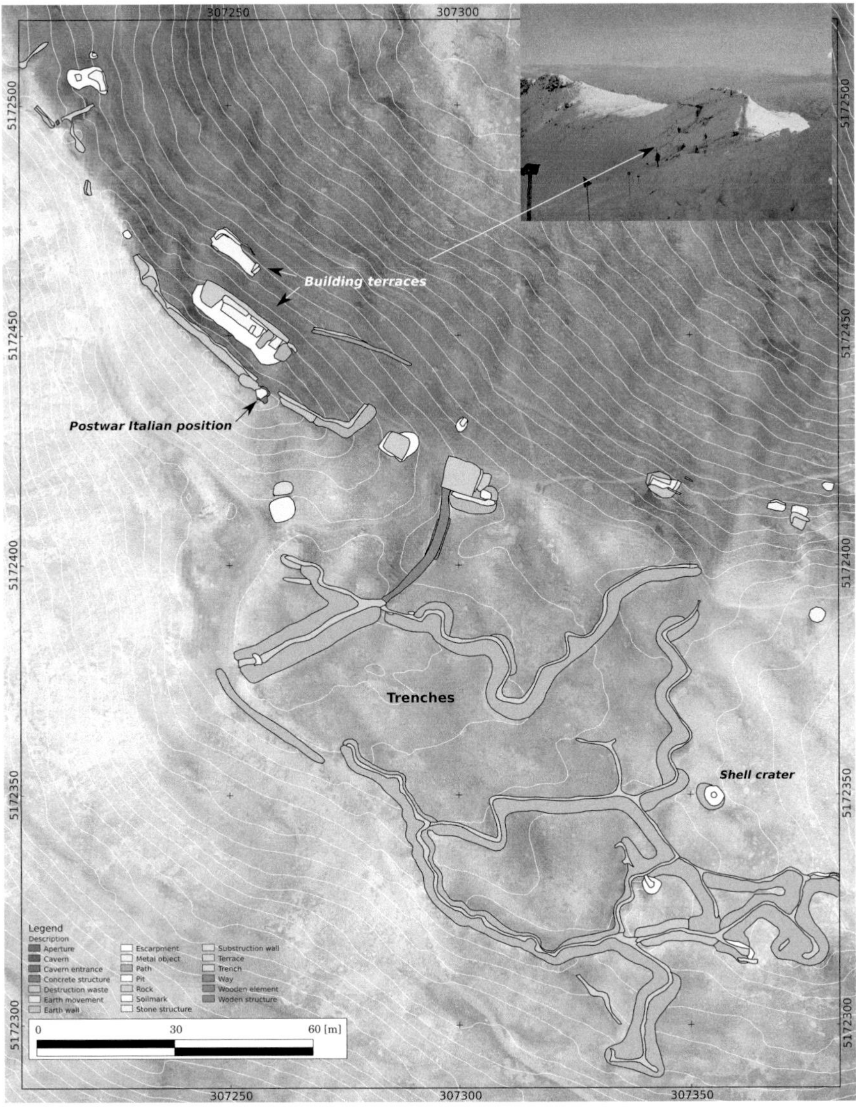

FIGURE 6.2 Results of the documentation work on the Austrian-Hungarian positions on the western Carnic Ridge. Source: © Arc-Team.

- All survey data are to be transformed into a uniform, higher-level coordinate system.
- The description of objects should be based on predefined categories.
- The data should be collected in such a way that it is suitable for 3-D applications and web GIS.
- The equipment in the field should be as light as possible.
- As a rule, a few minutes should be sufficient for the documentation of an object.
- The software for data processing should be open source.
- The data should be available to the general public as open data.

In order to obtain tangible data on the density of the front-line structures for the first time, the South Tyrolean Monument Office carried out a pilot project on the Plätzwiese (municipalities of Prags and Toblach) in 2012 and 2013, in which approximately six square kilometres of front were completely archaeologically recorded (Gietl et al. 2015: 11–18; ASFR 2017) (Figure 6.1). The area of the Plätzwiese was part of the *Sperre Landro* (Landro barrier). The area had already been expanded as a line of defence against the expected Italian attack in the pre-war period. It became a second line of defence and an important artillery base during the First World War due to the failure of the Royal Italian Army to advance.

The basis of the archaeological investigation was a survey using differential GPS, a description of the structures, geolocalized situation surveys and – for objects of particular interest – three-dimensional documentation using image-based methods. The result was around 1,000 geometrically recorded objects, recorded in around eight weeks by a two-man team. The project area was inspected systematically and all traces of human intervention in the area were mapped. A total of around 2,500 polygons were measured, which corresponds to around 1,000 objects. In addition, around 12,000 photos were taken, 1,500 geolocated images entered in an image database, and 138 3-D models generated (Figure 6.3).

The pilot project gave us valuable experience concerning the documentation method described above. The aim was to collect as much data as possible at a relatively low cost. The numerous caverns in the front area pose a particular challenge to the documentation methodology. In order to precisely measure the underground systems, a considerable amount of additional time and equipment would have been necessary. The problem could be solved with the help of the imaging technique structure from motion.[1] As has been shown in practical tests on site, this also delivers very good results in tight and enclosed spaces. In the course of data processing, it was therefore easy to obtain floor plans from the 3D models of the caverns. It took around one and a half hours to record an approximately 55-metre-long, angled tunnel system (Gietl et al. 2016: 9–15). In another project in 2018, we documented a 300-metre-long Italian cavern on Mt Doss Alto near Lake Garda in about six hours using the same method (Bezzi et al. 2018a: 205) (Figure 6.1).

Where there were structures in forested areas, it was no longer possible to measure with GPS, and so a total station was used. This led to a significant

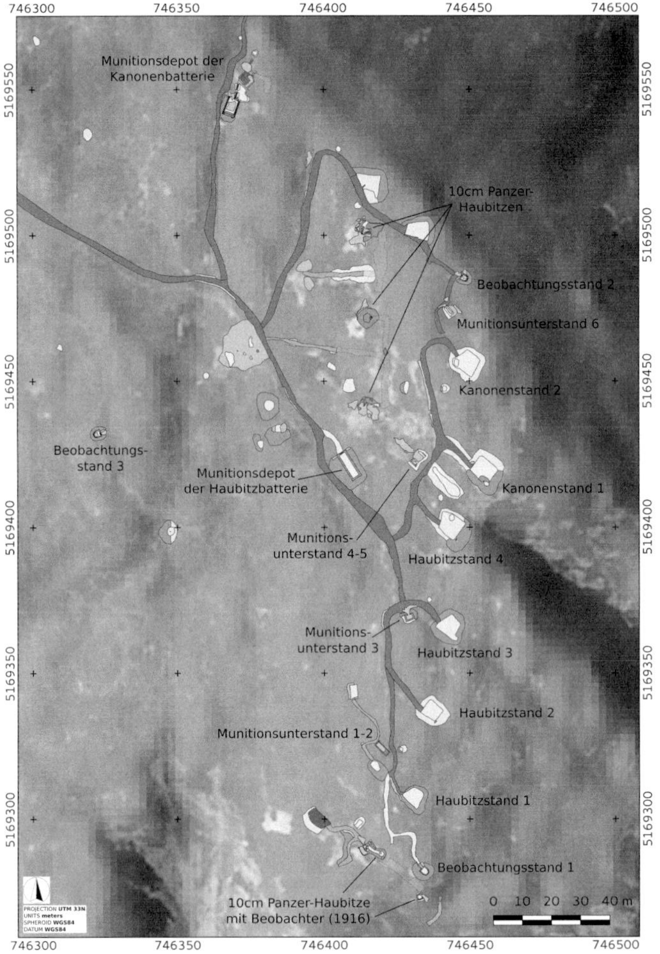

FIGURE 6.3 Results of the documentation work on the Austrian-Hungarian positions on Plätzwiese. Source: © Arc-Team.

slowdown in surveying and documentation. In order to increase the legibility of the monument ensemble, they were always photographed as parallel pairs of images, which can then be further processed into anaglyph scenes. This gives the viewer an additional (limited) spatial impression of the findings.

New technologies between wish and (augmented) reality

With modifications and adjustments, this methodology has now been used in 25 subsequent conflict archaeology projects along the Alpine front (Gietl 2019) (Figure 6.1). Most of these projects were standard archaeological investigations concerning construction projects that affected First World War remains. Some projects, however, included a component of more public interest, and here the potential of digital data could be fully tested. Namely, digital technologies can help solve some of the greatest problems by historically explaining the events in the many original locations. The first open-air museums in the front area were created in the 1970s with the aim of bringing the events of 1915–1918 closer to the interested public. But from the point of view of monument preservation and nature conservation, this approach was fraught with problems. Most of the time, original wartime positions were uncovered and some were also reconstructed, an activity which created a problematical hybrid layer of conflict landscape, because now, after several decades, some of these reconstructions can hardly be distinguished from the originals; this of course raises the issue of authenticity. Such actions almost always happened without the support of the responsible authorities, and were initiatives mostly supported by private associations, particularly committed individuals or veteran associations. Since costs are incurred every year for the maintenance of the open-air museums, many have not been able to maintain their original level of activity and preservation, a fact which has led to a degrading archaeological resource whose level of decay is due as much to its unofficial reconstruction as to normal processes.

Large parts of the Alpine front have been declared national parks or regional nature parks over the past decades. The Ortler front became part of the Stilfser Joch National Park in 1935. From the point of view of nature conservation, the remains of the war are a disruptive factor or a source of pollution of nature (e.g. from fuels, explosives, oils, tar paper, etc.). In addition, the parks' administrations want to avoid the creation of new tourist attractions, earth movements, reconstructions, display boards, and paths. However, it is difficult to explain the course of the front in the mountains and the complex events associated with it to people without excellent local knowledge. Even experts usually only know short sections of the front in intimate detail.

Digital technologies can offer solutions or support for all of these problems. WebGIS applications solve the problem of orientation and a lack of overview in mountainous terrain. At the same time, it is no longer necessary to put up display boards that have to be repaired regularly after the winter and disrupt the landscape and the view. Virtual reconstructions can replace on-site reconstructions and thus the original structures can remain unchanged. Finally, those not normally able to access original locations – due to age, disability, or lack of Alpine experience – can be offered virtual access via these technologies (see Carpentier et al. this volume).

Plätzwiese

During the pilot project on the Plätzwiese, the South Tyrolean Monument Office wanted the results to be presented on its website in order to provide a visible contribution to the commemoration years (Figure 6.1). We selected 15 interesting objects that had been three-dimensionally documented during the fieldwork. The models went online on the homepage of the monument office. As a framework for the creation of the visual presentation, we used 3DHOP, a web-based and open-source application designed to cope with the specific needs of the cultural heritage field (Bezzi et al. 2018b: 46) (Figure 6.4). The software

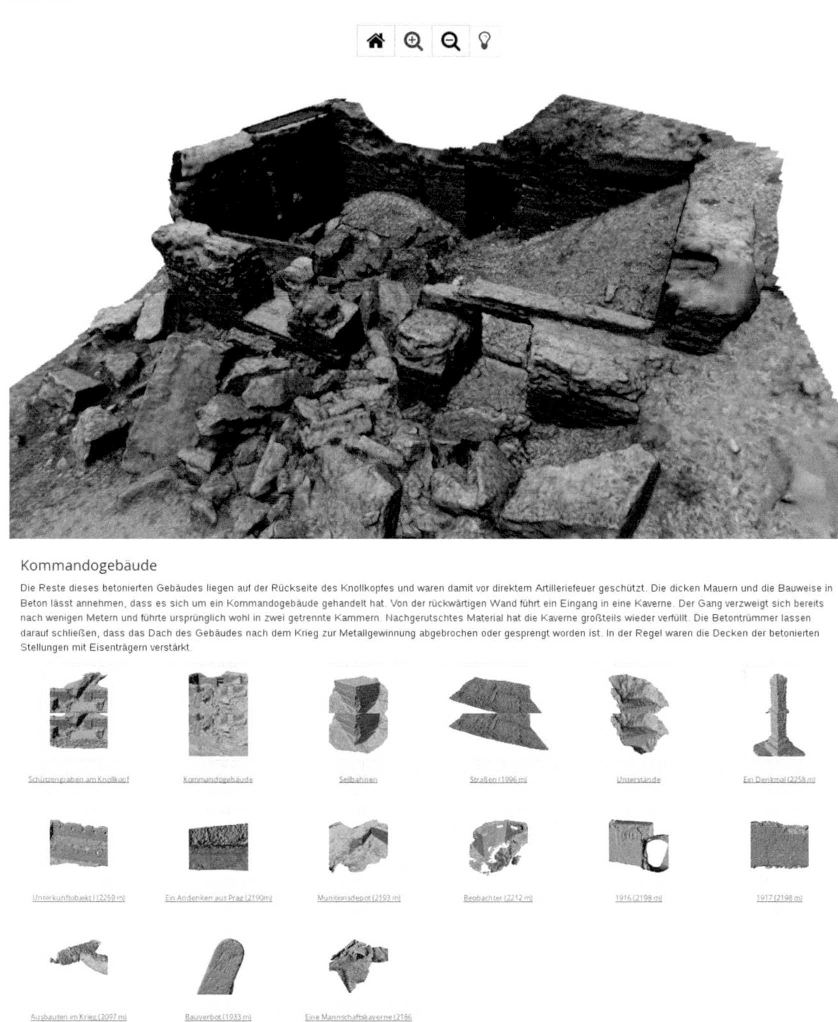

FIGURE 6.4 3-D presentation of 15 structures from the First World War on the homepage of the South Tyrolean Monument Office with 3DHOP. Source: Arc-Team / Screenshot www.provinz.bz.it/kunst-kultur/denkmalpflege/archaeologische-grabungsdokumentation.asp.

contains a number of functions that can be used to set up numerous possibilities for interaction between the user and the model. Public administration guarantees the long-term provision of server space and maintenance of the application. Unfortunately, due to limited funds, only the standard interaction functions could be implemented. The application is still online after five years.[2]

The Carnic Ridge

A project carried out on a section of the Italian positions on the western Carnic Ridge in 2015 had a special focus on the presentation and communication of the archaeological results (Figure 6.1). As a follow-up project to the inclusion of the Italian positions around the Knieberg (*Col Quaternà*) in 2014, the archaeological surveys were extended over a line of 3.7 kilometres across the so-called Cresta della Spina as far as Mt Col Rosson (2,300 metres) (Gietl 2017: 95–98), and around 4,200 objects were recorded. The work was carried out on behalf of the local Algudnei Museum in Dosoledo, with the aim of creating a historical hiking map that could be combined with the prototype of an app explaining this section of the Alpine front. The app can be downloaded using the QR code on the printed map and enables users to display their own position in a web GIS using GPS on an interactive map with the front structures. This allows hikers to orientate themselves accurately on the terrain and to target interesting points. Historical photos and informative texts on the events of the war complete the offer.

The application was well received by those who used it and has proven itself in practical terms. It was created with a very small budget of around 1,300 euros and is therefore very simple to set up. We used the MIT App Inventor online platform to program the application, and this works intuitively and easily and so can be mastered by beginners in a short time (Figure 6.5). One disadvantage, here and for similar applications elsewhere, however, is that an active internet connection is required.

In order to implement this prototype, we agreed to wait, update, and make the app available on our servers for the long term. Technical solutions such as apps and WebGIS not only generate costs when programming and generating content but also for maintenance. However, many local museums or associations neglect this aspect, which can mean applications no longer working after a few years, or projects not being implemented for fear of the consequential costs. For this reason, our current intention is to cease making data from the field recordings available on our own platforms, and instead to process them in such a way that they can be inserted into Open Street Map or other online map services, for example. However, the valid licences of the data must be taken into account. An unexpected problem was the misuse of the app for illicit excavations. Equipped with metal detectors, unknown individuals used the map to carry out targeted excavations for militaria. These events made it clear that using new technologies to research and communicate First World War issues had potential dangers as well as advantages, and thus had to be carefully controlled.

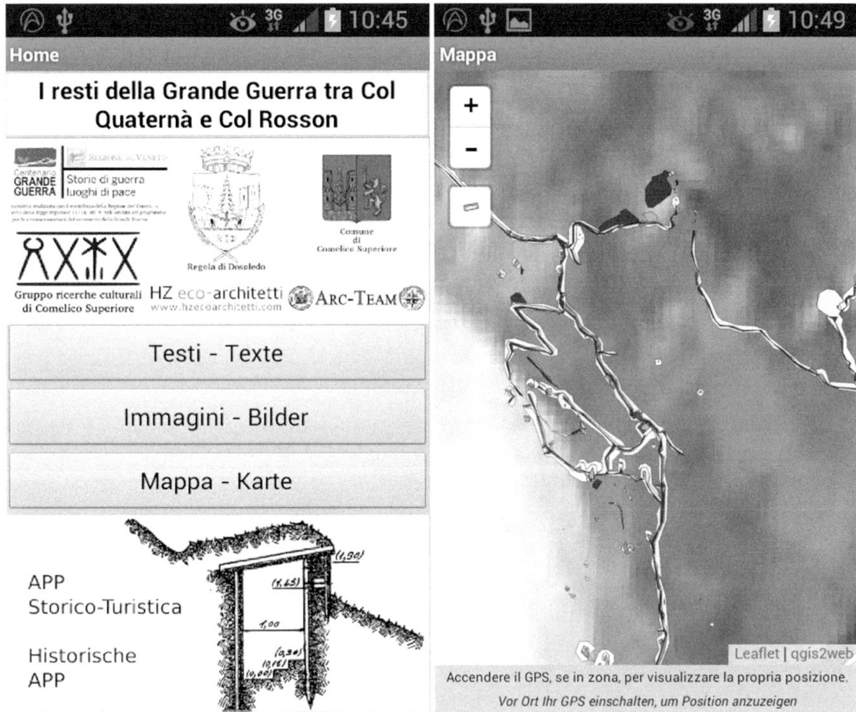

FIGURE 6.5 Two screenshots of the app with the war positions between the Knieberg and the Col Rosson. The start screen on the left, the WebGIS on the right. Source: © Arc-Team.

Schwalbenkofel

The opportunity for a purely conservative approach came in 2018–2019 when we were asked to document a very well-preserved ensemble of front structures on behalf of the South Tyrolean Office for Buildings and Art Monuments (Figure 6.1). The so-called *Kampfanlage Rautkofel-Schwalbenkofel* is very secluded at 2,500 metres above sea level in the municipality of Toblach in the Dolomites, with its origins in the pre-war period (Figure 6.6). Until a few years ago, the positions and buildings were well preserved, and numerous items of militaria were still on site. In addition, from a private photo album from the period 1915 to 1917, there are over 100 historical pictures of the site in its original condition. We documented the entire position in 3-D, from the ground and from the air, to capture the situation 100 years after the war. We also carried out some security work on one of the buildings. A short explanatory text was attached to this, but all other forms of presentation and publication were deliberately avoided in order not to expose the monument to increased pressure from looting.

FIGURE 6.6 The Austrian-Hungarian positions on the Schwalbenkofel lie around the top above the centre of the picture. Source: © Arc-Team.

Punta Linke

A completely different situation presented itself with a request concerning the open-air museum on Punta Linke (3,632 metres) (Figure 6.1). Between 2005 and 2012, the Trentino Provincial Monuments Office uncovered a cable car station built by the Austro-Hungarian Army on the glacier near the Vioz peak (3,645 metres) (Bassi et al. 2016). The facility consists of a 30-metre-long ice tunnel, an accommodation area, and the machine room of the cable car with a workshop and a position for a light gun. The structure has been partially reconstructed and is open for visits during the summer months. Because of its extreme location, only around 2,000 visitors reach the open-air museum every year.

For this reason, in 2017 we were asked to develop a prototype for a virtual tour of the site, which should also be compatible with future implementations (Bezzi et al. 2018b: 46–48). We decided to record the structure using image-based documentation methods (SfM, MVS) in order to obtain a high-resolution 3-D model, while at the same time panoramic videos of the interior were recorded with a 360° camera (Figure 6.7). The survey data was simplified and processed with a game engine in order to obtain an easy and network-compatible application. The interior of the site can be explored virtually, with hotspots allowing for additional information to be obtained.

The prototype remains on our servers and has not been published, in part due to the rapid development of the games industry and the constantly evolving

FIGURE 6.7 Punta Linke: On the left, the documentation work in the ice tunnel; on the right, a screenshot of the interactive model with a view from the door of the mountains to the north. Source: © Arc-Team.

demands of users. The graphics in the presentation are no longer likely to meet user expectations. Based on this experience, we are currently using the relatively simple technology of the Virtual Tour when a realistic representation of a situation is required. For this purpose, additional data is collected in the course of the archaeological recording with the help of 360° cameras. These are processed into 360° panoramas and linked together. In this way, an object can be easily explored inside and out.

Königspitze

Since 2015, we have been dealing with an object that has caused a sensation because of its exceptional location, its excellent state of preservation, and its history (Gietl 2019: D94).

On the Königspitze, the second-highest mountain on the Ortler front at 3,860 metres, there is an Austro-Hungarian army barracks (Figure 6.1). Due to global warming, it has been melting out of the ice piece by piece for around ten years. The interior is still filled with ice and, as a time capsule, completely preserves the situation of 3 November 1918. In a few years, if left to nature, the structure will crash over the 1,000-metre north flank of the mountain. To prevent this, we are melting the ice inside, documenting the situation, recovering the finds, and will finally dismantle the structure and bring it down into the valley (Figure 6.8). Yet, even if the building in the valley is reassembled, it will still have been removed from its historical context, highlighting the issue of authenticity where the actual landscape has had its key feature removed, and a new landscape has been created by the reassembling of the barracks. That is why it is all the more important to collect all possible data beforehand with all currently available technologies in order to create a basis for an appropriate presentation in the museum context. The original location changes year after year due to the glacial melt and

FIGURE 6.8 Königspitze: on the left, the situation of the barrack in 2015 from the helicopter; on the right, part of the 3-D model of the outer façade. Source: © Arc-Team.

soon our documentation will be the only thing that will remain of it. Sooner or later the same fate will overtake the entire front in rock and ice, and so 'preservation by record' is the best available option.

Summary and outlook

In the course of 25 projects between 2012 and 2019, the Arc-Team Archaeology company was able to map approximately 30,000 objects and structures along the front in rock and ice. The spectrum ranges from simple boards and nails to complex building findings, written documents, or excellent military and technical equipment for soldiers. Research initially focused on the immediate combat areas, but over time the entire conflict landscape of the Alpine front, up to 30 kilometres wide, became the focus of interest. We know today that, especially in the early stages of the war, positions were still being prepared up to 40 kilometres behind the main battle line. In addition, there are countless supply facilities, airfields, hospitals, and cemeteries, the traces of which remain largely undiscovered.

Every year, further traces of the high mountain front fall victim to the ravages of time or human hands. It is therefore important to examine other sections of the front in the same way in order to get a better and more complete picture of this important historical landscape. New technologies offer numerous options to make documentation even easier and faster in the future. The data should be recorded in such a way that it is suitable for communication to the stakeholders and can be easily further processed. In the early years, we tried to develop our own solutions for the digital presentation of the results (WebGIS, apps). Apart from in a few exceptional cases, this was not possible due to the high costs of programming and maintaining the systems. In recent years, our efforts have been to connect to the world's leading online map services and to process the data in such a way that they can be easily incorporated. We are also working on special forms of presentation, e.g. for museums.

For objects that are particularly outstanding and worthy of protection but difficult to access, the aim is to convey an impression of the situation on site for individuals with reduced mobility or without the necessary alpine experience with the help of virtual tours. Here too, technology is constantly changing and progressing.

In a second step, the digital archaeological results are brought together with archival documents from the Austrian and Italian armies, diaries, and the rich treasure of contemporary photographs. This step would be particularly important for the communication and historical evaluation of the results, but it has not yet taken place in most projects. Most of the time it is only through this process that we can interpret what we find in the field. At the same time, it also builds a bridge to the human experiences that underlie this conflict landscape, and which should not be forgotten. It remains to be seen what dynamic this research will be able to retain in the future, beyond the 2014–2018 commemorative years.

Acknowledgements

We thank all partners and colleagues who contributed to the success of the projects. In particular: the South Tyrol and Trentino Heritage Office, the Ortler Sammlerverein Erster Weltkrieg Association, and the Austrian Society for Fortification Research.

Notes

1 Structure from motion is a photogrammetric range imaging technique used to estimate 3-D structures from 2-D image sequences that can be joined with motion signals.
2 www.provinz.bz.it/kunst-kultur/denkmalpflege/archaeologische-grabungsdokumentation.asp

References

ASFR (Austrian Society for Fortress Research) (2017) 3D Models of Replacement Field Fortifications Plätzwiese. www.kuk-fortification.net/category/region-sudwest-southwest/sperre-landro-plaetzwiese/. Posted on September 16, 2017 by reklov.

Austrian State Archive (1917) AT-OeStA KA FA NFA BK ABrigKdo AKdo Hochgränten 3365. 12./XI.

Bassi, C., F. Nicolis and M. Vicenzi. (2016) Archeologia Della Grande Guerra in Italia. L'esperienza di Punta Linke (3.629 m slm) nel Gruppo Ortles-Cevedale. *Rivista di studi militari* 5: 348–352.

Berti, A. (1936) *Guerra in Cadore*. Rome: X Regg. Alpini.

Bezzi, A., L. Bezzi, F. Bonfanti, R. Gietl and G. Naponiello. (2018a) La Grande Guerra sul Garda Orientale. Un progetto di archeologia del conflitto. In F. Bonfanti and R. Ferrari (eds.), *La Grande Guerra sul Garda Orientale. Operazioni Belliche e Vicende Militari sul Lago e L'entroterra Montano*, pp. 173–207. Vicenza: Edibus.

Bezzi, A., L. Bezzi, Ch. Boscaro, K. Feistmantl, R. Gietl, G. Naponiello, F. Ottati and M. de Guzman. (2018b) Commercial Archaeology and 3D Web Technologies. *Journal of Field Archaeology* 43 (1): 45–59.

Giacomel, P. (2004) *1897–1901, Cortina d'Ampezzo: il forte austriaco Tre Sassi*. Udine: Gaspari.

Gietl, R. (2017) Frontgebiete unter der Lupe. Die Archäologie des Ersten Weltkrieges im Gebirge. Neue Ergebnisse der großflächigen archäologischen Dokumentationskampagne am westlichen Karnischen Kamm. In A. Jordan (ed.), 'Die kahlen, kalten Berge ...' Der Erste Weltkrieg im Alpenraum, die Deutsche Gebirgstruppe und das Württembergische Gebirgsbataillon. Rastatt: Museum Rastatt GmbH.

——— (2019) Sechs Jahre an der Front. Erfahrungen auf dem Feld der Konfliktarchäologie in Fels und Eis 2012 bis 2018. *Fundberichte aus Österreich* 56: D93–103.

Gietl, R. and H. Steiner. (2016) Restituzione tri-dimensionale delle gallerie della prima guerra mondiale usando l'approccio del FLOSS-Image Based Modelling. In F. Stanco and G. Gallo (eds.), *Free, Libre and Open Source Software E Open Format Nei Processi Di Ricerca Archeologica: VIII Edizione, Catania 2013*, pp. 9–15. Oxford: Archaeopress.

Gietl, R., H. Steiner and Ch. Terzer. (2015) Stumme Zeugen des 1. Weltkriegs. Dokumentation der Hochgebirgsfront des I. Weltkrieges im Pustertal. *Der Schlern* 89: 4–25.

Košir, U. (2019) Legacies of the Soča Front – From Rubbish to Heritage (1915–2017). In U. Košir, M. Črešnar and D. Mlekuž (eds.), *Rediscovering the Great War: Archaeology and Enduring Legacies on the Soča and Eastern Fronts*, pp. 181–198. London: Routledge.

Mlekuž, D., U. Košir and M. Črešnar. (2016) Landscapes of Death and Suffering: Archaeology of Conflict Landscapes of the Upper Soča Valley, Slovenia. In B. Stichelbaut and D. Cowley (eds.), *Conflict Landscapes and Archaeology from Above*, pp. 127–145. London: Routledge.

Nicolis, F. (2011) La Grande Guerra. Memorie sepolte nel Ghiaccio. Fra storia e archeologia. *Archeologia Viva* 147: 14–29.

——— (2017) The Scent of Snow at Punta Linke: First World War Sites as Sense-Scapes, Trentino, Italy. In N.J. Saunders and P. Cornish (eds.), *Modern Conflict and the Senses*, pp. 61–75. London: Routledge.

Reitmaier, Th. (2014) Bunker, Bomben und Baracken – Zeithistorische Archäologie in Graubünden. *Bündner Monatsblatt* 4: 355–375.

Saunders, N.J. (2010) *Killing Time: Archaeology and the First World War* (second edition). Stroud: History Press.

Schemfil, V. (1926) *Das k. u. k. 3. Regiment der Tiroler Kaiserjäger im Weltkriege 1914–1918*. Bregenz: Teutsch.

7

ENGAGING MILITARY HERITAGE

The conflict landscape of Val Canale, Italy

Anita Pinagli, Volker Pachauer, and Alexander J. Potočnik

Introduction

Val Canale is a strategic mountain passage in north-east Italy, with Austria to the north and Slovenia to the east. It mostly adheres to the topography of the valley of the River Fella, but also includes part of the Tagliamento River Valley and the Silizza (Italian) or Gailitz (Austrian) River Valleys. In a geostrategic sense, Val Canale connects the Mediterranean and Central Europe and is a secondary passage within the broader area of the Ljubljana Gap, parallel to the Ljubljana Gap proper (Potočnik et al. 2012: 13–21) which leads from Venice to Trieste, Ljubljana, and Graz. The Val Canale area contains many military and archaeological sites, especially on the summits and at the bases of the adjacent Julian and Carnic Alps. At the heart of this area, at the convergence of the major and secondary access routes of the valley is the municipality of Malborghetto-Valbruna, an area rich in the unstudied remains of historical as well as modern conflict.

The aim of this chapter is twofold: to introduce this comparatively unknown and un-investigated area and its conflict-related sites, and to demonstrate that landscapes of modern conflict must be investigated and understood with reference to their past lives, both natural and cultural. All landscapes are socially constructed, and as such are concepts as well as physical places. The terrains of modern conflict are 'not just a series of battlefields, but a palimpsest of overlapping, multi-vocal landscapes' (Saunders 2001: 37) which, because of their unchanging topography, often retain their strategic importance over time. Modern conflict landscapes, therefore, can be reconfigured versions of earlier historical battle-zones, with their present form and function a hybrid of past and present. It is our intention here to provide a diachronic account of the formation of the Val Canale conflict landscape, and thereby to explore and document how pre-modern war shaped twentieth-century conflict places, to what extent these have survived, and how they are viewed and engaged with today by local communities.

The complex challenges of investigating the Val Canale require the interdisciplinary approach of modern conflict archaeology (Saunders 2004, 2012; Schofield et al. 2002). As with any conflict landscape investigation, its study necessarily crosses the boundaries between archaeology, anthropology, cultural and military history, geography, heritage studies, and other disciplines, and is reflected in the different specialisms of the authors.[1] For the Val Canale, landscape investigation, military history, and ethnographic interviews with the local community between 2013 and 2019 reveal the richness and complexity of this conflict landscape, the potential for research, and the extent to which the local community is involved with its preservation. These investigations complement recent research carried out across (and indeed on) the border with Slovenia (Kozorog 2019; Zilli 2019).

Malborghetto-Valbruna: a strategic location

The municipality of Malborghetto-Valbruna lies in the region of Friuli Venezia Giulia in north-east Italy, whose triple-barrelled name reveals the cultural and geographical complexity of the area. Malborghetto-Valbruna itself covers an area of 119,900 square kilometres of mountainous terrain at the heart of the Val Canale (Domenig 2003). The area is characterized by the ancient Palaeozoic rock formations of the Carnic Alps to the north and by the Triassic rock formation sequences characteristic of the Julian Alps to the south (Padiero and Poldini 1991: 119). The lower valley has been shaped over time by the River Fella and its many lateral tributaries. From the locality of Malborghetto, the valley bottom widens, becoming an extended plain up to the limit of the town of Valbruna. The remaining part of the valley from Malborghetto to the western boundary of the municipality is characterized by poor sedimentary lands carried by the main river and its tributaries.

The Malborghetto area first saw major settlement in the Roman and Early Medieval periods, particularly during the sixth and seventh century CE (Faleschini 2010). Slavic tribes occupied the most fertile area of the valley – the plain of Ugovizza and Valbruna. Following Christianization, this area became a possession of the bishops of Bamberg in Germany in 1007, who considered it to be a strategic passage between the Adriatic and the lands north of the Alps. From the early medieval period onwards, the valley was known as '*Chanol*' (i.e. 'the Channel') (Jaksch 1904 cited in Domening 2003: 26). Towns such as Malborghetto developed into market centres specializing in ironworking. Other settlements in the area remained in the hands of Germanic and Slavic settlers, who were mostly shepherds and woodworkers.

The decline of the iron market, several incursions by the Ottoman Turks, and territorial claims made by the Republic of Venice marked a change in the political and military use of Val Canale between the fifteenth and seventeenth centuries. The bishops of Bamberg sold the valley to the Habsburg Empress Maria Theresa in 1759, thereby making it an important border region of the

Austrian Empire (Domenig 2003). This was the beginning of the conflict landscape which we analyze here.

The strategic military value of Val Canale became ever more evident during the Napoleonic Wars, when several important battles took place there in the campaigns of 1797 and 1809.[2] With this experience in mind, the Austrian military later fortified the valley in three stages: first during the 1840s, then in the 1880s, and finally in the 1900s. The fact that Italians never attempted any serious break-through along the Fella River Valley during the First World War has generally been attributed to the existence of Fort Hensel near Malborghetto, at the time the most advanced fortification system in the area (Weiss 2004)[3] (see Figure 7.3). The fort did not survive the pounding of Italian heavy artillery and as early as 1915 its armament was moved into underground caverns dug into nearby hills. Val Canale retained its importance throughout the twentieth century, and today this is attested by a motorway and high-speed railway defining this route as the main traffic corridor between Italy and Austria.

In describing this conflict archaeological landscape, it is important to recognize that Val Canale is a renowned convergence point of three ethnic groups – Italian, German, and Slavic – which had always lived together in the area. The two world wars and the colonization policies (applied by the Italian government between 1939 and 1942[4]) are among the causes of a changing sense of place and identity for these communities (Pinagli 2013). Changes also affected the sense of belonging and attachment to the visible local heritage, which differs even from village to village (Vavti 2005; Pinagli 2013).[5] Shifting military uses of Val Canale over the past 200 years have taken place against a multiethnic cultural background, and Malborghetto-Valbruna today retains this diversity of people and their senses of place.

Places are experienced and created through the human body, and perception will differ from person to person. 'We define ourselves not as creatures in the world, but as points of view upon it, as spectators looking at it from a distance or from above' (Wylie 2007: 145). In this way, places allow us introspection (Casey 1998). In Val Canale, these places are the remains of visible heritage and are perceived in different ways by its multiethnic community (Pinagli 2013), and thus as Chris Tilley (1994: 15) has observed, a group's 'experience of "being in" *their* landscape produces a sense of place and belonging'.

The local communities' ideas of local heritage and their form of attachment were investigated in a community-mapping survey conducted in 2013 (Pinagli 2013). Interviews sought to understand what aspect of the visible local heritage individuals felt engaged with. There were two constant responses: a desire to learn about the visible heritage of the native people who left the valley during the major conflicts, and a desire to understand the structures built for war purposes (those from the First World War to the Cold War), which today are left abandoned (ibid.: 169–170).

'Landscape is the world as it is known to those who dwell therein' (Ingold 1993: 156). For Italian scholars such as Vittorio Foramitti (2014: 112), understanding this border conflict area has to take into consideration the pathos and the intimate memories of the people who created and experience these places. Thus it is important to engage with community members, giving them the opportunity to understand, protect, and promote the heritage they themselves recognize. By considering and valuing local community needs, scientific investigations can acquire a deeper understanding of place, as well as lay the foundations for collaborative research.

The historic conflict landscape of Val Canale, 1500–1914

The municipality of Malborghetto-Valbruna, and especially the town of Malborghetto itself, offers an extraordinary range of conflict-related evidence, with many un-investigated archaeological sites. The authors chose it as a case study because it afforded the opportunity to investigate how a conflict landscape developed over 300 years. More theoretically, it enabled an analysis of the landscape relationship between twentieth-century modern conflict and earlier historical wars in the same places. The primary historical sources are Austrian and French – documentation which naturally reflects the perspectives of these 'outsiders'. Possibly the first local historian who attempted a complete historical description centred on this conflict landscape area was Maria von Plazer[6] (1899). Her work was referred to by local scholars and enthusiasts, including Raimondo Domenig (2003), Paolo Foramitti (1999), Ulrike Weiss (2013), and Leonardo Malatesta (2014). While most available literature provides a general historical account of recent conflicts, there is a notable lack of academic research on the archaeological landscape and architectural remains.

From the Middle Ages onwards, the Tarvisio and Predil Passes were important trade routes, allowing easy access to the town of Villach and the Drava River (Schaumann 1978). These strategic locations were accessible through secondary roads from the area of Malborghetto and especially from the Saisera Valley. The administration on behalf of the bishops of Bamberg developed a local subsistence economy and conferred importance on this passage by creating different customs stations protected by towers and fortifications. Most of these structures disappeared in an earthquake in 1348 and were subsequently forgotten (Domenig 2014: 73).

The first known attempt to build defensive fortifications in the area dates to the fifteenth century when the Ottoman army entered Val Canale. A two-storey tower was built in the locality known as Tabor[7] near the main church, possibly part of a series of inter-visual watchtowers. Historical documents refer to it as the S. Bernardino Tower[8] (Domenig 2003: 86), though it was later dismantled with only a basement corner on the northeast side of the hill surviving.

New defences were built in the seventeenth century. At this time, the border between the Bamberg administration and the Republic of Venice ran east–west along the Julian Alps up to the locality of Pontebba. Val Canale allowed direct access towards the Venetian plain (Bianco 1995: 23). Tensions between the villagers of the two powers destabilized the border and increased the need for defences. A section of this border passed close to the Saisera Valley. This was used by the Venetians as a direct corridor to enter Val Canale and plunder local villages, especially during the period of the Gradisca War[9](Manoli 1971: 55; Domenig 2012: 63). In 1604, a combined commission of Venetians and Bamberg representatives drafted a plan of the existing borders[10] which mentions the presence of a fortification located on a lower hill – known as *Monte Palla*,[11] located in the middle of the Ugovizza Plain and controlling access to the Saisera Valley. Historical accounts mention the presence of a wooden fort built on a promontory south of the town of Malborghetto, known as *Karl Schanze*.[12] Modern reuse of the land as pasture has destroyed any evidence of this structure (Domenig 2003: 33; Oman 2016).

The greatest changes in the military use of the valley, however, occurred after 1759, when Maria Teresa purchased the valley. Her military strategy had important consequences for reshaping the conflict landscape in Val Canale around Malborghetto. In 1797, during the first Napoleonic invasion, six earthen '*Schanzen*' (independent fortifications) and other defences were built in the north-east part of the plain close to Monte Palla, and nearby Camporosso.[13] In 1804, Erzherzog Johann von Österreich visited Val Canale and identified ideal positions to build fortifications in preparation for a new conflict (Leitner 1947: 31). The central focus of his choice was the *Tchalawai* promontory, a natural rock formation controlling access to the main communication route in the valley, the town of Malborghetto to the west, the Julian Alps to the south, and one of the strategic secondary passages towards Valbruna, the Saisera Valley and Vercella (also called the Nebria Pass).

Following von Österreich's plan, a fortification started to be built on a promontory east of Malborghetto in 1808 but remained unfinished in May 1809 (Leitner 1947: 41). It consisted of two blockhouses and wooden palisades built under the direction of Captain Friedrich Hensel. No accommodation was planned as soldiers lived in the village, billeted in rich families' houses or taverns (Foramitti 1999: 22; Domenig 2003). A small Austrian garrison defended the fortifications against the troops of Eugene de Beauharnais, though it was conquered on 17 May 1809. The French army easily surrounded the promontory, bypassing the main communication line of the valley by advancing up the Dogna Valley and entering Val Canale through the Saisera Valley and Valbruna.[14] After the siege and conquest, the valley became part of the district of Passiariano and the wooden fort was burned down in 1813 (Plazer 2012: 51). The archaeological evidence of this period is attested by some finds, but there are no recognizable structural remains.

The French understood the importance of using undefended secondary routes, a fact discernible in the first editions of a French cadastral map.[15] The first edition of the Malborghetto-Ugovizza map does not show a fort on the Tchalawai promontory. It does, however, mention a new fortification on top of the nearby isolated hill of Monte Palla, possibly already used for defence purposes in the seventeenth century.[16] An Austrian map from the same period (1806–1811) depicts a small wooden fort there.[17] This invites speculation that the French administration built new defences that replaced those destroyed in 1813 (Plazer 2012: 51).

After the 1814 Congress of Vienna, the valley was returned to Austria, though being so far from Vienna and the Habsburg Monarchy, nothing was done to re-fortify this key access to the Austrian heartland from the south. The south-western border seemed to be well protected by the so-called *Festungsviereck* or *Quadrilatero*[18] (Hackelsberger 1980; Biffart 1863). Revolutionary tendencies spreading from France across Europe prompted the Austro-Hungarian Empire to increase funding for fortifications in Tyrol (Franzensfeste-Fortezza), Venice, and Verona in 1830 (Hackelsberger 1980: 12–13).

The outbreak of revolutions across Europe in 1848 offered a much greater threat to the Empire. The Austrian general staff hastily ordered the construction of fortifications – including along the Val Canale. Due to the lack of time, almost exactly the same sites as in 1808–1809 were chosen, although the forts were larger with massive stone constructions, especially on the Tchalawai promontory.[19] The vulnerability of the free-standing 1809 blockhouses, so easily outflanked by the French Army at Predil and Malborghetto, was not lost on the high command in Vienna. For example, the latter's position did not even fully block Val Canale (Rosner 2009: 178, 184). Compensating for this, new blocking forts in Carinthia were planned as interrelated structures. Supported by obstacles and additional observation posts, these various elements formed a defence line of mutually supporting fortifications by making effective use of topography (Konold and Regnath 2014).

This fortification programme significantly impacted the landscape, shifting Austrian defences away from single fortifications and towards the concept of a barrier. The fortification captain and engineer Casimir Bielaswski was ordered to build the *Sperre Malborgeth* (i.e. the 'Malborghetto Lock') – a defence consisting of two blockhouses and other supporting defences (Weiss 2013; Malatesta 2014). In June 1848 construction works began in the Predil Pass, Tchalawai, and on Monte Palla.[20] The fortification on that latter hill was planned to block the exit from the Saisera Valley, and the Vercella Saddle south of Nebria Mountain, and therefore provide protection for Fort Malborghetto. However, due to a reduction of the military threat and lack of funds, construction at Monte Palla was stopped in 1849 (Jäger 1873; Plazer 2012) (Figure 7.1).

Although the reconstruction of Fort Malborghetto has received much scholarly attention, archival sources at the *Kriegsarchiv* in Vienna reveal plans for more complex fortifications between Malborghetto and Valbruna. The Austrians planned several batteries and blockhouses in order to overcome past tactical mistakes, such as a second fortification on the eastern side of Monte Palla (Figure 7.2). It would have consisted of a casemated semi-permanent battery on the southern slope of the hill and a blockhouse on top of the hill. On the north side, peace-time barracks and other elements would have completed the

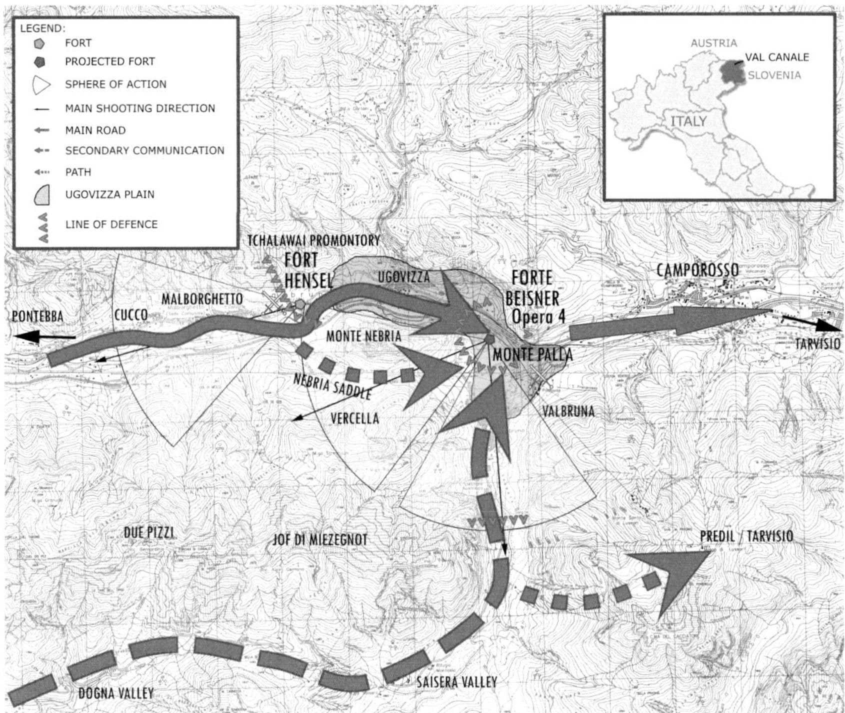

FIGURE 7.1 The modern Municipality of Marlborghetto-Valbruna, showing the military impact of the main fortified areas on the surrounding landscape. Source: © V. Pachauer.

structure. Archaeological fieldwork confirmed traces of both emplacements of the fort. The foundation remains of a structure on the highest point correlates with the ground section on the plan. This x-shaped blockhouse on top of the hill follows the general scheme of Austrian fortifications at that time.[21] The fort and battery were begun, but the works were left unfinished (Plazer 2012: 51).

In 1879, the railway Villach–Udine–Trieste was completed (N.N. 1879), thus giving Val Canale an increased strategic and military importance. This is a prime example of how technological development created a new 'modern' conflict landscape of industrialized warfare. One consequence was a commission set up in 1879 to decide the future purpose and layout of Fort Malborghetto (TAMK 1888: 3–4), which had been criticized by its own garrison officers for the huge resources of manpower and armaments it required for only a limited sphere of action (TAMK 1888: 2). Indeed, it had already been rendered obsolete by the development of siege armament. The original idea was to reinforce the existing structure and reduce its size, with the final decision recommending replacing the existing fortification with an entirely rebuilt structure.[22]

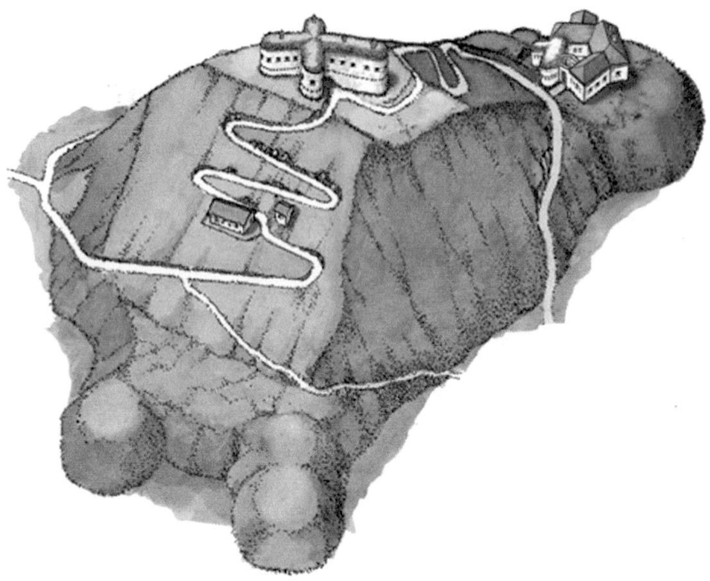

FIGURE 7.2 The fortifications planned on Monte Palla-Kugelberg, as they were supposed to appear according to the unrealized plan of 1848. Source: © A.J. Potočnik.

This new fortification was defended by the newly developed 12-centimetre breach-loader Model 1880 guns protected by steel armour and mounted on fortress carriages. 'Werk B' consisted of a battery of four casemated guns in a line, protected by massive cast-steel shields. Atop this was a secondary battery, with two heavy revolving turrets armed with two 12-centimetre guns each. This main part of the structure, officially named Fort Hensel after the defender of 1809, Captain of the Fortress Engineers Corps Friedrich Hensel, was designed to block the Tarvisio–Pontebba road and the Villach–Udine railway line as well as to withstand enemy siege batteries. The upper part of the fort, referred to as 'Werk A', consisted of the so-called *Rondell*, an open mortar battery and a barracks complex designed for infantry and close defence. A ditch, flanked by *caponiers* (protective access routes) gave additional protection to the fort's front side and right flank. Another novel feature was the use of tunnels dug through solid rock and connecting the flanking positions (Figure 7.3).

Although built as the most modern fortification in the Habsburg Monarchy (Figure 7.4) and probably in the whole of Europe, Fort Hensel soon became outdated due to the introduction of high-explosive shells. To compensate for this, the fort was repeatedly reinforced until 1914. In 1897–1898, 'Werk A' received an armoured battery of two Model 1880 15-centimetre mortars, two observation cupolas, and a machinegun battery,[23] and 'Werk B' received another two observation posts and a search-light position. During the following years, the

FIGURE 7.3 Reconstruction of Fort Hensel as it was in 1914. Source: © A.J. Potočnik.

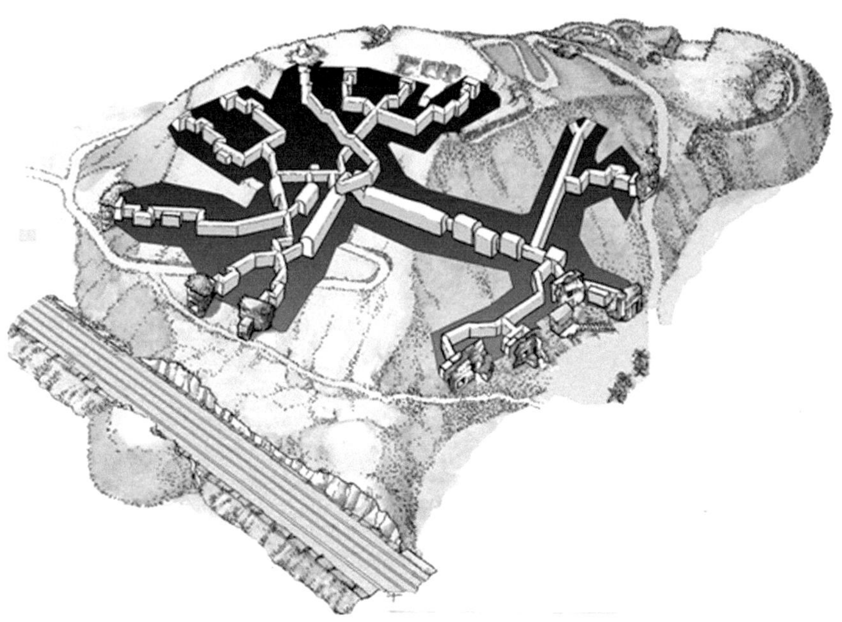

FIGURE 7.4 Opera 4 Ugovizza Gruppo 845 (Fort Beisner), a depiction of the present day situation including field fortifications (trenches) dating to 1848 and reused until the Cold War. Source: © A.J. Potočnik.

technical equipment was upgraded, and some of the roofs were reinforced by an additional layer of concrete. The threat of bypassing Fort Hensel through the Dogna and Saisera Valleys, or using the path south of Nebria Mountain (Figure 7.1) remained, however. Our research located several unfulfilled plans to fortify the 'Vercella Saddle'[24] in the Kriegsarchiv in Vienna, but none of them had been realized.

The modern conflict landscape of Val Canale, 1914–1945

In Val Canale, the First World War started in 1915. As the tension at the Austro-Hungarian Empire's official border between Pontebba and Pontafel increased, the bridge there was blown up and the Austrian forces retreated to Fort Hensel. The Italian Army took important positions atop the Julian Alps by conquering mountain peaks such as the *Jôf di Miezegnot* overlooking the valley and the important passage to the Saisera Valley. Soon, the conflict became a positional war. The Austrians had few regular troops available to send to the area, and its defence was based upon a volunteer militia known as the *Schützen*.[25] Initially, they constructed a first line of defence in the area of Cucco, defending the *Due Pizzi* mountain, and installed a 420mm howitzer near the Malborghetto train station (Schaumann 1978: 446).

Italian strategy focused on bombarding Fort Hensel, whose garrison resisted until 1916 (Ebner 2010: 20). The fort was reduced to ruins and the Austrians organized themselves on nearby Nebria Mountain and in two resistance lines in the Saisera Valley (ibid.: 9). The Austrian forces, with the help of alpine guides such as Julius Kugy,[26] transformed the Julian Alps into a high-altitude conflict landscape (Kugy 2008). Soldiers and volunteers built structures adapted to this new type of war. These were independent strongholds able to defend themselves and protect each other's flanks. Schaumann (1978: 476–479) describes three types of defensive structures: shelters, usually wooden structures with shingle roofs, stone basements, and tarred cardboard walls, serving as platoon headquarters; caverns (still visible today), located near the front line; and communication trenches which connected all these positions, and were dug into rock or earth.

The Italians and Austrians fought several battles for control of the nearby mountain peaks, during which many soldiers from both sides died from cold and disease. Between 1916–1917, villages such as Valbruna were heavily bombarded (ibid.). The Austrians built a base camp between Ugovizza and Valbruna known as *Lager Nebria*, geographically located between Nebria Mountain and Monte Palla. The latter, being exposed to enemy fire from higher Italian Alpine positions, did not have an important tactical function during this war. Trenches along its top edges suggest that it was used mainly for observation (Perderzolli 2007: 65).

In 1919, the Saint Germain Treaty assigned Val Canale to Italy. The demography of the valley had already been destabilized by a mass exodus amidst the chaos and destruction of the war years. A strong post-war acculturation and colonization phase by Italy has left a strong imprint in modern Val Canale.

The Italian government transformed the urban landscape of the valley through the construction of new military roads and bridges in order to restore the area's ancient function as a strategic passage towards the north (Bernasconi-Muran 2009). In this way, another layer was added to the centuries-old conflict landscape.

At the war's end, the Italians took possession of the Austro-Hungarian military positions. These became part of a new defence known as *Vallo Alpino del Littorio*.[27] In Val Canale, the wartime underground positions and fortifications facilitated the construction of this new Italian defence line. The Italian Army and hundreds of workers built more subterranean strongholds in the bedrock and reinforced concrete structures along the main communication lines (Bernasconi-Muran 2009).

There were two significant conceptual differences that distinguished Italian fortifications from other similar European systems of the interwar period. Rather than constructing massive fortifications, the Italians exploited the advantages of the Alpine terrain and drilled their positions into existing cliff-faces. In addition, due to areas of inaccessible terrain, they abandoned the principle of continuous, linear defence based on the interchange of flanking fire (Potočnik 2009: 82). Instead, they focused on blocking access routes, often in depth, as in Val Canale. This represented a distinctive break with the past, and dramatically reconfigured the conflict landscape.

Between 1931 and 1943, the design and construction of Italian border fortifications were dictated by the Italian Supreme Command, in circulars which prescribed the building of three defensive zones parallel to the border.[28] The fortifications in Val Canale did not follow this general pattern, however. The long, broad valley, lined by steep mountain peaks, dictated an in-depth defence with forts dotting the Fella River Valley along the entire 60 kilometres between Coccau, near Tarvisio, in the north and Tolmezzo in the south. South of Tolmezzo and Villa Santina, a mountain ridge, perpendicular to the converging valleys of the rivers Fella and Tagliamento, enabled the construction of the last Italian defensive line of *Invillino* (Silvestri 2005). Speaking later, during the Cold War, Sergio Silvestri, a civil engineer, author, and an authority on the *Vallo Alpino* fortifications in the Friuli Venezia Giulia region, summed up the logic of these Val Canale fortifications: 'In the eyes of the military the stony bed of the Fella river represented a broad highway for armoured vehicles which needed to be kept under control'.[29]

At the beginning of the Second World War, these *Vallo Alpino* fortifications played no role. After the invasion of Yugoslavia, they were disarmed and their units, called '*Guardia alla frontiera*', were moved and posted in garrisons on the occupied territories, mostly in Slovenia and Croatia.

Today, in the Municipality of Malborghetto, it is still possible to explore the remains of nine of these barriers, incorporating the more than 40 finished and unfinished shelter and defence barracks built between 1938 and 1940. Interestingly, from the perspective of the political shaping of conflict landscapes, some of Val Canale's *Vallo Alpino* positions were left unfinished because, in 1942, Hitler demanded that Mussolini stop constructing defensive structures against the Germans (Bernasconi-Muran 2009). The physical remains of this landscape also highlight changes in defensive concepts over time, as the old pre–First World War fort of Malborhgetto lost importance, while a new role was given to Monte Palla. Here, the Italians built the most important fort in the area, known first as 'Opera 1' and later 'Opera 4' (Fort Beisner), part of the Barrier 845 of Ugovizza (ibid.).

Fort Beisner and many other '*opere*' in the vicinity were built by Italian construction companies that also supplied the infrastructure providing access to the fortifications. One of these companies was Tarantelli (Archive Association 'Landscapes' 2016). After the German occupation of Northern Italy in 1943, the Germans re-armed individual forts and constructed new ones on the southern slopes of the Alps.[30] They were to become part of the so-called *Alpen Festung* (Alpine Fortress) (Domenig 2016). A survey aimed at evaluating Italian fortresses in the area by the German Captain Nobling in 1944[31] indicated that fortifications such as Fort Beisner in Ugovizza were judged appropriate for reuse (Archive Association 'Landscapes' 2018). However, the Germans preferred to build new defences oriented directly towards the Allies (Domenig 2016: 113–114).

The Germans occupied civil structures and military barracks such as the *Incau Solideo* Barracks in Ugovizza. Civil defences were built anew or converted from existing shelters. In the Val Canale area, there are still unexplored remains, such as the anti-aircraft shelter of *Bagni di Lusnizza* (no longer accessible), the underground system of Malborghetto, and another in Ugovizza located behind the church (Domenig 2016).

With the onset of the Cold War, interwar fortifications were repurposed again, exemplifying the legacy value of earlier defences, and simultaneously adding yet another layer to the conflict landscape. The end of the Second World War had brought further significant changes in national borders. The eastern and western parts of *Vallo Alpino* were now in Yugoslavian and French territory, respectively. They were disarmed and in many cases destroyed. In accordance with the peace treaty of 1947, even those fortifications that remained in Italy, such as those in Val Canale, had to be disarmed (Corino 1995; Corino and Gastaldo 1993: 364). This changed again with the Cold War. Neither Austria nor the then Yugoslavia belonged to the Warsaw Pact,[32] but the NATO[33] doctrine at the time assumed that neither country would be able to resist the advance of Warsaw Pact forces. Val Canale was therefore regarded as one of the main potential Soviet routes into Italy. As a result, NATO financed the restoration of existing forts along the border with Austria,[34] including those in Val Canale, and the construction of new ones along the border with Yugoslavia (now Slovenia) (Bernasconi, Muran 2009: 498).[35]

In 1976, fortifications along Italy's eastern border were still regarded as necessary (Bernasconi and Muran 1999: 47). This is well illustrated by the fact that the building of the new Udine–Tarvisio motorway (1973–1986) was accompanied by the construction of new corresponding fortifications (Cappellano and Chiaruttini 2015). One consequence of the dissolution of the Soviet Union and the Warsaw Pact was that Italian border fortifications were disarmed and sealed and the units operating them disbanded. Today, Fort Beisner is one of the few Val Canale forts maintained and open to the public.[36] These most recent historical developments have created new levels of conflict landscape, overlaying the already complex reconfiguration of war terrain dating back to the late eighteenth century.

While fortifications built during the twentieth century (the pre–Second World War *Vallo Alpino* and the post-1945 NATO-financed fortifications) were still in service, the militarized landscape of the entire Val Canale was in a sense undetectable. There is a certain irony in the fact that the real character of this heavily militarized landscape remained unknown until the abandonment of fortifications in the years 1991–1992.

The Italians were masters of camouflage and put this expertise to good use in building the *Vallo Alpino*. There was also secrecy, with construction sites being screened-off (Potočnik et al. 2012: 48). After the Second World War, simultaneous construction of a motorway and the last generation of fortifications made their construction virtually undetectable. Only the lack of maintenance during the last three decades and consequent deterioration of the camouflage shutters covering embrasures and cloches finally made them visible.[37]

For the authors, the realization that they had spent decades passing these *Vallo Alpino* fortifications without ever noticing them was a surprise. During the Cold War, it was only the presence of huge barracks like '*Caserma Lamarmora*' in Tarvisio, the munitions store in the Saisera Valley, and some anti-tank obstacles that indicated the strategic importance of the valleys converging on Tarvisio. The rest of the landscape had the appearance of a tranquil and undisturbed natural environment. In other words, the Italian interwar *Vallo Alpino* and the post-1945 NATO fortifications jointly formed a secret layer of the conflict landscape (arguably two layers) designed to be invisible, and integrated with the natural geography with a remarkable degree of technological sophistication. It is only now, decades after the conflicts of the twentieth century, that the real defensive character of this landscape and the extent of its militarization is being revealed.

Val Canale today: the insiders' landscape

Today, the various layers of conflict landscape in the municipality of Malborghetto-Valbruna are abandoned. Just a few sites have been rediscovered by volunteers with support from the local public administration. Fortifications left in ruins, such as Fort Hensel in Malborghetto, the *Vallo Alpino* pillboxes, and the Cold War barracks are visible and abandoned heritage that is only partially protected. Between May and July 2019, Pinagli undertook a new mapping project along the lines of the 2013 research in order to study locals' perception of this conflict landscape.[38]

While curiosity about the remains described above is still considered a niche interest in the area, 95% of those interviewed agreed that they are important (especially those from the First World War to the Cold War). Showing the power of material culture to bring together past, present, and future, these ruins represent local identity and are touristic resources for the area. Interviewees also indicated that memorial and military monuments, such as the Austro-Hungarian war cemetery in the Saisera Valley,[39] are important landscape markers in this area. Austrian and Italian residents visit these places to commemorate past events, even though they belong to a period when their forefathers were enemies. Fort Hensel, for example, is important for all three ethnic groups living in this area. Italian and Austrian volunteers, guided by the local administration, were able to clean the site and set up touristic information in 2018.[40] This was an example of an autonomous initiative which led to increasing the public awareness and rediscovery of the area.

A different approach has been taken by the volunteers of the Association 'Landscapes', who hired Fort Beisner, the largest *Vallo Alpino del Littorio* and Cold War fortification in the valley, from the Italian state (Figure 7.4) in order to save it from abandonment and looting, and to make it legally accessible (Rizzi 2014; Blasoni and Pinagli 2015). Since 2014, the Association has promoted the existence of a hidden Second World War and Cold War heritage at Fort Beisner. Most visitors are surprised that they have lived in proximity to these fortifications yet never noticed them. Nearly all are equally surprised to learn that their own Ugovizza Plain was one of the most important defensive lines during the Cold War.[41] Since the fall of the Berlin Wall in 1989, the abandoned military areas have been freely accessible, and visitors can discover a new type of archaeology. Interestingly, the first users of this heritage were the same soldiers who served in the army at this site during the Cold War. They helped the Association by providing primary sources about their experiences during this period[42] (Figure 7.5).

At present, the most important sites belonging to Malborghetto's Municipality are protected by the residents of the area. However, what do local people think and want? Among those interviewed in 2019, the general opinion can be summarized in the answer given by interviewee 48:

> All the forms of volunteering that are leading to the enhancement of the different historical sites are very important, but it is impossible to think that all have to remain in the hands of the volunteer alone… the experts are essential to coordinate the contribution of the volunteers – who may well be motivated by good intentions, but who, not knowing the appropriate approaches to take while carrying out their recovery initiatives, may inadvertently damage surviving artefacts (potentially irreparably) …

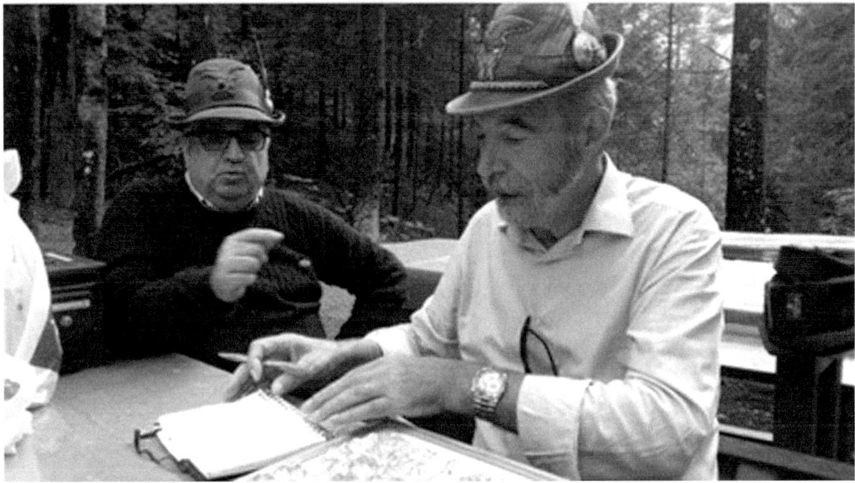

FIGURE 7.5 The last Captain in charge of Opera 4 (Fort Beisner) until 1991 during an interview in 2018. Source: © Archive, Association 'Landscapes' 2018.

communities, therefore, should not be left alone: organic interventions of protection are needed – even legislative ones.[43]

Conclusions

Conflict landscapes, like any landscapes, are ongoing processes, not stable entities or empty backdrops to human activities. Such processes implicate the lives of those who live within and constitute the landscape, with different groups engaging with their material surroundings in different ways over time. In this chapter, the authors (as representatives of the three different ethnic communities) cooperated for the first time with an interdisciplinary approach to investigate 300 years of conflict landscape layers in Val Canale, and especially within the municipality of Malborghetto-Valbruna.

It has been shown that this area contains many archaeological sites of historically recent conflict that need to be investigated and contextualized within a broader appreciation of modern conflict landscapes. While previous studies focused on establishing the importance of single monuments and artefacts, we have considered their diachronic relationship within the overall landscape. The valley's ethnic communities are aware of the importance of some landscape markers, such as Fort Hensel, while others, such as the Second World War pillboxes, are only now being recognized as heritage. Multiphase sites such as Monte Palla on the Ugovizza Plain, are examples of the hitherto unacknowledged palimpsestic nature of such landscapes.

Individual and community perceptions of, and participation in preserving their conflict heritage are essential, and require the support of local and state administrations. Understanding Val Canale's conflict landscape has to be a collaborative undertaking between professionals and locals, not least because the latter want to be in charge of their own heritage.

These sites are the consequence of Central Europe's most momentous conflicts over the last three centuries, and as such require modern scientific interdisciplinary investigation. Moreover, this heritage urgently needs official protection, providing a legal basis for their further preservation, in synergistic cooperation with the local population and volunteers. After all, we are all responsible for what is made of the past.

Notes

1 Pinagli is a local landscape archaeologist, Pachauer an expert in Austrian military architecture, and Potočnik a Slovenian historian.
2 Battle of Kluže (1797), clash at Venzone (1809), two battles of Tarvis (1797, 1809), Battle of Malborghet (1809), and Battle of Predil (1809).
3 The armament included two massive Gruson cupolas, each housing two 12-centimetre Mark 1880 cannons.
4 Option Treaty 1939 '1942: the agreement between Mussolini and Hitler to repatriate German-speaking families in the Reich territories (Magri 2012).
5 Today, some villages remain strongly attached to Slavic culture (e.g. the town of Ugovizza), others to an Italian-Friulian or a fading German identity (e.g. Tarvisio and Malborghetto). While the inhabitants of these villages feel Italian, their sense of place and identity today, as in the past, is influenced by the Germanic and Slavic remains in the environment. This has shaped their different understandings and perceptions of the surrounding landscape.
6 A local teacher (1842–1938) who lived in Malborghetto. Her archive is preserved in the Kärntner Landesarchiv in Klagenfurt.
7 Type of fortification built around churches (Potočnik et al. 2012: 26). It is also the placename given to the hill where the remains of this tower are located.
8 In 1559, this became the seat of the district judge. It was destroyed by Venetian incursions in 1616 and subsequently reused until 1809 (Domenig 2003).
9 The siege of Gradisca Fortress between the Venetian Republic and Austria occurred in 1616, and gave its name to a two-year conflict known as the 'Gradisca War'.
10 Biblioteca Nazionale Marciana Venezia Manoscritti Italia 491 (10060) dis.3- (Bianco 1995: 120).
11 Monte Palla, known in German as *Kugel Berg*. A recent pedestrian survey found no traces of this fortification, possibly because it was only planned on this document or perhaps destroyed by later fortification phases. (Pinagli and Pachauer 2018).
12 The fort was drawn on a map produced by Padre Coronelli in 1707, see Rui (2014: 130).
13 Kriegsarchiv Vienna AT-OeStA/KA – KSH IV A736-2 3 1797. On 25 March 1797, the French Army attacked the Austrian Army between Camporosso and Monte Palla on the Ugovizza (Jäger 1873).
14 The 22nd Light Infantry French Regiment entered Valbruna through the Saisera Valley in the night between the 14 and 15 May 1809 (Foramitti 1999: 58).
15 Kärntner Landesarchiv Klagenfurt FK Nr_23 Uggowitz Blatt 51 – Detail 1813.
16 Archivio di stato di Gorizia: French Cadaster Plans sec. XIX-XX Mappa Ugovizza JPG 3537 1811-1814. On this plan the hill has the place name '*al forte*'.

17 AT-OeStA/KA Kriegsarchiv Vienna KVIIB 80 1806-1811.
18 The fortresses of Verona, Peschiera, Mantua, and Legnano supported by bridgeheads at Borgoforte and later Rovigo as well.
19 Fort Malborgeth consisted of two blockhouses, five casemated batteries, several flanking elements and covered communications, and two courtyards serving also as gun emplacements.
20 AT-OeStA/KA GPA Inland CII Malborgeth Nr. 3, Situations Plan LittB. der im Bau begriffenen Thalsperre auf dem isolirten Berg-Kegel in der Ugowitzer Aue.
21 Austrian fortification with central, x-shaped blockhouses forming the reduit of the fort have been built around Mantua, Venice, Laveno, Cattaro, and Pula.
22 TAMK (1888: 5–8)
23 AT-OeStA/KA Kriegsarchiv Vienna – MBeh GGI Nr. 54 res. ex 1898: Reconstruction im Fort Hensel. Arbeitsrapport für den 14. Juni 1898.
24 e.g. AT-OeStA/KA Kriegsarchiv Vienna – KS GPA Inland CII Malborgeth Nr. 57 – Projektplan für das Blockhaus auf der Vercella Mure, Malborgeth 1881 – and Monte Palla as well AT-OeStA/KA Kriegsarchiv Vienna – ZSt KM Abt8 10-6/13 ex 1887, Attachment 'F'.
25 During the First World War, most of the Austrian soldiers were enrolled in the 4th Regiment of the *Landwehr* of Klagenfurt. However, at the beginning of the conflict, the Val Canale area remained almost without defences. Selected volunteers were recruited. These were known as *Kärntner Freiwilligen Schützen* (Tonazzi 2001: 17–16). See also, Brandauer (in prep).
26 Julius Kugy (1858–1944) acted as mountain guide for the Austrian troops in Val Canale during the First World War.
27 The *Vallo Alpino del Littorio* is a fortification system planned in 1931 by Mussolini. The eastern section, also called *linea non mi fido* ('I do not trust you'), was built after 1938 to defend the Italian border from a possible German invasion. In the Municipality of Malborghetto, there are nine of these barriers with more than 40 finished and unfinished hidden fortifications and barracks (Bernasconi and Muran 2009; Pederzolli 2007).
28 Circulars Number 200, 800, 7.000, and 15.000. Ministero della Guerra – Comando del Corpo di Stato Maggiore.
29 The statement made during one of the excursions organized by S. Silvestri between 2006 and 2014.
30 One of such German forts in vicinity of Osoppo was shown to A. Pinagli by Ing. Sergio Silvestri.
31 The Association 'Landscapes' obtained a copy from the German survey signed by Captain Nobling: Festungspioner Erkundung Staab- 'Erkundung und Auswertung der Ital. Alpenbefestigung- Abschnitt. Plezzo-Tarvis-Tolmezzo', v. 8.11.1944 sheet 479-667 ('Reconnaissance and Evaluation reports concerning the Italian Alpine fortification system in the Plezzo-Tarvis-Tolmezzo area. Nov 8, 1944'). National Archives of the United States.
32 A collective defence treaty (1955–1991) among the Soviet Union and seven Soviet satellite states of Central and Eastern Europe.
33 The North Atlantic Treaty Organization or North Atlantic Alliance.
34 Called *REIMPIEGATE NATO*, meaning 'reused by NATO'.
35 Newly built forts were simpler and usually consisted of a group of unconnected bunkers for a single machinegun (*Postazione M*), a single artillery piece (*Postazione P*), and a command post (*Postazione C*). Artillery pieces were usually turrets of M4 Sherman or M26 Pershing tanks (Bernasconi and Muran 1999: 47). The units manning the forts in Val Canale were '*Alpini d'Arresto*' (ibid.: 49).
36 By Association 'Landscapes'. www.landscapesvalcanale.eu/benvenuti/. Accessed Sep 2019.
37 One of us (AJP), obtained this data about construction from interviews conducted in the area of Idria (Iudrio) for the book Potočnik (2004). Locals still remembered how trusted Italian workers were brought from the interior, how they lived on site and

were then escorted away, all under armed escort in order to prevent any contact with the Slovenian and Croatian populations. They also remember sites being blocked off by large screens so no one could see what was being constructed.

38 Interviews made in 2019 consisted of multiple choice questionnaire sheets distributed to 50 people from the area of Malborghetto. Because of the confidential nature of the answers, interviewees are referenced with the interview registration numbers.

39 In the questionnaire, interviewees had to list those monuments in the landscape that are important to them: Fort Hensel and Fort Beisner scored the highest. Memorial monuments were also important, such as the 'Dying Lion of Malborghetto' which commemorates the Battle of Malborghetto in 1809.

40 Interviewee No. 35 stated that other locals acted independently in order to restore First World War trenches in the Saisera Valley without following a regular process of control conducted by the landscape-archaeological superintendent. (Interviewee No. 35, 23/06/2019, Archive Association. 'Landscapes' 2019.)

41 These are the results of interviews made with visitors to Opera 4 (Fort Beisner) between 2015–2017 (Archive Association 'Landscapes' 2019).

42 During the opening days, former soldiers belonging to the *Alpini d'Arresto* usually visit the site. They have begun to speak about their experiences in the fortification. The interviews are collected and published on social media: www.facebook.com/FORTEBEISNER/ (accessed September 2019).

43 Interviewee No. 48, 28/6/2019. (Archive Association 'Landscapes' 2019).

References

Bernasconi, A. and G. Muran. (1999) *Le Fortificazioni del Vallo Alpino Littorio in Alto Adige,Temi Trento.* Trento: Temi.

Bernasconi, A. and G. Muran (2009) *Il testimone di cemento – Le fortificazioni del 'Vallo Alpino Littorio' in Cadore, Carnia e Tarvisiano.* Udine: La Nuova Base Editrice.

Bianco, F. (1995) *Il Feudo Benedettino di Moggio (secoli XV–XVIII).* Udine: Arti Grafiche.

Biffart, M. (1863) *Venetien mit dem Festungsvierecke, eine militär-geographische Skizze.* Darmstadt-Leipzig: Eduard Zernin.

Blasoni, P. and A. Pinagli. (2015) Un Bunker del Vallo Alpino-Memorie nascoste, il Forte Beisner a Valbruna. *Wild-The Traveller's Magazine Estate.* Inverno: 22–26. Alpi Friulane Eds.

Brandauer, I. (in preparation) Forgotten War? Coping with the Trauma of the First World War and Strategies for its Centenary Commemoration in the Federal State of Tyrol. In P. Cornish and N.J. Saunders (eds.), *Curating the Great War.* London: Routledge.

Cappellano, F. and M. Chiaruttini (2015) Le fortificazioni del Tarvisiano. *Storia Militare* 257: 52–66.

Casey, E.S. (1998) *The Fate of Place, a Philosophical History.* Los Angeles: University California Press.

Corino, P.G. (1995) *L'opera in caverna del Vallo Alpino.* Borgone Susa: Piero Melli Editore.

Corino, P.G .and P. Gastaldo. (1993) *La montagna fortificata.* Borgone Susa: Piero Melli Editore.

Domenig, R. (2003) *Malborghetto-Valbruna, Comune in Valcanale.* Udine: Edizioni del Confine.

——— (2012) *Sotto il Pastorale Tedesco (1007–1759).* Udine: Museo Palazzo Veneziano Malborghetto, Arti grafiche Fulvio.

——— (2014) Tre Potentati a Confronto: Bamberga, Aquileia, Cilli. In M. Strassoldo (ed.), *Castelli e Fortificazioni del Canal del Ferro e della Valcanale*, pp 67–67. Udine: Forum.

——— (2016) *Tedeschi al confine orientale 1943–1945 Volume 2° Storia & Memorie*. Udine: Aviani & Aviani editori.

Ebner, K. (2010) *Fort Hensel – Il forte di Malborghetto durante la Prima Guerra Mondiale*. Valbruna: Edizioni Saisera.

Faleschini, M. (2010) Viabilità e insediamenti d'epoca romana nel territorio della Valle del Fella Mirta Faleschini. *Ce fastu?: Rivista della Società filologica friulana 'Graziadio I. Ascoli' 2: Normale 86* 2: 177–192.

Foramitti, P. (1999) *L'Assalto Malborghetto 1809 tra gli Asburgo e Napoleone*. Udine: Edizione del Confine.

Foramitti, V. (2014) Paesaggi di guerra e geografia militare in Friuli Venezia Giulia. In A. Quendolo (ed.), *Paesaggi di Guerra Memoria e Progetto*, pp 111–128. Udine: Istituto italiano dei Castelli, Gaspari Editore.

Hackelsberger, Ch. (1980) *Das k.k. österreichische Festungsviereck. Ein Beitrag zur Wiederentdeckung der Zweckarchitektur des 19. Jahrhunderts*. München: Deutscher Kunstverlag.

Ingold, T. (1993) The Temporality of Landscape. *World Archaeology* 25 (2): 152–172.

Jäger, G. (1873) *Turistenfuhrer im Kanaltal*. Wien: Verlag des 'Tourift' Salzgies 14.

Konold, W. and J. Regnath. (2014) *Militärische Schichten der Kulturlandschaft. Landespflege – Denkmalschutz – Erinnerungskultur*. Ostfildern: Jan Thorbecke Verlag.

Kozorog, M. (2019) On the Border: Perspectives on Memory Landscapes between Slovenia and Italy. In U. Košir, M. Črešnar and D. Mlekuž (eds.), *Rediscovering the Great War: Archaeology and Enduring Legacies on the Soca and Eastern Fronts*, pp 63–76. London: Routledge.

Kugy, J. (2008) *La mia Guerra nelle Giulie*. Valbruna: Edizioni Saisera.

Leitner, W. (1947) *Erzherzog Johann – Generaldirektor des Genie- und Fortifikationswesens 1801–1849* (Dissertationsschrift/PhD dissertation). Graz: Karl-Franzens-Universität Graz, Institut für Geschichte.

Magri, L. (2012) *Le Opzioni in Valcanale nel 1939*. Canal del Ferro e Valcanale: Quaderno n.2 Museo etnografico palazzo Veneziano – Malborghetto – Comunità Montana del Gemonese. Udine: Arti Grafiche Fulvio.

Malatesta, L. (2014) Forte Hensel nella 1° guerra mondiale. *Cè Fastu, Rivista della Società filologica friulana 'Graziadio I. Ascoli'* 1 (2): 93–118.

Manoli, P. and P.L. Piovesana. (1971) *Tarvisiano e Val Canale ieri e oggi*. Venizia: Ente nazionale per le Tre Venezie.

N.N. (1879) Die Eröffnung der Ponteba-Bahn. In M. Benedikt (ed.), *Neue Freie Presse, Morgenblatt*, p. 6. Wien: Verlag der Neuen Freien Presse.

Oman, A. (2016) *La toponomastica del Comune di Malborghetto-Valbruna*. Udine: Museo Etnografico Palazzo Veneziano, Arti Grafiche Fulvio.

Padiero, P. and L. Poldini. (1991) Flora e Vegetazione. In G. Bergamini and A. Merlo (eds.), *Guida del Friuli, VII. Val Canale*, pp 117–144. Udine: Società Alpina Friulana.

Pederzolli, E. (2007) *Rupi Murate Itinerari alla scoperta delle fortificazioni del Vallo alpino nelle Alpi Giulie dal 1938 a difesa del confine italo-tedesco e poi fino al 1992 come antemurale Nato verso il Patto di Varsavia*. Trento: Panorama srl.

Pinagli, A. (2012–2013) *The Valley Known as Val Canale: A Landscape of Convergence of Ethnic Groups and the Perception of Their Archaeological Heritage*. MA Thesis, Department of Archaeology, National University of Ireland, Galway.

Pinagli, A. and V. Pachauer. (2018) 1849: Questo forte… 'non sa da fare'. *Bollettino Società Friulana di Archeologia Onlus* XXII (Aprile): 13–14.

Plazer v. M. (2012 [1899]). Fort Hensel. In R. Domenig (ed.), *Il Forte di Malborghetto 1809–2009*, pp 20–63. Udine: Museo Etnografico Palazzo Veneziano-Malborghetto. Quaderno n.3. Arti Grafiche Fulvio.

Potočnik, A.J. (2009) *Rupnikova Linja in Alpski zid, odkrivanje utrdb ob Rapalski meji*. Logatec: Ad Pirum.

Potočnik, A.J., V. Tonić and M. Perpar. (2012) *Fortifying Europe's Soft Underbelly. The Rupnik Line, the Vallo Alpino and other Fortifications of the Ljubljana Gap*. Bennington, VM: Merriam Press.

Rizzi, R. (2014) La Fortezza Fantasma. Un passato segreto che rischia d'andar dimenticato. In M. Baccichet (ed.), *Fortezza FVG – Dalla guerra fredda alle aree militari dismesse*, pp 255–258. Monfalcone: Edicom Edizioni.

Rosner, W. (2009) Keine Ergebung ... Malborghet und Predil 1809. In C. Fräss-Ehrfeld (ed.), *Napoleon und seine Zeit. Kärnten – Innerösterreich – Illyrien*, pp 153–198. Klagenfurt: Verlag des Geschichtsvereins für Kärnten.

Rui, R.(2014) Il Fortino Veneziano di Pontabba. In M. Strassoldo (ed.), *Castelli e Fortificazioni del Canal del Ferro e della Valcanale*, pp 129–134. Udine: Forum.

Saunders, N.J. (2001) Matter and Memory in the Landscapes of Conflict: The Western Front 1914–1999. In B. Bender and M. Winer (eds.), *Contested Landscapes: Movement, Exile and Place*, pp 37–53. Oxford: Berg.

——— (ed.) (2004) *Matters of Conflict: Material Culture, Memory and the First World War*. London: Routledge.

——— (ed.) (2012) *Beyond the Dead Horizon: Studies in Modern Conflict Archaeology*. Oxford: Oxbow.

Schaumann, W., (1978). *Le nostre montagne: teatro di guerra IIIb: Alpi carniche orientali, Val Canale - Alpi Giulie occidentali*. Cortina d'Ampezzo: Ghedina and Tassitti.

Schofield, J., W.G. Johnson and C. Beck (eds.) (2002) *Matériel Culture: The Archaeology of 20th Century Conflict*. London: Routledge.

Silvestri, S. (2005) *Le fortificazioni del Vallo Alpino nel Parco delle Colline Carniche*. Villa Santina: Parco delle Colline Carniche.

TAMK (Technisches und administratives Militär-Komité). (1888) *Statistischer Bau-Bericht Nr. 4 über den Bau des Forts Hensel (:Thalsperre bei Malborgeth:) in den Jahren 1881–1883*. Wien: Kaiserlich königliches technisches & administratives Militär-Comité.

Tilley, C. (1994) *A Phenomenology of Landscape, Places, Paths and Monuments*. Oxford: Berg.

Tonazzi, D. (2001) *La Prima Guerra sul Fronte Carinziano- Settore Saisera Vol 1*. Rodeano Alto: Lito Immagine.

Vavti, S. (2005) 'Wir sind Kanaltaler!'- Regionale und lokale Identitäten im viersprachigen Valcanale in Italien. *Forum Qualitative Sozialforschung* 7 (1). Article 34.

Weiss, U. (2004) *Malborgeth 1881–1916 Fort Hensel*. Salzburg: Pallasch Sonderdruck 2, Österreichischer Milizverlag.

——— (2013) *K.(u) k. Befestigungsanlagen- vom Kanaltal über das Seebachtal Predil bis ins obere Socca (Isonzo) Tal*. Graz: Vehling Verlag Gmbh.

Wylie, J. (2007) *Landscape*. London: Routledge.

Zilli, S. (2019) Constructing the Italian Border: The First World War in the East of the Country. In U. Košir, M. Črešnar and D. Mlekuž (eds.), *Rediscovering the Great War: Archaeology and Enduring Legacies on the Soca and Eastern Fronts*, pp 77–89. London: Routledge.

Archival References:

Archive Association 'Landscapes' 2016 – Archivio Guido Tarantelli – Letters and unpublished pictures belonging to the Tarantelli Family, Rome.

Archive Association 'Landscapes' 2018 – Captain Nobling: Festungspioner Erkundung Staab, Erkundung und Auswertung der Ital. Alpenbefestigung-Abschnitt. Plezzo-Tarvis-Tolmezzo, v. 8.11.1944 sheet 479-667, document 544 note 2 (Reconnaissance and Evaluation reports concerning the Italian Alpine fortification system in the Plezzo-Tarvis-Tolmezzo area. 8 November, 1944). National Archives of the United States.

Archivio di stato di Gorizia, Italy.

Biblioteca Nazionale Marciana Venezia.

Kärntner Landesarchiv Klagenfurt.

Kriegsarchiv – Österreichisches Staatsarchiv, Vienna.

8

CONFLICT, MOBILITY, AND LANDSCAPES

The Arab Revolt in southern Jordan, 1916–1918

John B. Winterburn

The landscapes of southern Jordan[1] have a long history of conflict and militarization associated with transport and mobility. They are ancient desert regions through which traders and pilgrims have journeyed for millennia. They were militarized from at least the fifteenth century by the Ottomans and reached full-blown modern conflict landscape status in the early twentieth century during the 1916–1918 Arab Revolt. This remote corner of the Ottoman Empire was transformed initially by the construction of a telegraph line (Rogan 1998: 116) and then by the Hejaz Railway that conveyed Muslim pilgrims to Medina (and thence by camel caravan on to Mecca) (Nicholson 2005: 11).

The outbreak of the First World War in 1914 and, two years later, a Hashemite Arab uprising supported by the British and French against the Ottoman Empire, quickly escalated into significant conflict in the region. The Ottomans were determined to keep the railway operating as an essential link to their garrisons in Ma'an and Medina. They were defending a railway that followed the same route as the centuries-old Hajj pilgrimage road (Nicholson 2005: 14–15). Their tactics were similar to those employed in the past; a series of strong military points at regular intervals and military patrols between them.

A Bedouin Arab force accompanied by T.E. Lawrence[2] took the Red Sea port of Aqaba on 6 July 1917, surprising both the British and Ottoman high commands (Mousa 1966: 66–72). This changed the strategic game and galvanized the Ottomans into defending the landscape flanking the railway in an attempt to protect their lines of communications to the south. This intensified militarization of the landscape made the railway a target for British raids. This early twentieth-century conflict landscape was characterized by the deployment of Ottoman forces that were predominantly static, defending a terrain against highly mobile British and Arab forces during the Great Arab Revolt[3] of 1916–1918.

The British initially attacked the railway to disrupt its operation and ensure that Ottomans troops were tied down making repairs. However, they were resolute in their ambition to cut the railway in April 1918 and prevent Ottoman troops from threatening the British advance through Palestine and towards Damascus (Figure 8.1).

Archaeological investigations

Between 2006 and 2014, a 113-kilometre-long section of this landscape from Ma'an to the modern border with Saudi Arabia, just south of Mudawwara, was investigated archaeologically by the Great Arab Revolt Project (GARP n.d.; Saunders 2020) and with a focus by the author on landscape (Winterburn 2016,

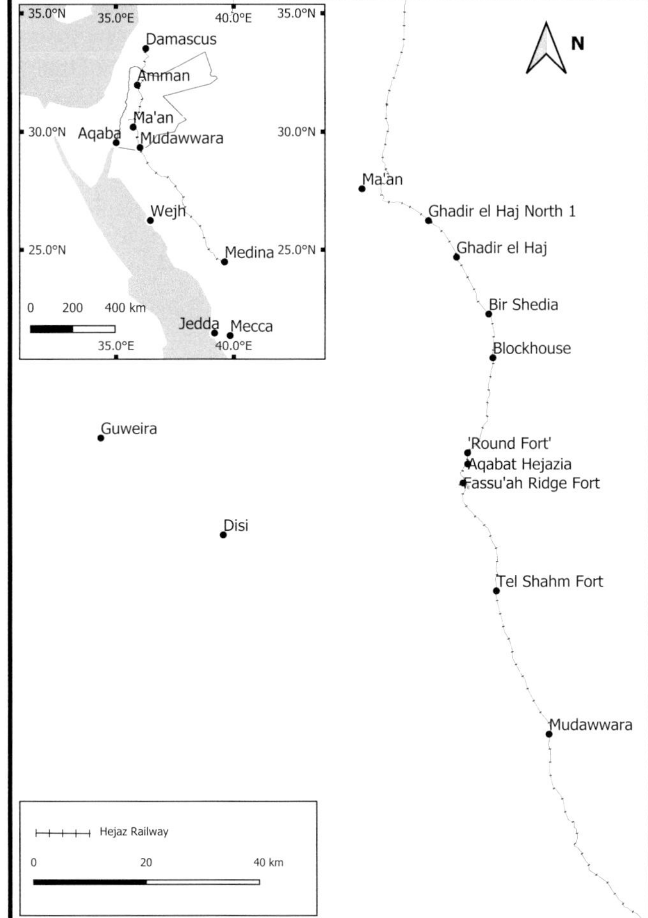

FIGURE 8.1 A map of Jordan showing the key locations mentioned in the text and the route of the Hejaz Railway. Source: © author.

in prep.). The over-arching methodology employed in this research was based on the principles of the sub-discipline of modern conflict archaeology – an interdisciplinary endeavour informed by anthropological theory and embracing a diversity of intellectual engagements including landscape, material culture, identity, and heritage (Saunders 2011: 45). The reasoning behind this was that the complexities of the archaeology of twentieth- and twenty-first-century conflicts were such that they required a robust multi-disciplinary response (Saunders 2012: x; Saunders and Faulkner 2010: 514).

The approach deployed here utilizes aspects of landscape, historical, documentary, and industrial archaeologies coupled with evidence from geology, physical geography, history, and remote sensing. Archival material[4] primarily from The National Archive, London, and the Imperial War Museum was combined with extensive fieldwork informed by the interpretation of satellite imagery and modern aerial photography (APAAME 1997–2020).

The last decade of the twentieth century witnessed a change in the anthropological investigation and analysis of landscapes, initiated in part by the publication of *Landscapes: Politics and Perspectives* (Bender 1993) and *The Anthropology of Landscapes* (Hirsch and O' Hanlon 1995). Hirsch equates landscape to the human body within anthropological discourses in that it has 'remained largely unproblematised' (Hirsch 1995: 1). He regards landscape as possessing a 'submerged presence and significance in anthropological accounts' in two interconnected ways. First, it is deployed as a 'framing convention', informing how studies are brought into view from an objective standpoint. Second, it is used to refer to the meaning given by local people to their 'physical and cultural surroundings' (ibid.)

Alternative views of landscape emerged where experiences of landscape are linked to political, social, and economic interactions and retain the 'notion of a hegemonic discourse' (Bender 1993: 246–248). These were a response to positivism and the overly empiricist approaches that dominated their study hitherto. Bender explores two propositions; first, that landscape is time materializing, and second, that landscapes can never be 'out-there'; they are always subjective, being based on or influenced by personal feeling, tastes, and opinions (2002: 103).

However, a theoretically nuanced view of conflict landscapes must also consider these places as seen and understood by both protagonists. Each will have their own view of the landscape – an Ottoman soldier guarding a hilltop redoubt overlooking the Hejaz Railway will have a very different perception of the landscape from the Bedouin raider or a British pilot flying above the same desert location.

Militarization and the landscape

The early trade and pilgrimage routes within GARP's study area were probably largely undefended during Nabataean, Roman, and Byzantine times.[5] However, by the fourteenth century, the Hajj pilgrimage itinerary of the famous Muslim traveller Ibn Battuta records several forts in southern Jordan, including those at Ma'an and Fassu'ah (Petersen 2012: 10–12). Although not explicitly built to protect the Hajj route, these pre-Ottoman forts fulfilled this role in addition to their primary function as regional military centres (Petersen 1989: 97–99), indicating that to a degree the landscape was militarized before Ottoman occupation.

The Sultan, as Caliph to all Muslims, had a duty to protect travellers on the Hajj pilgrimage route against Bedouin banditry and, by the eighteenth century, a series of 26 'Hajj Forts' along the *Darb al Haj*[6] had been built (Petersen 2012: 20–24). These were the nodal points of military power and were locations from which military forces could patrol the landscape, and they became route markers for pilgrims on their way to Mecca. They also served an essential function for imperial communications in an era when information travelled at the speed of a horse.

In southern Jordan, forts were built or reconstructed by the Ottomans in the eighteenth century at Ma'an, Fassu'ah, and Mudawwara to protect Hajj pilgrims against increasingly active Bedouin raiders; these forts became symbols of the empire, projecting its power, control, and influence across the region.

Damascus to Medina by telegraph and Hejaz Railway

In July 1898, Sultan Abdülhamid II issued orders for the construction of a 'telegraph line between Damascus and the cities of Medina and Mecca along the pilgrimage route' (Wasti 1998: 64), and it was fully functional by 1 May 1900. There had been conflict between the Ottoman Empire and the Bedouin tribes for centuries before the construction of the telegraph re-militarized the landscape. Its construction brought additional military personnel into the Bedouin tribal areas in order to protect the construction teams. The effect of building the telegraph was to increase access to the Hejaz region and to serve as an enabling technology for the building of the Hejaz Railway that began the same year. The military value of railways had been apparent to the Ottomans since their success in rapidly deploying troops along the Constantinople–Salonika railroad during the 30-day Greco-Turkish War of 1897. They had doubtless also noticed how the British had used a railway to control and supply its territory in Sudan in the late nineteenth century (Welsby 2011).

The Hejaz Railway was a 1,300-kilometre-long, single-track, narrow-gauge railway linking Damascus and Medina, though its original destination had been Mecca. Abdülhamid II issued an imperial order on 2 May 1900 for the construction of a Holy Railway, and this monumental feat of engineering and triumph of Islamic financing was completed by 1908.[7] The overt intention was to provide cheaper, faster, and safer transport for Hajj pilgrims to Mecca, reducing a typical 40-day camel journey to just four days (Shqiarat et al. 2011: 100).

As the Railway of Faith, the Hejaz Railway also aimed to enhance the status as Caliph of the world's Muslims of Sultan Abdülhamid II, who realized that as a tangible expression of pan-Islamism, the railway would bring him considerable political kudos (Nicholson 2005: 11). The British, however, were sceptical about the real purpose of the railway, as the route precluded tourist traffic, avoided the Mediterranean and the Red Sea ports, and followed the 'most sterile stretches of the country many miles to the east of the River Jordan' (Anon 1914: 75).

The evidence of defended railway stations in the south and elaborate siding facilities was cited by the British as proof that this was a military railway, a 'German highroad to Egypt' (Anon 1914: 75, 77), and ultimately a threat to the Suez Canal and British Imperial India. These predictions came close to reality when the Ottomans used the railway to mount attacks on the Suez Canal in late 1914 and early 1915 (Rogan 2015: 115–116, 312).

Anthropological studies have added to our understanding of the relationship between senses, the body, and landscape (e.g. Classen 2005; Howes 2005: 27–39). The telegraph and the railway were the first industrializations of the modern era in the landscapes in southern Jordan and Arabia. They were an example of how new technologies were used to project the power, control, and influence of the Sultan to the remotest parts of his empire, but at the same time created animosity and dissent among the traditional communities. The railway not only industrialized the landscape and the way of travel but importantly the mind as well. Elsewhere in the Ottoman Empire, industrial development was established and accepted. However, in the culturally and religiously conservative south, telegraphy and steam locomotion challenged centuries-old notions of the speed of communication and the deployment of military force. It was the industrialization of the sensorium, the sight and sound of steam locomotives' laboured 'breath', and the smell of smoke from Welsh coal.

Before the twentieth century, the dominant sense used to warn of possible danger in a conflict was sight – armies and troops would often have been visible before they could be heard. The arrival of modern weapons during the Arab Revolt recalibrated the capabilities for industrialized killing brought from the Western Front to Arabia. The sense of hearing became as important as sight, and the roar of Rolls Royce armoured cars, the rattle of machine guns, the artillery bombardment of high explosive, mines, and the drone of aeroplane propellers reinforced this lethal modernity. It was an industrialization that changed perceptions of time, space, and the conflict landscape. This assault on the senses heightened the awareness of the 'environment, sensing danger and staying alive' (Saunders 2011: 42).

The Hejaz Railway was a grand physical statement by the Ottoman Empire to its subjects and the governments of Western Europe. It signalled that the Sultan was in control of the remote regions of his realm, including Islam's most holy places, Medina and Mecca. The railway embodied and expressed Abdülhamid's imperial power and control. It also demonstrated, contrary to the views of the West, that the Ottoman Empire was capable of financing and building a railway without their financial or technical help, even though the aspiration to source all materials from within the empire ultimately proved impossible (Özyüksel 2014: 109–110).

The Great Arab Revolt

The Great Arab Revolt (GAR) was a remarkable uprising that contributed to the defeat of the Ottoman Empire and had a lasting impact on the Middle East. More specifically, for this discussion, it acted as a catalyst for the formation of a First World War conflict landscape along the route of the Hejaz Railway, with the Ottomans and their German allies pitted against the Arabs and their British and French allies.

The Revolt began on 5 June 1916, when tribal forces loyal to Sheriff Hussein, the Emir of Mecca, attacked the Ottoman garrisons in Mecca and Medina. It quickly spread to the Red Sea ports of Jedda and Wejh. From these bases, British, French, and Arab forces attacked Ottoman positions along the Hejaz Railway. In July 1917, a Bedouin Arab raiding party accompanied by Lawrence captured the Red Sea port of Aqaba, a fact which played a crucial role in creating the conflict landscapes dealt with here.

The capture of Aqaba enabled the British to establish a base at the head of the Gulf of Aqaba. Lawrence and his Bedouin irregulars moved northwards attacking Ottoman positions, and by late July they had captured the Ottoman defences at Waheida, causing alarm at the railway hub of Ma'an, 20 kilometres to the east (Lawrence 2003: 329). On 18 August 1917, Jafar al-Askari[8] and 800 Arab regulars arrived at Aqaba followed by 300 more two days later. A French contingent supplemented these and Emir Feisal, with 50 men, arrived on 23 August, making Aqaba the headquarters of his Northern Arab Army (al-Askari 2003: 120).

Throughout May and June 1918, Feisal kept up a 'relentless campaign' against the railway north of Ma'an (Allawi 2014: 122) and on 8 August 1918, a British operation that combined The Imperial Camel Corps (ICC) and the Royal Air Force mounted a successful attack on the important fortified southern station at Mudawwara. The final phase of the Arab Revolt coincided with General Allenby's Megiddo offensive in September 1918 (Murphy 2008: 75) and on 1 October 1918, Feisal's army entered Damascus, and the Turks[9] were pursued north to Aleppo. The Ottoman Empire signed an armistice on 31 October, and the Arab Revolt was over; its traces, however, survive in the wadis and hills of the southern Jordanian desert.

Defending the landscape

The Ottomans needed to protect the Hejaz Railway as the lifeline that supplied their large garrison in Medina; while the railway operated, it was also a potential military asset if they wished to re-capture Aqaba. From a British perspective, a functioning railway could transport thousands of Ottoman troops from the Hejaz north to Damascus and was a continued threat to Allenby's advance through Palestine. The scene was set for conflict between two very different imperial forces, each with their own strategies and objectives.

Before the Arab taking of Aqaba, the railway between Ma'an and Mudawwara was lightly defended. The only evidence of defence before 1917 are loop-holes in the masonry of the water towers at Ma'an and Mudawwara[10] Stations. The other railway station buildings, in Jordan and south of Ma'an, appear to have had no defensive features when built, but other defensive structures existed in the landscape south of Ma'an. One of the longest stretches of railway between stations can be found between Bir Shedia and Aqabat Hejazia Stations (Winterburn 2016: 145), and there are defensive structures here that are contemporary with the railway's construction and likely guarded against Bedouin attacks along this exposed section of track.

There is no available documentary evidence before 1917 for the fortification of the landscape within the study area. The British agent, F.R. Maunsell's[11] reports (IOR n.d.) do not include any mention of fortifications at Ma'an, or the section of the railway as far as Mudawwara, and only comments on those south of Tabuk, 215 kilometres further south. Had there been trench systems and fortifications surrounding Ma'an Station at this date then, as an experienced military officer and spy, it is inconceivable that he would not have seen and commented on them. D.G. Hogarth, a British Naval Officer and Director of Cairo's Arab Bureau produced a report on the Hejaz before the First World War (Hogarth 1917). Neither Maunsell nor Hogarth mention redoubts, hilltop forts, or other fortifications in the landscape to the south of Ma'an. It is possible that the forts were there and they failed to see them or that they did observe them but discounted them; they also failed to report the hundreds of 'tent-rings' that are such a characteristic feature of the railway's 1905 construction camps in this area.[12] As late as August 1917, the RFC mounted a bombing raid on Ma'an, but there were no reports of any fortifications being observed.

While there is scant evidence for any substantive defensive works along the railway between May 1900 and August 1917 (i.e. only enough to deter a Bedouin threat), there is far more evidence from summer 1917. The Turkish loss of Aqaba in July led in August to the arrival of the German military advisor General Erich von Falkenhayn in Ma'an to supervise a defence plan and fortify the garrison station by surrounding it with trenches (Lawrence 2003: 373; Rogan 1999: 233).

Falkenhayn made Ma'an a special command, and its commander was given 'six thousand infantry, a regiment of cavalry and one of mounted infantry' (Lawrence 2003: 373–374; Mousa 1966: 95). There were large supply dumps of military equipment, and air cover was supplied by a flight of aeroplanes (Rogan 1999: 233), whose impromptu airfield lay just east of the station. Lawrence noted that

> The Turks have made good use of their six weeks' peace. Falkenhayn has been down to advise them, and it has put new intelligence into their doings and made them much worthier of our new work … and that Ma'an had been entrenched until it was impregnable according to the standard of manoeuvre.
>
> *(Lawrence 2003: 373)*

The defences constructed on Falkenhayn's orders were the material culture of German Western Front–style trench warfare transplanted into a desert landscape, transforming in a matter of weeks low-level anti-Bedouin defences into an industrialized twentieth-century conflict landscape.

To the south of Ma'an additional fortifications were now constructed in the landscape. All the railway stations south to Mudawwara were equipped with defensive trench systems. Impromptu loop-holes were knocked through the station building walls, and mud-bricks were used to build curtain-walls to protect doorways and parapets on the roofs. Elaborate stone-built forts, hilltop forts, and earthwork redoubts were constructed on the plains north of Aqabat Hejazia Station between September 1917 and April 1918 (Winterburn 2016: 260–261, in prep.).

The conflict landscapes around Ma'an Station are the most comprehensive and best-preserved First World War landscapes in Jordan. The extensive trench systems represent an attempt by Falkenhayn to transform an unprotected garrison and centre of railway engineering into a fortress. His plan was successful and 'fortress Ma'an' survived an attack by the Northern Arab Army in April 1918. Despite being the most heavily bombed target in southern Jordan (Winterburn 2016: 211), Ma'an under its Turkish commander held out until the following September. Other defences along the railway proved to be less effective and yielded quickly to British and Arab attacks.

Hilltop forts

It is necessary to describe and analyze the components of conflict landscapes to understand their nature and development, the first of which is the category of hilltop forts. There are nine hilltop fortifications built at strategic locations along the route of the railway in GARP's study area and can be sub-categorized as 'small' and 'large' (Winterburn 2016: 116, in prep.). Small forts are built on isolated hilltops or rocky outcrops (e.g. Tel Shahm Fort, Figure 8.2) and, with a perimeter wall length of less than 175 metres, is too small in area to include campsites and other military structures. Large forts have perimeter walls up to 400 metres long and enclose other military structures such as gun emplacements, blockhouses, and tents (e.g. Fassu'ah Ridge Fort, Figure 8.3). These forts were close to the railway (within 1.2 kilometres), and the majority are located to the west of the line.

'The Ornamental Forts'

The second category of landscape components comprises three dry-stone-built forts guarding the flat plain and the railway between the Bir el Shedia and Aqabat Hejazia Stations, the longest section of track between stations. The forts are characterized by elaborate footpaths and walkways around their perimeters, their surfaces made from fine (less than 20 millimetres) black chert gravel that has

FIGURE 8.2 Tel Shahm Fort. Source: © author.

FIGURE 8.3 Fassu'ah Ridge Fort. Source: © author.

FIGURE 8.4 The Round 'Ornamental' Fort, 2009. Source: © author.

been selected from the surrounding desert, and consequently were named 'the Ornamental Forts' by GARP. Two of these found are rectangular in plan, and one, 'the Round Fort' (Figure 8.4) is circular.

The blockhouses and guardhouses

The third category is blockhouses and guardhouses. To the south of Bir Shedia is a building that has been described as 'the first great blockhouse below Shedia' (Lawrence 2003: 445), which intimates the presence of other blockhouses in the area. The building is similar in style to a station building. It has a mortared rubble, dressed-stone wall, segmental arch windows with vertically projecting keystones, and four loop-holes on the north, east, and south elevations. Additional firing positions have been cut through the masonry on the east elevation.

This blockhouse is the stone-built example described by Maunsell in 1907 (IOR n.d.), located at Kilometre 495,[13] referenced by Hülagü (2010: 86), and investigated by GARP in 2010 (Figure 8.5). Royal Flying Corps[14] reconnaissance reports from February 1918 indicate that there was a series of trenches around this building, although no traces of these were found. The orientation of the building and its firing loop-holes and windows suggests that it was designed to be seen both from the railway and to the east and was used for observing and protecting the railway to the north and south. It was probably contemporary

FIGURE 8.5 The blockhouse, showing the east and south elevations. Source: © author.

with the railway in this area (1904–1905). However, significant parts of the western wall have been rebuilt and the loop-holes may be later modifications.

A guardhouse is known only from Maunsell's report of 1907 (IOR n.d.) and described as 'two tents and water barrels'. No evidence for it has been found in the field at its given location at Kilometre 501. Another guardhouse is described and located, at Kilometre 507, to the south of a 'large valley bridge' supported by '20-foot stone arches' (Hülagü 2010: 87). This description enabled the location to be determined accurately and places it 13 kilometres south of the blockhouse. A structure comprising a circular, three-metre-diameter enclosure built from random stone blocks has eight courses of stones and is located on a slight rise, 450 metres to the west of the railway. As a defensive structure, it was too small to accommodate soldiers, who were provided with tents and water barrels (IOR n.d.).

Significantly, these Ornamental Forts together with the blockhouse and guardhouses are located on the second-longest section of railway between stations, and they may have been built at the same time as the railway in this area, 1904–1905 or shortly afterwards. The absence of documentary evidence for the Ornamental Forts indicates that these are probably contemporary with the guardhouses but were built after 1907.

Earthwork/redoubt fortifications

The fourth category of defensive features is composed of 12 small earthwork fortifications in locations overlooking the railway line between Ma'an and

Mudawwara. Excluding the extensive earthworks at Ma'an, these smaller earthworks generally comprise circular or oval trench systems surrounding a central gun position and sited to provide a defence of a strategic location such as a large multi-span railway bridge. An illustrative example is 'Ghadir al Haj North 1', an earthwork fortification mid-way between Ma'an Station and Ghadir al Haj Station. It is 22 metres in diameter with a central gun position with three concentric circles of 'wolf pits'[15] surrounding the earthwork (Figure 8.6). It guards the southerly approach to Ma'an Station, eight kilometres to the west, and overlooks a one-kilometre section of the line with eight bridges. This redoubt is probably one of Lawrence's 'enemy blockhouses' mentioned on 3 October 1917 (2003: 418). It was not recorded in reconnaissance reports from 13 March 1918 of a flight that included this area of railway line but is probably the one recorded by RAF pilot Lt. Siddons on 14 April 1918 (TNA 3 n.d.). Archive evidence suggests construction dates between mid-March and mid-April 1918 (Winterburn 2016: 261–262). However, it is possible that due to poor lighting conditions pilots on earlier reconnaissance flights failed to see it or did not commit it to memory for later inclusion in their reports: it could have been hiding in plain sight within the landscape.

Mobility and conflict

The Ottoman Turk fortification and defence of the landscape between 1917 and 1918 followed the same principles as deployed during the previous five centuries

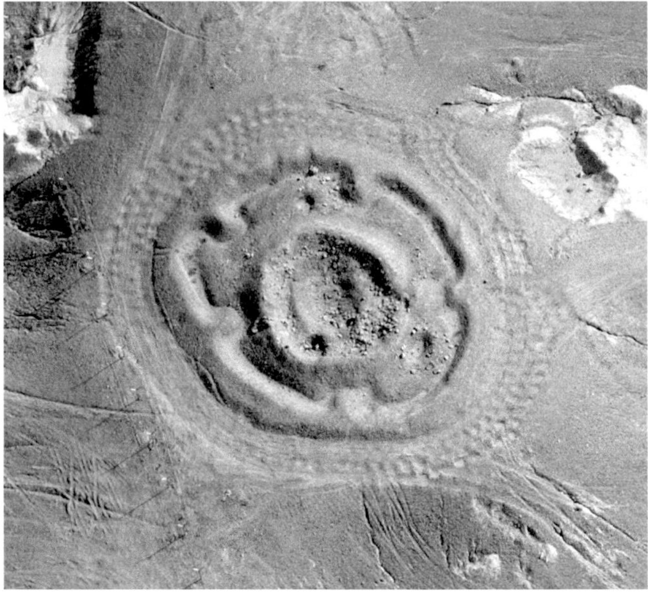

FIGURE 8.6 Aerial view of the 'Ghadir al Haj North 1' Earthwork fortification illustrating the 'wolf pits' surrounding the fortification. Source: © R.H Bewley, 2015. APAAME_20151006_RHB-0179.

– strong defensive points along a linear transport route. The Hajj forts of Ma'an, Fassu'ah, and Mudawwara, like others to the north and south, provided sparse militarization of the landscape. However, the density of militarization of the terrain significantly increased as a response to the Arab Revolt and the mobility of the British forces. The railway station buildings provided conveniently spaced nodes from which to militarize the landscape, and they offered additional locations (to the Hajj forts) from which Ottoman troops could send out their patrols.

For the Ottomans, the railway acquired functions beyond the self-evident; it was more than transport infrastructure. It was a lifeline, an umbilical cord. The entrenchment of the Ma'an garrison and the fortification of the landscape to the south confined the Ottoman forces to a linear deployment of their forces along the Hejaz Railway. Their role was defensive, protecting the railway and keeping open the supply lines to the garrison in Medina, 800 kilometres to the south. Their mobility was limited to travel north and south along the line, travel in one dimension in a three-dimensional world.

Conflict landscapes can often take unexpected forms and connect in unpredictable ways with other aspects of culture. The construction of the Hejaz Railway unintentionally created an eastern frontier marking the practical extent of the Ottoman Empire in the region. Beyond its zone of influence, for hundreds of kilometres, lay nothing but virtually uninhabitable desert (sparsely populated by Bedouin) known as *Al-Houl* (the Terror). In 1909, the British explorer and naturalist Douglas Carruthers was unable to travel east of the Hejaz Railway 'owing to the hostility of the Beduin [*sic*] and the watchfulness of the Turkish officials' (Carruthers 1910: 226). Eleven years later, in February 1918, an Anglo-Arab team led by RFC pilot Lt. Makins was returning from an expedition to salvage components from a crashed Turkish aircraft eight kilometres east of Uneiza Station and the railway line. Without escorting cavalry, which was obtained from the Bedouin leader, Auda Abu Tayi (TNA 2 n.d.), crossing the line was considered to be too dangerous due to Turkish forces based at the station.

These examples indicate that the railway was acting as a boundary or frontier before and during the Arab Revolt. However, no feature within a landscape 'is, of itself a boundary'. It can only become a boundary or the indicator of a boundary if it is recognized or experienced as such (Ingold 1993: 156). This was a frontier created, maintained, and controlled by the railway line itself and a series of fortified railway stations anchored by the two large garrison stations at Ma'an and Medina. Control of this frontier was achieved by patrols from these garrisons and fortified stations along the railway line, together with redoubts and trench systems guarding railway infrastructure.

Mobility

The different modalities of movement of British and Ottoman forces can be understood by examining their patterns of travel across the landscapes of the Arab Revolt and in a comparative perspective.

The Ottoman defence of the conflict landscape was a linear arrangement of fortified points, linked by a railway. Their forces were deployed at fixed points along a line, and the railway was used to project imperial forces beyond their normal operating areas. They had no other mechanized transport, and their movement was along a landscape corridor flanking the railway. They possessed three aircraft that were based at Ma'an (Nikolajsen and Yilmazer 2000: 105), but these were not used to counter British air superiority. German aircraft were 'rarely seen and attempted little more than tip-and-run raids' (Orange and Stapleton 1996: 17). By contrast, British forces initially had one base, Aqaba, supplied by the Royal Navy – an example of a maritime power projecting its 'influence inland beyond the littoral along which it was operating' (Boyle 2015: ix).

In August 1917 Rolls Royce armoured cars of the Hejaz Armoured Car Column arrived in Aqaba, along with Talbot wagons mounted with ten-pounder guns of the Royal Field Artillery Mountain Gun Section, under the command of Captain S.H. (Sam) Brodie (Lawrence 2003: 373). These allowed rapid movement, revolutionizing insurgent operations. Armoured cars especially were able to force their way through wadis, creating new roads as they progressed, and in areas of stony desert they were able to move unimpeded across the surface. They had the freedom to move across the area in two dimensions, and this afforded them their own defence in making use of natural features to hide from the enemy and to attack Ottoman forces from any direction at speed. The physical and existential extent of a conflict landscape was also forever altered by the speed and carrying capacity of transport that enabled long-distance, hit-and-run raids to be carried out against Ottoman forces along the railway.

The British approach was clearly a hybrid of different styles of movement, and this gave them the advantage over their enemy. Like most armies, they used the transport modality to convey their men and matériel from point to point, originally from Great Britain, then via Suez and along the canal to the Gulf of Aqaba – and Arab forces were moved from Red Sea ports to Aqaba.

The Rolls Royce armoured cars became wayfarers, no longer moving from point to point but roaming and hunting their enemy in a way similar to the Inuit hunting animals (see Ingold 2007: 75) 'laying a line of tracks through the expanse, looking for signs of another line that might lead you to your quarry' (ibid.). In this case, the Rolls Royces, as the first wheeled transport in the landscape, left their marks, cutting through the black chert surface stones exposing the cream-coloured limestone beneath. These guided the British on future missions. They were meandering in the landscape, through the two-dimensional space of the landscape surface, taking the best route through challenging terrain and remaining out of sight of the enemy (Lawrence makes references to tracks and lines made by vehicles and camels [Lawrence 2003: 212, 226, 692]).

It is useful here to consider fortifications and the deployment of forces as points, lines, surfaces, and volumes in a mathematical sense. Single fortifications in a landscape are points having individual dimensions that are insignificant when compared to the area in which they are located. Forces located at these features have no freedom to move; they are rooted in the landscape, and the structure provides their only defence.

The railway line and its flanking landscape corridor extending one kilometre on either side is a line with a width that is insignificant compared to its length. It is a mono-dimensional structure, and movement is only possible along the line. The orientation of the railway was predominantly north–south and so was readily located by the attacking British forces. Ottoman forces could only defend their fixed points, and their movements were limited to travel up and down the railway. Their mobility in the landscape was primarily dependent on the railway and reduced when the line was cut or damaged by enemy action.

The deployment of aircraft in southern Jordan was a crucial development in extending the conceptualization of conflict spaces into the third dimension. On 9 September 1917 a Special Duty Flight of the No. 14 Squadron, Royal Flying Corps (RFC), later re-named X-Flight, arrived in Aqaba (Orange and Stapleton 1996: 16–17) and established an airbase that was to remain until the end of the conflict. Initially, they operated solely from this base, but the increased mobility of the ground forces enabled them to break out from the confines of the mountains surrounding Aqaba and establish advanced landing grounds (ALGs) at locations that were closer to the enemy. By November 1917, an ALG and base were established at Guweira (TNA 1 n.d.), and a new ALG was established at Disi[16] by February 1918.

Aircraft required points in the landscape where they could take off, land, refuel, re-arm, and allow pilots time to rest and recover. Most significantly, these fixed points provided access to the three-dimensional airscapes above the desert surface and were portals from the two-dimensional to the three-dimensional conflict space or airscape.

As with the armoured cars, the RFC aircraft became wayfarers, roaming three-dimensional space above the earth's surface and perhaps leaving lines of exhaust smoke, an ephemeral, tangible artefact of their presence that endured for a few minutes. Their permanent 'lines' were the routes between landmark features, referenced to the railway line in the notes, sketchbooks, and memories of the pilots.

Conclusion

The landscapes of South Jordan have been militarized for centuries to protect their communications routes and Hajj pilgrims. The imperial response to low-level conflict and banditry was the construction of Hajj forts at points in the landscape where there was a military force that could patrol the area. The twentieth century brought industrialized technologies to the landscape, and the precedent for fixed points of military presence was continued with railway station buildings dispersed along the railway, many of them located close to the original Hajj forts. The requirement to maintain garrisons in Ma'an and Medina constrained the Ottoman response to the surprise loss of Aqaba. They no longer were able to advance through the landscape and threaten British interests, and they retreated to defend a linear corridor around the railway with historic roots spanning centuries. Their defence was grounded in principles derived from the German response to industrialized warfare on the Western Front.

The Arab Revolt pitted two empires against each other – the British and the Ottoman, though the latter was already in terminal decline and described as the 'sick man of Europe' (Finkel 2006: 459). However, it was still a potent military force that defeated the British at Gallipoli in 1915 and would do so again at Kut Al Amara in Mesopotamia in April 1916. By contrast, the British Empire was at its peak; controlling India and vast areas of Africa, it had the technology and the logistical support to conduct warfare in Arabia.

Supplied by land, sea, and air, British forces used their technology and mobility to exploit all three dimensions of the conflict landscape space to attack the Ottomans, who defended a mono-dimensional line in the sand rooted and routed in centuries of tradition and pilgrimage. The British too had their fixed points in the landscape: Aqaba, Disi, and Guweira. They built roadways that linked them, a linear arrangement with similarities to the railway. However, the British had the advantage of motorized vehicles and aircraft that broke free of the linear lines of communication that so constrained the Ottomans.

These British bases and advanced landing grounds demonstrate the asymmetry of the opposing forces based on their mobility in the landscapes of southern Jordan during the Arab Revolt. The British could deploy from any direction to within a few kilometres of their enemy without a real risk of being seen or engaged by the enemy. The Ottomans, however, were pinned to the railway, always in plain view, and capable only of north–south movement. This was asymmetry in action in a modern guerrilla landscape.

Notes

1 At the start of the twentieth century the study area was Ottoman territory within the Vilayet of Syria (Greater Syria). It became Transjordan in 1923 and The Hashemite Kingdom of Jordan (Jordan) in 1946.

2 Thomas Edward Lawrence, 1888–1935 (known as 'Lawrence of Arabia' in popular culture) held the military ranks of Lieutenant, Captain, Major, and Lieutenant-Colonel during the period 1916–1918. For clarity, he is referred to here as T.E. Lawrence or Lawrence.

3 Depending on personal and political views, some historians refer to this simply as the Arab Revolt (e.g. Mousa 1966).

4 It was not possible to access the Turkish Military and Strategic Studies Archive in Ankara which holds the most extensive collection of primary material on the First World War in the Middle East. Access to this archive is strictly controlled, often denied, and large parts of the collections are closed to researchers (Altay Atli, personal communication; see also Rogan 2015: xvi).

5 Nabatean period, 300 BCE–106 CE; Roman period, 64 BCE–324 CE; Byzantine period 324 CE–640 CE (Kennedy 2004).

6 The Syrian Hajj road between Damascus and Mecca.

7 The construction, history, and architecture are well documented (Aksay 1999; Fahmy 2001; Hülagü 2010; Nicholson 2005; Ochsenwald 1980; Özyüksel 2014; Tourret 1989; Wasti 1998).

8 Formerly an Ottoman Army officer but now a commander of Feisal's Northern Arab Army.

9 Turks refers to Turkish Ottoman troops. The terms *Ottoman Empire* and *Turkey (Turks)* appear interchangeable in many Western texts, and historical documents display a marked preference for the latter as the war progressed. I use the term *Ottoman* to refer to the Empire and *Turkish* in relation to the armed forces (see Anderson 2013: author's note).

10 The water tower at Mudawwara was destroyed on 8 August 1918. Photographs taken on that day show the loop-holes.

11 Francis Richard Maunsell was the former military attaché in Constantinople and was later employed at the Directorate of Military Operations (Satia 2008: 27–28).

12 Tent-rings are circular features constructed from locally available stones and rocks. They are approximately four metres in diameter and can be arranged in dual rows comprising up to 30 rings. They were built to protect the perimeter of 'bell-tents' in Ottoman construction and military camps.

13 Where 'Kilometre' precedes the figure, e.g. Kilometre 495, it denotes the distance along the railway from its origin in Damascus.

14 The Royal Flying Corps became the Royal Air Force (RAF) on 1 April 1918.

15 Wolf pits are circular pits up to one metre in diameter and two metres deep. They are designed to disrupt cavalry. They were first seen on Ottoman redoubts in Palestine by the Australian Light Horse Brigade (Idriess 1973 [1932]) and had similarities to those found in Jordan.

16 Disi is, today, a settlement near Wadi Rum. In 1917–1918 it was the site of a spring and Bedouin camping ground. It was also called Decie in some British archives.

References

Aksay, M. (1999) *The Hejaz Railway: Album of Photographs*. Istanbul: Albaraka.

al-Askari, J.P. (2003) *A Soldier's Story: From Ottoman Rule to Independent Iraq*. London: Arabian Publishing.

Allawi, A. (2014) *Faisal I of Iraq*. London: Yale University Press.

Anderson, S. (2013) *Lawrence in Arabia: War, Deceit, Imperial Folly and the Making of the Modern Middle East*. London: Atlantic Books.

Anon. (1914) For Pilgrimage or Invasion? *Navy and Arm* 2–13: 74–77.

APAAME (1997–2020) The Aerial Photographic Archive of Archaeology in the Middle East. Consulted 01/03/2020, www.flickr.com/photos/apaame/

Bender, B. (1993) *Landscape: Politics and Perspectives*. Oxford: Berg.

——— (2002) Time and Landscape. *Current Anthropology* 43: 103–112.

Boyle, J.R. (2015) Foreword. In J. Johnson-Allen (ed.), *T.E. Lawrence and the Red Sea Patrol*, pp. ix–xi. Barnsley: Pen & Sword.

Carruthers, D. (1910) A Journey in North-Western Arabia. *The Geographical Journal* 35: 225–245.

Classen, C. (ed.) (2005) *The Book of Touch*. Oxford: Berg.

Fahmy, A. (2001) Between Mystical and Military: The Architecture of the Hejaz Railway (1900–1918). *Proceedings of the 11th International Congress of Turkish Art* 1–22.

Finkel, C. (2006) *Osman's Dream. The Story of the Ottoman Empire 1300–1923*. London: John Murray.

GARP (n.d.) *Great Arab Revolt Project*. Consulted 11/2/2016, www.jordan1914-18archaeology.org

Hirsch, E. (1995) Landscape: Between Place and Space. In E. Hirsch and M. O' Hanlon (eds.), *The Anthropology of Landscape: Perspectives on Place and Space*, pp. 1–30. Oxford: Clarendon Press.

Hirsch, E. and M. O' Hanlon (eds.) (1995) *The Anthropology of Landscape: Perspectives on Place and Space*. Oxford: Clarendon Press.

Hogarth, D.G. (1917) *Hejaz before World War 1*. Cambridge: Falcon-Oleander.

Howes, D. (2005) Skinscapes. In C. Classen (ed.), *The Book of Touch*, pp. 27–39. Oxford: Berg.

Hülagü, M.M. (2010) *The Hejaz Railway: The Construction of a New Hope*. New York: Blue Dome.

Idriess, I. (1973 [1932]) *The Desert Column*. Penrith: Discovery Press.

Ingold, T. (1993) The Temporality of the Landscape, *World Archaeology*, 25: 152-174.

Ingold, T. (2007) *Lines: A Brief History*. London: Routledge.

IOR (n.d.) *IOR/L/PS/10/12*, File 3142/1903 'Hedjaz Railway', 1901–1908, India Office Records. British Library.

Kennedy, D. (2004) *The Roman Army in Jordan*. London: Council for British Research in the Levant.

Lawrence, T.E. (2003) *Seven Pillars of Wisdom, a Triumph*. Fordingbridge: Castle Hill Press.

Mousa, S. (1966) *T.E. Lawrence. An Arab View*. London: Oxford University Press.

Murphy, D. (2008) *The Arab Revolt 1916–1918: Lawrence Sets Arabia Ablaze*. Oxford: Osprey Publishing.

Nicholson, J. (2005) *The Hejaz Railway*. London: Stacey International.

Nikolajsen, O. and B. Yilmazer (2000) *Ottoman Aviation 1909–1919*. Arinsal: Nikolajsen.

Ochsenwald, W. (1980) *The Hijaz Railroad*. Charlottesville: University Press of Virginia.

Orange, V. and D. Stapleton (1996) *Winged Promises. A History of No. 14 Squadron, RAF, 1915–1945*. Fairford: The Royal Air Force.

Özyüksel, M. (2014) *The Hejaz Railway and the Ottoman Empire. Modernity, Industrialisation and Ottoman Decline*. London: I. B Taurus.

Petersen, A. (1989) Early Ottoman Forts on the Darb al-Hajj. *Levant* 21: 97–117.

——— (2012) *The Medieval and Ottoman Hajj Route in Jordan. An Archaeological and Historical Study*. Oxford: Oxbow Books.

Rogan, E.L. (1998) Instant Communication: The Impact of the Telegraph in Ottoman Syria. In T. Philipp and B. Schäbler (eds.), *The Syrian Land: Processes of Integration and Fragmentation: Bilād al-Shām from the 18th to the 20th Century*, pp. 113–128. Stuttgart: F.Steiner.

——— (1999) *Frontiers of State in the Late Ottoman Empire, Transjordan 1850–1921*. Cambridge: Cambridge University Press.

——— (2015) *The Fall of the Ottomans. The Great War in the Middle East, 1914–1920*. London: Allen Lane.

Satia, P. (2008) *Spies in Arabia: The Great War and the Cultural Foundations of the British Covert Empire in the Middle East*. Oxford: Oxford University Press.

Saunders, N.J. (2011) First World War Archaeology: Between Theory and Practice. In F. Nicolis, G. Ciurletti and A. De Guio (eds.), *Archeologia Della Grande Guerra: Atti del Convegno Internazionale 23/24 June 2006*, pp. 37–53. Trento: Stampalith.

——— (ed.) (2012) Introduction: Engaging the Materialities of 20th and 21st Century Conflict. In N.J. Saunders (ed.), *Beyond The Dead Horizon: Studies in Modern Conflict Archaeology*, x–xiv. Oxford: Oxbow.

——— (2020) *Desert Insurgency: Archaeology, T.E. Lawrence and the Arab Revolt*. Oxford: Oxford University Press.

Saunders, N.J. and N. Faulkner (2010) Fire on the Desert: Conflict Archaeology and the Great Arab Revolt in Jordan, 1916–1918. *Antiquity* 84: 514–526.

Shqiarat, M., Z. Al-Salameen, N. Faulkner and N.J. Saunders (2011) Fire and Water: Tradition and Modernity in the Archaeology of Steam Locomotion in a Desert War. *Levant* 43: 98–113.

TNA 1 Air1/2250/209/49/1 (n.d.) *X Flight RFC, War Diary October 1917*, Vol 1. London: The National Archive.

TNA 2 Air1/1667/204/100/1 (n.d.) *X Flight RAF War Diary February 1918*, Vol 5. London: The National Archive.

TNA 3 (n.d.) *Air1/1667/204/100/3, X Flight RAF War Diary, April 1918*, Vol. 7. London: The National Archive.

Tourret, R. (1989) *Hedjaz Railway*. Abingdon: Tourret Publishing.

Wasti, S.T. (1998) Muhammad Inshaullah and the Hijaz Railway. *Middle Eastern Studies* 34: 60–72.

Welsby, D.A. (2011) *Sudan's First Railway. The Gordon Relief Expedition and The Dongola Campaign*. London: SARS.

Winterburn, J.B. (2016) *The Conflict Landscapes of Southern Jordan*. Unpublished doctoral thesis, University of Bristol.

——— (in preparation) *Conflict, Command and Control: The Hejaz Railway and its Landscapes in the Late-Ottoman Period*. London: Routledge.

9

LIFE AND DEATH IN A CONFLICT LANDSCAPE

Visitor and local perspectives from the Western Front

Paola Filippucci

> Reading books about the war one forgets the emotional side, one thinks of it only as a technical fact – but going to the places where it happened, one realises once again that it really happened.[1]
>
> Throughout my childhood we picked lily of the valley in the [Verdun] forest. Only later I realised that it was strange to go pick lily of the valley on a battlefield. It seemed normal to see cemeteries everywhere, only later I realised that under the crosses there were people.[2]

The Western Front is one of the world's best-known and most-visited 'conflict landscapes'. Ever since the end of the Great War of 1914–1918, 'the places' where the war happened have attracted visitors. Initially, these were mainly civilian mourners and war veterans, especially as the vast majority of soldiers killed were buried close to 'where they fell' (Lloyd 1998; Winter 1995; Crane 2013; Sherman 1999). However, there were also many whose motivations were closer to those of ordinary tourists, curious to see at first hand the sights and sites of the war, which had already been brought to people's homes by newspapers, illustrated magazines, and film (Laqueur 2008). War tourism from all the combatant countries developed in the interwar period and has continued ever since (e.g. Lloyd 1998; Mosse 1990; Sherman 1999; Jansen-Verbeke and George 2013). In the twenty-first century many, such as my research participant cited above,[3] visit the Western Front battlefields not only to learn about a momentous historical event but also in order to feel 'close' to a conflict that is receding into the past chronologically yet lingers in social memory and imagination (Iles 2006; Saunders 2001; 2007; Offenstadt 2010). Less well known is the relationship with the Western Front conflict landscape of those who live there today, and in principle identify more closely with those who returned to it after the war to reconstruct a habitable landscape, rather than with the soldiers who were part of the war machine that devastated it. What does this landscape mean to them? What do they see and feel? As the second quote above suggests, for them the answer is less straightforward.

Lilies of the valley are both natural in a forest and troubling on 'a battlefield'; the ubiquitous war cemeteries are both an unremarkable feature of the local builtscape and tangible markers of the mass of people buried here. Such 'double' understanding of their surroundings is in my experience pervasive among local inhabitants, and I compare it in what follows to visitors' views of the stretch of the former Western Front where I conducted fieldwork. I show that visitors and many locals feel that the reconstructed landscape of the battlefield helps to access the 'war past' in a uniquely direct and realistic way through visible traces of conflict but especially through its material qualities, complementing and enlivening the commemorative message of monuments and cemeteries.

Locals, however, also use the reconstructed landscape and builtscape to evoke the local civilian experiences and losses of the war, not explicitly commemorated, and to explore imaginatively and articulate the relationship between place (identified with continuity, attachment, belonging) and the discontinuity, displacement, and disruption caused by mass death and destruction. Their understanding of their surroundings reflects and reveals the tension that is at the core of the Western Front 'conflict landscape' and inherent in all post-conflict reconstruction between restoring life and continuity and acknowledging and remembering death and destruction. More broadly, it shows that the restoration of a landscape after armed conflict is not limited to its material reconstruction but also has a symbolic dimension, insofar as a landscape can be the tangible ground for forging and negotiating the relationship between forgetting and remembering, between the living and the dead.

'The places where it happened': visitor perspectives

Following Jennifer Iles (2006), the reality effect on visitors today of going to 'the places' where the Great War happened can be understood as the ability to 'feel' the war, that is, 'to identify and empathize with its symbolic and commemorative spaces' (2006: 165). Iles points out that in the reconstructed landscape and builtscape of the former battlefields there is relatively little for today's tourists to see – past destruction and carnage have long since been replaced by farmland, settlements, war cemeteries, and monuments (ibid.: 163). This, however, intensifies the experience by providing a contrast between today's peaceful, ordinary, even beautiful appearance with the knowledge of past devastation and horror (ibid.). In a study of recent British battlefield tours, Iles shows that this is encouraged by tour operators and guides, who use narrative, photographs, objects, and performance (e.g. walking across a stretch of battlefield) to encourage visitors to imagine what the places that they visit would have looked and felt like during the war, and what the soldiers may have experienced (Iles 2006). This resonates with many if not most visitors' desire to feel a connection with these places and through them, with those who fought and died here. For Iles, in the case of British visitors, this desire is fuelled by family history and memory and the wish to remember and honour ancestors, and/or for some, by nostalgia for a 'better' past dominated by values of nationhood, courage and sacrifice (ibid.: 174–175).

Iles' account of visitor responses resonates with my own observations in the 'French' battlefields of Verdun and the Argonne, although here visitors are mainly French and, increasingly, German, as well as from nearby Belgium and Luxembourg, and much more rarely British.[4] Although there has been organized tourism here since the interwar period, unlike in the 'British' battlefields to the north, at Verdun or Argonne there has been no major surge in battlefield tourism since the 1970s and tourist development has been limited (cf. ibid.: 163). Site signage and information panels have been updated at various sites especially since the eightieth anniversary in the mid-1990s, but it was only for the 2014–2018 centenary years that more significant publicly funded interventions took place, such as the total refurbishment of the *Mémorial* museum on the Verdun battlefield (see http://memorial-verdun.fr). In Argonne in particular, restoration and tourist valorization of specific sites (Butte de Vauquois, Vallée Moreau, and Ravin du Génie) have largely occurred since 2000 thanks to the efforts and fundraising of local associations. Throughout my fieldwork in the area (2000–2014), I have never seen the crowds that are found, for instance, at the Last Post ceremony in Ypres throughout the year (Dendooven 2014). Nevertheless, there is a regular stream of visitors to the Argonne and Verdun battlefield sites, mainly during the summer, and in my observation, many of these express similar heartfelt impressions and connections with the battlefield landscape as those recorded by Iles.

Jean, the interviewee cited at the start of this chapter, was a man in his early thirties whom I met during an outing to war-related sites in the Argonne forest organized by one of the local associations devoted to restoring and retrieving Great War sites, the Amis de Vauquois. Jean admitted to a 'passion' for the Great War from a young age and had read everything he could find about the war, from history books to diaries to novels; he had seen every film and he visited the Argonne or other Great War battlefields almost annually. He had also undertaken genealogical research on his family and tracked a distant relative who had fought and died in Argonne and was buried in one of the local war cemeteries, which we visited together. Jean's passionate immersion in the topic was such that, as he put it, 'sometimes I feel as though I had done the war myself'. Nevertheless, as he also said, it is only 'when you go the places' that you 'realise that it really happened'. Like many other visitors I met during my fieldwork, he contrasted learning about the war from history books, school lessons, and even family history with being in the places themselves, which was widely said to 'bring the war to life' in a particularly poignant and direct way. Here, as another visitor put it, 'you see the war as it really was' – '*on voit la guerre comment c'etait*'. In spite of this reference to 'seeing', however, it is not primarily sight that brings the war 'to life' – as in Flanders and other sectors of the Western Front, there is not much of the war to see today at these locations.

The battlefield landscapes of Argonne and Verdun are very different from those of the northern stretch of the Western Front because they are dominated by forest, although in Verdun it is parkland. Argonne and Verdun were both demarcated as 'Red Zones' after the war, due to the extent of pollution by matériel, spent ordnance, military structures such as dugouts, trench systems, and, in Verdun, forts. At both locations, the very structure of the soil was severely damaged, in Argonne by mine explosions, and in Verdun by the intensity of artillery bombardment. Although similar levels of destruction occurred in Picardie, Nord, and Flanders, the bulk of the Red Zones there were reclaimed because the market value of the land offset the costs of reclamation (Amat 2015: 369).

At Verdun and in Argonne, upland locations with poor-quality land, it was not economical to return to farming, and consequently, large areas of Red Zone survived, managed as 'natural' forest environments (Amat 2015: 438–442, 486–490). Both areas thus contain a much greater number and density of war-related remains than any of the more northern battlefields; however, with the exception of some larger structures at Verdun (such as some of the forts) the remains are not easily visible or accessible to tourists. At both locations, tourist trails are limited partly because of the danger posed by unexploded ammunition, exacerbated by the passage of time as it continues to degrade (e.g. Saunders 2001: 46), and partly because of the management of both forests by the *Office National des Forêts* which is increasingly centred on environmental protection of biodiversity. So, although traces of the war are everywhere, they are not easy to see, especially to the untrained eye of casual visitors. On the other hand, visitors apprehend the war 'as it was' through their other senses.

A very frequent commentary among visitors to the Argonne and Verdun battlefields concerns the weather. Both areas are humid with frequent rain, and can be miserably cold in every season, as well as sometimes suffocatingly hot in summer. As a result, visitors often feel physically uncomfortable, and this almost invariably calls forth comments about how the soldiers must have felt: 'isn't it horribly cold and wet today – but nothing compared to what they must have endured!' In my experience, nearly every comment about the weather is followed and qualified by referring to the experience of combatants, as if the climate facilitates empathy and identification with the soldiers by bringing to life the conditions of their lives. Similar comments are made by visitors or also by tourist guides about physical aspects of the terrain: 'we may be struggling up this slope today but how much more they must have struggled under fire and with the weight of all that they were carrying!' I heard similar comments when people visited war-related structures such as forts, tunnels, and dugouts, which are usually quite dark, cold, and humid, the ground and walls often slippery and treacherous, and sometimes, in the case of narrower tunnels, for instance at the Butte de Vauquois or in the Argonne forest, physically oppressive.

In each case, visitors' expressions of discomfort and guides' warnings of danger are accompanied by more or less explicit comparisons with the living conditions of soldiers, bringing to mind and body 'the war as it was'. As in the cases analyzed by Iles, this is also encouraged by guides through taking visitors across the terrain and describing the present-day landscape by reference to the wartime, for instance speaking of going 'up the line' while walking along the remains of a communication trench, and going 'over the top' and towards 'enemy lines' when taking visitors across former no man's land. Guides also often remind visitors verbally, or via images or objects,[5] of iconic but now absent aspects of soldiers' sensations such as smells, the noise and impact of ordnance, hunger, thirst etc.

Another iconic aspect of the Great War experience, mud (e.g. Das 2005: 35 ff.), is instead easily available to visitors, especially in Argonne where the forest terrain is in all seasons very humid and consists of a type of limestone, *gaize*, that in wet and cold conditions (i.e. most of the time) degrades into an exceptionally sticky and slippery mass, causing significant discomfort to visitors not equipped with hiking clothes and shoes. Familiarity with these experiences among more regular visitors and guides, shown by their turning up better equipped and not complaining about the conditions, is also a way to claim a kind of 'insideness' in the landscape (Iles 2006: 165) which, as in the case of Jean, can translate into a feeling of 'having done the war', that is, insideness in the past (Figure 9.1).[6]

Overall, visitors to the Argonne and Verdun, as with Iles' research participants, rely on the landscape of the former battlefield less as a visual cue than as a physical trigger or immersive matrix of sensations which form the basis for triggering a 'feeling' about the past. This is understood as providing a more authentic

FIGURE 9.1 '*La guerre comment c'etait*'. Local guide and visitors, Ravin du Génie, Argonne battlefield, August 2008. Source: © author.

connection with the war past (*'la guerre comment c'etait'*) than that afforded by other sources of historical knowledge such as books and school instruction. A contrast is also drawn by some visitors and locals in Argonne and Verdun between the effect of 'being in the places' and that produced by memorials and monuments, described as mute: 'they don't say anything to me' [*ils ne me disent rien*]. Unlike British battlefield visitors, whom I have often heard praising the beauty of 'their' battlefield cemeteries and memorials, visitors to the 'French' sector of the battlefields seem to struggle to relate to or decode the interwar symbolism and aesthetics of monuments, by comparison with the attractive forest landscape. Nevertheless, the feeling for the past facilitated by the landscape is contained within the same commemorative logic and sentiments as those communicated by the monuments. Comments about and comparisons with soldiers' experiences are acts of imagination and empathy facilitated by the landscape (cf. Bloch 1998), but they are also moral acts, in the sense that they are acts of memory, affirming a moral commitment to past people by acknowledging the enormity of their suffering (cf. Lambek 1996; Bal et al. 1999):

> You realise what they have lived when you see the places – and note that we had good weather – how much worse it must have been then [during the war], in the rain and the cold! They really lived like animals, like the cows in the field, wet when it was wet, cold when it was cold.[7]

These words by a husband and wife visiting Verdun were spoken after a day out on the battlefield guided by the diary entries of the man's grandfather, who had fought and died at Verdun: 'for us it's not a holiday, it's a pilgrimage, it is for treading in their footsteps' [*aller sur leurs pas à eux*].

> The commemorative dimension was emphasised by their bed and breakfast host, present at our conversation and himself 'passionate' about the Great War because of the involvement of some of his own relatives. He explained about the man: 'He has come to fulfil the duty of remembering [*devoir du souvenir*] for his father who could never visit, and for his grandfather who never returned [home from the war]'.[8]

Similarly, local war heritage promoters, when they exploit the power of the local landscape to provide a 'heritage experience' for visitors, point out that this is not just 'Disney' (a common local shorthand to refer to shallow, theme park–type heritage entertainment) but is motivated by a moral obligation. For instance, costumed re-enactors stress that their performance is not just historically accurate entertainment but also undertaken to evoke and acknowledge the soldiers' suffering.

Participants in a reconstruction of scenes of war in the Argonne Red Zone said that their aim was to show visitors 'a bit of what happened here' but that this was moved by 'respect for the things that happened here 90 years ago'; theirs was 'a ceremony not a reconstitution'. So in his pep-talk to the 'troupe'/troops on the night of the dress rehearsal, a cold drizzly October night, the director said: 'it will be tough here tonight, but nothing in comparison to what they suffered here 90 years ago'.[9]

Similarly, the owner of a private Great War exhibit in Argonne, who collects and displays war-related materials gathered from the surrounding area, described his initiative as a 'pilgrimage for the soldiers' and his use of re-enactment for visitors as a way to bring home a moral message about the human aspects and costs of war:

> In the forest [schoolchildren] have to run with me up a hill and it's the same hill that the American [troops] captured with three thousand casualties [...] and at the top the children are knackered! They tell me it's not possible and I point out that they didn't have a gas mask on, were not carrying 40 kilos of backpack, there weren't bullets flying everywhere, explosions, barbed wire, and you hadn't just done another twenty hills and another thirty still to do! And in this way they get into the subject. [...] They get dirty, they arrive wearing trendy jeans and in ten minutes everyone is dirty, and this makes a group! After the visit they remain comrades [*copains*]! [...] It's to show them the soldiers, the humans, like you and me.[10]

In each case, practices currently used in heritage promotion to foster visitor engagement are presented as ethically charged acts of commemoration, in which remembering is a moral commitment to past people for their suffering, understood within the logic of 'sacrifice' (another word used really commonly to describe the soldiers) as an 'act of symbolic exchange between those who remain and those who suffered and died' (Winter 2006: 279; cf. Margalit 2002).

In particular, whereas monuments and formal commemorations help to remember the dead, practices that involve the battlefield landscape seem to facilitate something more akin to what Iles terms 'interacting with the dead' (Iles 2006: 172). Like some of Iles' research participants, especially those most familiar with the former battlefield landscape (e.g. regular visitors, tourist guides, re-enactors, and those involved in conserving war-related sites) speak familiarly about the soldiers. For example, they call the soldiers '*les gars*' [the boys] or use the affectionate term '*les poilus*' for the French combatants, with one group of volunteers who restore war sites and are also re-enactors sometimes referring to themselves as '*poilus*' and to the restoration work as '*la guerre*' (Figure 9.2). Many also alluded to feeling the soldiers' presence: 'sometimes when I am in the forest I see them running up the ravine, I hear them shouting', said a guide; while another confessed to experiencing 'a strange feeling, like a strong emotion, at certain locations in the forest'.

In line with modern sensibilities on the matter, no one spoke of 'ghosts' (see Stewart 2017: 9; Hurst 2017: 354; Carr 2017), but many associated the landscape with uncanny feelings or experiences ('there's no birdsong' was a recurrent one

FIGURE 9.2 Interacting with the dead? Costume re-enactors for the ninety-eighth anniversary of the battle, Verdun battlefield, June 2014. Source: © author.

both in Argonne and Verdun, although they both host many bird species[11]), signalling a perception of it as a bearer of unseen presences. The role of the battlefield landscape as a means for mourners to make contact with the dead, particularly the missing, is well documented in the interwar period (see Lloyd 1998; Sherman 1999). A century after the conflict, mourning has given way to more impersonal commemoration. But the cemeteries, monuments, and memorials perpetuate tangibly and signal symbolically the funerary nature of the reconstructed landscape as a whole, stemming from its post-war role as a material means for properly disposing of the war dead, most of whom were buried in the region 'where they fell' (Sherman 1999; Crane 2013; Mosse 1990). The link between the landscape and the dead is particularly explicit at Verdun, where the forest landscape created over the former battlefield after the war was explicitly designed both as an appropriate setting for the main cemetery and ossuary and as a means of giving dignified interment to the thousands of bodies that could not be retrieved (see Amat 2015; Filippucci forthcoming). Thus the Verdun forest is still today widely described and perceived as a 'vast cemetery' and a resting place for the missing: 'It's men who died, it's a cemetery, they all died for peace, French and also German. 300,000 dead. [...] he is missing so he is here' [points to the ground next to where we are standing].[12]

The imagery of the former battlefield as a 'vast cemetery' calling for a reverential relationship with the landscape and through it, with the fallen, recurs in Argonne, for instance, in an account of clearing vegetation from the hill at Vauquois:

> A certain morning as I was chopping down shrubs I saw a man advance towards me, red with anger: 'what the f*** are you doing there!' [...] 'What the f*** I am doing [...] you can see it, sir: it is to cut down the forest under which are asleep 1500 [*sic*] shattered dead! I don't want people to come here to make love or to answer a call of nature! It's an immense cemetery of heroes, here!'
>
> *(Platz 2007: 6)*

Living in/with a conflict landscape: local perspectives

Local inhabitants are not immune to the imaginative and emotional pull of the battlefield landscape: many of them are collectors of militaria, members of local or national commemorative associations, take part in costumed re-enactments, or work to retrieve and restore war sites. Those involved typically describe themselves as '*passionnés*' about the war, a term that implies an emotional/affective engagement with the past; and just like visitors, many account for their 'passion' by the memory of family members who died or fought in the war. As at other localities in France, Argonne villages, the city of Verdun, and its surrounding villages lost men in the Great War. However, unlike in the rest of France, for the populations of the war zone, the war also included displacement, the destruction or loss of property, and for those who returned after the end of the conflict, the process of reconstruction.

This aspect of the Great War is not as well documented or studied as the military aspects of the war (see Clout 1996). Civilian inhabitants of the war zone experienced 'a succession of displacements' between 1914 and 1919, as they moved away or were moved by the military authorities following the movements of the front; those caught behind German lines were in some cases interned in camps behind the front, or repatriated to France by the German authorities (Nivet 2004: 15). The extreme level of devastation in parts of the Argonne and Verdun made the return of local populations and the reconstruction of settlements and landscapes slow and arduous, and some of the pre-war population, as well as many businesses, never returned.[13] In both areas, some sectors were never fully resettled, including nine villages near Verdun that were not reconstructed and became memorial sites within the Verdun battlefield perimeter, receiving military honours for having 'died for France' like the soldiers.[14] Apart from these sites, the losses and experiences of the civilian populations of the former battlefields were not commemorated after the war, perhaps understandably given the enormity of the military losses. Villages and towns across the war zone erected war memorials for the military (and some civilian) victims of the war, but their iconography and symbolism was the same as that of war memorials elsewhere in France and virtually never depicted the destruction and the privations suffered by the local inhabitants.[15]

The issue of whether and how this aspect of the war is remembered locally a century after the Great War has been the focus of my ethnographic research in the Argonne and Verdun. By the time I began my fieldwork in 2000, only the very oldest residents born in the interwar period provided relatively detailed narratives about the wartime, the return, and reconstruction, based on parents' and grandparents' memories as well as their own as children. Younger inhabitants said more vaguely that 'everything was destroyed' but added that it was all 'reconstructed identical' to how it had been [*à l'identique*]. As discussed in detail elsewhere (Filippucci 2009), this broad, generic narrative was complemented by a commentary on the reconstructed builtscape made by using photographs of the pre-1914 villages that have survived in the form of postcards. These 'old postcards' [*vieilles cartes postales*] widely produced and circulated before and during the war (cf. Schor 1992) are locally displayed in houses and public buildings, and many collect and refer to them when asked about village history:

> 'Here is Cheppy before the war, the other side of the bridge, there, that's where you turned with the car, earlier. This one is the Mairie, it used to be a bit lower down, and we still have the foundations, the stones, we see them still. [...] So this is Cheppy again before '14, and earlier when we spoke in the street we were here. More or less at that spot there. And you turned there ... the church used to be just opposite. [...] And this is a panoramic view, you can see the whole of the high street. This photo, I took a picture from the same viewpoint, before they cut down the chestnut trees. And you can see the difference [between the pre-'14 and recent photos]: the growth of the trees. They had grown but not changed shape, the same shape'.

'And here Cheppy, always after the war, so, see, the only house that remained standing...'

'Yes when you go up there, in that neighbourhood, there's a house just around the back, which was partially destroyed but was rebuilt, it was the only one left from '14.'[16]

This excerpt is typical of many conversations I had with local residents as we looked at old images of their village. Here, two men evoke the pre-war appearance and wartime destruction of Cheppy (Argonne) but do not dwell on the destruction, instead comparing the pre-war and present-day builtscape as if to provide visual evidence that it was reconstructed '*à l'identique*' and of parts that survived the war. They also compare pre- and post-war layout as if to say that in spite of total destruction, those in the reconstructed village could still have found their way around the pre-war settlement. In this and many other similar conversations the focus was not on destruction: images of war ruins, when they were shown,[17] were only briefly mentioned, while pre-war images were scrutinized in detail for their connections with the present day. The postcards thus enable a commentary that makes the ruins of war fleetingly visible, minimizing them by contextualizing them with images of before and after, that visualize and make imaginable the continuities across this hiatus (Figure 9.3).

As is common with such 'topographicals', the images are used to compare past and present (Schor 1992; Crang 1996). Usually, this is in terms of a then/now binary, visualizing changes in the builtscape to fuel nostalgic longing for and attachment to 'home' places, with the images acting as 'souvenirs' in Susan Stewart's sense of objects which speak 'to a context of origin through a language of longing' (Stewart cited in Schor 1992: 200). In the case considered here, the commentary was sometimes nostalgic, especially when villagers pointed to the number of people and activities visible in pre-1914 images compared to the loss of local jobs, services, and population since then.[18]

However, as previously mentioned, it is more usually the *similarities* between pre-1914 images and the current village that are highlighted, while dramatic change is shown when, much more rarely, they are compared to the ruins of war. These images express attachment to home places, but the implicit temporal

FIGURE 9.3 'Old postcards' of the pre-war village on display in a guesthouse at Le Claon, Argonne, August 2008. Source: © author.

trajectory is less nostalgic than forwards-looking, about reconstruction and resettlement and remaking a living world in the aftermath of mass destruction. In the absence of a public narrative and commemorative discourse about the war's impact on local inhabitants and their privations, losses, and achievements, this imaginative work shows the central role of the landscape, in this case of the reconstructed builtscape of villages, in efforts to make war destruction part of place as a spatiotemporal construct and through it, of local identity.

It is not just the reconstructed builtscape that helps residents to link past, present, and future and connect unspeakable destruction and loss with reconstruction, continuity, and attachment. In the quote above about Cheppy, the relationship between change and continuity was also signified and visualized by the trees, which as my interlocutor pointed out, could be seen to have grown from 'before '14' to his own time 'but not changed shape, the same shape'. The idea of the persistence of 'natural' landscape features across the hiatus of war was also expressed about watercourses:

> [My grandfather] told me that when he returned [after the war] he had to check which way the water flowed in the stream, because he could recognize nothing at all – he had to check the direction of the water so he could say 'Malancourt was that way'.[19]

This quote hints at the stability and perhaps timelessness of the 'natural' landscape even in the face of mass destruction. In fact, in Malancourt as elsewhere in Argonne and in the Verdun uplands, the devastation was such that the very fabric of the soil was damaged and had to be reconstituted through levelling and tree plantation. As such, much of the apparently timeless 'natural' environment in these areas is in fact a historical human artefact. However, this has come to be masked by the intrinsic temporality of 'nature' itself: as Jean-Paul Amat has documented, mass destruction unleashed huge vegetative energy so that the former battlefield was rapidly re-colonized by new plant and animal species, and reforestation was a way to harness and manage this spontaneous regeneration (Amat 2015: 418–431).

In the longer term, the absence of cultivation has led the post-war landscape of the Argonne and, especially, of Verdun to develop unusual biodiversity for this part of Europe (Natura 2000). This is now central to the forestry management and tourist valorization of both former battlefields, and locals especially praise and enjoy the 'natural beauty' of the local landscape, and both battlefields are popular venues for outdoor pursuits such as hiking, riding, and mountain biking. This seems paradoxical because, as mentioned previously, it is especially the forest that holds war-related monuments and remains and is associated with the war past and the soldiers by visitors and locals. However, for the latter, the 'natural' aspect of the former battlefield landscape also holds particular potential for thinking about the *local* relationship between the war past and the present.

On the one hand, by focusing on the 'natural' landscape, locals more or less explicitly separate the present from the war past. For instance, when I described to some locals my excitement at seeing the war remains in the *Bois de la Gruerie*, in the Argonne, they dismissed this by saying that they 'only go to the Gruerie to collect mushrooms!'. More explicitly, a tourist officer in a village near Verdun spoke about his wish to turn the battlefield into a nature park because it's high time, as he put it, to use the 'green' aspect of the area to overcome its 'black' image associated with war, death, and destruction. On the other hand, the war is a powerful framework for interpreting the forest landscape: not only by people speaking of uncanny presences and feelings, but also by claiming that certain linear features visible in parts of the Argonne forest were Great War trenches when in fact they are eighteenth-century boundary ditches, and further, by describing any dip in the terrain as a shell hole regardless of its origin.

The 'natural' landscape thus makes the war past both invisible and visible, both nowhere and everywhere. Unlike in the case of builtscape, the relationship between the two is not linear (before/after); rather, they seem to coexist as two sides of the same coin, or perhaps two ways of seeing. As is evident in the quote at the start of this chapter, locals express a dissonant view of their surroundings in which they see the war everywhere and yet don't see it because it's a part of what's 'normal'. From a discursive as well as a physical point of view, 'nature' or 'environment' in their perceived timelessness help locals to background the historic aspects of this landscape. However, through landscape, the war past is also permanently 'there', unremarked and unremarkable but available to be foregrounded as a component of place (cf. Hirsch 1996).

Overall it is arguable that, for locals, mass destruction and mass death have come to be 'folded into' the ordinary day-to-day reality of the reconstructed surroundings (cf. Hastrup 2011), and thus are both invisible and visible through it. Landscape has both replaced destruction and kept it available to imagination and memory, as a permanent backdrop of place.

Conclusions

Anthropology has long recognized that landscape is not a passive, inert backdrop for human activity but a medium for social life, a means by which humans structure relationships and construct identities (e.g. Hirsch and O'Hanlon 1996). In this optic, the mass destruction of landscapes through war is not just a material loss but also affects issues of society and identity. For this reason, landscapes need reconstructing after war, and moreover, the reconstruction is not a simple matter of restoring physically safe and habitable surroundings. Instead, material reconstruction can be a central aspect of and medium for the reconstruction of identities after conflict (Sørensen and Viejo-Rose 2015). The interplay of material and symbolic aspects is clear in the case of the reconstruction of the devastated areas after the Great War. While the former inhabitants were keen to return and reclaim their properties as soon as possible (Clout 1996), there were those who argued that the war zone should be forever left in ruins, to testify for posterity to the horror of the war (Saunders 2001: 42). This view was abandoned, however, and the ruins of war were mostly cleared, partly under pressure from and through the efforts of the returning populations.

However, the Western Front was also reconstructed as a memorial and, especially, a funerary space, allowing for the proper disposal of the dead which, as theorized by anthropologist Robert Hertz, himself a victim of the Great War, is essential in order to allow society to reconstitute its integrity and identity (Hertz 2004 [1907]). The manner of death in the Great War, with tens of thousands of missing bodies, meant that the landscape as a whole came to be seen as a vast cemetery, a place where mourners could make contact with their dead in the absence of a known grave (cf. Saunders 2001). The Western Front landscape thus arguably helped survivors to make and manage a relationship with the war dead and through them, with each other (Winter 1995: 29–53). This way of viewing and experiencing the Western Front landscape is documented in the immediate aftermath of the war (Lloyd 1998; Sherman 1999) but arguably still shapes today's visitors' perceptions of and attitudes towards it, as described in this chapter.

Among those who needed to reconstruct their relationships and identities after the conflict and in relation to it were those who reclaimed the war zone as their home. They too needed to mourn their dead, but at the same time to restore living places where there had been so many deaths and so much destruction. Material reconstruction was virtually completed by the late 1920s, but the symbolic reclamation of the landscape has, in my view, taken much longer and indeed is still ongoing. As noted for the interwar period, the fate of the displaced populations was overshadowed by the military losses of the war and did not become a significant part of public commemoration. Nevertheless, those who resettled the war zone had to reconstruct their identities and sense of place in relation to the historical experiences of displacement, mass destruction, and mass death. I have suggested that they used and continue to use the landscape to imagine and negotiate affectively their relationship with the war past. The builtscape and, especially, the 'natural' surroundings help to make the war past at once invisible, truly 'past' (as, for instance, when villages are said to have been reconstructed 'identical'), and visible, always 'there', available to bring to mind as part of place and local identity. As with visitors, locals see 'double' in the surroundings of the Western Front, but where the former focus on the rural calm and beauty of today the better to see the chaos and horror of the past (Iles 2006: 163), the locals' gaze flicks between the two, as between 'figure' and 'ground' (cf. Hastrup 2011: 12). They do so in order to negotiate a tension between remembering and moving on, between honouring the dead and recreating ordinary, living places.

This tension dominated the reconstruction of identities, including local identities, in the interwar period and is even now not yet fully resolved, as successive generations strive to relate to a conflict that seems to 'never end' (Gauthier et al. 2008). Indeed, the disappearance of direct survivors may have intensified the memorial role of the former battlefields as current generations seek different means to forge an affective link with a conflict that continues to speak to European and global identities (cf. Winter and Prost 2005; Filippucci 2017). As former combatant countries continue to claim the former battlefields as 'theirs' in order to keep alive or to enliven the memory of the soldiers and of the war, the 'localness' of this landscape is not entirely a given but needs to be affirmed and negotiated. Mass destruction and death materially touched and arguably over-determined this landscape a century ago; a century on, they continue to over-determine it symbolically, shaping the perceptions and experiences not just of visitors but also of locals.

Notes

1 Interview. Jean, an Argonne battlefield visitor, 2002. Names of research participants, where cited, were changed to preserve their anonymity.
2 Interview. Resident, Bras-sur-Meuse, August 2011.
3 Ethnographic research was conducted in Argonne in 2000–2008 and in Verdun in 2008–2014.
4 No up-to-date figures on tourist numbers are available for Verdun or Argonne so this is based on my own observations and on comments I collected from local research participants involved in the tourist valorization of the battlefields.
5 In Argonne, guides of a tour branded 'On the footsteps of soldiers' evoked the smell of battle by burning up a small amount of gunpowder extracted from a shell detonator. Others were content to evoke this and other aspects of the battle experience verbally, but often by handing around war debris such as shrapnel, shell fragments, barbed wire, etc., which are easy to come by in some parts of both forests.
6 In Argonne and Verdun tour guides are usually local residents, including at least two German and one Dutch guides/war heritage promoters who had lived in the area for many years and regarded themselves and were regarded as part of the local scene (apart from the occasional tongue-in-cheek comment about '*Boches*' directed at the Germans). Tour guides also include employees of the national forestry agency *Office National des Forêts*, some of whom are from other parts of France but live locally, sometimes for several years or through their whole career. In these cases 'insideness' through familiarity with the war landscape can be seen as an expression of localness/local belonging, unlike the British guides discussed by Iles, whose claim to the war sites, like that of regular visitors, is to a sort of 'home from home' (Iles 2006: 175).
7 Interview. Bras-sur-Meuse, August 2011.
8 Interview. Bed and breakfast owner, Bras-sur-Meuse, August 2011.
9 Field notes. Re-enactment in the Argonne Forest, October 2005.
10 Interview. Private museum owner, Romagne-sous-Montfaucon, August 2011.
11 I heard the same comment about wooded war-related sites in other parts of the Western Front such as Belleau Wood and Thiepval Wood. Similar stories are told about the German Second World War camp at Auschwitz.
12 Field notes. Volunteer reader of soldiers' testimonies at anniversary event of the Battle of Verdun, Verdun battlefield, June 2014.
13 The post-war population grew faster in urban than rural areas, where more employment was available, and in relation to the level of devastation (see Amat 2015: 360).
14 '*Mort pour la France*' was the official terminology for soldiers who died in the war; villages that were not reconstructed were also awarded military medals; those reconstructed after severe damage received the official citation '*a bien mérité du Pays*' [deserves the country's praise].
15 In the villages of the Argonne and around Verdun where I conducted fieldwork, ruined villages and the exodus of the inhabitants are only depicted on some of the stained glass windows in churches reconstructed during the 1920s (see Laparra et Laparra 1998).
16 Interview. Residents of Cheppy, August 2005.

17 Postcards of war ruins were produced and widely circulated during the war, for propaganda and later tourism. See e.g. Henneman (2014).
18 The Argonne is classified by the EU as an area of 'rural decline'; as for Verdun and its hinterland, they have been weakened economically by the end of the Cold War that led to the final closure of military bases and facilities that had formed the core of the local economy of this former garrison town since the nineteenth century.
19 Interview. Resident of Malancourt, 2005.

References

Amat, J.-P. (2015) *Les Forêts de Guerre. Histoire, mémoire, patrimoine.* Paris: Presses de l'Université Paris-Sorbonne.

Bal, M., J. Crewe and L. Spitzer (1999) *Acts of Memory: Cultural Recall in the Present.* Hanover, NH: University Press of New England.

Bloch, M. (1998) *How We Think They Think. Anthropological Approaches to Cognition, Memory and Literacy.* London: Westview Press.

Carr, G. (2017) The Uninvited Guests Who Outstayed Their Welcome: The Ghosts of War in the Channel Islands. In N.J. Saunders and P. Cornish (eds.), *Modern Conflict and the Senses*, pp. 272–288. London: Routledge.

Clout, H. (1996) *After the Ruins.* Exeter: University of Exeter Press.

Crane, D. (2013) *Empires of the Dead.* London: William Collins.

Crang, M. (1996) Envisioning Urban Histories: Bristol as Palimpsest, Postcards, and Snapshots. *Environment and Planning A. Economy and Space* 28: 429–452.

Das, S. (2005) *Touch and Intimacy in First World War Literature.* Cambridge: Cambridge University Press.

Dendooven, D. (2014) Commemoration in Stone and in Silence: The Menin Gate and the Last Post Ceremony as lieu de mémoire. *The Low Countries: Arts and Society in Flanders and the Netherlands* 22: 20–30.

Filippucci, P. (2009) Postcards from the Past: Landscape, Place and the Memory of War in Argonne (France). In N.J. Saunders and P. Cornish (eds.), *Contested Objects: Material Memories of the Great War*, pp. 220–236. London: Routledge.

——— (2017) Témoins Muets/Mute Witnesses: Ethnography and Archaeology Encounter the Objects of the Great War. In M. Gellereau (éd.), *Témoignages et médiations des objets de guerre en musée*, pp. 15–25. Villeneuve d'Ascq: Presses Universitaires du Septentrion.

——— (forthcoming) 'These Battered Hills': Landscape and Memory at Verdun (France). In G. Wollentz and G. Di Maida (eds.), *Memory and Landscapes – Approaches to the Study of Landscapes as Places of Memory.* Oxford: Archaeopress.

Gauthier, C., Lescot, D. and Véray, L. (sous la dir. De) (2008) *'Une Guerre que n'en Finit Pas. 1914–2008, à l'ecran et sur la Scène.* Toulouse : Édition Complexe.

Hastrup, F. (2011) *Weathering the World. Recovery in the Wake of the Tsunami in a Tamil Fishing Village.* New York: Berghahn Books.

Henneman, I. (2014) *Shooting Range. Photography and the Great War.* Antwerp: Photo Museum.

Hertz, R. (2004 [1907]) A Contribution to the Study of the Collective Representation of Death. In R. Hertz (ed.), *Death and the Right Hand*, pp. 27–86. London: Routledge.

Hirsch, E. (1996) Introduction. Landscape: Between Place and Space. In E. Hirsch and M. O'Hanlon (eds.), *The Anthropology of Landscape: Perspectives on Place and Space*, pp. 1–30. Oxford: Clarendon Press.

Hirsch, E. and M. O'Hanlon (eds.) (1996) *The Anthropology of Landscape: Perspectives on Place and Space.* Oxford: Clarendon Press.

Hurst, S. (2017) The Senses: Battlefield Exploration, Drawing and Sculpture. In N.J. Saunders and P. Cornish (eds.), *Modern Conflict and the Senses*, pp. 344–360. London: Routledge.

Iles, J. (2006) Recalling the Ghosts of War: Performing Tourism on the Battlefields of the Western Front. *Text and Performance Quarterly* 26: 162–180.

Jansen-Verbeke, M. and W. George (2013) Reflections on the Great War Centenary: From Warscapes to Memoryscapes in 100 Years. In R. Butler and W. Suntikul (eds.), *Tourism and War*, pp. 273–287. London: Routledge.

Lambek, M. (1996) The Past Imperfect: Remembering as Moral Practice. In P. Antze and M. Lambek (eds.), *Tense Past. Cultural Essays on Trauma and Memory*, pp. 235–254. New York: Routledge.

Laparra, J. and J.-C. Laparra (1998) L'imagerie du Souvenir. In V. Péché (sous la dir. de) (ed.), *Monuments de Lumiere. Vitrail commémoratif de la Grande Guerre en Meuse*, pp. 47–83. Bar-le-Duc: Saint Paul France S.A.

Laqueur, T.W. (2008) Among the Graves. *London Review of Books* 30 (24): 3–9.

Lloyd, D.W. (1998) *Battlefield Tourism: Pilgrimage and the Commemoration of the Great War in Britain, Australia, and Canada, 1919–1939*. Oxford: Berg.

Margalit, A. (2002) *The Ethics of Memory*. Cambridge, MA: Harvard University Press.

Mosse, G. (1990) *Fallen Soldiers. Reshaping the Memory of the World Wars*. Oxford: Oxford University Press.

NATURA (2000) *Formulaire standard de données pour les zones de protection spéciale (ZPS), les propositions de sites d'importance communautaire (pSIC), les sites d'importance communautaire (SIC) et les zones spéciales de conservation (ZSC), FR4100171 – Corridor de la Meuse*. https://inpn.mnhn.fr/site/natura2000/FR4100171 (accessed 28 June 2018).

Nivet, P. (2004) *Les Réfugiés Français de la Grande Guerre. Les 'Boches du Nord'*. Paris: Economica.

Offenstadt, N. (2010) *14–18 Aujourd'hui. La Grande Guerre dans la France contemporaine*. Paris: Odile Jacob.

Platz, H. (2007) La resurrection de Vauquois (suite). *Les Amis de Vauquois et de sa Région. Bulletin de liaison des adhérents* 55: 6–11.

Saunders, N.J. (2001) Matter and Memory in the Landscapes of Conflict: The Western Front 1914–1999. In B. Bender and M. Winer (eds.), *Movement, Exile and Place*, pp. 37–53.Oxford: Berg.

——— (2007) *Killing Time. Archaeology and the First World War*. Stroud: Sutton Publishing.

Schor, N. (1992) 'Cartes Postales': Representing Paris 1900. *Critical Inquiry* 18(2): 188–244.

Sherman, D.J. (1999) *The Construction of Memory in Interwar France*. Chicago: University of Chicago Press.

Stewart, C. (2017) *Dreaming and Historical Consciousness in Island Greece*. Chicago: University of Chicago Press.

Stig Sørensen, M.-L. and D. Viejo-Rose (eds.) (2015) *War and Cultural Heritage: Biographies of Place*. Cambridge: Cambridge University Press.

Winter, J. (1995) *Sites of Memory, Sites of Mourning*. Cambridge: Cambridge University Press.

——— (2006) *Remembering War. The Great War between Memory and History in the Twentieth Century*. New Haven: Yale University Press.

Winter, J. and A. Prost (2005) *The Great War in History. Debates and Controversies, 1914 to the Present*. Cambridge: Cambridge University Press.

PART II
The Second World War

10

WHO OWNS THE 'WILDERNESS'?

Indigenous Second World War landscapes in Sápmi, Finnish Lapland

Oula Seitsonen and Gabriel Moshenska

> Maps are for tourists … [We] walk there to see.
>
> (a Sámi informant in Eanodat)

Introduction

Finnish Lapland lies on the northernmost shore of Europe by the Arctic Ocean. It is part of Sápmi, the transnational homeland of Europe's only indigenous people, the Sámi, stretching across parts of Norway, Sweden, Finland, and Russia (Figure 10.1). For outsiders, this barren arctic land can easily appear an empty and uninhabited northern wilderness. However, for the locals, it is an ancestral historical landscape and lifeworld imbued with centuries-old meanings and understandings. As Sámi academic Päivi Magga (2007a) has emphasized, Sámi landscapes are at the same time both natural and cultural, even if the cultural features are not immediately apparent to outsiders (see also Tervaniemi and Magga 2019). For the Sámi, people, animals, and inanimate entities coexist within the landscape in mutually reciprocal, respectful, and interconnected relationships (e.g. Helander 2000; Mazzullo and Ingold 2008). Parts of Sápmi have also been settled by Norwegian, Swedish, Finnish, and Russian settlers ever since the Early Modern Period, as part of an ongoing settler-colonialist process (see Helander 2000; Lehtola 2015; Ranta and Kanninen 2019). However, particularly in Finland, many of these settlers have adopted Sámi lifeways and environmental perceptions across the centuries in order to survive, such as reindeer herding, and there have been exchanges of cultural influences and intermarriage between Finns and Sámi (e.g. Ruotsala 2002: 385). Despite some recent encouraging developments, such as the ongoing repatriation of Sámi human remains and materials from museums and collections (Harlin 2019), the Sámi perspectives on landscape and heritage have often been neglected and erased by the dominant

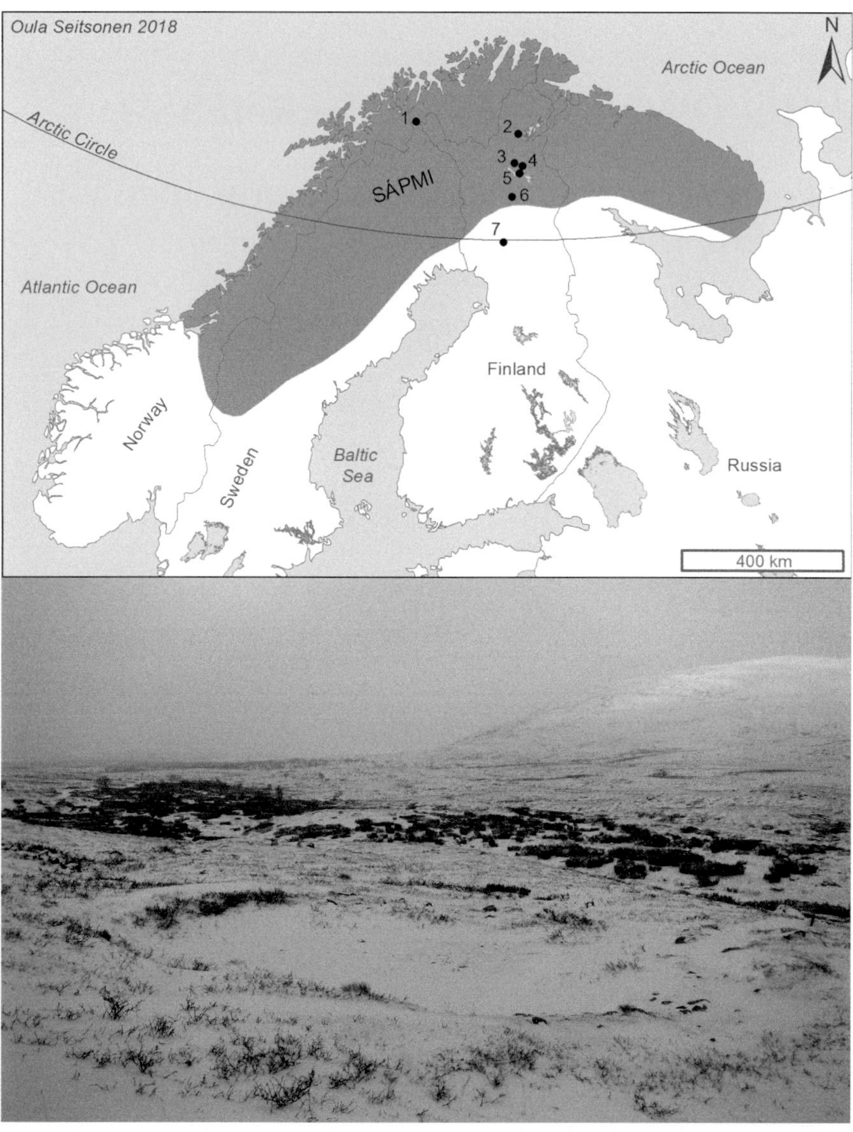

FIGURE 10.1 Top: map of Sápmi and the mentioned places: 1. Gilbbesjávri; 2. Anár; 3. Burdnomohkki; 4. Tankavaara; 5. Vuohčču; 6. Soađegilli; 7. Roavenjárga. Bottom: view over a German-run Second World War prisoner-of-war camp at Skirhasjohka, Gilbbesjávri, in mid-October; in the foreground is a prisoner tent placement. Source: map and photograph © O. Seitsonen.

(and biased) southern perceptions as part of an ongoing colonial process (Ranta and Kanninen 2019).

Over the past decade, Finnish cultural heritage professionals have started paying ever more attention to the material legacy of the Second World War (e.g. Fast 2017; Herva 2014; Seitsonen and Herva 2011), part of a global trend in the study of modern conflict (e.g. Myers and Moshenska 2011; Saunders 2004; Schofield 2009). In the northern half of Finland, the heritage of the wartime years was powerfully shaped by the heavy Nazi German presence, originally as Finland's co-belligerents in the fight against the Soviet Union in 1940–1944, and later as an enemy in 1944–1945. In these areas, the wartime histories and experiences, as well as their material remains, carry various kinds of meanings, closely intertwined with local and family histories (e.g. Koskinen-Koivisto and Seitsonen 2019; Seitsonen 2018; Seitsonen and Koskinen-Koivisto 2018). However, the Finnish national heritage discourse of the conflict has heavily marginalized and neglected the northern legacy, in large part due to the difficult and contested Nazi German heritage (e.g. Seitsonen and Herva 2011). The national-level lack of interest towards this heritage has also been coloured by its peripheral setting (from a dominant southern perspective) and an outsider's 'western gaze' (Bender 2002; Salmond 1992) that comprehends Lapland's landscape as an untouched wilderness.

In this chapter, we assess the Second World War German materialities and landscapes of the Arctic front and discuss how idiosyncratic northern environmental perceptions have affected, and continue to affect, the local views on this legacy. Firstly, we briefly present the Second World War history of Finnish Lapland and its material heritage. We focus on one prisoner of war (PoW) campsite as an example to which we tie various perspectives on Second World War memory and materiality. We then discuss the indigenous northern environmental perception and how it colours local understandings of the importance of wartime legacy. Finally, we explore questions of heritage ownership, custodianship, and the generation of transgenerational memories, drawing on the perspectives presented to us by Sámi interviewees[1] in different parts of Sápmi, mostly in the Anár (Inari) and Soađegilli (Sodankylä) areas but also in Gilbbesjávri, Eanodat (Kilpisjärvi, Enontekiö).[2] These provide a northern perspective on the ongoing international discussions on these broader themes of conflict heritage and landscapes of war (e.g. Gonzaléz-Ruibal 2008; Moshenska 2019; Saunders 2012) (Figure 10.1).

The Second World War on the Finnish Arctic front and its material traces

The German military presence in Finland was rooted in the Finnish Winter War of 1939–1940 against the Soviet Union. Finland suffered heavy territorial and other losses in the Winter War, and consequently joined forces with Nazi Germany. In the summer of 1940, the Finns allowed the German military to move into the northern half of the country as preparation for Hitler's attack on the Soviet Union, Operation Barbarossa (Kulju 2013; Mikkonen 2016).

When the Germans launched their attack in summer 1941 the Finns joined in, aiming to regain the lost territories and pursue a dream of 'Greater Finland' in the east (e.g. Kinnunen and Jokisipilä 2012). The fighting front in the northern half of the country was under German control. At the peak of their military build-up, there were over 200,000 German troops and about 30,000 prisoners and forced labourers from a variety of nations in the region, considerably outnumbering the local population in this thinly inhabited periphery (Kulju 2013; Westerlund 2008).

However, even the highly trained German Mountain Jaegers ('*Gebirgsjäger*') were ill-prepared for the difficult environmental conditions and poor infrastructure of the north, and there was little advance on the arctic front. Vast numbers of German troops and their prisoners were bogged down in projects on the poor and, in some places, non-existent infrastructure, such as building and improving roads, bridges, and railways. Most of this work was carried out using a PoW and forced/slave labourer workforce (e.g. Otto 2008; Westerlund 2008). The fates and material legacies of these marginalized groups have been especially neglected in heritage narratives through the post-war decades. The recent mapping of German-run PoW and work camps in northern Finland has revealed an astonishing number of sites, including nearly 200 camps (Seitsonen 2018: Appendix 1–2).

In September 1944 Finland was forced into a cease-fire treaty with the Soviet Union, after a major Soviet attack in the south. The terms of the treaty forced the Finns to drive their German allies out of the country on an unrealistic schedule. At first, the Finns and Germans worked together to evacuate civilians from the anticipated warzone, and then played mock war through September. However, under Soviet pressure, the half-hearted conflict turned hot and resulted in the so-called Lapland War between Finns and Germans. This resulted in widespread destruction of the northern half of the country by the retreating German troops, remembered widely as the 'Burning of Lapland' (e.g. Kulju 2013). Owing to this complex allies-cum-enemies and 'Lapland burners' relationship, as well as the post-war embarrassment of siding with the Nazis, Finno-German relations in the Second World War are still a rather difficult and sensitive issue in Finland (Herva 2014; Kivimäki 2012).

Ruins of thousands of overgrown German military sites can be found across Lapland's vast wilderness areas. Across the decades this difficult northern heritage has been mostly ignored and left alone. Owing to the continued national-level disregard towards it, any question of the cultural heritage value of this material legacy has been raised only recently and is still an open debate. Over the past decade an increasing amount of heritage-focused fieldwork has been directed to map this heritage, for instance, by the National Board of Forestry from 2010 to 2015, and by the large multidisciplinary project 'Lapland's Dark Heritage' based at the University of Helsinki (funded by the Academy of Finland 2014–2018; see

Koskinen-Koivisto and Thomas 2017). These mapping endeavours have been heavily influenced by local communities and local knowledge, since transgenerational memories have maintained the memory of sites through the decades, and remote sensing approaches have also been employed (LIDAR data and orthophotos, i.e. rectified aerial images; see Stichelbaut et al. this volume) (Figure 10.2).

The Burdnomohkki (Purnumukka) PoW camp shown in Figure 10.2 can serve as a starting point for exploring in more detail the material traces of the war and their connections to local long-term landscape perceptions. The physical

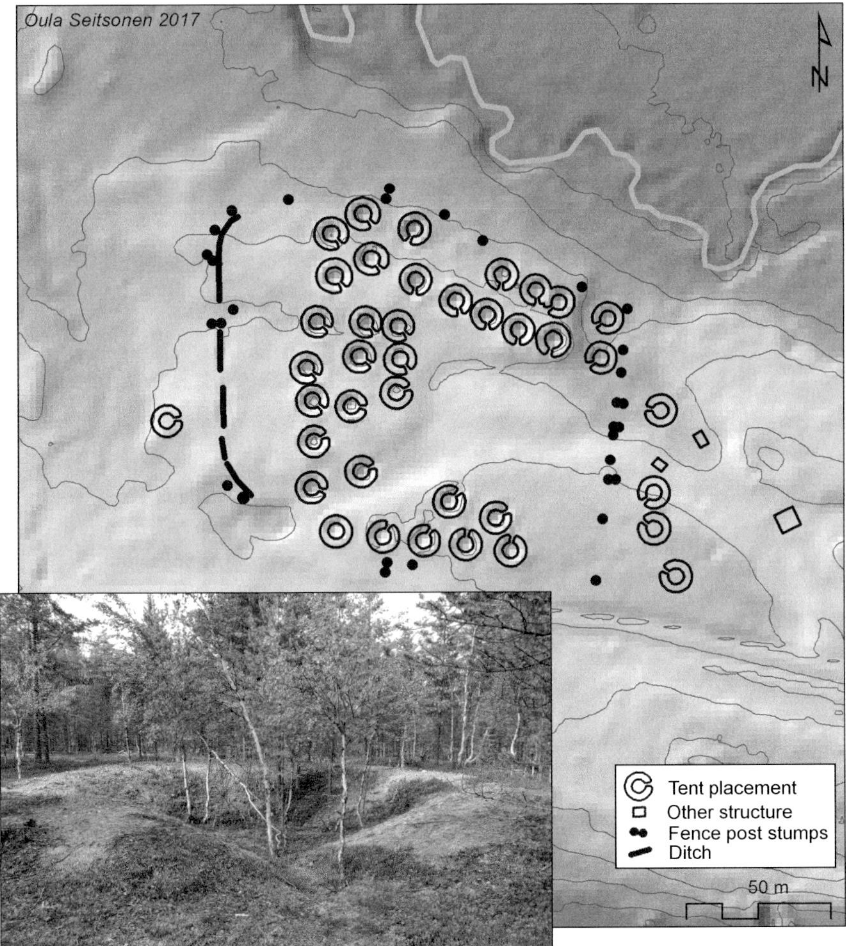

FIGURE 10.2 German-run Second World War PoW camp at Burdnomohkki, Soađegilli; background shows one-metre resolution LIDAR-based digital elevation model. Inset: a deeply dug prisoner tent placement. Source: map and photograph © O. Seitsonen; elevation model © and courtesy of Finnish Land Survey.

remains of this camp have always been known to the locals, despite their relative isolation, just as elsewhere in northern Finland people regularly use and encounter their surrounding landscapes during wilderness-based activities. The site is well-remembered in the transgenerational memories of the Sámi families that lived in the area before and during the war. However, it is little known to outsiders, and still not recognized by any Finnish heritage registers (despite our research and reports to the relevant authorities). The Burdnomohkki site is in fact one of the more regularly organized camps, with a clear internal division despite its 'organic' setting in the landscape and somewhat haphazard appearance on the map. Many of the PoW camps in the north do not exhibit any clear signs of camp architecture such as barbed-wire fences, but in contrast, this relatively large site had a double barbed-wire fence around it, highlighted by cut-down post stumps and ditches following its outline.

The deeply dug tent placements form a semi-circle with tent openings facing towards a central area, and the camp gates most likely located on the eastern edge next to one of the guard tents outside the fence. Guards' tents were not dug in the ground, and the entrenchment of PoW tents might have had a psychological effect, besides facilitating the visual dominance between the tents from outside the fence, with the prisoners descending into the 'bowels of the earth' when entering their accommodation (Seitsonen 2018: 88).[3] German guards' own accommodation was on the south side of the German-built road running next to the camp, with animal shelters next to the PoW camp. This clustering together of the animals and PoWs has been observed at several sites and might hint at the (conscious or subconscious) de-humanization of people categorized as lesser beings in the Nazi state's racist worldview (Seitsonen 2018: 112). The camp was burned down in 1944 during the German retreat and retains no standing structures apart from a few rotten barbed-wire entanglements on the eastern edge of the site. Besides the overgrown pit features, the site is marked nowadays by a scatter of surface finds, such as rusty tins and metal parts of plywood structures (see Seitsonen 2018: 64).

Many of the German sites in the north are even less well known than the Burdnomohkki camp (see Seitsonen 2018: 83–88) and reflect the considerable freedom that camp commanders apparently had in organizing their sites, scattered throughout the landscape. Often an uninformed passer-by walks past them without even noticing the sites, yet even some inconspicuous traces hold a place in local transgenerational memories. By contrast, at some places, heaps of German military material can still be found. Recently, a semi-official attempt was even made to 'clean' these remains from the landscape by a well-meaning but culturally ill-informed environmental organization. *Pidä Lappi siistinä* ('Keep Lapland Tidy') from Roavenjárga (Rovaniemi), the capital of Lapland, mounted a 'War Junk Project' in 2004–2010. This activity, strongly resisted and criticized by locals, was finally put on hold in agreement with the various heritage authorities, but not before over 100 tonnes of wartime material had been cleared from the landscape and sold as scrap metal (Seitsonen 2018: 118–123). Adopting an analogous standpoint, the Finnish media has frequently referred to German wartime remains as mere 'war junk', spoiling the 'pristine natural beauty of the Lapland wilderness'. But this statement rests on several questionable premises. Indeed, the media themselves reported the first author's recent research, which emphasized the heritage value of Second World War material (Seitsonen 2018), under headlines such as 'War junk left by Nazi troops on fjells evokes conflicting feelings – for Laplanders it is also cultural heritage' (Merimaa 2018). The notable disparities between the public perceptions of the 'pristine wilderness' and the values ascribed to wartime heritage by various stakeholders are one of the themes we explore in more detail below.

Northern 'wilderness': indigenous environmental perceptions and 'unseen' cultural environments

In the Sámi home region, no single, simple definition can be found for the English expression 'wilderness'. Neither the various Sámi languages (three Sámi languages are spoken in Finnish Lapland; Lehtola 2015: 23) nor the Finnish language has an exact equivalent to it. The Finnish word used for wilderness, '*erämaa*', is formed of the words '*erä*' (part) and '*maa*' (land), and means a section of land, literally a 'catchment area'. It has its roots in the hunter-gatherer past and emphasizes the importance and role of '*erämaa*' as a natural resource that belongs to someone based on the unwritten common law (Hallikainen 1998: 16–17; Länsman 2004: 99).

In Sámi languages the closest equivalent to wilderness is '*meahcci*', an area where natural resources are found but people do not live, yet it is intimately familiar to them and an integral part of people's seasonal activities (Länsman 2004: 99; Mazzullo and Ingold 2008; Schanche 2002; Tervaniemi and Magga 2019). It directly translates as 'forest' ('*metsä*' in Finnish), but '*meahcci*' does not need to have anything to do with any wooded expanse of land. Instead, it means a taskscape (Ingold 2000) that can be used to refer to, for example, reindeer herding on the open tundra or going fishing, which would then be described respectively as going to 'herding forest' and 'fishing forest' (Mazzullo and Ingold 2008). '*Meahcci*' thus always acquires its meaning in relation to the people encountering and using it (Mazzullo and Ingold 2008; Schanche 2002: 162–168). The opposite of '*meahcci*' is '*báiki*' ('place'), where seasonal or permanent dwellings and storage structures are situated (Länsman 2004; Mazzullo and Ingold 2008). '*Meahcci*' starts from where the built structures are no longer visible, although the borders between a 'place' and 'forest' are not fixed. The boundaries are blurred, fluid, and overlapping, and today's '*báiki*' can turn into '*meahcci*' tomorrow depending on the movement of people and their activities (Länsman 2004: 99). For example, the Burdnomohkki camp is within different '*meahcci*' taskscapes of locals residing some 20–30 kilometres away.

Movement and mobility are vital agents in the Sámi environmental perception. Landscape essentially unfolds and receives its meaning in the course of people's daily and annual mobility through it (Mazzullo and Ingold 2008). Movement along paths which diverge from a '*báiki*' tie the various landscape features into a tightly interwoven web of relations (Mazzullo and Ingold 2008). This tangle of interrelated pathways spreading through a landscape forms the extended home area for the Sámi, and '*meahcci*' used by people is as much part of their 'home' as the dwellings they live in at '*báiki*'. In the traditional, unwritten Sámi common law, family groups have the ancestral 'rights' ('*vuoigatvuohta*') to different '*meahcci*' taskscape and catchment areas extending from their '*báiki*' (Helander 2000; cf. the Finnish concept of '*erämaa*'). When we ask 'who owns the wilderness?' it is not only definitions of wilderness that we need to problematize, but also contested concepts of ownership, and particularly ownership of land.

Disregard for indigenous land claims is a hallmark of colonialism worldwide, just as the enclosure and theft of common lands in western Europe drove reactionary social change and the emergence of capitalism. In Sápmi, as in other colonized spaces, unwritten land rights embedded in practice and tradition leave communities vulnerable to expropriation, for example, by the capitalist system. This has surfaced recently in the intense debates surrounding Finnish-Norwegian-Chinese plans to build an 'Arctic Ocean Railroad' through the Sápmi from the coast, which would dissect the Sámi pasture lands and be disastrous to the culture. This has instigated active Sámi resistance and demonstrations against these plans under the slogan '*Eennâm lii eellim*' ('Land is life' in Anár Sámi language), for example in the village of Vuohčču (Vuotso) next to Burdnomohkki (Figure 10.3).

The traditional nomadic Sámi lifeways and land use did not necessarily leave any conspicuous marks in the landscape, which explains the fluidity of drawing boundaries between '*báiki*' and '*meahcci*'. In this sense the material remains of outsiders' activities, such as German Second World War sites or Finnish forestry camps, contrast strongly with the more subtle traces of locals' activities. The ancestors' campsites, herding structures, and pathways through the landscape are often practically 'unseen' by an outsider approaching the scenery with untrained eyes (see Seitsonen 2018: 155; Tervamäki and Magga 2019). Sámi heritage is thus at the same time material and immaterial – as fundamentally all heritage is (Smith 2006) – and cultural and natural. It lives on and gets its meaning through the transgenerational stories, songs ('*joik*'), and place names that tie together the past and the present and convey the ancestral legacy to the future. The northern landscapes attain their meaning, especially for the Sámi, subjectively, transgenerationally, and fluctuating in relation to people and their various spatio-temporal activities. Landscape perception depends thus on the context, perspective, and the activities that are carried out: through experiencing different phenomena, the places in landscape become meaningful for the experiencer (see Tuan 1977).

An important part of the Sámi worldview is a traditional cyclical concept of time, with eight seasons into which the rhythm of life is closely tied (Helander 2000; Mazzullo and Ingold 2008; Näkkäläjärvi 2000). Also, even today, the northern relational worldviews build strongly on an ancient animistic and

FIGURE 10.3 Demonstration against the 'Arctic Ocean railroad' at Vuohčču on 4 September 2018. The banderol says 'Our land, our future'. Source: © Jonne Sippola/Greenpeace.

shamanistic background, even if people (both insiders and outsiders) themselves are not aware of this (see Herva and Lahelma 2019). Sámi human–landscape relations have been described as reciprocal, and while people can affect their landscape through land use, the landscape can also affect people's self-understanding, identity, and legacy (Magga 2007b: 15; Schanche 1995). This worldview does not draw strict borders between the human and non-human or animate and inanimate realms but instead sees them all as part of the web of relations which forms the environment (e.g. Ingold 2000: 47). The all-encompassing environmental perception is illustrated, for example, by the deep embedding of wartime remains into the longer indigenous cultural continuum as observed in our fieldwork. Local peoples' cyclical, ancestral cosmology can explain some outwardly surprising chronological links made between the various temporalities through the wartime materialities. These include in particular the experiences of hauntings and ghosts that are commonly reported at wartime sites, offering an illustration of the 'porosity' of time and the active agency that material remains of the past still carry today. Thus, the past can affect the present through the medium of these material traces (Gonzaléz-Ruibal 2008; Herva 2014; Seitsonen 2018: 129).

To recapitulate, in the northern and specifically Sámi environmental awareness, any attempt at drawing a boundary between 'culture' and 'nature' or 'human' and 'non-human' is not meaningful, as has also been observed with other indigenous societies that live close to nature (e.g. Harrison 2015). There is essentially no equivalent to the English term 'wilderness' in either Finnish or Sámi languages (Länsman 2004: 98). Instead, in the Sámi perspective the landscape comes into being though people's corporeal everyday activities as they move through their familiar lands, which are part of their 'home', the extended '*meahcci*' activity area that spreads away from the dwellings situated at '*báiki*'. Locally, the landscape, the traces of human activity in it, and the ancestral stories together shape a fluid, embodied, and unified web of relations, a northern transgenerational, cognitively controlled lifeworld. The opening quote 'Maps are for tourists … [We] walk there to see' from a Sámi informant in Eanodat aptly describes many of the locals' corporeal, intimate, and physical active relationship with the landscape. Maps are often seen as distancing products of outside, uninformed instances that lack the vital connection with the land, and it is common for informants to describe places more often by relating their names and directions to them, instead of using maps.

Who owns the fjells and the forests?

Lapland's landscapes can appear to outsiders as uninhabited wilderness, as they did to the Germans during the war (see Seitsonen et al. 2019). However, for the locals, these very same settings are, due to the idiosyncratic northern perception of the environment, an intimately known, ancestral, embodied, and lived-in lifeworld loaded with meanings hidden from the outsiders. These hidden connotations can range from vast sacred landscapes, such as the sacred fjells, to the wide variety of meanings that are tied into the inconspicuous material remains of the Second World War. Our recent research on the perceptions of, and engagements with, the Second World War remains has illustrated how important these traces are to local people as part of the multi-layered historical landscape, and as material reminders of personal, familial, and communal pasts (e.g. Koskinen-Koivisto and Seitsonen 2019).

The significance of wartime remains on a local level became clear to us during our first excavations of a German camp in Anár in 2009 (Seitsonen and Herva 2011; Seitsonen et al. 2017), when the local media, and especially Sámi media, as well as history enthusiasts, took great interest in our pilot studies. This interest reflected opinions held by northerners in Finland regarding their past, which they feel has been side-lined and neglected by the southern authorities. Furthermore, the Sámi assert that their own particular histories have been subjected to even greater neglect at a national level (see Ranta and Kanninen 2019). As a result of the publicity following our first field studies, we received, in subsequent years, several invitations from locals across Lapland to visit and map the Second World War installations in their home areas. The villagers' hope was typically to receive some official recognition, and potentially protection, for what they perceived as their *own* local heritage situated on their *own* traditional lands and tied into the longer cultural continuity. Our work in Burdnomohkki started out with the locals contacting us and asking to map their heritage in order to protect it from National Board of Forestry land-use plans to cut down forest covering the Second World War ruins in the village. In this case, our joint efforts paid off, as the tree-felling plans were withdrawn following the heritage mapping. The sustained public interest also helped us to become involved in developing community and public archaeologies as new approaches to Lapland's wartime heritage, in 2016–2017 in Anár (Banks et al. 2018) and since 2019 in Gilbbesjávri (Stichelbaut et al. this volume).

The locals often express a strong sense of ownership and custodianship towards the German wartime sites and material remains, their 'own heritage'. From their point of view, these sites have acted, and continue to act, as witnesses to the local and family past(s), and have become an integral, embedded element of their long-term northern cultural landscape. The personal and often hidden memories that are tied to specific discreet traces in the landscape, or even memories of such traces, often surface in deeper discussions with locals. One example is recollections of a 'hanging pine' that used to stand in the corner of the Burdnomohkki PoW camp, which has been brought up by several locals. Some of our informants witnessed, as children, prisoners being hanged, whipped, and ill-treated there. Others learned about these atrocities through transgenerational stories keeping these memories alive. These violent images evidently left a stark recollection in the local memoryscape, which lives on even after the tree itself is gone. After the war, the tree became the scene of place-bound memorial acts, such as stopping and touching the tree when passing by, some continuing to stop at the place even after the tree had fallen. It is also said that somebody had carved a hammer and sickle on the tree, apparently to memorialize the sufferings of Soviet prisoners (Seitsonen 2018: 147).

Other hidden but locally important sites of memory nearby include a shallow overgrown pit east of the camp, where a local man, Piera Hetta, our informant's relative, stepped on a German landmine and died after the war (Seitsonen and Koskinen-Koivisto 2018), and a collapsed German dugout that was used by a local family as a residence during the post-war reconstruction period. These are also illustrated in the village history information boards erected at Burdnomohkki by a culturally active local reindeer herder-poet (funded by the European Union; Figure 10.4). However, these information boards are not signposted in any way from the main road, so one must know about their existence to visit them at the end of the small side road leading to the village.

Owing to the close familial and personal connections in these areas, the visible traces of war act as important agents of the transgenerational communal memories of the war, the German presence, and a host of other issues. The connotations that the German remains evoke in people's minds range from pre-war incidents (even from the 1800s) to modern political struggles, such as questions around Sámi rights (Seitsonen and Koskinen-Koivisto 2018). One theme that caught us by surprise was the common connection that many of our informants made between the wartime remains and the memories of Sámi families being 'employed' at fairs and zoos in southern Finland and abroad in the early 1900s.

FIGURE 10.4 The village history information boards at Burdnomohkki. Source: © O. Seitsonen.

An elderly Sámi lady at Vuohčču told us that seeing foreigners, electric light, and other novelties that came with the Germans did not have the same impact on her as on other villagers, as her family had been 'exhibited' in southern Finland and Germany before the war (Seitsonen and Koskinen-Koivisto 2018). Exhibiting Sámi families, their dwellings, herding dogs, and reindeer at fairs, zoos, and other places (e.g. Kivekäs 2015; Lehtola 2009) was part of the widespread phenomenon of the display of indigenous and non-white people as natural history 'specimens' in the west, a practice that endured into the twentieth century, and which was closely linked to the racial theories of the period (Andreassen 2015:9–11; McKay and Memmott 2016).

These memories of exhibitions are a powerful reflection of Lapland's long colonial past, its real or perceived marginalization by the southern authorities, and the enduring north–south confrontations in Finland (Lehtola 2015; Ranta and Kanninen 2019). The material traces of outsiders' activities are closely intertwined with a host of contemporary and historic issues in the landscapes, such as land-use rights and land ownership. These often cause tension in the North, with debates centring around, for example, the competing land-use demands of traditional reindeer herding and tourism, or plans imposed from outside such as the planned Arctic Ocean railroad.

The northern perspectives contrast clearly and notably with the established (southern) Finnish national narratives of the Second World War in the north, which typically emphasize the destruction following the Lapland War as the definitive aspect of the German presence (Seitsonen and Herva 2017). This emphasis on the devastation brought by the Germans also allowed Finland to present itself as a victim of Nazi aggression in the post-war years, rather than as a Nazi ally. At the same time, the powerful imagery of destruction and fire in Lapland has overridden on a national level the more subtle, multi-vocal, and marginalized subaltern indigenous voices (Seitsonen and Koskinen-Koivisto 2018).

The different local and outsider perspectives also promote differing attitudes towards, and engagements with, the material remains. This is represented, for instance, by the outsiders, typically from the south or even from abroad, who are involved in various alternative engagements with wartime heritage, such as metal detecting and memorabilia collecting (Thomas et al. 2016). Metal detectorists are commonly observed by locals at the Second World War sites. Many of these locals resent the removal of things from their 'own lands' and would prefer to see that they are 'left to be' where they have been resting for 70–80 years, 'where they belong' and 'witnessed' what happened, as one of the elders we interviewed described it. This illustrates how important the landscape setting is to the locals for creating and maintaining the meaning and importance of the past material remains (see Skandfer 2009). This emphasis on maintaining the landscape connection of the individual finds and structures to preserve their significance also explains the strong resistance that the 'War Junk Project' encountered in Sápmi. Despite its good intentions, the project was seen by the locals as an ignorant and careless eradication of their 'own history' from their 'own lands' by the 'southern' '*Pidä Lappi siistinä*' organization. This organization actually hails from Roavenjárga on the Arctic Circle, showing that for locals the 'south' is not so much a geographical entity or place, but something mentally opposed to, and potentially threatening to the 'north' and northern lifeways – an outgrowth of the region's long colonial history (see Ruotsala 2002: 18, 370; Seitsonen 2018: 149). Vuohčču and the neighbouring Tankavaara area were some of the first targets of these clearing activities, but Burdnomohkki escaped their attentions owing to its more remote location away from the main road to the north.

Roads have also attracted other kinds of potentially unwanted attention to the Second World War sites. One can find metal detectorists' pits and 'excavations' at almost all German camps situated within 4–5 kilometres of roads in Eastern and Northern Lapland. For example, at Burdnomohkki you can find pits and 'sorting stations', piles of leftover material scattered by the militaria collectors (see Herva et al. 2016). This contrasts with the Gilbbesjávri region in Northwestern Lapland, where we have so far located only one site showing digging by detectorists (Figure 10.5; see Stichelbaut et al. this volume). We do not know the reasons for this difference, but it might have to do with generally fewer people visiting and living in the extreme northwestern corner of Finland. Finnish metal detectorists know that they operate in a grey zone, since even if the Second World War sites are not protected as 'ancient monuments' (as, for example, First World War sites are in Finland), the National Board of Forestry, which is the biggest landowner in the north has forbidden metal detecting and collecting of memorabilia on their lands (Seitsonen 2018: 66). Despite this, detectorist finds

FIGURE 10.5 The only site with signs of metal detectorist activity so far located at Gilbbesjávri. Source: © O. Seitsonen.

can be found for sale at second-hand stores (in Roavenjárga, for example) and on internet forums, such as closed Facebook groups and metal detectorist discussion boards (Seitsonen 2018: 142; Thomas et al. 2016).

Conclusion

Our recent studies of German Second World War materialities in Lapland have demonstrated their importance as local heritage, as well as the complexity and multivocality of these local perceptions. These contrast notably and powerfully with the established national narratives that emphasize the 'Burning of Lapland' by the Germans in 1944. During our archaeological and ethnographic inquiries, it has become clear how important wartime material traces are for the local Sámi and Northern Finns. Local people often express a strong sense of heritage ownership and custodianship towards the material remains situated on their own ancestral lands. For them, the traces of war act as active agents of the transgenerational communal memories of war, destruction, and a host of other issues, all of them closely intertwined with pressing contemporary questions. These mirror Lapland's long colonial history, its mythification and marginalization – real or perceived – by the southern authorities, as well as the ongoing north–south confrontations, which surface especially concerning land ownership and use rights.

It appears that there are differences in how 'dark' the wartime remains in Lapland appear to different people based on their degree of familiarity with this heritage. People with personal ties or interests typically see the wartime remains in 'lighter' shades. For them, the sites and materialities communicate a variety of locally important issues, rather than solely the German presence and grievous war histories. On the other hand, for 'outsiders' with no relation to, or information about, the sites, they show up more easily as 'dark', threatening and haunting traces of an anonymous past, typically mirrored against the internationally replicated narratives of 'evil Nazis' (Herva 2014; Herva et al. 2016). This is an important corrective to scholarly narratives of 'dark' heritage that, while mostly and correctly taking a social constructivist approach to the 'dark' part, more commonly locate its truest or most representative form in the perspectives of local and historically most-affected communities.

Deep down, these contradictory attitudes towards the German ruins seem to correlate with the differing cosmologies and differing landscape perceptions of the different stakeholder groups. The 'insider', traditional, and indigenous Northern Finnish and Sámi environmental awareness is based on a relational ontology, on an embodied and cognitively controlled web of relations that does not try to separate 'culture' and 'nature'. In contrast, the 'outsider' perspectives present the more 'western' ontology of southerners, which approaches the landscape from the standpoint of a nature–culture split. This is particularly salient to the construction of concepts such as 'wilderness', and our understanding of so-called 'wildernesses' both in our understanding of Second World War history in the north and in approaches to the management of its heritage.

In studies of contested heritage, 'Who owns ...?' questions are as much about the authorship of historical narratives as they are about the ownership and control of spaces and materials. Most often, as in the case of German remains in Sápmi, the two are closely intertwined, with divergent perceptions of space, nature, and the value of conflict heritage both feeding and reflecting divergent narratives of war memory. These different perceptions connect closely with a host of wider issues, for instance, the continuing north–south dichotomies, land ownership questions, the so-called Sámi dispute, and Lapland's long and little-discussed colonial legacy. In a way, the highlighting of the local importance of German Second World War material heritage makes sense as a kind of indigenous reaction against the long-prevailing southern dominance and colonialism.

We would like to emphasize the importance of taking the locals and their indigenous perspectives into account in the study of conflict sites and landscapes. They have many roles, which in Lapland intertwine with myriad issues related to traditional land ownership and land-use rights. In Sápmi, the locals often see that their interests and interpretations are opposing the dominant southern perspectives, which are often seen as potential threats to the enduring northern lifeways and traditions. It might well be asserted, albeit from an unwritten, common law perspective, that these fjells, lakes, and forests are 'owned' as ancestral lands by the Sámi who, by the same token, are owners of the wartime material heritage embedded into their timeless cultural landscape.

Acknowledgements

Authors wish to thank the anonymous referees for their comments on an earlier draft and to express our gratitude to Áile Aikio, Iain Banks, Mirkka Hekkurainen, Vesa-Pekka Herva, Eerika Koskinen-Koivisto, Sanna, Sohvi, Elsa and Elvi Seitsonen, Suzie Thomas, and Wesa Perttola for taking part in fieldwork in different parts of Sápmi over the last decade and for discussions archaeological and beyond.

Notes

1 Altogether the project 'Lapland's Dark Heritage' has carried out over 40 thematic interviews in 2009–2019 with people related to the wartime heritage in Finnish parts of Sápmi.
2 Northern Sámi names are used, Finnish name in parenthesis.
3 This follows a pattern observed elsewhere on the Eastern Front where, due to the failure of their captors to provide shelter, Soviet and other PoWs in occupied areas, such as Norway and even in camps in Germany, were forced to dig holes in the ground, roughly covered, for example, with logs and cloth, to sleep in. Tents were a necessary addition in the arctic conditions to preserve the prisoners' health and thus their viability as a workforce – in this case for fortifying *Schutzwall-Stellung* at Tankavaara.

References

Andreassen, R. (2015) *Human Exhibitions: Race, Gender and Sexuality in Ethnic Displays.* London: Routledge.

Banks, I., E. Koskinen-Koivisto and O. Seitsonen. (2018) Public Engagements with Lapland's Dark Heritage: Community Archaeology in Finnish Lapland. *Journal of Community Archaeology and Heritage* 5 (2): 128–137.

Bender, B. (2002) Time and Landscape. *Current Anthropology* 43: 103–102.

Fast, J. (2017) German Transit Camp at Tulliniemi, Hanko 1942–1944. In J. Kaila and J. Knuutila (eds.), *Poetic Archaeology/Inside and Beside the Camp*, pp. 34–41. Helsinki: Academy of Fine Arts.

González-Ruibal, A. (2008) Time to Destroy: An Archaeology of Supermodernity. *Current Anthropology* 49 (2): 247–279.

Hallikainen, V. (1998) *The Finnish wilderness experience. Metsäntutkimuslaitoksen tiedonantoja 711.* Helsinki: Metla.

Harlin, E.-K. (2019) Sámi Archaeology and the Fear of Political Involvement: Finnish Archaeologists' Perspectives on Ethnicity and the Repatriation of Sámi Cultural Heritage. *Archaeologies* 15 (2): 254–284.

Harrison, R. (2015) Beyond 'Natural' and 'Cultural' Heritage: Toward an Ontological Politics of Heritage in the Age of Anthropocene. *Heritage and Society* 8 (1): 24–42.

Helander, E. (2000) Saamelainen maailmankuva ja luontosuhde. In I. Seurujärvi-Kari (ed.), *Beaivvi mánát. Saamelaisten juuret ja nykyaika. Tietolipas 164*, pp. 171–182. Helsinki: Suomalaisen Kirjallisuuden Seura.

Herva, V.-P. (2014) Haunting Heritage in an Enchanted Land: Magic, Materiality and Second World War German Material Heritage in Finnish Lapland. *Journal of Contemporary Archaeology* 1 (2): 297–321.

Herva, V.-P. and A. Lahelma (2019) *Northern Archaeology and Cosmology. A Relational View*. Abingdon: Routledge.

Herva, V.-P., E. Koskinen-Koivisto, O. Seitsonen and S. Thomas (2016) 'I Have Better Stuff at Home': Treasure Hunting and Private Collecting of World War II Artefacts in Finnish Lapland. *World Archaeology* 48 (2): 267–281.

Ingold, T. (2000) *The Perception of the Environment: Essays on Livelihood, Dwelling and Skill*. London: Routledge.

Kinnunen, T. and M. Jokisipilä (2012) Shifting Images of 'Our' Wars: Finnish Memory Culture of World War II. In T. Kinnunen and V. Kivimäki (eds.), *Finland in War II: History, Memory, Interpretations*, pp. 435–482. Leiden: Brill.

Kivekäs, J. (2015) *Lapista Saksaan. Lapinihmisiä Saksassa 1800 ja 1900-lukujen vaihteessag*. Helsinki: BoD.

Kivimäki, V. (2012) Between Defeat and Victory: Finnish Memory Culture of the Second World War. *Scandinavian Journal of History* 37 (4): 482–504.

Koskinen-Koivisto, E. and O. Seitsonen (2019) Landscapes of Loss and Destruction: Sámi Elders' Childhood Memories of the Second World War. *Ethnologia Europaea* 49 (1): 24–40.

Koskinen-Koivisto, E. and S. Thomas (2017) Lapland's Dark Heritage: Responses to the Legacy of World War II. In H. Silverman, E. Waterton and S. Watson (eds.), *Heritage in Action: Making the Past in the Present*, pp. 121–133. New York: Springer.

Kulju, M. (2013) *Lapin sota 1944–1945*. Helsinki: Gummerus.

Länsman, A.-S. (2004) *Väärtisuhteet Lapin matkailussa Kulttuurianalyysi suomalaisten ja saamelaisten kohtaamisesta*. Inari: Kustannus-Puntsi.

Lehtola, V.-P. (2009) Lappalaiskaravaanit harhateillä, kulttuurilähettiläät kiertueella? Saamelaiset Euroopan näyttämöillä ja eläintarhoissa. *Faravid* 2009: 321–346.

——— (2015) *Saamelaiskiista: sortaako Suomi alkuperäiskansaansa?* Helsinki: Into.

Magga, P. (2007a). Rakennuksia, kotasijoja, muistoja – saamelaista kulttuuriympäristöä inventoimassa. In T. Elo and P. Magga (eds.), *Eletty, koettu maisema: näkökulmia saamelaiseen kulttuurimaisemaan. Suomen ympäristö 34*, pp. 11–24. Rovaniemi: Lapin ympäristökeskus.

——— (2007b). Birrasis. Lapin kulttuuriympäristöt tutuksi – hankkeen SAAMELAISOSION LOPPURAPORTTI. Publication of Giellagas Institute 7. Vaajakoski: Giellagas Institute.

Mazzullo, N. and T. Ingold (2008) Being Along: Place, Time and Movement among Sámi People. In J.O. Baerenholdt and B. Granaas (eds.), *Mobility and Place. Enacting Northern European Peripheries*, pp. 27–38. Aldershot: Ashgate.

McKay, J. and P. Memmott (2016) Staged Savagery: Archibald Meston and His Indigenous Exhibits. *Aboriginal History* 40: 181–203.

Merimaa, J. (2018) Natsijoukkojen tunturiin jättämä sotaromu herättää ristiriitaisia tunteita – lappilaisille se on myös kulttuuriperintöä. *Helsingin Sanomat*, 2 March, www.hs.fi/tiede/art-2000005587168.html (Accessed 16 October 2018).

Mikkonen, K. (2016) *Parakkeja ja piikkilankaa*. Rovaniemi: Lapin maakuntamuseo.

Moshenska, G. (2019) *Material Cultures of Childhood in Second World War Britain*. Abingdon: Routledge.

Myers, A. and G. Moshenska. (2011) *Archaeologies of Internment*. New York: Springer.

Näkkäläjärvi, K. (2000) Porosaamelaisten luonnonympäristö. In I. Seurujärvi-Kari (ed.), Beaivvi mánát. Saamelaisten juuret ja nykyaika. Tietolipas 164, pp. 143–165. Helsinki: Suomalaisen Kirjallisuuden Seura.

Otto, R. (2008) Soviet Prisoners of War on the German Lapland Front, 1941–1944. In L. Westerlund (ed.), Sotavangit ja internoidut. Kansallisarkiston artikkelikirja. Prisoners of War and Internees. A Book of Articles by the *National Archives*, pp. 64–113. Helsinki: Kansallisarkisto.

Ranta, K. and J. Kanninen. (2019) *Vastatuuleen. Saamen kansan pakkosuomalaistamisesta.* Helsinki: S and S.

Ruotsala, H. (2002) *Muuttuvat palkiset. Elo, työ ja ympäristö Kittilän Kyrön paliskunnassa ja Kuolan Luujärven poronhoitokollektiiveissa vuosina 1930–1995. Kansatieteellinen Arkisto 49.* Helsinki: Suomen muinaismuistoyhdistys.

Salmond, A. (1992) Theoretical Landscapes: On Cross-Cultural Conceptions of Knowledge. In D. Parkin (ed.), *Semantic Anthropology*, pp. 65–87. London: Academic Press.

Saunders, N.J. (ed.) (2004) *Matters of Conflict: Material Culture, Memory and the First World War.* Abingdon: Routledge.

——— (ed.) (2012). *Beyond the Dead Horizon: Studies in Modern Conflict Archaeology.* Oxbow: Oxford.

Schanche, A. (1995) Det symbolske landskapet. Landskap og identitet i samisk kultur. *Ottar* 4: 38–47.

——— (2002) Meahcci – den samiske utmark. *Dieđut* 1: 156–171.

Schofield, J. (2009) *Aftermath. Readings in the Archaeology of Recent Conflict.* New York: Springer.

Seitsonen, O. (2018) *Digging Hitler's Arctic War: Archaeologies and Heritage of the Second World War German Military Presence in Finnish Lapland.* Helsinki: Unigrafia.

Seitsonen, O. and V.-P. Herva (2011) Forgotten in the Wilderness: WWII PoW Camps in Finnish Lapland. In A. Myers and G. Moshenska (eds), *Archaeologies of Internment*, pp. 171–180. New York: Springer.

——— (2017) 'War Junk' and Cultural Heritage: Viewpoints on the Second World War German Material Culture in Finnish Lapland. In A.K. Benfer (ed.), *War and Peace: Conflict and Resolution in Archaeology. Proceedings of the 45th Annual Chacmool Archaeology Conference*, pp. 170–185. Calgary: Chacmool Archaeology Association. https://prism.ucalgary.ca/handle/1880/52231

Seitsonen, O. and E. Koskinen-Koivisto (2018) 'Where the F… is Vuotso?': Heritage of Second World War Forced Movement and Destruction in a Sámi Reindeer Herding Community in Finnish Lapland. *International Journal of Heritage Studies* 24 (4): 421–441.

Seitsonen, O., V.-P. Herva, K. Nordqvist, A. Herva and S. Seitsonen (2017) A Military Camp in the Middle of Nowhere: Mobilities, Dislocation and the Archaeology of a Second World War German Military Base in Finnish Lapland. *Journal of Conflict Archaeology* 12 (1): 3–28.

Seitsonen, O., V.-P. Herva and T. Koponen (2019) 'Lapland's Roadway': German Photography and Experience of the European Far North in the Second World War. *Photography and Culture* 12 (1): 5–24.

Skandfer, M. (2009) Ethics in the Landscape: Prehistoric Archaeology and Local Sámi Knowledge in Interior Finnmark, Northern Norway. *Arctic Anthropology* 46 (1–2): 89–102.

Smith, L. (2006) *Uses of Heritage.* New York: Routledge.

Tervaniemi, S.E. and P. Magga (2019) Belonging to Sápmi: The Sámi Conceptions of Home and Home Region. In T.H. Eriksen, S. Valkonen and J. Valkonen (eds.), *Knowing from the Indigenous North: Sámi Approaches to History, Politics and Belonging*, pp. 75–90. Abingdon: Routledge.

Thomas, S., O. Seitsonen and V.-P. Herva (2016) Nazi Memorabilia, Dark Heritage and Treasure Hunting as 'alternative' Tourism: Understanding the Fascination with the Material Remains of World War II in Northern Finland. *Journal of Field Archaeology* 41 (3): 331–343.

Tuan, Y.-F. (1977) *Space and Place. The Perspective of Experience.* Minneapolis: University of Minnesota Press.

Westerlund, L. (2008) *Saksan Vankileirit Suomessa ja raja-alueilla 1941–1944.* Helsinki: Tammi.

11

OPERATION NORTHERN LIGHT

Remote sensing a Second World War conflict landscape in northern Finland

Birger Stichelbaut, Suzie Thomas, Oula Seitsonen, Wouter Gheyle, Guy De Mulder, Ville Hemminki, and Gertjan Plets

Introduction

The archaeological study of twentieth-century conflict landscapes emerged as a new field of research from the beginning of the twenty-first century (Dobinson et al. 1997; Freeman et al. 2001; Saunders 2007, 2012; Schofield et al., 2002). Initially, the majority of the research was carried out in the UK and followed the tradition of battlefield archaeology (e.g. Douglas et al. 2011). In addition, the temporal proximity of the Second World War in particular (and until relatively recently also the First World War) has allowed archaeologists to integrate ethnographic approaches to the study of memory and heritage-making (Camp 2016; Moshenska 2010).

Almost in parallel with these developments, there were also major advances in the fields of archaeological aerial photography and prospection. During both World Wars, literally tens of millions of aerial photographs were taken as a source of military intelligence. These collections were rediscovered and large digitization programs have made them available for research (Cowley et al. 2013; Cowley et al. 2012; Going 2002, 2009).

Thanks to the simultaneity between the historical remote sensing datasets and the holistic overview perspective they offer, historical aerial photographs present themselves as a privileged source for the study and reconstruction of historical warscapes. Their analysis provides an unprecedented insight into the diversity and spatial distribution of sites present at the time the aerial photographs were taken. The application of this historical aerial archaeology approach to the conflict landscapes of the First and Second World Wars (Hegarty et al. 2007; Hegarty et al. 2005; Passmore et al. 2008; Passmore et al. 2014; Pollard et al. 2013; Reeves et al. 2016; Stichelbaut et al. 2017b; Van Hollebeeke et al. 2016) has revealed an important benefit of this methodology: its non-discriminatory nature in mapping all visible features. This is especially important when analyzing a type of heritage that is influenced by memory politics and historical canonizations, which have over time produced a selective memoryscape (Macdonald 2013) where certain sites are actively remembered while more uncomfortable places tend to become forgotten or ignored.

In addition to developing a detailed historical reconstruction, new remote sensing techniques enable archaeologists to study the preservation of these features in the present-day landscape. Especially airborne laser scanning (ALS or LiDAR [light image ranging and detection]), an optical sensing technology which uses the measurement of reflected laser pulses to create high-resolution digital elevations of the earth's surface, have experienced unprecedented growth in archaeological applications (Hesse 2010). Its high resolution enables the detection of a wide range of subtly preserved surface features. Just as with historical aerial photography, the vertical perspective and scale of the data have ensured a shift from a site-directed approach to landscape-scale research in conflict archaeology (Gheyle et al. 2018; Hesse 2014).

Large parts of northern Finland have significant quantities of war matériel but conflict archaeology in this Arctic region is a relatively new field of study. As a consequence, conflict sites connected to the two World Wars possess only a limited cultural heritage status (Seitsonen 2017: 116–117; Seitsonen and Herva 2017). Combining archaeological methods with anthropological, ethnographic, and other approaches, the recent 'Lapland's Dark Heritage' was the first wider university-led research project to offer a multidisciplinary approach to the material legacy of the Second World War in Finnish Lapland (e.g. Seitsonen and Koskinen 2018; Thomas 2019). Recently, some initiatives have taken place alongside 'Lapland's Dark Heritage' to map the range of Finland's wartime remains. In 2010–2015, the Finnish National Board of Forestry mapped all heritage sites, including those of the Second World War, found within their forest regions, partly directed by LiDAR data (Koivisto and Laulumaa 2013). Historian Kalevi Mikkonen has mapped the wartime remains around the city of Rovaniemi (Mikkonen 2016), and in 2018–2019 an intensive field-mapping project was carried out by war history enthusiasts at the *Sturmbock-Stellung* south of Kilpisjärvi, also based on LiDAR data (Sillanpää et al. 2019). Outside Lapland, remains of a German transit camp have been studied in Hanko, in southern Finland (Fast 2017).

Most of these studies have been site-oriented, and in Lapland they are time-consuming due to the rugged nature of the terrain. So far, the research has focused mostly on the identification of individual sites – mainly prisoner of war (PoW) camps (Seitsonen et al. 2011) and German military bases (Seitsonen et al. 2017) – through survey campaigns based on leads given by local informants and an online public crowdsourcing initiative (Seitsonen 2018). Although remote sensing methods have been used to identify numerous sites (such as LiDAR data and orthophotos; see Seitsonen and Moshenska this volume), a systematic landscape-wide mapping approach has not yet been applied (but see Sillanpää et al. 2019). The identification and mapping of sites and gaining an understanding of the diversity, density, distribution, range, and preservation of preserved archaeological surface remains are of primary importance in this national heritage context (Seitsonen 2018: 62). They will provide a robust basis for data-informed discussions on the importance, preservation, and protection of this currently overlooked and often-ignored heritage.

This chapter presents the results of an interdisciplinary investigation of a Second World War conflict landscape in northern Finland. During the Finnish–German Lapland War (1944–1945) the German Army retreated towards Norway and made use of extensive defensive positions in northern Finland. This pilot project builds on extensive experience with First World War (Gheyle et al. 2018; Stichelbaut et al. 2017) and Second World War conflict heritage (Reeves et al. 2016; Van Hollebeeke et al. 2016) using both archival and open-data remote sensing datasets. The setup and methodology of the project are designed to meet the challenges of cost-effective mapping of the remote wilderness area in Finland.

The specific goals are: (i) to assess the potential of using wartime historical aerial photographs and (ii) LiDAR to study German field fortifications and military infrastructure in a novel research area in the Arctic; (iii) to gain an insight into the diversity, density, and distribution of Second World War heritage; (iv) to redirect archaeological research of Second World War material heritage in Finland away from a site-directed approach to a landscape scale of research; and (v) to evaluate how this systematically collected data can be used for heritage management and memory research.

Research area and historical setting

The research area is located near the small settlement of Kilpisjärvi (*Gilbbesjávri* in Northern Sámi) in the Kilpisjärvi region of Enontekiö, Lapland, on the north-western tip of Finland. It is on the border between Sweden and Norway. The area is part of the Northern Wilderness of Finland and is located 275 kilometres above the Arctic Circle, with an altitude ranging from 272 to 1,330 metres. The landscape consists of closed taiga and open tundra and there is a subarctic climate with long, very cold winters and short, mild summers.

During the Continuation War (1941–1944) Finland and Nazi Germany co-operated in northern Finland in the war against the Soviet Union. Finland had lost over 10% of its landmass in the Winter War of 1939–1940 to the Soviet Union, and joined in Hitler's attack to gain back the lost territories and to conquer a 'Greater Finland'. However, the Germans were unprepared for the poor northern infrastructure and harsh environment, and they struggled to make any significant advance. Consequently, a lot of German troops, along with a workforce of Soviet prisoners of war and other forced labourers, were deployed to improve the local infrastructure, such as building a road from Kilpisjärvi to Palojoensuu,

150 kilometres to the south-east, and connecting it to the Norwegian coast to facilitate a supply chain from the port of Skibotn.

A large number of German troops settled in the Kilpisjärvi region in 1942 due to the road-building and the planning of defensive lines. There was no village in Kilpisjärvi at that time; only two families lived there, and migrating Sámi seasonally herded their reindeer in the region. The Germans established several PoW camps in the area to accommodate the workers needed for road and fortification building. In September 1944, following a massive Soviet attack in the south, Finland made a ceasefire treaty with the Soviet Union. This treaty demanded that the Finns expel German troops from their country. At first, Finns and Germans, as former comrades-in-arms, evacuated the civilians from the anticipated warzone and engaged in a mock fight. However, increasing Soviet pressure forced Finland to attack the Germans who were retreating northwards to occupied Norway. In response, the Germans employed scorched earth tactics to slow down the pursuing Finnish troops.

In late October 1944, the Germans retreated in Western Lapland along the Swedish border to prepared positions at the *Sturmbock-Stellung* approximately 90 kilometres south of Kilpisjärvi, as part of their Operation *Birke* (Birch) (Kulju 2017: 146). The situation remained at a standstill until January 1945 when the Germans started retreating to the prepared positions of the *Lyngen-Stellung*, extending from the Lyngen Fjord in Norway to Kilpisjärvi, as part of the Operation *Nordlicht* (Northern Light) (Kulju 2017: 146). The last German troops left Kilpisjärvi for Norway on 27 April 1945 (Seitsonen 2018: 153) (Figure 11.1).

Historical aerial photographs

Historical aerial photographs are a rich and textured source of Europe's past (Cowley et al. 2012). From the First World War onwards, aerial photography quickly developed as a successful military intelligence method. Throughout all twentieth-century conflicts, aerial photography has played an important role in military intelligence and cartography. The resulting photographs have long been forgotten in archives but are now being rediscovered by archaeologists, geographers, and historians as a primary source (Stichelbaut et al. 2016). Because of the military context during which they have been taken they offer a privileged insight into conflict landscapes.

Extensive archives of Allied and German Second World War imagery are preserved in the two main global collections of historical aerial photographs at the National Collection of Aerial Photographs in Edinburgh (NCAP) and the US National Archives in Washington, DC (NARA) (Cowley et al. 2012; Going 2002; NARA 2008) as well as in smaller and more dispersed national collections in different countries. Targeted archival research revealed such a collection in the National Archives of Finland in Helsinki. Additional aerial coverage of the northwestern 'arm' of Finland is also held in the Finnish Military Archive (but is currently inaccessible due to security restrictions) and in NARA and NCAP.

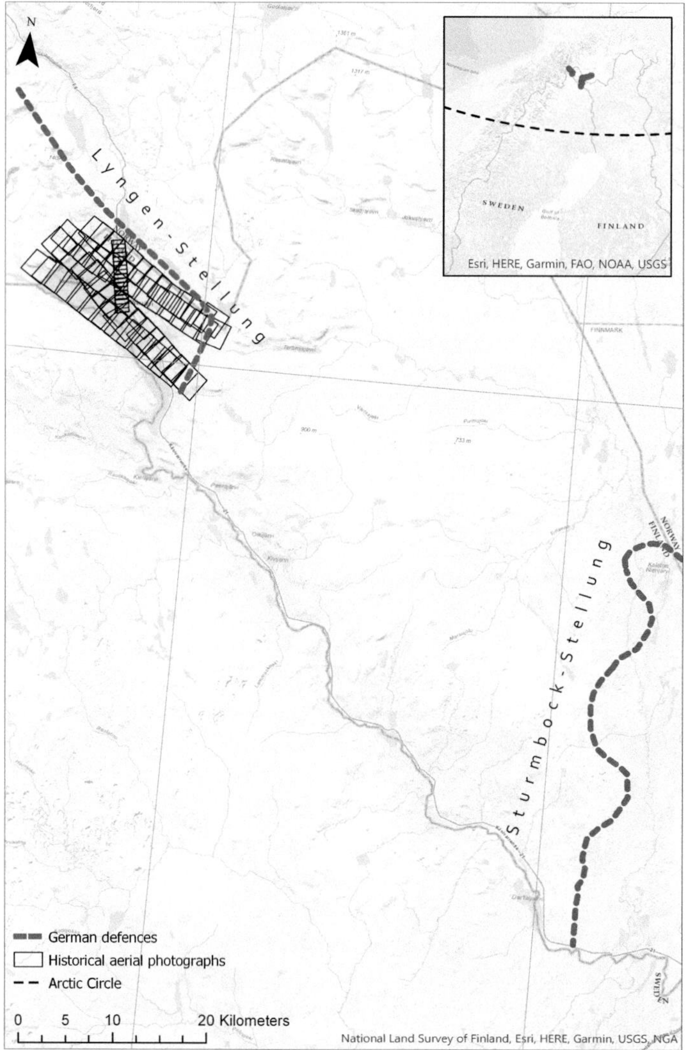

FIGURE 11.1 The study area.

Here, we focus on photographs originating from the National Archives of Finland. The first series of 54 undated aerial photographs covers four almost parallel strips with considerable overlap between consecutive frames (Figure 11.1). The flight plan of these Finnish Air Force (FIAF) aerial reconnaissance missions aligns with the boundaries of the country and focusses on Finnish territory, only slightly extending northwards into Norway. The total area covered is about 172 square kilometres. The recording of this series of photographs is not dated but probably took place in February or early March 1945. An additional strip of 22 aerial photographs, dating from 15 March 1945, has a larger scale and is provided with annotations. They were probably taken to evaluate a Finnish aerial bombardment on German positions.

One of the main challenges in processing aerial photographs in a remote and mountainous region such as Lapland is the geolocalization of the images. The extensive snow cover makes it almost impossible to select easily recognizable and clearly defined reference points. Natural features such as brooks, small bodies of water, and distinctive outcrops were used for localizing the pictures. Especially distinctive outcrops were highly visible on the historical images because of the low winter light. However, many of these outcrops are less visible on contemporary remote sensing images, making it difficult to geolocalize the historical images. Ultimately, LiDAR-derived digital elevation models (hillshades and other visualizations, see discussion below), showing the local topography more clearly, served as a reference set.

Based on a previously developed methodology (Stichelbaut 2011; Stichelbaut et al. 2017), the aerial photographs were interpreted and all visible traces were mapped in a geographical information system. Rather than a full, in-depth GIS analysis, in this chapter, we want to create an overview of the heritage potential of the research area and the application of a remote sensing approach. We mapped over 2,500 individual features; Table 11.1 provides a quantitative overview of the

TABLE 11.1 Overview of mapped features and comparison with their presence on present-day LiDAR and orthophoto

	Detected on WWII APs		*Visible on LiDAR/orthophoto*
Type and function	*Number (n)*	*Length (m)*	*Percentage of AP total (%)*
Defensive structures			
Trench		24,541	1.1
Fire position	30		6.7
Barbed wire		3,347	20.1
Bomb crater	47		0
Artillery emplacement	15		0
Accommodation			
Tent	199		5.0
Barrack/hut	50		14.0
Shelter	1,000		23.4
Circular shelter	121		14.0
Open shelter	126		17.5
Embankment	42		2
Transportation			
Path		19,360	0
Road		50,093	46.3
Walkboard		18,258	0
Snow fence		7,842	0
Sum	1,630	123,441	

different types of features encountered. The most important element in the landscape is the road between Muonio (Finland) and Skibotn (Norway), constructed by PoWs. The photographs show a great variety of structures, ranging from snow fences to keep the road clear from snowdrifts to extensive military camps and an elaborate network of trenches and dugouts or shelters. We can distinguish different functions: defensive structures, sites set up for accommodation and logistics, and transportation infrastructure.

All visible features on the aerial photographs are linked to the German presence in 1944–1945 (Figure 11.4). The German defences consist largely of isolated positions with short stretches of trenches (24.5 kilometres in total) and carefully located, isolated firing positions. The positions are located in the valley along the road, but also make use of the topography with numerous positions found on flat plateaus high in the mountains. Two defensive lines can be observed approximately six kilometres from each other. Both are almost perpendicular to the road and combine isolated positions in the mountains, larger concentrations of trenches close to the road, and isolated shelters and some trenches along the frozen Kierakasvuopio Lake.

The mountain strongpoints are located above the tree line and contain hundreds of dugouts and tents in which troops found shelter against the harsh winter conditions. The creative way in which trenches were constructed in the Arctic environment is interesting, as most seem to be made of above-ground walls of snow or ice. The positions are often surrounded by a thin barbed-wire fence. It is rare to see trenches carved into the rocks or permafrost. Access to them consists of wooden boardwalks, narrow mountain roads, and winding paths. Figure 11.2 shows three of these trench positions high up on the mountains. They are strategically positioned to overlook any potential advance of Finnish troops coming from the south along the main road and through the wilderness. Easily accessible and close to the main road, several possible gun emplacements show up as horseshoe-shaped ramparts that give cover to the artillery.

The largest concentrations of accommodations and logistic hubs lie just behind the second defensive line. They are mostly found in mountain birch groves closer to the roads. The first thing that stands out is the lack of structure, organization, and uniformity (e.g. Figure 11.3 A and B). A wide variety of small tents, large and sturdy dugouts, barracks and huts, sheds, and large circular cardboard tents were used in the camps. Some huts were even carved in the flanks of hills. Very often, there are shallow trenches to defend the perimeter or to seek shelter in case of Finnish bombardments, which occurred on at least one occasion (Figure 11.3 C). Transport and logistics proved to be very important, with some branches of the main road having shelters for parking cars (Figure 11.3 B). In some places, the shelters have been cut into piles of snow and look more like deep, wide communication trenches (Figure 11.3 B). Hundreds of metres of snow fences ensured that the road remained as accessible as possible.

The GIS dataset created by this research forms a robust basis for further research. For the first time, historical aerial photographs are used as a primary source to enhance and enrich our understanding of Second World War sites in

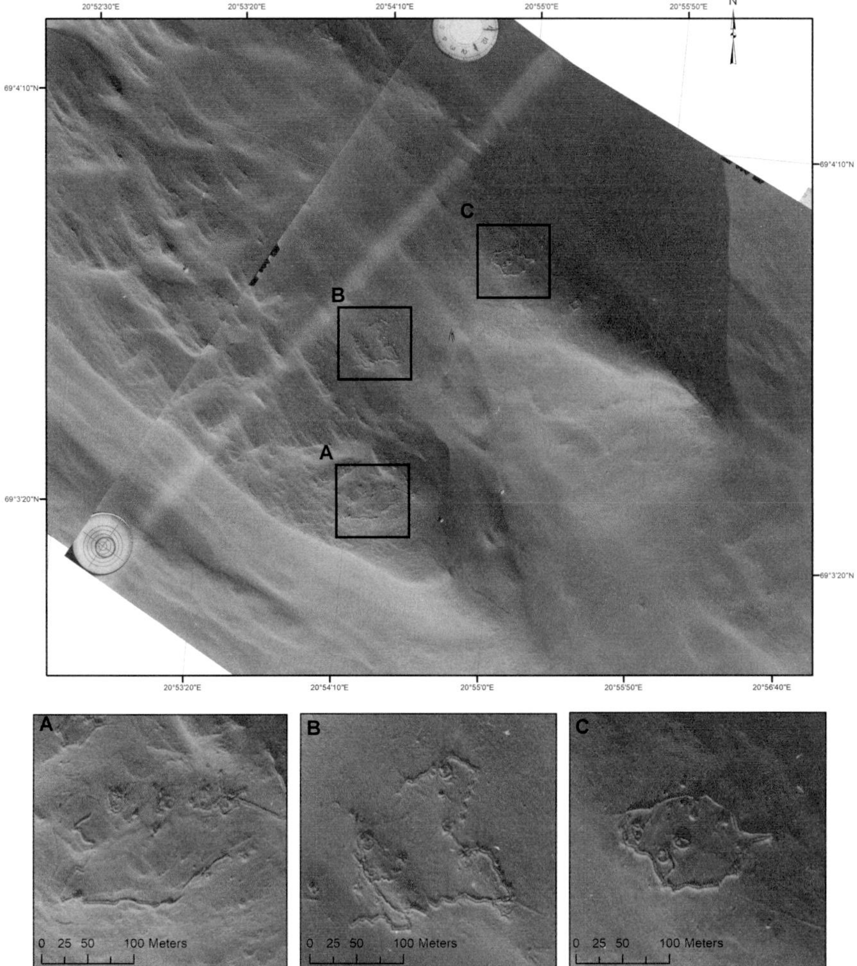

FIGURE 11.2 Three typical defensive positions near Kilpisjärvi, each consisting of trenches made with snow and ice-walls, dugouts, and some tents. Source: aerial photo, National Archives of Finland, scanned by O. Seitsonen, adapted by B. Stichelbaut.

northern Lapland. This approach supplements the existing heritage databases of the area and, above all, enables us to connect individual sites and to zoom out to a landscape perspective. A major limitation – in cases where the dataset is the only available source of information – is that the aerial photographs do not allow us to discern the current state of preservation of archaeological sites, features, or material culture. The data has to be combined with other non-invasive archaeological prospection techniques and/or ground-truthing to link it to the present-day situation.

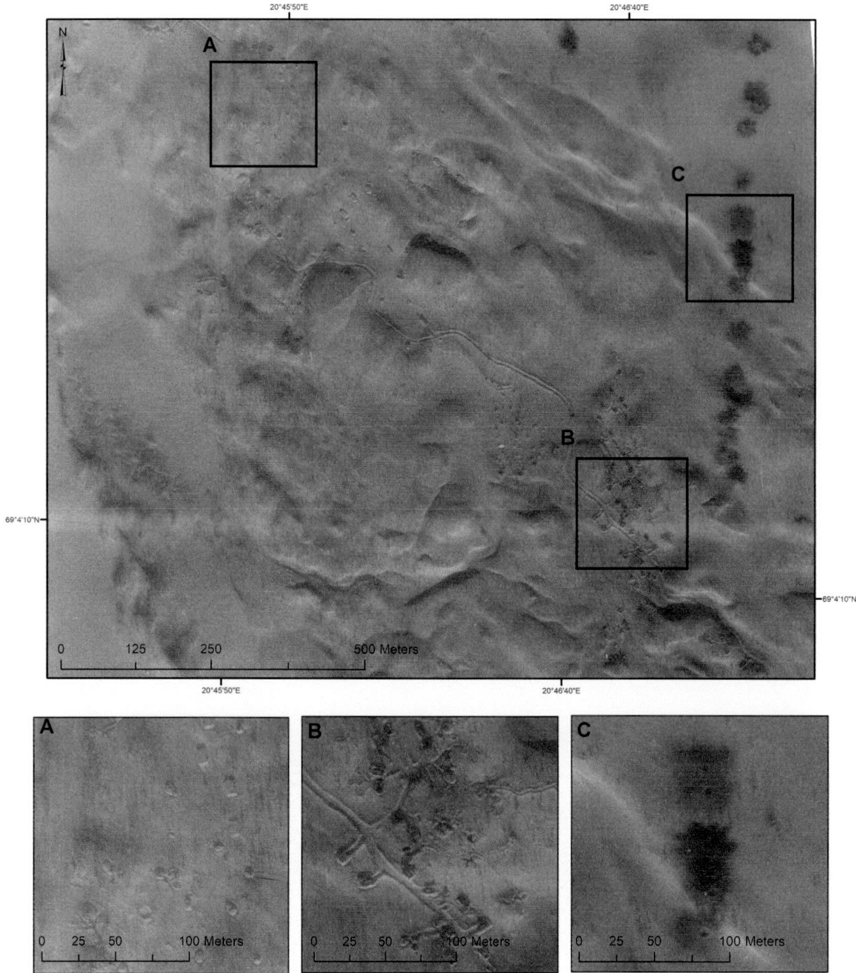

FIGURE 11.3 Historical aerial photograph of the accommodation area next to the main road (visible on the left and running from north–south). A: camp with rectangular huts and circular tents; B: open-air shelters for cars, shallow trenches, and a variety of dugouts/shelters; C: bomb craters of a Finnish bombardment. Source: aerial photo, National Archives of Finland, scanned by O. Seitsonen, adapted by B. Stichelbaut.

LiDAR, orthophotos, and field campaign 2019

In several European countries, high-resolution LiDAR datasets (with varying resolutions) are offered as open data by national or regional authorities (e.g. Flanders and Wallonia in Belgium, Finland, the Netherlands, Slovenia). This availability of big-data LiDAR has for some years opened up perspectives for the study of large-scale conflict landscapes in Europe. A disadvantage of LiDAR analysis is that we are looking at the contemporary landscape, a palimpsest of all traces of human activities from the past until the present. The difficulty lies in correctly interpreting subtle traces in the topography and attributing them to a certain period or function. However, when used in combination with historical aerial photographs, LiDAR-derived visualizations of warscapes can more easily be interpreted (Gheyle et al. 2018).

The character of the landscape in Lapland makes it an ideal case study for the use of LiDAR, as unlike more populated places in Europe, there are very few traces of modern human occupation. This facilitates the identification of Second

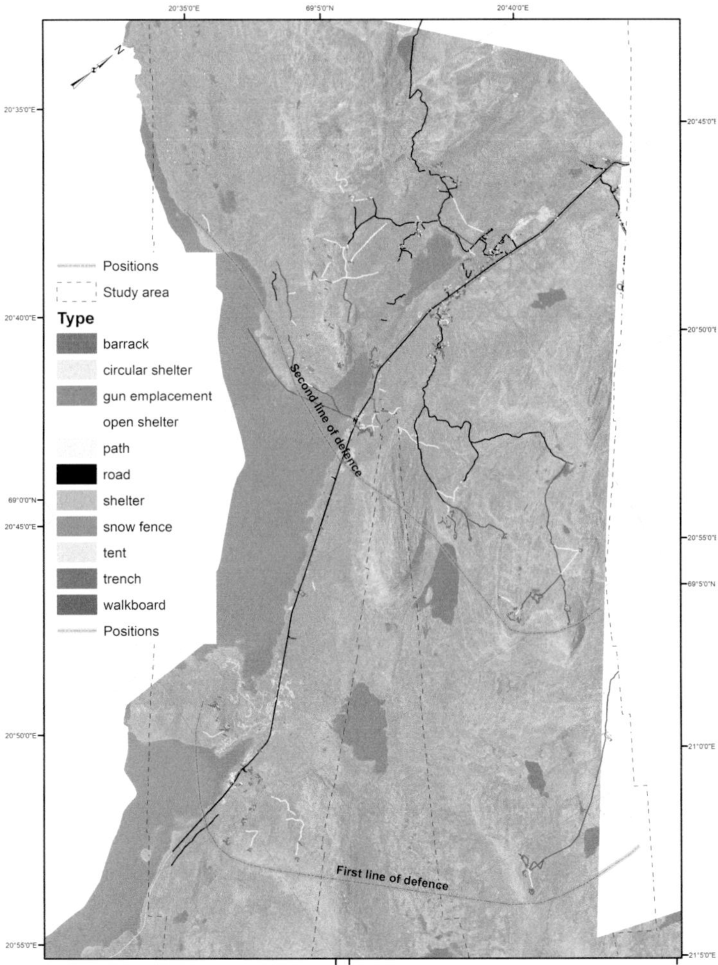

FIGURE 11.4 Cartography of war features in the study area. Source: orthophoto, National Land Survey of Finland open data CC 4.0.

World War archaeological sites (e.g. Figure 11.5) because there is very little confusion about the interpretation, especially in combination with available historical remote sensing datasets. Another major advantage of LiDAR – and aerial photography – is the ability to investigate large stretches of remote wilderness with few accessible roads and rugged terrain.

Through the Finnish National Land Survey, there is extensive open-data LiDAR coverage available for large parts of Finland with a minimal point density of 0.5 pixels per square metre. This resolution works to identify major structures. However, it must be borne in mind that smaller structures such as waste pits, narrow trenches, tents, etc., can only be identified in the field. This sparse point cloud was converted to a one-metre resolution raster digital elevation model of the bare earth. To reveal the archaeological topography on the terrain, specific visualization methods – sky view factor (Figure 11.5) and multiple hillshading – were applied by using the Relief Visualisation Toolbox (Kokalj et al. 2013). All traces visible on the LiDAR visualizations were inventoried in a two-stage process. In the first phase, the LiDAR-visualizations and modern-day orthophotos were checked. In the second phase, all features in the previously recorded GIS dataset (based on Second World War aerial photographs) were

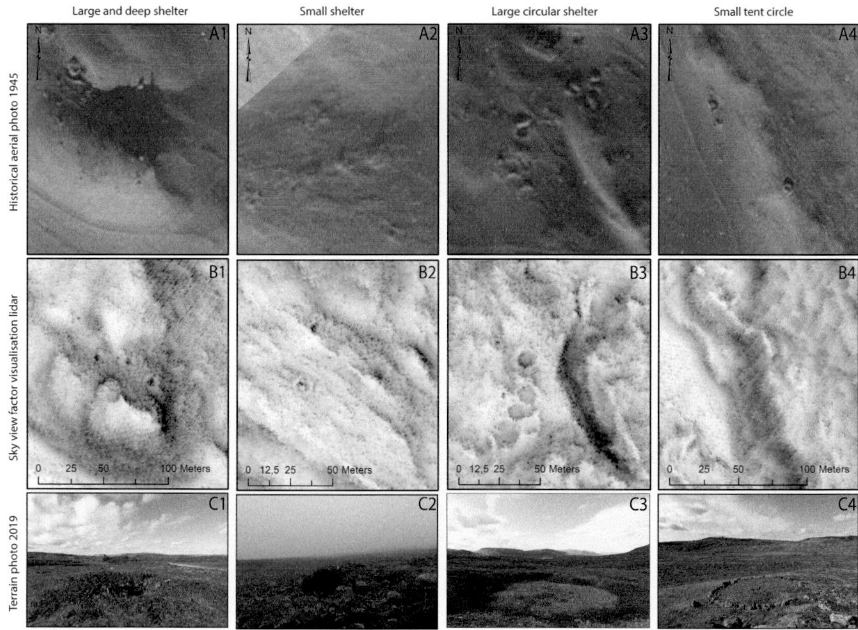

FIGURE 11.5 Comparison between historical aerial photograph, sky view factor visualization, and ground photograph of a variety of typical Second World War sites. Source: aerial photograph, National Archives of Finland, scanned by O. Seitsonen; factor visualization, National Land Survey of Finland open data CC 4.0; © B. Stichelbaut.

evaluated for whether they too could be identified by LiDAR. That appeared to be the case for a large number of features, pointing to good preservation in the present-day landscape. However, large parts of the military features showed in aerial photographs were not visible at all on the LiDAR data.

The resulting LiDAR cartography and aerial photograph mapping were used to produce a strategy for a ground-truthing campaign. The intention was to check the preservation of a selection of sites, to give an interpretation to a range of unknown anomalies on the LiDAR, black and white dots, and spots in the data (e.g. Figure 11.5) and to become familiar with the actual landscape conditions. In August 2019, a small field campaign investigated the remains of the Second World War heritage landscape. A wide range of sites was selected, with and without traces on the LiDAR data. With a mobile GIS, numerous sites were visited and documented. The targeted field walking was directed by the German network of roads and tracks visible on the aerial photographs. The addition of ground-truthing during an intensive field campaign aided in the further interpretation of both the LiDAR-derived visualization and the aerial photo mapping.

The first mapping of all the visible traces that had been set up before the fieldwork was refined after the experiences on the ground. Ground-truthing greatly helped to understand the snow-covered vestiges that manifested themselves on the aerial photo dataset. The interaction between historical aerial photographs and LiDAR, in combination with fieldwork, proved crucial for understanding this Arctic war landscape. After the fieldwork, a new phase of reinterpretation of the relics visible on LiDAR and aerial photo followed in order to integrate the knowledge gained on the ground. This was used to draft a preliminary typology of war features with information about their function and historical background.

On the LiDAR visualizations, the sites located high up in the mountains are particularly striking. These are large and deeply excavated structures, often with a rampart of excavated stones around it (15 by 15 metres is no exception) (e.g. Figure 11.5 B1). In some places, a wooden inner structure or metal roof is still in place (Figure 11.5 C1). Smaller shelters (roughly five by three metres) are made of curved corrugated iron sheets, often covered with stones (Figure 11.5 C2). Being well-camouflaged in this way, it is their entrances that make them visible (Figure 11.5 B2). Higher up in the mountains, structures seem to have been dug deeper, perhaps in order to provide better protection against the weather. The field research revealed many small firing positions for a single soldier made up of small walls of stacked stones. Also, numerous tent circles (Figure 11.5 C4) were found which were not previously visible due to the resolution of the LiDAR (Figure 11.5 B4).

The material culture is exceptionally well-preserved, littering the surface of the sites, and ranges from tin cans, glass bottles, ammunition boxes, *Organisation Todt* stoves, and even '*Frostschutzsalbe*' (frostbite salve) tubes. Many of the German roads and paths to the mountain positions are still in use today as hiking trails. While a large part of the features is still visible on the ground and on LiDAR, many other structures are difficult to discern today. Aerial photographs provide a clear view of the trenches in the mountain positions, but none of them can be seen on the LiDAR or in the current landscape. This reinforces the hypothesis that the trenches were built exclusively from snow and ice. No concentrations of war matériel have been found in these places. Wooden planks were found on the location of former ice-trenches only at one site.

At lower altitudes, a different picture emerges. Proportionally, there are far fewer traces visible on the LiDAR. However, large concentrations of features and material culture were encountered during fieldwork. Clearly, the low resolution of the open-source LiDAR data makes such an assessment far less instructive here. On the location of German camps and PoW camps, the foundation platforms of tents, huts, and large barracks were found (Figure 11.5 A3, B3, and C3). This forced a re-orientation of our LiDAR gaze to look for open spaces rather than dug-in features. In dozens of places, there are still small circular walls of stone and earth visible. These were formerly built around military tents. Wartime material such as bottles and cans of food can still be found lying around them. A possible hypothesis is that closer to the road there was more building material available and that there was not always the need to place shelters deep in the ground.

Table 11.1 gives a quantitative overview of the different types of structures observed on historical aerial photographs, comparing that with present-day traces observed through the analysis of recent orthophotos, LiDAR, and fieldwork. The number of preserved structures and the distribution of the war matériel is spectacular. It is so abundant, and lying in clear sight on the surface, that initiatives to clean up the 'war junk' in certain parts of Lapland have been initiated (Thomas et al. 2016; Seitsonen in press). In this region, this cleaning was carried out in the 1980s at first by the Finnish Association for Nature Conservation, and in 1989 by a Rovaniemi-based association 'Keep Lapland Tidy' ('*Pidä Lappi siistinä*') (Ylisirniö et al. 2014), which also cleared tonnes of war matériel elsewhere in Lapland in 2005–2010 (Seitsonen 2018: 120–121). Due to the excellent preservation of on-site artefacts in our study area, it is clear that some material has disappeared during these clean-ups.

Heritage valuation

In parallel with ground-truthing, interviews with local residents in Kilpisjärvi yielded a contextual understanding of how Second World War remains in the region are perceived. In addition to non-structured open-ended interviews, a community outreach event was organized in October 2019 to update residents on our research and to glean further local reflections on the wartime heritage. To chart the representation and management regimes of local and national heritage institutions, the heritage discourses of the municipal war museum (*Sturmbock-Stellung* museum of the municipality of Enontekiö), and the information infrastructure by the National Board of Forestry (the Finnish forestry authority) were analyzed. Representatives of the museum and National Board of Forestry were among the interviewees.

When comparing the memoryscape (i.e. that which is actively remembered by community members or promoted by local heritage institutions) with the archaeological landscape (i.e. all sites still visible on the ground and on the remote sensing imagery), a selectivity could be discerned. During conversations, respondents especially foregrounded the defensive positions, as well as the close and friendly interactions during the Finnish–German co-belligerence. Local imaginaries revealed some range in what different interest groups found important and worthy of note, sometimes contrasting with how the Second World War is curated on the ground. The *Sturmbock-Stellung* museum focuses on the German Army's activities in the region and enables visitors to visit a reconstructed system of trenches and shelters. Conservation work has similarly been geared towards these more visible defensive military structures. In 2017, volunteers of Lapland Society for Military History in collaboration with Finnish National Board of Forestry reconstructed a German shelter along a popular hiking trail and many information signs in the national parkland foreground a traditional military-historical narrative focusing on the German positions and everyday life of the soldiers.

In official information, the infrastructure of the significant Soviet PoW presence in the region from 1941 receives little attention, yet it was known among the residents of Kilpisjärvi. The multiple PoW camps and gravesites of PoWs and forced labourers connected to the construction of the defensive positions and the road were not explicitly mentioned in the official interpretation. One descriptive sign interprets the PoW camp, but besides discussing the site's morphology, little is mentioned about the inhumane working conditions and the significant mortality (Westerlund 2008). When we inquired about the large number of multinational PoWs and slave labourers that worked and died during the Continuation and Lapland Wars in the region, the community response was ambivalent and varied.

Some respondents indicated that they knew little about this history, while others shared knowledge about mass graves not known to the heritage authorities. One local history enthusiast mentioned that these gravesites and PoW camps are difficult spaces where he felt uncomfortable, and he did not like to visit them since they are imbued with death and suffering. This is in line with the feelings expressed by many people elsewhere in Lapland, where these kinds of sites are often surrounded by stories of ghosts and hauntings (Seitsonen 2018; and see Filippucci this volume; Carr 2017). Yet, despite the PoW camps and mass graves being absent from official interpretation, we learned that the school in Kilpisjärvi had arranged visits to a PoW mass grave in Malla for decades. These places seem well known locally, to the point that their locations have been visited by school-age children for many years as a part of their curriculum. Also, the fates of the thousands of PoWs working in the region are regularly speculated upon by the locals and also by Finnish national media (see Kulju 2017: 51). At the same time, the official interpretation – that which visitors to the region encounter – downplays and in some ways silences the 'darker' locations and their histories.

This emotionally charged and selective engagement with Second World War material remains correlates with earlier research about the 'dark heritage' values encoded in the warscapes of Lapland and eastern Finland (e.g. Seitsonen and Koskinen 2018). The distancing, by official heritage interpretation signage and by some of the informants, of the Soviet PoW narratives of death and suffering at the national level taps into the national war narrative of the small Finnish state forced into an alliance with Germany fighting the Soviet aggressors (Herva 2014; Kivimäki 2012). As the National Archives report by Westerlund shows, the nationalist reification of the war is connected with a national amnesia of the serious war crimes inflicted on Soviet PoWs (23,681 of the 64,000 Soviet PoWs died in Finnish camps due to forced labour and systemic starvation) and the active assistance the Finnish state provided to the Germans in their treatment of Soviet prisoners in the Lapland sector (at least 4,700 of the about 30,000 PoWs and forced labourers held by the Germans died in 1941–1944).

As Jay Winter (2010: 4–6) notes, 'silence' – particularly connected to violence – may be more nuanced than simply forgetfulness (see also Seitsonen et al. 2018). Rather, Winter posits, there are three different kinds of silence at play with regard to conflict: 'liturgical silences' connected to mourning; 'strategic silences' for political purposes; and thirdly, silence connected to 'considerations of privilege' concerning who has the right to discuss violent pasts (Winter 2010: 4–6). We speculate that more types of silence are at play in our study region. Although the national memory culture furthers a selective understanding of history, at the same time, some histories were probably privileged pasts that were not shared with us because of our outsider status. Remote communities in Lapland are closed and tightknit; elsewhere we have noted that particularly personal transgenerational memories, such as illegitimate children of German soldiers, have been kept from us during our interviews although they are well known in the community. Certainly, the tourists and other visitors to the Kilpisjärvi region are not invited to engage with the more painful aspects of the past, such as the incarceration and death of PoWs, beyond a few passing notions.

Conclusions and future perspectives

The research presented in this chapter is a pilot study to demonstrate the potential and preliminary results of a novel approach to Second World War conflict archaeology in the Arctic using a variety of remote sensing techniques. This landscape perspective on the German material legacy in Lapland is new and gives insight into the density, distribution, and diversity of the Second World War archaeological record on the Finnish part of the German *Lyngen* position. With the help of the GIS inventories created by this research, we gain a first insight into the war landscape that can be seen on the historical aerial photographs and the extent to which this landscape is still present today.

An archaeological assessment of the remote sensing data teaches us a lot about how the German Army, unprepared for Arctic warfare, improvised to provide adequate accommodation and defensive positions. Furthermore, the remote sensing research and subsequent fieldwork revealed a variety of accommodation types ranging from simple small tents to larger yurt-like cardboard structures, concrete and stone shelters, and even deep and very solid dugouts. These were integrated into a preliminary typology, establishing a baseline for a more elaborate typology of Arctic war features. The value of contrasting this data with the contemporary valuation of the heritage landscape has been that we have gained a deeper insight not only into this region's Second World War conflict archaeology but also into its contemporary status and values attached to it by local residents. In particular, the variable and nuanced engagements with memories of the PoW camps, a stark contrast with the clarity of their presence in our remote sensing imagery, underline the complexities in remembrance and the tensions between what happened and what is remembered.

Although most of our initial research questions were answered, the results raise even more pressing questions. For example, how should we deal with the huge number of sites scattered in the landscape? What considerations should we make in order to determine which sites should or should not be protected, excavated, or further investigated, and what is the potential for heritage tourism in this region?

We can conclude that the approach proposed here could be followed in several other areas of the Arctic region. In the first instance, of course, Norway is a prime target, as this is where the *Lyngen* position continues (*Norsk institutt for kulturminneforskning* 2019). But due to the increasing availability of Second World War aerial photographs in Finland due to the ongoing digitization projects in NARA and NCAP, we hope that this approach will also be deployed in Finnish conflict archaeology. Further availability of newly discovered series of historical aerial photographs will enable us to differentiate even more between PoW camps and the German military occupation of the region.

Acknowledgements

The fieldwork of 2019 was funded by the University of Helsinki Future Fund. We would like to thank Iain Banks (University of Glasgow), Vesa-Pekka Herva (University of Oulu), and Wesa Perttola (University of Helsinki) for their assistance during the fieldwork campaign in August 2019.

References

Camp, S.L. (2016) Landscapes of Japanese American Internment. *Historical Archaeology* 50 (1): 169–186.

Carr, G. (2017) The Uninvited Guests Who Outstayed Their Welcome: The Ghosts of War in the Channel Islands. In N.J. Saunders and P. Cornish (eds.), *Modern Conflict and the Senses*, pp. 272–288. London: Routledge.

Cowley, D. and B. Stichelbaut (2012) Historic Aerial Photographic Archives for European Archaeology. *European Journal of Archaeology*, 15 (2): 217–236.

Cowley, D., L. Ferguson and A. Williams (2013) The Aerial Reconnaissance Archives: A Global Aerial Photographic Collection. In W. Hanson and I. Oltean (eds.), *Archaeology from Historical Aerial and Satellite Archives*, pp. 13–30. New York: Springer.

Dobinson, C., J. Lake and J. Schofield (1997) Monuments of War: Defining England's 20th-Century Defence Heritage. *Antiquity* 71: 288–299.

Douglas, S. and A. McFeaters (2011) The Archaeology of Historic Battlefields: A History and Theoretical Development in Conflict Archaeology. *Journal of Archaeological Research* 19 (1): 103–132.

Fast, J. (2017) German Transit Camp at Tulliniemi, Hanko 1942–1944. In J. Kaila and J. Knuutila (eds.), *Poetic Archaeology. Inside and Beside the Camp*, pp. 34–41. Helsinki: Academy of Fine Arts.

Freeman, P.W.M. and A. Pollard (eds.) (2001) *Fields of Conflict: Progress and Prospect in Battlefield Archaeology*. BAR I.S. 958.

Gheyle, W., B. Stichelbaut, T. Saey, N. Note, H. Van den Berghe, V. Van Eetvelde, M. Van Meirvenne and J. Bourgeois (2018) Scratching the Surface of War: Airborne Laser Scans of the Great War Conflict Landscape in Flanders (Belgium). *Applied Geography* 90: 55–68.

Going, C. (2002) A Neglected Asset. German Aerial Photography of the Second World War Period. In R. Bewley and W. Raczkowski (eds.), *Aerial Archaeology. Developing Future Practice*, pp. 337, 23–30. Lesno: IOS Press.

——— (2009) Déjà Vu all over Again? A Brief Presentation History of Overseas Service Aerial Photography in the UK. In B. Stichelbaut, J. Bourgeois, N.J. Saunders and P. Chielens (eds.), *Images of Conflict: Military Aerial Photography and Archaeology*, pp. 121–134. Newcastle-upon-Tyne: Cambridge Scholars Publishing.

Hegarty, C. and S. Newsome (2007) *Suffolk's Defended Shore*. Suffolk: English Heritage.

Hegarty, C., S. Newsome and H. Winton (2005) The Greatest Battlefield That Never Was – Suffolk Aerial Archaeology. *Battlefields Annual Review*, pp 63–71 Barnsley: Pen & Sword.

Herva, V.-P. (2014) Haunting Heritage in an Enchanted Land: Magic, Materiality and Second World War German Material Heritage in Finnish Lapland. *Journal of Contemporary Archaeology* 1 (2): 297–321.

Hesse, R. (2010) LiDAR-derived Local Relief Models – A New Tool for Archaeological Prospection. *Archaeological Prospection* 17 (2): 67–72.

——— (2014) Geomorphological Traces of Conflict in High-Resolution Elevation Models. *Applied Geography* 46: 11–20.

Kivimäki, V. (2012) Between Defeat and Victory: Finnish Memory Culture of the Second World War. *Scandinavian Journal of History* 37 (4): 482–504.

Koivisto, S. and V. Laulumaa (2013) Pistepilvessä – Metsien arkeologiset kohteet LiDAR-ilmalaserkeilausaineistoissa. *Arkeologipäivät* 2012: 51–67.

Kokalj, Z., K. Zakšek and K. Oštir (2013) Visualizations of Lidar Derived Relief Models. In R. Opitz and D. Cowley (eds.), *Interpreting Archaeological Topography – Airborne Laser Scanning, Aerial Photographs and Ground Observation*, pp. 100–114. Oxford: Oxbow Books.

Kulju, M. (2017) *Käsivarren sota – lasten ristiretki 1944–1945*. Helsinki: Gummerus.

Macdonald, S. (2013) *Memorylands: Heritage and Identity in Europe Today*. London: Routledge.

Mikkonen, K. (2016) *Parakkeja ja piikkilankaa. Saksan armeijan rakentamiseen liittyvätoiminta Rovaniemen seudulla 1940–1944*. Rovaniemi: Lapin maakuntamuseo.

Moshenska, G. (2010) Working with Memory in the Archaeology of Modern Conflict. *Cambridge Archaeological Journal* 20 (1): 33–48.

NARA. (2008) *Web Version Based on Guide to Federal Records in the National Archives of the United States.* Compiled by Robert B. Matchette et al. Washington, DC: National Archives and Records Administration. Retrieved from www.archives.gov/research/guide-fed-records/groups/120.html

Norsk Institutt for Kulturminneforskning. (2019) *WWII Heritage in Arctic Europe.* Retrieved from www.niku.no/en/2018/03/wwii-heritage-in-arctic-europe/

Passmore, D. and S. Harrison (2008) Landscapes of the Battle of the Bulge: WW2 Field Fortifications in the Ardennes Forests of Belgium. *Journal of Conflict Archaeology* 4 (1–2): 87–107.

Passmore, D., S. Harrison and D. Capps Tunwell (2014) Second World War Conflict Archaeology in the Forests of North-West Europe. *Antiquity* 88 (342): 1275–1290.

Pollard, T. and P. Barton (2013) The Use of First World War Aerial Photographs by Archaeologists: A Case Study from Fromelles, Northern France. In W. Hanson and I. Oltean (eds.), *Archaeology from Historical Aerial and Satellite Archives*, pp. 87–104. New York: Springer.

Reeves, K., B. Stichelbaut and G. Plets (2016) Remembering Uncertainty: The World War II Warscape of the Australian Northern Territory. In B. Stichelbaut and D. Cowley (eds), *Conflict Landscapes and Archaeology from above*, pp. 167–184. Farnham: Ashgate Publishing.

Saunders, N. (2007) *Killing Time. Archaeology and the First World War.* Stroud: Sutton.

——— (2012) Introduction: Engaging the Materialities of Twentieth and Twenty-first Century Conflict. In N.J. Saunders (ed.) *'Beyond the Dead Horizon'. Studies in Modern Conflict Archaeology*, pp. 10–14. Oxford: Oxbow Books.

Schofield, J., W.G. Johnson and C.M. Beck (eds.) (2002) *Matériel Culture: The Archaeology of Twentieth Century Conflict.* Abingdon: Routledge.

Seitsonen, O. (2017) Crowdsourcing Cultural Heritage: Public Participation and Conflict Legacy in Finland. *Journal of Community Archaeology & Heritage* 4 (2): 115–130.

——— (2018) *Digging Hitler's Arctic War: Archaeologies and Heritage of the Second World War German Military Presence in Finnish Lapland.* Helsinki: Unigrafia.

——— (2021) *Archaeologies of Hitler's Arctic War.* London: Routledge.

Seitsonen, O., M. Hekkurainen, E. Koskinen and S. Thomas (2018) 'Voiko natsia rakastaa?': Lapin Maakuntamuseon Wir waren Freunde – Olimme ystäviä -näyttelyprosessi esimerkkinä vaikeasta kulttuuriperinnöstä. *Suomen Museo* 4: 112–132.

Seitsonen, O. and V.-P. Herva (2011) Forgotten in the Wilderness: WWII German PoW Camps in Finnish Lapland. In G. Moshenska and A. Myers (eds.), *Archaeologies of Internment*, pp. 171–190. New York: Springer.

——— (2017) 'War Junk' and Cultural Heritage: Viewpoints on World War II German Material Culture in the Finnish Lapland. In A. Benfer (ed.), *War & Peace: Conflict and Resolution in Archaeology. Proceedings of the 45th Annual Chacmool Archaeology Conference*, pp. 170–185. Calgary: University of Calgary.

Seitsonen, O. and E. Koskinen (2018) Where the F... is Vuotso?': Heritage of Second World War Forced Movement and Destruction in a Sámi Reindeer Herding Community in Finnish Lapland. *International Journal of Heritage Studies* 24 (4): 421–441.

Sillanpää, E. and A. Rikkinen. (2019) *Projekti Sturmbock.* Research Report. Loppuraportti: National Heritage Agency.

Stichelbaut, B. (2011) The First Thirty Kilometres of the Western Front 1914–1918: An Aerial Archaeological Approach with Historical Remote Sensing Data. *Archaeological Prospection*, 18 (1): 57–66.

Stichelbaut, B. and D. Cowley (eds.) (2016) *Conflict Landscapes and Archaeology from Above.* Farnham: Ashgate Publishing.

Stichelbaut, B., W. Gheyle, V. Van Eetvelde, M. Van Meirvenne, T. Saey, N. Note, H. Van den Berghe and J. Bourgeois (2017) The Ypres Salient 1914–1918: Historical Aerial Photography and the Landscape of War. *Antiquity* 91 (355):235–249.

Thomas, S. (2019) Locals, Incomers, Tourists and Gold Diggers: Space, Politics, and the 'Dark Heritage' Legacy of the Second World War in Finnish Lapland. In T. Lähdesmäki, S. Thomas and Y. Zhu (eds.), *Politics of Scale: New Approaches to Critical Heritage Studies*, pp 113–125 Oxford: Berghahn Books.

Thomas, S., O. Seitsonen and H. Vesa-Pekka (2016) Nazi Memorabilia, Dark Heritage and Treasure Hunting as 'Alternative' Tourism: Understanding the Fascination with the Material Remains of World War II in Northern Finland. *Journal of Field Archaeology* 41 (3): 331–343.

Van Hollebeeke, Y. and B. Stichelbaut (2016) A Bird's-Eye Perspective on Gold Beach. An Integrated Aerial Photographic Study of a Dynamic War Landscape. In G. Bird, S. Claxton and K. Reeves (eds.), *Managing and Interpreting D-Day's Sites of Memory. Guardians of Remembrance*, pp. 281–295: London: Routledge.

Winter, J. (2010) Thinking about Silence. In E. Ben-Ze'ev, R. Ginio and J. Winter (eds.), *Shadows of War. A Social History of Silence in the Twentieth Century*, pp. 3–31. Cambridge: Cambridge University Press.

Westerlund, L. (2008) *Saksan vankileirit Suomessa ja raja-alueilla 1941–1944.* Tammi: Helsinki.

Ylisirniö, A.-L. and A. Allén (2014) Toisen maailmansodan jäljet Mallan luonnossa. In A. Järvinen, T. Heikkilä and S. Lahti (eds.), *Tieteen ja taiteen tunturit*, pp. 131–140.Tampere: Gaudeamus.

12

POWER OF PLACE AND LANDSCAPE

The US 10th Mountain Division, from Colorado to the Apennines

John M. Scott

Introduction

This chapter presents and compares three military landscapes[1] encountered by the United States (US) Army's Second World War 10th Mountain Division[2] (the Division), the only wartime US formation dedicated to mountain warfare. The Division was primarily trained in the Colorado Rocky Mountains and had (self-described) good luck and success in the contested northern Apennine Mountains of Italy in 1945. The focus of this study is a fieldwork-based comparative investigation of the Division's Rocky Mountain training landscape and two sections of its Italian Campaign battle-zone landscape, Riva Ridge and Hill 913.[3] The Division's training centre at Camp Hale (the Camp) in the Colorado Rockies was a harsh, high-elevation mountain landscape, and at an elevation of 2,750 metres above sea level (ASL), was mostly more difficult to navigate and manoeuvre in than the 700 to 1,500 metres (ASL) of their Italian battle-zone landscape – the last defensive line of German military occupation in the northern Emilia-Romagna Apennine Mountains, from December 1944 to early April 1945.

The Division's training in the Rocky Mountains was more than adequate for their task of scaling mountain heights at the centre of the German *Wehrmacht*[4] Gothic Line in 1945. However, during combat, the Division suffered many casualties.[5] German weaponry clearly took its toll, but two well-known habits of the Division played a role: they were known for not turning back and they always held their ground (Isserman 2019: 16). Fortunately, these combat mountaineers had the benefit of being fresh to battle from two years of training in Colorado. They could also tap into combat experience and intelligence gained by the Allies during their attacks on Axis forces in Italy over the preceding 16 months. They benefited too from aerial photography and real-time combat updates from the Allied air forces that controlled their battle-zone airspace.[6]

Their mountain combat training, aided by the local inhabitants of the Emilia-Romagna Apennines, helped the Division move up to the front lines and ascend what the Germans considered impassable mountain winter landscapes to attack fortified German communications and observation posts on 18 February 1945. In combat, by early March 1945, the Division had taken 20–30 kilometres of mountains and hills and was considered a seasoned combat infantry, understanding the battle-zone landscape as well as any veteran combat unit. Later that spring, the Division was chosen to lead the American 5th Army out of their winter encampment (Imbrie and Imbrie 2004: 19), and on 14 April they attacked and took Hill 913.

Prior to the arrival of the Division, the Nazis had forced the Italian mountain inhabitants to construct the Gothic Line in the northern Apennines. These defences were built of strong points constructed on high ground commanding killing-zones created by mutually supporting machine guns, mortars, artillery, and mines. Global Navigation Satellite System (GNSS) data recently obtained during fieldwork on one of these high points, Hill 913, is presented and interpreted below.

Military landscapes and signs

This study is concerned with the military landscapes of specialized mountain training and mountain battle-zones. It proceeds from the view that landscapes are not just a material concept (Head 2010: 427) but exist also as memories which can be recalled to navigate physical as well as social landscapes. Generally, the physical landscape, or its symbols and signs, prompts the recall, but a memory of landscape can be triggered by any stimulus. Human repetitive interaction in physical and social landscapes strengthens and maintains people and their identity. Identity and culture (including military training) shape human perception and give meaning to the physical world with which people must interact. Landscape and culture are thus dialectically connected by feedback that creates and maintains perception. Military training is in many instances based on this type of mental imprinting and information exchange (Burchell 2019 this volume).

Signs and symbols associated with and found within the landscape are rarely universal; their meanings are culturally, contextually, and temporally determined. The reading of symbols and their association with landscape can be controlled because people often need to be trained to understand them. Thus, knowledge of the landscape can be used to inform or dominate others (Tilley 1994: 26). In contrast to the slow construction of memories and identity through normal daily life, the Second World War rapidly created new landscapes, with millions killed and wounded, and huge amounts of material produced and destroyed in a short time. Second World War battle-zones were intended to be deadly and confusing, and the Division was specially trained to recognize signs of danger and death in the cold and steep mountains, and how to react to them. In the Division's battle-zone landscape, buildings and travel routes could mean ambushes, snipers, machine gunners, mines, and explosive traps, or helpful noncombatant inhabitants, and sometimes both. To conquer the occupying forces, the soldiers had to pass through a series of deadly landscapes that quickly became peopled by the dead and wounded.

Power of place

The 10th Mountain Division developed a cohesion and group identity based on shared experience, and an intensive training regime in the high mountain landscape of central Colorado. That process mirrored Tilley's 'power of place' (1994: 26), where landscapes encountered in daily life through interaction with material and people and used in communication are invested with power or are seen as possessing power. People develop special meanings and symbols to understand and to be able to approach powerful landscapes such as mountains. In the case of the Division, the soldiers' intense daily training regimen, their isolation in the mountains, and their constant review by peers and trainers acculturated them to combat in this specific landscape in a short period of time.

The power of the mountain includes its height above the surrounding terrain, its ruggedness and slope, and this can be accentuated by the elements of elevation, darkness, and weather. Controlling the mountaintop or the high terrain gave soldiers a ground advantage over those below (Isserman 2019: 185); for much of the Second World War, the Germans had high ground advantage across the mountains of Italy. This facilitated easy observation of the battlezone and allowed weapon fire to be directed downwards on enemies struggling to manoeuvre upwards. German mountaintop defences encountered by the Division were powerfully constructed to occupy a particular position within a blocking defence system.[7] The Germans also had a more comprehensive view of and thus more control over the contested space. Mountaintops, therefore, can become a source of power and a place to be contested (see Cornish [this volume] for the analogous military importance of crest lines at lower altitude).

Training landscapes of the Camp

Camp Hale in Colorado (Figure 12.1) is located in the sparsely occupied Eagle Park along US Highway 24. Historically, this wide area of the Eagle River's valley bottom was known as Pando Valley, lying at an elevation of 2,800 metres, and characterized by potentially dangerous weather conditions for eight months of the year. It lies within a historic mining and railroad landscape surrounded by the towns of Red Cliff, Gilman, and Leadville. The Camp is a federal protected historic site listed on the National Register of Historic Places. It also, however, similar to modern battlefields, remains dangerous due to hazardous material dumps and unexploded ordnance. Above and south of the Camp, a granite monolith listing the names of 1,000 Division soldiers killed has been erected on Tennessee Pass at the entrance to the Division's original ski training area, now the Ski Cooper resort.

FIGURE 12.1 Google Earth oblique view of Camp Hale's central training area consisting of the Pando Valley floor and the immediate surrounding mountains. Source: © Google Earth Landsat/Copernicus.

The Camp was the equivalent of a small city, and essentially a wartime experiment to build a specialized infantry 'weapon', the 10th Mountain Division (Isserman 2019: 33). From 1942 to 1945, the Camp was the US centre of mountain combat training. At the time, it was considered ultra-modern due to the speed at which it was designed and built into the 'hazardous' mountain landscape and for its unique training facilities. When completed, it was well equipped with the capacity to house up to 20,353 mountain infantry trainees and with facilities for conducting basic training and combat mountaineering (Rottman and Dennis 2012: 10; Witte 2015: 46). At the time, it was the largest construction project undertaken in Colorado (Witte 2015), and once completed, the Camp's population peaked at nearly 17,000 soldiers and trainees (Rottman and Dennis 2012: 10).

Constructing a military landscape

In early 1942, the Pando Valley saw the construction of a contractor's camp, housing 10,000 workers. Between April and November 1942, civilian workers levelled the valley, straightened the Eagle River, and erected about 1,000 predesigned wooden and a few concrete buildings (Isserman 2019: 66). These would eventually house 16,800 individuals, stable approximately 4,000 horses and mules (Witte 2015: 81), and kennel about 200 dogs (Jenkins 2003: 51). Training facilities included a 457-metre-long rifle range, anti-aircraft weapon ranges, and several smaller ranges for pistol, grenade, machine gun,[8] and bayonet. Combat ranges for urban terrain as well as ranges utilizing zigzag trenches were also available. Rock faces for technical climbing were within walking distance at nearby higher and more difficult locations. Small downhill ski runs with rope tows were available at the Camp with a larger ski area about 300 metres higher in elevation just minutes away by vehicle. A short-lived artificial 'glacier' was also constructed nearby (Witte 2015: 85).[9] A soldier was able to step out of the Camp barracks and begin skiing at 2,800 metres and could traverse upward to as high as 3,660 metres; more rugged mountains reaching 4,270 metres were accessible beyond these lower mountains.

Recruits

Training at the Camp was conducted by American and international world-class mountaineers, skiers, and arctic explorers who were experienced in conquering mountains and cold landscapes. The National Ski Patrol (NSP) was involved from the beginning, and the Army made them the primary recruiter for the Division. Mountain experience or other types of outdoor experience with three letters of recommendation were initially required. The Army also ordered that the first recruits should be 18–19-year-old Colorado skiers and climbers (Witte 2015: 77–78). Out of 12,000 applications, the NSP eventually recommended 7,000–8,000 recruits (Isserman 2019: 40). Thus, more than half of the trainees knew something about mountain landscapes and had an alpine lifestyle in common prior to arriving at the Camp in 1942.

At the time, most ski racers and coaches were at northwestern and northeastern universities and colleges. This meant that many initial recruits had college degrees, making the Division one of the most highly educated US Army infantry units (Isserman 2019: 61). After recruitment of the initial 7,000 to 8,000 NSP-endorsed volunteers, more men were needed to fill the Division and recruitment was opened to general enlistment. The Army, not the NSP, recruited the remainder of the unit. Many of these later Army recruits were not able to ski or climb; they found the training and location miserable. From December 1942 to June 1944, the training dropout rate reached 55% (ibid.: 102).

All who completed training were changed physically and mentally by the regime and the landscape. At high elevation, becoming physically fit requires individuals to be properly acclimatized because intensive physical training at elevation can have deleterious physiological and psychological effects.[10] However, there is at least one known benefit of such training, and that is a temporary improvement of physical performances at lower elevations (Levine 2016). Although these advantages eventually diminish, trained individuals know that the lack of oxygen (hypoxia) while conducting intensive activities, whether at high or low elevation, can be overcome.

The D-Series at Camp Hale

The Camp was the only training location where the entire Division (all three regiments[11]) manoeuvred together as a single combat mountain unit of approximately 13,000 soldiers. The Army conducted this manoeuvre known as the 'Division-Level Series', or D-Series, to measure the ability of the three regiments to operate together in mountain combat simulations. During the D-Series, the Division, with a thousand mules, manoeuvred in simulated combat on steep terrain up to 3,960 metres in elevation during temperatures of 30 to 35 degrees below zero in nearly a metre of new snow during day and night (Isserman 2019: 129–133).

For three weeks in March and April 1944, the Division was pushed to its limits with minimal equipment and at times skiing continuously for up to 18 hours in extreme weather to reach their high mountaintop bivouac at 3,700 metres (Feuer 2006: 3). During the test, officers lost their soldiers; the location of entire regiments was at times unknown; and supplies were not delivered. Soldiers absent without leave (AWOL) numbered in the hundreds and had to be rounded up by military police from a nearby town (Isserman 2019: 130–131).

The Army declared the Division had proven itself and survived a worst-conditions scenario. Many of the graduates of the D-Series did not see the results in the same way.[12] They felt that they had barely survived, considering 195 cases of frostbite and 340 incapacitating injuries (ibid: 133). Several soldiers' memoirs and accounts (e.g. Dusenberry 1991; Whitlock and Bishop 1992: 42–44; Witte 2015: 175–182) recall that when combat in Italy became especially horrific, the soldiers would often say, 'yea it's bad, but not as bad as the D Series', or 'if this gets any worse, it's gonna be as bad as D-Series' (Witte 2015: 189). Notably, the D-Series was conducted on colder, higher, more expansive terrain than any of the ridges that the Division would eventually capture in Italy.

Mountain battle-zone landscape

When large military formations, such as a division, engage in combat on mountain landscapes, it is inevitable that they break into smaller elements because of limited usable ground surface, limited manoeuvrability, and limited communications. Mountain strongpoints are sought after because they provide a better view of the battlefield and control more space than they occupy. Line of sight and other forms of communication connect such points to each other to form a dynamic system of defence, which the Germans adopted against the Division. Combat units of company and platoon size were used by the Division to successfully attack both Riva Ridge and Hill 913.

At Riva Ridge, the Germans were unaware that the US Army had any substantial mountain combat capabilities, and so put too much faith in the steep and harsh landscape. Reinforcing this mistaken view was that no such specialized forces had been used in any of the three previous failed American attacks on Riva

Ridge and Monte Belvedere. In addition, American soldiers laying communication wires advanced up the ridge close behind their attacking units, providing critical communication between front line fighters and rear command. At Hill 913, however, sniping, booby traps, and mines quickly broke down the attacking American units, and forward momentum was maintained not by communication with rear command but by the initiative, bravery, and skill of a few soldiers.

More broadly in this context, civilian and military landscapes merge in battle-zones, and many multi-vocal overlapping accounts are produced at different times during, before, and after conflict, stimulated by confusion, fear, and trauma. In this sense, a conflict landscape is always in motion and in a process of becoming (Bender 2001: 4). Over time, art and monuments are created to memorialize the battle and the people, and these works are also manifestations of the different perceptions constructed during and after the conflict. Places, monuments, signs, and symbols evoke memory and emotion, and due to the interest of multiple stakeholders, they can become troubled and contested (Zalewska et al. 2017: 14). The Apennines of Emilia-Romagna offer a contemporary example of this. Interpretive signs at historical Division locations have been vandalized (Figure 12.2). Some signs providing information about local Italian resistance to the war have been damaged, with words and plaques scratched out, perhaps stemming from changing and conflicting interpretations of what Italian resistance fighters represented and accomplished (and see De Nardi 2017). In other words, signs as material culture are as volatile as the landscapes they announce.

10th Mountain Division battle-zone landscape

The 10th Mountain Division was one of the last combat units sent to the Italian Campaign, arriving in Naples in the winter of 1944–1945, itself heavily bombed due to being the principal Allied supply port (Ellis 1996: 99). Several soldiers described their arrival and paint a dramatic picture of sunken ships, bombed-out factories, piles of rubble, and broken and strafed walls and buildings. The Neapolitan poor were ever-present and consisted mostly of children and teenagers (Cossin 2001: 20).

Just prior to the Division's departure for Italy, on 6 November 1944, the US Army officially designated it the 10th Mountain Division.[13] However, on entering Italy their identity was kept secret: they told no one who they were and wore no identifying symbols or shoulder patches (Cousins 2001: 21). By mid-February, the entire Division had secretly moved to the frontlines of the US 5th Army by various routes, including a 28-kilometre march through un-reconnoitred snowy mountain terrain at night. In the 5th Army's front lines, they were positioned with the 442nd Infantry (composed of Japanese-Americans) about 40 kilometres to their left with rugged mountains between them. Within about three to four kilometres to their right was the Brazilian Expeditionary Force (BEF) and the all-black US 92nd Infantry, known as the Buffalo Soldiers. The Division was billeted in local homes and public buildings and allowed out only at night.

FIGURE 12.2 Interpretative sign on Monte Belvedere. Information on the Partisans has been removed from the upper half, and information on the Germans has been scratched out near the centre. Information on the Division is largely intact. Source: © and courtesy of Kelly J. Pool.

The soldiers developed a camaraderie and friendship with the *gente di montagna* on the front lines in the Emilia-Romagna Apennines in February of 1945. These locals had been living in a social landscape of terror created by the Nazis' commercial construction companies and the *Wehrmacht*, who were planning, building, and occupying the German Gothic line. Forced labour and terror were the German Army's tools to control rebellion and force compliance, and for that reason, since September of 1944, civilian areas in Italy outside of fascist control had supported Allied efforts to defeat the Nazis and Italian fascists (Jennings 2016: 117–120). Several murders and massacres were committed by the German Army in retaliation for partisan attacks within the Division's battlezone. Memorializing the victims of these atrocities, the administrative regions of Lizzano in Belvedere and Gaggio Montano in the Emilia-Romagna Apennines have erected monuments and plaques.

Riva Ridge and Monte Belvedere

The Division arrived at the front lines and led the limited action known as Operation Encore with the support of the Allied BEF and the US 92nd Infantry in reserve. This operation was to secure better positions for the planned Allied 1945 spring offensive towards the Po River Valley. Hill 913, discussed below, was part of the Division's battle-zone and a divisional objective, and consequently became one of many warscapes created and etched into divisional memory during the spring advance of 1945.

On the night of 18 February 1945, the Division prepared for their first attack, which would be the night ascent of Riva Ridge and then Monte Belvedere. On their front in the mountains to the north, they were opposed by troops of the Infanterie Regiment 232 (Isserman 2019: 137). In an irregular-shaped mountain bowl formed by three high ridges (Figure 12.3), the Division's soldiers were positioned with their backs to Monte Grande on the south; they faced the Germans on the north along all the high ground of the 5.6 kilometre-long Serriccia-Campiano Ridge line, designated as 'Riva Ridge'[14] and along the Belvedere-Torraccia Ridge. Riva Ridge (Figure 12.4) was an observation and communications post that controlled the German forward slopes of Monte Belvedere (Figure 12.5). A much more strongly defended mountain to the northeast, Monte Belvedere, was the southwestern-most peak of the southwest/

FIGURE 12.3 Google Earth oblique view northwards of the irregular-shaped mountain bowl with Riva Ridge on the northwest, Monte Belvedere on the northeast, and Monte Grande on the south. The Division's five attack routes on 18 February 1945 ascended Riva Ridge's southeastern slope. Source: © Google Earth Landsat/Copernicus.

FIGURE 12.4 View looking west at Riva Ridge from Monte Belvedere. Source: © author.

FIGURE 12.5 View looking east at Monte Belvedere from Riva Ridge. Source: © author.

northeast-trending Belvedere-Torraccia Ridge line. The German defensive system here epitomized the layout and organization of the deadly landscape that the Division encountered throughout the northern Apennines. The German Army controlled the high points and defended them with a concept of 'defence in depth', consisting of natural landscapes, built barriers, minefields, explosive traps, hidden snipers, and plunging fire from machine guns, mortars, and artillery.

Riva Ridge was less fortified than Monte Belvedere because the Germans believed its steep icy cliffs facing south towards the American lines protected the ridge-top from attack. The Germans were confident of their defences because the two ridges had already been assaulted unsuccessfully by Allied forces on three separate occasions. In preparation for the new attack, part of the Division moved under cover of night to the base of Riva Ridge and waited in the narrow valley of the Dardagna River. Riva Ridge above was a frozen finger-like mountain range with multiple snowy peaks and a river flowing below. The majority of the rest of the Division was hidden at the southwestern base of the slightly lower and less steep Monte Belvedere, about five kilometres east of Riva Ridge. All this high ground was occupied by *Wehrmacht* soldiers supported by their *Gebirgsjäger* – specialist mountain troops – who knew they were about to lose the war but nevertheless continued to fight from their high ground, manning machine guns, mortars, and artillery from behind ubiquitous barbed wire and mines.

At Riva Ridge, soldiers of the Division conducted one of the most daring mountain combat actions of the war. Weeks prior to the attack, Division climbers had secretly reconnoitred and selected five routes up the 2,000-foot-high (610 metres) ridge that they would use for their night attack. One of the few landscape advantages the Division's mountaineers had over the German troops entrenched above them was that they were fighting about 1,850 metres below the elevation of Camp Hale; they fought below that elevation for the rest of their combat in the Apennines. Unintimidated by the elevation and slope of these Italian mountains, the Division's soldiers were at one with their landscape.

In approximately ten hours of climbing (equivalent to a day's training at Camp Hale), the Division's mountaineers led several groups of more than 700 soldiers armed with small arms and hand grenades up the steep ice and snow-coated cliffs of Riva Ridge, immediately below German outposts. Two of the five routes required pitons and ropes. Conducted overnight, the surprise assault was completely successful, taking all enemy positions, and defending against all counterattacks.[15] Significantly, the defeat of these German counterattacks saw the Division triumph over some of its direct counterparts in the German Army, the *Gebirgsjäger* battalion, attached to Infanterie Division 232.[16] With German observers thus ejected from Riva Ridge, the rest of the Division could begin their uphill assault on Monte Belvedere and Monte Gorgolesco the following night. The Division broke the German mountain defences and, moving northeast, knocked them out until 6 March 1945; from then until 14 April, they regrouped and occupied the village of Castel d'Aiano and the high ground of Monte della Spe. During that time, they patrolled and probed their front, and prepared for the Allied spring advance to drive into the Po River Valley on 14 April.

The 1945 spring breakout and Hill 913

The first three days of the spring offensive (14–16 April 1945) were the worst of the war for the Division, with 1,336 casualties. On 14 April, Companies I, K, and L of the 85th Mountain Regiment on Monte della Spe had Hills 883 and 913 as their primary objectives and began their combat day watching the Allied air force bomb these and other hills to their north. Following the bombing, a 35-minute artillery and mortar barrage concentrated on the companies' main objectives, Hills 883, and 913, blanketing the area with smoke and dust. By the time Company L began their mid-morning advance across the valley separating Monte della Spe and Hill 913, most of the artillery smoke had dissipated. They took Hills 883 and 913 the same day.

Hill 913 was intensively mapped in 2019 as part of our fieldwork because it is a well-preserved example of the organization and layout of a Second World War German mountain defence (Figure 12.6). The data adds physical evidence to the historical documentation of the Division's battle-zone and training landscape. Our preliminary mapping results indicate that on the hilltop and around its slopes there are as many as 100 features associated with the Division's 14–15 April 1945 actions which captured it. Included here is Bunker A, a rectangular deep depression measuring approximately nine metres long, five metres wide, and five metres deep (Figure 12.7); four linear communication trenches – three averaging 20 metres long and one nearly 40 metres long – all terminating in circular pits at the south-facing slope edge; at least four U-shaped depressions likely representing mortar positions; and a mix of about 75 rectangular, circular, or irregularly shaped depressions representing artillery, mortar, and bomb hits, fox holes, and other unidentified combat features encircling the hilltop (Figures 12.6 and 12.8). When combined with historical documentation, these data from Hill 913 provide a detailed plan of the layout and organization of a specific German strongpoint within the Gothic Line battle-zone. Zones of fire and supporting minefields can be accurately determined and explored, and accounts of individual soldiers can be traced across today's landscape.

The German positions encountered by the Division at Hill 913 were similar to the 'Mountain Defence' diagrammed by Bull and Noon (2013: 28–29), and their information was used to interpret the GNSS-mapped features of Hill 913.[17] The mountain defence at Hill 913 (Figure 12.6) can be interpreted as consisting of forward slopes running down from the hilltop that contained isolated forward observers, snipers, and hidden machine-gun nests. The forward slopes were a German-controlled no man's land; patrols from both armies entered and exited this area, probing each other's defences and collecting intelligence. German machine guns were dug into the high point, just back from the forward slope's edge. On the rear slope, bombproof bunkers (Bunkers A and B in Figure 12.6;

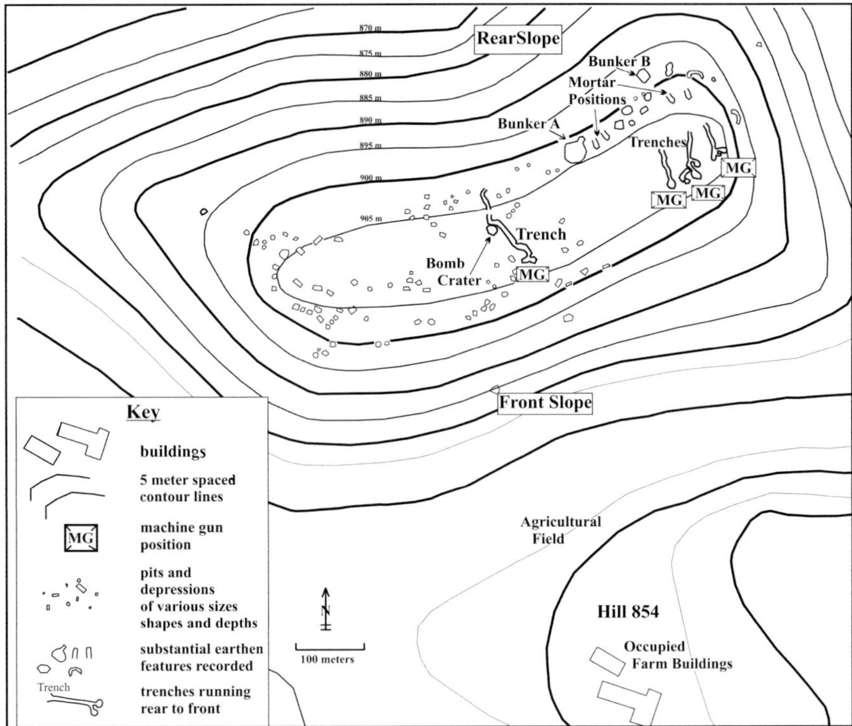

FIGURE 12.6 GNSS-produced sketch map of Hill 913 showing the defences. Soldiers of the Division attacked from the south and west, and the former had to capture Hill 854 first. Source: © author.

Bunker A in Figure 12.8) were constructed with communication trenches connecting them to the machine-gun pits at the front slope. Mortars and (most likely) artillery were also positioned in this rear area, and in combat, they concentrated arched plunging fire onto or beyond the front slope towards the enemy.

The Division's standard manoeuvre to defeat these strong points was to attract fire by attacking the German front slope. While the main body held fire to the front, one or more soldiers tried to flank the German position, attacking from the side. However, this type of attack in the Apennines had to coordinate with other forces advancing on the surrounding hilltop strongpoints to disturb and distract overlapping defensive fire. As part of the battle-zone landscape at Hill 913, the Division's John Magrath was awarded the Medal of Honor (posthumously) in part for successfully conducting this flanking manoeuvre at Hill 909 immediately east of Hill 913 on 14 April.

There are extensive first-person accounts as well as many military records that can be used to interpret the landscape of the Hill 913 battle-zone. However, the portion of the battle-zone presented in Figure 12.8 follows descriptions

FIGURE 12.7 View southwest of the remains of Bunker A on the rear (north) slope of Hill 913. In the foreground, boulders line a 100-centimetre-wide path and the scale marks the bunker's entrance. Source: © author.

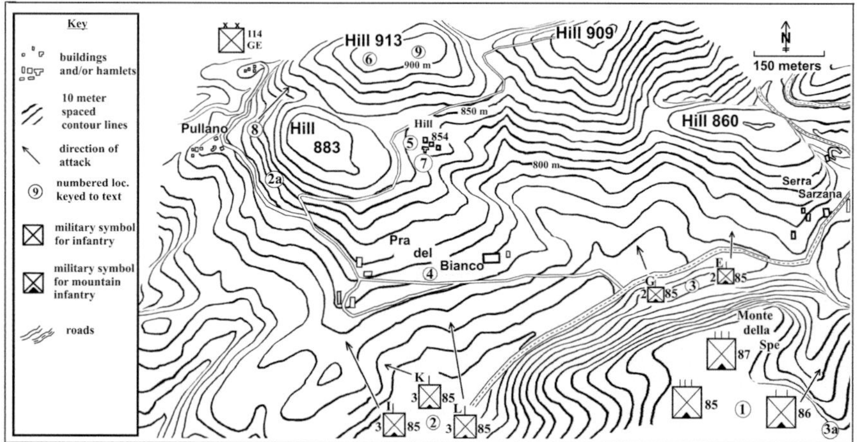

FIGURE 12.8 The Hill 913 battle-zone landscape on 14 April 1945. The Division (shown with military symbols) occupied Monte della Spe and confronted German-occupied Hills 883, 913, 909, and 860. The German 114th Infantry Division is shown as a military symbol upper left. Source: © author.

provided in the Division's history (Imbrie and Imbrie 2004), the 85th Mountain Regiment's history (Woodruff 1945), and W. Putnam's first-hand account (1991: 120–132).

Hill 913 conflict landscape

The following list of numbered points refers to locations in the landscape of the Hill 913 battle-zone presented in Figures 12.6 and 12.8.

1) Military symbols representing the Division's three mountain regiments of the 85th, 86th, and 87th on 14 April 1945 occupying the high point of the Hill 913 battle-zone, Monte della Spe.
2) Military symbols representing the three Companies I, K, and L (3rd Battalion, 85th Mountain Regiment) at mid-morning, coming from the west side of Monte della Spe to attack north towards Hill 913. L is to attack the front slope of Hill 913 via Pra del Bianco, a sloping agricultural field.
    a) I followed by K are to attack the left (west) approach of Hill 913 via Hill 883 and the hamlet of Pullano. Tanks that are supposed to support I, K, and L are delayed due to mines to the south (not shown). I and K continue to be stalled on the southwest slopes of Hill 883 because of steep terrain and minefields.
3) Military symbols representing Companies G and E of the 2nd Battalion of the 87th Mountain Regiment at the base of Monte della Spe on 14 April ready to attack hills 860 and 909 at the same time as I, K, and L attack hills 883 and 913.
    a) Elements of the 86th Mountain Regiment will attack to the northeast towards Rocca Roffino.
4) A platoon from L becomes pinned down in the Pra del Bianco near an east–west trending road and agricultural field. The field is mined, and machine-gun fire from above has stopped them. Lieutenant Putnam arrives and rallies a few other soldiers upward towards farmhouses on Hill 854 below Hill 913. This group of soldiers is later followed by others from the pinned-down platoon to the farmhouses.
5) A firefight occurs at the farmhouses, and several German soldiers surrender with Italian civilians also present. The German prisoners agree to go to the top of Hill 913, with Putnam calling out for other Germans to surrender.
6) As the Americans and their prisoners reach the top of Hill 913, dozens more *Wehrmacht* soldiers surrender. At the same time, the US Army begins shelling the hill, and American and *Wehrmacht* soldiers shelter together in a bunker (Bunker A, Figure 12.6). The shelling stops and the few Americans and their prisoners withdraw to the buildings at Hill 854. Later the Americans

return in force and occupy Hill 913, taking additional prisoners and remaining in control, under German artillery shelling.

7) By mid-morning, most of L Company have arrived at Hill 854 but I company is still 183 metres from Hill 883. Tanks remain stalled by mines.
8) At mid-afternoon, I Company is depleted due to casualties from minefields and machine-gun fire as they try to move up the southwest slope of Hill 883. K moves through I's position, making it onto the left flank of Hill 913 by late afternoon. Shortly thereafter, some American tanks arrive on the west flank of Hill 913, but others are still slowed by the large minefield on that slope.
9) At dusk, Hill 913 is occupied by K and L. By night, all the tanks have reached Hill 913. Hills 883 and 913 are occupied and held that night by several American companies. During this action, several thousand mines are removed from Hill 913.

Conclusion

There are several important differences between the conflict landscapes of the Camp in the Rocky Mountains and the Division's battle-zone in the Apennine Mountains. First, of course, Camp Hale was a facsimile battle-zone with no combat casualties. Second, as assessed during fieldwork, the Camp is a federally protected and administered historic site, while the Division's Italian battle-zone sites are officially unprotected due to the absence of Italian heritage laws governing landscapes, sites, and material culture from the Second World War. Despite this, the sites are generally well signposted and their material now professionally curated, identified, and interpreted by local private and community interests at the Monti della Riva and Iola di Montese museums. These actions have created several new contemporary landscapes – a partly cleared, partly annotated, but still undocumented battle-zone, and a new museological landscape. It is worth commenting that while the facsimile landscape of Camp Hale is protected by law, the real battle-zone landscape (with all its national, political, and emotional aspects) has no recognition or protection – the simulacrum appears more valued than the authentic.

Third, the Camp and its Rocky Mountains training landscape are both higher than the Division's actual battle-zones in the Apennines. The slopes of Riva Ridge, however, are actually steeper than that of the Pando Valley's east mountain slope (Figure 12.9) used daily for training at the Camp. The Rocky Mountain landscape actually prepared the American mountain soldiers to manoeuvre in a terrain that was more difficult than the one which confronted them in the Apennines. The only mountaineering skills needed by the Division in the Italian Campaign were for ski patrols conducted in the vicinity of their front when they first arrived, and for the Riva Ridge attack. However, of the five routes used in the Riva Ridge attack, only two required climbing equipment (Isserman 2019: 168). By the time the Division led the Allies' spring breakout in 1945 and

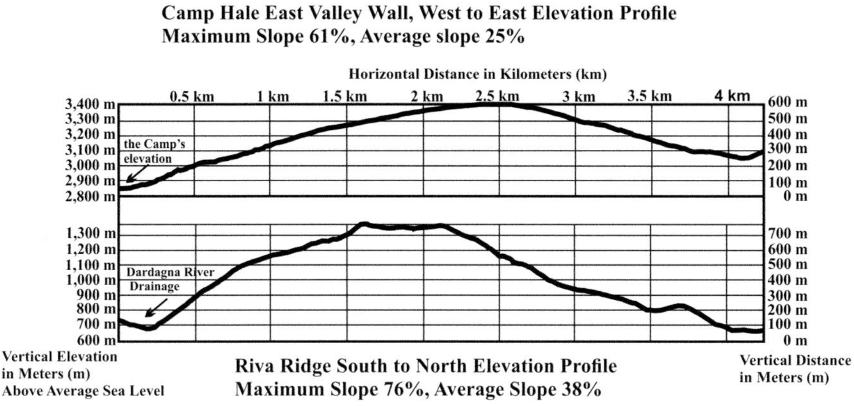

FIGURE 12.9 Graphs drawn from Google Earth elevation profile data for the west-facing mountain slope of Camp Hale and the southeast-facing mountain slope of Riva Ridge. Source: © Google Earth data; graph by author.

captured Hill 913, they were basically common infantry soldiers with no need for mountaineering skills.

Nevertheless, the relationship between these soldiers and their conflict landscapes was deeply formative, physically and psychologically. It was the intensity of their training and enculturation regime in the Rocky Mountains that allowed the US Army to create efficient specialized mountain infantrymen able to mount a successful operation in their designated terrain almost 'straight off the boat'. This was achieved despite the US Army having no tradition of mountain warfare – unlike their German opponents, particularly the *Gebirgsjäger* who counterattacked at the Riva Ridge. The 10th Mountain Division retained their dynamic identity after their mountain victory, successfully leading the US 5th Army into the Po River Valley.

Acknowledgements

I would like to thank Marco Belogi, Susan Daniels, Andrea Gandolfi, Amy Nelson, Kelly Pool, Massimo Turchi, Susan van Dyck, and John Winterburn. They all helped me map and map onto the landscape of the 10th Mountain Division in the Apennine Mountains of Emilia-Romagna, Italy.

Notes

1 The term 'military landscape' acknowledges the association between training sites and areas which saw fighting. Saunders and Cornish (2009: 5) use the term 'battlezone landscapes' for the First World War. Anthropologically, 'landscape' is commonly understood as a physical presence (i.e. the environment) and the socially and experientially constructed lives of people created from and within their environment.

These two aspects are in constant flux, and some investigators have argued for a more open-ended understanding of landscape, time, and space (Bender 2002). Landscape in this view is much more reflexive and reflective of social interaction and social knowledge than it is of the physical world, and the creation of various spaces and places by people are shaped and informed by the past and are continually renegotiated and redefined (Bender 2001, 2002; Tilley 1994). Military landscapes therefore are not only those of fighting, but also of memorialization and heritage.

2 The Second World War 10th Mountain Division was established and deactivated during that conflict. Surviving data makes clear the unusual nature of this highly trained, well-motivated, and (initially) civilian-inspired formation. The 10th Mountain Division of the twenty-first century is an all-terrain, all-theatre formation, connected to the original division only by the fact that it honours it by employing its name.

3 The fieldwork project, *Archaeology of the Night Climb: The Material Culture and Conflict Landscape of the 10th Mountain Division*, is a research consortium of Metcalf Archaeological Consultants, Inc. (USA), and the Iola di Montese and Monti della Riva museums of Italy.

4 The regular army of Germany during the Second World War.

5 Rottman and Denis (2012: 41) state that in 114 days of combat the Division suffered 4,086 combat casualties, including 952 dead. They calculated that the Division had 30% total casualties.

6 Aerial photography was provided by the Allied Mediterranean Airforce in 1945. Currently, the remaining photographs and negatives for Italy are stored in the 'National Collection of Aerial Photography (NCAP), Edinburgh, GB [sic]; Aerofototeca Nazionale, Rome, Italy; Centre C. Jullian, Aix-en-Provence, France. The original negatives, partially preserved by NCAP and National Archives and Records Administration (NARA), are currently being digitized by NCAP' (M. Belogi, personal communication, 17 February 2020). The limited archival information currently available online from NCAP includes no Division areas.

7 For a strongpoint to be truly effective, it must be part of an integrated system (Hill and Wileman 2002: 138).

8 In the 1983 Colorado OAHP site plan (White River National Forest Archive), there are four machine-gun ranges facing the cantonment's west valley wall, each having approximately 400 metres of narrow target range. Presumably, somewhere in the training area beyond the Pando Valley in the higher mountains, there were areas for longer-range target firing for machine guns.

9 According to Witte (2015), this was created by spraying water on the mountain side, and ice features such as 'seracs and crevasses' were constructed using logs and steep terrain coated with ice. The glacier would not stay frozen and was eventually abandoned.

10 Most effects of high elevation stem from poor sleep, likely due to difficulty in breathing, which causes daytime drowsiness. Acute mountain sickness (exposure to low oxygen at elevation causing headaches, nausea, sleeplessness, and dizziness) is the most common adverse neurological effect, with high-altitude cerebral oedema the most severe (swelling of the brain causing an extreme headache, disorientation, and lethargy).

11 A US Army Infantry Division of this period comprised three infantry regiments (each of three battalions), and further units providing artillery support, reconnaissance, transport, engineering, etc. An infantry division has three to five battalions, a battalion three to four companies, a company three to four platoons, a platoon three to four squads, and a squad six to ten riflemen.

12 The rigours of the D-Series hit divisional morale, which dropped even lower when, in May 1944, it was rumoured that the formation would be disbanded, though by November the Army had changed its mind again (Putnam 1991: 78–81). Morale remained low when the Division was transferred to Texas for training on lowland terrain, and only recovered when it embarked for Italy at the end of 1944.

13 Up to this time (i.e. from 15 July 1944), the unit had been called the 10th Light Division (Pack, Alpine) (Rottman and Dennis 2012: 18).
14 Isserman (2019: 157) infers that military intelligence renamed it Riva Ridge after a high point in the same Serriccia-Campiano Ridge line.
15 The mountaineers eventually placed .30- and .50-calibre machine guns, 60-millimetre mortars, and a 75-millimetre mountain howitzer (delivered by mule) on the ridge-tops, ensuring they could hold the position.
16 Sources vary as to the precise identity of this unit, which was either *Hochgebirgsjäger Lehr-Bataillon Mittenwald* or *Hochgebirgsjäger Bataillon 4*. As both units were attached to Infanterie Regiment 232, it is quite possible that men of both units were involved in the counterattacks.
17 Interpretive signs are present on the hill, but they provide only broad information about the attack.

References

Bender, B. (2001) Introduction. In B. Bender and M. Winer (eds.), *Contested Landscapes, Movement, Exile and Place*, pp. 1–18. Oxford: Berg.

——— (2002) Time and Landscape. *Current Anthropology* 43 (4): 103–112.

Bull, S. and S. Noon (2013) *World War II Winter and Mountain Tactics*. Oxford: Osprey Publishing.

Burchell, M.A. (2019) *Decoding a Royal Marine Commando: The Militarized Body as Artefact*. London: Routledge.

Cossin, C.V. (2001) *I Soldiered with America's Elite 10th Mountain Division of W.W.II*. USA: First Books.

De Nardi, S. (2017) *The Poetics of Conflict Experience: Materiality and Embodiment in Second World War Italy*. London: Routledge.

Dusenberry, H. and W. Ware (1991) *Ski the High Trail, World War II Ski Troopers in the High Colorado Rockies*. Portland: Binford and Mort.

Ellis, R. (1996) *See Naples and Die, A ski Trooper's World War II Memoir*. Jefferson: McFarland and Company.

Feuer, A.B. (2006) *Packs On! Memoirs of the 10th Mountain Division in WWII*. Mechanicsburg: Stackpole Books.

Head, L. (2010) Cultural Landscapes. In D. Hicks and M. Beaudry (eds.), *The Oxford Handbook of Material Culture Studies*, pp. 427–458. Oxford: Oxford University Press.

Hill, P. and J. Wileman (2002) *Landscapes of War: The Archaeology of Aggression and Defence*. Gloucestershire: Tempest Publishing.

Imbrie, J. and B. Imbrie. (Comps) (2004) Chronology of the 10th Mountain Division in World War II, 06 January – November 1945. *International Skiing History*. https://skiinghistory.org/chronology-10th-mountain-division-world-war-ii (accessed 31 December 2019).

Isserman, M. (2019) *The Winter Army. The World War II Odyssey of the 10th Mountain Division, America's Elite Alpine Warriors* (Kindle Edition). Boston: Houghton Mifflin Harcourt.

Jenkins, M. (2003) *The Last Ridge*. New York: Random House.

Jennings, C. (2016) *At War on the Gothic Line, Fighting in Italy, 1944–1945*. New York: Thomas Dune Books (St. Martin's Press).

Levine, B. (2016) *How High-Altitude Training Can Benefit Elite Endurance Athletes Like Runners and Swimmers*. University of Texas Southwestern Medical Center. https://utswmed.org/medblog/high-altitude-training/ (accessed 10 January 2020).

Putnam, L. (1991) *Green Cognac, The Education of a Mountain Fighter.* New York: AAC Press.

Rottman, G. and P. Dennis. (2012) *US 10th Mountain Division in World War II.* Oxford: Osprey Publishing.

Saunders, N.J. and P. Cornish. (2009) Introduction. In N.J. Saunders and P. Cornish (eds.), *Contested Objects: Material Memories of the Great War*, pp 1–10. London: Routledge.

Tilley, C. (1994) *A Phenomenology of Landscape: Places, Paths and Monuments.* Oxford: Berg Publishers.

Whitlock, F. and B. Bishop (1992) *Soldiers on Skis, A Pictorial Memoir of the 10th Mountain Division.* Boulder: Paladin Press.

Witte, D.R. (2015) *World War II at Camp Hale, Blazing a New Trail in the Rockies.* Charleston: History Press.

Woodruff, J. (1945) History of the 85th Mountain Infantry Regiment. *skitrooper.org.* www.skitrooper.org/85.pdf (Accessed 31 December 2019).

Zalewska, A., J.M. Scott and G. Kiarszys (2017) Introduction: Materiality of Troubled Pasts. Archaeologies of Conflicts and Wars. In A. Zalewska, J.M. Scott and G. Kiarszys (eds.), *The Materiality of Troubled Pasts Archaeologies of Conflicts and Wars*, pp. 11–20. Warsaw: Department of Archaeology, Szczecin University, Roadside History Lessons Foundation.

13

WAR IN THE NORMANDY *BOCAGE*

British perceptions and memory of a militarized landscape

Paul Cornish

> Awfully Stiff Country this ... If he attempts to take some of our big banked bullfinches in his stride, with a yawner on each side, will get into grief.
>
> Robert Surtees, *Mr Sponge's Sporting Tour*, 1853

The *bocage* country of the Calvados and Manche Departments of Normandy is an artefactual landscape, with its origins nowadays assigned (after a long academic debate) to late medieval times (Watteaux 2005). During and after the Second World War it gained unwonted notoriety as a conflict landscape, due to the bitter fighting that occurred in it following the 1944 D-Day landings. This paper does not seek to add yet another description of the military operations of June to August 1944 to an already congested field, but rather to investigate the impact of the terrain on the British soldiers who fought in it and the legacy of their experiences in terms of memory and historiography.

Encountering the *bocage*

Operation Overlord, the Allied invasion of German-occupied Europe in 1944, was the most complex military operation ever mounted. The primary task facing the planners was getting sufficient forces safely ashore in the face of German defences and fickle weather conditions. The beaches of Normandy were selected because they were less well-defended than those of the Pas-de-Calais, but still within the range of fighter aircraft operating from the UK. Mounting an invasion there also made the best use of Southern England's transport infrastructure (Davies 1946: 615). This was doubly important, as once a beachhead had been established the challenge principally became one of logistics – augmenting the newly landed forces and keeping them supplied. To the surprise of the Germans, no major port was encompassed in the initial landing area. This was because the

Allies brought their own port facilities in the shape of two floating Mulberry harbours. The plan for post–D-Day operations, personally outlined at a briefing given by the invasion force commander, General Sir Bernard Montgomery, on 7 April 1944, envisaged a steady advance to secure a 'lodgement area' from which mobile operations could be launched (D'Este 1984: 85–86).

The outer limit of the lodgement area, to be attained by D+17, was defined as 'the main enemy lateral GRANVILLE-VIRE-ARGENTAN-FALAISE-CAEN' (D'Este 1984: 86, 91). This is significant as that line lay across the breadth of the Normandy *bocage* country. The *bocage* was (and to a large extent remains) an agricultural landscape composed of small fields enclosed by hedges. Current thinking dates the origins of this manmade landscape to the fifteenth century, with continued development over the succeeding centuries, largely in response to the demands of the growing population of Paris for beef and dairy produce. From an anthropological perspective, it is therefore an early and quintessential example of a 'Western and capitalist' landscape (Tilley 1994: 20). The hedgerows built to confine cattle became, over time, a very solid feature of the terrain. By 1944 they sprouted from banks formed from earth and roots, which were flanked by ditches and studded with trees. Small, often sunken, roads and tracks wound between them. And through the *bocage* ran streams and rivers, frequently in steeply sided wooded courses.[1]

The D-Day planners were aware of the existence of this typically Norman terrain. Montgomery himself expressed the opinion that the Germans would adopt a

> roping-off policy, and must then hold firm on the important ground which dominates and controls the road axes in the 'bocage' country which are: the high ground east of the River Dives, the high ground between Falaise and St Lô between the rivers Orne and Vire, and the high ground west of the River Vire.
>
> *(D'Este 1984: 85)*

What they did not anticipate was the difficulty of attaining their proposed lodgement area. First, the Germans did not react as expected to the Allied assault. Instead of making the sort of limited withdrawals that the Allied planners assumed, they fought hard for every inch of ground and mounted numerous local counterattacks to regain territory that they had lost. The key to this struggle was the possession of commanding areas of high ground (see Buckley 2014: 66–183; Milner 2012). Second, the weather came to the aid of the defenders.

A violent storm on the night of 18–19 June destroyed one Mulberry harbour and damaged the other. This severely hampered the build-up of the Allied forces. It proved to be the nadir of a spell of poor weather that prevailed until late July, significantly reducing the availability of air support to the Allied ground forces (Belfield et al. 1965: 19; Davies 1946: 631). These factors combined to ensure that the process of establishing the planned lodgement area was much slower and bloodier than had been expected. Before reaching the line of the high ground on which Montgomery had expected German resistance to crystallize, the Allies were obliged to fight their way through much of the *bocage* country. The heaviest burden of fighting in this terrain fell upon the American First Army, with the British-Canadian Second Army only partially engaged in this type of country. Nevertheless, the costly, close-quarter struggle for the *bocage* had a lasting impact on both the British soldiers who fought there and on those who have subsequently recorded and analyzed their experience and actions.

Fighting in the *bocage*

The unique nature of the battles fought in the *bocage* between June and August 1944 by Montgomery's 21st Army Group[2] was quickly established in the immediate post-war literature on the campaign. The first books to appear were written by eye-witnesses. The former Allied supreme commander, Dwight D. Eisenhower, writing in 1948, recalled

> the prevalence of formidable hedgerows in the bocage country. In this region the fields have for centuries past been divided into very small areas, sometimes scarcely more than building-lot size, each surrounded by a dense and heavy hedge which ordinarily grows out of a bank of earth three or four feet in height. Sometimes these hedges and supporting banks are double, forming a ready-made trench between them, and of course affording almost the ultimate in battlefield protection.
>
> *(Eisenhower 1948: 294)*

In 1954, former war correspondent Chester Wilmot described this

> area of undulating hills broken by steep-sided valleys of innumerable streams. The hills become more rugged and more heavily covered with woods and thickets as you move south-west along the few straight, tree-lined highways or the countless tortuous side-roads … Its dominant characteristic is the hedgerow – a bank three or four feet high with a ditch on either side and topped by a line of thorny bushes whose deep roots bind the earth into a wall which will rebuff even bulldozers.
>
> *(Wilmot 1954: 329–330)*

Curiously, the person who might be expected to have been most closely concerned with the problems caused by this terrain, Field Marshal Montgomery, makes only passing references to it (Montgomery 1947: 21, 66, 71; Montgomery 1954: 239). All subsequent accounts of the campaign make 'sometimes florid' references to the Norman terrain (Badsey 2006: 50). Among the plethora of recent popular studies on the subject, the centrality of the *bocage* to the fighting in Normandy is a common trope. A quick glance at the titles alone of currently in-print books yields *The Battle of the Hedgerows* (Daugherty 2001; Zaloga 2017), *Dying for Saint-Lô: Hedgerow Hell* (Lodieu 2007), *Normandy 1944: The Battle of the Hedgerows* (Forty 2018), and *Bocage: The Battle for Normandy* (Pisani 2018). The difficulties caused by this 'terrible' terrain are often presented as proof of a failure in Allied planning and training, in that insufficient attention was given to preparing to fight in it (Hastings 1985: 43; D'Este 1984: 104; Horne 1994: 147).

The existence of the *bocage* was of course well known, as the specific mention of it in 'Monty's' briefing makes clear. His British Army superior, Field Marshal Sir Alan Brooke, was remembered by two fellow members of the Allied high command as being pessimistic about traversing this country, of which he had personal knowledge (Tedder 1966: 563; D'Este 1984: 87). Marshal of the Royal Air Force Lord Tedder claimed that Brooke told him that 'I know the bocage country from my boyhood days and they will never get through it'. Given that Brooke's childhood was divided between the foothills of the Pyrenees and County Fermanagh this seems a dubious recollection (Fraser 1982: 10–22). Anthony Beevor makes the more believable suggestion that Brooke passed through the *bocage* during 1940; by which time he would have been looking at it through the eyes of a soldier rather than those of a schoolboy (Beevor 2009: 253). We know from Brooke's diary that, during his brief command of British forces in France post-Dunkirk, he was driven from Cherbourg to Le Mans (Danchev and Todman 2001: 79). One likely route, passing through St Lô and Vire, would have taken him through the heart of the *bocage*.

The original planner of Overlord, Lieutenant-General Frederick Morgan, did not record such undiluted pessimism from Brooke. Among his own staff, the prevalent thinking was that the *bocage* had the potential to offer advantages to both sides (Morgan 1950: 163–164). This analysis underlies a pre-invasion appreciation conducted by Supreme Headquarters Allied Expeditionary Force (SHAEF):

> Generally speaking the area will not be an easy one for forces to advance through rapidly in the face of determined resistance, but it will likewise be most difficult for the enemy to prevent a slow and steady advance by infiltration. Bocage country may not be suitable for the employment of tanks in mass although tanks can penetrate most of the hedgerows and could no doubt work in small groups with infantry to good advantage … It is difficult to judge whether such terrain favours defending or attacking infantry … The tactics to be employed in the fighting through bocage country should be given considerable study by formations to be employed therein.
>
> *(National Archives WO 205/118)*

It appears clear, however, that few of the formations scheduled to fight in Normandy did in fact give sufficient thought to the potential problems posed by the *bocage*. With regard to the Americans, one authority states that the military characteristics of the *bocage* 'seem to have taken First Army by complete surprise' and that 'despite Allied planners' awareness of the nature of the *Bocage*, American commanders had done little to prepare their units for fighting among the hedgerows.' (Doubler 1988: 21). Most British formations were little better prepared. For example, the 7th Armoured Division, famous from the North African campaign as the 'Desert Rats', did its pre–D-Day training on the open heaths of the Norfolk Breckland. It was not, as one officer recalled, 'tuned-up to the conditions that we had to fight in the first few months in the *bocage*' (IWM Sound 10896: Reel 3). Other formations trained in equally unhelpful areas, such as the North York Moors and Salisbury Plain. There was at least one exception, in the form of 43rd (Wessex) Division, which trained in West Kent where,

> the enclosed country around Stone Street strikingly resembled the Normandy Bocage. Without realising the fact, therefore, the Division, in contrast with those accustomed to the Western Desert, became particularly well attuned to the conditions it had to face from the very moment it landed in France.
>
> *(Essame 1952: 55)*

This recollection reminds us that there was actually no shortage of potential training areas in England and Wales that resembled the Norman *bocage*, much of Devon and the High Weald of Sussex and Kent being prime examples. The failure to make use of them may have stemmed from reluctance to disturb vital agriculture (Buckley 2004: 83). However, this recent summing up of the question rings true:

> Everyone expected and trained for the best case – quick breakthrough leading to mobile war – and ignored the prospect of having to fight through the bocage, which seemed pessimistic and old fashioned. This issue fell through that gap in intelligence, planning and training.
>
> *(Ferris 2006: 195)*

The upshot was that formations finding themselves engaged with the enemy in the *bocage* were obliged to adapt their tactics and techniques on the spot. The steepest learning curve was that followed by the US First Army. Fighting in the very densest part of the *bocage*, around St Lô and across the middle of the Cotentin Peninsula, the Americans initially struggled badly. This was a type of terrain that none of them had experienced in either peace or war. The man in charge of providing tactical air support, General Elwood 'Pete' Quesada, put it bluntly: 'We were flabbergasted by the *bocage*. Our infantry had become paralysed. It has never been adequately described how immobilized they were by the sound of small-arms fire among the hedges' (Hastings 1985: 289). But the Americans adapted their tactics to meet the challenge, and also cut the tactical Gordian Knot by introducing a device that allowed tanks to cut passages through the hedgerows (de Lee 2006; Doubler 1988).

It is clear also that formations of the Second Army revised their tactics and patterns of deployment to cope with the *bocage*. Particular attention was devoted to improving the level of cooperation between infantry battalions and the armoured units deputed to support them (Buckley 2004: 98–102). Infantry divisions generally received the support of independent armoured brigades (with American Sherman tanks) or tank brigades (with British Churchill infantry tanks). An example of the importance of this inter-arm cooperation was provided by the 15th (Scottish) Division, whose interaction with the 31st Tank Brigade during Operation Epsom (26–30 June) was seen as poor, but which worked excellently in harness with 6th Guards Tank Brigade, with whom it had previously trained in the UK, during Operation Bluecoat (30 July–7 August) (Buckley 2014: 87, 153). Armoured divisions fielded both an armoured brigade and an infantry brigade, but efforts were made to break down this binary structure and to integrate the deployment of the individual units that made up the two brigades (Buckley 2014: 131; Daglish 2009: 57; French 2000: 269-70). Major B.E.L. Burton of the 1/5 Queen's Regiment recalled this occurring in the 7th Armoured Division between 6 and 16 July, when 'intensive training' in a 'technique for coping with the Germans in the Norman *bocage* country' was undertaken. This necessitated integration at the sub-unit level, as it involved 'the closest possible cooperation between the individual tank and the infantry working with it' (IWM Documents 2558a: 19).

Experiencing the *bocage*

So how did British soldiers experience the *bocage*? The overwhelming impression gained from the testimony of those who fought in it is that it was perceived as a landscape of lurking danger, where restricted views concealed a variety of threats to life and limb. The embanked hedges offered superb cover for defending infantry. Troops advanced in a state of extreme tension, awaiting the sounds that spelt danger, the crack of a hidden sniper's bullet or, worse, the 'tearing cloth' rasp of a fast-firing German machine gun (Buckley 2014: 135).[3] An officer of the Durham Light Infantry recalled, 'You were just walking blind, until somebody opened fire … they were initiating everything … that was why everyone felt nervous because we were walking along and we go on until somebody shoots at us' (IWM Sound 28699: Reel 6). The trees that lined the hedges, and the copses and woods that dotted the landscape, harboured other dangers. The effectiveness of German mortar bombs (already the chief threat to British soldiers) was enhanced by this leafy canopy. The foliage and brushwood were dense enough to actuate the sensitive impact-fuzes of the bombs, causing showers of deadly fragments from 'air-bursts' – significantly more deadly than the same effect when a mortar bomb exploded on, or in, the ground (IWM Documents 2558a: 16; IWM Sound 10415: Reel 4; IWM Sound 10599: Reel 20).[4] Conversely, the closeness of the country hindered the ability of British mortar crews to observe the fall of their own fire. They were forced to fire 'off the map' – i.e. by using map references only (Picot 1993: 80; IWM Sound 10599: Reel 20).

Infantrymen bore the chief burden of these threats. Overall, the Allied armies in Normandy suffered 200,000 casualties in the course of the campaign. Over the years of planning for the invasion Allied leaders – particularly the British, and none more so than Winston Churchill – had been desperate to avoid a static bloodbath like the Western Front of the Great War (Buckley 2014: 297; Fraser 1982: 521) The fighting in Normandy temporarily made their fears a reality, with casualties being sustained at a higher rate than that endured by the British at the 1917 Battle of Passchendaele. By far the largest proportion of these losses was visited upon the infantry. Just 14 per cent of the men in the British 2nd Army served in infantry companies, but these men at the 'sharp-end' suffered 70 per cent of its casualties (Sheffield 2006: 121). Their morale and mental state deteriorated accordingly – although it should be noted that not all of their losses and setbacks occurred in the *bocage* (Buckley 2014: 140–143).

Armoured vehicle crews were safer but appear to have found the *bocage* even more intimidating. An infantryman of the 43rd (Wessex) Division retained the following impression: 'It was a debatable question – whether you was a "tankie" or an infantryman – neither side would say that their side was better off, but nobody would want to swap' (IWM Sound 21548: Reel 6). Trooper Ernie Marlow of the 7th Armoured Division described it as 'the last place for tanks to be in, but there we were' (IWM Documents 26095: 79). Lack of visibility was the central problem for tank crews. Seeing the outside world from the claustrophobic interior of a tank was never easy; in the *bocage* it became much harder. A trooper of the 8th Armoured Brigade recalled

> It was walking in the dark … it was like walking in a minefield … The fear of the unknown – what was around the corner? … I can feel it now, after all these years … No wonder we drank the calvados … We were so pleased once we got through that *bocage* country.
>
> *(IWM Sound 17632: Reel 15)*

This was particularly challenging for men who had done the bulk of their previous fighting in the open spaces of the North African littoral. One of them told Trooper Arthur Reddish,

> you'll get a shock after the desert … we could see the buggers in the desert and they could see us. Here they could see us but I'll buggered if we could see them. This country's ideal for defence but attacking through it gives you the bloody creeps.
>
> *(Buckley 2014: 64)*

Normally tank commanders fought with their heads exposed through their hatch – enabling them to stay aware of the position of other tanks of their own unit and nearby friendly infantry, and to be ready to spot the appearance of enemy tanks (Buckley 2014: 129). In the *bocage* this behaviour risked death at the hands of a sniper concealed in a tree or, with less finality, a pelting with hard cider apples dislodged by the passage of the tank (Buckley 2014: 129; Crosthwaite 1996: 53; Daglish 2009: 52). The drivers and gunners inside the tank were less exposed but almost blind in the *bocage*. In Ken Tout's memoir *Tanks Advance*, he looks through his gunner's periscope to see 'a close-up of a square yard of prolific bramble' (Tout 1989: 88). The restricted vision from inside a tank could combine with the enclosed nature of the *bocage* to create a double sensation of isolation, as when Tout recalls his tank sitting in

> A tiny field. Not big enough to kick a football in. Certainly not the space for a game of cricket. A tiny grazing area defended by high ramparts of hedgerow. And nothing to see. Another tiny private world of our own. Conquered by us. And nobody the wise.
>
> *(Tout 1989: 88)*

Tankmen were afflicted with particular fears unknown to the infantry. First among them was the threat of enemy tanks or anti-tank guns. At the close ranges imposed by the *bocage*, a hit from one of these was capable of penetrating the thickest armour of any Allied tank (Buckley 2004: 125). Furthermore, the dense cover gave an advantage (both material and psychological) to whichever side was able to fire the crucial first shot from a concealed position (Buckley 2006: 86). At a tactical level this could be anyone, but the fact that British tank crews were obliged, at an operational level, to be on the offensive, made them feel acutely vulnerable to such attacks. This sensation was heightened when hedges had to be traversed. If a hedge was low enough for a tank to cross, it meant potentially exposing the thinly armoured underside of the tank to concealed anti-tank guns as it rose up over the earth bank. Ken Tout subsequently described the sensation for the crew as 'rather horrific' (IWM Sound 21286: Reel 3).

The *bocage* also had obvious potential for harbouring German infantrymen armed with short-range shaped-charge anti-tank weapons (the *Panzerfaust* and the *Panzerschreck*). These were generally referred to by British tankmen as 'bazookas' and it is clear that they loomed large in their thinking (Buckley 2004: 87–89; IWM Sound 20370: Reel 8; Tout 1989: 88). Ernie Marlow recalled an officer being upbraided by his more experienced Troop Sergeant for the slow progress of his tanks down a hedge-lined road, with the words 'this is bazooka speed' (IWM Documents 26056: 80). However, statistically at least, this anxiety, though very real, appears to have been exaggerated, as this weapon type caused only six per cent of tank kills in Normandy (Buckley 2004: 89). Nevertheless, it is easy to understand these men's fear of a munition that could, with no warning, send a hypersonic jet of explosive through the cramped confines of their tanks[5] (Figure 13.1).

FIGURE 13.1 A Sherman tank enters a sunken lane during Operation Bluecoat. Source: © IWM B 8271.

This neurotic engagement with the *bocage* as a landscape of deadly hidden threats has been well recorded and the quotations in the preceding paragraphs represent but a tithe of those available from both primary and secondary sources. However, there was another perspective on the *bocage* that is yet to be investigated, this being how it was perceived – with or without the presence of the enemy – as a piece of countryside. Frequently, investigations of conflict environments lay stress upon their strangeness to soldiers compelled to fight in them, with the consequent necessity of rapid adaptation (Breithoff 2017; De Nardi 2017a; De Nardi 2017b: 139–162; Macdonald and Cimprić 2011: 9–20; Seitsonen 2021). However, this was not entirely the case with the *bocage* (Figure 13.2).

Two historians of the campaign writing in 1965 made the point that in many respects its fields and lanes provided a familiar rural setting for British soldiers, who experienced 'a deep sense of affinity with the Normandy countryside'; although the various quintessentially French manmade additions to the landscape meant that 'this sensation of being at home was only spasmodic' (Bellfield et al. 1965: 19).[6] For many West Countrymen of the 43rd (Wessex) Division, in which one of these two authors had commanded a brigade, this was quite likely to have been the case. However, due to the nature of Britain's demographics,

FIGURE 13.2 Men of the Seaforth Highlanders advance during Operation Bluecoat, through a landscape that could as easily be Devon or Sussex as Normandy. Source: © IWM B 8595.

the Army – or at least its 'other ranks' – was composed primarily of men from an urban background. Three-quarters of inter-war recruits to the regular Army were unskilled urban labourers (French 2000: 49). The huge wartime expansion of the Army by means of conscription made new soldiers from men who were 'mostly townsmen: open country and darkness, the natural environments of the soldier, were entirely alien' (Fraser 1983: 98). Actually, the latter comment puts it too strongly, as few of these men would have been wholly ignorant of the countryside; nevertheless, seaside trips or hiking on moors, dales, or peaks would not have prepared them for the *bocage*. Even for country-born soldiers like Trooper Jack Edwards, raised in the shadow of the Peak District, the *bocage* stood out as 'difficult country' consisting of 'hedges, hedges and more hedges' (IWM Documents 25976: 30 July 1944).

This does not mean that men would necessarily have been predisposed to dislike such terrain. The 1930s had witnessed the rise of rambling. This leisure activity was encouraged by the ready availability of Ordnance Survey one-inch maps and by rail and bus company posters urging people to take advantage of their services to get out into the countryside. Furthermore, in an army with high levels of literacy, and in an era where learning poetry by heart was encouraged, the works of Clare, Wordsworth, Keats, and their ilk would have contributed to a reservoir of positive images of enclosed pastoral landscapes. However, the work of a contemporary poet, Peter Young, shows how, by the summer of 1944, this idyllic picture had been inverted. His poem 'Recce in Bocage Country' (Butts and Selwyn 1992: 106) begins 'Pinned down in the sunken lane we waited / pressed into the hedgerow's shadows'; before addressing the deadly consequences of advancing up the lane:

> So we climbed in and drove up the lane
> past the laddie with his thumbstick under a cloud of flies
> and the rest of the platoon sprawled untidily
> where they'd been dropped.

This a thoroughfare far from Keats's half-dreamt 'winding mossy ways' and the hedges are certainly no longer Wordsworth's 'little lines of sportive wood run wild' (Keegan 2001: 554, 663).

Many officers would have surveyed the *bocage* with a very specific eye for the landscape – that of the fox-hunter. A high proportion of British officers, particularly in the Royal Artillery, the Guards, cavalry regiments, and Yeomanry regiments (the last three categories all represented by armoured units in Normandy), rode to hounds. Some did not even let the war interfere with their sport. My own father recalled a Somerset Yeomanry major bringing half a pack of hounds along when his unit was posted to a Devon town (Cornish 2004: 8–9). Ivor Crosthwaite, who fought in Normandy with 6th Guards Tank Brigade, enjoyed umpiring an exercise in 1942 because it allowed him to crash around the 'lovely hunting country' of the 'Warwickshire, Bicester, Pytchley and Grafton' hunts on the back of a tank (Crosthwaite 1996: 46). In their book *Fire-Power*, former Gunners Dominick Graham and Shelford Bidwell asserted that wartime artillery officers were 'hippophils to a man … if they read at all they preferred Surtees to Liddell Hart and *Horse and Hound* to the *Army Quarterly*' (Bidwell and Graham 1982: 288). These men would have seen the *bocage* as a bad sort of place even without the presence of the enemy, with (to borrow from Surtees himself) its 'banked bullfinch' hedges making it 'awfully stiff country'.

One way or another, the *bocage*, despite its somewhat English bucolic charm, firmly established itself as a forbidding landscape in the eyes of British soldiers who fought in it. Most probably they were aware of both aspects simultaneously, as it is perfectly possible for a person to 'more or less in the same breath, understand a landscape in a dozen different ways' (Bender 2002: 106). Such conflicting impressions might even in themselves have been a source of unease (Sheffield 2006: 120). So it is hard to pin down the point at which adverse impressions began to outweigh the positive ones. The negative engagement was certainly uppermost in the mind of veterans after the war. To repeat the words of Ronald Henderson above, 'The fear of the unknown … I can feel it now, after all these years' (IWM Sound 17632: Reel 15). Former infantry officer Geoffrey Picot wrote of his impressions on a post-war visit to his unit's old battlefields: 'still those little fields, thirty or forty yards square, bordered by thick tall hedges; still those winding, half-sunken roads; still the claustrophobic atmosphere' (Picot 1993: 281).

Most significantly for our present-day envisioning of the Normandy campaign, this dystopian conceptualization has transmitted itself to historians of the campaign who, seemingly without exception, find space to detail the difficulties and perils faced by men fighting in what one goes so far as to describe as 'A tangle of squalid woods and muddy lanes embodying all the nastiest elements of Nature at her worst' (Crang 2000: 3). However, I feel that it is worth stepping back and asking two things about the basis of this collective memory of landscape. First, was the fighting in the *bocage* as terrible as has been routinely portrayed? Second, how sustained was the British soldier's actual engagement with this landscape?

War in the *bocage,* real and recollected

In general terms, the Norman *bocage* was very far from being the most difficult terrain fought over by British and Empire troops during the Second World War. Normandy had neither high mountains nor jungle. While it did at times afflict soldiers with heat, dust, and swarms of flies, these were minor inconveniences compared with the analogous phenomena experienced in Libya and Egypt. There was nothing to compare with the bitter cold of winter in the Apennines, the sandstorms of North Africa, or the sweltering climate of Burma. Supply lines were short, making it easier to provide soldiers with the necessities, and even comforts, of life there than on any other front. Admittedly, the *bocage* was first-class terrain for the Germans to fight a grim, infantry-based defensive struggle in. However, it should be realized that this was not necessarily what they themselves wished to do. Circumscribed by Hitler's insistence that no retreats should be made, German commanders in Normandy found themselves fighting on a defensive line that was not of their choosing (Buckley 2006: 81). While they adapted well to fighting in the *bocage*, they railed against its propensity for stopping them from mounting coordinated armoured counterstrokes.

The successive lines of hedgerows certainly assisted them in their standard practice of creating multiple defensive lines, and the tree-cover offered the opportunity of moving troops unobserved between them. But for the German commanders, the *bocage* was not an end in itself. Instead, it served as a defensive perimeter for the higher (and often barer) fragments of ground that offered fields of observation that were key to dominating the battlefield (Buckley 2014: 77, 153). Furthermore, their policy was not merely one of passive defence. Ordered into incessant counterattacks in the face of ferocious Allied artillery fire, the German infantry sustained terrible and irreplaceable losses. In fact, the *bocage* became even more of a charnel house for the Germans than it did for their foes (Buckley 2014: 143–144). Finally, it is clear that, at least on occasion, the prediction of the Allied planners that the terrain would offer opportunities to both sides was borne out, when the British exploited the concealment offered by the terrain to employ their superior mobility to outmanoeuvre their opponents (Daglish 2006: 96–98; IWM Documents 2558a: 32).

The broad, rolling hills south and south-east of Caen were, in many respects, the antithesis of the *bocage* in terms of military geography. Here lay an 'open' landscape wherein, it seemed, large scale armoured attacks might be mounted, or even a breakout achieved. Indeed, Montgomery received considerable criticism at the time, and has done since, for not making more headway there (Lamb 1987: 138–140; Milner 2012: 9). However, the Germans were no less willing to contest this landscape. What it lacked in concealment it gained in fields of fire for their anti-tank guns and tanks. The nucleated villages that studded this arable farmland were marvellously suited for conversion into defensive strongpoints (Badsey 2002: 358). It was, frankly, *more* dangerous to be a British (or Canadian) soldier fighting here than in the *bocage* (Milner 2012: 13–14). In Operation Goodwood, a large offensive mounted south-east of Caen over three days (18–20 July 1944), the British lost 400 tanks and sustained around 5,000 casualties. By comparison Operation Bluecoat, in which even larger forces drove into the heart of the *bocage*, was carried out with the loss of 250 tanks and much the same number of casualties, but lasted *three times as long* as Goodwood. Indeed, the success of the initial attack by the VIII Corps during Bluecoat was partially due to the defenders having denuded a key part of the front of anti-tank weapons, as they considered the *bocage* there to be too dense for tanks to negotiate (Buckley 2014: 161; Daglish 2006: 95). The Churchill tanks of 6th Guards Tank Brigade proved capable of crashing over or through the hedges and, as one of its officers recalled 'as in foxhunting, there were gateways and weak places' (Crosthwaite 1996: 53) (Figure 13.3).

During the Normandy campaign, Second Army mounted 11 major offensive operations.[7] Of these only two, Perch and Bluecoat, involved the wholesale commitment of forces to the *bocage*. Perch (10–14 June) was an abortive strike from the beachhead area into the *bocage* around Villers-Bocage. Bluecoat (30 July–7 August) saw an attack by two Corps south and south-east of Caumont, into terrain that the British official history described as 'even more difficult than any … yet encountered – bocage at its worst, a jumble of tree-clad hills and valleys' (Ellis 1962: 387). In addition, Operation Epsom (26–30 June) did entail fighting in some *bocage*-like terrain, but its main aim was to cross the River Odon and seize the dominating open ground south of Caen (Ellis 1962: 275, Odon Battlefield map). Operation Pomegranate (16–17 July) was mounted to pin German forces in place prior to Operation Goodwood, and involved fighting in the fringes of the *bocage* around Vendes and Noyers-Bocage (Ellis 1962: 275, Odon Battlefield map).

The Normandy campaign is generally considered to have lasted 72 days. British, Canadian, and eventually, Polish troops could be found fighting a major offensive action on 51 of these.[8] However, only 17 days of this fighting can really be considered to have taken place in the *bocage*.[9] Obviously, troops held the line in

FIGURE 13.3 The equal dangers of 'open' terrain. A British ammunition truck is hit by a mortar bomb during Operation Epsom. Source: © IWM B 6017.

the *bocage* in between offensives; especially in the Hottot-Noyers sector between 17 and 30 July. Of the 16 divisions available to Second Army, nine – all British – fought in the *bocage* at some point, along with four of the nine independent brigades deployed.[10] Thus it is clear that experience of fighting in the *bocage* was far from universal among British soldiers in Normandy, and that those who did fight in it frequently only endured its unique cocktail of dangers for a few days. Only the 7th Armoured Division and 56th Independent Infantry Brigade were committed more than once to offensive operations in the *bocage*.

Of course, none of these statistics does anything to minimize the fear and suffering of the men who were called upon to fight in the *bocage*. The dangers were all too real and the impact on those who fought there was plainly lasting. Furthermore, it should be noted that, if this chapter addressed the US Army experience of the *bocage*, its conclusions would probably be very different. But, as the preceding paragraphs make clear, the British soldier's engagement with the *bocage* was both partial and evanescent. It was also, statistically, a less dangerous environment to fight in than the more open terrain that characterized the other flank of the battlefield. It is extraordinary, therefore, that recollections and analyses of fighting in this unique militarized rural landscape should have so dominated post-war engagements with the campaign. It is also worthy of note that this fixation with the *bocage* is particularly thoroughly ingrained in accounts of armoured warfare there – despite the statistics showing that by far the greatest risks were faced not by tank crews, but by the infantry.

The sunken lanes of *Basse Normandie* have been tramped by generations of military tourists, battlefield visitors, and historians (BAOR 1947; Daglish 2009). The 'claustrophobic' atmosphere of the *bocage* has loomed large in personal testimonies of the fighting, and the challenges of fighting in it feature prominently in almost every book on the subject. At its extreme, this focus has made '*bocage*' synecdochic shorthand for the entire Normandy theatre of operations. More commonly the distinctive features of this landscape-form are projected onto areas that were not (and probably never have been) *bocage*. But, after all, what are landscapes but 'constructs of the imagination projected onto wood, water and rock' (Schama 1995: 61). One is driven to wonder whether the prominence given to the fighting in the *bocage* in post-war writing is something that stems not just from soldiers' memories, but from the attraction of the authors themselves to such a (in peacetime at least) charmingly bucolic landscape? Or perhaps the attraction is in the piquancy of such a landscape – such an *English* landscape perhaps – being the scene of such bitter fighting?

Landscapes in general might quite rightly be comprehended as 'time materializing' and, like other landscapes, the *bocage* has not stood still (Bender 2002: 103). Indeed, it offers us a similar sort of 'palimpsest' to that presented by the First World War Western Front – as defined by Nicholas Saunders – although with few of the 'tombs' that he identifies as one of the multiple temporal layers that characterize that landscape (Saunders 2001: 37).[11] And, of course, the limited duration of the fighting there did not engender a comparable level of 'destruction/creation' (ibid.: 38). This warscape is now undergoing a new phase in its 'social life' as the object of archaeological investigation (Carpentier and Marcigny 2019; Carpentier et al. this volume).

The wartime military engagement with the *bocage* also fits within a further anthropological understanding of landscape. From the initial planning of the campaign onwards, the landscape of Normandy was clearly the object of the 'ego-centred' 'Western Gaze', both by commanders poring over it in map form and by soldiers coping with its challenges (Bender 1999: 31). And the notion that the 'Western Gaze is about control' can be applied in this case to the desire to establish military control, with both sides striving to secure commanding ground.

Notwithstanding these various processes, the memory, or imagined memory, of the war in the *bocage* has taken on a life of its own, which has developed independently of the landscape itself. The realities in which this phenomenon originated remain rooted in the summer of 1944 but, to get to them, one must hack through a dense growth in which memory and historiography have become entangled with one another. Simon Schama seems to put his finger on the nub of the matter when discussing a very different bosky landscape, far to the east:

> once a certain idea of landscape, a myth, a vision, establishes itself in an actual place, it has a peculiar way of muddling categories, of making metaphors more real than their referents; of becoming, in fact, part of the scenery.
>
> (*Schama 1995: 61*)

I will content myself with the more prosaic observation that this small region of hedges, hills, streams, and woods – fought over for just two months of a six-year-long war – has punched well above its weight in the imprint that it has left on the personal, collective, and public memory of the fighting in Normandy.

Notes

1 Despite changes in agricultural practice and other post-war development, modern satellite views still reveal the general extent and heavily enclosed nature of the *bocage*.
2 Comprising the US First Army and the Anglo-Canadian Second Army.
3 The German MG42 had a cyclic rate of fire of 1,200 rounds per minute, making the individual reports of its discharged cartridges almost indistinguishable from one another.
4 Mortar fire caused over 70% of British casualties in North Western Europe (Buckley 2014: 80, 253).
5 Shaped charge weapons focus their explosive energy into a narrow jet, which can punch its way through armour.
6 My own first impressions on teenaged visits to this land of mini-golf and gastronomic epiphanies were remarkably similar.
7 'Major' defined as involving multiple divisions; the operations in question being Perch, Epsom, Charnwood, Jupiter, Greenline, Pomegranate, Goodwood, Spring, Bluecoat, Totalize, and Tractable.
8 On 23 July the Canadian First Army became active, incorporating Canadian and British formations along with (from the end of the month) the 1st Polish Armoured Division. The Second Army now became effectively an all-British formation.
9 That is to say the *bocage* as defined elsewhere in this paper. Other definitions may vary. For example, the US official history contains a map which shows no *bocage* in the British Second Army's sector (Blumenson 1961: 12).
10 The latter comprising five armoured brigades, three tank brigades, and the 56th Independent Infantry Brigade.
11 There are only two military cemeteries in the *bocage* country, both German. They are at Marigny and Orglandes in the Cotentin Peninsula. The remains of Allied soldiers killed in the *bocage* were re-interred at Bayeux (British) and Colleville-sur-Mer (US).

References

National Archives

WO 205/118 Operation Overlord: Appreciation on Possible Developments of Operations to Secure a Lodgement Area

IWM Documents Archive

2558a Private Papers of Major B.E.L. Burton

25976 Private Papers of Jack Edwards
26056 Private Papers of Ernie Marlow

IWM Sound Archive interviews

10415 G. Chambers
10599 I. Roger
10896 P. Victory
17632, R. Henderson
18515 A. Carter
20370 R. Forbes
21286 K. Tout
21548 K. Baker
28699 J. Casey

Secondary sources

Badsey, S. (2002) Terrain as a Factor in the Battle of Normandy, 1944. In P. Doyle and M. Bennett (eds.), *Fields of Battle: Terrain in Military History*, pp. 345–363. Dordrecht: Springer

——— (2006) Culture, Controversy, Caen and Cherbourg. In J. Buckley (ed.), *The Normandy Campaign 1944, Sixty Years On*, pp. 48–63. London: Routledge.

Beevor, A. (2009) *D-Day: The Battle for Normandy*. London: Viking.

Belfield, E. and H. Essame (1965) *The Battle for Normandy*. London: Batsford.

Bender, B. (1999) Subverting the Western Gaze: Mapping Alternative Worlds. In P. Ucko and R. Layton (eds.), *The Archaeology of Landscape: Shaping Your Landscape*, pp. 31–45. London: Routledge.

——— (2002) Time and Landscape. *Current Anthropology* 43 (4): 103–112.

Bidwell, S. and D. Graham (1982) *Fire-power: British Army Weapons and Theories of War, 1904–1945*. London: Allen and Unwin.

Blumenson, M. (1961) *Breakout and Pursuit*. Washington, DC: Department of the Army. Office of the Chief of Military History.

Breithoff, E. (2017) The 'White Death': Thirst and Water in the Chaco War. In N.J.Saunders and P. Cornish (eds.), *Modern Conflict and the Senses*, pp. 213–228. London: Routledge.

British Army of the Rhine, G (Training) HQ. (1947) *Battlefield Tour: Operation Bluecoat: 8 Corps Operations South of Caumont 30–31 July 1944*. British Army of the Rhine.

Buckley, J. (2004) *British Armour in the Normandy Campaign 1944*. London: Frank Cass.

——— (2006) British Armoured Operations in Normandy, June – August 1944. In J. Buckley (ed.), *The Normandy Campaign 1944, Sixty Years On*, pp. 74–98. London: Routledge.

——— (2014) *Monty's Men*. New Haven: Yale University Press.

Butts, D. and V. Selwyn (eds.) (1992) *Poems of the Second World War*. Walton-on-Thames: Nelson.

Carpentier, V. and C. Marcigny. (2019) *Archéologie du Débarquement et de la Bataille de Normandie*. Rennes : Éditions OUEST-France/Inrap.

Cornish, C.T.R. (2004) *A Small Town at War*. Holsworthy: Cornish.

Crang, J. (2000) *The British Army and the People's War 1939–1945*. Manchester: Manchester University Press.

Crosthwaite, I. (1996) *A Charmed Life*. Pangbourne: TWM Publishing.
Daglish, I. (2006) Operation BLUECOAT – A Victory Ignored? In J. Buckley (ed.), *The Normandy Campaign 1944, Sixty Years On*, pp. 9–103. London: Routledge.
——— (2009) *Over the Battlefield: Operation Bluecoat*. Barnsley: Pen & Sword.
Danchev, A. and D. Todman. (2001) *War Diaries, 1939–1945: Field Marshal Lord Alanbrooke*. London: Weidenfeld & Nicolson.
Daugherty, L. (2001) *The Battle of The Hedgerows: Bradley's First Army In Normandy, June-July 1944*. Shepperton: Ian Allan.
Davies, A. (1946) Geographical Factors in the Invasion and Battle of Normandy. *Geographical Review* 36 (4): 613–631.
de Lee, N. (2006) American Tactical Innovation in Normandy, 1944. In J. Buckley (ed.), *The Normandy Campaign 1944, Sixty Years On*, pp. 64–73. London: Routledge.
De Nardi, S. (2017a). Emplacing the Italian Resistance: The Dystopian Fight against Nazism and Fascism (1943–1945). In N.J. Saunders and P. Cornish (eds.), *Modern Conflict and the Senses*, pp. 142–154. London: Routledge.
——— (2017b). *The Poetics of Conflict Experience*. London: Routledge.
D'Este, C. (1984) *Decision in Normandy*. London: Pan.
Doubler, M.D. (1988) *Busting the Bocage*. Fort Leavenworth: US Army Combat Studies Institute.
Eisenhower, D. (1948) *Crusade in Europe*. London: Heinemann.
Ellis, L.F. (1962) *Victory in the West. Vol 1: The Battle of Normandy*. London: HMSO.
Essame, H. (1952) *The 43rd Wessex Division at war, 1944–1945*. London: William Clowes.
Ferris, J. (2006) Intelligence and OVERLORD: A Snapshot from 6 June 1944. In J. Buckley (ed.), *The Normandy Campaign 1944, Sixty Years On*, pp. 185–200. Abingdon: Outlook.
Fraser, D. (1982) *Alanbrooke*. New York: Atheneum.
——— (1983) *And We Shall Shock Them*. London: Hodder and Stoughton.
French, D. (2000) *Raising Churchill's Army*. Oxford: Oxford University Press.
Hastings, M. (1985) *Overlord*. London: Pan.
Horne, A. (1994) *The Lonely Leader: Monty 1944–1945*. London: Macmillan.
Keegan, P. (ed.) (2001) *The New Penguin Book of English Verse*. London: Penguin.
Lamb, R. (1987) *Montgomery in Europe 1943–1945*. London: Buchan and Enright.
Lodieu, D. (2007) *Dying for Saint-Lo: Hedgerow Hell, July 1944*. Paris: Histoire and Collections.
Macdonald, J. and Ž. Cimprič. (2011) *Caporetto and the Isonzo Campaign*. Barnsley: Pen & Sword.
Milner, M. (2012) Reflections on Caen, Bocage and the Gap: A Naval Historian's Critique of the Normandy Campaign. *Canadian Military History* 7 (2): 7–17.
Montgomery, B. (1947) *Normandy to the Baltic*. London: Hutchinson.
——— (1954) *Memoirs*. London: Companion Book Club.
Morgan, F. (1950) *Overture to Overlord*. London: Hodder and Houghton.
Picot, G. (1993) *Accidental Warrior*. Lewes: Book Guild.
Pisani, A R. (2018) *Bocage:The Battle for Normandy*. Reading, PA: Aperture Press.
Saunders, N.J. (2001) Matter and Memory in the Landscapes of Conflict: The Western Front 1914–1999. In B. Bender and M. Winer (eds.), *Contested Landscapes: Movement, Exile and Place*, pp. 37–53. Oxford: Berg.
Schama, S. (1995) *Landscape and Memory*. London: Harper Perennial.
Seitsonen, O. (2021) *Archaeologies of Hitler's Arctic War*. London: Routledge.
Sheffield, G. (2006) Dead Cows and Tigers: Some Aspects of the Experience of the British Soldier in Normandy, 1944. In J. Buckley (ed.), *The Normandy Campaign 1944, Sixty Years On*, pp. 118–130. London: Routledge.

Surtees, R. (1853) *Mr Sponge's Sporting Tour.* London: Methuen.
Tedder, A. (1966) *With Prejudice: The War Memoirs of Marshal of the Royal Air Force Lord Tedder G.C.B.* London: Cassell.
Tilley, C. (1994) *A Phenomenology of Landscape, Places, Paths and Monuments.* Oxford: Berg.
Tout, K. (1989) *Tanks Advance!* London: Grafton Books.
Watteaux, M. (2005) Sous le Bocage, le Parcellaire. *Etudes Rurales* 175/176: 53–79.
Wilmot, C. (1954) *The Struggle for Europe.* London: Reprint Society.
Zaloga, S. (2017) *St Lô 1944: The Battle of the Hedgerows.* Abingdon: Osprey.

14

ARCHAEOLOGY, D-DAY, AND THE BATTLE OF NORMANDY

'The Longest Day', a landscape of myth and materiality

Vincent Carpentier, Emmanuel Ghesquière, Benoît Labbey, and Cyril Marcigny

Since the emergence of preventive archaeology in France at the end of the 1980s, Normandy's coastline and soil have yielded up many remains of the battle that took place from 6 June to the end of August 1944 between the Allies (Americans, British, and Canadians) and the Occupation forces of the Third Reich. Since 2014, these discoveries have been the subject of scholarly interest, and are included in the Ministry of Culture's national archaeological research programme (Carpentier and Prilaux 2018). These investigations relate to the material and anthropological history of twentieth-century conflicts, as well as to the memory and heritage that derive from that history; they have entailed also the protection and management of sites that are important for the collective memory. These include the artillery battery of the Pointe du Hoc, the artificial port of Arromanches, and military cemeteries such as those of Colleville-sur-Mer/Omaha Beach (USA) and Ranville (UK). Even the D-Day beaches themselves are candidates to join UNESCO's World Heritage List.

Following an initial overview in 2014 (Carpentier and Marcigny 2019), several studies and inventories are currently underway at sites as varied as maritime shipwrecks, concrete structures of the Atlantic Wall, military camps and installations, subterranean shelters for civilians during the Battle of Caen, and camps for German prisoners. More than 75 years after the end of the Second World War, these diverse material traces remain ever-present in Normandy. The sites have seen varied fates and transformations: some were simply destroyed or reconfigured after the war, following mine clearing, cultivation of fields, or the rebuilding of cities, ports, and industries. However, the French authorities sacralized other sites from as early as 1946 to pay homage to the sacrifice of soldiers of all nations involved in the struggle for the Liberation of France. More recently, a memorial was built in memory of the conflict's numerous civilian casualties in Falaise at the location of a house obliterated by Allied bombs. These memorials, which have become emblematic of the Battle of Normandy, represent the numerous less spectacular remains, whose fate was to permanently fall into oblivion; archaeology is bringing these remains to light during the development of infrastructure on French soil.

Erasing material evidence of the war began the day after Liberation. Local or national priorities focused on rebuilding and mine-clearance, in particular in coastal areas, which had been heavily booby-trapped by occupying Axis forces or bombed by the Allies. Many Atlantic Wall bunkers were destroyed after the war to make way for infrastructure related to seaside tourism; others were used for exploding the innumerable shells, mines, ammunition, and ordnance spread over the battlefields. Reconstruction work, which was suffering from chronic material shortages, reused the recovered shrapnel and steel; bunkers were bought cheaply and transformed into annexes, bars, or nightclubs. Concrete bunkers were also the object of intense looting as early as the 1960s on behalf of and by militaria collectors; both groups (where there was a difference) were often baby boomers, i.e. born immediately after the war. These relics – the most desirable ones being of German origin – have fed an increasingly global market, their prices sometimes fetching astronomical levels. Many objects have also entered private collections or, in the best-case scenario, the storerooms and exhibitions of the many community museums dedicated to the Battle of Normandy.

The archaeological community and public authorities only realized the importance of recording surviving Second World War remains in the first decade of this century; stimulated in large part by the recording of First World War remains in northern and eastern France (e.g. Desfossés et al. 2008; Schnitzler and Landolt 2013). The first archaeological investigations dedicated to the Second World War were in Normandy, one of the regions most affected by the conflicts' battles and massive bombings. A team of British scholars (Gaffney et al. 2004) carried out a pioneering survey in the early 2000s on an isolated site of the Atlantic Wall. A few years later, in 2009, an excavation was requested by the *Service Regional de l'Archéologie* (Regional Archaeological Service) to clear part of the prison camp of La Glacerie, near Cherbourg (Early 2012; Fichet de Clairfontaine 2013, 2016). Although they were still present in the memories of the oldest locals, urbanization had erased these remains from the landscape, which led to them being almost completely forgotten by the end of the 1940s.

While such historically recent investigations are marginal activities for the region's archaeologists and scholars who focus on earlier periods, they revealed gaps in historical documentation and highlighted the absence of protection of war sites as historical monuments. In 2015, the *Service Régional de l'Archéologie* of Normandy, the University of Caen, the *Institut National de Recherches Archéologiques Préventives* (INRAP, National Institute for Rescue Archaeological Research), and local authorities (the three *départements* of Calvados, Manche, and Orne, as well as the Lower Normandy region) launched a major project for the comprehensive inventory of war remains in order to fill in these gaps. The aims of this new programme were to make an inventory of all preserved, decaying, or buried material remains on land and at sea, and to map them by creating a database coupled with a geographical information system (GIS). This chapter aims to present the more recent results of this survey.

The Atlantic Wall revisited by archaeology

The inventory has revealed that, although the most important constructions of the Atlantic Wall, such as coastal artillery batteries, are relatively well known, detailed plans have not been drawn and little is known of other structures that form entire sections of defence lines. These include kitchens, cisterns, sanitary installations, and even premises for leisure like tennis courts built for German soldiers at Fermanville, all of which related to the everyday lives of the German Occupation forces. Observations made during soundings, excavations, and field surveys show that many Atlantic Wall constructions were hastily built using a restricted range of available materials despite the war's massive economic production of war matériel. Contrary to German propaganda, concrete was used more sparingly than brick, wood, and stone. Moreover, it is now quite clear that the state of preservation of this heritage varies in different sectors of the coastline. Surprisingly, however, certain sites, for instance the Utah Beach sector on the east coast of the Cotentin Peninsula, still possesses many well-preserved works, despite having been subjected to major destruction during D-Day.

Other portions of the Atlantic Wall, located inland, have been unearthed in areas around Caen that were already urbanized or in the process of being so. These include a bunker uncovered near the University of Caen, or a flak position (for German anti-aircraft guns) to the southwest of the city, at Bretteville-sur-Odon, east of the Carpiquet airfield, which is to be excavated in the near future. Moreover, the chronology of these military constructions has two distinct phases. An initial phase of construction occurred from June 1940 to September 1943. This was followed by a rise in construction under the increasing threat of an Allied landing that translated into the increasingly anarchic use of various materials and in the (often incomplete) construction of V1 and V2 missile-launching ramps. Finally, the inventory includes another meaningful and under-exploited component: the recording of the many inscriptions, drawings, and signatures (i.e. graffiti) left by soldiers.

It has also become apparent that the documentation of even the largest and most emblematic sites is incomplete as regards either their mapping or the interpretation of remains. This is the case, for instance, for the large coastal artillery batteries of Merville-Franceville-Plage, Longues-sur-Mer, and the Pointe du Hoc, all three visited each year by thousands of international tourists. Two diagnostic soundings at Merville-Franceville-Plage revealed parts of the complex that had not been mapped. The Pointe du Hoc, located to the west of Omaha Beach (with its memorial built for American forces) was subjected in 2019 to an archaeological multidisciplinary survey entrusted to INRAP by the American Battle Monuments Commission (ABMC) (Figure 14.1). The archaeological

FIGURE 14.1 Digital model of the site of the Pointe du Hoc, made by l'INRAP at the request of the American Battle Monuments Commission. Criqueville-en-Bessin, Calvados. Source: ©V. Carpentier, INRAP.

investigation focused on the building methods of pillboxes and the location of the artillery pieces, the degree of completeness of works on 6 June, and the techniques and materials employed. These were often very different from the official standards detailed in the archives, which led to a rigorous and quantifiable comparison between observations in the field and the plans, photographs, and archives of the Third Reich or the American Army.

Beyond this last example, and more generally, the mapping of the remains of the Atlantic Wall has resulted in a more objective knowledge of the diversity of military presence in the area. Surveys carried out in recent years have uncovered hundreds of installations, in particular, logistical works meant for equipment and supplies, vehicle maintenance, the use of construction materials, or the billeting of troops, of which little was known or which had been buried by sand dunes or vegetation. Their discovery has refined chronology and typology. Essential aspects of the military presence are still unknown, however. This is the case for telecommunication sites, telephone relay installations, and cable networks, as well as radar stations and radio jamming installations. Other aspects are better documented and are taken into account within a wider framework: for example, V1 launching pads, which until now had never been the focus of an overview, or large-scale logistics, such as the bypass road around Bayeux, built by the Allies in conjunction with the gigantic rear base necessary to support successive American and British offensives.

This increase in archaeological research into the sites and remains of the Battle of Normandy, and particularly the Atlantic Wall, has stimulated much public interest. D-Day sites are visited by increasing numbers of tourists, and information centres provide space for archaeological information that completes, slightly modifies, or enriches the historical accounts. A recent exhibition on the archaeology of the Second World War, organized by INRAP at Longues-sur-Mer for the *Journées Nationales de l'Archéologie* (National Days for Archaeology) and the seventy-fifth anniversary of the D-Day landings, was visited by more than 650,000 people in a period of five months.[1]

Underwater D-Day shipwrecks, a unique component

The remains of the D-Day landings and the Battle of Normandy also include a large number of underwater sites and shipwrecks. As of 2009, the Normandy region's project of adding the D-Day beaches to the UNESCO list of World Heritage sites has encouraged the *Département des Recherches Archéologiques Subaquatiques et Sous-Marines* (DRASSM, Department of Underwater and Submarine Archaeological Research) to undertake a comprehensive inventory of submerged D-Day installations and shipwrecks located off the five beaches, where American, Canadian, and British forces landed on 6 June 1944 (Sauvage et al. 2019).

A 2016 inventory dealt with the entire set of data recorded by the DRASSM and various societies of divers such as ADRAMAR (Association for the Development of Maritime Archaeological Research) which, since the early 2000s, have been in charge of a census of shipwrecks in cooperation with American and British archaeologists and hydrographers (Atcheson et al. 2015). After completing the census, the DRASSM carried out three research expeditions onboard its ship (the *André Malraux*) to verify the information. The ship was equipped with a multi-beam sounding machine used in the underwater mapping and gathering of relief images of shipwrecks. Diving campaigns gathered accurate information on the mapped remains. More than 150 D-Day sites have been recorded off the Normandy beaches. Half are the wrecks of transport boats, and the other half are warships, armoured vehicles, and artificial port components. Seventy-five years after D-Day, this submerged heritage seems to be not only fragile but also very modest in comparison to the 1,200 Allied warships and 5,700 transport units sunk during Operation Neptune. Erosion, the recovery of steel, mine removal, and looting by amateur archaeologists and divers have all resulted in the removal of much of these remains, of which only a fraction survives, requiring urgent measures to protect and preserve it.

Though the inventory does not fundamentally challenge the history of D-Day, it nevertheless facilitates the management and value assessment of these remains. It also allows a better understanding of the varied means used by the Allies and emphasizes the naval character of D-Day, which has sometimes been obscured by a more land-based vision of this historical event. Moreover, despite their outwardly modest nature, the results are quite remarkable, as on a global scale, no other historical event has left more traces than D-Day, thanks to these submerged remains.

Traces of fighting, as seen from archives buried in the ground

Apart from the Atlantic Wall and shipwrecks, the remains of the Battle of Normandy (6 June to the end of August 1944) consist of innumerable material testimonies left by belligerent forces in the region. These are either directly related to fighting (shelters for combatants, artillery positions, areas of parachute landing) or bear witness to the immense logistics of the Allied invasion (landing strips and airports, Bailey bridges, ammunition depot areas), and even the consequences of this campaign (provisional burials, bomb craters, destruction). In addition, shelters for civilians and the infilling following carpet-bombing and internment camps for prisoners all contribute to making this chapter of history a new field of research for archaeologists of the recent past.

Several sites excavated near the D-Day beaches and the American and British parachuting areas bear the marks of the first fighting during the Battle of Normandy. Recent archaeological research has included the initial theatre of operations of the 6th British Airborne Division northeast of Caen, which yielded considerable new data. At Bénouville, at the site of the famous Pegasus Bridge (captured by a British airborne commando in the first minutes of D-Day), an archaeological diagnostic made it possible to complete the plan of the German defences of the *Wiederstandnest* (WN) 13 on the banks of the Orne Canal and in the bridge's vicinity. This 'legendary' site, made famous by the 1962 Hollywood epic *The Longest Day*, was in effect quite poorly documented in the absence of preserved German archives. Archaeological fieldwork has thus provided an opportunity to put together and crosscheck available sources from photographs and testimonies, and to complete this information with fieldwork data. Not far from this location, the landing areas intended for British gliders were also documented archaeologically in advance of construction at Ranville on the Orne's right bank. The discoveries range from small individual finds to more consequential material and installations, which were identified by crosschecking historical sources.

Other battle locations have also yielded archaeological information of comparable importance. At Langune-sur-Mer, for instance, in the Juno Beach sector, recent excavation has exposed a group of objects left behind by No 48 (Royal Marine) Commando in the wake of tough fighting for the village's liberation (Figure 14.2). At Fleury-sur-Orne, to the south of Caen, part of a large regrouping camp for the Canadian Second Infantry Division was mapped and excavated. Many shelters were dug in the soil by Canadian infantrymen and artillerymen. Archaeologists have discovered a wide range of objects in these shelters, including items of weaponry and military equipment, kitchen utensils and medical

FIGURE 14.2 Remains abandoned on the spot by men of No 48 (Royal Marine) Commando at Langrune-sur-Mer, Calvados. Source: © E. Ghesquière, INRAP.

gear, rudimentary heating devices made on-site with recycled materials, kitchenware, bottles, and even personal effects, some marked with a name, such as a bracelet inscribed 'Harry Fox'. Following research by Denis Renaud of Ottawa University, who was in contact with the excavation supervisor Denis Ghesquière of INRAP (Figure 14.3),[2] the bracelet was subsequently returned to the family in Canada.

Military installations from the battle also survive, ranging from simple excavations (foxholes, slit trenches) to larger state-of-the-art logistical infrastructure, such as artificial ports and airstrips. Though foxholes – these being soldiers' shelters dug for protection against bullets and shells – are mostly simple pits the size of a man lying on the ground, other larger and deeper bunkers on relatively static front lines held for several weeks or months were meant to be more permanent; these were roofed and connected to trenches. When considered on a larger scale (thanks to topsoil removal on a vast scale during archaeological excavations), these individual installations sometimes reveal tactical front line organization. The finds, such as utensils linked to the everyday lives of troops, have enabled

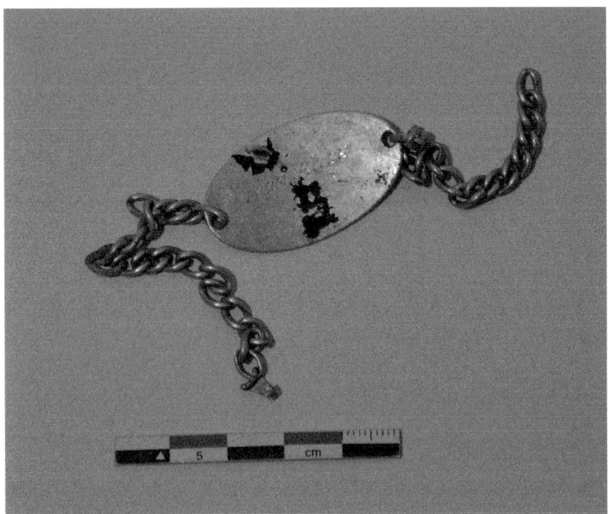

FIGURE 14.3 Chain bracelet inscribed with the name of Harry Fox, a Canadian artilleryman, unearthed at Fleury-sur-Orne, Calvados, to the south of Caen. Source: © E. Ghesquière, INRAP.)

a study of the behaviour of fighters in wartime. For instance, in Normandy, the presence of alcoholic beverage containers has revealed differences between nationalities, reflecting habits from civilian life, military traditions of soldiers at war, and even the supply and tastes of troops on the front, where cider and calvados have often left a deep impression on the memories of foreign soldiers (see Cornish this volume).

From a broader and more accurate perspective, modern archaeology is able to investigate specific but varied aspects of a war operation theatre, which reveals a wider spectrum of remains. These vary from the coastal strip where Allied forces landed to the wooded countryside of Normandy where the 'Battle of the Hedgerows' (see Cornish this volume) took place (a battle that was very costly in human lives) to villages defended by German troops and finally, post-war reconstruction in urban areas devastated by Allied bombs. Apart from the aforementioned landing sector of the 6th Airborne Division and British troops at Sword Beach, the sector of the Battle of Caen, lasting from 6 June to 20 July 1944, is now documented by several sites excavated since 2014 on the city's periphery, at Fleury-sur-Orne, Cagny, Bourguébus, Soliers, Bretteville-sur-Odon, and Tilly-sur-Seulles.

In Caen's city centre, excavations at the castle have uncovered evidence of bombing and liberation by the British infantry. Some of the remains unearthed during the excavation are somewhat unexpected, such as a Japanese sabre; some finds stir the imagination, for instance, a gas metre that froze in the aftermath of one of the most violent aerial bombings on the city in the spring of 1944. Sites which have been infilled after destruction are also a source of information that reflects a town that was destroyed and rebuilt. Recent archaeological projects in Caen's centre that take war strata into account have resulted in a reappraisal of collective representations prevalent since the end of the war, notably the idea of a martyred city rebuilt on a heap of ruins. Fieldwork data has revised previous images of the destruction (Carpentier et al. 2019) and accords with the most recent analyses by geographers, particularly those of Romain Stepkow, which are based on the study of aerial coverage and land registry archives. Without minimizing the considerable impact of destruction caused by Allied bombing, the city was not totally destroyed and was not rebuilt directly on its ruins, as gravel, stones, and other materials were removed by thousands of German prisoners held in Caen until 1948.[3]

A broader concept of war remains: logistical installations, shelters, prison camps, human remains

The many discoveries made during the last few years have resulted in a significant broadening of the notion of war remains to include new categories of objects and installations with connections to conflict.

The Second World War witnessed military innovation on an unprecedented scale, marking a turning point in modern warfare. As regards the Battle of Normandy, the two artificial ports set up on 6 June at Saint-Laurent-sur-Mer and Arromanches by the Allies, as well as the huge logistical platform created around Bayeux (including workshops, vehicle parks, warehouses, hospitals, and airstrips), were investigated archaeologically in the early 2000s. Other innovations brought by Allied military engineers have also had a long-term legacy: for example, the Bailey bridges on the Orne River and canal, created by a British engineer who arrived in Normandy in June 1944. They were later used throughout liberated Europe to compensate for the destruction of bridges by Allied bombs and German army mines. Once more, archaeology has located the last surviving remains of these bridges on the banks of the Orne – stakes and stone heaps forming abutments, remains rendered fragile by the tides. Their survival will probably not exceed a few more decades (Figure 14.4). Logistical works sometimes cover considerable areas; this is the case for ammunition or fuel depots created by the German army in the forested uplands of northwestern Europe. In Normandy, surveys by David Capps-Tunwell, David Passmore, and Stephen Harrisson on such sites have made possible the reconstruction of an entire and, until now, largely ignored part of German war infrastructure (Passmore et al. 2014; Passmore et al. 2017).

To the south of Caen, archaeologists have recently identified refugee shelters, remarkably preserved since the Liberation. Subjected to massive Allied bombings during the summer of 1944, thousands of Caen's inhabitants fled to the underground quarries that had formed a belt around the city since the Middle Ages. One of them, a former quarry at Fleury-sur-Orne, which, by 1944, had

FIGURE 14.4 The remains of one of the Bailey bridges built by the British Royal Engineers on the Orne and its canal, the day after 6 June, the earliest example of a category of bridges imported on the continent. Source: © V. Carpentier, INRAP.

become the cellar of a brewery,[4] was recorded in 3-D during a series of investigations begun in 2014 (Carpentier et al. 2016). INRAP archaeologists and a team of topographers from INSA (*Institut National des Sciences Appliquées de Strasbourg*) focused on gathering archaeological information over a five-year period, applying an innovative recording protocol associating lasergrammetry (scanner), photogrammetry, and relational databases (Figure 14.5). With the conclusion of this programme, archaeologists now possess a complete digital record of the quarry in three dimensions, providing a unique heritage archive that ensures the protection and preservation of the site for future generations. While the quarry itself is now inaccessible, the public can make virtual visits, touring the site through a 3-D model which also allows archaeologists to develop their interpretations without damaging this exceptional site.

To this can be added the pioneering excavation of a prison camp for German soldiers at La Glacerie near Cherbourg and other prison sites in France, particularly in Normandy. Between 1944 and 1948, thousands of detainees rebuilt

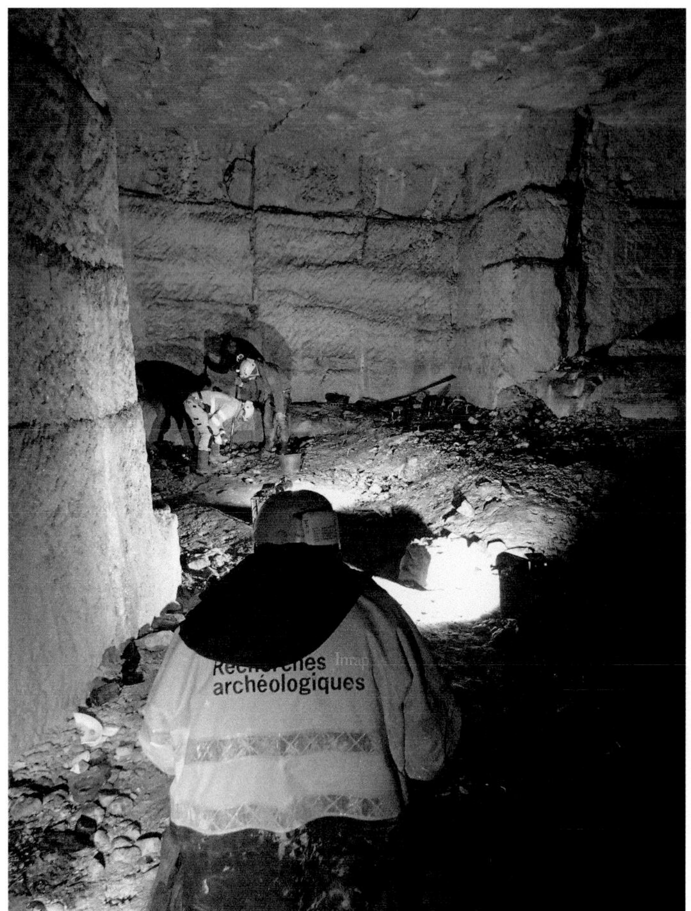

FIGURE 14.5 Archaeological study of the shelter-quarry of the Saingt brewery at Fleury-sur-Orne, Calvados. Source: © C. Marcigny, INRAP.

infrastructure or cleared mines at these sites (Carpentier and Marcigny 2014). Portions of camps were excavated at Mosles, La Glacerie, Nonnant-le-Pin, Urville-Nacqueville, and Fleury-sur-Orne. When combined with archives and testimonies of detainees or French people living near the camp, the excavations have provided information on the detention conditions of thousands of soldiers, some of whom settled in Normandy after 1948, blending into the local population.

Another component of archaeological research relates to human losses, both civilian and military, which were extremely high in Normandy not just because of the fighting but also due to large-scale Allied bombing and German repression against the civilians suspected of being resistance fighters. Large military cemeteries were created after the war by France and the other combatant nations so as to group together most of the casualties previously scattered across the battlefields. However, preventive archaeology sometimes uncovers forgotten temporary cemeteries and even the remains of abandoned soldiers of all nationalities. Such provisional burials of German soldiers were discovered at Cagny, and a temporary cemetery for British and Canadian soldiers was found at Colomby-Anguerny. Archaeologists recently discovered the remains of British soldiers, whose burials had been summarily recorded, and the body of a German *Panzergrenadier* obviously buried in haste after receiving a mortal wound at Maltot, next to the 'Hill 112' battlefield, during the excavation of Iron Age Occupation levels (Figure 14.6). Following legal protocol, these fortuitous

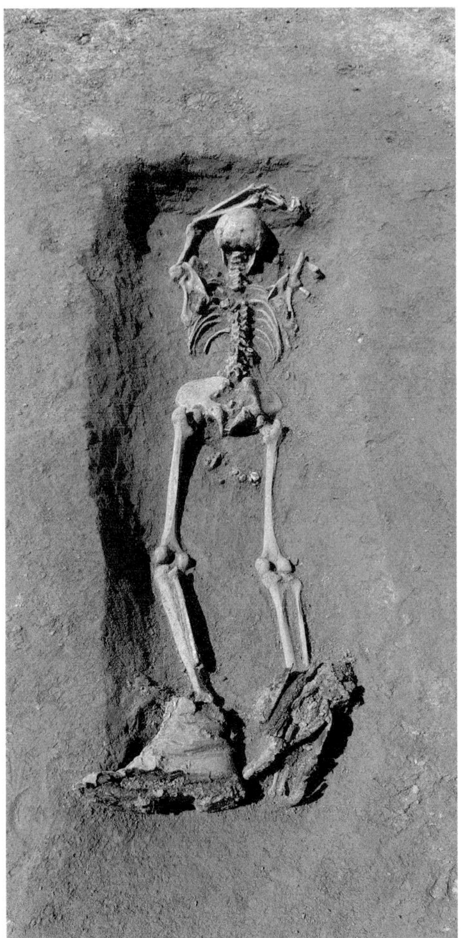

FIGURE 14.6 The body of a forgotten German *Panzergrenadier* soldier on Hill 112 at Maltot, Calvados, discovered in May 2019. Source: © V. Carpentier, INRAP.

discoveries were declared to the *Gendarmerie*, and various commissions in charge of national military cemeteries recovered the remains. Archaeologists participated in the process whenever possible, focusing on recording or consigning all elements likely to enable the identification of casualties or the establishment of the causes of the death and burial. Seventy-five years after the end of the conflict, these discoveries confirm that many bodies of soldiers and civilians are still awaiting discovery in Normandy.

Beyond myth: a new and objective contribution to the understanding of the conflict

In a relatively short time, archaeology has contributed substantially to our knowledge and understanding of D-Day and the Battle of Normandy. By presenting new documentation and complementary historical, textual, photographic, and sound archives, it has shed new light on otherwise seldom or untouched aspects of the conflict. This enables a reconstruction of the real magnitude of war and the devastation it caused, and which is very different from the heroic myth of *The Longest Day*. Archaeology provides a unique and irreplaceable material testimony to the extent of operations launched on the D-Day beaches, as well as other theatres of the Battle of Normandy. The variety of these material traces (many of them having escaped the historian's eye) is indeed quite remarkable: bomb craters, shipwrecks, foxholes, airstrips, remains of Bailey bridges, forgotten provisional cemeteries, personal effects belonging to soldiers, underground shelters for civilians, and the remains of prison camps for German soldiers. By analyzing these remains at various scales, while distancing itself from national or partisan narratives, archaeology has revealed the buried traces of a giant cycle of construction–destruction–reconstruction typical of twentieth-century war. Beyond the memory of 'heroic' deeds of the Battle of Normandy, archaeology has exposed the profound human reality of war, responding to a demand by the public, in its quest for new and more objective narratives. In turn, archaeologists have the duty of memory regarding these war remains, threatened by erosion, looting, and land development. The deaths of the last direct witnesses have made this major episode of the Second World War a bygone past, but with the work of archaeologists, it has become a new research topic with the aim of preserving the memory of these times for future generations.

Notes

1 www.inrap.fr/une-exposition-longues-sur-mer-sur-l-archeologie-du-jour-j-et-du-debarquement-14372
2 www.insidehalton.com/community-story/7380608-archeologist-digs-for-clues-in-quest-to-identify-owner-of-lost-bracelet/
3 www.canal-u.tv/video/la_forge_numerique/que_reste_t_il_du_caen_d_avant_guerre.49785; https://caen.fr/sites/default/files/2019-02/caenmag184.pdf
4 www.normandie-attractivite.fr/a-44-quarry-shelter/

References

Atcheson, B., B. Neyland and A. Catsambis (2015) Retour en Normandie: Prospections archéologiques de l'US Navy sur la flotte immergée de l'opération Neptune. *Revue d'Histoire maritime* 21: 85–124.

Carpentier, V. and C. Marcigny (2014) Les camps de prisonniers allemands. Un nouveau champ de recherche pour l'archéologie française. *Archéopages* 39: 64–69.

——— (2019) *Archéologie du Débarquement et de la Bataille de Normandie*. Rennes: Ouest-France [1st ed. 2014].

Carpentier, V. and G. Prilaux (2018) L'archéologie des grands conflits mondiaux. In J.-P. Demoule, D. Garcia and A. Schnapp (eds.), *Une histoire des civilisations, Comment l'archéologie bouleverse nos connaissances*, pp. 516–521. Paris: La Découverte/Inrap.

Carpentier, V., L. Dujardin and C. Marcigny (2016) Archéologie du refuge ou de l'enfermement volontaire. La carrière-refuge de la brasserie Saingt à Fleury-sur-Orne (Calvados). *Les Nouvelles de l'Archéologie* 143: 59–63.

Carpentier, V., D. Flotté and C. Marcigny (2019) Un puzzle à grande échelle ? Caen, sa plaine et la vallée de l'Orne du Néolithique au XXe siècle: Retour critique sur 20 ans d'expérience, de l'acquisition à la modélisation des données archéologiques. In P. Brun, C. Marcigny, J. and Vanmoerkerke (eds.), *L'archéologie préventive post-Grands Travaux. Traiter de grandes surfaces sectionnées et discontinues: de l'instruction des dossiers d'aménagements aux modèles spatiaux. Bulletin de la Société archéologique champenoise* 110 (4): 5–30.

Desfossés, Y., A. Jacques and G. Prilaux. (2008) *L'archéologie de la Grande Guerre*. Rennes : Éditions Ouest-France.

Early, R. (2012) Excavating the World War Prisoner of War Camp at La Glacerie, Cherbourg, Normandy. In H. Mytum and G. Carr (eds.), *Prisoners of War, Archaeology, Memory, and Heritage of 19th- and 20th-Century Mass Internment*, pp. 95–115. New York: Springer.

Fichet de Clairfontaine, F. (2013) *Le camp de travail de prisonniers de guerre allemands 112A*. Caen: DRAC Basse-Normandie (Archéologie en Basse-Normandie 2), https://journals.openedition.org/nda/3410.

——— (2016) Pourquoi fouiller les camps d'enfermement de la Seconde guerre mondiale ? Le camp de La Glacerie (Manche). *Les Nouvelles de l'archéologie* 143: 48–53.

Gaffney, C., J. Gater, T. Saunders and J. Atcock. (2004) D-Day: Geophysical Investigation of a World War II German Site in Normandy, France. *Archaeological Prospection* 11 (2): 121–128.

Passmore, D.G., D. Capps-Tunwell and S. Harrison. (2014) Landscapes of Logistics: The Archaeology and Geography of WWII German Military Supply Depots in Central Normandy, North-west France. *Journal of Conflict Archaeology* 8 (3): 165–192.

Passmore, D.G., D. Capps-Tunwell, M. Reinders and S. Harrison. (2017) Towards an Archaeology and Geography of Second World War German Munitions Storage Sites in North-West Europe. *Journal of Conflict Archaeology* 12 (1): 46–71.

Sauvage, C., C. Billard, V. Carpentier, C. Marcigny, S. Lamache and B. Labbey. (2019) Les 75 ans de la bataille de Normandie. Les révélations de l'archéologie des conflits. *Archaeologia* 577: 18–25.

Schnitzler, B. and M. Landholt. (2013) *A l'est, du nouveau! Archéologie de la grande guerre en Alsace et en Lorraine*. Strasbourg: MAM.

15

'AN EXAMPLE OF NAZI KULTUR'

Paradigmatic and contested materiality at Bergen-Belsen concentration camp

Caroline Sturdy Colls and William Mitchell

Introduction

> This is the site of the infamous Belsen concentration camp *liberated by the British on 15 April 1945*. 10,000 unburied dead were found here. Another 13,000 have since died. All of them victims of the German new order in Europe. And an example of Nazi kultur.
>
> (a sign posted by the British army at the entrance to Bergen-Belsen concentration camp [United States Holocaust Memorial Museum, courtesy of Madalae Fraser])

Since it was liberated by the British military forces on 15 April 1945, Bergen-Belsen (Germany) has been perceived by many as an archetypal example of a concentration camp and one synonymous with the cruelty of the Nazi regime (Schultze 2006, 2015). Shocking images and film footage of bodies piled high and being bulldozed into mass graves embedded the 'horror camp' (Berney 2015: 4) into British consciousness providing 'a constant reminder to the British people of the menace they have beaten' (*Daily Mail* cited in Reilly et al. 1997: 4; Haggith 2006) (Figure 15.1). This evidence of so-called 'Nazi kultur' revealed that tens of thousands of people died as a result of starvation, ill-treatment, and disease during the concentration camp period alone (Gedenkstätte Bergen-Belsen [GBB] 2019).

As recent scholarship has shown, in reality, Bergen-Belsen was far from a 'typical' concentration camp and the iconography that has developed around it portrays only the events of the final few months of its existence (Stone 2020b; Cesarani 2006). Many scholars have argued that these representations meant that the camp 'became separated from what the people held in this camp had had to

FIGURE 15.1 Images of Bergen-Belsen at liberation. Left: a camp inmate, reduced by starvation to a living skeleton, delouses his clothes, 17–18 April 1945. Right: German SS guards and a bulldozer fill in a mass grave. Source left: © IWM BU 3766; source right: © IWM BU 4273.

endure, and why they had been incarcerated in the first place' (Schulze 2015). At different times since the war, it has been used as what Kushner (1996: 181) has termed a 'crude metaphor' for 'the universal horrors of war and man's capacity for evil', Jewish suffering, Nazi/German atrocities, and/or the 'decency' and thoroughness of those who 'exposed [these crimes] to the outside world' – a contested site where different victim groups and certain narratives have been emphasized at the expense of others.

Therefore, because of Bergen-Belsen's place in 'British imagination' and international consciousness (Kushner 2017: 364), there has been little discussion concerning the extent and nature of the mass graves on the site, the various methods of body disposal employed, and what might have happened to the thousands of individuals whose bodies have never been found. Images of the clean-up operations which were broadcast around the world contributed to the notion that the burials and numbers of those who died in the camp were fully documented. This belief was affirmed further after the creation of the well-tended memorial and museum that now exist in the former camp area where the locations of known mass graves are marked. Historians researching the site have, by their own admission, not dedicated a great deal of time to the issue of body disposal practices, as it was assumed that all remains that could be found had been found (Seybold 2017; GBB 2019). Since the materiality of destruction was so evident at liberation, first within the camp and then within the images taken, the misconception persists that the form and function of Bergen-Belsen are fully understood. Only a handful of scholars and practitioners have challenged this view, drawing upon archaeological, historical, and augmented reality (AR) methods to highlight the importance of analyzing physical evidence and space, not least because few traces of the camp survive above ground (Pacheco et al. 2014; Sturdy Colls 2015a; Schute et al. 2014; Hummel 2008).

This chapter outlines the results of the most recent of these archaeological investigations which used historical research, non-invasive technologies, and the novel fusion of 3-D data to map the terrain of Bergen-Belsen and generate new digital educational tools.[1] The main focus of the discussion centres on how this work complemented and challenged established narratives surrounding the site, something which was an unexpected consequence for historians working at the associated memorial museum. The ethical challenges involved in these investigations – as well as the contestation that surrounds the issue of unmarked burials – are also discussed, thus highlighting both the value and some of the dangers of utilizing archaeological methods at sites of conflict and genocide (Figure 15.1).

Brief history of the camp

Numerous publications and testimonies exist concerning Bergen-Belsen which document its various functions and prisoner groupings (e.g. Rahe 2012; Wenck 2000), landscape and architecture (Cole 2016), liberation (e.g. Stone 2020b; Berney 2015; Eeles and Konig 2015), place within cultural memory and British society (e.g. Stone 2020a; Kushner 2006; Reilly et al. 1997), and contested aspects of its history (e.g. Schultze 2006; Kushner 1996; Rosensaft 1979). Therefore, only a brief overview of the camp's history is provided here as context for the remainder of the article.

The first camp to be established at Bergen-Belsen was a military camp constructed by the German army in 1935. This complex was expanded leading up to and after the start of the Second World War, resulting in the creation of several military bases and prisoner of war (PoW) camps in the area (GBB 2019). In June 1941, Stalag 311 was created south of the main military base at Hohne to house 20,000 Soviet PoWs. Starvation, ill-treatment, and disease were common from the beginning, resulting in 19,500 deaths by January 1945 (ibid.; Cesarani 2006).

From spring 1943, the southern section of this camp was taken over by the SS Business-Administration Main Office (WVHA) and 'detention camp (*Aufenthaltslager*) Bergen-Belsen' was created. This camp was unusual as it housed Jews due to be exchanged for Germans captured by the Allies, although in reality just over 200 people were actually exchanged (Rahe 2012: 278).[2] Although the majority of people held in the new detention camp were Jewish, other detainees included Romani, homosexuals, Jehovah's Witnesses, criminals, 'asocials', and political prisoners (USHMM 2019). In this early phase, inmates generally experienced better conditions than in other concentration camps (depending upon which sub-section of the camp they were housed in and their perceived status) and survivors 'recalled a place of order rather than a place of disorder', dominated by roll calls, barbed wire, and work (Cole 2016: 207).

In March 1944, Bergen-Belsen was designated as a recovery camp (*Ehrholungslager*). From this point onwards, sick and dying prisoners from other camps were transferred there, as were women en route to other German satellite camps (Wachsmann 2015: 565). However, it was not until after December 1944 – when an increased number of transports arrived from evacuated camps such as Auschwitz – that the completely overcrowded, disease-infested, corpse-ridden Bergen-Belsen that was documented by the liberators came into existence (Lavsky 1993: 37). The increase in prisoner numbers was dramatic; rising from 15,000 in December 1944 to 22,000 in February 1945 and 41,250 in March (Rahe 2012: 280). By the time of liberation in April 1945, around 55,000 people were imprisoned in a space designed to hold just 10,000 prisoners. The number of deaths at Bergen-Belsen also peaked at this time. Testimonies paint a picture of the appalling conditions as accommodation was limited, sanitation was absent, and illness rife. The prisoners of the camp were left to fend for themselves. They no longer worked and all basic human survival needs – food, water. and room to sleep – were withdrawn: 'Those too weak to move [to the cookhouse] died of starvation' (*The Illustrated London News* 1945). Instances of cannibalism were documented by witnesses (Lees-Milne 1977: 192), and lice, typhus, and typhoid were commonplace (Blitz n.d.).

Unlike other concentration camps, the infrastructure of Belsen was not equipped to deal with the overwhelming numbers of sick and dying people: 'it did not have the "Facilities" of Auschwitz, where bodies were "processed" with comparative ease. Auschwitz was a place where people were MURDERED. In Belsen they PERISHED' (Lasker-Wallfisch cited in Lattek, 1997: 70). As Dan Stone (2020a:76) has argued 'in its last days, and whatever the Nazis intended it to be for, Belsen was in fact a death camp'. According to research undertaken by Gedenkstätte Bergen-Belsen (2019), the anticipated death toll during the concentration camp period stands at 53,000 people, around 14,000 of which perished after liberation when they failed to recover from medical conditions acquired whilst incarcerated.

When the British forces liberated Bergen-Belsen, their priority was understandably to care for the living and to repair, and then ultimately destroy, the 'infrastructure' of the camp to prevent the spread of disease (Eeles and Blitz Konig 2015). Bodies were quickly buried in mass graves and, once all surviving inmates had been evacuated, the camp was burnt down and levelled. Unlike in other camps where the Nazis had time to hide their crimes, irrefutable proof of atrocities was evident; hence, the British government felt that there was no need to conduct lengthy investigations or collect material remains for use in legal trials. Capturing the evidence on film and in photographs before the site was destroyed was deemed sufficient. Since the permanent memorial was constructed in the early 1960s, a peaceful, green landscape, almost entirely devoid of any obvious traces of the camp, has defined the site.

Bergen-Belsen archaeology project

In 2015, the UK Holocaust Memorial Foundation initiated a project which sought to map the terrain of Bergen-Belsen in three dimensions, identify surviving buried remains, and generate new digital educational tools. As a result, the Centre of Archaeology at Staffordshire University and ScanLAB Projects were commissioned to undertake a survey in the spring of 2015.

An interdisciplinary non-invasive methodology was employed which accounted for the ethical issues involved in examining Holocaust sites. One important consideration was the fact that Jewish law (*Halacha*) strongly discourages the disturbance of human remains of Jewish victims buried within graves, since it states that to disturb a grave is to disturb the soul of an individual (Sturdy Colls 2015b; Schudrich 2015). As Bergen-Belsen has been designated a cemetery and there was the possibility that unmarked mass graves may exist, traditional methods of archaeological investigation were rendered inappropriate. Data was therefore generated via desk-based assessment (DBA), the application of terrestrial LiDAR (to generate a topographic model of the modern landscape and identify surface indicators which may indicate the presence of buried remains), photogrammetry (to further document above-ground remains and the current memorial from the air and at ground level), surveying tools (such as GPS and total station survey to record surface materials), and ground-penetrating radar (GPR) (to identify and characterize buried remains) (e.g. Carrick Utsi 2017; Opitz and Cowley 2013; Egels and Kasser 2002). This methodology has been successfully applied by the authors at several other Holocaust sites where excavation was not permitted, or desirable, on religious grounds (e.g. Sturdy Colls 2012, 2014, 2015b).

Whilst the whole of the former camp terrain was surveyed using the airborne methods, targeted survey areas were selected for terrestrial laser scanning and GPR survey based on the size of the site and specific research questions (Figure 15.2). Even though the aim of the project was not to search for burial sites per se, it became apparent during the DBA that 70 years after the liberation of Bergen-Belsen, questions still remained about the extent and nature of some areas of the camp, and what happened to the bodies of almost half of the known victims. Therefore, the western end of the camp, near the crematorium, was targeted since historical research suggested this was where many of the deceased bodies were disposed of. Part of the Men's Camp was also examined to determine the configuration of barracks in this area, alongside a potential sewage line and barrack in the south-west of the concentration camp area (Sturdy Colls 2015a). The collected data was synthesized with documentary, cartographic, and photographic resources to generate a novel 3-D representation of the site, allowing both researchers and the public the opportunity to analyze both above- and below-ground remains within a digital space (Figure 15.3).

As a result of this survey, several new discoveries were made that offered the opportunity to record, identify, and characterize buried evidence connected to

FIGURE 15.2 Map of Bergen-Belsen showing key features of the concentration camp in early 1945 in relation to the survey areas. Source: © Centre of Archaeology, based on analysis of aerial photographs and research by Gedenkstätte Bergen-Belsen 2012.

the former Nazi camp at Bergen-Belsen within selected pilot study areas (Sturdy Colls 2015a). The remainder of the chapter will focus on three of these discoveries relating to (1) the crematorium, (2) potential unmarked burials relating to the post-liberation period, and (3) potential unmarked burials dating to the concentration camp period.

The crematorium

It is well documented that during the early stages of Bergen-Belsen's operations as a concentration camp, the bodies of those who died were cremated. A purpose-built crematorium was located within its own building, surrounded by a fenced compound. This area was physically distinct from the prisoner barracks and was separated from the rest of the camp by additional fences to the north, south, and east. Surviving photographs taken by the British liberators

FIGURE 15.3 An example of a scene from the 3-D model of Bergen-Belsen showing a memorial obelisk (background) and two of the marked mass graves (foreground). Source: © ScanLAB Projects.

demonstrate that it consisted of a metal oven(s) housed within a wooden structure (Figure 15.4).

Analysis of documentary sources confirms that the crematorium building was dismantled by the liberators along with the rest of the camp structures; hence, popular narratives suggest it was totally destroyed. However, the archaeological survey demonstrated that elements of the structure and its surrounding compound survive. GPR revealed both a square feature, measuring approximately 6.15 by 6.15 metres, and a semi-circular feature nearby. When the GPR data and historic aerial photographs of the camp were georectified in GIS onto modern satellite imagery, it became apparent that the square feature likely represented the foundations of the main crematorium building (Figure 15.5). The structure likely continued to the east underneath a memorial constructed in 1964–1965 to protect an area where burnt human remains and ashes were recovered (Archiv Lüneburg 11320/3.2; Seybold 2017: 5–6). This suggests that the crematorium's precise location was forgotten after it was demolished in the absence of detailed maps of the camp. Although this discovery presented new information, it was not viewed as contentious by historians and educators working at the site (Stephanie Billib, personal communication). Rather, it was seen as useful information that could aid educational and conservation efforts in the future.

Unmarked burials?

The memorial landscape at Bergen-Belsen centres on the presence of mass graves; 13 stone memorials (11 of which are inscribed with the number of dead)

FIGURE 15.4 The remains of the Bergen-Belsen crematorium after liberation, 1945. Source: © IWM BU 4004.

cover the burial sites dug by the liberators, giving the impression that all of those who died in the camp are buried there (GBB 2012). However, more detailed analysis of the landscape and the processes of burial reveals not only that there is a disparity between the predicted death toll and the number of bodies that are believed to have been found (54,000 dead versus only 23,200 in marked burials), but also that seemingly the British did not mark all of the graves that they found or created. In the first instance, this is evidenced by the fact that two of the body deposition sites were marked in the 1950s and 1964–1965 respectively, long after the British had burnt down the camp (GBB 2012; Seybold 2017). Although the unknown number of bodies residing in these two locations does reduce the margin between the death toll and body count, as does the fact that other people were cremated or buried in mass graves in Camp II (Hohne barracks), recent research by Seybold (2017) (initiated after the archaeological research described here) suggests that around 15,000 people remain unaccounted for. Historical and archaeological research by the authors revealed that these victims are likely buried in mass graves – some of which relate to the period when the camp was operating and others to after liberation.

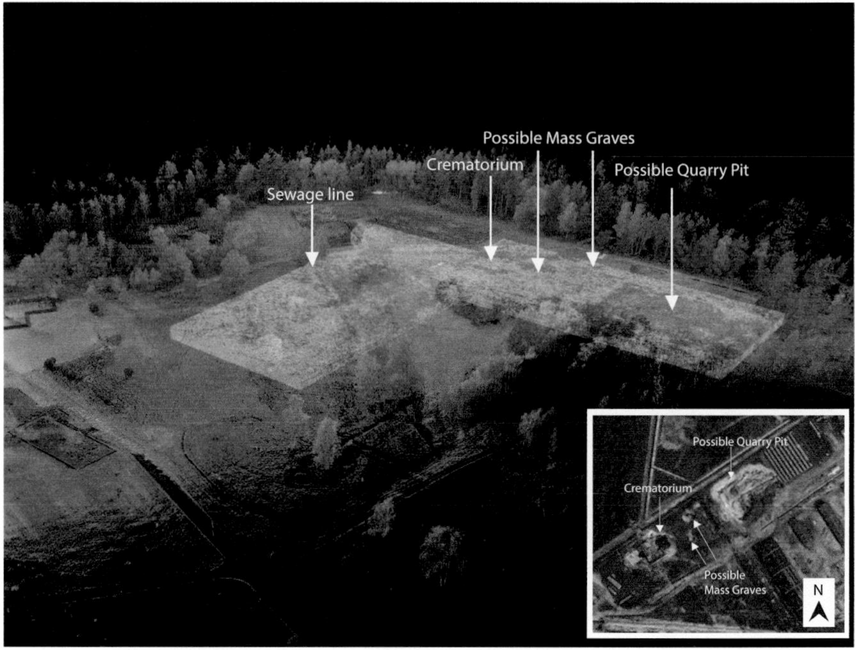

FIGURE 15.5 GPR data showing the locations of the crematorium, possible mass graves, and a quarry pit overlaid onto terrestrial LiDAR data. Inset: aerial photograph from September 1944 showing the corresponding features. Source: © Centre of Archaeology and ScanLAB Projects; inset © NCAP.

Burials after liberation

When the liberators arrived at Bergen-Belsen, the number of dead was so staggering it left them unable to comprehend the unfolding scenes (IWM 8996). As journalist Patrick Gordon Walker (1945) described 'corpses in every state of decay were lying round, piled up on top of each other in heaps. There were corpses in the compounds in the blocks. People were falling dead all around – people were walking skeletons'. The scale of the disaster – which saw a further 14,000 people die after liberation (5,000 in the first five days) – and the risk of disease meant that the British needed to excavate many pits to dispose of the corpses (Walker 1945). Speed was imperative. Trailers were soon used to gather up the bodies and SS guards were then made to put them into the graves (IWM 32374). Bulldozers – immortalized in the iconography of Bergen-Belsen via photographs shown in the media – were occasionally used to push in the corpses (see for example Levy 1995: 11–12; Riches 1987 in IWM 9937). In almost all cases, identification of individuals was impossible in the absence of possessions on the bodies or relatives to identify them (TNA WO235/13). As François-Poncet recalled, 'as most of the survivors could not even give their own names … it was useless trying to obtain information as to the identity of the dead' and few had personal belongings in their possession (cited in Stone 2020b: 170–171; Walker 1945).

Lime was placed on top of the bodies and then soil, forming 76-centimetre-high mounds, used to cover the graves. A service was then held by the various chaplains and a 'notice board was erected stating the approximate or actual numbers buried, and the date the pit was closed' (British Zone Review 1945). The lack of precision and record-keeping is described in various sources, including one by a British NCO: 'a lot of the pits we just put on number unknown. But some pits we put 5000, 8000 and that's how it went on. But we weren't really sure how many 'cause nobody counted them. They was just buried, that was the only way we could do it' (IWM 32374). The lack of precision in counting the dead likely explains some of the disparity between the anticipated number of people who died in Bergen-Belsen and the numbers marked on the graves.

Contemporary records show that there was concern at the time that the initial exercise to cover and mark these pits was not enough to ensure their commemoration:

> At present, the sites of the mass graves at the former BELSEN concentration camp are marked by the presence of several large mounds. There is, however, a danger that with the passage of time the significance of these mounds may come to be overlooked, since there is little to show that they conceal the unrecorded graves of thousands of former camp inmates.
>
> *(TNA FO 1032/2308)*

As already mentioned, these concerns appear to have been valid as historical records show that two body disposal locations were not located until the 1950s and early 1960s, respectively, suggesting that either they were never marked by the liberators or that their markers had been lost (GBB 2012).

Testimonies suggest at least one other location that the British possibly recognized and reused as a mass grave. This area, located west of the crematorium, has been referred to as a bomb crater by Gedenkstätte Bergen-Belsen (2012). However, aerial photographs and a camp survivor suggest that it may have been a quarry or gravel pit in which the British buried 2,000 bodies after liberation (Cheim 1945) (Figures 15.2, 15.5, and 15.6). GPR survey over this area confirmed the presence of a large feature measuring a minimum of 63 by 58 metres, originating at 0.47 metres below ground (the likely ground surface at the time the concentration camp was operating) and extending beyond the five-metre depth of the survey (Figure 15.6, marked A). It appeared consistent with a backfilled pit, most likely containing redeposited sand and silt, and its overall form matched that of an area of disturbance visible in aerial photographs taken in 1944. Several associated features were also located. The first was a likely ramp into this feature, thus supporting the theory that it was a pit that required access (Figure 15.6, marked B). The second was a rectilinear feature – seemingly structural – which enclosed an irregular feature: an apparent backfilled pit measuring

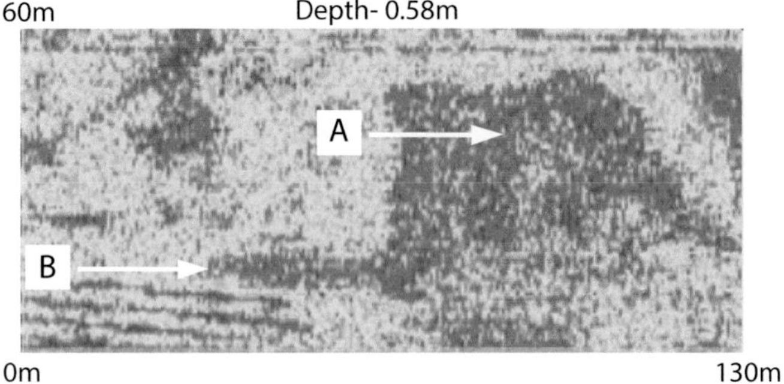

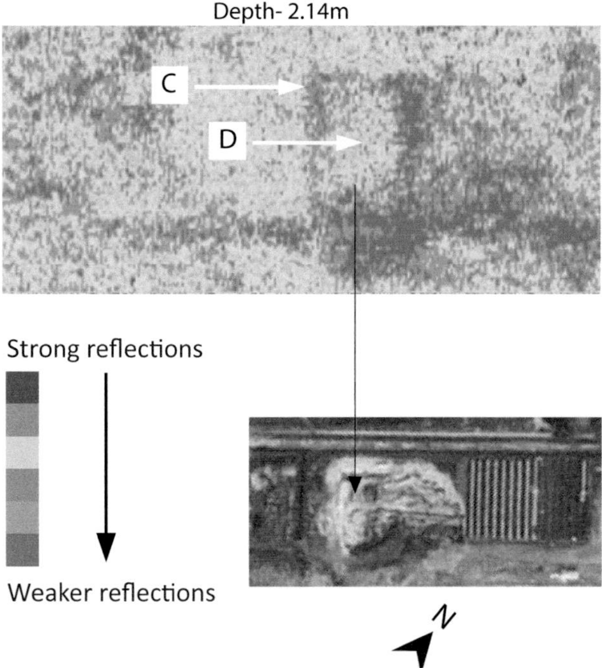

FIGURE 15.6 GPR time-slice results (birds-eye data view) at 0.58-metre depth and 2.14-metre depth showing the possible quarry pit and associated features. A: possible quarry pit; B: ramp; C: rectilinear feature; D: possible backfilled pit. Source: © Centre of Archaeology.

approximately 17 by 14.8 metres (Figure 15.6, marked C and D). The former was visible in aerial photographs taken whilst the camp was in operation. The latter was not, but this is likely because it was present at a greater depth. Interpreting the exact nature of this and associated features remains difficult because witness testimony is limited and excavation is not possible out of respect for Jewish law.

However, the archaeological and historical information does present a plausible theory that additional burials and a quarry could exist in this locality.

Concentration camp–era burials

When the camp was under SS control, archive research shows that the crematorium at Bergen-Belsen was insufficient in size and the number of ovens was too few to have managed the number of dead, particularly in its final months (Leo 1945; examples in Cole 2016). The escalating death toll and the advance of the British brought about the need to build cremation pyres and then to excavate mass graves, something that inmates were forced to do under SS supervision (Le Druillenec 1945, Winwood 1945a). Identification and documentation of the deceased had to be dispensed with to prevent further chaos (Reilly 1998: 17).

As already noted, the graves marked by the British in 1945 contained only the bodies of the 10,000 unburied dead they found around the camp and those who died after liberation. Therefore, it appears that the graves dug by the SS were not located, or at the very least they were not marked, by the time the British left the camp. Whilst some of these 'large pits', 'excavations', 'open mass graves', and 'burial pits' may not have been evident to the liberators, others were certainly observed by them (TNA WO171/4604; Burger 1945; Winwood 1945b). For example, Brigadier Glyn Hughes noted that: 'near the crematorium were signs of filled-in mass graves, and outside to the left of the bottom compound was an open pit half-full of corpses' (Lattek 1997: 38), yet only a memorial covering scattered burnt bone fragments exists near to the crematorium and this was erected in 1964–1965 (Seybold 2017: 6). Jean-Pierre Renouard showed the liberators another grave which was not 'yet filled to the brim, far from it. But there are already thousands of bodies' (Renouard 2012: 86). Therefore, it is necessary to pose the question: where are the concentration camp–era mass graves located?

The possibility that the British reused open graves, burying the recently deceased on top of those interred by the SS, cannot be ruled out, meaning that some of the graves could be those already marked. If this is the case, it remains unclear whether these bodies were included in the death tolls written on the grave markers. Two other possible options exist in the form of open pits, east of the crematorium, which are visible in aerial photographs taken in September 1944 (Figure 15.7). When GPR was carried out in this area, two anomalies were discovered 0.5 metres below the surface, originating at what was believed to have been ground level when the concentration camp was in operation. The first anomaly – measuring approximately 30.5 by 8.5 metres, and exceeding 4.5 metres in depth – matched the size and location of one of the pits shown in the aerial photographs (Figure 15.7, marked A). The second – which was approximately 30 by 12.5 metres, and also exceeded 4.5 metres in depth – was considerably larger than the pit visible in the aerial images and only partially matched its

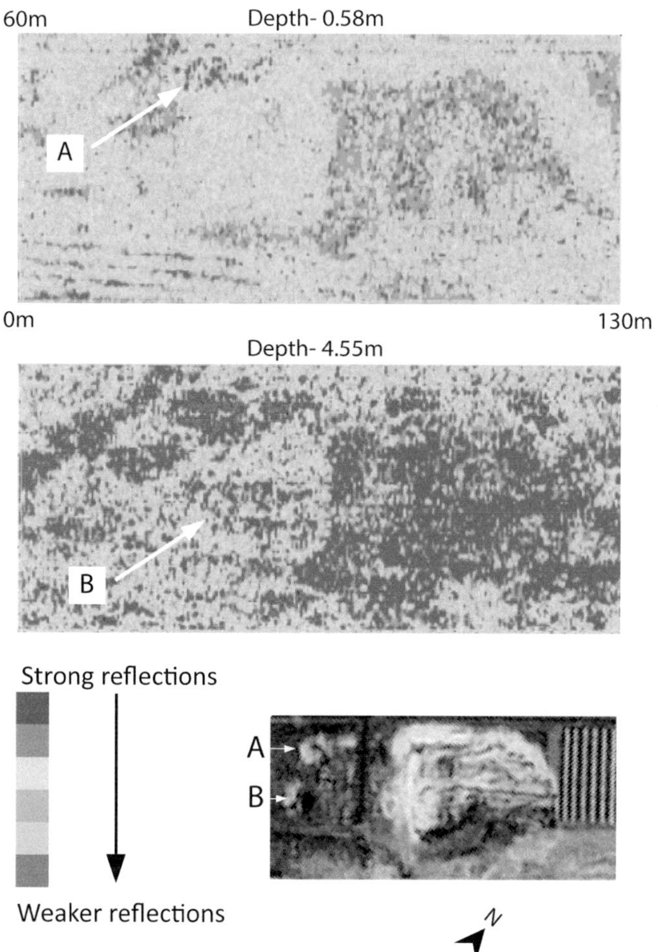

FIGURE 15.7 GPR data showing two possible mass graves, marked A and B. Source: © Centre of Archaeology.

orientation, suggesting it was either partially filled in when the September 1944 photograph was taken or, more likely, that it was enlarged for the purpose of continued use after liberation (Figure 15.7, marked B). The latter may be supported by the testimony and map of survivor E. van Lambaart, which refer to a mass grave to the east of the crematorium into which he reportedly buried a friend shortly after liberation (Schute et al. 2014).[3] Considerable ground disturbance was visible in this area in aerial photographs taken after liberation, seemingly confirming the long-term use of these pits. Once again, excavation is not possible to confirm the exact nature of these features. To rule out the possibility of other burial sites, further archaeological research is also required to the south and west of the crematorium.

Contentious findings

The discovery of evidence relating to unmarked mass graves at Bergen-Belsen was an unexpected and contentious consequence of the archaeological investigations for the museum at Gedenkstätte Bergen-Belsen (Stephanie Billib, personal communication). By their own admission, the specifics of body disposal practices before and after liberation had not been a topic that the museum's historians had extensively researched. After controversial proposals for exhumations were put forward by a French Mission in the 1950s, the decision was taken that the dead should remain undisturbed in perpetuity and no further searches were carried out (Rosensaft 1979; Anstett and Dreyfus 2017). Archaeological works in 2014 (Schute et al. 2014) and 2015 (by the authors) reopened the debate about what happened to the dead during and after the camp was operating. Several ethical questions arose for both the memorial and the archaeologists involved in the research: what further investigations (if any) should take place? Could the existence of graves ever be confirmed and memorialized solely based on non-invasive data? At what point should survivors/descendants be informed of the findings and how might they react to such news? Does a site which is already seen as a cemetery need additional markers? What might the implications be of disrupting the established narrative of the site?

Ultimately, the archaeological research inspired a new research project at the Bergen-Belsen memorial relating to body disposal practices (Seybold 2017) which the historians at the museum felt was the only way to confirm the plausibility of additional graves. As this process is ongoing, no further action has yet been taken with regards to officially recognizing the existence of the sites identified by the archaeological works.

Concluding remarks

Given its status as a 'deathscape', Bergen-Belsen forms part of a group of places that are both 'intensely private and personal … while often simultaneously being shared, collective, sites of experience and remembrance; each place mediated through the intersections of emotion, body, belief, culture, society and the state' (Maddrell and Sidaway 2010). The former camp is quite rightly viewed as a cemetery by survivors, whilst judicial and museum authorities have stressed its importance as a 'landscape of memory' which embodies lived and recalled experiences (Anstett and Dreyfus 2017). As a *lieux de memoire* (Nora 1989), Bergen-Belsen's contemporary landscape and paradigmatic aspects of its history were formed as a result of 'the selective preservation, construction, and obliteration of ideas about the way things were in the past' (van Dyke 2006: 277). Via these selection processes, the dead are both everywhere and nowhere, ingrained in international consciousness via media portrayals and survivor recollections, and simultaneously forefronted and anonymized within the landscape by prominent mass grave memorials referring to numbers and not names. Bergen-Belsen is a landscape defined by the absence of people, but also of materiality, as its buildings were demolished by the British liberators. As Wolschke-Bulmahn (2001: 300) argued of the current heath-like landscape developed in 1961, 'on the one hand, it reflects an attempt to recall the Nazi past but, on the other, it may be interpreted as an attempt to conceal historic events behind a façade of a comforting landscape'.

To date, this 'façade' has served to detract attention from the fact that questions remain about the camp's operations and, in particular, the issue of what happened to the dead. The research outlined here has clearly shown that, faced with thousands of corpses to dispose of and a rising death toll, the British liberators focused on the rapid burial of bodies, as opposed to detailed investigations regarding the identities of the victims or the specifics of the Nazis' crimes. It is evident from archaeological readings of historical sources that many bodies were never found and non-invasive methods have indicated possible locations where they may have been buried, whilst also accounting for Jewish law (Sturdy Colls 2015b). This project has revealed important new evidence regarding the nature of buried remains and generated novel 3-D tools, which have the potential to enhance visitor experiences, provide new foci for commemoration practices, and generate new information and tools for use in education and research. The archaeological work has also complemented and challenged narratives in a way that historical research alone cannot (Gonzáles-Ruibal 2008).

However, it is precisely for this reason that some of the work at Bergen-Belsen was considered contentious. Whilst the identification of the crematorium building as well as barrack foundations and a sewage line (not described here, see Sturdy Colls 2015a) were welcomed because they complemented historical narratives, the suggestion of further mass graves was contested because it challenged them.[4] Even though there has been a recent 'forensic turn' and a growing recognition of the value of archaeological methods at sites of mass violence, non-invasive archaeological research within Holocaust studies remains in its infancy (Dziuban 2017; Sturdy Colls 2015b). Although the combination of historical research and non-invasive archaeological data has been a central part of efforts to memorialize previously unidentified killing sites away from the camps, e.g. in the fields and forests of Poland and Ukraine, as part of projects led by the authors and others, what the example of Bergen-Belsen shows is that, at well-established memorials, there remains a reluctance to accept that historical research might not be the only way to understand sites and events. This undoubtedly also stems from the fact that archaeological evidence – and the marking of graves that it might inspire – has the potential to (physically and metaphorically) disrupt 'comforting landscape[s]' and well-established narratives, evoking a wide range of difficult ethical questions about approaches to Europe's conflicted past.

Acknowledgements

The authors are extremely grateful to the UK Holocaust Memorial Foundation (in particular Tim Kiddell and Andrew Morris) for providing the opportunity and funding for the Bergen-Belsen survey project. Special thanks are also due to ScanLAB Projects (especially Will Trossell), who coordinated the fieldwork and undertook the terrestrial LiDAR and drone survey work described in this chapter. We are grateful also to Atlantic Productions for providing funding and logistical support for the project. The work would not have been possible without the support of Gedenkstätte Bergen-Belsen, in particular Stephanie Billib, who provided invaluable assistance with fieldwork logistics, the acquisition of archive material, and feedback on our work. Thanks also go to the fieldwork team from Staffordshire University: Janos Kerti and Czelsie Weston. We are grateful to the historians at Gedenkstätte Bergen-Belsen and to archaeologist Julianne Hummel for their help and advice. Thanks are also due to Dr Ivar Schute and Professor Paul Verschure, who provided information about their research which paved the way for our own survey and to Katja Seybold, who undertook the historical review concerning burials at Bergen-Belsen after our fieldwork was completed. Further research for this chapter would not have been possible without funding from the Humanities in the European Research Area (HERA) Network and the European Union Horizon 2020 fund under grant agreement 649307 (Accessing Campscapes: Inclusive Strategies for Using European Conflicted Heritage [IC-ACCESS] project).

Notes

1 Further analysis of the fieldwork data and additional research concerning the issue of unmarked burials was carried out under the auspice of the Accessing Campscapes: Inclusive Strategies for Using European Conflicted Heritage (IC-ACCESS) project. For more information about this project see www.campscapes.org.

2 Around 1,400 Hungarian prisoners were also exchanged in late 1944 as a result of separate negotiations between the SS and a Zionist aid committee (see Rahe 2012: 278).

3 In 2014, based on the information provided by E. van Lambaart, his grandson (a respected neuroscientist) and archaeologists from RAAP in the Netherlands conducted resistance and metal detecting surveys over part of the terrain to the east of the crematorium (Schute et al. 2014). Although they were successful in identifying shallow disturbances within their targeted area, their survey was neither large nor deep enough to target the pits shown in the aerial photographs. This work was another motivating factor in proceeding with the GPR survey over this area.

4 Since 2010 Gedenkstätte Bergen-Belsen have utilized an Augmented Reality (AR) app that 'allows visitors to physically visit the former campsite and perceive and experience the historical spatial structures and details of fences, buildings and camp sections as part of the landscape', demonstrating a clear commitment to the inclusion of materiality within their educational offerings (Future Memory Foundation 2019; Pacheco et al. 2014). Hence, this reaffirms the view that it is the mass graves that remain the most contentious.

References

Anstett, E. and J.-M. Dreyfus (eds.) (2017) *Destruction and Human Remains. Disposal and Concealment in Genocide and Mass Violence*. Manchester: Manchester University Press.

Archiv Lüneburg, 11320/3.2, Cf. letter from the district president in Lüneburg to the Lower Saxony Minister of the Interior, 6.8.1964 (copy: GBBA).

Berney, L. (2015) *Liberating Belsen Concentration Camp: A Personal Account*. Middletown, DE: CreateSpace Independent Publishing Platform.

Blitz, N. (n.d.) www.annefrank.org/en/downloads/filer_public/08/b3/08b3ff12-d8c1-4964-b9ec-e17a7b035a76/one_day_they_simply_weren.pdf (accessed 23 September 2019).

British Zone Review (1945) *Belsen. An Account, Based on Official Reports, of the Uncovering by the British Army of the Belsen Concentration Camp and of the Action Taken during the Vital Days to Minimise the Suffering of the 60,000 Inmates, Supplement to the British Zone Review, 13.10.1945*. Hamburg: Information Services Division, Control Commission for Germany.

Burger, P. (1945) Transcript of the Official Shorthand Notes of 'The Trial of Josef Kramer and Forty Four Others – Seventeeth Day, Friday 5th October 1945'. www.bergenbelsen.co.uk/pages/TrialTranscript/Trial_Day_017.html (accessed 24 September 2019).

Carrick, U.E. (2017) *Ground Penetrating Radar. Theory and Practice*. Oxford: Butterworth-Heinemann.

Cesarani, D. (2006) A Brief History of Bergen Belsen. In D. Cesarani and S. Bardgett (eds.), *Belsen 1945: New Historical Perspectives*, pp. 13–21. Middlesex: Valentine Mitchell.

Cheim, M.R. (1945) *Diary of Rudolf Martin Cheim, June 1945, S. 16*. New York: YIVO Institute for Jewish Research.

Cole, T. (2016) *Holocaust Landscapes*. London: Bloomsbury.

Dreyfus, J.M (2017) The Mass Graves at Hohne and the French Attempt (and Failure) at Exhumation (1958–1969). *Accessing Campscapes: Inclusive Strategies for Using European Conflicted Heritage* 4: 6–13.

Dziuban, Z. (ed.) (2017) *Mapping the 'Forensic Turn': The Engagements with Materialities of Mass Death in Holocaust Studies and Beyond*. Vienna: New Academic Press.

Eeles, N. and N. Blitz Konig (2015) *Liberating Belsen Concentration Camp*. Middletown, DE: CreateSpace Independent Publishing Platform.

Egels, Y. and M. Kasser (2002) *Digital Photogrammetry*. London: Taylor and Francis.

Future Memory Foundation (2019) www.futurememoryfoundation.org/ (accessed 24 September 2019).

Gedenkstätte Bergen-Belsen. (2012) *Bergen-Belsen Geschichte der Gedenkstätte/History of the Memorial*. Celle: Stiftung niedersachsische Gedenkstätten Bergen-Belsen/Gedenkstätte Bergen-Belsen.

——— (2019) https://bergen-belsen.stiftung-ng.de/en/ (accessed 23 September 2019).

González-Ruibal, A. (2008) Time to Destroy: An Archaeology of Supermodernity. *Current Anthropology* 49 (2): 247–279.

Haggith, T. (2006) The Filming of the Liberation of Bergen-Belsen and its Impact on the Understanding of the Holocaust. *Holocaust Studies* 12 (1–2): 89–122.

Hummel, J. (2008) *Quellen zurtopografie Bergen-Belsen 1938–1945*. Bergen-Belsen: Stiftung niedersächsische Gedenkstätten Gedenkstätte Bergen-Belsen, R. S. R. T.

Illustrated London News, April 28, 1945-No. 3027-Vol. 116, pp. 458–459.

Imperial War Museum (IWM) 8996. 1/09/1985. Dixey. John Roger Bertram (Oral History). www.iwm.org.uk/collections/item/object/80008788 (accessed 24 September 2019).

——— 9937. 19/09/1987. Riches, Frederick Alexander (Oral History). Francois-www.iwm.org.uk/collections/item/object/80009720 (accessed 24 September 2019).

——— 32374. British NCO (n.d.) Served with 113th Light Anti-Aircraft Regt, Royal Artillery during Liberation of Bergen-Belsen Concentration Camp, Germany, 4-5/1945. www.iwm.org.uk/collections/item/object/80031034 (accessed 24 September 2019).

Kushner, T. (1996) The Memory of Belsen. *Journal of Holocaust Education* 5 (2–3): 181–205.

——— (2006) From 'This Belsen Business' to 'Shoah Business': History, Memory and Heritage, 1945–2005. *Holocaust Studies* 12 (1–2): 189–216.

——— (2017) The Holocaust in British Imagination: The Official Mind and Beyond, 1945 to the Present. *Holocaust Studies* 23 (3): 364–384.

Lasker-Wallfisch, M.S. and C. Lattek. (1997) Bergen-Belsen: From 'Privileged' Camp to Death Camp. In J. Reilly, T. Kushner, D. Cesarani and C. Richmond (eds.), *Belsen in History and Memory*, pp. 37–71. London: Frank Cass & Co, Ltd.

Lavsky, H. (1993) The Day After: Bergen-Belsen from Concentration Camp to the Centre of the Jewish Survivors in Germany. *German History* 11 (1): 36–59.

Le Druillenec, H.O. (1945) Bergen-Belsen Trial 1945, TNA, WO 235/13.

Lees-Milne, J. (1977) *Prophesying Peace*. London: Chatto & Windus.

Leo, F. (1945) Transcript of the Official Shorthand Notes of 'The Trial of Josef Kramer and Forty Four Others – Eleventh Day, Friday 28th September 1945'. www.bergenbelsen.co.uk/pages/TrialTranscript/Trial_Day_011.html#Day011_Leo (accessed 24 September 2019).

Levy, I. (1995) *Witness to Evil. Bergen Belsen. 1945*. London: Peter Halban in association with The European Jewish Publication Society.

Maddrell, A. and J.D. Sidaway (eds.) (2010) *Deathscapes. Spaces for Death, Dying, Mourning and Remembrance*. London: Routledge.

Nora, P (1989) Between Memory and History. *Representations* 26: 7–24.

Opitz, R.S and D.C. Cowley (2013) *Interpreting Archaeological Topography: 3D Data, Visualisation and Observation*. Oxford: Oxbow Books.

Pacheco, D., S. Wierenga, P. Omedas, S. Wilbricht, H. Knoch and P.F. Verschure (2014) Spatializing Experience: A Framework for the Geolocalization, Visualization and Exploration of Historical Data Using VR/AR Technologies. In: *Proceedings of the 2014 Virtual Reality International Conference*, p. 1.

Stone, D. (2020b) *Fascism, Nazism and the Holocaust: Challenging Histories*. London: Routledge.

Rahe, T. (2012) Bergen-Belsen Main Camp. In G.P. Megargee (ed.), *The United States Holocaust Memorial Museum, Encyclopaedia of Camps and Ghettos 1933–1945, Vol.1, Early Camps, Youth Camps, and Concentration Camps and Subcamps under the SS-Business Administration Main Office (WVHA)*, pp 278–281. Bloomington: Indiana University Press.

Reilly, J. (1998) *Belsen: The Liberation of a Concentration Camp*. London: Routledge.

Reilly, J., D. Cesarani, T. Kushner and C. Richmond (eds.) (1997) *Belsen in History and Memory*. London: Taylor & Francis.

Renouard, J.P. (2012) *My Stripes Were Earned in Hell*. Lanham, MD: Rowman and Littlefield.

Rosensaft, M.Z. (1979) The Mass-Graves of Bergen-Belsen: Focus For Confrontation. *Jewish Social Studies*, 41 (2): 155–186.

Schudrich, M. (2015) Jewish Law and Exhumation. In International Holocaust Remembrance Alliance (ed.), *Killing Sites: Research and Remembrance*, pp. 79–84. Berlin: Metropol.

Schulze, R. (2006) Forgetting and Remembering: Memories and Memorialisation of Bergen-Belsen. *Holocaust Studies* 12 (1–2): 17–235.

——— (2015) Why Bergen-Belsen's 1945 Liberation Is Ingrained in British Memory. *The Conversation.* https://theconversation.com/why-bergen-belsens-1945-liberation-is-ingrained-in-british-memory-39956 (accessed 1 September 2019).

Schute, I., W.J. Verschoof and N. Warmerdam (2014) *Locating a Mass Grave in Camp Bergen Belsen, Lower Saxony, Germany. A Geophysical Survey.* RAAP Report 2851. Leiden: RAAP Archeologisch Adiesbureau BV.

Seybold, K. (2017) The Dead of Bergen-Belsen. Number and Burial Places of The Victims of The Bergen-Belsen Concentration Camp. https://bergen-belsen.stiftung-ng.de/en/research-and-documentation/currentresearchprojects/ (accessed 7 January 2018).

Stone, D. (2015) *The Liberation of the Camps: The End of the Holocaust and its Aftermath.* New Haven: Yale University Press.

——— (2020a) Belsen and the British. In T. Lawson and A. Pearce (eds.), *The Palgrave Handbook of Britain and the Holocaust*, pp 153–180. London: Palgrave Macmillan.

Sturdy Colls, C. (2012) Holocaust Archaeology: Archaeological Approaches to Landscapes of Nazi Genocide and Persecution. *Journal of Conflict Archaeology* 7(2): 71–105.

——— (2014) Gone But Not Forgotten: Archaeological Approaches to the Landscape of the Former Extermination Camp at Treblinka, Poland. *Holocaust Studies and Materials* 3: 239–289.

——— (2015a) *Bergen-Belsen: An Archaeological Assessment.* Field Investigation Report. Centre of Archaeology Staffordshire University.

——— (2015b) *Holocaust Archaeologies: Approaches and Future Directions.* New York: Springer.

The National Archives (TNA). FO 1032/2308. Letter to the 229 'P' Mil Gov Det. Hannover from Office of the Chief of Staff (British Zone), 10th October 1945.

——— WO171/4604. Montague, C.H. Belsen. Report by HQ Garrison on 18–30 April 1945.

——— WO235/13. Brigadier Glyn Hughes British Medical Officer. The Belsen Trial, 1945, pp. 31–32.

United States Holocaust Memorial Museum (USHMM) (2019) *Bergen-Belsen.* https://encyclopedia.ushmm.org/content/en/article/bergen-belsen (accessed 23 September 2019).

Van Dyke, R.M. (2006) Memory, Place, and the Memorialization of Landscape. In B. David and J. Thomas (eds.), *Handbook of Landscape Archaeology*, pp. 277–284. London: Routledge.

Wachsmann, N. (2015) *KL: A History of the Nazi Concentration Camps.* New York: Straus and Giroux.

Walker, P.G. (1945) Personal Notes Friday April 20th, 1945. www.bbc.co.uk/archive/patrick-gordon-walker--belsen-facts-and-thoughts/zdsvxyc (accessed 24 September 2019).

Wenck, A.-E. (2000) *Zwischen Menschenhandel und ‚Endlösung': das Konzentrationslager Bergen-Belsen.* Paderborn: Schöningh.

Winwood, T.C.M (1945a) Transcript of the Official Shorthand Notes of 'The Trial of Josef Kramer and Forty Four Others – Forty Sixth Day'. 8 November. www.bergenbelsen.co.uk/pages/TrialTranscript/Trial_Day_046.html (accessed 24 September 2019).

——— (1945b) Transcript of the Official Shorthand Notes of 'The Trial of Josef Kramer and Forty Four Others – Nineteenth Day'. 8 October. www.bergenbelsen.co.uk/pages/TrialTranscript/Trial_Day_019.html (accessed 24 September 2019).

Wolschke-Bulmahn, J. (2001) *Places of Commemoration: Search for Identity and Landscape Design.* Washington, DC: Dumbarton Oaks Research Library and Collection.

16

CAMPSCAPES AND HOMESCAPES OF THE MIND'S EYE

A methodology for analyzing the landscapes of internment camps

Gilly Carr

Introduction

When one thinks of landscapes of war, one imagines muddy battlefields or bombed cities, yet it is easy to forget that internment camps formed their own conflict landscapes, most especially for those trapped inside them. Such places were often purpose-built barrack block camps, but civilian internees were also placed in old *Schlösser* or castles, in institutional buildings such as hospitals, or in requisitioned hotels or old military barracks.

Those interned in such camps during the Second World War added a new chapter to the biography of these buildings. They also had their own perceptions of the camp and landscape outside the camp that differed from that of both the previous inhabitants and those living outside the camps, reminding us that 'people, differently engaged and differently empowered, appropriate and contest their landscapes' (Bender 1993: 17, 2001). Landscapes are, after all, multi-vocal, seen in different ways by different people in the same moment (Bender 2006: 303). They are not inert; people engage with them and rework them (Bender 1993: 3), if only in the mind's eye, as we shall see. By recognizing the political dimensions of landscape, we are able to acknowledge the element of contestation and appropriation over its use, and reterritorialization and interpretation by different groups. By also seeing camps through a biographical rather than palimpsestic lens, we are able to keep within sight 'the various long-term effects of crucial events and the often explicit or deliberate re-awakening and re-use of earlier meanings' of place (Sørensen and Viejo-Rose 2015: 13). The war-time role of the sites of the camps today, which are now repurposed and much changed, is periodically re-awakened and invoked in annual visits by former internees, something we will touch on below.

This chapter explores the camp landscapes (or 'campscapes') as depicted in the material culture produced during these years of captivity, and as seen through the eyes – and mind's eye – of civilian internees, analyzing these vistas at the levels of analysis of space and time attempted here. The campscape as I define it here encompasses all of these vistas, both looked at *then* and remembered *now*; everything within the purview or gaze, both inwards and outwards, of the internees. It stretched from the camp itself to the horizon, and in the mind's eye and memory of the internee, carried forwards with them as they grew old.

At the first level, I look at the space of the camp grounds, inside the barbed wire, and how it was perceived by the camp's inhabitants. The second level lifts the eyes beyond the wire to the wider landscape, also within the purview of the extended campscape as I define it here, to examine the camp hinterland. At the third level, the internees turned inward to depict remembered landscapes of home – their 'homescapes'. Finally, we move forwards in time to the present, to examine our fourth level: the remembered campscapes in the mind of internees in their old age.

Deportation and internment

In order to set the scene of the civilian internment camps examined here, some historical context is necessary. In 1942 and 1943, during the German occupation of the Channel Islands, around 2,200 civilian Islanders were deported to southern Germany for the rest of the war (Cruikshank 2004 [1975]). They were sent to four main camps: the neighbouring towns in Baden-Württemberg of Biberach and Wurzach, which I will focus on predominantly in this chapter, and which held family camps for people from Guernsey and Jersey respectively; Liebenau, in the same state, which held a women's camp; and the Bavarian town of Laufen, which housed male internees. These represented the final destination for the vast majority of Channel Islander internees, although the transit camps of Dorsten (in North Rhine-Westphalia) and Compiègne (outside Paris) also received Islanders for a few months en route. During their years of incarceration, the Islanders passed the time by making a range of artefacts from the contents of their Red Cross parcels and by painting the views inside and beyond the barbed wire.

The Channel Islanders were deported from their homes in two waves as a reprisal for British action in Persia (modern Iran) in the autumn of 1941, during which German subjects working in Iran were rounded up, deported, and interned in Australia. The Islanders targeted for reprisal deportation in the first wave of September 1942 comprised men born outside the Islands aged between 16 and 70 and their dependents. Most of these were English as opposed to indigenous Islanders, and the German forces assumed that this segment of the population would be more likely to stir up later resistance. However, a good number were actually indigenous Islanders who happened to be born outside the Channel Islands.

Further deportations took place in February of the following year, which this time targeted those who had somehow evaded deportation the first time around, as well as people who had spent time in prison for resistance offences, former officers, British Jews, and large families from Sark (thought to be a drain on resources), in retaliation for a British commando raid which took place in Sark in October 1942. The deportation order stated that people were allowed to take with them a few scant possessions: warm clothes, strong boots, meal dishes, a drinking bowl, and a blanket.

When the Islanders arrived in their camps after passenger-train journeys lasting several days, they found that Biberach camp (made up of old barrack buildings), like Wurzach (an old *Schloss*), had problems with flies and mosquitoes, was overcrowded and infested with vermin, and was very cold in winter; but the Islanders cleaned their camps as best they could and, with time, conditions did improve. As at Wurzach, a school was set up for the children at Biberach, and a makeshift theatre and a small orchestra was organized. There was also a small area for sports, a place for church services and for dances, and classes were held on a small number of subjects for the adults. Many of these entertainments were also organized at the other camps. After a while, in some of the camps, internees were allowed now and again, depending on the weather, to go on country walks, escorted by their guards. On these occasions, wood was collected for firewood for cooking, heating water, and warmth, until the residents of the local towns complained about this practice. This wood was also used, on occasion, for whittling, painting, and making artefacts.

The Red Cross located the Islanders in December 1942, reversing increasing problems with malnutrition. After that time, the food situation improved greatly. German rations had been small and mouldy and of such poor quality that the coffee was used to fill hot water bottles and the tea was used to clean the tables. Later in the war, the Islanders were able to barter the contents of their Red Cross parcels with local townsfolk, exchanging tinned food for rabbits, chicken, and eggs (Harris 1979: 62). Islanders could also be sent next-of-kin parcels from the UK, and the contents of these were also useful for recycling and craftwork.

Apart from food worries, concerns about family and friends in the UK and Channel Islands, and intense anxiety about their own fate, other problems for the Islanders included the petty squabbling and the spreading of malicious rumours caused by the overcrowding, frayed nerves, and lack of privacy. Such concerns affected morale badly and were responsible for a number of cases of mental ill-health (Harris 1979: 82). Some sufferers ended up in asylums (Harris: 125).

Countering 'lageritis or fedupness' as the inmates of Laufen named it in the camp publication *The Birdcage* (Ilag VII Laufen: 18), and finding ways to pass the time, to 'forget their troubles and difficulties, circumstances and surroundings, if only for a short while' (ibid.: 32) were the chief problems of the internees of all camps. The Red Cross and YWCA were able to play a more crucial role than they realized in this respect. They were able to deliver to individuals supplies of paper, paint, writing materials, 'occupational therapy materials', and sewing materials (Garland n.d.a: 8; n.d.b: 19) which, supplemented with items sent in next-of-kin parcels, helped internees cope with imprisonment and separation from loved ones, afforded short periods of 'oblivion of internment', and 'evaded the barbed wire' (Ilag VII Laufen: 56). The Red Cross parcels themselves were recycled and turned into various objects by internees to pass the time, as detailed below; such diversions from their circumstances helped Islanders to survive, both mentally and physically (Carr and Mytum 2012a: 5–6). As Garfield Garland, the Biberach camp leader, said in his report to the British Red Cross in September 1944, 'had it not been for the regular supply of food parcels and tobacco from the British Red Cross, we could not have regarded anything with the same philosophical outlook and endeavour to overcome difficulties' (Garland n.d.a: 8).

Campscapes and homescapes of space and time

The campscapes and homescapes created in internment camps were fashioned, as mentioned above, from recycling the raw materials of Red Cross parcels. The food tins were cut open and rolled out and the panels hammered together to make cups and plates; the parcel string was variously untwisted, dyed, plaited, and woven to make handbags; the cardboard from the parcels was cut into various shapes and employed for uses such as shoe soles; the coloured cellophane strips used for packing material were woven and crocheted, and the wooden crates that the parcels arrived in were soon sawn up and made into anything from armchairs to children's toys and chess sets. As with other similar accounts of artwork and artefacts made by internees (e.g. Archer 2004; Cresswell 1994; Becker 2004; Carr 2009; Dusselier 2008), many themes and meanings can be seen within the types of artefacts which have been discussed in detail elsewhere (e.g. Carr and Mytum 2012b; Myers and Moshenska 2011; Mytum and Carr 2013).

All of these items fall into the long-established category of trench art, more recently defined and conceptualized academically by Saunders (2003: 11). Archer and Jeffreys (2012: 25–26) take issue with the masculine, military implications of the nomenclature of this term. Although the category of trench art was identified and named before Saunders, who himself observes that the terminology is misleading (2003: 9), Archer and Jeffreys argue that while Saunders' definition appears to 'give parity to soldiers, civilian internees and other non-military personnel', the 'use of the word "trench", with its male, military and First World War connotations, belies this parity' and 'illustrates the male, military supremacy in the historical record and historiography'. This, they argue, renders invisible the female experience of war, and especially items made by women in camps such as embroideries. Although Saunders does discuss such works by women (e.g. 2003: 202, 219–220), Archer and Jeffreys fail to offer an alternative nomenclature or definition for camp art and crafts. Nonetheless, I heed their call in not overlooking women's needlework, instead treating it with deserved parity with other items made by internees. Although most (but not all) of the process of making trench art in camps by Islanders was gendered, with the men making items out of wood and metal and the women knitting, crocheting, and embroidering, generally people used their pre-war skill set. This was augmented by a pamphlet published by the Red Cross, which showed people how to make objects from tins.[1]

These items, as an assemblage, soon supplemented the spartan rooms of the camps, pre-furnished only with bunk beds, wooden tables, and stools. This process has been identified by Dusselier as one of 'remaking inside spaces' where 'shoddily built, crowded and barren inside living spaces' of Japanese American internment camps were 're-territorialized' into 'spaces of survival' during the Second World War (Dusselier 2012: 82).

Previously I have looked at the hidden worlds and meaning of space in the Channel Islanders' camps (Carr 2013), examining the multiple levels of embodied and nested space within a camp. While this earlier work focused on how space was structured within the camp buildings according to class, power, gender, and age, here I step firmly outside the buildings to foreground the levels of perception of the landscape. The point of overlap with the earlier work is the first level of analysis presented here: that of the camp grounds within the barbed wire.

Many of the artworks of this area of the camp grounds seem to emphasize how grey and dispiriting the area inside the perimeter was. The collection of over 60 cartoon 'camp personalities' drawn by Arscott Dickinson in Biberach show many of the internees marching around the perimeter looking comically grumpy or frozen stiff (Figure 16.1).[2] Depictions of the camp's watch-towers were also popular in camp art, both types of images acting as testaments (and muted complaints) about the circumstances of incarceration. Yet other artworks attempted to soften the view out of the barrack-room or *Schloss* windows. A watercolour by Harold Hepburn made in Wurzach focuses on the barbed wire, the main gates of the camp with the swastika flag flying high, and the town's buildings beyond. Yet in the foreground are children playing in the sandpit and on a see-saw; a couple saunters past, arm in arm, and a girl relaxes on the grass.[3]

Attempts to add colour to the grounds of Biberach camp are clear in two particular paintings. Sidney Skillett clearly had his back to the barbed wire in his watercolour of the camp grounds. This shows busy flowerbeds bursting with large cabbages and patriotically coloured red, white, and blue flowers.[4] Sark watercolour artist Ethel Cheeswright was able to use productively the time that weighed heavily on her hands in camp. Her image of the camp grounds ostensibly has as its focus the barbed wire and watch-tower, and yet these fade away through her addition of colourful flowers around the perimeter fence, and flower beds outside the camp buildings.[5] Cheeswright perfected her ability to banish the sting of the barbed wire in a birthday card for a child, Stephen Matthews. The barbed wire of the camp morphs into a garden fence, and Mickey Mouse stands outside a barrack block, looking at a bird and a rabbit that have hopped into view.[6] These kinds of images show the internees' agency at resisting the sting of the camp architecture of enclosure and surveillance, choosing to inject colour, beauty, imagination, and even a little humour into the camp grounds.

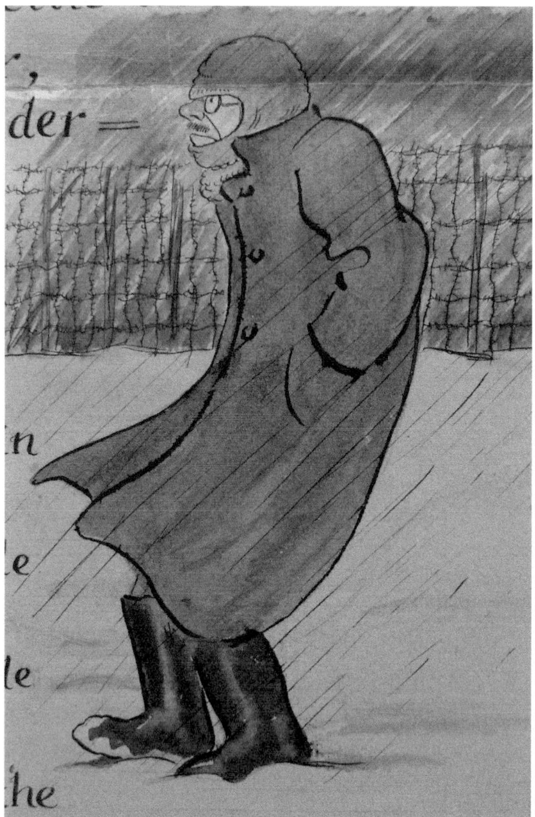

FIGURE 16.1 A cartoon caricature of an internee inside the perimeter fence of Biberach by Arscott Dickison. Source: courtesy of Jersey Heritage ref. L/C/177/A, reproduced by kind permission of Jersey Library.

As if stepping into one of Arscott Dickinson's greetings cards, we see a view out of the barrack window on the card front, covered in cellophane from a cigarette packet, and decorated with barbed wire (Figure 16.2).[7] We open the card to step out of the camp and into the landscape beyond, entering our second level of analysis: the view to the horizon beyond the barbed wire. This is a theme most clearly illustrated in images of Biberach camp, where landscapes 'come into being only at the moment of their apprehension by an external observer, and thus have a complex poetics and politics', as Cosgrove (2006: 50) puts it. Whether these particular views of the extended campscape existed as such before being depicted by internees from their particular vantage point is unknown, but Biberach camp afforded four very specific vistas which we see depicted multiple times.

These were the village of Birkenhard (and, in the distance, trees which the internees referred to as the 'Black Forest'); a little hill crested along its spine with trees (with the alps in the distance on a clear day); the *Wieland Linde*, a linden tree

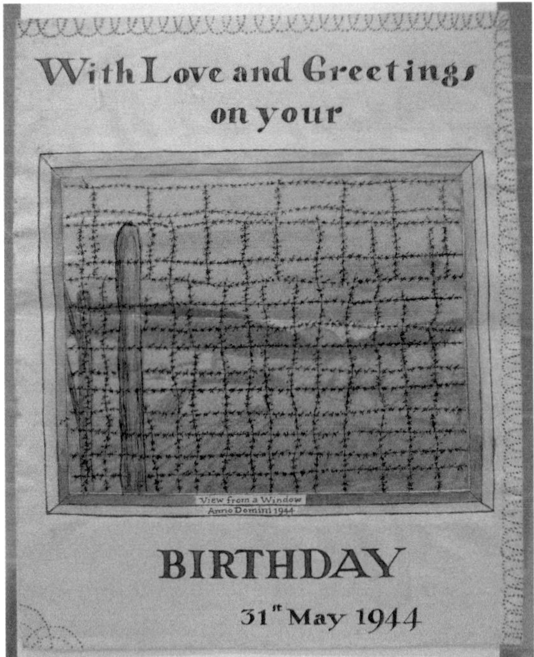

FIGURE 16.2 Greeting card by Arscott Dickinson. Source: courtesy of Jersey Heritage ref. L/C/177/A, reproduced by kind permission of Jersey Library.

planted in the eighteenth century to mark the engagement of Biberachian poet and writer Christophe Wieland; and undulating meadows dotted with trees. These images are repeated on camp-issued mugs engraved by Byll Balcombe, an inmate who also carved shell cases at the time of the liberation of the camp, a skill no doubt learned while fighting in the trenches during the First World War.[8] These mugs were sold or bartered to other internees in the camp and given as gifts for special occasions such as Christenings, wedding anniversaries, and birthdays, and even, eventually, liberation. Most of the mugs are, today, in the possession of former internees or their children.

The extended campscapes as viewed from the camp also occur on other items of material culture, such as in an early example from Biberach camp: a painted wooden plate with the hill crested by trees in the background, barbed wire, and a watch-tower in the middle of the picture. Below this is a collection of 27 signatures of internees, no doubt wanting to create a record of their presence in this new landscape.

The same views occur again in many of the paintings and drawings done in Biberach, most notably by the camp's most talented artists, John Merry and Henry Sandwith. While these artists' gaze sometimes includes barbed wire at the base of the image, their chins were set determinedly higher and their eyes looked towards the horizon. By inventing their own names, such as the 'Black Forest', for the hinterland of these extended campscapes, the internees were 'turning a locale in the landscape into a piece of social memory', with all the insight this gives us into the 'nature of space and place in the landscape' (Johnson 2007: 148) and the agency involved in creating and claiming places in German spaces.

Such agency in claiming German spaces for their own is seen most clearly in the maps, plans, and bird's-eye views of the camps drawn by a number of internees. Preston John Doughty in Wurzach made one such blue pen and ink sketch,[9] with the exact positioning of the barbed wire, the guardhouse, and the watchtowers clearly marked (Figure 16.3). Parts of the *Schloss* were labelled to indicate where the men's and women's sleeping quarters were, where the bread store and hospital ward were positioned, as well as the location of the washing lines, the football field, the potato and coal stores, and the moat separating the internees' space from that of the nearby Hitler Youth huts. As well as being a historian's dream for its level of detail, this degree of mapping, labelling, claiming space, and naming place is another form of re-territorialization. A vividly colourful version of such work can also be seen from Biberach, where an embroidery of the camp grounds was made by a male internee, Mr Wakeham.[10] The wool for the embroidery came from unravelled jumpers, but the barbed wire was stitched in black cotton, picking out the camp perimeter as it weaved around the barracks and looped from fence post to fence post.

FIGURE 16.3 Bird's-eye view of Wurzach by Preston John Doughty. Source: courtesy of Jersey Heritage ref. L/C/46/B/12.

To travel to the third level of analysis, we journey via another mug engraved by Byll Balcombe, on display in La Vallette military museum in St Peter Port, Guernsey, which shows the *Wieland Linde* on one side. Intruding into this extended campscape is a map of the south-east corner of England (including Balcombe's natal Suffolk). This map is labelled 'Bhliti' (Blighty), and the caption at the top of the mug reads 'coming nearer every day', showing not only Balcombe's desire for liberation by the British but his desire for the landscape of home.

This landscape of home or what we might term a 'homescape' is one of the strongest themes to emerge from the camps and is paralleled in the large amount of artwork and artefacts produced by the internees. These seem to speak to the desire which must have dominated every person in the camp – to get beyond the barbed wire and go home, whether that was England, Jersey, Guernsey, or Sark. By bringing these images inside the camps, they were attempting to bring a concept, a vision, a landscape of home, wherever that might have been, closer: close enough to touch. These homescapes were not the bombed and devastated British cities of reality, nor the coastal scenes of the Channel Islands, ruined by concrete German bunkers. Rather, they represented a peaceful and beautiful, idealized, traditional, pre-war home.

Focusing on items made in Wurzach camp, the English (rather than Channel Island) origin of many of the internees, or perhaps their patriotism, is clear from their stitched and painted idealized images. One of the internees of this camp, Joan Coles (who later published her internment memoirs *Three Years Behind Barbed Wire*) (Coles 1985), was skilled in embroidery and needlework, and regularly produced items for the camp exhibitions of arts and crafts. At least three embroidered miniature pictures by Coles still survive in the archives of Jersey Heritage. One is the size of a postcard and the other two are little brooches. They show idyllic English country cottages, complete with thatched roofs, leaded windows, and flowers around the doorway.[11] A similar image can be seen in the centre of a watercolour. The picture comprises four roundels, three showing the three armed forces in action, and the fourth showing a Red Cross ambulance. At the top and bottom of the painting are the flags of the Allies, and in the centre is a man arriving home (no doubt, from internment), walking through the wooden gate at the end of the garden path, which leads up to a traditional English thatched cottage: an idealized vision of a peaceful home, which is what the Allies were fighting for.[12] In fact, paintings and greetings cards showing thatched cottages and traditional English villages were among the most popular scenes created at Biberach and Wurzach, and it is clear that, as the internees were not able to go home, they did the next best thing, which was to bring 'home' into the camps by depicting it.

Greetings cards, by their very nature, are designed to be gifts to others (as were many other paintings and artefacts made in the camps); thus, the meaning of the gift becomes all the more poignant when we consider that internees were giving each other the most meaningful one possible: the gift of home. The significance of this helps us to understand the decidedly non-festive theme of many Christmas cards, such as one painted in Laufen, which depicts a traditional English country village apparently in the middle of summer, with hollyhocks in full bloom.[13]

Many interned artists passed their time in painting views of the Channel Islands from memory. Ethel Cheeswright painted an achingly beautiful watercolour of the Sark coast for the German camp doctor, Anton Fleischer, to thank him for his help in treating internees (Figure 16.4). The Guernsey cliffs were the inspiration for some of the scenes in the greetings cards made in Biberach by Henry Sandwith.

In Wurzach, as in Biberach, internees were allowed out on walks, chaperoned by their guards. Although frequency and length of walks varied, at its peak, 125 internees at a time were allowed out as much as five times a week (Harris 1979: 78). Whilst on the walks, many internees collected firewood, and some were able to save little scraps of wood with which to make artefacts. These include knots of wood turned into badges and painted with famous Jersey landmarks: the Corbière lighthouse and Janvrin's Tomb.[14] Another source of wood

FIGURE 16.4 Frau Fleischer in 2006 holding a watercolour by Ethel Cheeswright. Source: © author.

used in the camp came from Red Cross parcel crates. A Mr Butler fashioned a jewellery box for his wife Alice using a table knife and broken glass as his only tools, as noted in an inscription inside. The box was decorated with the image of a cobbled path leading through a garden to the front door of a half-timbered house.[15]

In the brief skirmish that accompanied the liberation of Biberach and Wurzach by the Free French in late April 1945, the German army retreated, abandoning their weapons and ammunition. Upon their liberation, the internees were, at first, free to wander at will around the town and landscapes that they had for so long only viewed through barbed wire. A photograph owned by a former internee, Tom Remfrey, shows his father standing among a heap of abandoned ammunition and shell cases. It was probably one such shell case that Byll Balcombe took as a souvenir and engraved with a view that had been painted many times already in the camp: that of the Weberberg (weavers') district of Biberach, a pretty area of traditional buildings. This view was no longer seen through interned eyes but seen through the eyes of the liberated, and it represented the first stage of the long journey home. As such, it was important for Balcombe to draw or engrave it, as if to claim this stage as his own. For him, it marked a line drawn in the sand: a refusal to return to a life behind barbed wire.

After waiting for almost six weeks in their liberated camps, the Islanders were flown by the American Air Force to the UK in June 1945, where those without relatives in the UK waited in Displaced Persons camps. By August, the internees were at last allowed to travel back to the Channel Islands, many of them still carrying the objects and greetings cards made in the camps. That a large number of these items have survived to the present day attests to their continued importance to the deported.

It is interesting that, just as images of England, the Channel Islands, and the views beyond the barbed wire were so important to internees whilst interned, at least half of all images observed on surviving greetings cards and in paintings show the camps or barrack rooms themselves. These images, also found on artefacts such as Balcombe's mugs, were seemingly just as important to bring home. On preparing to leave the camps, there was obviously no 'weeding out' of images of campscapes; they were as important as the others.

Although the number of Channel Islands' internees still alive today is rapidly dwindling, I have observed many commonalities between those I have interviewed over the last 14 years. Nearly every former internee has kept, as a minimum, the camp-made greetings cards exchanged during the 30 months of internment. Many also have autograph books filled with sketches, portfolios of artwork made in the camp, and some small items of camp-made objects. As the internees I have met were all children or teenagers in the camps, or at the very least were (more rarely) young adults who accompanied their deported parents, the items they have kept were mostly the possessions of their parents. Just as much as a memory of the camp, these objects represent a memory of their deceased parents.

These artworks are not kept framed on walls or on mantle-pieces as daily reminders of the war years; instead, they are shut away safely in cupboards. The excellent preservation of many of these items suggests that they have not been handled frequently in the years since the war and the homecoming of the internees. They are memory objects that few wished to be reminded of daily, so eloquently did they exclaim the conditions under which they were made and the emotions of the maker. Their colours are still bright, their condition good, and their ability to function as a potent 'memory bridge' (Saunders 2001) is still wholly intact. This bridge, composed of 'materiality, emotion and memory' (Saunders 2001: 478) has the power to transport the living internees to a bitter-sweet time when their parents were still alive, but their family was imprisoned behind barbed wire, with all of the trauma inherent in that experience.

More than providing a memory bridge to the period in the camp, these art-works are also aspects of the camp that reached forwards into the present and can be seen as part of the physically detached 'distributed personhood' of the campscape (Gell 1998: 104). These powerful fragments of the camp and the mixed emotions that they evoked were often too dangerous to call to mind or too private to share. This meant that, during interviews, I was often left alone to examine these objects while the former internee bustled in the kitchen. We are reminded of Bjørnar Olsen's words of advice for those who examine landscapes (or, in this case, campscapes): we should consider not just how we create or change the landscape, but how landscapes affect us; for 'there seems to be little concern for the properties ... possessed by the landscape itself ... what *difference* do they make to the way we live, think, and act?' (Olsen 2010: 31, emphasis preserved). For former internees, the campscape of the 1940s continues to impact them into their old age, and it is this vision in the mind's eye that I recognize as my fourth level of analysis.

I have found that the children and grandchildren of internees are rarely able to explain to me the full context, source of raw materials, or stories associated with the objects and artwork of the camp, testifying to long-term storage and a lack of airing within the family. These 'testimonial objects' (Hirsch et al. 2006) carry testaments from the past that those in the present are unable to read with-out significant effort. This has led to these items being undervalued or sold by the second and third generations. But we might ask why these objects were kept at all by the former internees. No matter how potent they are as negative or powerful reminders of the past, they are also part of the distributed personhood of their long-deceased parents, and act as memory objects from the past that simply do not function (at least in the same way) for later generations who did not share the same formative experiences.

Revisiting the sites of the camps is a pilgrimage that not all former internees have wished to take. Today, *Lager Lindele*, the proper name of Biberach camp, although it was never used by internees, has been dismantled and replaced with a police training camp; a wing of *Schloss* Wurzach is now a hotel. St Helier, capital of Jersey, has been twinned with Bad Würzach (as the town is now named) since

2002, and there are strong links and regular exchange visits of the twinning association of both towns. In Guernsey, the Deportee Association, the Guernsey Friends of Biberach, and Biberach Friends of Guernsey have all been involved in arranging regular exchange visits between former internees in Guernsey (sometimes accompanied by local dignitaries) and local families in Biberach, some of whom befriended internees more than 75 years ago. The main theme of these visits is reconciliation, forgiveness, and friendship, and it is often a deeply conflicting, emotional, and cathartic experience for former internees who make the journey. Disconcertingly, the vistas of the extended campscape remain much the same, even though they hold different emotional weight for those who view them today.

The campscape itself is, for many, filled with 'ghosts', or 'the sense of the presence of those who are not physically there' any longer (Bell 1997: 813). The act of visitation threatens to liberate these ghosts and to replace the remembered campscape in their minds with a new space, filled with rose bushes instead of barbed wire, and empty rooms instead of places filled with parents, siblings, and friends. The offer of replacing a conflict landscape with one of reconciliation and forgiveness can sometimes be too much to ask.

Conclusion

At Christmas 1945, after the men of barrack 20 of Biberach were safely back in their island homes, they exchanged a folded-up greetings card designed by fellow internee Henry Sandwith (Figure 16.5). It depicted the snow-covered clock tower of the administration block of the camp, a part of the camp which dictated the camp routine and was occupied by the guards and German camp staff. Inside, the card referred to the event of leaving the barrack the previous June, where most had given 'the Camp and most of its inmates a well merited raspberry'. Opened up, the card also gave the names and addresses of the 47 men who had shared the barrack together. The conflicting emotions redolent in this card can still be felt 75 years later and show the almost-unavoidable act of invoking the campscape (and, notably, a reclaimed piece of German-occupied space) and bringing it into the homes of former internees. This mixing of landscapes is an inverted example of the third level of analysis described above, or perhaps an early invocation of the fourth level at a time when the memory bridge was very short indeed, and events too recent to trigger much of an Olsenian reaction in the internees.

This chapter has proposed four levels of analysis in order to understand the conflict landscape of the internment camp as perceived by internees: a three-level perception of the campscape comprising the area within the barbed wire, the vista of the extended campscape viewed by internees and reaching to the horizon, and the distributed campscape that they carried home with them after the war in their memories and their art and craft work. These perceptions of landscape were supplemented by the distributed homescape, a landscape of pre-war

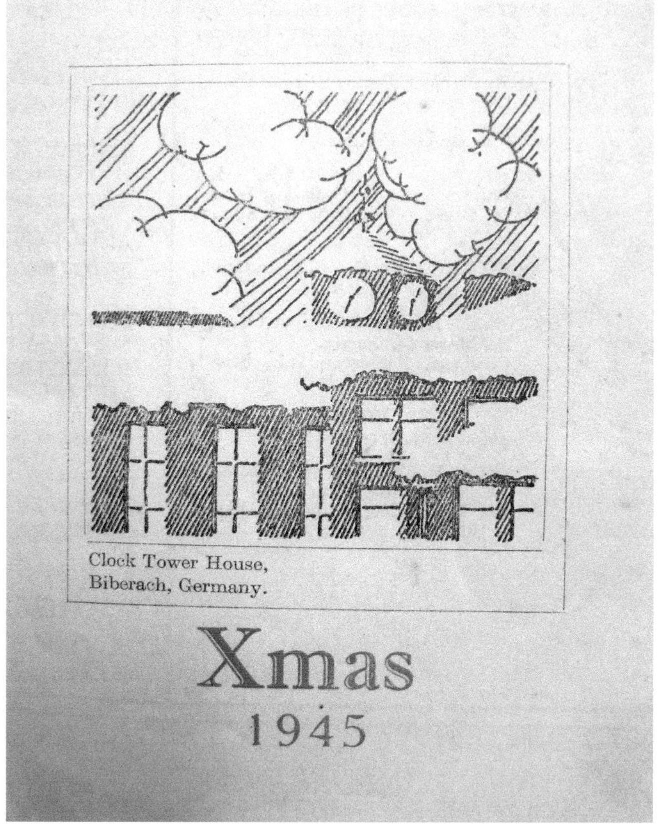

FIGURE 16.5 Greeting card by Henry Sandwith. Source: courtesy Damien Horn.

home brought into the camp to facilitate an emotional escape and to fulfil a constant longing that every internee held dear. By making the landscape our lens of analysis, we can more clearly understand the extent to which internees sought to carry both campscapes and homescapes with them and why, both during and after internment, despite – and because of – the emotional impact that they held.

Acknowledgements

I would like to thank the past and present members of the Guernsey Deportee Association and Jersey ex-Internee Association, and the museum owners and curators of the German Occupation Museum, Guernsey; La Villette Military Museum, Guernsey; Guernsey Museum; Jersey Museum; Jersey War Tunnels; the Channel Island Military Museum; the Island Archives, Guernsey; Jersey Archives; and the Red Cross Archives, London.

Notes

1 British Red Cross Archives Library ref. 95/50. *Useful Articles from Empty Tins: Hints on how to make them.*
2 Dickinson collection, Jersey Archives ref. L/C/177/A.
3 Jersey Archives ref. L/D/25/E1/2.
4 In private ownership.
5 Private archival collection of owner of German Occupation Museum, Guernsey.
6 In private ownership.
7 Dickinson collection, Jersey Archives ref. L/C/177/A.
8 I am indebted to John Cadot for contacting me regarding his discovery of some of Balcombe's correspondence from 1908-1918 within a wall cavity in Balcombe's former residence in Hauteville, St Peter Port, which Mr Cadot subsequently owned. This correspondence gives a brief insight into Balcombe's First World War army career. He saw active service in the trenches, and it seems likely that he learned how to engrave there.
9 Jersey Archives ref. L/C/46/B/12.
10 In private ownership.
11 Joan Coles collection, Jersey Archives ref. L/D/25/E1/2 and L/D/25/E1/4.
12 Jersey Archives ref. L/D/25/E1/2.
13 Private archival collection of owner of German Occupation Museum, Guernsey.
14 Jersey Archives ref. L/D/25/E1/4.
15 In private ownership.

References

Archer, B. (2004) *The Internment of Western Civilians under the Japanese 1941–1945: A Patchwork of Internment.* London: Routledge.

Archer, B. and A. Jeffreys. (2012) The Women's Embroideries of Internment in the Far East 1942-1945. In G. Carr and H. Mytum (eds.), *Cultural Heritage and Prisoners of War: Creativity Behind Barbed Wire*, pp. 244–260. London: Routledge.

Becker, A. (2004) Art, Material Life and Disaster: Civilian and Military Prisoners of War. In N.J. Saunders (ed.), *Matters of Conflict: Material Culture, Memory and the First World War*, pp. 26–34. London: Routledge.

Bell, M.M. (1997) The Ghosts of Place. *Theory and Society* 26: 813–836.

Bender, B. (1993) Landscape – Meaning and Action. In B. Bender (ed.), *Landscape: Politics and Perspectives*, pp. 1–17. Providence: Berg.

——— (2001) Introduction. In B. Bender and M. Winer (eds.), *Contested Landscapes: Movement, Exile and Place*, pp. 1–18. Oxford: Berg.

——— (2006) Place and Landscape. In C. Tilley, W. Keane, S. Küchler, M. Rowlands and P. Spyer (eds.), *Handbook of Material Culture*, pp. 303–314. London: SAGE.

Carr, G. (2009) *Occupied Behind Barbed Wire.* Jersey: Jersey Heritage.

——— (2013) 'My Home Was the Area Around My Bed': Experiencing and Negotiating Space in Civilian Internment Camps in Germany, 1942–1945. In H. Mytum and G. Carr (eds.), *Prisoners of War: Archaeology, Memory and Heritage of 19th- and 20th-Century Mass Internment*, pp. 189–204. New York: Springer.

Carr, G. and H. Mytum (2012a) The Importance of Creativity Behind Barbed Wire: Setting a Research Agenda. In G. Carr and H. Mytum (eds.), *Cultural Heritage and Prisoners of War: Creativity Behind Barbed Wire*, pp. 1–15. London: Routledge.

——— (2012b) *Cultural Heritage and Prisoners of War: Creativity Behind Barbed Wire.* London: Routledge.

Coles, J. (1985) *Three Years Behind Barbed Wire: The Diary of a British Internee in Schloss Wurzach, Germany, 1942–1945*. Jersey: La Haule Books.

Cosgrove, D. (2006) Modernity, Community and the Landscape Idea. *Journal of Material Culture* 11 (1): 49–66.

Cresswell, Y. (1994) *Living with the Wire: Civilian Internment in the Isle of Man During the Two World Wars*. Douglas, Isle of Man: Manx National Heritage, Manx Museum & National Trust.

Cruikshank, C. (2004 [1975]) *The German Occupation of the Channel Islands*. Sparkford: Sutton Publishing.

Dusselier, J.E. (2008) *Artifacts of Loss: Crafting Survival in Japanese American Concentration Camps*. New Brunswick: Rutgers University Press.

——— (2012) The Arts of Survival: Remaking the Inside Spaces of Japanese American Concentration Camps. In G. Carr and H. Mytum (eds.), *Cultural Heritage and Prisoners of War: Creativity Behind Barbed Wire*, pp. 81–97. London: Routledge.

Garland, G. (n.d.a) *Report to the British Red Cross Society, 1944*. Unpublished manuscript in archives of German Occupation Museum, Guernsey.

——— (n.d.b) *A Brief History of the Guernsey Deportees to Germany, September 1942 to June 1945*. Unpublished manuscript in the Priaulx Library, St Peter Port, Guernsey.

Gell, A. (1998) *Art and Agency: An Anthropological Theory*. Oxford: Clarendon Press.

Harris, R. (1979) *Islanders Deported*. Ilford: Channel Islands Specialists Society Publishing.

Hirsch, M. and Spitzer, L. (2006) Testimonial Objects: Memory, Gender and Transmission. *Poetics Today* 27 (2):353–383.

Ilag VII Laufen. (1945) *The Birdcage*. Hälsingborn: Aktiebolaget Boktryck.

Johnson, M. (2007) *Ideas of Landscape*. Malden, MA: Blackwell Publishing.

Myers, A. and G. Moshenska (eds.) (2011) *Archaeologies of Internment*. New York: Springer.

Mytum, H. and G. Carr. (2013) *Prisoners of War: Archaeology, Memory and Heritage of 19th- and 20th-Century Mass Internment*. New York: Springer.

Olsen, B. (2010) *In Defense of Things*. Lanham, MD: Altamira Press.

Saunders, N.J. (2001) Apprehending Memory: Material Culture and War, 1919–1939. In P. Liddle, J. Bourne and I. Whitehead (eds.), *The Great World War 1914–45. Volume 2: The Peoples' Experience*, pp. 476–488. London: HarperCollins.

——— (2003) *Trench Art: Materialities and Memories of War*. Oxford: Berg.

Sørensen, M.L.S. and D. Viejo-Rose. (2015) *War and Cultural Heritage: Biographies of Place*. Cambridge: Cambridge University Press.

PART III

Beyond world wars

17

IMAGINING MARITIME CONFLICT LANDSCAPES

Reactive exhibitions, sovereignty, and representation in Vietnam

Graeme Were

During the summer of 2014, a wave of reactive exhibitions was launched across Vietnam that responded to the political crisis in Bien Dong or the South China Sea.[1] These exhibitions were quickly orchestrated by museums under direction from the Vietnamese Ministry of Information and Communications to show public support for Vietnamese claims to sovereignty over the Paracel Islands (Hoàng Sa) to the north and Spratly Islands (Trường Sa) to the south. The crisis escalated when China placed a drilling rig close to the waters of the Paracel Islands which led to a series of skirmishes between Chinese and Vietnamese shipping vessels and calls for restraint by Beijing and Hanoi in a bid to defuse military tensions in the region.[2]

In this chapter, I am interested in how this offshore episode of military confrontation provided the catalyst for a series of reactive exhibitions to take place.[3] These reactive exhibitions were designed to communicate to Vietnamese and international tourists sovereignty rights over the islands by making them visible and to expose the Chinese as aggressors in the region. An analysis of these reactive exhibitions will reveal the power relations at play in their construction and display, and provide a means to be able to understand how conflict landscapes are imagined and brought into view in a highly volatile and contested geographic zone which lies off the east coast of Vietnam. What is important in terms of understanding maritime conflict landscapes is that these are imagined zones, areas that remain at the margins of borders and territory and which few Vietnamese have ever visited or could identify. Exploring how these landscapes are made visible through curatorial techniques of silencing and foregrounding combined with calls for public participation in collecting and ceremonies demonstrates the complex and political processes taking place in museums to make conflict landscapes real and so galvanize national and international support. By asking what processes of formation are at stake in museum methods (Thomas

2010), this chapter contributes original research to discussions about how museums are deployed as resources to symbolically shore up territorial borders by making visible the nation's geo-body (Winichakul 1994).

Conflict, national narratives, and museums in Vietnam

Vietnam is firmly fixed in the popular imagination as a place that has been afflicted with conflict and destruction, propelled by Hollywood films and US political narratives about American military intervention in the region. The memory of the war never dies, as the Vietnamese scholar Nguyen (2016: 39) argues, though he also reminds us how the fragments of it offer a precious resource from which the country's reconstruction and future could be built. Indeed, this process of reconstruction has already commenced as Vietnam has become a major international destination for conflict heritage with tourists offered the opportunity to experience battlefields and trails, tunnel complexes, and military prisons used by the North Vietnamese army in conflicts against the French and Americans (Henderson 2000). Coupled with this growth in dark tourism, many of these sites have also become pilgrimage destinations for ex-American servicemen, who make return trips to Vietnam to visit places where they were stationed or battlefields where they fought (Bleakney 2006; Schwenkel 2009).

The decades of conflict against the French and Americans form a dominant political discourse, continually evoked by both Vietnamese media and state organizations in television programmes and anniversary commemorations. As Pelley (2002) describes, the rhetoric of victory and resilience over foreign invaders (the Chinese, the French, and the United States) has unified the country so much that military heroes who sacrificed themselves for the state have been transformed into martyrs and worshipped at commemorations organized by the state (Malarney 2001). Tai (2001) calls Vietnam the 'country of memory' given the upsurge in commemorative activities since unification in 1975, though these narratives have been exclusively controlled by the Vietnamese Communist Party, with its power base in Hanoi.

The centralist control of history is most evident in state-funded history museums.[4] There, museums generally organize national history through a Marxist-Leninist chronology of linear time following epochal events in the development of the state before and after the August Revolution in 1945. Their objective is to relay the achievements (*thành tựu*) of the Vietnamese Communist Party and the progress of the state under its stewardship.[5] In its exhibition form, this stands accused of blatant propaganda though it functions as a tool for patriot training of schoolchildren, political cadres, police, and military cadets. In effect, this dogmatic approach to history can also be viewed as a distortion as it tells an idealized or mythical version of events according to those in control (Anderson 1983; Hobsbawn and Ranger 1983; Tai 1998; Trouillot 2015; Watson 1994). Typically, historical displays tell the Vietnamese state version of history, centred on breaking down stereotypes in Western media of Vietnam and at the same type homogenizing Vietnam as though the country had one experience of the past. Nguyen (2017), for example, observes how the War Remnants Museum in Ho Chi Minh City – a challenging museum that depicts in graphic detail the atrocities of the US–Vietnam war and the effects of Agent Orange on infants – promotes Vietnamese history and anti-colonial resistance through a more humanitarian representation of Vietnamese people. She argues that this is an attempt by the museum to counter negative foreign stereotypes of the Vietnamese and thus enable the Vietnamese to tell their own story and truth about the conflict and its impact on them. This process reinforces the state strategy of placing the Vietnamese as victims of foreign aggression (Pelley 2002), eliding any discussion of divisions within Vietnamese society or of diverging versions of history (Tai 1998).

Yet, more recent scholarly attention has focused on how museums are agents for transforming historical consciousness. These approaches place Vietnamese museums in a superior role for understanding the shifting politics and policies within the Vietnamese Communist Party. Through the interpretation of historical events by analyzing exhibition content, tone, and narrative, state attitudes towards historical events can be revealed publicly. For instance, Sutherland (2005) observes how exhibitions at Hoa Lo Prison Museum – a heritage site that depicts the incarcerated lives of Vietnamese revolutionaries during the French colonial period as well as the detention of American airmen during the US–Vietnam conflict – have taken on a strong anti-French tone, while sentiments towards the Americans have been toned down. Similarly, Schwenkel (2009) also notes how exhibitions focused on the atrocities committed by American forces during the US–Vietnam conflict have been reworded, making them more palatable to American tourists who now visit the country. Schwenkel adds that this process ties into the wider objectives of the Vietnamese state in its diplomatic relations with the United States. Thus, with the onset of the Doi Moi reforms of 1986 in Vietnam, which allowed the state to enter into normalized diplomatic relations with other countries, museums reflect this policy of openness in the way other countries are portrayed in exhibitions.

The idea that museums are agents of change in Vietnam is most succinctly captured in the outcomes of an exhibition at the Vietnam Museum of Ethnology in 2006. This exhibition – *Life in Hanoi the Subsidy Period 1975–1986* – received much critical acclaim because it was the catalyst for promoting discussion for the first time in Vietnamese society of a period of economic hardship called *bao cấp* (the subsidy era) that the government wanted to forget. Maclean (2008) argues how the exhibition – through its public display and discourse – was a watershed moment in establishing the subsidy period officially (since no official name existed beforehand) and shaping how this period was known and understood by Vietnamese society.

Yet what is absent from the scholarly literature on museums in Vietnam (as well as Asia in general) is a question of how territorial sovereignty is represented and imagined through state-funded museums.[6] This is surprising given the current dispute in the South China Sea which – as a maritime conflict landscape – is at the centre of competing legal claims to sovereignty not only by China and Vietnam but also by the neighbouring states of Malaysia, the Philippines, and Taiwan. As China has gradually increased its military presence in the region, most notably by the building of military airstrips and fortifications on individual islands in the Paracel Islands, there have been increased tensions in the region which almost spilt over to a military confrontation between Vietnam and China in 2014.

At present, most of what we know about sovereignty and nationalism in Vietnam has come from historians (e.g. Tai 1998, 2001; Pelley 2002), political scientists (e.g. Amer and Nguyen 2005), or anthropologists working with minority communities (e.g. Taylor 2014; Scott 2009). While most of the literature on museums and sovereignty either focuses on colonialism and empire (Macdonald 2003; Andermann 2007; Knell 2011; Preziosi 2011) or the sovereign rights of First Nations and indigenous peoples (Kelly and Gordon 2002; Lonetree 2012; Tsosie 2009), little if any research has addressed the question of sovereignty and museums in Vietnam, particularly how such claims are expressed through reactive exhibitions. What makes any discussion of conflict landscape so interesting in the Vietnamese context is how maritime borders become liminal spaces that can only be seen in the imagination or in museum exhibitions. Thus, during periods when sovereign borders are under threat, how do states mobilize museums and in what form are these landscapes represented? Drawing on ethnographic fieldwork conducted over several visits to the museum since 2013 and during 2014 at the height of the tensions, I use the Museum of Da Nang in central Vietnam as my case study to explore how conflict landscapes are imagined and understood in Vietnamese society.

Reactive exhibitions, the Museum of Da Nang, and sovereignty claims

Opened in April 2011, the Museum of Da Nang stands on a site which is a microcosm of some of the key historical milestones that have taken place in Vietnam over the last century and a half (Figure 17.1). The museum is built adjacent to the historically significant Dien Hai Rampart – the national historical monument marking the first conflict where General Nguyen Tri Phuong fought the French when they were on the way to invade Vietnam in 1858. In one corner of the museum's site stands a US Bell 'Huey' helicopter – an icon of the US–Vietnam war – and just outside the perimeter of the museum grounds stands a large glass skyscraper, the impressive Da Nang City Hall – a 34-storey development run by the People's Committee of Da Nang – an emblem of the country's rapid economic growth and embracing of the modern market economy. Almost unnoticed, positioned at the foot of the steps leading into the museum is a water feature labelled with the names of individual islands of the Paracel Islands. Da Nang is a centrally controlled municipality with administrative control over the Paracel Islands.

FIGURE 17.1 Museum of Da Nang. Source: © author.

The Museum of Da Nang is a purpose-built space with a display area of 3,000 square metres, divided into three floors. The main hall of the museum has a curved shape, which symbolizes the terrain of the city like a great arm holding the sea. On the wall of the entrance foyer, there are five sail-shaped plaques representing the marine city rising from the ocean. The content of the bas-reliefs on the plaques represents the historical development of Da Nang, which includes images of conflict, modernity, minority communities, and mythology. The galleries introduce more than 2,500 objects, photographs, and documents about natural history, history, the culture of Da Nang City (including its rich maritime and fishing heritage), and the surroundings. These include eclectic displays of archaeological implements, musical instruments, ethnic minority cultures, and military history, including graphic photographs and dioramas of battlefields from the US–Vietnam War.

During the summer of 2014, at the height of tensions between Vietnam and China over the South China Sea, the Museum of Da Nang put together two exhibitions asserting Vietnam's maritime sovereignty over the Paracel and Spratly Islands. These two exhibitions, one displaying maps and documents, and the other, colour photographs, are the focus for this discussion of conflict landscapes.

Maps, territorial claims, and continuous sovereignty of the Paracel and Spratly Islands

The first exhibition was called: *Paracel – Spratly Archipelagos: The inseparable territory of Viet Nam* and displayed a diverse assortment of historical documents, photographs, atlases, and maps collected from China, Europe, and Vietnam. The exhibition was neatly arranged in semi-circle formation on a set of wooden easels in the entrance hall of the museum so that museum visitors, including Chinese tour groups, could file past to witness what the museum (and the Vietnamese state) consider as the incontrovertible truth (Figure 17.2). Many of the maps dated back to the sixteenth century and had captions explaining their significance in Vietnamese, English, and Chinese, clearly marking the islands as separate from Chinese occupation. The maps and historical documents presented an image of continuous territorial occupation through the use of chronology, multiple perspectives (the use of Chinese, Vietnamese, and European maps), and photographic testimony (using both French colonial and Vietnamese ones), often using yellow highlighter to draw attention to significant information or facts.

Maps legitimate political authority over territory and empire; they help create myths that assist in the maintenance of borders and are an 'aggressive complement' to speeches, texts, and patriotic songs (Harley 1988: 282). In the Museum of Da Nang, the map is intimately linked to maritime sovereignty claims, which invokes important questions about national identity and world views (Whitehead 2011: 110). Winichakul (1994) demonstrates how the map was a modern tool introduced to communicate and enforce territorial control over a region in the face of foreign expansion into Southeast Asia; it serves to make bounded spaces a reality. Similarly, in Vietnam, the map is deployed as a political tool for asserting Vietnam's claims of territorial sovereignty over the archipelagos. The map is a dominant form of visual culture in heritage sites and museums across the country. For example, in the UNESCO World Heritage Hue Citadel, an antique map displays the dynastic lineages of Vietnamese rulers on the Paracel Islands, affirming the continuity of Vietnamese presence on the islands over Chinese presence. Here the imperial past is usurped to make claims to sovereignty. Similarly, in the

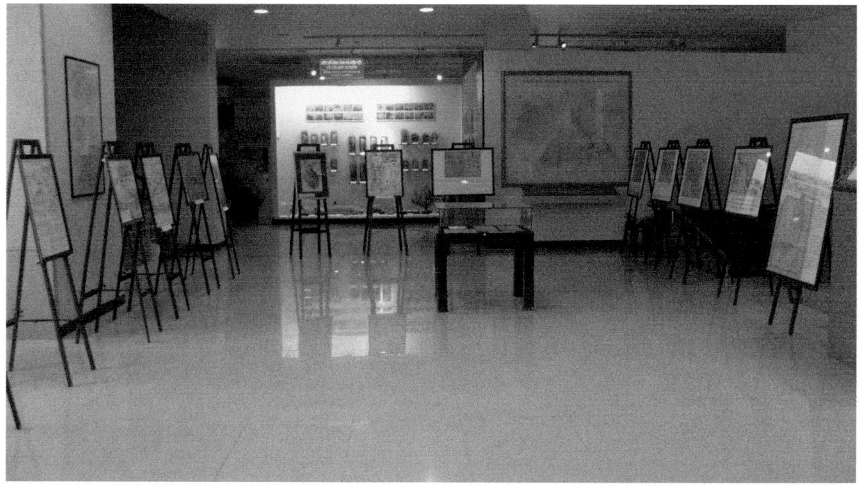

FIGURE 17.2 Map exhibition at the Museum of Da Nang, 2014. Source: © author.

Museum of Nature in Hanoi, visitors are directed around a large gallery space tracing out human evolution. The final section displays a large interactive map featuring Southeast Asia; visitors are informed by the museum attendant how the Paracel and Spratly Islands have always been part of Vietnam. Here, claims of sovereignty are expressed through autochthony, the inalienable relation of the land to its original inhabitants.

Commenting on the silences of maps, Harley (1988: 209) remarks how hidden political messages may be communicated in maps through what is omitted as much as what is depicted and emphasized. This control of the visual imagery is akin to what Hall (1999) terms 'selective canonisation' – and exposes the way Vietnamese state institutions invest in developing their own truth and writing history. In the Museum of Da Nang, the curatorial intent imposed a particular significance on the maps in the exhibition as it presented the map as indisputable evidence of Vietnam's claims over the disputed islands: it represents the geo-body of the nation in concrete form, identifying the limits of territory and othering what lays beyond (Winichakul 1994). The strength of this evidence rested on historical documents which were produced in the pre-revolutionary past and then used to assert visual evidence of continuous territorial sovereignty of the islands. For instance, the maps on display in the exhibition conceal the very fact that during the conflict between North Vietnam and the United States, it was the South Vietnamese navy that challenged the Chinese navy and tried to force them into withdrawal from the Paracel Islands. The omission of this historical fact neatly evades the issue of continuous territorial sovereignty and avoids heaping praise on the enemy, the South Vietnamese army – who are marginalized in dominant political narratives as puppets (*ngụy*) of the American regime. Moreover, the maps – presented as evidence of territorial sovereignty – relate to the pre-revolutionary period. This is a period that does not fit easily into official histories of national unity and is often neutralized in Vietnam. Similarly, another map presented at the exhibition is titled 'A map of China published by the U.S. Central Intelligence Agency in 1979'. Thus, the exhibition reactivates the past to serve the political demands of the state. Activating this past also mobilizes competing narratives and memories.

At first glance, the Museum of Da Nang's exhibition appears to be the result of a political directive from the City of Da Nang's Ministry of Information and Communication to produce a cogent political message supporting state claims of sovereignty over the disputed islands. From the outside, this may appear to be true as the museum curators endorse an official state narrative of continuous occupation of the islands through the chronological arrangement of maps, photographs, and documents in order to defend the state's territorial integrity. However, a closer exploration of the process of exhibition will reveal much more about the complexities of how this reactive exhibition shapes historical consciousness.

In acknowledging how museums operate through global networks and relations, Basu (2011) describes a collaborative museum project that encouraged expatriate Sierra Leoneans to repatriate knowledge by engaging with a digital heritage project focused on documenting Sierra Leone collections in British ethnographic collections. The return of object knowledge, claims Basu (2011), can be understood as a form of cultural remittance – supporting the return of dissipated objects and associated knowledge in digital form – and then deployed in nation-building after a period of devastating civil war.

In Vietnam, museums are also linked to these global networks and relations from which they are able to garner support and resources. In the case of the sovereignty exhibition, ordinary citizens were invited to contribute in support of the sovereignty crisis by donating maps and documents that maintain Vietnamese maritime sovereignty over the Paracel Islands. This form of cultural remittance – unlike Basu's (2011) apparent return of cultural knowledge – is politically complex. This is because the call to actively acquire maps and documents relating to the disputed islands reveals other interesting insights about the complexities of history in Vietnam, as those complicit in its production hold competing narratives about the past. I make this claim because these materials (maps, atlases, photographs, and documents) were collected from various donors, nationally and internationally. Some were collected from individual map collectors and scholars in Vietnam; others were acquired by expatriate Vietnamese (*Việt Kiều* who were not necessarily supporters of the Vietnamese state) who donated them to the research institutes and museums, most likely as a public show of support and patriotism – a form of cultural remittance – which may one day be recognized in the event of reconciliation between the Vietnamese state and expatriates who left after 1975. Others were collected by government bodies, such as the City of Da Nang, who acquired them from antique auctions. There were also many ancient maps relating to Vietnamese cartography stored in national libraries or archives in Belgium, Holland, the UK, the US, Spain, and Portugal. The government and researchers had contacted these collecting institutions to copy maps or atlases which were then displayed in the exhibition. Thus, the process of collecting the maps and documents on the South China Sea reveals conflicting ideologies and complex motivations. While expatriate Vietnamese may not support the single-party system and the Vietnamese Communist Party, they respond to the nationalist call for support because Vietnamese sovereignty over its own borders is of much greater significance to them.

Photographic exhibition documenting the sinking of fishing boat DNA 90152

Running concurrently to the sovereignty exhibition was a second exhibition of photographs housed in the large glass atrium that stands at the front of the Museum of Da Nang (Figure 17.3). Titled *Pictures about the fishing boat DNA 90152 sunk by Chinese vessel on May 26th 2014*, the exhibition featured around 20 large colour photographs documenting Chinese aggression in the South China Sea and the sinking by a Chinese vessel of Vietnamese fishing boat DNA

FIGURE 17.3 Photographic exhibition at the Museum of Da Nang, 2014. Source: © author.

90152 near the oil rig which Chinese authorities had placed in the disputed region. The photographs – stills from actual video footage of the incidents which had been aired on state media outlets – told a story of how the fishing boat was rammed and then sank, which led to the rescuing of the Vietnamese fishermen in the South China Sea.[7] This story of violence is portrayed as a kind of sacrifice and points to what Girard (1972) proposes, that the constitution of modern nation-states depend on the sacrifice of one of one's own community or group.

The photographic exhibition clearly emphasizes the dynamic and reactive nature of many Vietnamese museum exhibition programmes that respond to rising tensions in the South China Sea. In the aftermath of the incident, these photographs were reproduced in various media formats for the public to witness. Through their strategic deployment in public display (in the exhibition, newspapers, World TV news, and so forth), the photographs became active agents in the Vietnamese struggle for continued sovereignty of the island archipelagos. As Caswell (2014) has pointed out in relation to photographs displayed in the Tuol Sleng archives in Cambodia of prisoners detained and tortured under the Pol Pot regime, the images perform the act of bearing witness as they capture the very moment of aggression and violence.

The exhibition opening at the Museum of Da Nang was orchestrated to coincide with an international workshop by the University of Da Nang and Pham Van Dong University called *Paracel-Spratly Archipelagos: Historical Truth* (19–21 June 2014). Over 100 scholars attended from countries such as the United States, Australia, and France to discuss China's placement of a drilling rig in Vietnamese waters. Scholars attending the opening ceremony were also invited to sign their names on a large map of Vietnam placed in the courtyard in front of the museum. The signing ceremony took place in front of a crowd of prominent officials, academics, museum staff, and local school children next to the statue of General Nguyen Tri Phuong, who repelled the French colonial soldiers in 1858, affirming the Vietnamese spirit of resistance.

This form of spectacle plays an active role in the nationalist agenda which involves transforming visitors into witnesses of Chinese aggression and territorial incursions. As Caswell (2014) has commented in relation to the documentation photographs of prisoners in Tsol Sleng prison in Cambodia during the Khmer Rouge regime, visitors to the exhibition are secondary witnesses who share in the process of remembering. Caswell states how the photographic mug shots of prisoners are incorporated into new archival records that document the act of witnessing, revealing both how photographs specifically are an active part of the performance of human rights in Cambodia, and how records in general are dynamic performative entities whose meaning and context change as they travel through space and time with reuse (Caswell 2014: 99). While, in the Vietnamese case, domestic visitors like school children and local people were shepherded past the displays, placed in the most prominent area of the museum, resources in the form of state media, military personnel, international experts, and local dignitaries transformed the exhibition into a spectacle.

The signing ceremony could be seen as an inscriptive protest towards territorial incursions, a call for intervention and international justice. The participants witnessing the signing of the map of Vietnam (and the disputed archipelagos) stand in for larger constituencies; the foreign academics are a symbol of the international community; the Vietnamese school children (unintended victims of Chinese aggression) are a symbol of the next generation of Vietnamese. In the case of the photographs, maps, and documents, this future generation is witnessing the international community witness the sinking of the fishing boat and the territorial incursions committed by the Chinese. Here, witnessing the photographs, maps, documents, and the signed map is an antidote to forgetting. These images – mass-produced as a form of what Nguyen (2016) calls 'weaponized memory' – reflect the creation of new records in the form of media that documents the act of looking at the map and photographs. They provide an opportunity for viewers of these images, school children, museum visitors, foreign academics, and others, to enable another layer of looking. In this way, the photographs and maps are performing sovereignty claims by making maritime conflict landscapes visible. The exhibitions become a vehicle through which the conflict becomes real, and people can document bearing witness to the aggression of the

Chinese state and garner international attention for the assertion that such incursions should not be repeated.

These images gain another life through media attention of the opening events, being widely covered in Vietnamese newspapers and online media. In the photographs of people looking at maps and documentary evidence (digital and paper, video and still), the maps and photographs are transformed from records of political aggression to records of justice; the narrative is transformed from one of the helplessness of victims (the fishermen rammed and injured by Chinese vessels) in the face of territorial incursion from a regional superpower to one of the agency of survivors in the act of witnessing. This political spectacle mobilizes emotional responses: outbreaks of violence such as the burning of factories suspected of being run by Chinese owners, and acts of philanthropy in the donation of maps and documents, or through the gifting of fishing boat DNA 90152 to a new exhibition hall dedicated to the Paracel Islands, planned for construction close to the beach in Da Nang.

Conclusion

Harley (1988: 301) states that maps are 'preeminently a language of power, not of protest'. However, in the case of the South China Sea, maps perform as both: as a selective process of foregrounding and silencing, together as agents of international rights, calling out for justice and intervention from the international community for territorial incursions. As a collection of maps and documents, they reveal hidden meanings and sentiments as they embody diverging ideas of history and conflicting political ideologies, nationally and internationally. On the one hand, the issue of territorial sovereignty unifies, drawing together people on a global scale in opposition to foreign (Chinese) aggression; and on the other, it glosses over differences of historical interpretation by creating an emotional response to territorial incursions and the threat to Vietnamese sovereignty.

The maps and photographs became the focal point of the Museum of Da Nang, whose displays were used to assert claims over the archipelagos. The maps and photographs were then deployed to attract international attention to the incursion of the Chinese drilling rig in the face of Western indifference. These maps not only provide historical evidence to the sovereignty claims of the Vietnamese state; the photographs also bring ashore the reality of conflict between the Chinese navy and Vietnamese fishing boats by documenting hostilities and the sinking of the fishing boat for domestic and international visitors to the exhibition to witness.

Seen in this light, museums play a pivotal role in making conflict landscapes real and knowable. By putting on reactive exhibitions and mobilizing audiences (school children, workers, officials, cadres, and state media), museums create witnesses to maritime incursions and implore their audiences to communicate messages of territorial sovereignty to increasing circles of listeners. Therefore, rather than simply reflecting state policy on the South China Sea, the museum becomes a site for political action to shore up its geo-political body by mobilizing larger constituencies in transmitting the nationalist message. By asserting sovereignty over the islands and ensuring that incursions will be remembered, these public records of witnessing affirm territorial rights in the face of a local and international political climate that favours forgetting. In this way, the reactive exhibitions are a museological strategy on the part of the museum to manage and produce conflict landscapes, foregrounding maps, documents, and photographs as the truth to what lies offshore and unseen, while also playing down and silencing certain aspects of the reality of the current occupation of the islands.

Notes

1 Bien Dong means East Sea in Vietnamese.
2 For more details of sovereignty issues and conflict resolution in the South China Sea, see Buszynski (2013), Valencia (2007), and Yahuda (2013).
3 Reactive exhibitions are displays which are put on rapidly, with minimal time for planning, research, and preparation, and which solely serve a particular issue, such as a political crisis or social agenda. In general, I distinguish them from other types of exhibitions which have lead-in time and which fit into a particular institutional programme and agenda, rather than being guided externally by state policies and political ideology.
4 Museums – as an institutional phenomenon – have a long history in Vietnam. Under the French Indochina colonial period, the first museums were established in the early twentieth century. The Museum of Imperial Antiquities in the ancient capital of Hue, the Louis Finot Museum in Hanoi (now the Vietnam National Museum of History), and the Musée Henri Parmentier in Da Nang (now known as the Museum of Cham Sculpture) were the early forerunners before a new wave of building took place in the late twentieth century, squarely focused on nation-building and promoting the achievements of the ruling Vietnamese Communist Party. See Tai (1998) for an overview of the colonial formation of museums in Vietnam and their development.
5 Under one party rule, national and provincial museums fall under state control with the Ministry of Culture, Sport, and Tourism responsible for managing museums and heritage sites nationally. Others, such as the Vietnam Women's Museum or the Vietnam Museum of Military History come under the governance of the Women's Union and the Vietnamese Ministry of National Defence respectively, though these are both state organizations. Recent heritage legislation permitting the establishment of private museums has been the catalyst for growth, though these institutions generally expand rather challenge nationalist ideology and there still exists some form of control and checking by the state to attain the legal rights to open a museum.
6 See Humphrey (2007) for an insightful overview of anthropological approaches to sovereignty.
7 In May 2019, the fishing boat was put on display at a newly built exhibition centre on the coast of Da Nang that focused on asserting sovereignty over the Paracel and Spratly Islands. The boat was donated to the Da Nang city government by its owner and then displayed with its prow facing out towards the sea.

References

Amer, R. and T.H. Nguyen. (2005) The Management of Vietnam's Border Disputes: What Impact on Its Sovereignty and Regional Integration? *Contemporary Southeast Asia* 27 (3): 429–452.

Andermann, J.(2007) *The Optic of the State: Visuality and Power in Argentina and Brazil*. Pittsburgh, PA: University of Pittsburgh Press.

Anderson, B. (1983) *Imagined Communities: Reflections on the Origins and Spread of Nationalism*. London: Verso.

Basu, P. (2011) Object Diasporas, Resourcing Communities: Sierra Leonean Collections in the Global Museumscape. *Museum Anthropology* 34 (1): 28–42.

Bleakney, J. (2006) *Revisiting Vietnam: Memoirs, Memorials, Museums*. New York: Routledge.

Buszynski, L. (2013) ASEAN, the Declaration on Conduct, and the South China Sea. *Contemporary Southeast Asia: A Journal of International and Strategic Affairs* 25 (3): 343–362.

Caswell, M. (2014) *Archiving the Unspeakable: Silence, Memory, and the Photographic Record in Cambodia*. Madison, WI: University of Wisconsin Press.

Girard, R. (1972) *Violence and the Sacred* (transl. P. Gregory). London: Continuum Books.

Hall, S. (1999) Whose Heritage? Un-Settling 'the heritage', Re-Imagining the Post-Nation. *Third Text* 49: 3–13.

Harley, J.B. (1988) Maps, Knowledge and Power. In D. Cosgrove and S. Daniels (eds.), *The Iconography of Landscape*, pp. 277–312. Cambridge: Cambridge University Press.

Henderson, J.C. (2000) War as a Tourist Attraction: The Case of Vietnam. *International Journal of Tourism Research* 2 (4): 269–280.

Hobsbawn, E. and T. Ranger (eds.) (1983) *The Invention of Tradition*. Cambridge: University of Cambridge Press.

Humphrey, C. (2007) Sovereignty. In D. Nugent and J. Vincent (eds.), *A Companion to the Anthropology of Politics*, pp. 418–436. Oxford: Blackwell.

Kelly, L. and P. Gordon. (2002) Developing a Community of Practice: Museums and Reconciliation in Australia. In R. Sandell (ed.), *Museums, Society, Inequality*, pp. 153–174. London: Routledge.

Knell, S. (2011) National Museums and the National Imagination. In S.J. Knell, P. Aronsson and A.B. Amundsen (eds.), *National Museums: New Studies from Around the World*, pp. 3–28. London: Routledge.

Lonetree, A. (2012) *Decolonizing Museums: Representing Native America in National and Tribal Museums*. Chapel Hill, NC: University of North Carolina Press.

Macdonald, S. (2003) Museums, National, Postnational and Transnational Identities. *Museum and Society* 1 (1): 1–16.

MacLean, K. (2008) The Rehabilitation of an Uncomfortable Past: Everyday Life in Vietnam during the Subsidy Period (1975–1986). *History and Anthropology* 19 (3): 281–303.

Malarney, S.K. (2001) 'The Fatherland Remembers Your Sacrifice': Commemorating War Dead in North Vietnam. In H.-T.H. Tai (ed.), *The Country of Memory: Remaking the Past in Late Socialist Vietnam*, pp. 46–76. Berkeley, CA: University of California Press.

Nguyen, K.H. (2017) A Postcolonial Museum of War: Curating War and Colonialism at Vietnam's War Remnants Museum. *Interventions* 19 (3): 301–321.

Nguyen, V.T. (2016) *Nothing Ever Dies: Vietnam and the Memory of War*. Cambridge, MA: Harvard University Press.

Pelley, P. (2002) *Post-colonial Vietnam: New Histories of the National Past*. Durham, NC: Duke University Press.

Preziosi, D. (2011) Myths of Nationality. In S.J. Knell, P. Aronsson and A.B. Amundsen (eds.), *National Museums: New Studies from Around the World*, pp. 56–66. London: Routledge.

Schwenkel, C. (2009) *The American War in Contemporary Vietnam: Transnational Remembrance and Representation*. Bloomington: Indiana University Press.

Scott, J.C. (2009) *The Art of Not Being Governed: An Anarchist History of Upland Southeast Asia*. New Haven, CT: Yale University Press.

Sutherland, C. (2005) Repression and Resistance? French Colonialism as Seen Through Vietnamese Museums. *Museum and Society* 3 (3): 153–166.

Tai, H-T H. (1998) Representing the Past in Vietnamese Museums. *Curator: The Museum Journal* 41: 187–199.

——— (ed.) (2001) *The Country of Memory: Remaking the Past in Late Socialist Vietnam*. Berkeley, CA: University of California Press.

Taylor, P.A. (2014) *The Khmer Lands of Vietnam: Environment, Cosmology, and Sovereignty*. Singapore: NUS Press.

Thomas, N. (2010) The Museum as Method. *Museum Anthropology* 33 (1): 6–10.

Trouillot, M-R. (2015) *Silencing the Past: Power and the Production of History*. Boston: Beacon Press.

Tsosie, R. (2009) Native Nations and Museums: Developing an Institutional Framework for Cultural Sovereignty. *Tulsa Law Review* 45 (1): 3–24.

Valencia, M.J. (2007) The East China Sea Dispute: Contexts, Claims, Issues, and Possible Solutions. *Asian Perspectives* 31 (1): 127–167.

Watson, R.S. (1994) Making Secret Histories: Memory and Mourning in Post-Mao China. In R.S. Watson (ed.) *Memory, History, and Opposition Under State Socialism*, pp. 65–86. Santa Fe, NM: School of American Research Press.

Whitehead, C. (2011) National Art Museum Practice as Political Cartography in Nineteenth-Century Britain. In S.J. Knell, P. Aronsson and A.B. Amundsen (eds.), *National Museums: New Studies from Around the World*, pp. 105–122. London: Routledge.

Winichakul, T. (1994) *Siam Mapped: A History of the Geo-Body of a Nation*. Honolulu: University of Hawaii Press.

Yahuda, M. (2013) China's New Assertiveness in the South China Sea. *Journal of Contemporary China* 22 (81): 446–459.

18

PEOPLE, BARRIERS, MOVEMENT, AND ART

Contested sandscapes of Western Sahara

Salvatore Garfi

On the Atlantic coast of northern Africa, and at the far western edge of the Sahara, lies Western (formerly Spanish) Sahara. Spain claimed the territory as a colony in 1884 and established the trading post of Villa Cisneros at the inlet known as Rio de Oro. The inhabitants of the region were Bedouin of Berber and Arab ancestry and known then as 'Moors' (Hodges 1983: 8). This is anachronistic today, and the people of Western Sahara refer to themselves, quite simply, as Saharawis.

Villa Cisneros was established peaceably by negotiation with the local tribes, but hostilities soon developed between them and the Spanish, and the garrison fled to the Canary Islands (Pazzanita 2006: 89–90). This was the starting point of the contest over Western Sahara that has continued up to the present. And though the nature of the contest has changed, it has culminated, in the last quarter of the twentieth century, with the imposition of a monumental territorial partition, literally impressed upon the desert sands by a new colonizing power in the region – Morocco.

Creating a Spanish colonial space

The trading post at Villa Cisneros was soon re-occupied and transformed into a substantial fort. Through the efforts of Francisco Bens, its energetic governor and veteran of the Spanish–American War (1898), the Spanish acquired two further footholds along the coast, first at Cape Juby to the north (1916) and then at La Guera to the south (1920). The garrisons were small and the Spanish rarely ventured inland. As a consequence, the territory became a haven, and base of operations, for tribes in the far west of the Sahara in their opposition to French imperialist expansion in neighbouring Mauritania and Algeria. From deep within Spanish territory, they would attack the French in long-distance raids (Arabic, *ghazi*), sometimes travelling more than 1,000 kilometres across the whole of Spanish Sahara. In response, the French counter-raided from bases in Mauritania, hitting the tribes in their sanctuaries in the Spanish colony (Bonte 1993: 73).

By 1934, the territory was deemed 'pacified', and the French established a cordon of forts along the border with Mauritania and in Algeria, and linked by a track serving a similar function to the *limes* of the Roman Empire (Isaac 1988). Designated as the *Piste Imperiale No. 1,* it unequivocally exemplified the colonial spirit of France writ large on the desert sands (Trout 1969: 348; Beslay 1993: 30). The Spanish territory was thereby girdled with Spanish posts on the coast and French forts inland – creating the first militarized enclosure of Western Sahara (Figure 18.1).

After decades of fighting, the pacified tribes were forced to accept the dominance of the better-armed and organized Europeans, eventually welcoming

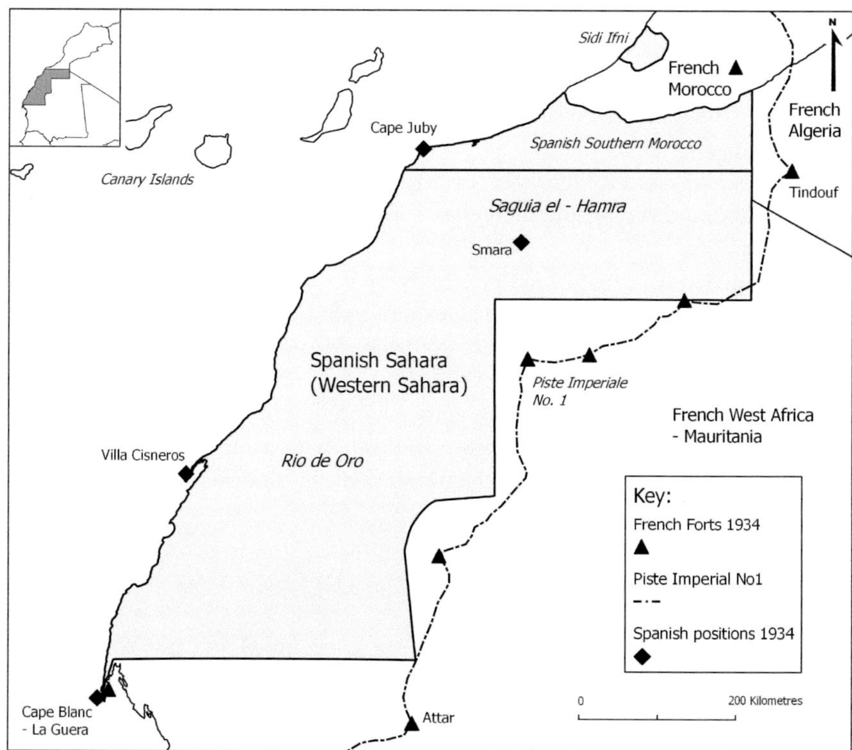

FIGURE 18.1 Western Sahara in 1934, including Spanish Southern Morocco and the Spanish enclave of Sidi Ifni. Spanish coastal forts and settlements are shown, along with French forts and the *Piste Imperiale No. 1*. Upper left insert shows the location of Western Sahara in northwest Africa. Source: © author.

what became a durable peace (Caro Baroja 1966: 69 cited in San Martin 2010: 33). The Spanish finally occupied the town of Smara in 1934, where they created their first desert outpost. They secured the coast and by 1938 founded El-Ayoun (La Ayoun), the future capital of the territory (San Martin 2010: 32–33). They also occupied and settled at Guelta Zemmour, Bir Gandus, Tichla, and Zug by 1946 (Hodges 1983: 69).

An insurgency erupted in the region in 1956 (Pazzanita 2006: 32–33) in an attempt to oust the French and Spanish from the western Sahara. Known as the 'Forgotten War' (San Martin 2010: 69), it lasted well into 1958, when finally, the 'Saharawi Liberation Army' was defeated by the joint, and very substantial efforts of France and Spain (Pazzanita 2006: xxvii, 31). As a result, this second pacification of the territory generated a new colonial impetus previously unmatched, and in the deeper desert areas, it created a new militarized space imposed on the landscape.

There were already sizeable military establishments attached to the main settlements in the territory since the pacification, but by 1961, with the potential for a further insurgency, the Spanish military extended its presence throughout Western Sahara (Mercer 1976: 226). The new Spanish bases included a new type of small desert outpost, such as the fort at Tifariti (Figure 18.2), which was indicative of the type. There were at least six of these posts constructed throughout the territory, and most were positioned in the north, presumably, in case of conflict with Morocco over Spain's continued occupation of Sidi Ifni. There were also tensions between Algeria and Morocco which could have spilt into Western Sahara.

Spain finally relinquished its control over Western Sahara in November 1975, but ceded the northern two-thirds of the country to Morocco, with the southern third being handed over to Mauritania. This arrangement – the 'Madrid Accords' – was contrary to a recent International Court of Justice ruling that clearly affirmed the right of self-determination for the Saharawi people, and Moroccan and Mauritanian troops very quickly occupied the country well before Spain's military finally left it in January 1976 (Hodges 1983: 230). This precipitated an exodus of Saharawi refugees, mainly to camps in Algeria, and open war with the Polisario Front, an acronym for the 'Popular Front for the Liberation of Saquia el-Hamra and Rio de Oro', which had been agitating for Saharawi independence from Spain since 1973 (Pazzanita 2006). The conflict is not over, and hostilities only ended in 1991 with a United Nations–brokered cease-fire.

Many of the Polisario fighters came from Spanish colonial units, like the *Tropas Nómadas*, and they proved to be highly effective desert warriors. By reviving the tactics of the *ghazi*, and by using land rovers instead of camels, they forced Mauritania out of the conflict in 1979 and pushed the Moroccans up into the far northwest of the territory. To counter this, and to regain their almost lost colony, Morocco embarked on the creation of a series of great earth and rubble fortifications, which would literally sculpt the desert in a hitherto unseen way. Between 1981 and 1987, the brute force of simple earth-moving machines (Zunes and

FIGURE 18.2 The fort at Tifariti. The upper image shows the fort as it looked up to 1975. The lower photograph, taken in 2007, shows damage created by a Moroccan air strike in 1991. Source for upper image: courtesy *Tercio 'Don Juan de Austria' 3° de la Legión*, available online at www.amigosdeltercertercio.com/ifni/html/Page2.html. Source for lower image: © author.

Mundy 2010: 21) carved out a new Moroccan colonial space, enclosing Western Sahara for a second time.

These earthen fortifications, called berms in contemporary military jargon, have created a new and dramatic kind of conflict landscape – a contested space bounded by huge linear monuments. With a conceptual strategy similar to the vast trench systems of the Western Front during the First World War, Morocco embarked on building, through excavating and earth-moving, a series of six earth and stone defensive walls which extended in enveloping waves from the northwest corner of the territory. These partitioned Western Sahara with the aim of denying the fighters of the Polisario access to virtually 80 per cent of the country.

Figure 18.3 shows the sequence and dates of the Moroccan berms constructed across Western Sahara. There are no reliable, published maps of the berms; therefore the plots shown here have been digitized from Google Earth imagery – thereby presenting a unique depiction of this contested space. The total lengths of the berms, including compartmentalization where it exists, and those portions where only forts exist with no linear barriers, can be calculated from the plots

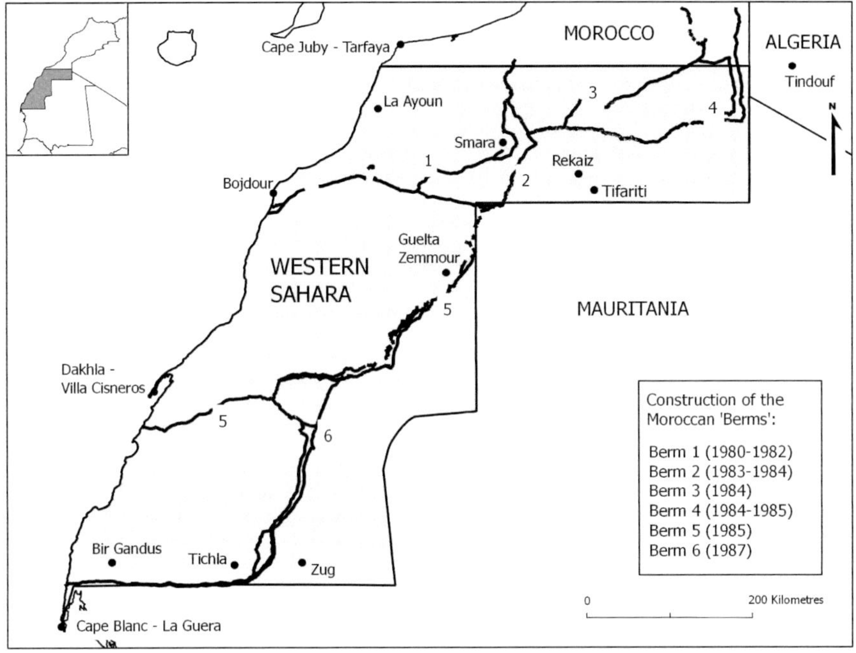

FIGURE 18.3 Map showing sequence and distribution of the Moroccan berms. Places mentioned throughout the text are also shown. Source: © author.

at approximately 4,000 kilometres. This runs counter to their published lengths, which can vary from 1,500 kilometres (Pazzanita 2006: 91) to 2,720 kilometres (UPES 2008). Although the barriers vary in height from around two to four metres, they consist of sections of single and multiple embankments with ditches, while portions in the northern part of the territory include dry-stone walling. There are approximately 2,000 military installations on or immediately behind the walls, and these too have been estimated from Google Earth. These include forts (strongpoints), mustering locations, observation posts, fire support artillery bases, and un-enclosed garrisons. There are extensive minefields with barbed wire fronting the barrier.

Confronting the desert and the berms

The barrier dividing Western Sahara cannot be approached – it is a heavily militarized zone. This has not, however, stopped Saharawi youths and activists from approaching the berms and staging demonstrations, and literally taunting the armed troops on the Moroccan side (Touballi interview). More importantly, the fortified nature of the barrier has not stopped some Saharawis from taking the extreme step of escaping by foot from the Moroccan-occupied zone, walking over the barriers and through the minefields, and into the Polisario 'liberated' zone. Many have been activists who would have faced imprisonment for their political activities, such as Malainin Larkhal and Hamdi Touballi, or they have been idealistic teenagers like Salek Labaidi Bachir. These individuals have had a very direct experience of the Moroccan barriers, and not as military personnel cosseted within defended camps and positions, but as vulnerable civilians, pedestrians, facing first the open desert, and then the complete panoply of the fortified berms.

Salek Labaidi's 'story' began in 2004, when as a teenager of 17, he and some friends were appalled by the treatment of corralled camels by the Moroccan army in the city of Smara, in the occupied zone. As Salek recounted in an interview:

> [The] Moroccan soldiers had caught the camels close to the Moroccan wall, and they were taken to Smara where I lived. The soldiers didn't feed or water them, but the camel means our [Saharawi way of] life, our culture. We, and the people of Smara, felt strongly that the soldiers did something bad.
>
> *(Bachir interview)*

So Salek, with four friends, broke into the camel compound and freed the animals, and as a result, the friends found themselves crossing the desert and escaping into the liberated Polisario-held territory southeast of Smara. What is striking is that this was not an obviously political act; instead, the teenagers were moved by a perceived societal imperative to liberate an animal which represented the essence of Saharawi culture. The camel is the animal upon which their traditional, nomadic, pastoral society depended, and since there are no oases as such in Western Sahara (save for the valley of the Saguia al-Hamra), the following of the rains by camel across vast ranges to seek out pasture and temporary water sources was integral to the centuries-old lifeways of the Saharawi tribes. This was why the largest of the Saharawi tribes, the Reguibat, used to be known as 'the people of the clouds' (Thompson and Ardloff 1980: 309), meaning that they would follow the clouds that bring the rains, and this could only be done by camel.

This act of 'animal liberation' caused Salek and his companions to walk 70 kilometres, towards and across the berms that surround Smara, and into the Polisario liberated zone. They passed a rear support base, and then ten kilometres further, to the south-southeast, they stood on a hill overlooking the barrier. 'After a short walk, we saw the berm, it was very big, like a snake' (Bachir interview). It was one o'clock in the morning and the moon was out. Salek described the land around the berm as barren, and there were lights from the small bases along the barrier. Upon encountering the barrier, Salek was initially confronted by a dry-stone wall around one and a half metres high by three-quarters of a metre thick. Then at about three metres distant there was a two-metre-high earthen bank, followed again by a second similar bank with a single fence of barbed wire in the front. There was a military base nearby, encircled with barbed wire, and Salek remarked that there was something which he interpreted as a radar installation. The teenagers had stopped to rest between the second and third barriers, but when they thought that they were seen by a Moroccan soldier, only a few metres away, they ran over the third barrier and through the barbed wire. Surprisingly, Salek could not remember how he got through the wire, but he obviously did, and he and his companions made it safely through the minefield. The five youths eventually made their way to Bedouin grazing their camels in the liberated zone. Their journey took four days, and they eventually moved on to the Saharawi refugee camps near Tindouf, Algeria, where Salek is now a journalist (Bachir interview).

Malainin Larkhal's case was different. He was a high-profile activist in the Moroccan-occupied capital of Western Sahara, El-Ayoun (he is now a highly respected Saharawi journalist and commentator). Speaking in an interview, he recounted how he had been arrested a number of times and even tortured, so for his own safety, and for that of his fellow activists, he left the occupied territory in the summer of 2000 when he was threatened with a further arrest.

He travelled southwards, towards Mauritania, with his brother and a friend, first by car to Bojdour, and then by another car driven by a smuggler who agreed to take them close to the berm by the border with Mauritania. They were then to travel southwards on foot, but their trek to the wall was much longer than expected. Malainin knew that he and his friends were at a disadvantage being, as he said, 'city boys'. They didn't know the 'ways of the desert', and they were travelling in the southwest of the country where there are many sand dunes which made walking very difficult, but luckily, they had the 'strength of youth' on their side. When they made it to the berm, they first came upon a Moroccan base where they saw Moroccan soldiers milling about, and Malainin even took the time to note the base's mud-brick buildings. The smuggler had told the three that when approaching the berm, they would first come across a track that the Moroccans maintained and swept clear, so as to detect the footprints of people approaching and trying to cross the barrier. They located the path and afterwards came upon a sand embankment. After this, they found the larger frontal embankment of the barrier, but between the two the ground was strewn with flat stones and this created a distinctive tactile experience for the refugees. In Malainin's words:

> I remember that they were also using rocks between the small embankment and the first big wall [embankment]. They were putting some kinds of rocks, like flat rocks, and the problem was that when you're walking, you make noise, because they start hitting each other ... it was unnatural, their presence was unnatural, and I remember that. Walking on these walls, when you're walking under these conditions, you think that everyone is looking at you, and that any sound you make will bring soldiers.
>
> *(Larkhal interview)*

Malainin encountered no barbed wire in front of the barrier and made it safely through the land mines in front of it. After crossing the border into Mauritania, the three refugees eventually made their way northwards to the Saharawi camps near Tindouf.

Seven years after Malainin Larkhal crossed the berms, the young Saharawi activist Hamdi Touballi was compelled to leave his home in El-Ayoun for the Polisario-controlled free zone. Hamdi had become very involved in protests in the capital and was arrested on the first day of the Saharawi civilian uprising (or intifada) that started in the occupied territories in May 2005. He was subsequently arrested a number of times and kept under surveillance, so in January 2007 he decided to leave his home and cross the berms. A friend first drove him into the desert southeast of Dakhla and then walked with him part of the way towards the berm. They got within 30 kilometres or so of the barrier, and Hamdi then walked on by himself. Hamdi recounted to me his crossing of the barrier:

> I remember, it was maybe half past two or three in the morning [when] I found myself at the wall. When I was close to the wall I could hear Moroccan soldiers talking near to me, but I was lucky because I was alone. I was very, very scared, not from the soldiers, but from the mines. I thought, that if I exploded a mine the problem was that no one was with me, no one could help me. And of course, the Moroccan soldiers would not help me.

Hamdi described the barrier he crossed as consisting of two earthen banks, with the frontal barrier higher than the rear embankment, around eight metres behind it. There was barbed wire in front of the berm, but Hamdi could not recall how he got through it (Touballi interview).

Malainin, Hamdi, and Salek all made it successfully across the berms. In the locations in which they crossed, they all describe a line of parallel barriers, though the first of these was made of stone in the north of the country. The barriers could be climbed and walked over easily, but they were obviously designed (essentially as steep-sided sandbanks) to stop vehicles – the motorized raiding parties of the Polisario/SPLA. It is striking that the barbed wire, noted in all published descriptions of the berms, was meagre in the sections crossed by Salek and Hamdi, and non-existent in the south, near the Mauritanian frontier. It is also noteworthy that the minefields were easily and safely crossed by foot. Malainin Larkhal is of the opinion that the minefields and barbed-wire fences have not been maintained by the Moroccans, because over the years, Polisario soldiers have removed the mines and barbed wire in many places (Fadel and Larkhal interviews).

These three accounts give us an experiential view of the Moroccan barriers, and for the duration of their journeys, Malainin, Hamdi, and Salek became immersed in their undertakings, and 'dwelled' (Ingold 1995) in the hostile environment of the desert and the berms. They had to confront the barriers they crossed in an undeniably direct, bodily way. They had to carefully navigate across an unknown space, as Ingold (2007) would say as 'wayfarers', using all of their senses to make their way, in a 'kinesthetic interplay' of the tactile, sonic, and visual (Feld 2005: 181), while filled with fear and other strong emotions. Tilley (2004) would describe their visceral experiences as 'holistic' and even 'carnal', though in the real-life context of individuals facing the possibility of death in a hostile environment (from armed soldiers and land mines) these terms might appear inadequate, perhaps even trite. Trying to understand a landscape, especially a contested one, through the experiences of intimately involved individuals 'is much more than an academic exercise – it is about the complexity of people's lives, historical contingency, contestation, motion and change' (Bender 2001: 2).

Salek's distinctive description of the barrier as a large 'snake' is reminiscent of the sinuousness of the trenches and wire entanglements of the First World War. In fact, when viewed from above, via Google Earth, for instance, the berms can appear graceful. They can appear serpentine or angular, to sweep or glide, and the forts can appear organic in form (Figure 18.4). But when viewed from the ground, Malainin had this to say about Morocco's 'great' wall:

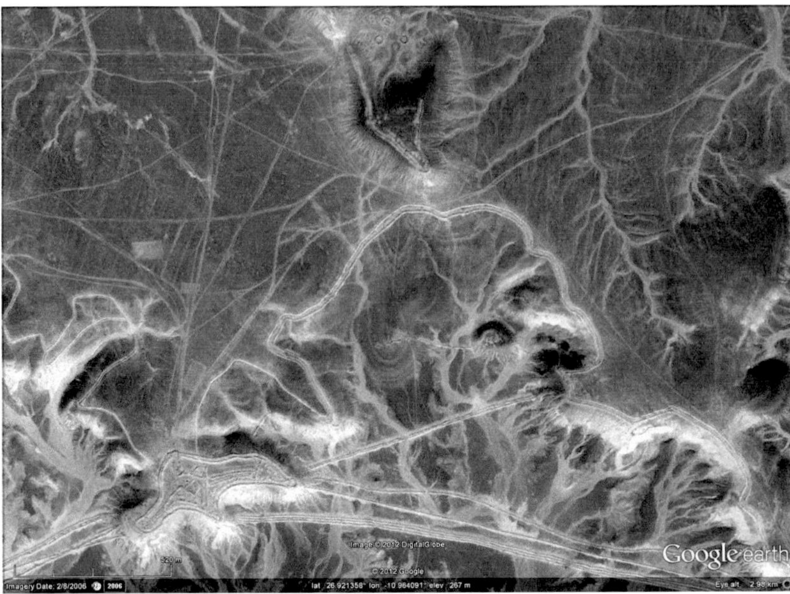

FIGURE 18.4 This image shows the complexity and 'organic' quality of one of the Moroccan berms (berm 3). A large mural fort follows the contours of a ridge with natural embayments. Radiating berms cut across the lower ground. A fire support base is visible at the top of the image, positioned behind a spur. At middle-left are two rectangular cleared areas that probably represent helicopter landing zones. Source: courtesy and © 2012 Google Earth and © 2012 DigitalGlobe.

> It is very ugly. When I've seen, for example, the Berlin wall, you can draw graffiti on it, you can express yourself, it is something physical … I mean, when you see the Israeli wall, it's similar, it's very imposing and big, this one is just a berm, it's just dirt, some embankment. Even if you take it in photos it isn't interesting.
>
> *(Larkhal interview)*

Polisario and the berms

When the British journalist, Jeremy Harding, approached the berm for the first time in 1986, he could barely make it out.

> I had heard any number of stories about the wall, its size, its character and aspect, but none of them prepared me for this cryptic blemish on the body of the desert. I had imagined a structure that would be visible from a long way off; the bases situated … along its length would surely dominate the landscape. The whole thing would rise out of the desert, effortless and magisterial. But... it required hard work with the binoculars and guidance from the local Polisario commander to pick out the defence at all. In the event, it was a thin band of pallor standing out from the rest of the terrain, which was darker by a shade. At the crest of a hill where the defences rose with the contours of the land, there was a base, a wide circle of ground, paler still.
>
> *(Harding 1993: 124–125)*

His Polisario guide, Nuruddin, though able to speak a number of European languages, often condemned the wall with the French term 'la pourriture', referring to the barrier as something rotting, something in decay. His view was simple and contemptuous. If the wall were left alone, it would just crumble away – it would return to the desert from which it was made (Harding 1989: 25). But the archaeology of the berms tells a different story, and in time, traces of the walls will be indelibly inscribed onto the desert's surface, save perhaps in those extremely sandy regions where the desert winds are their strongest.

Polisario insurgents undoubtedly had the upper hand in their fight against Mauritania and Morocco, and then Morocco on its own, in the vast desert spaces of Western Sahara. Like T.E. Lawrence's camel-mounted raiders in the First World War and the Long Range Desert Group in the Second World War, they would exploit their intimate knowledge of the desert to harass and attack Moroccan positions. Their guerrilla tactics were finely honed, and with small groups of armed Land Rovers they would always attack Moroccan positions, on the move, and then quickly withdraw. Additionally, when Polisario forces occupied a Moroccan position they would not stay long, but again withdraw, and rapidly attack another Moroccan strongpoint. Such continued harrying of the Moroccans improved Polisario's fighting abilities, and the Moroccans were even more vulnerable when the attacks occurred in the hotter times of the year, with the Saharawis being much more comfortable in the summer heat than the majority of Moroccan soldiers (Fuente Cobo and Mariño Menéndez 2005: 77–78).

Although Saharawi tactics could include large columns of tens of vehicles, even up to 100 or more at a time (also including armoured vehicles), in the end, their strength lay with their own modern and mechanized form of the smaller-scale *ghazi*. Initially, these tactics were highly successful, but when the berms were constructed, for all of Nuruddin's contempt, the Moroccan barriers did put a substantial brake on Polisario's offensive effectiveness (Zunes and Mundy 2010: 23). This being the case, Jon Anderson, an American journalist who visited Western Sahara between 1988 and 1991, sardonically described the war with Morocco as turning into a 'kind of military pantomime', where appearing to be at war took the place of real hostilities. To Anderson, Polisario's offensives merely became orchestrated 'displays of their military prowess'. The berms made a 'mockery' of the war, forcing the Saharawis to symbolically continue to assault the barriers, to breathe life into the conflict as a sort of 'bellicose ritual or blood sport. Like a family seeking to retain the semblance of a nobler lineage than present appearances suggest'. Anderson additionally observed that Saharawi participants in these actions talked about them for months after the fact. He went on to say:

> Indeed, these battles amount to precious heirlooms, material for the carefully tended oral history of a war that now exists mostly in name. Guerilla veterans like Moulay [Anderson's guide] are discernibly wistful, speaking as if their best times were behind them, back in the days before the wall.
>
> *(Anderson 2006: 158–159)*

Contrary to this, Polisario combatants were still able to occasionally attack the berms in a relatively conventional way and bloody the Moroccan defenders. One very bad year for Morocco was 1987 when substantial Polisario forces attacked the Moroccan military in 16 locations. A common Polisario attack on the barrier, according to Fuente Cobo and Mariño Menéndez (2005: 112–114), could target two mutually supporting mural posts at the same time, approached at night to avoid detection. The first phase would be a mechanized incursion across the barrier followed by a second phase of further vehicular and tank attacks on the two posts. While holding the forts, the force that crossed the berm would wait and engage the Moroccan rapid reaction force that would be called into the battle (in a third phase), and deal them as fatal a blow as possible. Another Polisario motorized unit would give back-up to the attackers and take captured material and prisoners to the rear. Such a surprise attack could only shock the Moroccans, cause them to deploy forces away from other positions, destroy material, and give the Moroccans a 'bloody nose'. But a territorial inroad would not be made. These were essentially harrying attacks, and that was all that Polisario was able to do to a lesser or greater degree. But the Saharawis could be mischievous in their relationship with the berms. Besides removing mines from in front of the berms, Polisario soldiers would often cross over the barriers and rebury them on the Moroccan side, behind manned Moroccan positions (Zunes and Mundy 2010: 22). Such a simple attritional tactic could only add to the spectre-like quality of the Saharawi insurgents.

Moroccan soldiers and the berms

The Moroccan forces manning the berms – and numbering up to 120,000 (Pazzanita 2006: 92) – have mainly been conscripts, save for the officer class, and many came from the more temperate parts of Morocco north of the Wadis Draa and Sus, and including the very clement Rif and Atlas mountain regions (Hodges 1984: 103). Because of this, they were not used to the extreme heat of Western Saharan summers – when Polisario would increase their operations – and this definitely took its toll on them (Jensen 2013: 35). Although this chapter has mainly considered the Western Sahara conflict from a Saharawi perspective, there is at least one Moroccan soldier who has spoken publicly about his experiences manning the berms. This was an infantry officer named Abdelilahou Issou who was interviewed in 2010 by the journalist and writer on Arab affairs, Anouar (Anwar) Malek, for the Algerian newspaper Echourak.

Issou was commissioned in 1988 and rose to become the head of an infantry company. Stationed along one of the berms facing Polisario territory, he explained that an infantry company could be spread out and stationed at different posts along the barrier, between which were unmonitored lengths of berm fronted by land mines and barbed wire. The minefields and barbed wire failed to prevent Polisario fighters from infiltrating the barrier, and, according to Issou, the Moroccan units facing a Polisario attack would often flee 'in disarray' (Malek 2010). This might be an exaggeration, but it tallies with some of the comments made by Polisario informants – that Moroccan soldiers would easily give up after a fight and that Polisario tactics were a psychological strain on them (Deya and Breica interviews). Issou claims to have thwarted a number of such incursions between 1988 and 1990, but he became bitter with the army when his resources were reduced.

Issou never mentioned where he was stationed along the berms, but he talked about continual attacks by Saharawi forces, saying that 'Polisario fighters pounded daily our positions with heavy machine-guns causing many casualties among the Moroccan troops'. He added that the soldiers' lives became a 'nightmare' from Polisario's 'relentless and ill-fated attacks'. He also claimed that Saharawi 'commandos' would sneak into Moroccan army barracks and slit the throats of sleeping soldiers, which made him very fearful and kept him up at night (Malek 2010). This last point is out of keeping with the way in which Polisario have presented themselves as behaving throughout the 16 years of war. As Anderson (2006: 159–160) noted:

> Polisario has refrained from using terrorism to strike at Morocco beyond the wall. Because it pretends to nationhood, the Polisario affects the sober

> demeanor seemingly appropriate for a sovereign state: Its fighters aren't called guerrillas, but soldiers – and soldiers, of course, don't commit acts of terrorism. This is war with a sense of honour, fought on the battlefield.

But a sense of honour was not apparent on the battlefield, according to one Moroccan army doctor captured by Polisario during the fighting at Lebouirate in 1979, and who recounted that he saw Polisario fighters kill wounded Moroccan soldiers in their hospital beds (Hollowell 2009: 37–39). Honest accounts of all wars will show that extreme brutality can occur on all sides. Even Malainin Larkhal, who has maintained that Polisario fought honourably since it was against their 'Saharawi culture' to do otherwise, has commented that if hostilities resumed, the younger fighters of today, frustrated with the political impasse over Western Sahara and the maltreatment of Saharawis in the occupied territories, would fight with greater brutality than might have occurred before the 1991 cease-fire (Larkhal interview).

ARTifariti

Soon after Google Earth went online in 2005, the Spanish artist, Fernando Peraita, found himself looking at its imagery over Western Sahara and was astounded at the land art quality of the berms (Figure 18.4). To borrow from Roland Barthes (2000: 27), he experienced a punctum; he felt 'pierced' by the image, 'bruised' even. Here was a design etched upon the surface of the earth, extensive and bold – one large and graceful work of sculpted art – and in his own words, 'a piece of [land] art tied to death, to suffering, and to separate the people, terrible, no? Culture [art] is usually used for peace, for good things' (Peraita interview).

Peraita was so moved that he decided to gather together a group of Spanish artists who would go to Western Sahara to create a piece of land art situated opposite the berms, in the liberated zone. But of course, this was impractical, so he and his colleagues changed tack:

> Instead of making one land art we [were] going to create a centre of contemporary art [dedicated] to peace and human rights that can be a weapon [against the wall], in the middle of the desert, in a no-man's land. We can create a centre of art in a city [Tifariti] that has been bombed by Moroccan planes, and where a lot of fighting has taken place, but nobody in the world knows about it, and, near the archaeological rock art sites of Rekaiz.
>
> *(Peraita interview)*

And so, the ARTifariti art festival was inaugurated, and from 2007 to 2010, groups of artists (mainly Hispanic but including other nationalities and Saharawis) congregated in the settlement of Tifariti – one of the outposts founded by the Spanish in the 1960s – adding a stratum of contemporary archaeology in the form of art interventions on top of the strata of earlier occupations and archaeological periods. These include the field defences created by Moroccan troops between 1977 and 1979, the earlier Spanish colonial fort and settlement of the 1960s and 70s, and earlier still, the prehistoric funerary landscape in which Tifariti is embedded.

The festival (now held solely in the Saharawi refugee camps in Algeria) is not just an encounter between peoples – between foreign artists and Saharawis. It is also an encounter between the visiting artists and the vast Sahara itself (Figure 18.5). As the participating artist Federico Guzmán wrote when he took part in ARTifariti for the first time,

> The first impression of the desert is light. Everything is flooded with light, Sun, clarity, heat. Then there's the immensity of space, silence and emptiness … [I am] Standing on a limitless flat plain where four thousand years ago flourished a green savannah, I open my arms to the ten million square kilometres of infinite sand. Space is so enormous it erases time …
>
> The desert [changes] colors and texture [like] an animated painting. [While travelling] we have crossed all the hues of ochre, red, white, and … green. Once in a while, we pass a [car tyre] stuck in the ground, the only sign of [any] … human presence. Hamdi, our … driver keeps on navigating the changing signals on the … sand routes where the map is blank. He lights his pipe and plays [music] and the electric piano mix[es] with

FIGURE 18.5 The artist, Federico 'Fico' Guzmán, lying down in the desert in Western Sahara illustrating his views on the vastness of the Sahara. Source: courtesy and © ARTifariti.

> the speed, the bumps, the stones and the infinite horizon in a continuous trance.
>
> We see wonderful petroglyphs of human figures, symbols of Mother Earth, giraffes and deer … [inscribed on] … rock[s] … I imagine when this was a green savannah and now there's only earth and sky … We … discover how the … landscape of the desert is actually full of life and that even in [this] most inhospitable land a paradise can be born … [We] stop to eat under the protecting shade of … [an acacia tree] and the bread and cheese has never tasted so good.
>
> (*Guzmán n.d.*)

Such was Fico Guzman's prelude to Western Sahara. He was entranced by the desert, and his sentiments can be found in myriad accounts and travelogues describing experiences in the deserts and wild places of the globe. His sense of wonderment and awe was also expressed by other artists taking part in ARTifariti. One such artist was María Ortega Estepa, whose approach to art tries to reflect the relationship of people with nature. She sees her art as a dialogue with the environment (Estepa n.d.), and at Tifariti she painted an outdoor mural that represented a green, wooded glade – part of a forest – representing what is, to her, a paradise (Figure 18.6). In her own words:

> I wanted to bring what I consider to be my own kind of paradise; therefore I've worked with colour to paint a forest, so that a person here [in the Sahara], can dream and forget a little about the reality in which they

FIGURE 18.6 María Ortega Estepa, with Saharawi children, in front of her mural showing a wooded glade, entitled *Travelling Paradise*. Source: courtesy and © ARTifariti.

> are living in. Well, I believe that paradise can be anything that you want it to be ... and I leave with that sensation, with the conclusion that this country – the people who inhabit the whole Saharawi Nation – is, for me, a paradise.
>
> (*ARTifariti 2009*)

This is in contrast to Fico Guzman's raw sense of wonder with the vastness of the desert, while her sense of wonder is with the Saharawi people. Nevertheless, the sentiments that both she and Guzmán earnestly feel are shared with all of the other artists who have taken part in ARTifariti. By realizing their art in the open desert, exposed, and in the liberated territory, they see their work as an act of solidarity with the people of Western Sahara. The founders of ARTifariti and the participating artists see their creations as agents that can mediate change and as positive, contributing additions – weapons even – to the arsenal of the Saharawi people in their struggle over the fate of their nation. The artworks are manifestations of the collective sub-culture, or community, that the artists belong to (at least while they are in Western Sahara). They work together as an aggregate and their creations (Figure 18.7) are a manifestation of their individual and group sentiments (Rampley 2005). To borrow from Alfred Gell (1998), the ARTifariti artworks are 'enculturated beings' and examples of 'distributed personhood'. However, this enculturated group entity, consisting of artworks imbued with

FIGURE 18.7 A composite of some artworks created during the ARTifariti art festivals held in Tifariti from 2007 to 2010. Source: upper right courtesy and © Nick Brooks, the other three courtesy and © ARTifariti.

the sentiments of their creators, individually and as a community, is not high art. By the very nature of the interventions created, they are highly ephemeral and they do not fare well when exposed to the extreme conditions of the Sahara. Nevertheless, the festival is a way of re-appropriating the Saharawi patrimony, even if, carried out mainly by foreign artists, it is a form of re-appropriation by proxy.

Conclusion

Western Sahara has been a contested place for over 100 years, and this has created a conflict landscape specific to the territory and its people. For decades, the Spanish colonizers stayed holed up in their coastal forts and outposts, and only confronted the deeper desert after 1934 when the region was pacified by the French. Both the French and Spanish marked out their presence in the western Sahara through a series of outposts and forts, only connected by tracks and *wadi* route-ways. But this was to change after Western Sahara's northern neighbour – Morocco – occupied the whole of the territory, and after severe military setbacks, they partitioned Western Sahara by constructing thousands of kilometres of fortified earthen barriers – the berms.

This chapter has presented some of the ways in which people, in particular, Saharawis, soldiers, journalists, and artists have interacted with and responded to the berms. Refugees fleeing over the barriers and through the minefields have been forced to confront the deep desert and the berms in a way that affected all their senses. Crossing the barriers was a challenging, fearful, and emotional undertaking, forcing inexperienced young men to become 'wayfarers', with limited food and water in the vast Sahara in a way that could only be described as visceral. On the other hand, Saharawi soldiers have shown a marked contempt of the barriers, confident in their sense of being at home in the desert, while Moroccan soldiers, especially those from the more temperate north, found themselves bombarded by uncertainties, and with a fear of what were to them the spectre-like fighters of the Polisario Front. Foreign journalists reporting on the Western Sahara conflict have been confounded by the berms. Morocco's 'great wall' did not live up to expectations, even though its potency held Polisario fighters in check.

But perceptions of the berms changed dramatically with the advent of Google Earth. For the first time, anyone could actually view the berms in their entirety, spreading over thousands of kilometres of desert and literally corralling a country. Appearing like a sinuous and graceful work of land art (belying its martial purpose), artists have been moved by the berms, and through the ARTifariti festivals, they have responded to the inequity of the barriers. They have gone into the Western Sahara desert and, being moved by its immensity and its effect on their senses, they have expressed themselves through sculptures, installations, and murals in the open air, and as a group in solidarity with the Saharawi people in their struggle for self-determination and independence from Morocco.

References

Anderson, J.L. (2006 [1992]) *Guerrillas: Journeys in the Insurgent World*. London: Abacus.

ARTifariti (2009) ARTifariti Parte 2. *YouTube Video*. www.youtube.com/watch?v=w09WIRZQ6_E&feature=player_embedded (accessed 3 April 2014).

Barthes, R. (2000) *Camera Lucida*. London: Vintage Books.

Bender, B. (2001) Introduction. In B. Bender and M. Winer (eds.), *Contested Landscapes: Movement, Exile and Place*, pp. 1–18. Oxford: Berg.

Beslay, F. (1993) Les confins algero (mauritano) marocains. In E. Bernus, P. Boilley, J. Clauzel and J.L. Triaud (eds.), *Nomades et commandants: Administration et societes nomades dans l'ancienne A.O.F.*, pp 29–33. Paris: Editions Karthala.

Bonte, P. (1993) L'emir et les colonels, pouvoir colonial et pouvoir emiral en Adrar mauritanien (1920–1932). In E. Bernus, P. Boilley, J. Clauzel and J.L. Triaud (eds.), *Nomades et commandants: Administration et societes nomades dans l'ancienne A.O.F.*, pp 69–79. Paris: Editions Karthala.

Caro Baroja, J. (1966) Los Nomadas y su Porvenir: conferencia pronunciada en el salon de actos del CSIC en dia 19 de febrero de 1965. *Archivos de Institutode Estudios Africanos* 78:61-71

Estepa, M.O. (n.d.) *María Ortega Estepa*. www.mariaortegaestepa.com/obramenu.html (accessed 14 May 2013).

Feld, S. (2005) Places Sensed, Senses Placed: Toward a Sensuous Epistemology of Environments. In D. Howes (ed.), *Empire of the Senses: The Sensual Culture Reader*, pp 179–191. Oxford: Berg.

Fuente Cobo, I. and F.M. Mariño Menéndez (2005) *El Conficto Del Sahara Occidental*. Madrid: Ministerio de Defensa de España.

Gell, A. (1998) *Art and Agency: An Anthropological Theory*. Oxford: Clarendon Press.

Guzmán, F. (n.d.) *Salam Aleikum*. salamailekum.blogspot.co.uk/ (accessed 18 December 2012).

Harding, J. (1989) Polisario. *Granta* 26 (Spring): 19–40.

——— (1993) *Small Wars, Small Mercies*. London: Viking.

Hodges, T. (1983) *Western Sahara: The Roots of a Desert War*. Westport, CT: Lawrence Hill & Co.

——— (1984) The Western Sahara File. *Third World Quarterly* 6 (1): 74-116

Hollowell, T. (2009) *Allah's Garden: A True Story of a Forgotten War in the Sahara Desert of Morocco*. Urbana: Tales Press.

Ingold, T. (1995) Building, Dwelling, Living: How Animals and People Make Themselves at Home in the World. In M. Strathern (ed.), *Shifting Contexts: Transformations in Anthropological Knowledge*, pp 57–80. London: Routledge.

——— (2007) *Lines: A Brief History*. London: Routledge.

Isaac, B. (1988) The Meaning of the Terms Limes and Limitanei. *The Journal of Roman Studies* 78: 125–147.

Jensen, G. (2013) *War and Insurgency in the Western Sahara*. Carlisle, PA: Strategic Studies Institute, U.S. Army War College.

Malek, A. (2010) Moroccan Army Deserter Abdelilahou Issou to Echorouk: The Ceasefire Saved the Moroccan Army from Debacle at the Hands of the Polisario Front Fighters. *Echorouk Online*. www.anouarmalek.com/?p=3891 (accessed 10 March 2014).

Mercer, J. (1976) *Spanish Sahara*. London: Allen & Unwin.

Pazzanita, A.G. (2006) *Historical Dictionary of Western Sahara* (3rd ed.). Lanham, MD: Scarecrow Press.

Rampley, M. (2005) Art History and Cultural Difference: Alfred Gell's Anthropology of Art. *Art History* 28(4): 524–551.
San Martin, P. (2010) *Western Sahara: The Refugee Nation*. Cardiff: University of Wales Press.
Thompson, V. and R. Adloff. (1980) *The Western Saharans: Background to Conflict*. London: Croom Helm.
Tilley, C. (2004) *The Materiality of Stone: Explorations in Landscape Phenomenology: 1*. Berg: Oxford.
Trout, F.E. (1969) *Morocco's Saharan Frontiers*. Geneva: Librairie Droz.
UPES (2008) *The Wall of Shame, a Crime Against Humanity (TECHNICAL FILE) 20/03/2008*. Sahrawi Journalists and Writers Union (UPES). www.upes.org/bodyindex_eng.asp?field=sosio_eng&id=885 (accessed 8 March 2014).
Zunes, S. and J. Mundy. (2010) *Western Sahara: War, Nationalism, and Conflict Irresolution*. Syracuse: Syracuse University Press.

Interviews

Bachir, Salek Labaidi. [Saharawi journalist and activist.] Interview in English (at Rabuni, Tindouf). 19 October 2011.
Breica, Habua. [Head of the 1st Artillery Regiment, SPLA, 2nd (Tifariti) Military Region.] Interview in Arabic, interpreter: Malainin Larkhal (at Tifariti). 2 November 2011.
Deya, Muhammed. [Mayor of Tifariti, and former SPLA soldier.] Interview in Arabic, interpreter: Malainin Larkhal (at Tifariti). 27 October 2011.
Fadel, Muhammed. [Long term SPLA soldier, Chief of Reconnaissance in the Tifariti Military Region.] Interview in Arabic, interpreter: Malainin Larkhal (at Tifariti). 30 October 2011.
Larkhal, Malainin. [High profile Saharawi journalist and activist.] Interview in English (at Tifariti). 2 November 2011.
Peraita, Fernando. [Artist and founder of ARTifariti.] Interview in English (at 27th February Refugee Camp, Tindouf). 17 October 2011.
Touballi, Hamdi. [Saharawi journalist and activist.] Interview in English (at 27th February Refugee Camp, Tindouf). 15 October 2011.

19

A PARTHIAN CITY IN THE IRAN–IRAQ WAR

Incorporating the ancient site of Charax Spasinou into a modern conflict landscape

Mary Shepperson

Historical background

The Iran–Iraq War, which lasted eight years, from 1980–1988, is by far the largest and bloodiest conflict ever fought in the Middle East. It is often compared to the First World War due to the similarities it has with the Great War's Western Front in terms of tactics, casualties, mud, and the battlefield use of poison gas (Razoux 2015: 471; Murray and Woods 2014: 212).

Iraq, under Saddam Hussein and the Ba'ath party, invaded Iran in 1980 with the intention of waging a short war and suing quickly for an advantageous peace. By the end of 1982, Iraqi forces had been pushed back to the pre-war border and faced defending their own land against a numerically superior and highly motivated Iranian army, whose goal was the annihilation of the Ba'athist state and export of the Islamic Revolution. The Iraqi response was to dig in, constructing vast and elaborate defensive earthworks along the 1,500-kilometre border. For the remaining six years of the war, the Iranians would throw hundreds of thousands of troops in human waves against these prepared defences but achieve little more than a bloody stalemate. The war would end with no clear winner, with the border exactly where it had been in 1980, and with around a million Iranians and half a million Iraqis dead (Tucker-Jones 2018: 98; Hiro 1989: 250; Razoux 2015: 568; Khakpour et al. 2016: 2). The war enduringly transformed the landscape of the Iran–Iraq border area, including its archaeological sites.

Landscape

The landscape of the border area between Iran and Iraq varies greatly from north to south. In the north it winds through the high Zagros Mountains; here the Iraqis laid mines in the mountain passes, and in the valleys and plains every vantage point, including ancient tells, was topped with a command post or artillery position. The central section of the border runs through the western foothills of the Zagros, passing Baghdad at a distance of little more than 100 kilometres.

However, the focus here is on the southern front, where the border runs across the southeast side of the huge alluvial plain of the Tigris and Euphrates rivers. The two rivers join at the town of al-Qurnah to form the Shatt al-Arab waterway, which runs southeast for 200 kilometres, past the city of Basra, to empty into the Gulf at al-Fao.

The landscape here is utterly flat, relieved only by man-made features. Settlement and agriculture are concentrated close to the rivers, but away from the Shatt al-Arab, the landscape becomes increasingly empty. The ground is not sand but dull, beige alluvial clay and silt, which during the winter rains becomes a slippery, cloying morass, extremely challenging for the movement of men and vehicles. The land is low-lying and marshy in places, but north of al-Qurnah it becomes true marshland, passable only with boats or pontoon bridges.

War of the bulldozers: military transformation of the landscape

The flat alluvium of the southern front, which would be the most heavily contested sector of the war, presented military engineers with an almost blank canvas on which to shape a militarized landscape. Both armies were accompanied by hundreds of bulldozers for the construction of defensive positions, and their use was so ubiquitous that Iraqi generals complained that their troops had no concept of digging their own defensive positions if bulldozers were not available (Murray and Woods 2014: 300). The Iranians even incorporated bulldozers into their offensive activities; during night attacks, bulldozers would advance behind attacking troops and rapidly construct new berms, behind which the attackers could retreat when repulsed without relinquishing all the land seized (ibid.: 230–231).

The largest and most intensive earthworks were constructed by the Iraqis along the Iraqi side of the international border. As the war turned in Iran's favour through 1981–1982, Iraqi military engineers applied themselves to the question of how to stop the Iranian advance and defend Iraqi territory. The important southern city of Basra, with its oil fields and access to the Gulf, was dangerously exposed; there were just 18 kilometres of flat land between the Iranian border and the outskirts of Basra. To defend the city, enormous engineering works were undertaken, including a 60-kilometre-long, ten-metre-wide earth embankment and the construction of a huge artificial canal between Basra and the border. This canal was 30 kilometres long, two kilometres wide, and four metres deep, designed to be impassable for tanks and vehicles (Razoux 2015: 188). The border area was also extensively mined.

Defending Basra did not simply mean fortifying the city itself but required the defence of its main supply line – the Basra to Baghdad highway. Between

1982 and the end of the war, the Iranians tried repeatedly to capture the highway north of Basra in order to cut the city off from reinforcements and supplies (Karsh 2002; Tucker-Jones 2018). Consequently, the Iraqis constructed evermore elaborate defences between the border and the highway, stretching from Basra up to al-Qurnah, north of which the waterlogged marshes were thought to provide an impassable natural barrier. Major defensive lines were established parallel to the border, studded with bunkers and artillery positions, and augmented with minefields, barbed wire, and electronic monitoring systems. A secondary line of defence was constructed parallel to the highway and the Shatt al-Arab (Figure 19.1). Much of this huge defensive system remains visible today and is clear on satellite imagery.

At the latitude of al-Qurnah the border makes a large step westwards towards the highway and the Shatt al-Arab. The border here lies within 20 kilometres of the road, its closest approach to the highway. Close to this potentially vulnerable point lies a large archaeological site which was once the great Parthian port city of Charax Spasinou.

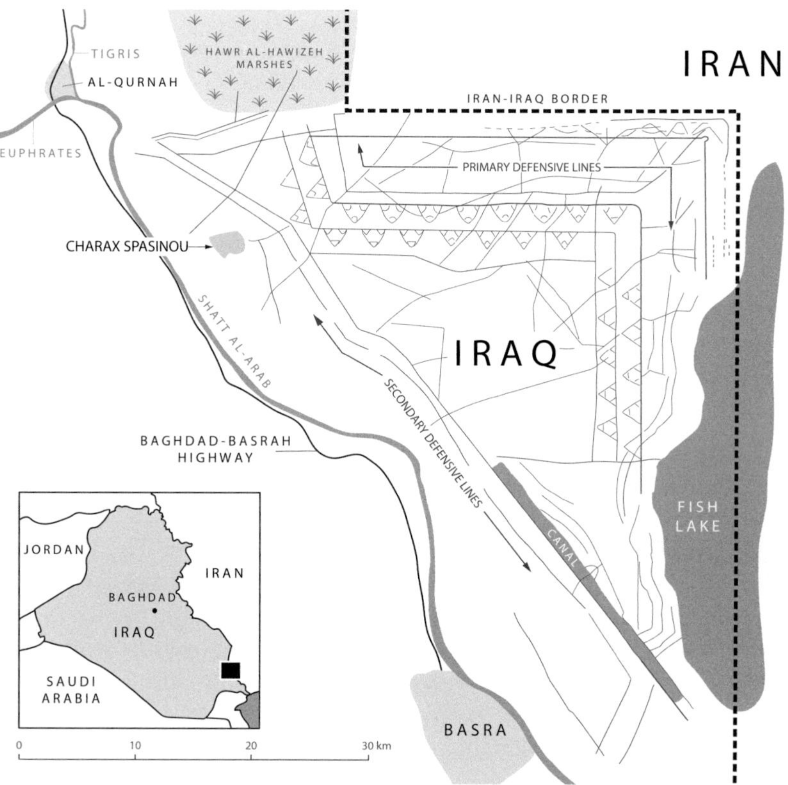

FIGURE 19.1 Iraqi defensive earthworks north of Basra. The canal east of Basra is now dry and the extent of Fish Lake, expanded by the Iraqis during the war, is now much reduced. Source: © author.

Charax Spasinou

The ancient city was founded by Alexander the Great in 324 BC as Alexandria-on-Tigris. It reached its peak during the Parthian period (247 BC–224 AD) under the name Charax Spasinou, when it was the major port at the head of the Gulf. For three centuries the city thrived on trade, connecting the maritime trade routes of the Arabian Gulf and Indian Ocean with the overland caravan routes through Petra and Palmyra to the Mediterranean world. It declined through the Sassanian period as trade decreased and the coastline shifted southwards, being finally abandoned sometime during the Islamic period.

The Charax Spasinou Project (University of Manchester) is an archaeological survey aimed at mapping and recording the site through drone survey, magnetometry, and test trenching (www.charaxspasinou.org/). The archaeological site covers at least six square kilometres, reflecting the ancient city's wealth and importance. Magnetometry survey has revealed an extensive classical city grid, residential neighbourhoods, and large palatial buildings. The only standing ancient structure is the city's northern and northeastern rampart, which runs for a combined length of 3.4 kilometres, incorporating three baked-brick bastions. The rest of the site is generally flat with some areas under occasional cultivation and the ancient remains visible as only slightly raised ground and scatters of pottery and baked-brick fragments. The only upstanding features inside the ramparts are earthworks from the Iran–Iraq War (Figure 19.2).

The war around Charax Spasinou

Given the position of Charax Spasinou, in a critical area for the Iraqi defensive system, it is unsurprising that the site was significantly impacted by the war. According to local representatives of the State Board for Antiquities and Heritage (SBAH), Iraqi government archaeologists were opposed to the occupation of Charax Spasinou by the military, but given the desperate nature of the conflict at the time, it is unsurprising that heritage concerns were not prioritized.

According to a local landowner, Ali Wehayib Abdul Abbas, the army arrived at the site in 1984 and the local villagers were evacuated. This suggests the occupation of Charax Spasinou may have been a response to Operation Kheibar, also known as the Battle of the Marshes, an offensive launched by the Iranians in late February 1984. The Iranians surprised the Iraqis by attacking across the supposedly impassable Hawr al-Hawizeh marshes using a flotilla of small boats. Their aim was to then turn south and seize al-Qurnah and the Baghdad–Basra highway which passed through the town, but the Iranians' initially successful advance was bloodily halted on the outskirts of al-Qurnah by Iraqi tanks, artillery, air attacks, and the large-scale use of mustard gas (Murray and Woods 2014: 228–230; Hiro 1989: 103–104). The Iraqis also resorted to running a 200,000 V high-tension electricity line into the marshes close to the Iranian bridgehead, electrocuting thousands of Iranian troops (Razoux 2015: 226–227).

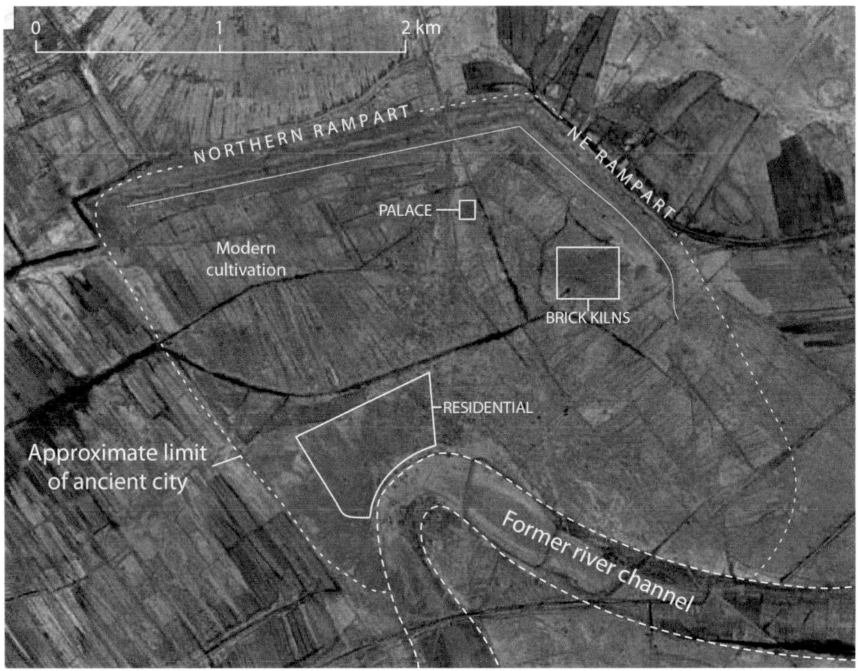

FIGURE 19.2 The site of Charax Spasinou today, illustrating the position and extent of the 3.4-kilometre-long ancient ramparts and indicating other important features of the ancient city so far identified. Source: © author; map data Google, Maxar Technologies.

The Iranians lost around 20,000 men, but they had come far closer to their goal than the Iraqis were comfortable with. Consequently, the Iraqis probably sought to reinforce the sector around al-Qurnah, in which Charax Spasinou lies. The Iranians launched a similar offensive, Operation Badr (the Second Battle of the Marshes), in March 1985. They briefly succeeded in capturing al-Qurnah, and with it the highway and bridge across the Euphrates, but again were defeated by superior Iraqi armour and air power with the loss of around 10,000 Iranian troops (Razoux 2015: 319–324; Pelletiere 1992: 88–90). This was the closest that the fighting would ever come to the new fortifications at Charax Spasinou. The site was never seriously attacked during the course of the war, but it was just within artillery range of the Iranian front lines and may have taken part in the sporadic artillery exchanges which characterized the day-to-day conduct of the war.

The refortification of Charax Spasinou

Unlike the utterly flat surrounding landscape, the ancient site presented the military engineers with some useful pre-existing topography; chiefly the

3.4-kilometre-long city ramparts. Conveniently for the Iraqis, the ancient ramparts were oriented very suitably for the tactical situation in 1984. The northern and northeastern ramparts faced towards the vulnerable gap where the main defensive lines met the marshes, which the Iranians had just attempted to exploit in Operation Kheibar, and would soon attack again in Operation Badr.

The ancient ramparts are 13 to 16 metres wide and around three to five metres high, making them larger than the average berms thrown up by the engineers, which are generally five to nine metres wide in the area surveyed. Charax Spasinou's ramparts are closer in dimensions to the largest military embankments which form the main defensive lines; part of the major embankment of the secondary line of defence was surveyed by drone and is around 17 metres wide. It can be seen on satellite images to run for 60 kilometres southeast to meet the canal protecting Basra.

The manner in which the ramparts were fortified by the engineers is similar to how these main embankments were furnished. The infantry dug foxholes, each big enough for between one and three men at irregular intervals along the crest of the earthwork. At Charax Spasinou almost 250 foxholes remain detectable along the top of the ramparts, suggesting an infantry strength of 500–600 men for the defence of the ramparts, or 15–20 men per 100 metres of rampart. In some places, these were connected by a narrow infantry trench running behind the foxholes on the earthwork's reverse slope, but these trenches do not survive well and many have probably been lost to erosion. Along Charax Spasinou's northeastern rampart the infantry trench was dug along the foot of the reverse slope with a small additional berm behind it. At its southeast end, this rampart also has a small berm eight metres in front of the base of its forward slope (Figure 19.3).

Vehicle positions were built against the reverse slope of the embankments for tanks and more lightly armoured vehicles. In some cases, these were simply protective, consisting of two small berms perpendicular to the embankment to protect the sides of vehicles parked behind it. Other emplacements facilitated a more active defence in providing positions from which tanks or self-propelled artillery could fire towards the enemy. In the case of the army-built embankments, these consist of a ramp of compacted earth against the reverse slope of the embankment, up which tanks could be driven until their guns could bear over the top of the earthwork. In the case of Charax Spasinou, the tank emplacements set into the ancient ramparts varied from this model in that the tank positions were embedded right into the top of the rampart rather than being just a ramp to the rear of the embankment.

This variation is likely due to the difference between the newly made embankments, which were built up using freshly disturbed surface material and were therefore relatively soft, and the ancient rampart which is made of heavy river clay, compacted through the course of two millennia. While the army embankments probably wouldn't have held the weight of a tank without risking collapse, the rock-hard ramparts provided a solid firing platform. In total, 51 tank positions were cut into Charax Spasinou's ramparts, constituting the most visually dramatic military intervention at the ancient site.

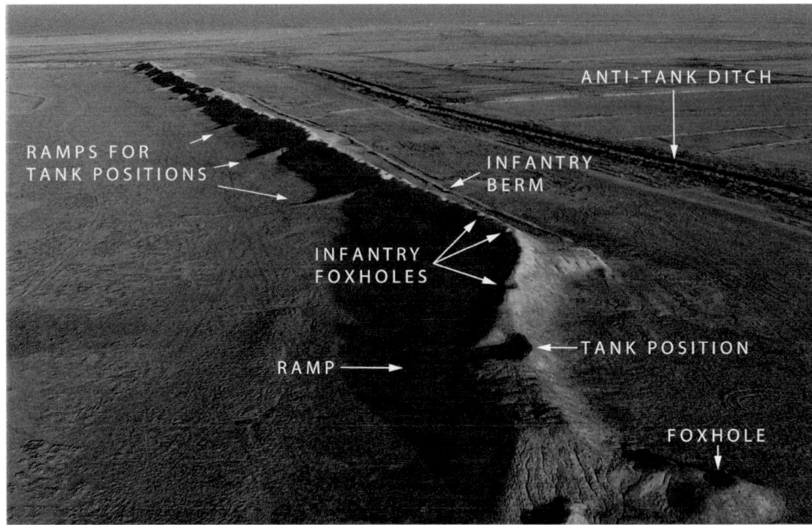

FIGURE 19.3 The northeast rampart of Charax Spasinou with military alterations, notably tank positions and their ramps. Drone photo, facing north. Source: © Charax Spasinou Project.

The northern rampart has a large number of protective vehicle emplacements adjoining its reverse slope, growing increasingly dense towards the western end of the rampart. These consist of a series of three-sided bays which do not offer firing positions, only protection from enemy fire. This is perhaps an area in which transport, supply, and communications vehicles could shelter, but could also have been used for storing supplies needed on the ramparts.

As well as refortifying the ancient rampart itself, additional parallel layers of defence were added both in front and behind the rampart. Two hundred metres in front of the northern rampart, an eight-metre-wide anti-tank ditch was dug, retaining traces of vehicle entrenchments along its rear edge. A similar ditch protected the northeastern rampart, although at a distance of only around 100 metres. Part of this ditch has been more recently re-cut as a drainage ditch for the adjacent cultivation. The northern rampart had a secondary, smaller ditch between the anti-tank ditch and the rampart along much of its length. Overall, the ancient ramparts of Charax Spasinou were transformed into a defensive obstacle as formidable as any purpose-built earthwork produced by the army engineers.

Military interactions with the archaeology

Archaeological landscape

Although the refortification of the city's ancient rampart is by far the most significant example of the reuse of archaeological features by the military, there is one other example, which demonstrates the willingness of the army to take advantage of archaeological topography on a much smaller scale. Inside the eastern rampart, there is an area of low mounds, which are formed by a series of ancient brick kilns (Figure 19.4). Magnetometry survey and limited test trenching suggest this is an industrial area of the city, with the brick kilns arranged along the side of a large linear feature, which is probably a canal. The line of kilns thus forms a low ridge of raised ground running northeast–southwest and the Iraqi army was quick to fortify this as one of many short irregular lines of defence established within the ancient city. A low berm was added on top of the pre-existing ridge of kilns and vehicle emplacements were embedded along its southeast side. One emplacement retains large fragments of a lightly armoured vehicle.

The fact that the Iraqi army used this low ridge of kilns demonstrates that those in charge of laying out the defensive earthworks were not oblivious to the underlying ancient city. The new military landscape was not simply imposed over the pre-existing landscape as a rigid system, as appears to have been the case in the highly regular front line defences along the border (see Figure 19.1). Rather, the military landscape at Charax Spasinou was moulded around the archaeological landscape. The refortification of the ancient ramparts turned the site into a defensive strongpoint, which in turn impacted the Iraqi defensive organization in this part of the sector. A concentration of anti-aircraft and artillery positions,

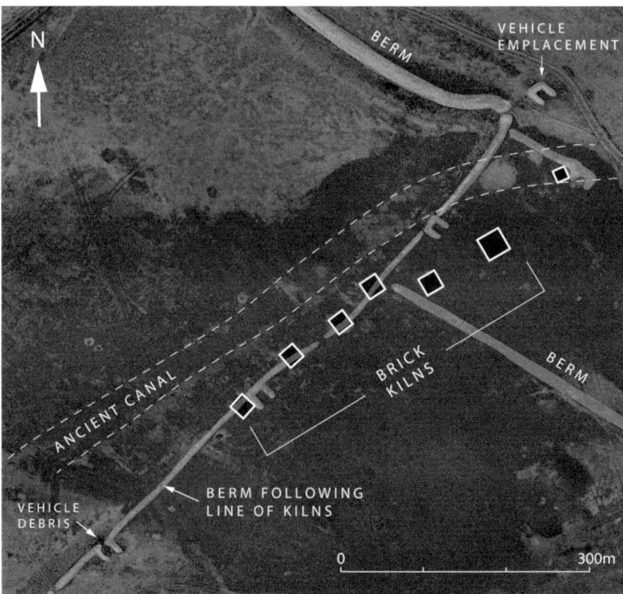

FIGURE 19.4 The positions of the underlying brick kilns, with 1980s Iraqi military features highlighted, including a long berm with integrated vehicle emplacements. From magnetometry results. Source: drone photo ortho-mosaic © Charax Spasinou Project.

vehicle emplacements, and other earthworks at the centre of the site suggests that the interior of the ancient city, protected by the ramparts, became a command post or staging area for Iraqi forces. A large conical mound in this central area is most likely the support for a communications array. As well as the strategic importance of its location, Charax Spasinou's role in the war was determined by its archaeological remains, chiefly the substantial standing ramparts. Such activities are a feature of twentieth-century conflict, where ancient places retained their strategic significance despite the passage of millennia. One example amongst many is the Early Bronze Age site at Tell el-Hesi in southern Israel, captured and entrenched by Jewish forces in the 1948 Israeli War of Independence, and unsuccessfully attacked seven times by the Egyptians (Toombs 1985).

Archaeological materials

There is no question that the military personnel occupying Charax Spasinou during the war were aware that they were entrenched on an ancient site. Archaeological material is obvious on the surface in many areas, generally in the form of sherd scatters and concentrations of baked brick. Ancient coins are not uncommon as surface finds, and pieces of carnelian show up particularly well after rain. Such objects have value locally and would certainly have drawn the attention of soldiers posted to the site for any length of time.

The main source of interaction between military personnel and archaeological material was of course through the construction of earthworks. Almost 1,000 military earthworks have been mapped within the approximate area of the ancient city, with a combined area of over 116,000 square metres. An insightful comment on the relationship between modern conflict and archaeological knowledge is that it is unlikely that archaeologists will ever excavate Charax Spasinou to the extent that the Iraqi military did in the 1980s.

Approximately half of the mapped features were dug into or against the ancient ramparts, but the soldiers and engineers would probably have found few artefacts while digging their foxholes and tank emplacements here. The main body of the rampart is made of re-deposited natural: heavy river clay heaped up in basket loads. It is almost sterile in terms of cultural material. The only other structures along the ramparts are three large baked-brick bastions, approximately 15 metres square and standing up to several metres high. However, these were mostly left untouched by the military as they were too hard for even bulldozers to make much impact, and certainly too tough for hand-dug foxholes to be sunk. Archaeological encounters along the ramparts were more or less limited to interaction with the gross structures themselves.

Around 450 earthworks have been mapped across the interior of the ancient city and these excavations are far more likely to have brought soldiers into contact with archaeological material. The majority of the mapped earthworks are above-ground bulldozer-constructed features, such as berms and emplacements for vehicles and artillery. The most common features are vehicle emplacements, which number around 150 within the site, made by pushing surface material into banks around three sides of a vehicle to form a U-shaped earthwork (see Figures 19.4 and 19.7). At Charax Spasinou, the archaeology lies just below the surface in many areas, and it is clear from sherds and bricks embedded in these embankments that many are made from archaeological deposits. In some areas, military earthworks cut down into more substantial ancient structures. There is at least one example where the construction of a vehicle emplacement cut into a large palatial residence just beneath the surface, throwing up large blocks of carved limestone, which remain embedded in the side of the earthwork (see Figure 19.5). Such stonework is extremely rare at Charax Spasinou due to the city being remote from any stone sources.

As well as the work of the bulldozers, many soldiers would have had the opportunity to dig into the ancient deposits by hand. The interior of the city is scattered with rows of foxholes and arrays of mortar positions and machine-gun posts. These were often substantial dugouts involving the disturbance of considerable material (Figure 19.6).

There is no direct evidence that Iraqi military personnel engaged in anything which may be termed archaeological enquiry while stationed at Charax Spasinou (or any other site) during the Iran–Iraq War, as occasionally happened in other conflicts where soldiers were dug into an archaeological landscape for an extended period, such as during the First World War (Saunders 2007: 4–9). However, it would be surprising if soldiers did not pick up artefacts from the site, either as souvenirs and curiosities to take home or as saleable objects. During the

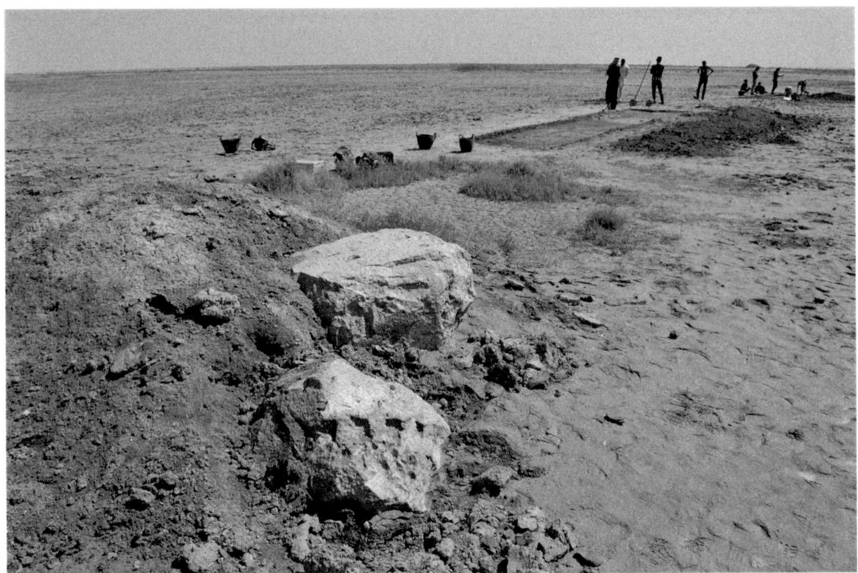

FIGURE 19.5 Limestone blocks from a high-status building, disturbed by bulldozers during the construction of a military earthwork (left). Source: © Charax Spasinou Project.

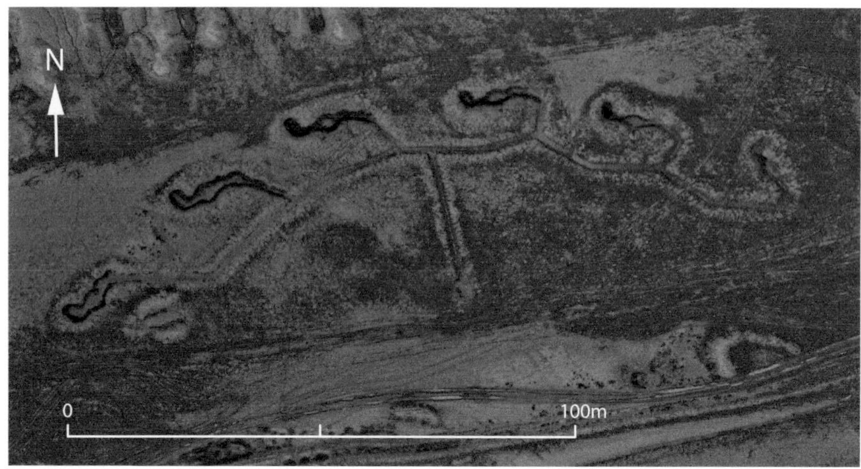

FIGURE 19.6 A battery of mortar positions linked by an infantry trench dug within the ancient city. This represents the excavation by hand of a large volume of archaeological deposits. Source: © Charax Spasinou Project.

war, it was certainly common for soldiers to take home military souvenirs, such as shrapnel and shell casings, as keepsakes and gifts (Dehqan 2006: 21–22), so perhaps a Parthian coin or a carnelian bead may have added some variety to these souvenir assemblages. Such 'souveniring' activities were widespread also during the First World War, and not just along the Western Front; in northern Greece, Gallipoli, and the Middle East, ancient and modern items were variously collected, sold, bartered, left behind, or taken home.

In the case of collecting objects to sell on, it is likely that such activities by the military at Charax Spasinou may have acted as the forerunner to refreshed looting efforts after the war, which continue to this day. The construction of military earthworks brought a huge quantity of ancient material to the surface, which could be combed through by local villagers after the military had left. Secondly, the spread of military earthworks across the whole site would have acted almost as test trenches for would-be looters, providing soundings across the site to identify the richest areas. Otherwise, the vast, flat expanse of the ancient city gives few clues as to where the best places to dig might be. This phenomenon of military excavations acting as a catalyst to civilian looting is known from other sites such as Thessaloniki (Saunders 2007: 7).

Archaeological interactions with military remains

As well as being recording as the latest period of occupation at the site, the features and remains left by the Iran–Iraq War have impacted the work of our archaeological survey project in several ways. First, there is the problem common to most sites of modern conflict: that a quantity of ordnance remains at the site, some of which could still be live. The surface of the site is littered with debris such as bullets, shell casings, mortar components, vehicle debris, and communications wiring. Fortunately, the majority of unused munitions at the site were disposed of by the Iraqi army at the end of the war, and any metal left exposed at the surface since the 1980s is now degraded beyond any danger, due to the extremely harsh surface environment. However, there remains a small degree of risk from any ordnance which has become buried, and consequently, the survey team avoids entering depressions, dugouts, and trenches left from the war. The Iran–Iraq War detritus impacts the magnetometry survey in two respects; firstly, the large amount of metal debris remaining at the surface causes considerable interference due to its strong magnetic signal, and secondly, gaps have to be left un-surveyed where military earthworks either make it impossible to walk with the magnetometer or have left potentially ordnance-bearing depressions.

However, there are some ways in which the remains of the Iran–Iraq War have assisted the study of the ancient remains at the site. One example mentioned above is the stone blocks brought to the surface in one area by a bulldozer-built vehicle emplacement (Figure 19.5). This is the only architectural stonework found so far at Charax Spasinou and this single indication of the presence of stone architecture is helpful in the interpretation of the magnetometry results, as well as providing us with information about the nature of the underlying building prior to any excavation. As mentioned above, the 450 earthworks across the interior of the city in many respects act as a crude set of test trenches, bringing samples of buried archaeological material to the surface all over the site.

A further example of the military earthworks proving archaeologically helpful came during our investigation of the ramparts. As discussed above, the ramparts are made of extremely tough clay, which is very difficult to dig with hand tools. This, combined with a reluctance to cause visible damage to the site's only standing structure, made examining the ramparts through excavation highly problematic. Fortunately, the military interventions in the ramparts had left us with several pre-cut sections through at least the upper structure where vehicle access points had been cut. Much of our knowledge of the structure and materials of the ramparts comes from cleaning up one of these military-made sections.

As a final comment on the interaction of the archaeological project with the military landscape, members of the team are constantly reminded of the men who lived at the site in the 1980s by the objects left on the site. Common finds include ration cans, uniform buttons, helmet liners, and occasionally clothing; army socks appear to survive particularly well. Although military debris is not collected as survey material, several team members have accumulated small collections out of personal curiosity.

The erasure of the military landscape

Much of the military landscape shaped by the Iran–Iraq War is likely to endure long into the future. The front line defences, close to the border, are largely protected from human interference due to restricted access to the still sensitive border, the remoteness of much of the land from roads and settlements, and extensive uncleared minefields. Only wind and rain are slowly acting to wear down the berms and fill in the ditches. However, this is not the case for the area surrounding Charax Spasinou. The site lies relatively close to the Shatt al-Arab, is easily accessible by road, and is in an area of rapidly expanding settlement and cultivation. This means that, as well as natural erosion processes, the military landscape is being erased by human actions, in some cases at a rapid rate.

Much of the area around Charax Spasinou, including parts of the site, has come under cultivation at some point or another since the end of the Iran–Iraq War. Although some larger berms and emplacements, which were clearly too much trouble to level, have been ploughed around, drone photos reveal the scars of ploughed-out military features on the site and in surrounding fields. At least 34 ploughed-out features can be identified within the archaeological site. A further agricultural issue for the Iran–Iraq War remains is that, in several cases, what appear to be military ditches have been re-cut, in total or in part, for irrigation or drainage purposes. This practice destroys the character of the military features and frequently throws into doubt the original age and extent of many of these ditches.

By far the greatest threat to the integrity of the military landscape surrounding Charax Spasinou is the deliberate removal of upstanding earthworks for building purposes. There is a substantial amount of house-building and development underway in the local area as the surrounding villages expand. Due to the low-lying, semi-waterlogged nature of the ground, it is necessary to build up a platform of earth under new houses to keep the structures dry during the wet winter months. The earth cannot simply be pushed up from the surrounding area without effectively digging out a lake around the new building, so the earth has to be brought in from elsewhere. The favoured source of building earth in this area seems to be the Iran–Iraq War earthworks. The practical basis for this is that, because the earthworks lie above the surface, the earth in them tends to be drier than earth dug from below the surface, but also it is practically easier to scoop the upstanding earthworks into a truck with a JCB than to dig down for the material. It is also likely that this practice is encouraged by landowners who may consider it beneficial to clear the land of earthworks with an eye to possible future cultivation. The result is that the military earthworks are rapidly disappearing from a large area around the expanding settlements. The use of bulldozers is forbidden on the archaeological site, meaning that the earthworks at Charax Spasinou are so far almost untouched by this process, but we have observed the process in action nearby during off-site survey and the tide of clearance can be clearly mapped in sample areas surveyed in the surrounding area (see Figure 19.7).

A war to forget

The remains of the Iran–Iraq War are treated with little reverence in Iraq, as illustrated by the ease with which they are trucked off for building material, but

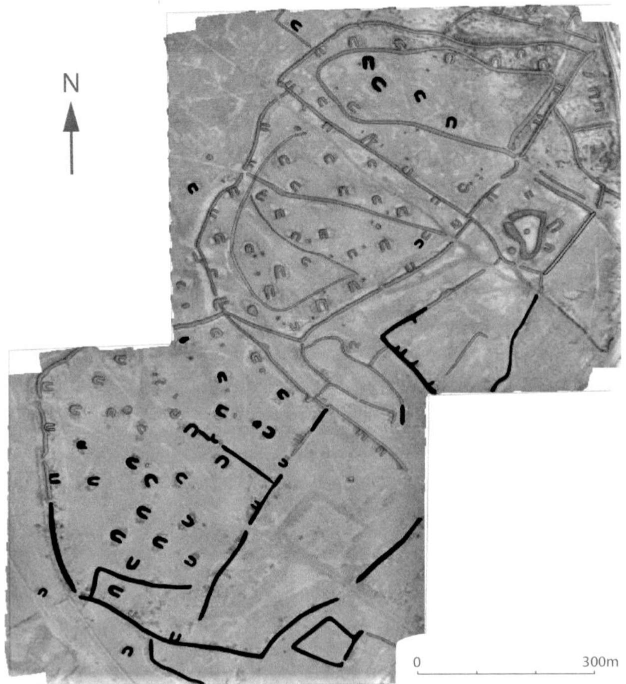

FIGURE 19.7 An area some four kilometres southeast of Charax Spasinou, showing vehicle emplacements protected by a series of berms. The military features in the southern part of the surveyed area, indicated in black, have been recently removed. Standing military features are shaded to make them more visible. Source: drone photo ortho-mosaic © Charax Spasinou Project.

this is not the case in Iran. The war is remembered very differently on the two sides of the border. For Iran, the war was the fire in which a new Iranian national identity was forged following the Islamic Revolution of 1979. The war, in which Iraq was the initial aggressor, was used by the new regime to generate huge patriotic and religious fervour in defence of Iran, Shia Islam, and the Revolution. Martyrdom in the war was elevated to a supreme religious virtue. The conflict is revered as a great national struggle defined by heroism, religious virtue and terrible, but glorious, sacrifice (Khakpour et al. 2016; Moosavi 2015).

In Iran, the war is known as the Holy Defence and is heavily memorialized. There is an entire week of commemorations each September, and in 2017 Iran opened a huge new museum: the Holy Defence Museum, which covers 21 hectares (Daftari 2017). Important battlefields on the Iranian side of the border are preserved as sites of pilgrimage, traditionally visited in the spring during the Nowroz New Year festival. Even the earth of the battlefields, imbued with the blood of martyrs, is considered sacred and is brought back by pilgrims to plant in gardens (Wellman 2015: 576), a practice also known from inter-war pilgrimages to the Western Front (Saunders 2007: 75), and most recently in the inclusion of soil from the Somme battlefield in the production of Remembrance Poppy pins made from melted-down shell cases (YAM 2016).

Attitudes to the war in Iraq are far more mixed. One issue is that the memory of the Iran–Iraq War has been pushed into the background by subsequent conflicts; the invasion of Kuwait, leading to the Gulf War in 1990–1991, then the US invasion of 2003 and the insurgency which followed, and finally the war with Islamic State, which has barely ended at the time of writing. In the face of almost continuous conflict and turmoil, Iraq now has little opportunity for reflection and memorialization of a war that has become eclipsed by more recent tragedies.

Probably of more significance, however, is the way in which the causes and motives behind Iraq's part in the war have come to be viewed in the present. While Iran can cast itself as the victim of an unprovoked attack, Iraq acted as the initiator of the conflict under the direction of Saddam Hussein, and it is his legacy that looms large over the memory of the war in Iraq. For Iraqis, the war with Iran was wrapped up in Ba'athist propaganda and the personality of its leader. While, fundamentally, most Iraqis who fought did so to protect their homeland from foreign invasion, they did it under the banner of Saddam Hussein and their efforts were presented in terms of the defence of the Ba'athist regime (Moosavi 2015: 11). It would be grossly simplistic to say that the memory of Saddam Hussein is now universally despised by Iraqis, but the legacies of his rule and the horrors he inflicted on large sections of the Iraqi people have coloured perceptions of the Iran–Iraq War to the point where it is broadly considered to have been a bloody and unnecessary conflict, fought in a bad cause.

This Ba'athist taint which hangs over the Iran–Iraq War has resulted in a minimal culture of remembrance and memorialization in Iraq, compared to the rich legacy of commemoration on the Iranian side of the border. During the Ba'athist post-war years, there was a state-sponsored programme of events and memorials to the war, including Martyrs Day, celebrated on 1 December, and a series of national monuments. However, these commemorations were all thickly packaged in Ba'athist propaganda and most were abandoned after 2003 when the trappings of the former regime were cast down.

An illustrative microcosm of the conflicting emotions surrounding the Iraqi perception of the war is the Victory Arch, the famous monument in Baghdad consisting of a pair of huge bronze arms crossing two curved swords. This was commissioned by Saddam Hussein, reportedly being of his own design, in 1986 as a monument to his yet-to-be-attained victory over Iran and as a memorial to the Iraqi martyrs of the war. After the fall of Saddam, the new regime in Baghdad began to purge the capital of Ba'athist monuments, of which the Victory Arch was considered a particularly egregious example (Whitaker 2004). Demolition of the arch had actually begun in 2007 before it was halted by a disparate group of mostly Iraqi individuals and organizations who argued that the Victory Arch should be preserved as an important historical monument, no matter what its political connotations (Semple 2007). It is this latent understanding that the Ba'athist era's material manifestations mark a key period in Iraqi history and are meaningful for the country's cultural memory that may hold out some hope for the future study, and perhaps preservation, of the material remains of the Iran–Iraq War. There are already organizations, such as the Iraq Memory Foundation (IMF n.d.), working to record and preserve the history and monuments of the Ba'athist era, along with the memory of all its horrors.

Conclusions

The site of Charax Spasinou is an evocative example of the unpredictable interaction of modern conflict processes and ancient remains in the formation of an archaeological landscape. While on a superficial level, the military occupation of the site might simply be seen as damage to the archaeological record, viewed in a wider context and in greater depth it can be seen as a creative, or even a regenerative as well as a destructive, process. The long-abandoned defensive ramparts of the ancient city returned to military relevance and were re-fortified. The city, in some respects, reverted briefly to being a living settlement, with a defined role in the newly reorganized landscape of military defence, a role which was substantially shaped by its ancient archaeological remains. The Iran–Iraq War features and material at the site can be considered as a true occupation phase, which represents an extremely important period in twentieth-century regional history.

Charax Spasinou is also an example of the difficult but sometimes rewarding relationship between conflict remains and modern archaeological research in a palimpsest landscape. The intrusion of military earthworks into earlier archaeological deposits can provide data as well as destroy it. In a site as vast as Charax Spasinou, where archaeological resources will never be equal to the area, military excavations may prove the only window possible onto subsurface deposits over much of the site.

During the current period, in which there is little enthusiasm for the memory of a war tainted by a political past which Iraq is striving to put behind it, the military landscape is being rapidly erased from this area. In a further example of the sometimes-surprising interaction between modern archaeology and landscapes of conflict, the heritage management measures now in place to protect the ancient city will also preserve a bubble of the Iran–Iraq War landscape after it has been cleared from the surrounding area. Perhaps in the future, with a longer historical perspective, Iraqis will find as much interest in the remains of this pivotal conflict as they do in the ancient remains of the great Parthian city below.

Acknowledgements

The Charax Spasinou Project is supported by the British Council's Cultural Protection Fund. The project is made possible by the collaboration and kindness of our colleagues from the State Board for Antiquities and Heritage.

References

Daftari, A. (2017) Holy Defense Museum in Tehran – Iran's War Memorial for the Digital Age. *CNN Travel*, 2 April. https://edition.cnn.com/travel/article/iran-holy-defense-museum/index.html

Dehqan, A. (2006) *Journey to Heading 270 Degrees* (transl P. Sprachman). Costa Mesa, CA: Mazda Publishers.

Hiro, D. (1989) *The Longest War: The Iran–Iraq Military Conflict*. London: Grafton Books.

IMF (n.d.) Iraq Memory Foundation. Website. www.iraqmemory.com/en

Karsh, E. (2002) *Essential Histories: The Iran–Iraq War 1980–1988*. Oxford: Osprey Publishing.

Khakpour, A., S. Vatanabadi and M. Khorrami (2016) Introduction. In A. Khakpour, S. Vatanabadi and M. Khorrami (eds.), *Moments of Silence: Authenticity in the Cultural Expressions of the Iran–Iraq War, 1980–1988*, pp. 1–8. New York: New York University Press.

Moosavi, A. (2015) How to Write Death: Resignifying Martyrdom in Two Novels of the Iran–Iraq War. *Alif: Journal of Comparative Poetics*, 35: 9–31.

Murray, W. and Woods, K. (2014) *The Iran–Iraq War: A Military and Strategic History*. Cambridge: Cambridge University Press.

Pelletiere, S.C. (1992) *The Iran–Iraq War: Chaos in a Vacuum*. Santa Barbara, CA: ABC-CLIO.

Razoux, P., (2015) *The Iran–Iraq War*. Nicholas Elliot (trans.) London: Belknap Press of Harvard University Press.

Saunders, N.J. (2007) *Killing Time: Archaeology and the First World War*. Stroud: Sutton.

Semple, K. (2007) Iraq Confronts Hussein Legacy Cast in Bronze. *New York Times*, 7 April. www.nytimes.com/2007/04/08/world/middleeast/08monuments.html

Toombs, L.E. (1985) *Modern Military Trenching and Muslim Cemetery in Field I, Strata I–II. Tell el-Hesi*, Vol. 2. Waterloo, ON: Wilfred Laurier University Press.

Tucker-Jones, A. (2018) *Iran–Iraq War: The Lion of Babylon, 1980–1988*. Barnsley: Pen and Sword.

Wellman, R. (2015) Regenerating the Islamic Republic: Commemorating Martyrs in Provincial Iran. *The Muslim World* 105: 561–581.

Whitaker, B. (2004) Fate of Saddam Relics Sparks Debate. *Guardian*, 16 June. www.theguardian.com/uk/2004/jun/16/arts.iraq

YAM (2016) 19,240 – One for Every Soldier. *Yorkshire Air Museum Website*, 4 May. yorkshireairmuseum.org/latest-news/19240-one-for-every-soldier/

20

ABSTRACT LANDSCAPES

Learning to operate in conflict space

Mark A. Burchell

Introduction

The motto of Britain's Royal Marines is *Per Mare, Per Terram*. This chapter discusses the second of these two environments in relation to Royal Marine training. It will show how the Corps both creates conflict landscapes and imposes a military perspective on existing environments.

Conflict on a scale that impacts landscapes is rarely, if ever, an unplanned act. Even such a minute element as a single stride propelling a soldier's body forwards will comprise a complex history of training and preparation. Each combatant, or operator, is meticulously trained and skilled to understand the mechanical potential of their body, resulting in weaponized organic energy. This chapter will focus on the kinetic relationship between body and landscape as a central aspect of bodily weaponization during preparatory phases of armed conflict.

Creating an effective operator is not as straightforward as placing a weapon in hand and teaching to shoot. Operating a rifle effectively comes much later in a training programme. What is more, firearms are ancillary to the body itself. A soldier entering conflict is, in fact, a weapons system, combining weapons, ammunition, and communications equipment with a human brain and muscle. Naturally, the equipment is relatively useless without an effective operator. The soldier must be rendered sturdy and resistant to fatigue so that effective manoeuvrability and deployment of weapons can be achieved when required.

Central to the preparation of troops is the training environment which transforms them into battle-ready operators. This transformation is complex and dependent on recruits being able to recognize their metamorphosis as they proceed through training, assimilating their eventual new identity as a skilled combatant (Burchell 2019: 114). Fundamental to this process is the relationship created between a recruit's body and the military's material culture such as, but not limited to, obstacle courses and other physical training grounds. Here, 'active' and 'passive' obstacles during basic training are essential for the development of movement and momentum, strength and the formation of a relationship between body and kit, and how all can be considered component parts of a training conflict landscape.

From human-engineered obstacles in a training camp environment, recruits will progress to hybrid training landscapes where they will learn to move synergistically across natural and man-made obstacles. Finally, they will learn endurance on natural landscapes such as Dartmoor National Park. Here they will move across landscapes of greater distances as well as learning the art of camouflage and concealment. Here, I will show how recruits are taught 'landscape language' which equips them to communicate effectively in any environment about the environment.

Obstacle course

Training in artificial and abstract environments such as obstacle courses deserves close examination due to their multifaceted role in the production of weaponized bodies. Numerous human responses, or layers of process, are simultaneously occurring before during and after recruits engage with them. I begin by describing what an obstacle course is and then a recruit's relationship with it.

Military obstacle courses are situated in outside spaces, usually within the confines of a training centre. Individual obstacles, set out in succession, together comprise the 'obstacle course'. However, within a training centre the term 'obstacle course' may denote an area wider than just the obstacles themselves. At Commando Training Centre (CTC) where Royal Marines are trained, there is an area called 'Bottom Field' in which the obstacle course is located along with various other rope training apparatus and an open space for physical activity such as warm-ups prior to engaging the obstacles. The Bottom Field area is characterized by physical activity which is controlled meticulously by a highly skilled training team. Within obstacle courses, time and space can become highly defined through a bodily commitment to intense physical labour, which is measured by the requirement for a relatively high number of exacting movements to be performed over a given frame of space, and within the prescribed measurement of time (Burchell 2019: 56–64). Nigel Foster says that 'instructors put continued pressure on the recruits in order to simulate the high-pressure environment of the battlefield' (Foster 1998: 51) (Figure 20.1).

Obstacle courses and other training landscapes are used to prepare recruits for armed conflict, where a combatant's ability to negotiate conflict landscape is a key skill. Military training grounds are designed to resemble challenges that war environments present to soldiers. The resemblance is not a recreation of terrain or landscape but an abstract representation of obstacles and challenges encountered in a conflict space. In addition to physical hardships, obstacle course training teams create stress and fatigue through the orchestration of bodily

FIGURE 20.1 Bottom Field obstacle course. Source: © author. Figure note: Images in this chapter are blurred for the Ministry of Defence security reasons.

movements. Recruits are kept in a high state of physical and mental stress before, during, and immediately after an obstacle course training session. With continued engagement and practice, they will develop skill, strength, speed, and momentum. Repetitive training will provide a means by which recruits can comprehend their development and growth through multiple distinct physical performances merging into one memory, or 'synthesised performance' (Burchell 2019: 113). They will experience their bodies becoming faster and more agile over the obstacle course and will get progressively closer to completing it within the required time allowance.

To achieve the required standard of obstacle course completion the recruits build skill and knowledge. At their introduction to the obstacle course, the training team will demonstrate each of the obstacles explaining technique while recruits watch. Recruits will then go over the obstacles in slow-time and practice the correct techniques. This introductory phase is done without carrying a rifle or wearing belt-kit. The number of different movements and postures they assimilate represent a steep learning curve. When determined by the instructors to be ready the recruits will 'run' the course with belt-kit only. This is a crucial adaptive phase: learning to move with agility whilst carrying what is essentially dead weight. Eventually, the recruit's kit to be carried will include their rifle. From this point onwards they will always train with belt-kit and rifle (Figure 20.2).

Once recruits have adjusted to carrying kit, they begin 'timed runs' which are recorded by the training team. During the early stages, it is unusual for recruits to complete the course within the given time allowance and some are considerably slower. With practice, the recruits grow stronger and quicker and,

FIGURE 20.2 Recruit with full belt-kit and rifle. Source: © author.

importantly, learn how their bodies move and what they are capable of achieving without 'breaking'. Over the course of basic training, they will build an extensive vocabulary of body 'rhetorics' (Bourdieu 1999: 75) and the mental agility to adapt one body posture to the next with little requirement for conscious reasoning.

The abstract nature of obstacle courses stimulates the development of a repertoire of body movements. The obstacles are stand-alone structures which I refer to as active and passive. Active obstacles include those that move whilst the recruits engage them, such as a 'swing bridge' for striding across or 'cargo net' for climbing up. The logic here is about learning to manoeuvre the body not only to conquer the moving obstacle but to work with the dead weight (belt-kit and rifle) being carried. A swing bridge obstacle that moves forwards and backwards challenges recruits to stride across in a forward direction whilst judging the swinging momentum of the bridge in accordance with each strike of the foot. Done correctly the combined momentum propels the body forwards, which, with the weight of kit, develops control whilst moving at speed. Without the correct momentum, the bridge will work against the recruit's forward momentum or sway side to side, causing them to be thrown out of kilter by the heavy kit.

Multidirectional movement such as climbing a cargo net presents a different form of logic. Here the net construction will not allow a perfect rhythm of movement. As recruits climb up and down the other side the net will move and sway in all directions, with rapid direction changes exaggerated further by the weight of the kit being carried. This obstacle and other rope-based obstacles like it develop an awareness of the influence kit will have on the body, teaching recruits to incorporate that influence into their calculations of momentum and movement.

Passive obstacles are those made of solid and immovable structures such as brick walls for climbing over and concrete tunnels for crawling through. These obstacles develop the extra strength required for the incorporation of the kit to the body. Solid brick wall structures, for example, have zero movement. On the approach to a five-foot (1.5 metres) wall, as is the case on Bottom Field, recruits will run at it with maximum speed. As they make full-body contact with the wall, energy in their forward momentum is stopped dead and degenerated. They are left reliant on raw strength to pull themselves up and over the wall top. When this obstacle is near the beginning, such as in the Bottom Field Assault Course at CTC, recruits can scale the wall with some ease. On another Royal Marine assault course, the high-level rope-based 'Tarzan Assault', this type of obstacle is placed at the end (Burchell 2019: 74). Consequently, it is encountered when the body is already greatly fatigued. In this instance, recruits experience the weight of their kit differently and feel it many times heavier, adding to their understanding of the relationship between their body and kit.

Combining body with kit is not simply about developing strength and fitness to carry it or being able to move with it across a variety of terrains. In order to do that, recruits must learn to synchronize body movement with the momentum of the load being carried. Kit is essentially dead weight and the laws of physics determine that propelling that dead weight in any particular direction will cause it to continue on that course. Therefore, if a combatant is running forwards and needs to change direction, allowance has to be made for the momentum of kit that will work against the body's intended new direction of travel. The obstacle course provides an essential mechanism for recruits to 'pair' body with kit and learn how to move in and out of multiple postures and change the direction of movement without losing balance or fluidity of movement. Overcoming active and passive obstacles often requires an intense burst of aggression and total-body strength, forcing recruits into an inseparable relationship with their kit regardless of the burden caused by it. The development of these skills weaponizes the body and builds the momentum of movement through conflict space.

Recruits practice in-camp assault courses for the duration of their training programme, strengthening the relationship with their kit whilst gaining power and speed of movement. In time, recruits are required to develop longer-distance endurance over less abstract terrain as they begin to identify with naturally formed obstacles. Royal Marine recruits make this transition on the Endurance Course – a seven-mile-long (11 kilometres) assault course.

Hybrid training landscapes

Hybrid landscapes are a step away from the purely abstract landscapes like training camp obstacle courses. One such transformative training landscape, the

Endurance Course at CTC, is set in an open landscape on nearby Woodbury Common. The Endurance Course is comprised of three parts: first, an assault course around three miles (five kilometres) long followed by a four-mile (6.5-kilometre) road run back to the training centre. On arrival, assuming the allotted time has been achieved, there is a shooting test.

The first part of the Endurance Course will further develop momentum and movement over terrain and obstacles by adding to the skills learned on the in-camp obstacle course. Instead of a short five-minute burst, the obstacles are drawn out over three miles (five kilometres) incorporating naturally formed mud, stagnant water, and decaying and rocky pathways as well as human-engineered tunnels such as 'smartie tubes'.

The course begins with a series of smartie tubes which, in contrast to the concrete tunnel found on the Bottom Field assault course, incorporate elements of natural terrain. They are underground tunnels walled with corrugated iron, allowing just enough room for recruits to crawl through. During winter months some can be three-quarters filled with trapped water turning stagnant. After the series of tubes and tunnels, the course opens onto muddy and rocky pathways weaving through natural formations in the landscape up and down steep hills (Figure 20.3).

Recruits will eventually arrive at the 'sheep dip', which is another tunnel obstacle fully submerged in a water hole. To complete this obstacle the recruit going through the tunnel takes a deep breath and forces himself underwater to the entrance of the tunnel. As he does so, one of his comrades who is in the pool with him will grab his trouser belt and force him forwards into the tunnel. Left there unassisted, he will likely drown. Waiting at the exit end of the tunnel is a third recruit. He is deep in the water with an arm fully stretched out into the

FIGURE 20.3 Endurance Course pathways weaving through the landscape. Source: © author.

FIGURE 20.4 The clay pit. Source: © author.

tube, waiting to feel some part of the recruit's body so he can grab it and pull him the rest of the way through and up to the surface of the water (Burchell 2019: 68–69).

The final obstacle in the assault course section is the 'clay pit'. Recruits crawl through a naturally formed sump of heavy and sticky clay which has similar characteristics to quicksand, so they must keep moving. The clay pit is exhausting, leaving the body feeling depleted of energy. In addition, kit, body, and particularly boots are caked in heavy clay, adding tremendous weight as the recruit crawls out and up a slippery slope only to begin the four-mile (6.5-kilometre) road run back to CTC (Figure 20.4).

On completion of this run back, recruits go straight to the 25-metre range for their shooting test. After a considerable effort, all can still be lost if recruits are not successful at the shoot. By this point in their training, it is less likely they will fail due to missing the required number of hits on target than due to their rifle failing to fire because of soiling whilst crawling through the smartie tubes and clay pit.

The progressive nature of Marines training develops a recruit's skill at movement and momentum, starting in human-engineered environments and moving on through hybrid landscapes to culminate in the final Commando test: the Thirty-Miler (48 kilometres).

Natural landscapes

At the end of a long and intense training programme, Marine recruits will face their ultimate test, a 30-mile run across Dartmoor National Park. This is carried out across an entirely natural landscape and requires recruits to navigate their way. On completion, they are awarded the coveted Green Beret, a part of Marines material culture that symbolizes elite forces status and that is so iconic that it can often be a metaphor for the Marine himself (Saunders 2004: 6).

Having gone through a multitude of final tests leading up to the Thirty-Miler, recruits' bodies are exhausted, sore, and bruised as they begin the run. The natural formations of terrain on Dartmoor and the challenges posed by unpredictable weather provide a final conversion from abstract landscapes to operating across natural landscapes. During this test recruits will draw on all their enculturated knowledge of their body's dynamics so as to maintain the required momentum of movement and overcome the multitude of challenges such as the terrain, the weather, and pathfinding.

Terrain

The route across Dartmoor will cover a multitude of terrain types. Recruits encounter gravel tracks providing a relatively comfortable ground on which they can find a shared sensorial cadence of boots striking the ground. Most of the route is grassland, starting off flat and turning to small hills with taller vegetation causing more resistance to rhythm. In addition to small hills, there are steep ones that, combined with the weight of the kit being carried, will fully fatigue the legs. Depending on the time of year, recruits will also encounter soft boggy terrain which, like the clay pit, saps their energy and increases the weight of each boot.

The most challenging aspect of the run is two-fold. First, due to the natural and varied terrain, recruits will be unable to establish and keep a comfortable rhythm. They must constantly adjust to the changing vegetation underfoot and the peaks and troughs in altitude. Second, their teamwork will be severely tested. They will carry out the run in a team of eight, all of whom must cross the finishing line together within the required time in order to pass. If one fails, they all must re-run the course. Due to the distance and endurance required, all recruits will tire – some sooner than others. The temptation during extreme exhaustion can be for individuals to think of themselves first instead of the group. As they are increasingly under strain, they will visibly start to focus inwards to the detriment of the weakest lagging behind. To succeed, the recruits must maintain group solidarity, bring the weakest to the front, and ensure the punishing environment does not get the better of them.

Weather

The landscape of Dartmoor is very exposed to the elements. There is no respite from the heat on a warm day and, in the winter, the weather can be treacherous. A winter Thirty-Miler carries the constant threat of hypothermia caused by severe and changeable weather conditions. Recruits can begin marching onto the Moors in glorious sunshine and in less than half an hour be covered in snow and 'cold to the bones'. For this reason, they must apply the survival skills that they have learned to constantly assess and re-assess the appropriateness of clothing being worn. If they get this wrong, they can dehydrate as quickly as freeze.

They carry one Bergen rucksack between each sub-group of four. This contains essential survival equipment, such as an arctic-quality sleeping bag for use if one of the team 'goes down' due to severe weather or injury. The Bergen will be rotated around the group and is an additional burden to the belt-kit and rifle they all carry as standard. All types of weather conditions have the potential to add to the discomfort of kit.

Pathfinding

Distance, the weight of kit, and the addition of weather conditions require skilful use of landscape and pathfinding over it. On the Moors recruits will learn essential techniques such as maintaining elevation whilst traversing hillsides and identifying routes of least resistance on the approach to steep climbs. They will learn to identify natural pathways through rocks and dense vegetation and avoid troublesome surfaces that conceal swamps and bogs. As well as learning to use energy-efficient natural pathways, they will need to know when not to do so; in enemy territory, these will be avoided due to the likelihood of enemy ambush.

In abstract training environments, the energy between the body and harder surfaces can work somewhat synergistically; when throwing a ball against a hard surface, it will bounce off as energy is returned. In a natural environment, however, body energy is soaked up by the softer landscape and environment being passed through. This makes it increasingly difficult for a recruit to find a rhythm and cadence not just with comrades but with his or her own relationship to the ground.

Bodily endurance is the key to the Thirty-Miler. It is not uncommon for recruits to hobble to the start line, having already endured relentless testing against a number of environment types. The required standard of endurance is not inherent to the recruits' bodies. It is created and developed externally through continued relationships with landscape. That is to say, environmental conditions of military operations will determine the level of fatigue caused to the body and in response, the operator's effort to survive it. When exhausted in training, the body will develop physically but is still paralyzed without the correct command signals from the brain. The tough testing enables recruits to psychologically push themselves further and for longer than previously possible. This is a key part of their final preparation for operating in and surviving conflict landscapes.

Training in landscape synergy

Operating in and surviving conflict landscapes requires a degree of knowledge about making one's way through and over terrain as well as concealing and camouflaging body and equipment. Recruits are taught to look out across landscapes to spot the enemy as well as to conceal themselves from the enemy gaze. Being able to communicate effectively about the environment is also essential. This I refer to as landscape synergy.

Entering a conflict space requires a period of acclimatization where operators get a feel for the natural conditions of the environment. This is vital in order that an unusual shape or movement can be detected – especially in a patrolling scenario. Recruits are taught not just to look at vegetation but to look into and beyond it. The gaze of an untrained eye will rest at the object surface. Recruits are trained to look past the surface and scan for shapes, textures, or movement that would not occur naturally. This skill to detect is enhanced by knowledge about formations of landscape and vegetation that provide likely 'cover' for the enemy.

In addition to eye detection, skilled operators learn to recognize noises that are unnatural in a given environment. Patrolling in high-risk conflict spaces requires concentration and a sense for 'atmospherics', a term that refers to the feeling that something isn't quite right. This is a skill that requires the operator to become highly attuned to the surrounding landscape and environment. If something suspicious is detected, it must be communicated immediately to comrades.

Likewise, an operator can camouflage and conceal himself from onlookers by attaching local vegetation to kit and body. A number of principles are central to successful concealment such as 'breaking up' the human shape. Typical camouflage clothing has a 'patchy' pattern to disguise the body's outline. In addition, cam-cream (or face paint) is applied to the face and hands to break up the outline. Recruits are taught there are no straight lines in nature, so the rifle is also painted or dressed with vegetation and cloth to disguise it (Figure 20.5).

Applying local vegetation to the body and kit requires a practised skill at being able to recreate a natural look. Unskilled recruits might begin by attaching plant matter the wrong way up or by causing it to move in an unnatural way. They must also learn to recognize when vegetation changes as they move through it. Emerging from a long grassy plain and entering bushland will require a change of vegetation camouflage. This is a particularly important skill for reconnaissance and setting up observation posts (OPs) that overlook enemy strongholds. Here, natural land and shrub formations will provide cover and concealment.

Having mastered the basics of blending with surrounding environments, recruits will learn to effectively communicate about them. It is imperative that communication in a conflict environment is clear, concise, and well practised. Preparation for conflict narrative begins in basic training when new recruits learn Corps-specific words such as 'yomp', meaning marching with a heavy load, or 'oolu' (or ulu), meaning jungle or area of heavy vegetation. Because recruits join from all regions of the UK, Corps-specific words provide a single language with one meaning. In the absence of specified words, recruits are taught to identify and define their surroundings according to principles relating to basic

FIGURE 20.5 Recruits learning to use local vegetation to build a concealed look-out position. Source: © author.

characteristics of the situation or thing being described. In this way, the narrative is informed and shaped by the physical and material cultural environment.

Recruits begin to communicate their surroundings when in abstract landscapes inside training camps. On the Bottom Field Assault Course at CTC, the obstacles are named according to how they look and any peculiar characteristics, however obvious these may sometimes be. For instance, the five-foot-wall (1.5-metre) obstacle is a wall standing five feet tall, and the zigzag wall is a wall in a zigzag formation along the top of which recruits have to run. Abstract obstacles are identified by describing their character, and this changes the mindset of recruits from using local or colloquial language to using shared descriptions (Figure 20.6).

As recruits progress to hybrid training landscapes they encounter obstacles such as the sheep dip – a process of being fully submerged into an underwater tunnel and pulled out the other end by a comrade. Similarly, the clay pit is exactly as it sounds. If the sheep dip were called 'obstacle 8' and the clay pit 'obstacle 9', this would likely cause recruits to make mistakes about which is which. For this reason, logical naming conventions are used to prevent any ambiguity in clear, concise communication about what, when, and where.

Simple naming conventions become increasingly logical as recruits familiarize themselves with natural landscapes where there is an absence of human-engineered features to navigate. When looking out over a human-populated landscape, navigating the gaze of another individual to a particular point can be achieved by referencing landmarks such as 'the tall building' or 'the thatched cottage'. By contrast, when looking out over a featureless expanse of ocean, the absence of identifiable 'places' is overcome by the clock method – imagining

FIGURE 20.6 Recruit climbing over the five-foot-wall. Source: © author.

a clock face on the water's surface with the 12 o'clock position straight ahead. Assuming 12 o'clock is north, the three o'clock position will be east. This method enables signalling to a general area or direction of gaze.

On natural landscapes, recruits are taught how to direct the gaze of comrades to a specific point. The scenario might be that they are patrolling when they come under fire from a sniper. They take cover and look out over the landscape until one has spotted the hidden enemy position. The spotter then guides comrades to the enemy so they can train rifles onto that position. This is a well-practised skill not only for the one communicating but also for those listening and following the guidance.

Reading a seemingly featureless landscape and being able to communicate a precise point without being able to gesticulate requires recruits learn to identify features and describe them with a straightforward narrative. Instead of being taught what an oak tree looks like, a tree will be described according to its distinctive features. Noting techniques in military sketching, Paul Gough (1995, 2009) considers methods of guiding the eye to relevant points in the landscape by referencing key devices in the terrain such as an isolated chimney, a single red roof amongst black roofs, or three silhouetted bushes on a crest line. These serve as markers that point to targets or tactically vital features whilst avoiding complex drawing frames.

Whilst looking out over the landscape range, once a recruit has spotted the enemy location, as an example, the following instructions will be given to comrades:

> At the one o'clock position there is a big lone tree in the middle of field. To the right of the tree there is a hedgerow. Follow the hedgerow along the twelve o'clock position to the bushes. Look to the right of the bushes to the

small copse of trees. There is a tall skinny tree and at the base to the right side as you look at it, movement has been seen.

Recruits do not learn a taxonomy of things; instead, they use simple naming conventions informed by characteristics of the object being described. Once they have progressed from training and are operating in a conflict environment overseas, they will be effective at describing the landscape around them regardless of having limited knowledge of the local plant and fauna. In this way, operators will have a universal language that at any point is informed by the local environment.

Conclusion

Prior to conflict, combatants' bodies are trained and weaponized through bodily engagement with abstract landscapes. During basic training, recruits are taught anew how to walk, run, and carry themselves (Hockey 1986) as they begin the education of their bodies inside training camps on purpose-built landscapes such as obstacle courses. These and other training apparatuses are not designed to resemble any particular conflict space. They are abstract environments created to obstruct bodily momentum. This challenging enculturation of the body has been developed to provide practical outcomes aimed at preserving life and gaining tactical superiority in a conflict situation.

To master these challenging artificial environments, recruits do not need to apply intellect but rather need to absorb practical knowledge of how best to employ and comport their bodies to overcome obstacles, both physical and psychological. The aim is to gain alternative strategies within the given symbolically structured space (Bourdieu 1999: 75). Recruits are taught rhythm, timing, and the correct use of energy expenditure because for ground troops in conflict, skilful movement across the landscape and what is referred to as 'battle momentum' are essential to overthrow an enemy position. Ground troops, or raiding troops like Marine Commandos, will aim to win a firefight through momentum and a heavy weight of advancement. The power of highly skilled and muscular bodies moving across the ground tactically in unison is overwhelming (Burchell 2014: 213).

Obstacle courses are the start of a recruit's landscape and environmental education and are constructed to maximize bodily coding and shaping (Goffman 2009: 16) of the postures recruits must adopt to be successful. Obstacle course logic prescribes a time limit within which recruits must complete the succession of obstacles and this dictates their momentum. Each obstacle will interfere with their momentum, causing them to learn new positions, movements, and different ways of harnessing and expending energy.

Recruits learn to negotiate both passive and active obstacles differently. In the case of an active obstacle, they will synergize energy and bodily movement to work with or counter the frequency and direction of an obstacle's movement. Passive obstacles, on the other hand, will require recruits to overcome them by exerting 'explosive' directed energy which is usually referred to as controlled aggression. In the case of elite forces such as the Royal Marines, this training is undertaken whilst carrying rifle and belt-kit at all times. As the recruits progress through their training, they will become increasingly efficient at moving 'over' the obstacle course, working towards completion within the required time. The difficult-to-achieve completion time ensures they continue to maximize their effort at each course engagement.

Attempting in-camp obstacle courses requires short but intense physical and mental commitment, developing the recruit's strength and fitness, often understood as the raison d'être for this training. However, the obstacle course will enable recruits to develop a vast vocabulary of movement while carrying their rifle and kit. Herein lies the logic of pairing the body with the military's material culture such as weaponry and ancillary items whilst undergoing training. The kit that elite combatants such as the Royal Marines Commandos must carry into conflict is weighty and recruits must therefore synergize their body with kit to feel natural.

Having developed the relationship between body and kit on 'short-burst' in-camp training landscapes, recruits begin their endurance training over more naturally formed landscapes outside the training centre. This teaches them how to convert energy and momentum from a short, explosive form to a longer, enduring form. Establishing these skills is essential for longer-distance manoeuvres over conflict space, which will further develop the synergy between soldier and kit.

The key principle to winning a tactical engagement or firefight is constant movement. The in-camp assault courses build the power and fitness required for constant short bursts of movement. While two Marines are on the ground providing covering fire, two others will be bounding forwards towards the enemy with maximum speed in a zigzag pattern, making them harder targets. The Endurance Course will begin to prepare the recruits for battle across larger and less well-defined grounds.

The Royal Marines Endurance Course prepares recruits for landscape realities such as mud, adding significant load to kit, and wet conditions, causing well-fitting clothes to rub the body sore. In addition, the relationship with kit is strengthened because there is a shooting test at the end which can only be passed with the correct number of hits on target. It is essential that whilst crawling through the smartie tubes and clay pit, recruits are fully conscious at all times not to allow the rifle to become so soiled that it will not fire, as this counts as an Endurance Course failure.

A soiled rifle failing to fire can have fatal consequences during conflict. For this reason, weapons cleaning is carried out meticulously and rifles are kept immaculate. The Endurance Course provides recruits with an increasingly close relationship with kit and fundamentally teaches them to 'care' for their rifles (and kit). The Endurance Course and the associated fear of 'failure to fire' creates a rifle-consciousness and subsequently an increased bonding with it. Human, object, experience, and landscape become inextricably fused in this process and are inseparable (Saunders 2009: 42).

Recruits become increasingly aware of the necessity for kit-consciousness and that their survival depends on a well-formed relationship with it as well as with comrades. Here, landscapes are as much a threat as the enemy, and hybrid training landscapes bridge the gap between learning the basics in abstract landscapes and surviving in natural landscapes.

The 30-mile run over an entirely natural landscape across Dartmoor is the hardest challenge. It is never rehearsed prior to recruits attempting it as their final test that accumulated training has prepared them for. It is the final transition recruits make towards operating in natural conflict landscapes and tests their adaptability to conflict spaces where the terrain is unknown. Recruits will draw on their knowledge and practised body dynamics to make way overland whilst maintaining momentum. This action is a union of bodily movement and perception, and every action is skilled (Ingold 2011: 94).

Recruits are required to learn to ceaselessly attune their movements to perturbations in the perceived environment without interfering with the flow of action. This level of skill, rather than being innate, must develop as a part of growth and development in a given environment (ibid.). The Thirty-Miler is a gruelling test of their ability to show they have mastered the skill of movement over distance and unknown terrain regardless of weather conditions, the weight of kit being carried or their exhausted body.

Bonds between recruits also develop due to sharing the highs and lows and, in particular, the experience of pain and discomfort. Individuals will experience the same highs and lows with their kit and in a similar vein will form a bonded relationship with it. The Thirty-Miler, as with all Commando tests, demonstrates skill and effort. Whether the test is abstract or natural, the training and subsequent testing are about unifying body with kit and testing mastery of movement over landscapes, which is not a simple kinetic application. Recruits must learn 'the development of skilled ways of moving through the landscape' (Tilley and Cameron-Daum 2017: 94), which requires the knowledge to 'read' natural formations. Pathfinding must include decisions about safe passage as well as concealment. What might appear the fastest and easiest passage may be the most dangerous. Making their way along a hilltop, for instance, will often present terrain that is easy underfoot but expose a silhouette to the watchful enemy.

Synergy requires that recruits learn to 'blend' with landscapes. Camouflage and concealment are essential skills in a conflict environment. Done right, the body will blend so well with surroundings that an enemy can walk past without seeing the camouflaged operator. This requires recruits to learn about natural vegetation and how to apply it to kit and body not only to go unseen but to make it difficult for an enemy shooter to hit on target.

Any preparation for conflict involves forging a relationship between human activity and landscape. Beginning with human-engineered abstract landscapes, recruits learn to bond body with kit. They acquire the basics of movement over multi-surface terrain and of simple environmentally informed descriptive language. In hybrid landscapes, they learn to engage their body and maintain the tempo of movement over natural terrain and describe it according to its peculiarities. As recruits progress to natural training landscapes, they train their bodies for endurance against elements of the open environment and perfect a universal form of descriptive narrative that equips them to communicate about the environment.

This relationship with landscape occurs throughout a training programme and is central to transforming civilians into battle-ready operators, experts at movement through and survival within multiple terrains. They communicate clearly and effectively in any environment, regardless of the challenges. Elite forces train to synergize with their surroundings. They do not become landscape experts to appreciate natural beauty but to deliver lethal force.

References

Bourdieu, P. (1999) *The Logic of Practice* (transl. R. Nice). Cambridge: Polity Press.

Burchell, M.A. (2014) Skilful Movements: The Evolving Commando. In P. Cornish and N.J. Saunders (eds.), *Bodies in Conflict: Corporeality, Materiality and Transformation*, pp. 208–218. London: Routledge.

——— (2019) *Decoding a Royal Marine Commando: The Militarised Body as Artefact*. London: Routledge.

Foster, N. (1998) *The Making of a Royal Marines Commando*. London: Pan Books.

Goffman, E. (2009) *Asylums: Essays on the Social Situation of Mental Patients and Other Inmates*. London: Aldine Transaction.

Gough, P. (1995) *'Tales from the Bushy-Topped Tree': A Brief Survey of Military Sketching*. http://paulgough.org/bushy.htm (accessed 14 July 2020).

——— (2009) 'Calculating the Future': Panoramic Sketching, Reconnaissance Drawing and the Material Trace of War. In N.J. Saunders and P. Cornish (eds.), *Contested Objects: Material Memories of the Great War*, pp. 237–250. London: Routledge.

Hockey, J. (1986) *Squaddies: Portrait of a Subculture*. Exeter: Wheaton & Co Ltd.

Ingold, T. (2011) *Being Alive: Essays on Movement, Knowledge and Description*. London: Routledge.

Saunders, N.J. (2004) Material Culture and Conflict: The Great War, 1914–2003. In N.J. Saunders (ed.), *Matters of Conflict: Material Culture, Memory and the First World War*, pp. 5–25. Oxford: Routledge.

——— (2009) People in Objects: Individuality and the Quotidian in the Material Culture of War. In C.L. White (ed.), *The Materiality of Individuality: Archaeological Studies of Individual Lives*, pp. 37–55. New York: Springer.

Tilley, C. and K. Cameron-Daum (2017) *An Anthropology of Landscape*. London: UCL Press.

INDEX

Note: Page locators in italic refer to figures and bold refer to tables.